THE WILEY SERIES ON NET-ENHANCED ORGANIZATIONS
Transforming the Organization Through Internet Technologies

RICHARD T. WATSON
Series Editor

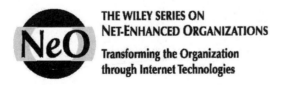

**THE WILEY SERIES ON
NET-ENHANCED ORGANIZATIONS**
Transforming the Organization
through Internet Technologies

FOREWORD

Dear Reader,

We live in a world of ubiquitous high bandwidth networks and mobile Internet connections. New technologies, new strategies, and new terminologies are rapidly developing in the field of e-business.

NEO, Wiley's Series on Net-Enhanced Organizations: Transforming the Organization through Internet Technology, will provide you with the resources you need to respond to the latest changes and trends in the field. The books in this series will help you to develop a comprehensive understanding of e-business and its technological underpinnings, essential knowledge in the Internet age of the neo-modern business.

As the series editor, I will be working closely with Wiley's editorial staff and authors to bring you textbooks specifically designed to meet your need to understand how Internet technology supports the Net-Enhanced Organization.

We are proud to present you with the second book in this groundbreaking series: Foundations of Net-Enhanced Organizations by Detmar Straub, an highly accomplished information systems scholar and one of the field's thought leaders.

I am sure you will enjoy reading about the net-enhanced organization and learning how it is changing the nature of business. Because this form of organization is so new and in its formative stages, this book (and the series) will position you at the forefront of business knowledge. And keep an eye out for upcoming texts in this exciting new NEO series.

Best regards,
Richard T. Watson, Series Editor
J. Rex Fuqua Distinguished Chair for
  Internet Strategy
Director of the Center for
  Information Systems Leadership (CISL)
University of Georgia

Foundations of Net-Enhanced Organizations

DETMAR STRAUB

Georgia State University

JOHN WILEY & SONS, INC.

Acquistions Editor   *Beth Lang Golub*
Marketing Manager   *Gitti Lindner*
Assistant Editor   *Lorraina Raccuia*
Editorial Assistant   *Ailsa Manny*
Senior Production Editor   *Ken Santor*
Cover designer   *Karin Kincheloe*

This book was set by Publication Services and printed and bound by Malloy, Inc. The cover was printed by Brady Palmer Printing Company.

This book is printed on acid free paper.

0471-44377-8
WIE 0471-42940-6

Printed in the United States of America

10 9 8 7 6 5 4 3 2 1

PREFACE

PURPOSE OF THIS BOOK

This book is designed to aid and abet the study of e-commerce or e-business. It also intends to show how current and future managers can take actions to bring into reality initiatives using the Internet and other high-speed networks as the transport and communications vehicles. The differences between such e-terms will be discussed later in the book, but for now we will use them interchangeably to mean *commercial activity via electronic (computerized) networked connections.*

Organizations that are deploying e-commerce or e-business systems are seeking to become *Net-enhanced organizations* (NEOs). We shall use the terms NEO and NE (Net-enhancement) to refer to this transition to networked enterprises in addition to the term e-commerce (and occasionally e-business).

The knowledge being developed is specifically on organizations. One could design many books on the impact of the Internet and e-commerce on individuals, and how it changes the way persons learn, think, and interact. How individuals are gaining direct access to other individuals, for business and other purposes, could be another interesting subject for study. But that is not the focus of this book.

Or one could stress community use of e-commerce—how towns, cities, federal governments, and entire regions exploit their strengths through effective use of Web sites. Again, this is a worthy area of inquiry, but it is not the subject of this book.

This book concentrates on organizations and, particularly, on profit-making institutions. The intention is to explore ways in which an organization can become technically and operationally proficient in e-commerce. And, of course, no organization can become proficient unless its human capital—its employees and its future employees—is proficient. For this reason, the range of topics covered by the book is broad. In that regard, the book is intended to be introductory in nature.

The intended audience of the book is also fairly broad. This book serves as an introduction to Wiley books of a more specialized nature delving into Net-enhancement. Therefore, the intended audience is general managers or those studying in academic programs to be general managers but also those who are preparing to be specialists in chosen areas of e-commerce. Restated, there is no expectation that readers will have a strong technical background and already understand, for example, the intricacies of the Internet protocols, nor are they supposed to be marketers with many years of marketing experience, including online markets.

Just to be perfectly clear, students in MBA programs or specialized master's programs in business or management schools are a primary target audience. Improvement of the basic understanding of graduate students for conducting business in cyberspace is a goal of the book.

ORGANIZATION OF THIS BOOK

The philosophy underlying the structure of the book may be of interest to readers or potential readers. There are five major topics in the book: fundamental concepts of NE, basic NE technologies, strategy and organizational designs for NEOs, implementation issues and opportunities, and looking forward.

In the fundamental concepts topics, it is made clear that Net-enhancement is a phenomenon whose time has come. In a certain sense, it was an inevitable consequence of the evolution of computing and networking; Chapter 1, "The Migration from Traditional to Net-Enhanced Organizations and Systems," makes this argument. Readers need to understand why the e-commerce revolution makes sense from an economic standpoint, and Chapter 2, "Principles of Networked Economy Businesses," presents the economic justification for making the huge investments that are required to be NE-proficient. As a groundwork for the rest of the book, Chapter 3, "Structures, Frameworks, and Classes of Net-Enhancement," presents readers with the NE terms, acronyms, and concepts that will be used throughout the rest of the book.

At its heart, the e-commerce revolution is a technological innovation, or better said, a host of technological innovations. Chapters 4 through 6 are, therefore, a layperson manager's view of how the underlying information technologies actually work. Chapters 4 and 5, "Basic NE Infrastructure" and "Middleware Technologies and Applications," respectively, introduce the reader (or level the playing field somewhat) to how open networks and the Internet works and show how distinctly different this is from proprietary networks. Security is a topic in its own right, and will be considered along with trust issues in this commercial space. Online payment issues fit in nicely here too. These appear in Chapter 6, "NE Security, Trust, and Payments."

The chapters that discuss strategy and organizational designs for NE cover corporate strategies, business models, and marketing strategies for introducing successful e-commerce systems. Chapter 7, "Competitive NE Strategy," deals with this topic at the highest level in the corporation, exploring how NEOs should strategize e-commerce. It probes questions such as: What are the ways to be successful in an organizational evolution to NE? Following this seventh chapter is a chapter on creating business models that define the opportunities in e-commerce distinct from traditional business settings (Chapter 8, "Business Models and Strategic Planning"). The roles of brokerage, agency, and other forms of intermediation in e-commerce are discussed in Chapter 9, "Intermediation and Cybermediation." A crucial element in corporate strategic planning and business modeling is for managers to redesign their organizations through partnering and contractual arrangements that call for broad and wide electronic communications. A chapter that discusses these "virtualizing" designs is Chapter 10, "Strategic Partnering, Outsourcing, and Virtual Organizations." Chapter 11, "Strategizing for E-Markets," shows how managers can exploit marketing concepts in both the consumer and organizational buying online environments.

The chapters that focus on implementation issues and opportunities cover what is required to phase in an NE initiative, both from a technical and project management standpoint. How one gets feedback to learn from the effort is also an important topic in Chapter 12, "Deploying NE Solutions." Hurdles to successful implementation are also a knowledge base that every well-educated manager should have and that is dealt with in Chapter 13, "Challenges to Implementation." The social and global environments are important in successfully implementing online solutions. These are delineated in Chapter 14, "Social and International Issues (available online at http://www.wiley.com/college/straub."

Chapter 15 (available online at http://www.wiley.com/college/straub) discusses topics for looking forward, examines a few absolutely central key trends, and reflects on how the NE evolution will interact with these movements. A helpful glossary can also be found there.

Persons who are just beginning their serious study of electronic commerce are the audience for this book. All that it takes to gain value from this book is the willingness to learn and the ability to apply that learning.

SUPPLEMENTS

All supplements are on the book's Web site, www.wiley.com/college/straub. Supplements that accompany the text include:

- Instructor's Manual
- Lecture slides in PowerPoint
- Test Bank

Detmar Straub
Atlanta, Georgia USA

Contents

▶ **CHAPTER 6** NE Security, Trust, and Payments   **159**

▶ **CHAPTER 7** Competitive NE Strategy   **197**

▶ **CHAPTER 8** Business Models and Strategic Planning **235**

▶ **CHAPTER 9** Intermediation and Cybermediation **267**

▶ **CHAPTER 12** Deploying NE Solutions **381**

▶ **CHAPTER 13** Challenges to Implementation **423**

ONLINE AT WWW.WILEY.COM/COLLEGE/STRAUB

ONLINE AT WWW.WILEY.COM/COLLEGE/STRAUB

ONLINE AT WWW.WILEY.COM/COLLEGE/STRAUB

▶ Glossary

CHAPTER 1

THE MIGRATION FROM TRADITIONAL TO NET-ENHANCED ORGANIZATIONS AND SYSTEMS

MANAGING NET-ENHANCED ORGANIZATIONS TODAY AND TOMORROW

Why do managers need to understand the profound changes that are occurring in electronic interconnections between organizations? Isn't this something that the technical and information systems (IS) people can and should be handling? Networking, the Internet, HTML, browsers—aren't these technical matters that the general manager does not need to learn about or be informed about? The answer is that general managers cannot help but be versed in these technologies and their actual and potential applications. Managers are charged with overseeing firm investments and information technology (IT) investments are among the largest and most critical investments the firm can make. So why is it valuable to be versed on how these technologies are changing the underlying business processes? These are the kinds of questions that we will attempt to answer in this chapter.

LEARNING OBJECTIVES FOR THIS CHAPTER

- To argue for or against the proposition that the terminology currently used for a phenomenon, terms such as "e-commerce," are much less important that the underlying phenomenon and its influence on society
- To enumerate and explain the drivers of this twenty-first century electronic revolution in organizations and society
- To explain the main trends in the migration from traditional commerce to e-commerce
- To identify the organizational and environmental drivers of e-commerce

- To explicate a comprehensive definition of e-commerce and Net-enhancement
- To evaluate how a business can reduce its costs and transform its business model as technology is implemented
- To explain emerging trends and the second wave of e-commerce
- To judge relevance, timeliness, reliability, integrity, and accuracy of internet sources
- To perform simple statistical analysis on data sets
- To evaluate peer performance and presentation of information
- To design and develop full-channel multimedia presentations
- To communicate electronically both synchronously and asynchronously
- To demonstrate use of a variety of software applications
- To efficiently conduct internet research
- To strengthen creative writing skills
- To design multimedia presentations
- To communicate in cyberspace
- To network electronically

▶ *CASE STUDY 1-1*

RAPIDLY SHRINKING CYCLE TIMES AT GRAND & TOY

Grand & Toy is known for its leadership as an office products supplier and is recognized today as one of Canada's leading players in business-to-business (B2B) e-commerce. As the largest supplier in Canada, Grand & Toy's business challenges require that they deal with very large volumes of data, be able to analyze and manage profitability, measure product performance, and monitor retail versus commercial results.

In response to these challenges, Grand & Toy implemented a state-of-the-art national distribution and supply chain infrastructure via an Internet platform. The system services eight distribution centers, 21 sales offices, and 75 stores. It also utilizes an existing B2B network that represents 75% of the company's revenues. The enterprise-wide system ensures that customer orders are seamlessly sent to the closest distribution point, streamlining the order process. Live inventory availability allows customers to verify that the product they are ordering is in stock in their immediate area prior to submitting their order. The display of thumbnail images during the product selection process offers users the ability to view and verify their selection while ordering. The result is that Grand & Toy is able to reliably offer consistent next-day delivery, real-time inventory availability, accurate order fulfillment, and overwhelming customer satisfaction. The characteristics of a robust distribution network and key associations with e-commerce partners have proved so successful that Grand & Toy doubled its size in just five years. With an increase in Internet sales of 244% between 1999 and 2000, Grand & Toy's Internet business has drawn the attention of many other B2B e-commerce providers resulting in important strategic alliances and partnerships.

Grand & Toy is better able to manage products and profitably, make better decisions, and has overall increased performance due to its innovative e-commerce solution. In 2000, Grand & Toy was awarded Canada's E-commerce Award of Excellence, which recognized Grand & Toy as a visionary organization employing effective and innovative e-commerce solutions.

Discussion:

1. Implementation of Grand & Toy's enterprise wide system provided unique opportunities for changing business processes. How were basic processes changed and what impact did the changing of business processes have on the cycle times of core business functions?

2. Identify the environmental and organizational drivers that enabled Grand & Toy to develop their successful B2B network.

3. In what ways have Grand & Toy's e-commerce solutions influenced their strategic alliances and partnerships?

Sources:

Bakos, Y. "The Emerging Role of Electronic Marketplaces on the Internet." *Communications of the ACM*, 41, 8, August (1998).

Information from Rick McKay, Vice President, Marketing, Grand & Toy, Toronto, Ont.

Grand & Toy, Toronto, Ont., http://www.grandandtoy.com/CorporatePages/en/corporate_retail_locations.asp.

1.1 INTRODUCTION

1.1.1 Fads and Fashions

Business studies are plagued with "fads" and "fashions" that occupy our attention (and academic courses) for a while, and then they seem to quietly fade from view.[1] TQM (total quality management) was the trumpet call during the late 1980s when it seemed that Japanese strategies and management practices has conquered the world. Before that MBO (management by objectives) had its heyday. Lately, it has been BPR (business process reengineering) and ERP (enterprise resource planning) systems, and even more lately, the term being substituted for ERP, which is EAI (enterprise application integration).

What is the problem with management practices being constantly altered according to fashion? Organizations make tremendous investments in both financial and human terms when one of these "principles" becomes popular and companies begin to imitate the behavior of other firms without necessarily thinking through the consequences of the change.[2] Moreover, if elaborate restructuring of the organization occurs and the anticipated benefits do not materialize, then the losses in both micro- and macro-terms is gigantic.

Will e-commerce or Net-enhancement (NE), that is, commercial activity via electronic (computerized) networked connections, be one of these soon-forgotten fads?[3] Will the Internet not become the transforming and revolutionary phenomenon it is widely predicted to be? There are legitimate concerns that need to be addressed before we devote our energies to learning how to deploy and infuse NE into our organizations.

The argument made below is that NE is not just another "fad" or "fashion"— it will become one of the central transforming innovations of the twenty-first century, and is worthy of our serious consideration.

1.1.2 NE, E-Business, and Other E-Terms

Before discussing the influential social and organizational drivers that suggest that NE is an inevitable technological revolution (or evolution), it is important to discuss terms that are being used to describe the main subject of this text. One widely used term is e-commerce. Another of the most viable contenders to represent the phenomenon is e-business. Proponents of this term argue that e-commerce is limited to transactions and external exchanges between businesses whereas e-business is a broader and more inclusive term.

---

[1]Abrahamson (1996); Abrahamson (1991).
[2]Ang (1997).
[3]This term was introduced by Straub et al. (2002).

4

Focus on NE: Fad or Fashion?

In June of 2000, the U.S. Government Electronic Commerce Working Group officially declared the digital economy a reality, not just a fad! In their third annual report entitled, "Leadership for the New Millennium, Delivering on Digital Progress and Prosperity," significant findings were released reporting the promotion of e-commerce. Important findings include:

- Internet access had increased by 78% over the previous year. The number of people with Internet access has reached an estimated 304 million worldwide.
- One-third of real U.S. economic growth was contributed by the information technology industry between 1995 and 1999.
- Computer prices declined by 12% per year from 1987 to 1994, and 26% per year from 1995 to 1999.
- Falling IT prices have directly pulled down inflation by an average of 0.5 percentage points per year.
- Computers with a unique Internet address ballooned from 1.3 million in 1993 to 93 million in 2000.
- The number of Internet users increased by 423 million from 1993 to 2000.
- The number of Americans online has grown 1135% since 1993.

The Internet is also experiencing tremendous international growth. Although North America accounted for 45% of worldwide users in 1999, within five years this region will account for just 29%. Of the roughly 100 million new users who logged onto the Internet in the study year, three-quarters were located outside the United States.

Sources:

Third Annual Report, http://www.usembassy.it/pdf/other/ec2000.pdf

http://www.computerworld.com/news/2000/story/0,11280,45562,00.html

E-Business is a proprietary term originally promulgated by IBM. Clearly, it has now moved beyond IBM consulting practice and into the mainstream. But it is important to recognize that the term has no *inherently* larger meaning than e-commerce. It is, after all, just a word. A Webster's dictionary definition of "commerce" is buying and selling, but that definition implies that there would be activities to support that buying and selling, otherwise how could one ever buy and sell? So, it can easily cover an intranet and also cover industrial buying, that is, business-to-business (B2B) exchanges, and specific terms like extranets that describe forms of electronically facilitated commerce.

The term e-business, however, is suspect as a representation of commercial activity enhanced or supported by the Internet and other networks precisely because it is a company-invented term. Computer services and consulting firms have a proprietary interest in promulgating the use of the term "e-business" rather than other terms like "e-commerce," "Net-enablement," or "Net-enhancement." At some point, there may be complete consensus in languages worldwide on what these terms mean. For the moment, though, such is not the case.

Nevertheless, the terms e-commerce and e-business have some currency, to be sure. There would not seem to be universal concurrence on the meaning of these or any of the terms being bandied about. It is a matter of usage.

What are possible solutions? We could employ the term "e-everything" if we were interested in how governments, nongovernmental organizations, and nonprofits use networks and the Internet in their lives. And if we extended our topic to individual usage, an unusual term like e-everything would still be appropriate.

In fact, there are virtues to using the term "e-commerce" to stand for the entire phenomenon of supporting businesses through networked connections. As it is used in one of the early works describing the phenomenon of interest, Kalakota and Whinston's *Frontiers of e-Commerce*, there is no such limitation. In this seminal book, e-commerce covers the range of online activity, including customer service, B2B, and internal activities of the firm in support of Internet business.

A simple extension of the argument offered by proponents of the term e-business points out the deficiencies of both e-commerce and e-business. Surely, there are many parallels between the uses of the Internet to serve business customers and government clients, for example. But the term e-business is clearly not broad enough to cover e-government activities nor those of nonprofits or nongovernmental organizations (NGOs).[4] If these activities are of interest, and they certainly are of some interest in this textbook, then we may be forced immediately to a term like e-organization. Moreover, if proprietorships are buying and selling over the Internet, in venues like e-Bay, one would be tempted to call this C2C activity something broader than e-organization. What would that be? E-World?

Let's review the terms we have intimated may be at the heart of the revolution thus far:

- Net-enablement
- Net-enhancement
- E-Commerce

---

[4] The term net-enhanced organizations (NEOs) is employed in this book in order to broaden the concept to all organizations, not just profit-making organizations. It also is related to the nature of the activity and not what it applies to. Nevertheless, because the term does not imply an organizational domain, net-enhanced can and does apply to all types and sizes of organization.

- E-Business
- E-Organization
- E-World

The solution we have adopted in this book is to adopt the two coined, hyphenated words Net-enablement or Net-enhancement[5] The components of the terms convey the exchanges over open networks that we are focusing on in this text. Distinctions in these terms will be raised later, but for the moment we can say that the term Net-enhancement is not company invented, and does not have the taint of a proprietary connotation. Thus, for the sake of simplicity, this text has been named *Foundations of Net-Enhanced Organizations.*

1.2 ORGANIZATIONAL AND ENVIRONMENTAL DRIVERS OF NE

Keeping in mind a temporary, working definition of "Net-enhancement" as "commercial activity via electronic, networked connections," we now need to explore the possibility that Net-enhancement was inevitable, once certain organizational and environmental conditions were in place, and, moreover, that it represents a permanent change in the way commerce will transpire on planet earth.[6]

First, what are these drivers? There are at least eight that need to be recognized (see Table 1.1). We need to consider them carefully for the ways in which they make the movement to the Internet inevitable.

1.2.1 Driver 1: Digitization

Media are generally thought of as the means by which people (and computers) communicate. "Content" is generally thought of as the information, art, or evaluation that is the value-added component of media exchanges. Digitization is a process of capturing content in bits rather than in a physical form in a particular medium. Sounds coming across a telephonic medium, for example, can be captured as analog signals on a tape, as in many home voice mail or answering systems, or they can be rendered as bits and stored on any medium for later reproduction. With digitization, the medium for storing the content is not important. Only the accurate storage of the bits is important, as shown in Figure 1.1.

---

[5]Straub et al. (2002) advance the term "Net-enhancement." This term has a somewhat broader meaning even than "Net-enablement" because it applies equally well to organizations that are using the Internet in extremely modest ways, that is, not just as an enabler but as an enhancer.

[6]I owe the listing and basic reasoning behind most of the drivers in this section to Dr. Richard Welke, Director of the Electronic Commerce Institute at Georgia State University. I thank him for his permission to adopt and express his concepts.

Table 1.1: Drivers of Net-Enhanced Organizations

#	Source	Driver
1	Environment	Digitization of media
2		Inexpensive telecommunications
3		Widespread diffusion of computers
4	Organization	Increasing pressure on costs and margins, including globalization and commoditization
5		Changing organizational models, including empowerment of workers, informating of key business activities, outsourcing and downsizing of many firms, partnering, cross-functional business processes, virtual teams
6		Rapidly shrinking cycle times
7		Intelligent products and services
8		Demand for customized products and services

The movement away from media content embedded in physical forms to digits makes a huge difference in our future capability for technological innovation, as Negroponte argues in his book *Being Digital*.[7] It means that the use and reuse of that content is not dependent on the limitations of a given medium. Negroponte points out that atoms restrict the number of ways that content can be expressed, transferred, and altered. Digits do not.

A concrete example may help to make this clearer. Traditional photography allows a negative to be produced, or a slide, or a plate, but all of them have the content of the picture embedded in the physical form. To change the form involves an expensive, time-consuming, and imperfect conversion. If you have an old print of your great-great-grandmother (and that is all you have), for example, you might, using traditional media, have to have another picture taken of the print, and from there chose a medium in which to re-embed the content. Once that choice of a new medium was made, let's say a slide, you would be restricted to that format until you went through another conversion, for example, to a larger photo print. Another conversion at this point from the print-of-a-print would result in loss of detail and coloration. And all of these efforts call for specialized equipment. In other words, in traditional media, the content and the medium are not now and never were independent of each other.

[7]Negroponte (1995).

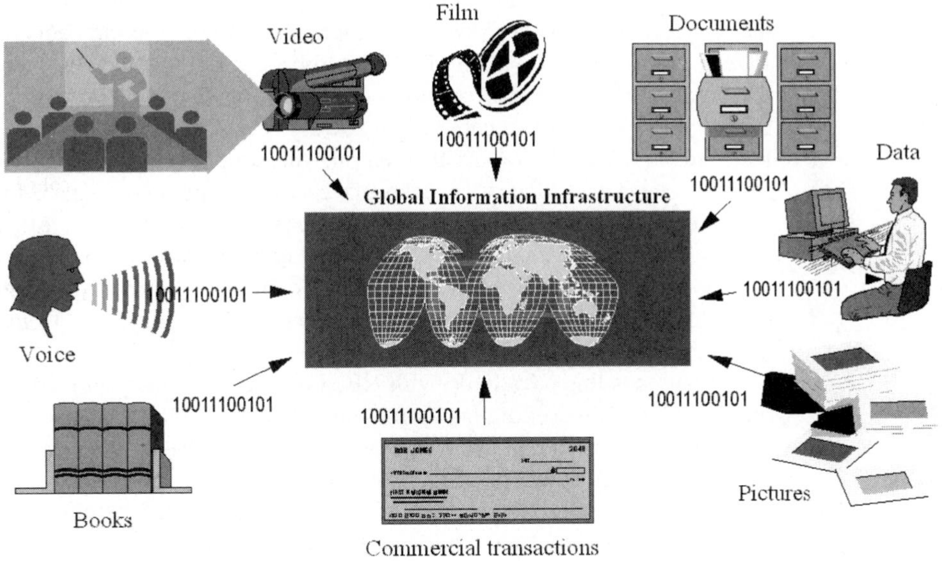

Figure 1.1 Digital Convergence of Media into Bits. (Copyright 2002, Richard Welke. Permission to reproduce granted.)

Now let us imagine a high resolution digital photo that has been taken of your great-great-grandmother by a time traveler. The content of the photo is represented as digits, and not embedded in atoms, except as a readily changeable storage medium. The medium of choice at this point is completely dependent on the equipment you have available. If you want a photo print, you can create that easily. If you want a slide, one would usually send the digits representing the photo to a service that will return a slide to you. The point is that the content of the photo—your great-great-grandmother's dress, her hair, her old-fashioned swing—are not restricted to a particular medium. The digits themselves are medium-free and can be readily moved into any medium you choose.

This transference of atoms into digits (or symbols) is proceeding at a pace few would have predicted years ago. The large film studios will likely stop shooting film in the very near future, if they have not already done so. The granularity that can be captured in digital motion picture cameras exceeds or certainly matches that of celluloid film, and digitizing in the original shooting allows special effects to be integrated into the final product easily and with no medium degradation.

Libraries are another case where organizations are moving toward digital formats very quickly today. Storing digital information as extensive as the entire text of the Judeo-Christian Bible on a storage medium the size of the head of a pin is not an unreachable goal. Moreover, storage media for gigabytes and terabytes of data are becoming very affordable for many individuals, let alone major institutions. So moving diverse physical sources such as books, articles, maps, blueprints, music, and poetry to a digital form allows them to be reconfigured and expressed in a mind-boggling variety of formats. Books can be read on e-book devices. Maps can be visualized on computer screens, and zoomed in to any level of meaningful detail. Poetry can be retrieved in written form or as spoken by the poetess or poet.

Other examples might include the Chicago Board of Trade, where a conversion from the physical "open outcry" system, depicted in the climatic moments of the film *Trading Places,* with Dan Aykroyd and Eddie Murphy, could, conceivably, endanger the future of the board. Selling futures, or future contracts for commodities, has historically been a highly physical process where sellers vocally "cry out" their offers, and bidders "cry out" their bids in what is known as an open pit. The digitizing of these contracts allows another form of electronic "outcry" to take place where computers engage in the by-play. The medium on which the computers' sell ranges and bid ranges are stored is irrelevant, because they can be manipulated to be displayed, by user choice, on computer-connected screens or in print, or they can be projected onto a large screen. The digits themselves are everything. The medium formed by atoms becomes insignificant. Atoms are bound; digits are free to "morph."

What does this have to do with NE? For one, networks can readily move content for organizations if it is in digital form. And, when received, the digits can be used immediately or kept waiting until they take on a new form. The choice is granted to the receiver, rather than dictated by a physical medium.

The digitizing of most new media content (and a lot of the old content, an example of which is American Movie Classics digitizing of old films) has led to an environment where content is fluid and can be readily remade for new uses. This characteristic makes digitization an important precondition for NE.

1.2.2 Driver 2: Inexpensive Telecommunications

It is no secret that the cost of using the telecommunications networks worldwide has fallen dramatically over the last decade. In the United States, the critical event spurring this was the deregulation of the telecommunications industry, which had been dominated by the AT&T government-sanctioned monopoly. The same tendency to privatize the PT&Ts (Post, Telegraph, and Telephone Systems) in Europe and around the globe is beginning to yield more competitive markets where prices are falling precipitously.

In Egypt, for example, the number of ISPs (Internet service providers) rose from 26 to 50 to 76 in a three-year period. Fixed monthly rates of U.S. $20 were available by the spring of 2000, rates which had been available in the United States for several years prior to this.

The cost of making telephone calls also dropped over the decade of the 1990s. By the year 2002, long distance calls in the United States could be made for as little as U.S. $.05 per minute, for domestic connections.

Still, consistently low rates for most telecommunications services are not yet available worldwide. The barriers to affordable telecommunications are primarily the huge costs to replace outmoded telecommunications infrastructures and the inefficient, government-run monopolies that still operate in many countries throughout the world. Deregulation of this industry should create a competitive marketplace where low cost provider economics will eventually play out. One solution to the outdated or insufficient infrastructure may be to leapfrog to wireless for even the basic services. Wireless services are extremely popular in Europe, to the point where one in two Finns now carry a cellular phone device.

In any case, enough economies can afford Internet connections to make it a truly worldwide phenomenon, indicating that the cost of telecommunications has not been not a disabling factor everywhere.

The effect of low cost, widely available telecommunications connections on NE is obvious. As long as connecting to a network was prohibitively expensive and not readily available, relatively little traffic passed over networks. Once it was simple, easy, and of low cost, the possibilities for usage of the network mushroomed, especially after the development of the Internet and the World Wide Web, topics that will be discussed in a later chapter.

1.2.3 Driver 3: Widespread Diffusion of Computers

Computers, both personal computers and those used for enterprise-level computing by organizations, have become omnipresent in our postmillennium world. The growth of use of personal computers in the United States has been exponential, from 25% of homes in 1995, to 33% in 1998, to 50% in the year 2000, as Figure 1.2 illustrates. There is no reason to believe that this growth will stop anywhere short of the 90%+ level, which is a reasonable approximation of the penetration of televisions in the United States.

Rates of growth in other parts of the world have been equally impressive in industrialized and developed countries in Europe and Asia, although they do tend to lag the United States by a few years. Because of the cost of computers and the tariffs placed on imports by governments, the diffusion of computing in many developing countries (DCs) has been much slower. Figure 1.3 shows the typical ratios that we have come to expect in penetration of computing in industrialized countries such as the United States, Singapore, and Canada, and DCs such as China.

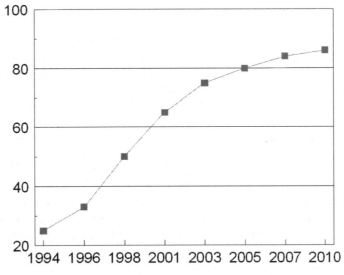

% of US Homes with Computers

Figure 1.2 Real and Projected Growth of Home Computing in the United States

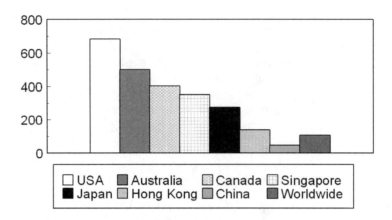

Figure 1.3 Typical Ratios in International Diffusion of Computing

Clearly, NE cannot reach consumers without penetration of the population at large. But there is no reason why businesses cannot communicate with other businesses, even in countries with a largely illiterate population, like Egypt. So the argument is straightforward in that NE depends on the availability of both transmission capabilities (driver 2, inexpensive telecommunications) and the machines to send and receive transmissions (driver 3, widespread diffusion of computing).

Without a critical mass of users, no communications technical advance can succeed, but it appears that the critical mass is now present as a result of drivers 2 and 3.[8]

1.2.4 Driver 4: Increasing Pressures on Costs and Margins: Globalization and Commoditization

Costs and margins are under pressure because of two factors: (1) globalization and (2) commoditization. Globalization means that businesses operate freely and with minimal restraints across national borders. The ability of firms to do this has increased dramatically over the last decade and is as potent a phenomenon as computerization in all of its forms. Giant trading blocks such as NAFTA (North American Free Trade Agreement) in the Americas and the European Union (EU) in Europe have reduced or eliminated custom procedures, taxes, tariffs, and other constraints on free trade. Trading agreements between nations, such as designations like "favored trading status," have also opened up markets and allowed multinational corporations (MNCs) to set up operations in foreign countries.

Because of globalization, firms find today that they must pay attention to their margins when they are conducting business on a global basis. The firms against which they are competing may have the advantage of scale economies,[9] and the only way they can compete is to be more effective at NE.

Commoditization, on the other hand, is the standardization of products and services such that differences between them are not perceived by customers as differentiating characteristics. At one point in the personal computer (PC) revolution, for example, it became clear that there was little difference between manufacturers of products with the same con-

[8]Markus (1987).
[9]Bartlett and Ghoshal (1998).

figuration. As a result, prices plummeted and the producers with excellent economies of scale, like Dell Computers, began to dominate the industry. The movement of products and services from being differentiated to being commoditized is important because it opens up markets.

Why are these significant as organizational factors that encourage the development of electronic commerce? In brief, if firms felt that they could not readily buy and sell abroad, they would be less inclined to use the Internet and NE. The Internet, in particular, has international reach. Uniform Resource Locators (URLs) express locations for virtually any spot on the globe. Governmental regulations are the only impediment to being able to access Web sites globally, so the trend in globalization is nicely matched by the capabilities of the Internet to transact business anywhere on the planet.

Commoditization, by the same token, spurs economic growth and opens up more opportunities for international sales. It allows new firms (many of them off-shore) to enter a market, because products and services have become standardized. The outsourcing of software component-building and assembly to India is a case in point. If it were not for the international connectivity afforded by the Internet, it is difficult to see how the high level of activity in India could be sustained. The Indian software factories are supplying a great deal of the world's application components and NE is a critical link in the efficiency of this operation.

1.2.5 Driver 5: Changing Organizational Models

Organizations are changing and, by happenstance or in dynamic interaction with the capabilities of NE itself, the ways in which they are changing are readily supportable by NE. These new models include the following: (a) empowerment of workers; (b) informating of key business activities; (c) de-layering, that is, downsizing and outsourcing; (d) partnering; (e) telework; and (f) virtual teams.

Empowerment: As greater decision-making authority is vested in workers on the "front lines," the need for increased exchange of information among workers within and across work groups also increases.[10]Hence, the need for closer attention to appropriate choices of networked communication media, such as e-mail, voice-over IP, or video conferencing, becomes paramount.

Informating: Automated processes spin off data that can be reshaped as information for managerial decision making.[11]The amount of information that can be produced from a clickstream of data exchanges between a firm and its customers in cyberspace is enormous. It is clear that managers will need to find new ways of managing this data flow, tools like data mining coming instantly to mind.

De-layering: As organizational layers are removed (often by eliminating supervisory or middle-manager ranks), spans of control increase.[12]This means that managers must communicate with more subordinates, creating greater pressure for communication efficiency as well as greater potential for stress, because of the increase in potential incidences of incomplete communication sequences. De-layering leads naturally to outsourcing because the work must still be done.

---

[10]Keller and Dansereau (1995).
[11]Zuboff (1988).
[12]Zeffane and Mayo (1994).

Partnering: Strategic alliances are the rule today, rather than the exception. Firms are partnering with those who can complement their internal core competencies. Sometimes this is via an arm's length transaction or a long-term contract, and other times it is through a loose cooperative arrangement.[13]Coordinating these numerous tasks is greatly facilitated by networked connections and the applications that run on the Internet.

Telework: More and more, knowledge workers are performing their work in locations remote from a central office. This change in organizational form is, in fact, only made possible with the advent of high-bandwidth communications.[14]

Virtual teams: In order to achieve rapid-cycle product design and get to the root causes of nettlesome quality problems, reconfigure business processes, and so on, many organizations are turning to ad hoc task forces, teams, and committees, whose membership are often virtual, comprised of workers in different functions and different locations.[15]Provision of appropriate communications tools to support these temporary organizational structures is now, and is going to continue to be, a key to successful organizations.

1.2.6 Driver 6: Rapidly Shrinking Cycle Times

There is a nearly universal need in business to reduce cycle times for production and fulfillment processes. The improvements in cycle time that companies like UPS and FedEx were able to accomplish with their delivery schedules is as impressive as those in the design of automobiles or chips. In all cases, the amount of time it took to complete certain cycles were halved, and then halved again. Each time the cycle time improved, customers were more satisfied and costs went down.

Decreasing cycle times requires a tight integration between tasks in the critical path, and NE applications are being used to create that seamlessness. As we shall see next, this has been accomplished through electronic data interchange (EDI), but lately this coordination is being worked through XML. Because the Internet is a time- and space-free medium, coordination can take place on a basis of 24 hours seven days a week (24x7).

1.2.7 Driver 7: Intelligent Products and Services

Miniaturization of computers is a benefit of the space age. Computers needed to be both powerful and small to be carried into space, and the chip was the result. Today, chips are found in everything from automobile dashboards to cereal boxes. Chips can be used to identify pets, such as dogs and cats, and they can be used to record the time of a runner in a footrace.

The intelligence of products goes far beyond identification. GPS systems are being installed in rental cars so that renters can be given detailed directions to find their way to any part of visited destinations. Cellular phones are evolving into hand-held computers and being amenable to Web surfing. E-Book devices not only can display large numbers of electronic books, but they can bookmark pages and serve as an amanuensis for information that you wish to highlight and store.

[13]Heeks (1996).
[14]Watad and DiSanzo (2000).
[15]Maznevski and Chudoba (2000)

Sometimes the intelligence is not embedded in the products and services themselves but is so closely associated with them that it seems as if the products and services are, indeed, more intelligent. Don Tapscott, who comments on the ability of the producers of goods to track consumer buying patterns, refers to bread as being "smart."[16] And bread can, indeed, be smart, if the firm's databases and tracking applications know that a customer typically buys certain kinds of bread with a regular frequency. The firm can induce sales if and when consumers break out of these buying patterns. E-Mail is an excellent conduit to help to induce such sales. The process of sending the e-mails can be easily automated, and the customer given "bail-out" options, should they not wish to receive such "friendly" reminders.

Intelligent products and services of the future will increase the capabilities of NE and extend its penetration into our daily lives. Cell phones are just one example of intelligent devices that will be net-ready. PDAs, or personal digital assistants, such as Palm Pilots can be linked through wireless connections into the Internet, as well as to LANs (local area networks) in the office. Flows of information from client to producer to customer to provider will be taking place in the next few years as if that process were the most natural we have ever known.

1.2.8 Driver 8: Demand for Customized Products and Services

Customers have had their appetites whetted by the ability of manufacturers and service providers to tailor their offerings to the specifications of the customer. In physical products, the examples are legion. Dell Computer offers a configurator on its online Web site that allows one to precisely specify the computer or peripherals one wishes to purchase and have delivered. This is known as working with mass customization or markets-of-one, as illustrated in Figure 1.4. In other situations, more and more often, it is possible for customers to indicate their exact requirements and have an automobile, for example, built to their specs and delivered rapidly.

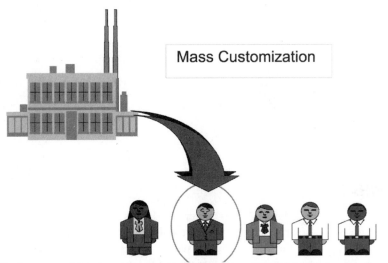

Mass Customization

Figure 1.4 Dell Computer Manufacturing for Individual Consumers through its Configurator Engine (Creates feedback from customer via Web-page screen)

[16]Tapscott (1996)

In the services arena, Ernst & Young developed an online service for small businesses that used an expert system interface to their best practices knowledge management system.[17] Because small business customers cannot afford the full, premium prices of Ernst and Young's consultants, they are able to gain access to tailor-made consulting advice via this service. This is an interesting solution in that E&Y have turned their differentiated product, their knowledge base, into a commodity to be delivered via an intelligent computerized system.

The fact that the examples in this section are already Net-enhanced products and services is an indication of the extent to which NE is required to personalize the response to the client and to build-to-order. It is possible to do this with physically driven processes, but the costs and prices are much higher and the market is not likely to be a mass market, but rather a niche market. The days of the Rolls-Royce handmade automobile are gone. However, with NE, we are truly seeing the markets-of-one that Gilmore and Pine speak of.[18] The cyberspace markets of the future will be targeted to anyone, anytime, and anyplace.

Focus on NE: Always Up

A world dominated by NE will mean that systems will always be available to process orders and that firms will no longer have the luxury of natural "breaks" in their corporate rhythms. Day and night, weekends, holidays, festivals, and vacations will no longer be wedded to a particular locale or culture, because the clientele for all firms will be global. New organizational designs will be required to adapt to this new environment—designs such as virtual organizations, telecommuting, global work teams, and flexible working hours.

1.3 WHAT IS NE?

We define NE as commercial activity via electronic (computerized), networked connections, a definition which will serve well enough to get us started but will not be sufficient for the long term. By placing NE in a historical context, however, we can begin to see some of the characteristics of the current phenomenon that set it apart from computing and networking revolutions of the past.

[17]Jaworski et al. (1998).
[18]Gilmore and Pine (2000); Pine and Gilmore (1993).

Before we discuss this evolution, we need to be sure that the concept of a network itself is well understood. Networks were first conceived in the late 1940s as the simple exchange of information between a sender and a receiver computer. Information theory, first formulated in 1948,[19] articulated the idea of minimal bit exchange in order to perfectly complete a transaction. With this concept, the essential intellectual groundwork for networking was in place. Once three additional features are added to this model, the features of (1) remoteness of senders and receivers, (2) the possibility of multiple senders and/or receivers, and (3) the possibility of multiple networks, the vision of a modern-day telecommunications network was present. These essential linkages and exchanges are shown in Figure 1.5, "Generic International Telecommunications Network."

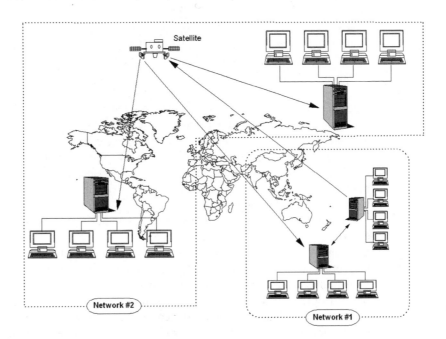

Figure 1.5   Generic International Telecommunications Network

How did computing systems and networking finally converge in NE? In one sense, there were certainly elements of NE in the unveiling of the first IBM computer dedicated to business processing in the early 1960s. Commercial activities were never the same after that event in that many business manual processes, especially those associated with traditional accounting and bookkeeping systems, could now be electronified. The original large firms who invested in computers, moreover, soon began connecting their home bases, with the mainframe computers, to remote job locations, which typically held printing devices for reports and other transaction processing. These connections were created via networks.

Why wouldn't this set of technological configurations and business processes be considered NE? As we shall see shortly, NE is unique in the intelligence of its network(s)—that

[19]Shannon and Weaver (1948)

is, the ability of networks to operate by making dynamic, local decisions about the routing and rerouting of information, and the ability of endpoints to have complete information processing capabilities in their own right. These capabilities were simply not present in the early days of computing.

As the concept developed during the 1990s, electronic commerce came to be strongly associated with distributed computing intelligence, such that both processing and data storage could be dispersed across the network. This distribution makes these networks "robust," or capable of continuing to operate even when sections of the network fail. As we shall see later in this chapter, there are also differences in organizational goals that can be cited for why we had not arrived at the era of NE by the year 1964.

For all intents and purposes, the development of smart networks grow out of PC advances, in the early 1980s. At first, PCs were typically stand alone, and it was not until later in the 1980's that PCs were being heavily used as smart input-processing and output devices not located at the same physical location as the mainframe computers. Distinctions between different forms of mainframe computers, mini-computers, and high-end workstations started to blur in this period as well.

Intelligence in networks, thus, began to be associated with the smarter and smarter machines of many varieties that are placed at various strategic points around the networks. By the end of the 1990s, the technical landscape was ready for NE, but the organizational and interorganizational landscape still was not. Organizations had to be able to see that the exchange of information with other business entities was not only desirable for creating efficiencies in accounting for and producing goods and services, and assisting in decision making, but could also be instrumental in creating new strategic capabilities and networked linkages for the firm.

Harvard's Jim Cash discusses three stages of the evolution of organizational needs (see Table 1.2). In the first era of computing, organizations used computers to run their transaction processing systems (TPS) and to create the standard reports that were generated off of these, their so-called management information systems (MIS). Seeing that more sophisticated analysis of this internally generated information was possible, firms began to produce decision support systems (DSS) and rule-based decision aids in the form of expert systems (ES). By the early 1980s, firms like airlines were using information systems as competitive weapons.[20] The first airline customer reservation systems (CRSs) connected travel agencies with certain airlines, notably United and American, and the systems allowed these firms to grow larger and faster than their rivals. It is critical to note at this juncture that these systems were not available on publicly accessible networks. The networks and the network protocols were proprietary. Although the computers that were used to access information were more than sending and receiving devices (i.e., they were "smart" terminals), their intelligence was limited to interface control and a few other functions.

---

[20]Ives and Learmonth (1984).

Table 1.2: The Three Eras of Computing (Adapted from Jim Cash's Harvard lecture series on IT, 1988.)

Era	IT Focus	Generic Systems	Purpose	Primary IT
I: (1950s–1960s)	Organization	TPS, MIS	Efficiency	Mainframes
II: (1970s–1980s)	Individual	DSS, ES	Effectiveness	Minicomputers
III: (early 1980s–1990s)	Intra-industry	Customer Reservation Systems (CRS)	Strategic/ Competitive Systems	Proprietary network connections; smarter terminals

From the standpoint of reaching beyond the boundaries of the firm to industry agents, such as travel agents, these early airline computer reservation systems partake of some of the characteristics of later full-fledged NE applications, in principle. In being proprietary in nature, though, they failed to break away from the traditional internal, and closed focus of systems in eras I through III.

How does NE differ from the first three eras of computing and networking with respect to organizational purposes? The argument in this text is that NE breaks out of the straitjacket of the first three eras by finally leaving firm boundaries behind. As Table 1.3, "The NE Era vis-à-vis Traditional Computing/Networking," shows, Era IV refocuses the organizational targets from intra-industry systems (such as the airlines and travel agents communicating among themselves) to truly inter-industry and consumer-oriented systems. As we shall see later in this book, firms are stretching far beyond their traditional partners to include new suppliers and intermediaries in their domain of contacts, not to mention, of course, the end-consumers. The purposes of Era IV systems are varied; however, they are intended not for simple internal efficiencies, but to give the firm overall competitive advantages in all respects, including opening the doors for the firm to enter entirely new lines of business. These systems are increasingly being based on a network hand-shaking protocol (sender-receiver standardized format) known as TCP/IP (Transmission Control Protocol/Internet Protocol). The exact nature of this protocol must wait for a later elucidation in a chapter dealing with technical issues. For the moment, it is sufficient to point out that TCP/IP is the open systems protocol universally used by the Internet and the World Wide Web.

Table 1.3: The NE Era vis-à-vis the First Three Traditional Eras of Computing

Era	IT Focus	Generic Systems	Purpose	Primary IT
I: (1950s–1960s)	Organization	TPS, MIS	Efficiency	Mainframes
II: (1970s–1980s)	Individual	DSS, ES	Effectiveness	Minicomputers
III: (early 1980s–1990s)	Intra-industry	Customer Reservation Systems (CRS)	Strategic/Competitive Systems	Proprietary network connections; smarter terminals
IV: (1990s–present)	Inter-industry; ultimate consumers	Browsers, WWW, and Web page applications	Market penetration; new marketing channels; ventures into new businesses	Internet; servers; client software

▶ **CASE STUDY 1-2**

THE FDIC'S JOURNEY THROUGH THE FOUR ERAS OF IT

The banking industry has made significant strides in the utilization of information technology. It has migrated from pen and paper ledgers to punch-card tabulation machines to Internet-based applications. The Federal Deposit Insurance Corporation (FDIC) insures deposits at the 10,101 banks and savings associations in the United States. When one of those institutions fails, the FDIC returns assets to solvent financial institutions to avoid a collapse in the banking system. Because all federally insured institutions must report to the FDIC, the banking industry has had to keep pace with the use of information technology. The journey of the FDIC, from the systems of the 1950s and 1960s to an organization committed to today's deployment of internet-based applications, illustrates how information systems within the banking system have evolved.

In the 1950s and 1960s, during the first era of computer systems, the systems were focused on generating standard reports and on transaction processing for the organization. Organizations used mainframe computers, and the purpose of the existing MIS systems was to enhance efficiency throughout the organization. Decisions were made in a top-down fashion with all processes being regulated by the IT manager. Until 1965, when the FDIC purchased its own computer, the FDIC borrowed the Federal Reserve Board's IBM computers. Processing time was scheduled by the Federal Reserve in specific windows that the FDIC had to adhere to. The FDIC-owned computer was not up and running until 1967, at which time batch processing became the standard form of operation for analyzing bank data.

The second era of IT began in the 1970s and ended in the early 1980s. Information systems were built on time-sharing concepts, and, with the introduction of minicomputers, processes were filtered down from mainframe computers. In 1974, the FDIC installed remote terminals for selected supervisors to view online data. Batch processing continued at the FDIC until the mid 1980s when the system was upgraded to an online processing system. Minicomputers were purchased for specific employees to analyze data. The primary aim of these systems was to improve individual effectiveness.

During the late 1980s and 1990s, the third era, systems provided businesses with competitive advantage through IT. Internal organizations and functions were restructured to take advantage of IT's capability. The FDIC began networking computers in the late 1980s. As PCs were connected to the network, various geographic locations could be served simultaneously. Recognizing the expanded capabilities that a network provided, personal computers were purchased for most of the staff, and restructuring took place to take advantage of the IT network.

Today, the FDIC is testing cutting-edge "third-generation" wireless technology for high-speed transfer of data over mobile devices. This new technology will allow the FDIC to manage the due diligence process mandatory for troubled bank franchises from any location. David Sequeira, chief of corporate telecommunications at the FDIC, envisions doing away with the whole idea of an office in the future. The FDIC is developing communication strategies that will enable communication with customers of failed financial institutions, procedures of Internet Financial Institution Closings, and consulting and advisory services. Wireless technology and Internet-based solutions will allow the FDIC to secure online environments for project and transaction management and allow documents to be securely and instantly deployed to participating organizations.

Discussion:

1. The FDIC strategically partners with organizations from many sectors and many industries. How has the adoption of technology by partner organizations impacted the technological journey of the FDIC over the past 50 years?

2. How will the move to Era IV systems impact the services offered by the FDIC?

3. How will the implementation of wireless technology impact FDIC field workers in the future?

Sources:

Cash, Jr., J., F. McFarlen, J. McKenney, and L. Applegate. "The Challenge of Information Technology: Issues in Information Technology." in *Corporate Information Systems Management*. Richard D. Irwin, Inc., 1992, 10–11.

Inscoe, D. "Milestones in the Collection and Use of Data for Federal Deposit Insurance 1934–2001," FDIC. September 4, 2001. [Online] Available: http://www2.fdic.gov/hsob/milestones.pdf.

Metavante Providing FDIC With E-Commerce Technology Consulting. September 17, 2001. [Online] Available: http://www.metavante.com/newsroom/press/091701_1.jsp.

FDIC to Test "3G" Wireless Technology, http://www.washingtontechnology.com/news/16_8/business/16860-1.html

1.4 DEFINITIONS OF NE

We have placed NE in a historical context, which gives a lot of clues as to how one might ultimately define it. But to derive a single, comprehensive definition, there are definitional perspectives that stress the technical evolution of the phenomenon and others that look to its symbols, that is, the information-substitution principle that will be highlighted over and over again in this book. Finally, the organization itself will need to be redesigned to accommodate NE, and this transformation is another definition that must be weighed.

1.4.1 Technology-Based Definition of NE

It is appropriate to inaugurate a fuller definition of NE with a definition that hinges on the technology itself. The (r)evolution that has led to NE grew out of certain technical advances, and, as we just saw, these advances to a large extent defined the boundaries of the phenomenon. NE involves exchanges of information that are governed by the rules of open protocols such as the TCP/IP protocol. Although certain EDI and electronic funds transfer (EFT) exchanges have, and will continue to, take place using protocols that are not TCP/IP, these largely proprietary protocols will be replaced, over time, by TCP/IP. The universality of TCP/IP is what makes it so attractive as a network exchange language. No single firm or country owns it.

1.4.2 Information-Based Definition of NE

To flesh out our inclusive definition of NE, we need to consider additional aspects of what happened when computer systems evolved from Era III to Era IV. As firms extended their boundaries, they found that they were replacing informational processes for physical processes. This, it turns out, is a critical reason for why these systems were so dramatically different from traditional computing and networking. An example may help to illustrate what is meant here.

Dell Computers went online with their consumer sales in 1996.[21] Although they manufactured many of the components themselves to fill these online orders, they outsourced the making of monitors to Sony. The Dell NE system not only allows the firm to interact directly with consumers, but it also allowed them to tightly coordinate the orders so that monitors arriving from the Sony factory could be combined by third-party logistics firms such as UPS and FedEx with the rest of the customer's hardware and software order and delivered as a single unit. There are significant informational substitutions for physical processes that Dell employs. The need for a physical storefront where the hardware and software are displayed, and from which the customers choose products, has been eliminated. Instead, customers rely on the Dell online configurator system to assist them in choosing a set of components that work well together. Item specifications and pictures substitute for the physical elements.

Information can also enhance traditional products and services in ways that suggest that we are moving into radically different ways of thinking about where the real value of a customer connection lies. If, for example, the product that one sells is only a preliminary to a long-term relationship, where customer loyalty and belief in the firm and its brands are sustained, then the information that allows the firm to track the use of a product

---

[21]Rangan and Bell (1999).

through its life cycle could be more valuable than the original sale. Ives and Learmonth's customer resource life cycle suggests that product ownership passes through stages and that the firm can manage this relationship, as depicted in Table 1.4.

Table 1.4: Customer Resources Life Cycle (Ives and Learmonth 1984)

Customer Stage	Name	Description
1	Search	Helping the customer find how to acquire your product or service
2	Selection	Assisting customers in choosing your offerings
3	Acquisition	Making it easy and convenient for customers to acquire your product or service
4	Stewardship	Aiding customers in keeping track of your offering
5	Disposal	Helping customers salvage your product

Hewlett-Packard (HP) sells printers, but large profits to the firm do not materialize from the initial sale, which is not a high-margin proposition. The ability to track the product from its initial sale to later customer needs, such as printer toner and repair, allows HP to retain a competitive advantage. Online registration of the product during software installation is one way the firm develops a database of customer information for future use.

The electronic connection between an Otis elevator and a monitoring station allows the organization to take advantage of the "smart" product and to ensure that facilities run smoothly. This ability to remotely monitor the product, and help the customers act in the role of "stewards" of the product, serves both parties. Otis retains customer loyalty. The customers receive rapid servicing and proactive repairing of their elevators.

"Smart" products can be much simpler, however, and exploit connectivity even further. For instance, digital products and services downloaded from the Internet are, perhaps, inherently "smart" in that the organization can readily track the installation and registration of these products. A simple online registration (which also can gather highly useful customer information) accompanies most such programs and, in operational mode, the products can "report" back to the vendor when they are in need of updating or new versioning. AOL is a good example of a service that maintains the latest version of its products. When a customer is online, the software communicates with the AOL host; if enhancements are needed, the software informs the client that the service is being maintained. Of course, a dialogue box informs the client that no online minute charges are involved while the downloading of the upgrade and the installation is taking place.

Finally, "smart" products can be thought of as an extension of the information substitution principle discussed earlier. If AOL did not have "smart" software that knows to inquire about updates, updates would require a physical process. Customers would need to be sent CDs or disks in the mail. Or, even if the capabilities of the Internet were used, the customer would have to initiate the upgrade and its installation. "Smart" products and services "fix" themselves, and substitute for physical actions on the part of customers.

Tracking information as an information enhancement in the package delivery business is another example. UPS customers, for example, did not realize that they wanted this kind of information until they were presented with it. That is why the provision of new information to a customer is an experimental process in NE. Focus groups often elicit on what the customer thinks he or she needs, but are not useful in extracting information about their potential and future needs. NE systems can be built rapidly and beta-tested in the target population with lower risks and a greater return of information about the usefulness of the product or service.

To the firm, the substitution produces enormous cost advantages. In many cases, it can substitute for physical processes, which will be discussed at greater length in Chapter 2, "Principles of Networked Economy Businesses."

What is the overall definition of NE that combines the various perspectives we have been exploring? We have reached a point in the discussion where the definition can be advanced:

> Net-enhancement is commercial activity utilizing open network protocols like TCP/IP, in which information is typically substituted for physical processes.

Although it is likely that, over time, TCP/IP will decline, and possibly disappear, as the underlying network protocol for internal LANs and the Internet, the important point emphasized in this definition is that the protocol be universally available and not proprietary. We shall see later in Chapter 4, "Basic NE Infrastructure," that there are major advantages to the world economy if the Internet remains "open" from a technical standpoint. In Chapter 14, "Social and International Issues," the same matter will be investigated from a governance perspective.

1.4.3 Organizational Structure-Based Definition of NE

A third definition of NE focuses on how firms organize to do business. With respect to the structure of NE organizations, there is an obvious tie-in to the physical-informational dichotomy that we have been working with. NE firms are predisposed to focusing on informational core competencies and to outsourcing noncore physical assets and capabilities. Clearly, some firms are by their very nature heavily involved with the physical movement of goods and their transformations. Manufacturers such as auto companies and logistics firms such as overnight delivery services are inherently more labor- and equipment-intensive than firms like Yahoo. But this simple distinction misses the point.

Auto manufacturers are increasingly altering their internal business processes by making processes more information-intensive.[22] Firms that are not moving rapidly toward robotics and automated warehouses are simply not going to be competitive by the second decade of the twenty-first century. Toyota has successfully experimented with entire factories that have substituted machines for most of the processes involved in the assembling of autos. One of their plants in Japan was reputed to have only eight employees, most of whom were robotics maintenance engineers.

Leading-edge thinking in firms like UPS and FedEx has also led to advances in the use of information. Package tracking systems are legion in this industry, but the ability of these firms to coordinate orders from different sources and to deliver them as though they

[22]Autonomous (1999).

were a single purchase are just other small pieces of evidence about how quickly this industry is moving toward NE.

The following definition synthesizes all of the concepts we have been discussing thus far:

> Net-enhancement is commercial activity utilizing open network protocols like TCP/IP, in which information is typically substituted for physical processes, a transformation that leads to firms that are more and more virtual in their organizational structures.

1.4.4 Other Distinguishing Characteristics of NE

A firm that intends to adopt NE needs to consider the following "ideal type"[23] of a firm that has dedicated itself to a full-blown NE deployment. NE in such a firm will:

1. Adopt a global focus, both in terms of sourcing/supplying and selling.
2. Closely tie its IT to the organization's strategic positioning.
3. Avoid proprietary solutions and technologies whenever possible.
4. Examine the concept of full information visibility and selectively deploy it.
5. Create strong links to its customers through its proprietary data, which will be its main competitive advantage.

Many of these concepts will be discussed throughout the book. They are briefly mentioned here to give the reader a preview of coming attractions and to encourage thinking along these lines.

1.5 SCENARIO: ELECTRONICALLY WRINGING OUT COSTS IN AN AIRPORT VEHICLE RENTAL BUSINESS

To illustrate the ideas we have been discussing so far, let us imagine a typical firm operating worldwide and, assuming that top management and the board of directors were committed to the firm transforming itself, see how this firm would begin to evolve into an NE firm.

Internationally, most airports have vehicle rental companies. These firms often operate off-site, requiring customers to check in at a location on the airport grounds and then to shuttle to an off-site station where they are directed to their rental vehicle and given the keys. To ensure that thieves do not "shrink" the inventory of rentable vehicles, security guards are frequently posted at exits to check credentials and proper paperwork. This may be backup security in the case where keys are issued to the customer at check-in, but it is especially necessary when keys are left in vehicles that are inventoried in fence-enclosed lots.

There are many aspects of this business that are physical. The provision of vehicles, their cleaning and regular maintenance, the locales for check-in and pick-up, emergency road services, and ancillary products and services such as cell phone rental. Physical processes in

---

[23]"Ideal types" are Weberian descriptions of a "most like" form of a concept. Not all firms will demonstrate all characteristics of an "ideal type," but the more of these characteristics they do demonstrate, the closer they are to a true embodiment of the concept of NE.

many or most cases require human agents, so the more physical processes there are, the larger the personnel cost. For instance, check-in counters require check-in clerks. Provision of vehicles requires security guards at exits, for backup security, at least.

How can the firm take advantage of NE and its tendency to completely invert business models? If the top management understands principles of information substitution, they will begin to look for ways to replace physical processes with information that can be made available system-wide through the Web, for example. Disregarding their supply chain for the moment, a set of processes with which they could extract minimal prices in NE trading for new automobiles or maximal prices for salvage autos,[24] the interaction with the customer is a process that is already heavily laden with information. What is not efficient, though, is that this information is typically being gathered and regathered, confirmed and reconfirmed, all through labor-intensive processes and human intervention at particular physical locations.

Check-in is an information-gathering and confirmation process that does not have to be tied to a physical site or to a human assistant. Once customers have arrived at the airport, they are increasingly capable of communicating with the rental car firm either through kiosks distributed around the terminals or through the wireless Web. The firm's Web site must have a simple interface so that customers can navigate quickly to the page that relates to the reservation they have placed or, lacking a reservation, to the available vehicles at that location. But this is eminently doable.

What is being replaced is the check-in counter at the airport and the staffing of that counter. Ultimately, the number of check-in clerks at the off-site location will also be severely reduced. The information that clerks typically gather in person can either be entered by the customer via the Web or, preferably, simply be transferred over from the customer's reservation and history of transactions with the firm.

Once customers have reviewed an order online and confirmed choices such as the make and size of vehicle, options for gasoline purchase, extra insurance, cell phone, and the like, the order may be accepted via the digital signature issued by the customer's client software or via a light-pen at a kiosk.

Kiosks that are currently in service in many U.S. airports now issue a physical key to the customer. One can envision a day not far off when no physical keys or key cards are issued, but car entry devices read finger- or voice-prints to authenticate customer identities. Or, alternatively, the car could communicate via infrared signals with the customer's client machine or device, which would unlock the automobile as the customer was making his or her final approach to the vehicle.

Readable chips placed in scannable locations on each car in the fleet would allow firms to track when specific cars were leaving the lot and when they were arriving back in the lot. This kind of automated inventory control would greatly reduce the risk of in-lot security, for one; more to the point, it would allow the firm to utilize the fleet to its maximal capacity. The exact positioning of the vehicle in the cleaning and maintenance process as well as computer estimates as to its availability for renewed service (given the staffing on particular days, for example) should open up the inventory and allow management to derive maximal advantage for the fleet.

Competitive advantage would derive from more than customer perceptions of quicker and faster service, although this would certainly be a tangible benefit. In addition, it would come from more than lower costs in overhead and personnel. The real benefit of NE is the

---

[24]McKeown and Watson (1999).

new business model that emerges for interacting with customers and in binding customers to the firm. Web-based systems can deal with customers on a 24x7 basis and respond to them in a more "personal" way than human agents. If a good customer (a fact which a firm's computer systems can know and use in its interactions) wishes to change an order, and the new vehicle choice is not available, the system can be programmed to upgrade the vehicle based on available stock. Although human clerks can also be empowered to make such decisions, it is unlikely that they would still be physically present in the airport terminal at the moment of late arrival of Flight 542 from Stockholm at 3:00 A.M. A kiosk that simply dispenses keys or key cards would be available, and, what's more, it would be able to print out exact directions for retrieving the vehicle from a shared after-hours lot maintained by the consortium of rental companies in the terminal itself, for example.

It is obvious in such a scenario how a move toward removing physicality from the process could carry the firm into new competitive territory. Suppose that a group of cars cleaned were available at 6:00 P.M., but that the keys could only be rushed to the kiosk for deposit at 6:20 P.M. A good customer arriving at the kiosk at 6:01 P.M. could have been assigned or upgraded to the vehicle of his or her choice, but the physical key was not present, so the request had to be denied.

Vehicles entered and operated by unique identifying characteristics of the driver, such as finger- or voice-prints, would require neither check-in nor kiosk. The authenticating code would be directly beamed to the assigned vehicle via the wireless Web after the customer confirmed the order. This could be carried out during deplaning or during the walk down the halls of the terminal. Exact directions for picking up the vehicle could be forwarded directly to the customer's Web communicator.

The Star Trek feel of this extended scenario may not be as far-fetched as one might believe, as we shall see later. The important point at this stage in learning about NE is that top management needs to think in terms of giving customers direct access to information that will both improve quality of the service they are getting and, at the same time, represent this new plateau of customer relationship. Customer needs should be foremost so that rapid response systems that are Web-based and computer-orchestrated must be available to global customers at all hours and in all places. Access through the firm's Web site will allow customers to adjust their own orders or, if needed, contact and speak, in either online text or online voice, with call center associates. These call center associates can assist by redirecting or pushing relevant pages to the customer or explaining these in a one-on-one chat session tied to particular pages. Call centers will be in operation 24x7 for global firms, and will be labor-intensive, but the result will be heightened customer loyalty and new business.

What is the business model of this reengineered firm? The business model focuses on a direct-to-consumer model that puts resources in place to ensure that customers can move directly from the door of their airplane to the door of the rental vehicle with a bare minimum of physical steps or stages in between. We would argue that this is the NE vision that should drive change in avant-garde firms in this industry.

1.6 KEY TRENDS

There are a number of trends in the development of NE that will place the scenario we have just discussed in its proper perspective. Microlevel trends change so rapidly and such forecasts are so unreliable that it make sense to discuss only fundamental or long-term trends in a textbook such as this.

1.6.1 Resistance to Change

There is little doubt, for example, that resistance to new information systems will continue to characterize adoption decisions in the future as they have in the past. There is an inherent conservatism in people's psychosocial makeup that makes resistance to change feel natural.

Clearly, if top managers are reluctant to adopt new procedures and the accompanying information systems that radically reform and reshape their businesses, the NE revolution will be hindered.[25] Likewise, knowledge workers must warm to using the Web for gathering information and for interacting with other firms and customers. In the study that we will be reporting on in Chapter 3, resistance to the use of Web-based systems characterized both managers and knowledge workers. They were willing to admit that NE was a dominant trend and that it would inevitably change their industries, but they were clear in their feelings that they did not approve of, nor did they like, this change. Moreover, they were adamant that their organizations were not changing quickly into virtual organizations, which they admitted were necessary to foster the move to NE.

One of the undeniable consequences of resistance to change is that transitions take much longer than expected. The migration from traditional business models to NE models is going to take a great deal longer than most people predict. Even when resistance is minimal, the conversion of legacy systems is nontrivial. As we shall see in Chapter 12, the meshing of systems geared to traditional physical processes and those geared to informational processes is not always easy.

Is being ready to embrace change necessarily or always a good thing? There are reasons to believe that some changes are not useful and can actually lead to harmful outcomes in an organization.[26] The concept of Internet speed will be discussed at greater length later in the book. What we can say at this point is that Internet "speed" is a concept that innovations on the Internet occur more rapidly than in traditional business environments. This may be true, but it also means that many traditional organizations are not going to be caught up in fads and fashions that will burn brightly and then fade as their inability to produce value becomes clear. An example of such a fad is "push" technologies. These technologies send unsolicited Web pages to users. The pages may be in response to a general user profile of desired information, but the specific pages themselves are not called for by the user.

Whereas some inventions fail once and for all, other innovations find a second life. The timing for their introduction was initially not right, and the critical need they fulfilled only became obvious later. FAX is a good example of this. FedEx spent over U.S. $100 million promoting their FAX service only to find that it took another three years after they shut down this line of business for fax machines to become a rage. For these reasons, push technologies are discussed later as a promising technology, even though they have already been tried once and have failed.

The real downside to resistance to change is that resisters to change are typically late in adopting innovations. The mean time to consider a new approach to doing business is shrinking, and the late adopters will not just be late, but will never get in the game. There are reasons to believe that "late adopters" of technological innovations will never be able to accept the level of failure that may be required for a true NEO (Net-enhanced organiza-

[25]Straub and Klein (2001).
[26]Straub and Karahanna (1998).

tion). Therefore, the ability to innovate quickly requires firms to accept failure as part of the process of doing business. Organizations that are not able to accept a true R&D (research and development) mentality, which expects a certain percentage of failures, will ultimately not succeed in the Internet Age.

1.6.2 Moore's Law

Over the last few decades, computer systems have demonstrated a relationship between price and performance that has become known as Moore's Law.[27] Figure 1.6 demonstrates a logical extension of this relationship.

Over any given 10-year period, the capabilities of computers appear to increase tenfold, while the pricing for those capabilities decreases tenfold. If this law had applied to automobile manufacturing and sales, a Cadillac in the year 2000 would cost about $5. With the exception of quantum size limitations, which are still not in the immediate future, we can expect that this relationship will continue to persist through at least the first half of the twenty-first century.

What are the implications of this trend for NE? Network routers and servers, fiber optic transmission lines, clients and servers equipped with wireless functionality, and NE software, including application software, should all be subject to this same law. This means that bandwidths will increase at the same time that prices for these services will fall. There can be little doubt that the pricing of international calls over the Internet, for example, are just a fraction of what they were several years ago. This trend is also revealed in the extremely low cost of e-mail in the present era.

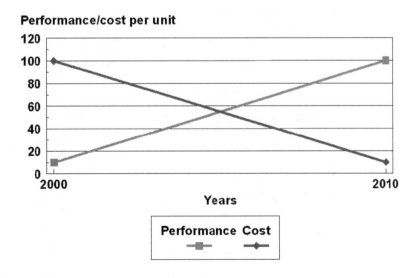

Figure 1.6   Cost-Performance Relationships in Computing Power

[27]Schaller (1997)

Focus on NE: Global Positioning Satelite (GPS) Applications

According to strategic research (Frost & Sullivan "North American Global Positioning Satellites Applications Market") the total North American global positioning satellite (GPS) application markets are estimated to grow from $366.2 million in 1996 to $3.5 billion by 2003. The GPS market is expected to more than double within the next three years as a result of the federal government removing selective availability. GPS receivers are becoming accurate to within 20 meters. The expanding technology will benefit consumers who use location data by increasing efficiency with GPS-based digital maps. This increase in efficiency will permit more-accurately pinpointed 911 calls, locate mobile equipment, and monitor supply-line product movement. GPS can provide services for more personal locator applications also. How would you feel about having a dime-sized computer chip implanted under your skin that uses a GPS to track your travels? Engineers are working on a prototype of this technology, called Digital Angel, that could help to locate escaped criminals, soldiers in combat, or even your wandering pet. The body heat–powered chip can also monitor the wearer's heartbeat and other vital signs. If your grandmother had a medical emergency, Digital Angel (www.digitalangel.net) would alert a medic instantly. The technology consists of a miniature sensor device, designed to be implanted just under the skin, that captures and wirelessly transmits the wearer's vital body-function data to an Internet-integrated ground station. In addition, the antenna receives information regarding the location of the individual from the GPS satellite. Both sets of data—medical information and location—are then wirelessly transmitted to the ground station and made available on Web-enabled desktops, laptops, or wireless devices.

Sources:

http://www.spacedaily.com/news/gps-97c.html

http://www.aero.org/publications/GPSPRIMER/EvryDyUse.html

http://www.findarticles.com/cf_0/m1590/12_57/72868720/p1/

article.jhtml?term=%2BGlobal+%2BPositioning+%2BSystem+%2BUsage

How does Moore's Law impact the definitions of NE that we have developed? The ability of firms to substitute information for physical processes with greater and greater power for less and less money means that this element of NE will continue to be viable for years to come. TCP/IP is the dominant transmission protocol, and a great deal of research and development in this protocol will result in incremental and large-scale improvements that will drive progress in NE. TCP/IP will eventually be replaced, in all likelihood, but that may take a long while and, in the meantime, improvements will speed up the Internet. Finally, the ability of firms to use advances in technology (at lower absolute costs of investment) will permit them to use Web-based systems to switch rapidly between suppliers and to coordinate large-scale projects. This will heighten the desirability of making the firm more virtual.

1.6.3 Growth in NE Sectors

There is little doubt that all sectors of NE activity are growing. The only issue is whether B2B will remain the source of the greatest investment or if B2C (business to customer) will eventually overtake it. The growth rates have, in all likelihood, tapered off to mere double-digit growth rates, but these still healthy rates indicate continuing strength.

The growth of the Internet, for example, has been primarily in the more-industrialized societies, but at some point in time there will be a large-scale infusion of this technology in the developing world. Double digit rates have characterized the phenomenon for the last several years, and forecasts are that this represents sustainable growth. By the same token, sales of PCs and servers vary over the years, but were steadily rising even in downturns of the industry as a whole. In the year 2001, PC sales may have actually declined, but the long-term prospects of computing are still strong.

What are the ramifications of this Internet growth for NE? On the one hand, there is an indication that a first-mover advantage cannot be maintained long-term in the Networked Economy, partly because of the wide availability of basic infrastructure technologies implied by these across-the-board growth rates. If technology is cheap, robust, and widely available, the competitive advantage conferred by technology alone is not significant. This subject will be explored in much greater detail in Chapter 7, "Competitive NE Strategies." For the moment, it is sufficient to note that there is certainly a critical mass of equipment and software[28] to enable NE and that these growth rates will insure its long-term diffusion through the world.

[28]Markus (1987).

1.7 SECOND OR CONSOLIDATING WAVE OF NE (2000-?)

One trend that needs to be dealt with separately is the fall-off in dot.coms in the worldwide stock markets in the year 2000. The list of major and minor failures is too long to enumerate. Some of these firms were well capitalized, such as boo.com with over U.S. $100M. Others were well connected in a marketplace that was surely not saturated. The U.S. NAS-DAQ index, which is heavily laden with technology sticks, declined 40% from the turn of the year to the fall of that year.

It is tempting to overinterpret short-term stock market variability as meaningful. Nevertheless, there is probably enough evidence about this fall-off to picture this as an indication of the larger phenomenon of stages of growth of technological innovations. In the early days of computer mainframes, Harvard's Nolan offered an explanation for the S-curve of growth that had been noticed in the technology infusion or internalization rates in corporations.[29] As Figure 1.7 shows, an initial exponential growth period is followed by an era of consolidation and control, where investments are more carefully scrutinized and rationalized. A second spurt of growth is followed thereafter by another period of reflection and caution, and so on.

The initial phase of technology innovation in NE could be characterized as a period of "contagion," because dot.coms were springing up all over the world and initial public offers (IPOs) for nearly any Internet stock were inevitably oversubscribed.

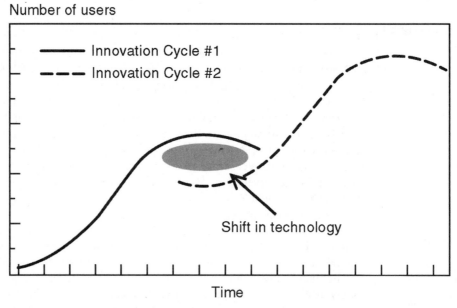

Figure 1.7   Nolan's Stages of Growth Model

[29]Nolan (1973). Such S-curves are common as descriptions of product cycles and are used by marketers to describe the cycle of product sales. After a slow initial period, sales move briskly, taper off, and start to fall when the next version of the product or a brand new product design is introduced.

Once the period of "contagion" has passed, organizations move into a mode of controlling the technology and dispersion to users until there is a technology transition. Following the "dot.bomb" failures, it was inevitable that organizations would engage in heavier-than-usual control of these investments. The danger then was in underinvesting and letting the competition leapfrog with new technical capabilities.

One thing is clear. We will have business cycles in the future, which, much like the past, will impact levels of business investment and innovation. NE offers an opportunity to give companies that are willing to take risks an edge. Downturns are times when most businesses are contracting. Innovating in NE in these times is countercyclical and could distinguish the strategy of a firm as far-sighted and lead to long-term competitiveness.

1.8 SUMMARY

Chapter 1 follows the migration of firms from traditional commerce to NEOs or e-commerce. Certain organizational and environmental conditions were necessary before this phenomenon could occur. Important environmental drivers include the digitization of media, an increase in the availability of inexpensive telecommunications, and widespread diffusion of computers. Organizational drivers include globalization and commoditization, changing organizational models, rapidly shrinking cycle times, development of intelligent products and services, and demand for customized products and services.

Originally, the concept of networks and information theory laid the essential groundwork for NE to evolve. Important features such as the distance between senders and receivers, the possibility of multiple senders and/or receivers, and the possibility of multiple networks provided the technical factors necessary for success. However, organizations had to adapt to the idea that the exchange of information with other organizations could create efficiencies in tracking goods and services, producing goods and services, and decision making. It could also be instrumental in creating new strategic and network alliances.

Three eras of computing existed before the stage was set for NE to develop, as Table 1.5 shows.

Table 1.5: The NE Era vis-à-vis Three Traditional Eras of Computing

Era	IT Focus	Generic Systems	Purpose	Primary IT
I: (1950s–1960s)	Organization	TPS, MIS	Efficiency	Mainframes
II: (1970s–1980s)	Individual	DSS, ES	Effectiveness	Minicomputers
III: (early 1980s–1990s)	Intra-industry	Customer Reservation Systems (CRS)	Strategic/Competitive Systems	Proprietary network connections; smarter terminals

Table 1.5: The NE Era vis-à-vis Three Traditional Eras of Computing (Continued)

Era	IT Focus	Generic Systems	Purpose	Primary IT
IV: (1990s–present)	Inter-industry; ultimate consumers	Browsers, WWW and Web page applications	Market penetration; new marketing channels; ventures into new businesses	Internet; servers; client software

NE breaks through the limits of the first three eras by leaving organizational boundaries behind. Era IV systems are designed to improve market penetration and diversify existing businesses into new businesses. These systems are intended to give a firm overall competitive advantage in all respects.

To derive a single, comprehensive definition of NE or e-commerce, one must look at three basic dimensions. The technology-based definition involves the governing rules of the TCP/IP protocol. The information-based definition includes the substitution of informational processes for physical processes. The organizational-structure-based definition includes an organization's ability to create a virtual organization. Other distinguishing characteristics of NEOs are firms that are dedicated to full-blown e-commerce deployment.

Key, long-term NE trends to consider include resistance to change, the inverse relationship between price and performance (Moore's Law), growth in B2C and B2B e-commerce sectors and the inevitability of business ups and downs, as illustrated by the fall-off in dot.coms in the worldwide stock markets.

KEY TERMS

B2B: Business-to-business commerce—commercial transactions enacted between two businesses.

B2C: Business-to-consumer commerce—commercial transactions enacted between a business and an individual.

Commoditization: The standardization of products and services so that differences between them are not perceived as differentiators by customers.

De-layering: As organizations are downsized, managers must communicate with more subordinates, creating greater pressure for communication efficiency and greater potential for stress caused by increased miscommunication.

Digitization: The process of capturing content in bits rather than in a physical form in a particular medium.

E-Commerce: Commercial activity utilizing open network protocols, in which information is typically substituted for physical processes, which leads firms toward virtual organizational structures. Terms used in this text for e-commerce are "Net-enablement" and "Net-enhancement."

Empowerment: Increased exchange of information among workers within and across work groups and governance rules that allow delegation of decision making to lower levels of the organization.

Globalization: The ability of businesses to operate freely and with minimal restraints across national borders.

Moore's Law: Computing power increases tenfold over a decade as the cost of computing drops by the same value.

Informating: Managing the data flow that results from data exchanges between a firm and its customers.

Partnering: Forming strategic alliances with partners who can complement core competencies.

TCP/IP: Transmission control protocol/Internet protocol, the suite of communications protocols used to connect hosts and clients on the Internet.

Telework: Performing work in locations remote from a central office.

Virtual teams: Ad hoc task forces, teams, and committees, comprised of workers in different functions and in different locations.

REVIEW QUESTIONS

1. Organizations should avoid fad or fashions in strategies and management practices. List at least two reasons why organizations should avoid such practices.
2. List three environmental drivers of e-commerce.
3. What are the organizational drivers responsible for e-commerce? List four.
4. Define the difference between "media" and "content."
5. How will digital media affect our capability for technological innovation?
6. What is the major difference between traditional media and digital media?
7. Why is digitization an important prerequisite for e-commerce?
8. What are the barriers to worldwide affordable telecommunications?
9. Why has diffusion of computing been slower in developing countries?
10. Why is globalization an important factor of e-commerce?
11. How does commoditization impact e-commerce?
12. Why does empowerment of workers require increased exchange of information?
13. Define what is meant by *informating*.
14. How does de-layering impact an organizational model?
15. Why do organizations seek strategic partnering?
16. Define a virtual team.
17. How can e-commerce affect business process cycle times?

TOPICS FOR DISCUSSION

1. Management practices for e-commerce organizations differ in some ways from traditional firms. Discuss the implications of new forms of organizations and changing organizational practices on the way in which e-commerce firms organize themselves, relate to their employees, and network with other firms.

2. A key component of the organizational adoption of technology is the background and attitude toward technology of top management. Discuss how management decision making for e-commerce organizations affect innovation and productivity in firms and how they shape growth in e-commerce organizations.

3. Organizations are changing the traditional organizational models that were used in previous eras of computing. Describe the strategies, technological capabilities, and management skills required in today's e-commerce organizational models.

4. A critical success factor in developing successful B2B e-commerce organizations is forming strategic alliances. Discuss how strategic alliances impact innovation and diffusion of technology in organizations.

5. Knowledge and human assets are widely viewed as a key competitive factor in determining performance and growth in organizations. How will Era IV systems accomplish the management of these assets in the future?

6. Digitization of media is causing a revolution in the electronic transmission of data. Discuss ways in which this development will impact further convergence of existing and future technologies

7. A key trend in e-commerce is the falloff of dot.com organizations. With world events, unanticipated economic shifts and the rise and fall of major players constantly reshaping the business environment, discuss how an e-commerce organization can achieve execution of strategy when the "givens" keep changing.

8. Cybernetics is the science of communication and control. Discuss how an organizational model for a NEO would implement principles of communications and control in the design of enterprise-wide systems.

9. Discuss the impact of resistance to change on the ability of organizations to adapt to the adoption of new technologies and business practices.

10. Consider the entertainment industry and the distribution of entertainment products. Discuss the ways in which this industry could utilize full e-commerce deployment, and describe the barriers to achieving this goal.

INTERNET EXERCISES

1. Choose three countries of your choice. Create an Excel chart showing the change in number of ISPs over the last three years.

2. Choose a destination and plan a trip! Prepare a spreadsheet to compare costs for your trip from two Internet sources.

3. Configure your new networked home computer system from the Dell Web site.

4. Find a "smart" product on the Internet and describe its capabilities.

5. Locate excerpts from Nicholas Negroponte's book *Being Digital* on the Internet. Choose an available online chapter and summarize the content.

6. Choose a company Web site on the Internet. Describe the information given on the home page.

7. Visit the Census Bureau E-status Web site and determine which industry has the highest e-commerce percent of total value.

8. Wells Fargo has existed for over 150 years. In that time, it has transformed itself to keep pace with the needs of its customers. Align the historical timeline with the four eras of IT.

9. Visit an auto rental Web site. Investigate the services offered.

TEAM EXERCISES

1. Have your group choose an industry. Prepare a report describing how the environmental and organizational drivers discussed in this chapter have affected that industry. Include predictions about how the industry may continue to change because of these factors.

2. Select a company currently not engaged in e-commerce and analyze how the company can be transformed into a NEO. Outline how the human factor can be reduced or eliminated. Describe the types of technology that can be implemented and the potential savings. Present your recommendations as if you were a team of consultants hired by the company to look into the company's NE capabilities.

3. Determine how a potential merger between AOL/Time Warner and Sony Records can transform the media-related industry (i.e., movies and music) into a profitable business using e-commerce to satisfy the originating artist, the customer, and applicable copyright and intellectual property laws. What existing component will be most negatively affected by the merger?

4. Visit the Circuit City, CompUSA, and Office Depot Web sites. Prepare a comparative analysis of the products and services offered at each Web site.

5. Resistance to change can be a major factor in the rate of adoption of technological innovations. Prepare a PowerPoint presentation on the factors of resistance to change in e-commerce. Include suggestions on how to overcome this resistance.

INTERNET RESOURCES

System On a Chip (http://www.lsilogic.com/about/stw/lsiprocess/intro.html): This presentation by LSI Logic will guide you through the process of creating an ASIC (application specific integrated circuit) chip. These chips are used for many of the "smart products" we have today.

Unisys (http://www.strategic-alliances.org/slideshows/Summit2001Scottsdale/CurtisUnisys/ index.htm): A PowerPoint presentation by Cheryl Callahan of Unisys on Corporate Alliances/Joint Partner Planning

Data Indicators for "Coopetition" in the New Economy (http://www.neweconomyindex. org/section1_page07.html)

REFERENCES

Abrahamson, E. "Management Fashion." *Academy of Management Review,* 21, 1 (1996), 254–285

Abrahamson, E. "Managerial Fads and Fashions: The Diffusion and Rejection of Innovations." *Academy of Management Review,* 16, 3, July 1991, 586–612.

Bartlett, C.A., and S. Ghoshal. *Managing Across Borders: The Transnational Solution*, Harvard Business School Press, Boston, 1998.

Heeks, R. "Global Software Outsourcing to India by Multinational Corporations." In Palvia, P., S. Palvia, and E. Roche, eds. *Global Information Technology and Systems Management: Key Issues and Trends*, Ivy League Publishing, Nashua, NH, 1996, 365–392.

Ives, B., and G. P. Learmonth. "Information Systems as a Competitive Weapon." *Communications of the ACM*, 27, 12, December 1984, 1193–1201.

Jaworski, B., E. Litwin, W. Miller, and K. White. "The Evolution of Ernie—The On-Line Business Consultant." Produced by Marshall School of Business and Ernst and Young LLP, 1998. [Online] Available: http://www.trinity.edu/rjensen/000aaa/ernie.htm and http://ernie.ey.com/

Keller, T., and F. Dansereau. "Leadership and Empowerment: A Social Exchange Perspective." *Human Relations*, 48, 2, February 1995, 127–146.

Markus, M. L. "Toward a 'Critical Mass' Theory of Interactive Media Universal Access, Interdependence, and Diffusion" *Communication Research*, 14, 5, October 1987, 491–511.

Maznevski, M. L., and K. M. Chudoba. "Bridging Space over Time: Global VirtualTeam Dynamics and Effectiveness." *Organization Science*, 11, 5 (2000), 473–492.

Nolan, R. L. "Managing the Computer Resource: A Stage Hypothesis." *Communications of the ACM*, 16, 7, July 1973, 399–405.

Negroponte, N. *Being Digital*, Knopf: Distributed by Random House, New York, 1995.

Rangan, V. K., and M. Bell. "Dell Online." Case Study 598116, Harvard University, March 1999.

Shannon, C. E., and W. Weaver. *The Mathematical Theory of Communication*, University of Illinois Press, Urbana, IL, 1949.

Straub, D., and R. Watson. "Transformational Issues in Researching IS and Net-enabled Organizations." *Information Systems Research*, 12, 4, December 2001, 337–345.

Straub, D. W., D. Hoffman, B. Weber, and C. Steinfield. "Measuring e-Commerce in Net-Enabled Organizations." *Information Systems Research*, 13, 2, June 2002, 115–124.

Tapscott, D. *Digital Economy: Promise and Peril in the Age of Networked Intelligence*, McGraw-Hill, New York, 1996.

Watad, M. M., and F. J. DiSanzo. "Case Study: The Synergism of Telecommuting and Office Automation." *Sloan Management Review*, 41, Winter 2000, 85–96.

Zuboff, S. *In the Age of the Smart Machine*, Basic Books, New York, 1988.

2

PRINCIPLES OF NETWORKED ECONOMY BUSINESSES

APPRECIATING THE UNDERLYING ECONOMICS OF THE NETWORKED ECONOMY

Why do managers need to understand the economic factors that will be driving the economy of the future? What are these factors? There are principles that seem to be at the heart of what we will be referring to as the Networked Economy that mean that managers must become aware of the changing cost structures and substitution effects brought about by the Internet. How can firms and other organizations begin to rethink their strategies to accommodate these inevitabilities? These are some of the questions that will be dealt with in this chapter.

LEARNING OBJECTIVES FOR THIS CHAPTER

- To understand the economic paradigm shift taking place in the Networked Economy
- To understand the three principles of emerging economic realities for e-commerce
- To describe novel sources of income in the Networked Economy
- To explain returns of scale in the Networked Economy and the Old Economy
- To compare and contrast features of a Networked Economy firm with an Old Economy firm
- To analyze production, transaction, and exchange costs for NEOs
- To recognize novel sources of income for Networked Economy firms

▶ *CASE STUDY 2-1*

STAPLES, INC., AND B2C MARKETING

The first Staples store was founded and opened in May 1986 in Brighton, Massachusetts. The company has nearly 1400 stores worldwide, a Web site (staples.com), catalogs, and Staples Direct. From the beginning, Staples marketed aggressively to consumers and small businesses; however, Staples Inc., faced the challenge of marketing to their customers through three sales channels: (1) online, (2) catalog, and (3) direct sales. Staples, Inc., needed a system that allowed marketers to analyze, monitor, and predict what products were bought through all three channels. They were also interested in learning customer buying trends and in determining response to promotions. The information was vitally important to the company because it would allow the company to target promotions of specific products, through a specific channel, to a specific customer.

Staples's marketing division invested in a combination of SAS software and Hewlett-Packard servers to conduct sophisticated tracking and analysis of customers' buying habits. The company currently has accumulated information on about 10 million customers from previous business transactions and manages hundreds of thousands of records. Through analysis of this information, they are able to predict which products their future customers will buy and in what quantity. They are also able to analyze how customers find out about products and can more effectively decide the best way to market their products.

The dynamic activities involved in marketing allow for other areas of improvements. For instance, sales forecasts can be completed on a daily basis for the nearly one thousand stores located in the United States. Inventories can be stocked with the right products. Revenue projections and growth strategies are more accurate. New locations for stores can be located and marketed to specific areas.

Any business with a B2C marketing strategy must focus on satisfying customer needs and pleasing customers. Mr. Fuller, director of marketing analysis at Staples, understands this important principle and states: "Our goal is to understand our customers better so that we can provide the products they want with the marketing vehicle that they respond to best." This perspective provides a strategic advantage over the competition and provides a win/win situation for the customer and Staples, Inc. The customers take advantage of the promotions and the business becomes more profitable. In addition, customers get better service and feel that they are receiving better service because promotions are better matched to their buying trends.

Customer loyalty and relationship building is an important aspect of a business to customer-oriented organization. Staples, Inc., has been able to achieve customer loyalty and relationship through the building of a marketing system designed to provide customer satisfaction.

Discussion:

1. Describe the role of information technology in running Staples's business.

2. What are some of the advantages of B2C marketing in an organization in the Networked Economy?

Sources:

Chung, S., and M. Sherman. "Emerging Marketing." *The McKinsey Quarterly*, 2 (2002).

Fuller, W. "Staples: Loyal Customers and Killer Marketing." *SAS Com Magazine*, October, 2001. Retrieved September 14, 2002, from the World Wide Web: http://www.sas.com/news/success/staples.html

May, P. "Customers Relations for E-Commerce." in *The Business of Ecommerce: From Corporate Strategy to Technology*, published by Cambridge University Press, 1 (2002), 214–220. Retrieved September 14, 2002, from the World Wide Web: http://www.fathom.com/fks/catalog/feature.jhtml?story_id=35060&featurePageNumber=2

2.1 INTRODUCTION

This chapter will discuss the underlying economic principles of Net-enhanced businesses and processes. Many of these have already been implied in the definitions of NE above. Nevertheless, it is critical to understand these principles in order to see why e-ventures represent an economic paradigm shift and why they ultimately succeed or not.

2.2 THE ECONOMIC PARADIGM SHIFT IN NE

Paradigm shifts occur when the very basis of doing business changes. For example, the industrial revolution brought about a paradigm shift when machines replaced human labor in the production process. In the information revolution that we have seen unfold over the last several decades, a particular hybrid of machines and human intelligence, that is, computers, replaced humans in repetitive processing of information. As we have discussed earlier in Chapter 1, physical processes in the NE revolution are being replaced by information shared via networks.

The NE paradigm shift has resulted in two major changes to be discussed in this chapter. First, the cost of doing business has been lowered by orders of magnitude. By this we mean that it is frequently possible to dramatically lower the cost of carrying out a business process in the value chain, to less than 1% of what it cost previously, for instance. Cost savings of this magnitude are perhaps as incredible at this time as the ability of machines at the beginning of the industrial revolution to deliver, for a similar size and cost, one hundred times as much power as a human being. We know today that this machine-human ratio in machine tools has grown to differences in orders of magnitude in the hundreds of thousands.

The NE revolution elevates differences in orders of magnitude to the millions and even billions. Not only are computers that much faster at processing digits than human beings, but they are capable of perfect accuracy, a statement which is not true of mechanical devices (machine tools) compared to humans. Cost savings are not yet in this range, but they are certainly dramatic. The first signs of this are in the small staffs of the surviving and successful dot.coms and the large number of customers they are serving. The economic indicators of this trend would be in the ratio of revenue to employees, for example.

The second major change in economics is the complex interrelationships between organizations and their stakeholders. The simple model of the firm relating to suppliers and customers has completely broken down in the NE era. Firms now have intricate linkages to those supplying them with raw goods and those who are performing some parts of the value chain for them. They also hire phalanxes of intermediaries to assist in fulfilling the order and delivery processes. Competitors are not ruled out as possible partners in given enterprise initiatives. And customers are now viewed in the larger light of sometimes being customers, sometimes outsourcers, sometimes investors, and sometimes suppliers. In short, the modern virtual organizations are a patchwork quilt of core competencies that include the ability to coordinate multiple partners in creating products and services, moving them to the customers, and delivering after-sales support. A detailed discussion of virtual organizations and their economic power is found in Chapter 10.

What is the Networked Economy? The Old Economy is often identified with firms that focus on traditional sources of revenue, such as manufacturing and value-added services associated with physical goods. Heavily information intensive, Networked Economy firms focus on information value-added services, ICT (information and communications technologies), or other high technology offerings. If there is a paradigm shift, then it must be occurring in the domain of the changes to intellectual creation and substitution of information for physical processes that we have talked about.

It is clear that the production and servicing of physical goods and machines will be with us for the foreseeable future. But even firms that are now locked into making money through physical assets can become more flexible by forming relationships with other firms that have certain physical processes as their core competency. UPS specializes in delivering packages the last logistical mile. The vast majority of firms are incapable of performing this service half as well or as cheaply as UPS. UPS is becoming a virtual warehouse for other firms and, again, unless a firm has a core competency in inventory management, Networked Economy firms will shed these physical assets and hire package delivery firms to handle these kinds of deliveries.

Not every firm can or should become entirely networked, eliminating all or most of its physical processes. Even if a machine for converting energy directly into products and services were to be widely available, we would still need machines to make the machines to make the machines, in an infinite regression. But where information can short-circuit material processes, it should.

What is different in the current milieu is that information is not merely supplementing physical processes; it is replacing it. In the four eras of computing discussed in the last chapter, the first era was the attachment of information to transactions. The automation of clerical functions with an electronic cash register, for example, does not mean that the check-out process is still not highly physical. The addition of computerized information about the items sold meant that management was able to more carefully track inventory levels and to avoid stock-outs.

The replacement of the physical activities in the check-out process that is occurring in the Internet age is wholly different from simple automation. When a file server acts in the role of the clerk, the physical activity has been dramatically reduced. There is no physical bar code scanning required on a transactional Web site, for instance, nor human presence needed for electronic payment unless there are serious problems with the electronic side of the transaction. If the product or service being acquired is digital in nature, the computer can also handle the delivery of the items. The replacement of the physical process with symbolic manipulations and file transfers by a computer represents a many million-fold increase in capabilities.

This is the quintessential shift in economics with the coming of the Internet.

Focus on NE: Chip Technology

Smart products! Are you ready for your refrigerator to tell you that you've had too many calories for the day? Or a house that runs your bath for you on your way home from work? Maybe a robotic pet? All are possible with embedded software. In layman's terms, embedded software is software that has been etched onto a chip. It is also referred to as a "System on a Chip." Embedded software appears in everything from telephones and pagers to systems for medical diagnostics, climate control, and manufacturing. Embedded software constantly interacts with the environment by way of audio, visual, tactile, and radio sensors to perform tasks based on the decision-making program embedded on the chip. Embedded software has the advantage of being robust, compact, resistant to virus attacks or other bugs, low cost, capable of rapid processing, and miniaturist. And it can easily be networked!

2.2.1 Dramatic Reductions in Production and Exchange Costs

The most obvious economic difference between Old Economy traditional bricks and mortar business processes versus Networked Economy "clicks" or "clicks and bricks" business processes is the lower cost of doing business. The terminology here helps us to sort out one main difference. The overhead in running a warehouse or a retail business is directly tied to the "bricks" that are required to shelter goods and personnel, and upon which one must maintain security, insurance, and so forth. Physical facilities and machines are expensive, as are the personnel needed to staff such facilities.

Now imagine an online storefront where sale goods are displayed on virtual shelves and questions about these goods are answered through an expert computer system. Theoretically, the store can be selling to hundreds and thousands of customers with computer systems that cost little more than a few dozen employees, at most. Assuming for the moment that the systems are "flexible," "robust," and "scalable" (these terms will be explored later in the Chapter 4, "Basic NE Infrastructure"), customers can be served on a global basis 24 hours seven days a week (24x7). It is clear that the physical experience of shopping in stores is not equivalent to shopping at hp.com, for instance. Nevertheless, there are trade-offs that make the online experience as viable as a physical experience, and if these can be substitutes or better than substitutes in the customers' mind, then the costs of running a business are astonishingly lower for firms at their end of the exchange.

Besides the substitution of information for physical facilities, another way to lower production costs occur through the intensive substitution of information for physical processes. Let's take the example of the Dutch flower industry. The method of grading and inspecting flower lots is shown in Figure 2.1.

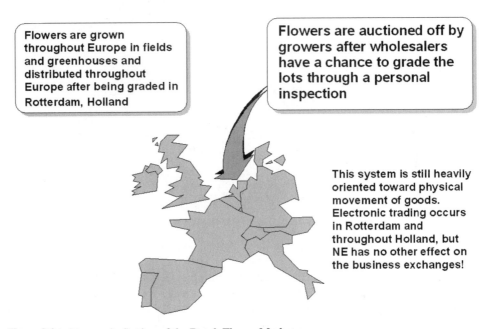

Figure 2.1 Economic Setting of the Dutch Flower Market

In this industry, flowers are flown from the locale of production (i.e., where the flowers are grown) to the auction in Rotterdam, Holland. At this point, they are graded and priced for the market. Buyers can inspect the quality of the flowers and determine their bids for certain lots. Once the flowers are purchased, they are flown to destinations for sale by retailers.

The physical elements of this process are illustrated in Figure 2.2. The process is labor- and capital-intensive in that people move from lot to lot, and the investment is delayed until lots are purchased and delivered.

The Dutch Flower Market is in the process of reengineering this cycle to eliminate the need for the physical inspection by buyers. A computerized auctioning system known as buyer-at-a-distance auction (BADA) has been successful in permitting off-site grading and pictorial displays of flowers via network connections.[1] Coupled with ratings by trusted sources who are on-site, the BADA application gives inspectors enough information to bid on the lots remotely and to negotiate other terms online.

---

[1] Van Heck and Ribbers (1997).

Figure 2.2   Example of Movement of Goods in Dutch Flower Market

Figure 2.3 shows how the online system can eliminate part of the physical chain by substituting information about flower lots for the in-person inspection. The Dutch flower industry profits by facilitating broader participation as well as greater velocity in the cycle.

How can information substitution continue driving economies in this industry? Figure 2.3 indicates a possible avenue that would carry the transformation on to a logical extension. If information can be substituted for onsite physical inspection, flowers can be flown directly from production to market, cutting out one expensive physical link in the value chain. The quality of imaging would be a key factor in whether these inspections can be conducted remotely. Alternatively, local trusted sources could rate the lots, and this information could be associated with each lot. As technology progresses, there is little left to the imagination if there comes a time when holographic images of the flowers can be beamed across the Internet and inspectors can evaluate their bids in any corner of the globe. Such dreams are now just that, dreams, but in the not-too-distant future, they will be realities.

Given this scenario, where are the real monetary savings for such an organization? As transactions become more virtual, that is, taking place through the assistance of electronic networks, the economies of the Internet take over. Transactions over the Internet are measured in cents and pence, not in dollars and pounds. The transportation of bits is radically less costly than moving atoms, as Negroponte points out in his book *From Atoms to Bits.*[2]

[2]Negroponte (1995).

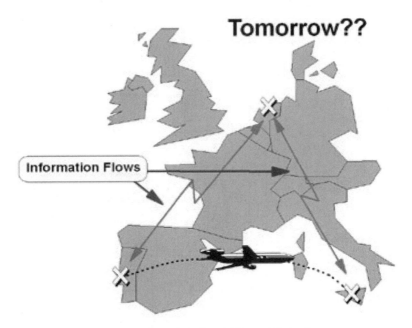

Figure 2.3 Future Movement of Goods in Dutch Flower Market?

Operating at Internet speed is another consideration. The time that it takes an inspector to view lots and enter bids over an online system is drastically lower than in a physical system. Moving a group of inspectors around a warehouse from flower lot to flower lot is physically demanding and time-consuming. Other buyers are also eager to "look over the goods" and there is time lost in waiting for a good view of the lots. The final part of the buying cycle is the entering of bids. Again, the physicality of this process limits the efficiency with which this can be carried out. Time is lost as the sellers sort the bids, and perhaps even enter them into a computer system for analysis and decision making.

Physical transactions are different in orders of magnitude from Net-enhanced transactions in nearly all cases. If the firm's costs for completing the transaction drop by 99%, and the velocity of transactions is increased by some factor at the same time (meaning that the elapsed minutes to complete transactions is lowered), then the firm has the financial capacity to do at least 100 times as much business as previously. Figure 2.4 shows some of the dramatic cost savings compiled by Andersen Consulting (now Accenture) in the banking, securities, and travel industries.[3] Assuming that computer systems can replace manual activities, a technology infrastructure can affect productivity in numerous and varied ways.[4]

---

[3] These reductions are based on a presentation by Steve Freeman, Andersen Consulting, on March 11, 2000, Atlanta. Ritz Carlton.
[4] Malone et al. (1987).

Figure 2.4   Cost Savings from NE

The exchange of business information between parties, either between business and business or between business and consumer represents a cost, but this cost is broader in concept than the transaction costs that are the object of study in transaction cost theory.[5] Transaction cost theory will be discussed later in this chapter, but for the moment it is sufficient to indicate that transaction costs are the costs of moving from an internal provision of a good or service to external provision in the marketplace. These include costs such as searching for a vendor or provider, negotiating a contract, monitoring the external provider, and so forth. Figure 2.5 illustrates how the Web could be used to replace some of these physical costs.

Business exchanges also have a value chain. Lowering the costs of a business exchange are outlined in Malone et al. (1987). Networks give managers access to information about products and services that are expensive to acquire in a more physical world. These transaction costs are dramatically lowered in a world of electronic connections between firms and other firms and between firms and customers.[6] Another part of the exchange that lowers the cost, theoretically, is the time-saving for the parties.

The range of exchange costs includes transaction costs, but both have a distinct impact on e-commerce. Exchange costs are part of the fulfillment process, as shown in Figure 2.5. They accompany production costs and are certainly part of the overall costs of goods or services sold in the accounting sense.

---

[5] Malone et al. (1987) perhaps mean "exchange costs" rather than "transaction costs" when they discuss the desirability of moving to online exchanges of information in order to lower costs. The issue here is not really a choice between costs of an internal hierarchical provision versus external market provision, which is what "transaction costs" usually refer to.

[6] Malone et al. (1987).

- (Web) search for products and services
- Interactive demos and reviews of products/services
- Details of company, links to customers
- Email and FAQ for further information

- Item(s) selection and ordering
- Delivery selection and ETA
- Secure payment transactions (SET, SHTTP, Digicash, etc.)
- EDI over net for purchase orders, invoices, contracts, etc.

- Transmission over network of information content of product
- Support information and follow-up
- Automatic registration of product/service
- Follow-up information

- Upgrade/maintenance notification
- On-line support for problem queries
- Part purchase and upgrades
- On-line media for training, use, repair

Figure 2.5 Web Reductions of Transaction Costs in a Purchase. (Copyright 2002, Richard Welke; Permission granted to use copyrighted graphic.)

2.2.2 Manipulation and Global Dissemination of Symbols

Networked Economy businesses manipulate symbols rather than physical objects. And these businesses are able to disseminate these symbols throughout their cyber domain for further manipulation.

Substituting information for physical processes is different from this manipulation. In the case of the Dutch flower example, flowers can be flown from Spain to England because information has replaced physical inspections and approvals. But the representation of these flowers, down to the minutest level of detail, means that we have abandoned physical counting systems and replaced them with symbols that can be manipulated for further managerial decision making.

Let's take the example of flowers again to illustrate this principle and the differences between doing business in the Networked Economy and doing it traditionally. Flowers may be physically transported, as lots, from greenhouses and fields in Spain to Rotterdam, and then onto England. Taking advantage of the substitution effect, Networked Economy businesses can avoid the physical transference to Rotterdam. As we discussed in the last section, this saves the time and expense of a complete leg of the journey of the flowers from supplier to retailer.

But suppose the flowers are on a fast boat to England from Spain when a last-minute rush order has negotiated a premium price for particular lots of the shipment bound for England. The fast boat on the following day would still be timely enough for the majority of lots in the shipment, but not all.

The substitution of information for physical processes has allowed a direct movement of goods from producer to consumer (retailer, at least). But it does not inherently allow for the further manipulation of the physical objects, flowers, to dynamically reprogram the order en-route.

The only physical way to accommodate the rush-order customer would be to physically match each arriving order with a physically sorted and calculated list of lots or sublots that were not time critical. In short, the lot of flowers retain a physicality that does not permit the process to manipulate them readily.

If the lots were represented by symbols rather than by their own physical existence, a Networked Economy business could manipulate the symbols and dispense instructions for sorting and handling to the landing dock yard, or, if there were sorting devices available, aboard the ship itself.

Figure 2.6 illustrates how sub-lots that matched the requirements of the rush order could be segregated from physical flower lots to maximize the value for all current customers.

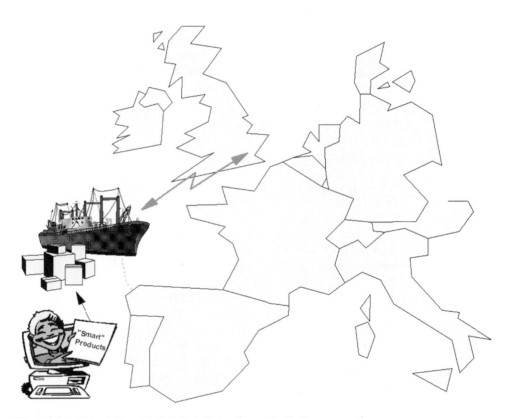

Figure 2.6   Ship at Sea with Sub-Lots Being Dynamically Reprocessed

What would be required for such a process to collect data, repurpose the order, and vet the change order? Flowers would have to be sorted into sub-lots, which, based on historical change options, would be marked with meaningful symbols for future manipulation. Bar codes have been a traditional physical way of marking such products. Inexpensive, barely discernible chips, however, have the ability to be read from any position and angle by unobtrusive scanners.[7]

Modularization is the key to this dynamic rearrangement of shipments and orders. But modularization is only possible to the extent that the data is captured, manipulable, and communicable to the parts of the network that need it.

The creation of symbols as stand-ins for physical goods has been a long-term process that has evolved over the century and more. Figure 2.7 shows the growth of information work in the United States during the 100 years from 1890–1980. It is clear that information as the inputs and outputs that knowledge workers deal with has been at the expense of workers engaged in physical processes, such as manufacturing jobs and farm jobs. Technology uses information to carry out physical processes with orders of magnitude of improvements in efficiency, and this has resulted in a dramatic shift in where human labor can be most effectively employed. Needless to say, the industrial revolution has also contributed to this transformation, but our main concern here is in the effects of information substitution.

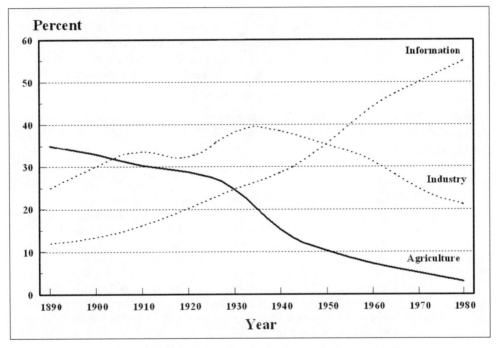

Figure 2.7   Distribution of Knowledge Workers in the United States, 1890–1980

To understand the long-term consequences and meaning of such changes, one has only to think of the difference between the railroad-spike-nailing abilities of John Henry and the machine in the traditional American ballad. In the ballad, John Henry wins the contest with the machine, but then dies of exhaustion. A modern computer-controlled

[7] Chip readers or scanners are capable of picking up identifying numbers from chips embedded in the shoelaces of runners in races, from the windshields of cars whizzing down the highway, and from other obscure and buried locales. They represent the next logical and Networked Economy extension of bar codes, which still depend on physical representations, the physical lines that are inscribed on the bar. If these lines become physically marred or removed, the code is unreadable. Chips are clearly still physical, but they are closer to the symbols themselves. They embed digits directly, rather than analogs of those digits, as in bar codes.

machine for spike driving would be programmed to treat all aspects of the task with precision and speed, each spike would be pounded with the exact amount of pressure needed to hold the rail in place, and the machine would be able to manage its inventory of spikes and spike coating so that there would be no delays in material required to do the work. Finally, there would be no contest with a human opponent. The computer-controlled machine would be hundreds or thousands of times as efficient because of its ability to treat the parameters of the job as symbols and to use this information to carry out the task almost perfectly again and again.

The ability to manipulate symbols on a global basis greatly expands the reach and range of product offerings and markets. Firms are able to extend their markets to an international audience without maintaining branches or warehouses or factories throughout the world. Distribution is still an issue for firms going global, but this can be outsourced, as we shall see in Chapter 10.

Cost reduction is a huge advantage for Internet-based firms. But revenue acceleration is perhaps an even greater economic opportunity in an era where a single well-thought-out Web site can be designed in a culturally sensitive manner for global sales. There are numerous implementation issues to position the firm for a broad reach and range to be sure, but there can be little doubt that the economies of globalization are different in an online environment than in a traditional, physical environment.

▶ CASE STUDY 2-2

CINEMANOW

CinemaNow is an Internet distribution company for feature-length movies, with exclusive rights to over 1200 titles. Consumers can view advertising-supported films free as streamed or downloadable files; they can choose a pay-per-view transaction for two or three dollars, or they can pay $10 a month for an all-you-can-watch subscription. The site has 1000 subscribers and delivers 10,000 pay-per-view films each month. About 20% of CinemaNow's customers access films via dial-up connections.

CinemaNow faced many unique challenges in offering downloadable films. Initially, CinemaNow was dealing with complicated licensing rights to distributed films. Each film can hold dozens of licensing agreements, and filmmakers can sell distribution rights to theatrical releases, home video, and syndication. The complex regulations are further complicated by territorial rights of separate licensing jurisdictions.

CinemaNow also needed to make sure that customers received the highest quality digitization possible. Bandwidth constraints impact the quality of streamed media, and profit was dependent on the customers' ability to download and view the film.

In addition, CinemaNow needed to fully safeguard all its licensed films from piracy, assuring that the films could be accessed only by authorized customers and used only according to licensing restrictions. The foremost reason that Hollywood has not eagerly embraced online film distribution is its concern for security.

CinemaNow desired simple and efficient customer access to locating, paying for, and watching movies over the Internet. To accomplish this, the company would need a fully Net-enhanced, user-friendly Web site that combined films and their respective licensing agreements. Because digital media, particularly firms, are resource intensive, the company's Web site would also need to be equipped to handle surges in usage.

The company invested in a Microsoft-based system called PatchBay, which provided solutions for the managing the commercial site, designing the Web interface, converting films to digital format, and distributing films online. CinemaNow can concentrate on core business functions rather than the complicated licensing and distribution regulations inherent in the film industry.

Moreover, CinemaNow can also consider scaling up to worldwide marketing and distribution because of the Networked Economy. The reach and range of NEOs is vastly greater than that of bricks and mortar firms. Once a film has been digitized, there are no limits to the markets that can be targeted (assuming legal and jurisdictional issues can be managed), nor is CinemaNow restricted to considering only one product type. Information technology can allow them to bundle products and to even include service options for those who might be eager and willing to pay for installation and set-up.

Discussion:

1. Explain how information processing and the Internet have replaced physical processes in the online distribution of films.

2. What is the impact of open architecture and open structures on the online film distribution industry?

3. How can business improve for CinemaNow by enhancing services offered with information gathered from the consumer data base.

Sources:

http://www.microsoft.com/windows/windowsmedia/content_provider/casestudies/
    cinemanow/default.asp

http://www.microsoft.com/windows/windowsmedia/content_provider/profiles/
    cinemanow/default.asp

http://www.informationweek.com/story/IWK20011108S0015

http://www.internetnews.com/ec-news/article.php/894361

2.3 MOVING TO THE MARKET FOR SUPPLIERS, COMPLEMENTORS, AND SUPPLEMENTORS AND INCURRING NEW TRANSACTION COSTS

Theorists contrast the decision of firms to build or manufacture products themselves versus purchasing these goods from others. The terminology that is often used to characterize this decision is "build versus buy." In the Networked Economy, this decision is much more complex in that it also includes services. The terminology in this case contrasts internal provision of a service ("in-house provision") against hiring or external provision ("outsourcing"). What is the decision-making process in the Networked Economy that leads firms to build versus buy, and insource rather than outsource?

The form this debate took in the 1990s was informed by transaction cost theory. More restricted in scope than the transaction costs described in Malone et al. (1987), transaction costs for Networked Economy businesses are the extra costs associated with moving to the marketplace to acquire goods and services. If a firm decides to purchase externally, there are processes and procedures that must be followed to ensure that the firm has done its "due diligence." A sampling of "transaction" costs are shown in Table 2.1.

Table 2.1: Sample Transaction Costs

Transactions Costs	Description
Search	Costs to find firm able and willing to sell desired goods and services
Decision making	Costs to determine relevant bidders
Negotiating	Costs to determine mutually agreed upon deliverables and pricing
Bonding	Costs to ensure against failure to deliver or sub-performance levels
Legal	Costs to investigate and formulate contracts
Monitoring	Costs to monitor ongoing outcome performance

Transaction cost theory argues that the firms will choose to "move to the market" when it is less expensive to achieve its goals by purchasing from the marketplace than it is by provisioning internally. The following simple formula represents this concept:

$$\text{Internal production costs}[8] > \text{Transaction costs} + \text{External price of goods/services}[9]$$

Old Economy firms are just as subject as Networked Economy firms to the theoretical pressures to build or buy as expressed in transaction cost theory. If the move to electronic markets to fulfill firm needs is less expensive (and especially if it is *much* less expensive), then both Old and Networked Economy firms could decide to cease provisioning themselves.[10] For the moment it is only important that we recognize that transaction costs necessarily create expenses when a firm buys from the marketplace.

2.3.1 Transaction Costs versus Business Exchange Costs

For these reasons, transaction costs are certainly relevant to Networked Economy firms, but business exchange costs are even more germane. The cost of business exchanges can be much lower using networks like the Internet because the physical costs of carrying out the searching, negotiating, and so on that are part of the transaction are expensive (See Table 2.2). Networked Economy firms will go to the Internet to save these physical costs, especially in the B2B setting, as we shall see in Chapter 3.

---

[8] Termed a "hierarchy" in transaction cost theory for the typical firm structure that is capable of producing goods and services internally.

[9] See Ang and Straub (1998) for an empirical analysis of this trade-off in information systems decisions.

[10] Chapter 10 discusses these issues in greater depth.

Table 2.2: Physical versus Net Business Exchange Costs

Physical Business Exchange Costs	Description	Net Business Exchange Costs	Description
Transaction costs	Physical costs to find bidders, negotiation, guarantees, writing contracts, and monitoring	Transaction costs	Internet costs to find bidders, negotiation, guarantees, writing contracts, and monitoring
Invoicing	Costs to handle a physical bill	Invoicing	Costs to handle an electronic bill
Payment	Physical costs to pay	Payment	Internet costs to pay
Movement of goods/services	Physical movement of goods/services	Movement of goods/services	Digital movement of goods/services

Let us consider the case of two firms in the auto body repair business, one operating according to Old Economy principles (Call-Around Auto Body) and one according to Networked Economy principles (Surf-the-Net Body Shop.com). The physically oriented body shop Call-Around Auto Body will make phone calls to locate auto parts necessary to make repairs. Because there are a limited number of suppliers that can be reached given the margins expected from a single repair, a full search can never be undertaken. Theoretically, therefore, a sub-optimal price[11] for supplies results from such labor-intensive searches as well as the higher personnel costs from the search process. Finally, the physical movement of the parts from the suppliers to the firm and the physical invoicing and payment processes also raise the overall business exchange costs.

Surf-the-Net Body Shop.com not only advertises its service over the Web, but it also uses the Web to find the suppliers and parts it needs. Price adjustments, if any, are negotiated online. This Networked Economy firm has much lower overall exchange costs. Its transaction costs are lower and it finds more optimal prices for its parts.[12] Furthermore, it uses the Internet to complete the exchange by electronically handling the bill and paying the charges. If Surf-the-Net Body Shop.com were also in a business that involved intellectual property, that is, if it sold digital goods or services, it could also choose to deliver these online. Companies like software manufacturers frequently offer the option for delivery of the software over the Internet. Consulting firms like Ernst & Young are also offering their services online.[13]

Therefore, even though transaction costs are higher when one goes to the marketplace, this is true for both e-commerce firms and those that are more physically based. The major difference in economics between the two types of firms is the much higher business exchange costs of the traditional firm. The formula below expresses this relationship.

E-Commerce business exchange costs < Physical business exchange costs

[11] These limitations on search costs are known as "bounded rationality" and were discussed in Herbert Simon's work. See Simon (1965), Simon (1957), and Simon (1956).
[12] To see how this works in actual firms, see Choudhury et al. (1998).
[13] Jaworski et al. (1998).

Focus on NE: Dutch Flower Auction Simulation

 In the Networked Economy, auctions can take place online, as we have discussed above. One such auction, the Dutch auction, derives its name from the wholesale flower market in Holland, the largest worldwide exporter of cut flowers. Because a primary concern is damage and exposure to the flowers, this auction technique is chosen because it provides the most time-efficient scheme of getting the cut flowers to market. In the Dutch auction, a seller (auction house) sets a price. Using a clock, the price falls until a buyer bids (presses a button to stop the clock). The first bid is the winning bid.

Try this yourself by running a simulation of the flower auction at the Web site http://www.batky-howell.com/~jb/auction/.

Sources:
http://www.dutchflowermarket.com/
http://www.batky-howell.com/~jb/auction/

2.4 THREE PRINCIPLES OF E-COMMERCE TIED TO THESE EMERGING ECONOMIC REALITIES

There are three principles of digital business that drive the Networked Economy:

Principle #1: Substitution of less expensive, more effective information-driven processes for physically-driven processes
Principle #2: Use of open systems architectures and standards
Principle #3: Enhancing products and services with information

A brief description of each of these principles follows. What is important to remember is that the NE revolution is not occurring in a vacuum. Businesses would not be moving to e-commerce unless there were convincing economic realities that support these decisions. Managers need to be aware of the economic impacts of these decisions so that they can accurately forecast the benefits from the change and exploit all advantages available to them.

2.4.1 Principle #1: Substitution of Information for Physical Processes

As discussed above, networked organizations are able to displace physical activities. It is not just the cost savings that are important here, although these are not inconsequential. A firm that has information at its command can short-circuit long and cumbersome physical systems in order to respond more effectively to customers.

Let's take the example of the Dutch Flower Market once again. Suppose that there is a pressing need for certain varieties of flowers in Sicily, but that the physical fulfillment process requires that this less popular variety must be inspected and graded first in Holland. The physical process of shipping the flowers to the Netherlands is not only more expensive, but likely to result in the loss of sales in the case where a specialized order calls for speed. The ability to grade and immediately ship flowers directly from Spain, where the flowers are grown, to Sicily maximizes the information-rich capability of a process enabled by networks, and, specifically, the Internet.

2.4.2 Principle #2: Use of Open Systems Architectures and Standards

For the moment, we can define "open" systems architectures and standards as those technical features of a network that allow for free and open exchange between all parties in a market. More will be said about the value of these architectures and standards in Chapter 4, "Basic NE Infrastructure."

The economic impact of architectures and standards on a marketplace is related to competitive power. If certain players in a marketplace control the technical standards, they can also control prices and availability of products that utilize those standards. With 90% of the microcomputers in the world using the Wintel platform, for example, Microsoft through its Windows operating systems and Intel through its patented central processing unit (CPU) chips are in a dominant economic position. The effect of this market dominance is to suppress competition and to exploit a monopoly position. This, and reasons below, are why the U.S. Department of Justice pursued an anti-trust legal case against Microsoft during the Clinton administration.

At one time, standards for Web browsers were more competitive, with Netscape as the leader in browsers and Microsoft's Internet Explorer a distant second. Microsoft has, however, gained a commanding lead in the browser market as they did in PC operating systems. This, the U.S. government argued, resulted in restraint of trade and a noncompetitive business climate.

In spite of the "closed," proprietary standards of many of the basic infrastructural elements of the client side of e-commerce, the rest of the industry structure is much more competitive. There are dominant players, for example, Cisco in routers and Dell and Compaq in servers, but none enjoy the monopolistic power of Microsoft and Intel in their respective industries. The telecommunications industry is highly competitive in the United States and is becoming deregulated elsewhere at a blistering pace, so that access to the Internet is universally less and less expensive. Telecommunications privitization is also a phenomenon that is playing out worldwide.

In order to retrieve and display Web pages, browsers read HTML (hypertext mark-up language) code and that of a group of other programming languages like Java sharp, C sharp, and so forth. HTML is an open international standard, as is its successor XML (extensible markup language). No single firm has a proprietary hold on the selling or licensing of this standard.

We shall see many other cases of "open" Net-enhanced systems and standards in Chapter 4. The economic principle that is being argued here is that the more open systems and standards are, the more competitive the marketplace. This should lead to a more vital and innovative e-commerce industry and better products and services for consumers and businesses.

2.4.3 Principle #3: Enhancing Products and Services with Information

Embedding information into what businesses trade on allows for more informed processes throughout the entire system. A product that can be tracked back to specific times, machines, labor, shipments, and so forth can lead to improvements in manufacturing. Defective lots can be linked to defective machines or work habits, for example. Service provision can be much more efficient and of higher quality, especially when maintenance is involved. Linking repair work with parts and the replacement of defective parts can inform the entire business process of after-sales support.

From a marketing standpoint, information embedded in products (and services) allows managers to forecast demand and quickly respond to changes in the marketplace. The Reynolds Aluminum Supply Company's (RASCO) sharing of information with its suppliers was only possible because each product was coded in the inventory, and this information could then be used to implement just-in-time (JIT) systems with their customers.[14]

Tapscott's "smart" bread is a classic example of the essential meaning of this principle.[15] No bread is truly "smart," of course. But if information about the purchasing of certain kinds of bread at certain times is utilized, a firm can learn a great deal about customer behavior. If a customer regularly purchases a speciality bread every Friday, then this helps to forecast demand, most immediately, and to cross-sell, more indirectly. Speciality breads may accompany gourmet dinners, and customers may be induced to buy with promotions sent by e-mail over the Internet, or "pushed" as a Web page when they are online. We will examine the circumstances under which a firm may want to pursue this strategy later in the chapter on "e-marketing." For now, it is enough to see that without embedded information, none of this advanced marketing would be possible.

One final observation is relevant here. Products and services that can be tracked, monitored, and dynamically rerouted or repurposed depend on information visibility. "Information visibility" is a term that represents the amount of sharing of internal information, much of which is embedded in systems, with suppliers, strategic partners, and customers. The concept of "full" information visibility has been bandied about in the trade press, and, for the sake of discussion, it calls for a working definition, at least. It appears to mean that information about goods and services are "visible" to all parties up and down the value chain. If a wholesaler is clued into the sales of retailers, this party can ensure that stockouts do not occur, assuming that the wholesaler can acquire merchandise. If the manufacturer is aware of the sales of the wholesaler, and even the sales of the retailers, plant capacity will be better planned, and wholesalers will be well supplied.

---

[14] Pontoon (1990).
[15] Tapscott (1996).

As we shall see in later chapters, there are reasons why "full" information visibility may or may not develop among firms, or within an industry. Distributors do not want to be disintermediated, and hiding information may be perceived as part of their value added. Moreover, few firms will be sharing their internal cost structures, because this will signal how low a price for their offerings can be made. Furthermore, not all partners and other entities interacting with the firm need to know everything. Information visibility should probably be on a "need-to-know" and "need-to-tell" basis, lest it lead to information overload or loss of strategic information to competitors.

The point of this discussion is that information can enhance services and products in such a way that it goes beyond a simple substitution for physical processes.

2.4.4 Novel Sources of Income in the Networked Economy

Loebbecke et al. (1999) present four income sources for Net-enhanced profit-making organizations:

1. Increased revenues via products or services from a larger global market, from more effective product marketing on the Web
2. Increased margins from lower internal costs (low-cost computers deal with the customer and the delivery of goods and services) from higher prices because of value-added services to the customer (information attached to product)
3. Increased revenues from selling cyberspace, from becoming a portal
4. Value-added content sold from selling searches, access to data, and electronic documents

Whereas the first two of these income sources do not differ from traditional business sources of income, the latter two do. All firms try to expand their markets and increase the margin between cost and sale price, but traditional Old Economy firms are not able to sell in cyberspace itself nor are they able to sell content over the Web. Also, as argued earlier, Loebbecke et al. emphasize that there are economic efficiencies inherent in Internet commerce.

Web content offers a unique presentation format, accessible worldwide and 24x7, but in other respects it is not terribly different from print media. Income source (3) from the previous list, however, is unique to e-commerce and represents an e-commerce business model that has no analog in the brick and mortar world.

2.5 INCREASING RETURNS TO SCALE IN THE NETWORKED ECONOMY

2.5.1 Marginal Costs Approaching Zero

Economies of scale mean that a firm can produce such high volumes of goods that its production costs are minimized. Why would this be so? When manufacturers in a free market buy raw materials from suppliers in bulk, they are able to negotiate the lower costs because the suppliers can make their profits on the volume of materials sold. Larger volumes on all sides result in lower prices all around.

The concept of the low price producer readily moves up and down a value chain in that each intermediary can pass cost savings onto their own customers in order to induce larger volumes of sales. The fundamental principle is that a larger scale of production leads to lower costs of production and thinner margins, which are made up in volume.

The ability to fully use the production capacity of a plant is another example of economies of scale. If the overhead needed to support a plant pays for only one eight-hour shift, then the plant is only being utilized one-half (or even one-third) of the workday. Adding shifts increases the efficient use of the physical assets.

As another example, think about the economies of scale in the airline industry that occur when there are slack resources[16] in fleet utilization that would allow flights to depart rather than be canceled. Smaller airlines do not have a large enough fleet to have resources that can be repurposed at a moment's notice. By not having such degrees of freedom, smaller firms will have to pass up sales opportunities and deal with maintenance impacts on the means of production in other, less-efficient ways.

Networked Economy producers of intellectual goods experience the same economies of scale, but it is sometimes manifested in a slightly different way. In software, for example, companies do not need factories with certain machine tools to design and make software, but they need cadres of qualified professionals who can turn out well-formed code that is error-free. Because machine tools are not involved in the creation of products, the relationship between productivity and the intellectual capital required to innovate is present, even though it is not physically derived. Large pools of expertise to draw on and large libraries of reusable code should equate to production efficiencies.

The terminology used in economics to stand for this concept of production efficiency is "returns to scale." Returns to scale can be either constant, decreasing, or increasing. Economies of scale suggest that as the scale of production goes up, the efficiencies of production also go up (as in costs of goods going down). Figure 2.8 depicts these as increasing returns to scale. Constant returns represent that equilibrium point where adding quantities of production does not yield economic advantages. Supplier prices may have been driven to their absolute minimum, and increasing the scale of production does not affect these costs. Also known as the "law of diminishing returns," decreasing returns to scale occur,[17] for example, when the labor capacity of a plant is maxed out, and additional units of production require paying workers overtime, or one and half times their usual wages.

Or if, for instance, Intel needs to build another plant in order to keep up with demand on its new chip, the cost of building the plant could result in diminishing returns, given that there is not enough time to recover the investment in the physical asset. The alternative to building is not very desirable either because not satisfying customer demand can hardly be called a good strategy for a thoughtful company. So a firm that is subject to diminishing returns is often in a difficult strategic position and needs to be very creative (or a monopoly) in order to continue to be profitable.

---

[16] Bourgeois (1981).
[17] Nguyen (1990).

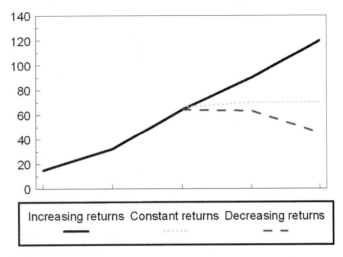

Figure 2.8   Scale Economies

The average cost of a production unit determines when the economies change,[18] but all that is crucial to know at the present time is that in Old Economy, physical, traditional manufacturing firms reach a point where adding productive capabilities and production will not help the firm's bottom line.[19] Networked Economy firms, however, may offer exceptions to this rule in certain cases.

Let us consider the case of Microsoft as a firm selling various forms of intellectual property in the Networked Economy. Whereas there may well be economies of scale involved with the human assets needed to develop software (and, therefore, decreasing returns at some point), as argued above, the marginal cost of producing a unit of Microsoft Word 2003 once the research & development fixed costs have been recovered is very low, to the point of approaching zero.Software can be distributed online, and payment for the product can also be handled electronically through various e-payment options. Once the distribution application has been set up and the code for payment established, the same application can be used for a variety of software products, and it can be used over and over again, millions of times.

To service 1000 customers a month certainly requires a certain level of expenditure for hardware, but to service 1000 time this number, a million customers a month, does not require a proportionately larger hardware investment for Microsoft. The hardware must have the capacity to handle 1000 times the volume, but the cost of larger servers drops exponentially with size and so there are palpable savings for firms distributing their own intellectual property over the Internet.

If the firm's marginal cost is nearly zero for new units of production (which is the cost of creating and distributing one additional unit of, say, Windows 2003), then a firm that is not in a smokestack industry can, conceivably, reap huge profits from increasing returns to scale. The more closely a firm resembles smokestack industries, with huge facilities for production, the less true this will be, in general.

---

[18] Nguyen (1990).
[19] Varian (1996).

2.6 CAPITALIZING NE INITIATIVES?

How much does an NE effort cost a firm? From the standpoint of basic hardware, system software, and networks, the costs are not high. Powerful server- and client-side systems can be set up for relatively small investments, and the marginal cost of adding a supplier or partner or customer to an existing base is very small.

The major software and hardware investments in e-commerce are twofold: (1) creation of initial and ongoing "stickiness" in their business-oriented or consumer-oriented Web sites and (2) links to legacy systems. Legacy systems are the application infrastructure of a firm, the computer systems that record and manipulate order, operational, logistical, and marketing functions. Integrating these systems, which may not be connected among the various product lines or divisions of the firm to begin with, must be tied into the new net-enhanced systems for both supplier-facing and customer-facing activities. This is a nontrivial investment.[20]

The economics of doing business in the Networked Economy require managerial due diligence to estimate the costs and benefits of implementing certain e-commerce strategies. Links to legacy systems are going to be one of the highest costs.

The second major capital cost is the functionality of the Web site. As we shall see later in Chapter 7, "Competitive NE Strategy," there are options to bring different parts of the value chain online. There are trade-offs with each of these as well as costs. A site that offers only brochureware is not expensive to put up, but the advantages it offers and its ability to hold customer interest is minimal. First-time visitors are one measure of success, but if users never return to the site, then the site may be actually counterproductive for the firm.

Web sites should be "sticky" for first-time and return visitors alike. The costs of maintaining up-to-date and valuable content is substantial and not an expense that many firms are willing yet to wholeheartedly embrace. The firm Web site is not the only way e-commerce expresses itself in a networked organization, but it is one of the most visible ways. Sites that are ghost towns of never-visited hyperlinks will not serve the organization well. Sadly, many firms are in the position of having many ghost towns on their Web sites, however, and this does not bode well for their future.

2.7 SUMMARY

Paradigm shifts occur when the basis of doing business changes. The e-commerce paradigm shift has caused the cost of business to be lowered by orders of magnitude and has also changed the complex interrelationships between organizations and their stakeholders. Old Economy firms focus on traditional sources of revenue. In the Networked Economy, firms focus on information value-added services and information and communications technologies. The most obvious economic difference between Old Economy firms and Networked Economy firms is the lower cost of doing business.

---

[20]Consulting firms have estimated that an initial investment for a large firm may be on the order of U.S. $1 million. This includes a fairly elaborate connection to legacy systems for processing orders. Clearly, the extensiveness of the initial Web site has a lot to do with the size of the required investment. A site for inquiry by customers, partners, and prospective employees is not nearly as expensive as one that performs end-to-end order fulfillment.

The decision of firms to build or manufacture internally versus purchasing goods from others is called the "build versus buy" decision. Firms will choose to move to the market when it is less expensive to achieve its goals by purchasing from the marketplace than it is by provisioning internally. Transaction costs are higher when one goes to the marketplace. Traditional firms have much higher business exchange costs than a Networked Economy firm.

Three economic principles drive the Networked Economy:

Principle #1: Substitution of less expensive, more effective information-driven processes for physically driven processes

Principle #2: Use of open systems architectures and standards

Principle #3: Enhancing products and services with information

Income sources for NE are a combination of traditional sources (1 & 2) and those unique to the Internet (3 & 4):

1. Increased revenues via products or services from larger global market from more effective product marketing on the Web
2. Increased margins from lower internal costs from higher prices due to value-added services to the customer
3. Increased revenues from selling in cyberspace, from becoming a portal
4. Value-added content sold from selling searches, access to data, and electronic documents.

Success for NEOs requires investments. The major investments required for e-commerce should lead to return customers on their business or consumer-oriented Web sites and links to legacy systems. Critical costs are for the creation and maintenance of the Web site and the functionality of the Web site.

KEY TERMS

Build versus buy: This terminology is used when firms make a decision to manufacture products, software or applications themselves rather that purchase from the marketplace.

Business exchange costs: Exchange costs are the costs of carrying on a business activity. If a computer system can substitute for humans in business exchanges, then the exchange costs of building and buying a computer network would be contrasted with the physical costs of these activities.

E-Commerce: E-Commerce is defined as commercial activity via electronic or computerized network connections where information substitutes for physical processes.

HTML: Hypertext markup language. It is the language for publishing hypertext on the World Wide Web. HTML is read by browsers sitting on clients like PCs.

Information visibility: Represents the level of sharing of internal information, most of which is embedded, with suppliers, strategic partners, and customers.

In–house provision: In-house provision is defined as providing products or services internally, within the organization

Legacy systems: Legacy systems are computer applications of a firm (and other requisite technology support) designed to record and manipulate ordering, operational, logistical, and marketing functions.

Networked Economy: The Networked Economy is comprised of firms focusing on information value-added services, information and communications technologies, or other high-technology offerings.

Old Economy: The Old Economy is comprised of firms that focus on traditional sources of revenue such as manufacturing and value-added services associated with physical goods.

Open systems architecture and standards: Technical features in a network that allow for free and open exchange between all parties in a network.

Outsourcing: Outsourcing is hiring others external to the firm to provide a service or product.

Overhead: Overhead is defined as the costs incurred when maintaining a business, for example, storage of goods and shelter of personnel, security, insurance, and so on.

Transaction costs: Transaction costs are costs incurred when moving from an internal provider of goods or a service to external providers in the marketplace.

REVIEW QUESTIONS

1. What causes a paradigm shift?
2. How can production costs be lowered via networks?
3. What is the Networked Economy?
4. Explain what a BADA is.
5. What are transaction costs?
6. How can networks lower transaction costs?
7. What is a "build or buy" decision?
8. Define transaction costs for the Networked Economy.
9. What are search costs, and what would be some examples?
10. Give examples of decision-making costs within transaction costs.
11. Describe some negotiating costs.
12. Explicate bonding costs within the transaction cost framework.
13. What are legal costs in this framework and monitoring costs?
14. List and elaborate on the three principles of digital business that drive the Networked Economy.
15. What are "open" systems architectures and standards?
16. Define information visibility and discuss why a firm would want it.
17. Enumerate and describe the four Loebbecke et al. income sources for e-commerce.
18. What are economies of scale and returns to scale? What are increasing, constant, and decreasing returns to scale?
19. Make a case for the major investments necessary for a successful NE initiative.
20. What are legacy systems?

TOPICS FOR DISCUSSION

1. One major change that has resulted from the NE paradigm shift is that the cost of doing business has decreased significantly. Discuss how this paradigm shift is responsible for decreased costs of doing business. Give examples of specific industries in which these changes have made a major impact.

2. Old Economy firms focus on traditional sources of revenue, such as manufacturing and value-added services associated with physical goods. Networked Economy firms focus on information value-added services. Compare and contrast the economic similarities and differences between the Old Economy and the Networked Economy.

3. All firms face "build or buy" decisions. Compare the decision-making process for the "build or buy" decision for an Old Economy firm versus a Networked Economy firm.

4. The cost of business exchanges can be less expensive for a Networked Economy firm as compared to an Old Economy firm. Describe why these costs can be less expensive and outline the differences in business exchange costs for the two types of firms.

5. Physically driven processes can be replaced with more effective information-driven processes. Describe how information-driven processes can be more effective than physically driven processes and the ways in which costs can be saved. Give examples.

6. Open architectures and standards in a marketplace are vital to competitive power of an organization. Discuss the benefits of open architectures and standards and relate the way in which they increase competitiveness.

7. Discuss why information visibility is important to suppliers, strategic partners, and customers.

8. Economies of scale mean that a firm can produce high volumes of goods and minimize costs. How do economies of scale impact the production capacity of an organization?

9. Explain the concept of returns to scale and discuss how the law of diminishing returns affects a firm's economic advantage.

10. Outline the major investment and costs necessary for success associated with establishing an e-commerce site in the Networked Economy.

INTERNET EXERCISES

1. Go to a Web page hosting site. What services do these providers offer? What are the costs? Create a spreadsheet comparing two different hosting sites.

2. Go to download.com. Choose one of the applications from the Most Popular link. Write an analysis of the application, its purpose, its feature's, and its cost.

3. Call a local florist and ask the price of a dozen red roses. Can you get a better price on the Internet?

4. Compare the process of ordering a dozen roses from your local florist with ordering a dozen roses on the internet.

5. Locate a Networked Economy firm. Evaluate how the firm substitutes information for physical processes.

6. Visit the UPS Web site. Evaluate the services offered.

7. Research the internet for information on the growth of information workers in the United States. Prepare a graphic to illustrate your findings.

8. Look in your local newspaper for a car of your choice. Compare the price to the price of the same make, model, and year of the same car on the Internet.

9. Compare the number of users for Microsoft Internet Explorer and Netscape browsers.

10. Use the Internet to find out how holograms will be used in the future.

TEAM EXERCISES

1. Investigate both sides of the issues involved in the Microsoft antitrust case. Debate the issues and include specific information on the violations and the laws.

2. Analyze a local Old Economy company. Determine how NE could change the business operations of the organization. Also, investigate the plans and projects that this company has, if any, to adopt and adapt this new way of conducting business.

3. Determine who the leading regulatory and supervisory agencies are for e-commerce. Include information on possible regulations and legal initiatives for e-commerce. Do not limit your search to taxation or economics issues. Describe the regulations being discussed at the present.

4. NE is a view of business that can lead to virtual stores. With this, corporations can expand their market and increase their market share. A wide range of features is available, ranging from catalogs to online ordering. Locate two companies that use an NE capability and discuss their strategies.

5. Find out how NE creates new security issues for companies. An example may be protecting the firm's Web site against hackers. With your team, find out three possible security issues and discuss how companies can protect against them.

6. Each group should find three publications online. These publications should have articles discussing NE issues. Locate these publications and give a brief review of them. Your review should include the site's URL, nature of the publication, subscription fees (if any), and so on.

INTERNET RESOURCES

System On a Chip (http://www.lsilogic.com/about/stw/lsiprocess/intro.html): This presentation by LSI Logic will guide you through the process of creating an ASIC (application specific integrated circuit) chip. These chips are used for many of the "smart products" we have today.

Unisys (**http://www.strategic-alliances.org/slideshows/Summit2001Scottsdale/Cur-tisUnisys/index.htm**): A PowerPoint presentation by Cheryl Callahan of Unisys on Corporate Alliances/Joint Partner Planning

**Data Indicators for "Coopetition" in the New Economy
(http://www.neweconomyindex.org/section1_page07.html)**

REFERENCES

Ang, S., and D. W. Straub. "Production and Transaction Economies and IS Outsourcing: A Study of the U.S. Banking Industry." *MIS Quarterly*, 22, 4, December 1998, 535–552.

Bourgeois, L. J., III. "On the Measurement of Organizational Slack." *Academy of Management Review*, 6, January 1981, 29–39.

Boynton, A. "Rasco: The EDI Initiative." Case UVA-IT-001, University of Virginia, 1990.

Choudhury, V., K. S. Hartzel, and B. R. Konsynski. "Uses and Consequences of Electronic Markets: An Empirical Investigation in the Aircraft Parts Industry." *MIS Quarterly*, 22, December 1998, 471–507.

Jaworski, B., E. Litwin, W. Miller, and K. White. "The Evolution of Ernie—The On-Line Business Consultant." Case written by Marshall School of Business and Ernst and Young LLP, (1998), http://www.trinity.edu/rjensen/000aaa/ernie.htm; http://ernie.ey.com/.

Loebbecke, C., P. Powell, and C. Callagher. "Buy the Book: Electronic Commerce in the Booktrade." *Journal of Information Technology*, Fall 1999.

Malone, T. W., J. Yates, and R. I. Benjamin. "Electronic Markets and Electronic Hierarchies: Effects of Information Technology on Market Structure and Corporate Strategies." *Communications of the ACM*, 30, 6, June 1987, 484–497.

Negroponte, N. *Being Digital*. Knopf: Distributed by Random House, New York, 1995.

Nguyen, S. V., and A. P. Reznek, "Returns to Scale in Small and Large U.S. Manufacturing Establishments." Report by Center for Economic Studies, U.S. Bureau of the Census, 90–11 (1990).

Simon, H. A. "Rational Choice and the Structure of the Environment." *Psychological Review*, 63 (1956), 129–138.

Simon, H. A. *Models of Man: Social and Rational*. Wiley, New York, 1957.

Simon, H. A. *The New Science of Management Decisions* Harper & Row, New York, 1965.

Tapscott, D. *Digital Economy: Promise and Peril in the Age of Networked Intelligence*. McGraw-Hill, New York, 1996.

Van Heck, E., and P. M. Ribbers, "Experiences with Electronic Auctions in the Dutch Flower Industry." *International Journal of Electronic Markets*, 7, 4 (1997), 29–34.

Varian, H. "Differential Pricing and Efficiency," *First Monday*. 1996. Peer-reviewed Internet journal, accessed in 2001. http://www.firstmonday.dk/issues/issue2/different.

STRUCTURES, FRAMEWORKS, AND CLASSES OF NET-ENHANCEMENT

UNDERSTANDING TYPES OF NET-ENHANCED ACTIVITIES

Every field has structures and kinds of things that are important to the core body of knowledge. Accountants have their "Generally Accepted Accounting Principles," and other fields have similar structures. The core body of knowledge of NE is growing and not established yet, but it is equally clear that there are many organizational principles and ways of subdividing the knowledge of the field that are essential to further and more sophisticated understanding. This chapter surveys these basic structures and classes.

LEARNING OBJECTIVES FOR THIS CHAPTER

- To discuss differences between the supply and demand sides of the NE industry
- To enumerate the categories of supplier, and what each has to offer the industry as a whole
- To describe the user side of NE, and the interrelationships between these players
- To compare and contrast the types and modes of e-commerce and NE activities, especially with respect to their separate capabilities
- To define varying types of media richness and media examples of each type
- To present an argument for why it is important for managers to understand the different classes of NE activity
- To be able to fit structures, classes, and modes of NE activity to successful and not-so-successful examples of organizations

UPS

The period from 1990 to 2000 saw enormous growth for UPS. With its distinctive brown trucks and its effective advertising slogan of "Think Brown," UPS now dominates this industry worldwide. In foreign markets, UPS's growth was based on mergers and acquisitions (M&A) and strategic partnering. They bought regional firms that were delivering packages and formed business connections with other third-party logistics (3PL) providers on a country-by-country basis. This deployment was in marked contrast to some of their competitors who had to withdraw from parts of the world because they were not able to execute.

In spite of their past success in logistics, UPS is also stepping outside of its traditional businesses and developing innovative supply chain and e-commerce solutions for clientele. As Vice Chairman and incoming CEO (2002) Mike Eskew says:

> Out of every dollar spent on logistics, 6 cents is spent on moving small packages. The other 94 cents is the other part of the supply chain. It's fulfillment, it's warehousing, and it's the cost of goods. So we have been moving into the other 94 cents.

Besides offering new products and extensions to existing products, UPS devised new channels for reaching customers. The Web was added as another means of tracking with supplemental bail-out chutes to call centers. Alliances with Oracle and SAP allowed customers to use these application forms to exchange information with UPS. PDAs and other mobile devices were also viable ways to download the latest information.

UPS's tracking system for packages is available on the Web for anyone who has sent mail or packages through their system. One of the reasons this system has been so successful is that the in-vehicle technology, which has moved over the years from version Diad I to Diad II to Diad III, allows drivers to input the status of the order directly to the database through satellite links. Without such technology support, it would be physically impossible to create, in a timely manner, the level of detail required by customers. But with such support, volume has mushroomed from 50,000 packages a day in 1992 to roughly 6 million a day in 2002.

The firm has moved aggressively into businesses that complement their core businesses and, at the same time, enable global commerce. Subsidiaries are set up to explore and exploit these investment opportunities, and those that work in these subsidiaries earn a position as integral parts of the firm.

In the area of automating the supply chain and the return supply chain (reverse logistics), UPS has developed supply chain solutions capable of calculating optimal inventory levels, best holding locations, and inventory carrying costs. Through information systems, they are able to manage other firms' procurement and fulfillment and to help a firm substitute information for physical processes.

As we shall see later in this chapter, UPS works both the supply and demand side of the e-commerce industry. They are now and will continue to work closely with suppliers in the e-commerce industry in helping them transport components to assembly points. They are also delivering the last mile to consumers of NE products such as hardware, software, and network devices.

Even though UPS is itself still heavily involved in the storage and movement of objects, they are utilizing information to reduce business exchange and transaction costs for themselves and their clients—and the Internet is a key part of this strategy.

Discussion:

1. Discuss the advantages, from the customer's point of view, in tracking package status data via the Web.

2. Describe the ways in which UPS now utilizes networks to manage customer needs. How could they use the Web even more in the future?

Sources:

Ross, J. W., W. Draper, P. Kang, S. Schuler, O. Gozum, and J. Toll. "United Parcel Service: Business Transformation through Information Technology." Case, WP-331, MIT Center for IS Research (CISR), 2002.

Shah, J. B. "UPS Creates In-house Parts Planning Team." *Electronic Buyers' News*, 1308 (2002), 4.

3.1 INTRODUCTION

Before proceeding to technologies and applications that make up the NE space, we need to pause and consider critical terms and concepts that will frame the discussion of NE principles in the remainder of this book. These acronyms, or abbreviations (one letter is taken from the beginning of each word in the term), such as EDI for electronic data interchange, are found each and every time one even begins to discuss NE, e-commerce, or e-business. Therefore, it is essential that managers be aware of what structures, frameworks, and classes mean as well as where they can be applied.

This chapter begins with comparing and contrasting (1) the providers or industry side and (2) the user or demand side of e-commerce. The structure of each side is presented through a model. First is the NE Industry Provider Structure (NEIPS) Model, a model that shows the key elements of the NE industry. Next is the Hex Model, which shows how dyads, or pairs, of partners interact on the user side of *Net*-enhancement. Both models have implications for managers.

Classes of NE activity are frequently described by acronyms, such as B2C (business to customer), B2B (business to business), and so forth. In fact, NE also falls into this category of useful acronyms. Learning the acronyms themselves is important because the terms will often not be defined in management meetings, and well-educated managers need to know what the terms mean in order to be able to understand issues in these meetings. What is even more significant is the meaning of the terms and the way in which these concepts inform NE practice and management.

Knowing that EDI stands for electronic data interchange would be a basic level of understanding and is the first thing a manager must learn. Comprehending that EDI is a technical description of transactional data delivered across networks between the computers of business partners is the second, and decidedly more sophisticated, level of meaning. Managerial implications can only be intelligently debated, however, when a manager also knows that EDI will probably migrate to XML (another acronym and term!), and the transactions will have to be in this format when they are sent over the Internet to other businesses. Finally, knowing that EDI is a form of business-to-business exchange, and therefore a part of all B2B-type exchanges, will allow a manager to understand many conversations in which she or he would otherwise have been left out. All such terms need to be framed within classes, structures, and frameworks so that intelligent discourse, and, ultimately, intelligent planning, can take place.

Finally, there are many modes of interaction that are enabled by networks and the Internet. Each of these modes has meaning for how businesses and other organizations can possibly interact with clients, customers, and strategic partners. In short, these modes scope out the strategic possibilities. Once again, the framing of this dialogue is critical before we can talk about the particulars.

Focus on NE: Electronic Villages

The Blacksburg Electronic Village, one of the most famous Internet-equipped towns in the world, is an example of the user or demand side of the e-commerce industry. It is the result of a partnership between Blacksburg Electronic Village (BEV), an outreach project of Virginia Tech, and the town of Blacksburg, Virginia. More than 87% of its 38,000 citizens use the Internet on a regular basis. The BEV offers a wide variety of Internet-based services to citizens, civic groups, and nonprofit organizations in the Blacksburg area. Individual mail accounts are available to anyone in the community for personal or noncommercial use. They also offer personal Web sites, mailing lists, online calendars, newsgroups, and online forums for citizens. Civic Web sites, DNS service, and online small-group collaboration, is available for organizations and groups. BEV is also experimenting with providing streaming audio and video as a community service. Local schools in Blacksburg Virginian were the first in the nation to have broadband Internet access in every classroom. New jobs and work opportunities have been created. Twenty-four new technology companies have been started in Blacksburg in the last five years. Over 500 business listings, almost every business in town, is using the Internet for advertising. More than 150 community, civic, and nonprofit groups participate in the Electronic Village.

Sources:
http://www.bev.net/project/digital_library
http://www.newconnections.gov.au/Article/0,,0_2-1_1-2_5-4_100912,00.html
http://www.bev.net/

3.2 SUPPLY-SIDE AND DEMAND-SIDE STRUCTURES

The interaction between the supply and demand sides of electronic commerce is an important first step in appreciating how to fully utilize the power of this technological transformation. The supply side includes all the makers of hardware that allow for connections between senders and receivers, secure the network and the ends of the networked connections, and design, install, and manage the entire system. They include, at one end of the scale, the Suns, Microsofts, and ASPs and, at the other end, governance bodies like the Internet Society.

The demand side includes the various individuals, businesses, consumers, intermediaries, suppliers, and complementors who use the technologies provided by the industry. Figure 3.1 illustrates how this division in the market space plays out, showing also that there is a dynamic at work in supply and demand responding to each other.

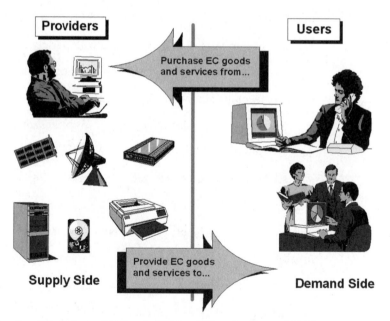

Figure 3.1   Provider Industry (or Supply Side) and User (or Demand Side)

3.2.1 The Dynamic between Industry and Usage

The NE industry builds underlying technologies, including networks, hardware and software, and commercial software packages. If there was no interest in purchasing these capabilities, the industry would decline, consolidate structural elements (perhaps), or (conceivably, but not likely) disappear. A strong demand pulls new products from this marketplace.

Innovation in the NE industry also pushes new products onto the market that have not been conceived before and, therefore, have untested demand. This is a standard push-pull phenomenon that is found in nearly all technology-driven markets.

An efficiently functioning NE industry will also solve problems that are inhibiting the future development of this information industry. As Rose et al. (1999) point out (discussed in greater depth in Chapter 13), download delay is a serious technical problem because it impacts the willingness of consumers to buy online. Solutions such as download accelerators are being pushed to consumers to speed up downloads by factors of 4 to 8.[1] By rank ordering the most popular applications, sites such as download.com are encouraging consumption of certain kinds of software. Eventually, through word-of-mouth and other mechanisms such as third-party evaluation sites like epinions.com, consumers begin pulling these same products from the marketplace.

Users stimulate innovations by being willing to, first, try out and then, later, to purchase software. The NE industry, in turn, recapitalizes these investments by developing new and better software and hardware. As we shall see in Chapter 11 on e-marketing, the Web can be thought of as the greatest marketing focus group in history, composing any and all current and potential users of a product or service. This runs counter to the history of business, certainly, where small samplings have most often determined the future shape of offerings.

3.3 STRUCTURE OF THE PROVIDER INDUSTRY

The parts that compose the NE infrastructure are simple enough to list, just as we did above—makers of NE hardware, Web security firms, Internet management organizations, and so forth. Unfortunately, a comprehensive list of such industry structural elements would run to several pages and would not help us to visualize the underlying structure of the industry. To understand the underlying structure, we need to look at relationships between components.

What are the fundamental units of the NE industry, and how do they fit together? A study by Storey and colleagues at Georgia State University (2000) indicates that it looks something like Figure 3.2. To determine the underlying structure, technologists who were knowledgeable about NE infrastructure were asked to physically sort index cards which held examples, or objects, related to various aspects of NE.

The graphical depiction of their findings in Figure 3.2 shows that 10 categories or classes of providers describe the industry. The relationships between them suggest that the central feature of the structure is a client-server model, with client software and hardware being provided by the industry for users, and server software and hardware being provided for business Web sites.

Client-server models will be discussed in Chapter 4, but, for our purposes in this chapter, it is sufficient to indicate that a client is a piece of software running on a PC, a high-end workstation, or another device, such as a thin client or a network computer. Network computers have just enough software on them to be able to readily access the Internet and process browser software and plug-ins. Clients fit nicely into e-commerce because they can run browser software and network-accessing software and send a request for a Web page over a network like the Internet, as shown in Figure 3.3. Sitting at nodes on the Internet, servers, as their name indicates, serve the request by finding the page on their systems and sending it back across the network to the client. Details about how this process works will be covered in somewhat greater detail in Chapter 4.

---

[1]For an example of this software, see http://downloadaccelerator.com/ for Download Accelerator Plus 5.0.

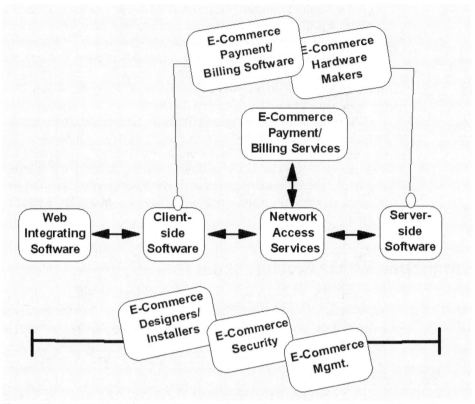

Figure 3.2   NEIPS Model. Lines with arrows in the diagram represent flows of information or programs/applets; lines without arrows represent applicability.)

Placing these 10 classes within the context of an industry value chain, we can see that consumers are users of "client-side" software and hardware. Businesses offering their goods and services via e-commerce are envisioned as users of e-commerce on the "server side" (see Figure 3.5). Principal intermediaries in the process are services for processing, certifying, and handling billing and payments of e-commerce transactions. Certain activities— e-commerce management, security, and design, installation, and maintenance services— play a role throughout the relationships and are represented in that manner. Software required for e-commerce payment and billing, as well as hardware, apply to both server and client sides.

Before proceeding to discuss each of structural elements of the industry, a word or two needs to be said about the Georgia State University (GSU) study just referred to. This ongoing research provides insight throughout the book into what is happening in NE and e-commerce, and it is appropriate for readers to understand the basis for its data, inferences, and conclusions.

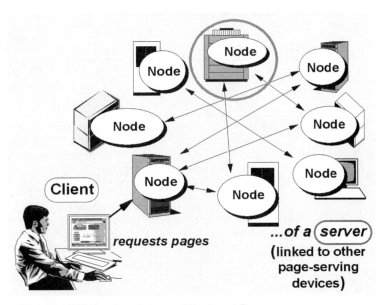

Figure 3.3   Nodes and Connections between Clients and Servers

3.3.1 GSU Study Background

Many of the observations set forth in this book are based on an ongoing program of study at GSU, Atlanta, Georgia, dealing with NE activities of firms and the success and failures they are encountering in this technological (r)evolution. This particular research began as an investigation of the structure of the e-commerce industry, as reported in the present chapter, but quickly expanded to critical research questions on the nature of firm NE efforts. To find out exactly how firms were approaching the transition to NE, the research team conducted extensive interviews with senior executives, middle managers, and information technology (IT) managers in a wide variety of firms.

As the sample of respondent organizational titles in Table 3.1 indicate, a large portion of the participants were strategists in their organization. Approximately 150 individuals were interviewed in the study, and over 100 organizations, half with over $1 billion in annual sales, participated. So there was a balance between large firms and small- and medium-sized enterprises (SMEs). Data was gathered throughout the United States and in one developing country, Egypt.

Table 3.1: Makeup of Respondent Organizations and Roles in GSU Study

Organizational Type	% of Participants	Representative Titles
Insurance	35	President, CIO, Executive VP, Director of E-Commerce, VP of E-Commerce Marketing
Computer services	16	President, CEO, VP of Technical Operations, VP of Information Systems, Director of Internet Marketing
Manufacturing	9	President, CIO, Director of Telecommunications, EDI Manager, Director of Customer Information Services
Professional services	9	CIO/VP, Global Practice Director of E-Commerce, Senior Consultant, Web Developer
Financial services	9	CEO, Exec. VP of Information Systems, Project Manager, Vice President of Multimedia Resources
Education/government	14	Agency Head, Senior Advisor, Dean, Director of Departmental Computing, Programmer Analyst
Other (hospitality, health care, food/beverage, transportation)	8	President, CIO, Director of Emerging Technologies, Senior Network Analyst, Director of Information Systems, E-Commerce Development Manager

There were five primary research questions explored. Table 3.2 shows these questions as well as the scientific methods used in gathering data.

Table 3.2: Resarch Questions and Methods Used in GSU Study

Question Explored	Scientific Methods Used
1. What is the structure of the emerging e-commerce industry?	Q-sorting techniques with managers and technologists; analysis of technology literature
2. What are the key technological impediments to e-commerce?	Analysis of technology literature
3. What are the key trends and developing business patterns in e-commerce, especially in insurance?	Literature review and analysis; on-site interviews with over 100 key informants

Table 3.2: Resarch Questions and Methods Used in GSU Study (Continued)

Question Explored	Scientific Methods Used
4. What are the key issues in public policy and regulation affecting e-commerce, especially in insurance?	Literature review and analysis; on-site interviews with relevant key informants
5. How can organizations become successful in e-commerce	Literature review and analysis; on-site interviews with over 150 key informants

Sponsored by insurance and computer firms, there was a stress in the study on the insurance industry. Sponsors were Sedgwick, North America; Policy Management Systems Corporation; EDS; Sun Microsystems; Centers for Digital Commerce; and Risk Management, GSU.This heavier emphasis on the insurance industry was not thought to be a significant drawback because the financial services industry as a whole is being so dramatically impacted by networks and the Internet.

Class 1: Client-Side Software Providers

As shown in Figure 3.4, respondents in the Storey et al. study saw browsers and other server-client software in a pragmatic rather than a technical light. Technically, browsers connect network, server, and client processes, but participants chose to view them as client-side applications. Also included in this class were organizations that create software for multimedia content, interactive TV, video-on-demand, Web-casting development, and Internet information retrieval. Then, too, firms that offer plug-ins and those that develop Web browsers were thought of as being similar. Interestingly, applications or e-commerce sites, such as Yahoo, that appear on client software were perceived as being in this class.

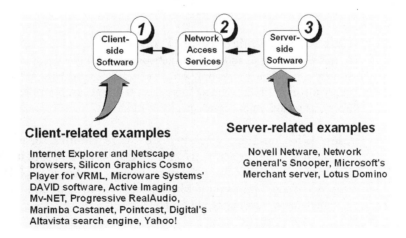

Client-related examples

Internet Explorer and Netscape browsers, Silicon Graphics Cosmo Player for VRML, Microware Systems' DAVID software, Active Imaging Mv-NET, Progressive RealAudio, Marimba Castanet, Pointcast, Digital's Altavista search engine, Yahoo!

Server-related examples

Novell Netware, Network General's Snooper, Microsoft's Merchant server, Lotus Domino

Figure 3.4   Clients and Servers

Class 2: Network Access Services Providers

In the network access services class were common carriers such as AT&T and British Telecom, as shown in Figure 3.5. These telecommunications firms can be placed in the same industry subgroup as ISPs and cable companies. Interestingly, value-added services that are involved in creating electronic communities also appeared in this category. The telecommunications links between clients and servers completes the client-server model that describes the basic, underlying NE infrastructure. This model is helpful when thinking about the way Web pages are "pulled" from the server by requests from the client. It is possible for servers to "push" Web pages to clients, also, but we will reserve this discussion until later, in the chapters discussing NE technologies.

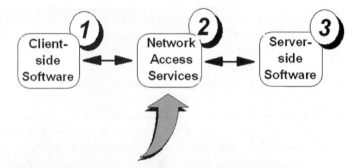

Network Access-related examples

AT&T, Sprint, AOL, Compuserve
Comcast, Media One, Prodigy
Chat, Tripod, GeoCities

Figure 3.5   NE Industry Structure as Client-Server Model

Class 3: Server-Side Software Providers

In this class we find software for network operating systems or administrative support and software that clearly runs only on the server itself. Although the Storey et al. study did not query the use of NE-oriented languages, resident JavaScript would likely fall into this category, as would other server-specific languages.

Class 4: E-Commerce–Related Hardware Manufacturers

Classes 4 and 5 apply across the entire client-server model of the industry (see Figure 3.6). NE hardware makers were the most clearly defined part of the industry, according to respondents. PC and server hardware were seen as being similar as were network computers, modems and point-of-sale devices.

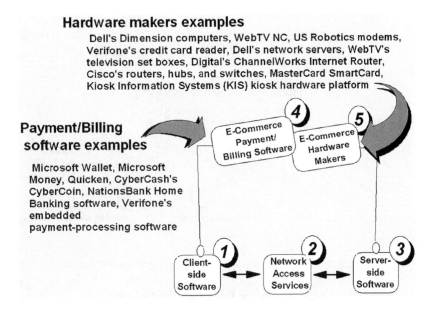

Figure 3.6 NE Hardware Providers and Payment Software

Class 5: E-Commerce Payment/Billing Software Providers

Firms that create software for electronic money, electronic billing and payment, overpayment, electronic banking, and point-of-sale processing were found in this single class (Figure 3.6). The various software types were seen as residing on either the client or the server.

Class 6: E-Commerce Payment/Billing Services Providers

Including major new intermediaries in e-commerce, such as banks and information providers, these organizations will process electronic payments, provide electronic receipt and payment of bills, and offer electronic money services and electronic banking services (see Figure 3.7). Third-party guarantors of transactions, such as certificate authorities will also participate in this category (see Chapter 7 for more information on this topic).

Class 7: Web-Integrating Software Providers

Participants did not view back-end software such as ColdFusion as belonging in this class. Web-casting Web-browsing software were, likewise, not found in this class. These providers create software that allows one to convert documents, images, or multimedia to Web pages. The makers of Dreamweaver and FrontPage would be good examples of firms falling into this class (Figure 3.7).

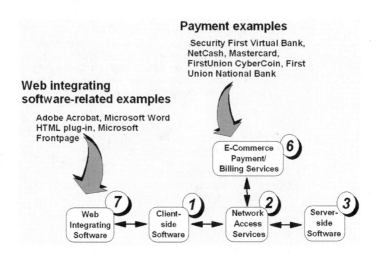

Figure 3.7   Payment Services and Web-Integrating Software

Class 8: E-Commerce Designers/Installers

As purely NE service organizations, these firms install corporate intranets, network hardware and software, EDI, and Web-oriented software (see Figure 3.8). Maintenance firms that host Web, EDI, or auctioning activities would fall into this category. Finally, Web design services are critical to the building of the NE infrastructure.

Class 9: E-Commerce Security Providers

Security was such an important factor that it was thought to be a separate category and one that spanned the industry (see Figure 3.9). NE security covers not only clients and servers but also the Internet and EDI proprietary networks. Providers that bundle asset protection, privacy, and security standards as well as those that offer and sell Internet security systems, firewalls, communication security services, digital signatures, and network security fell into this category. Finally, providers who set standards for encryption, Internet security, Internet privacy, and digital signatures were thought of as being on the security side of the industry.

Class 10: Providers of E-Commerce Management

The second support category was governance oriented. Organizations that manage the Internet and set communication protocol standards were major objects in this class. Sometimes these are bodies that involve partnerships between the public and private sectors, as in establishing standards for Web programming languages or network protocols. At other times, these management groups are intended purely for governance, and groups such as the Internet Society—both the International Society and the country-level Internet societies—fit into this segment.

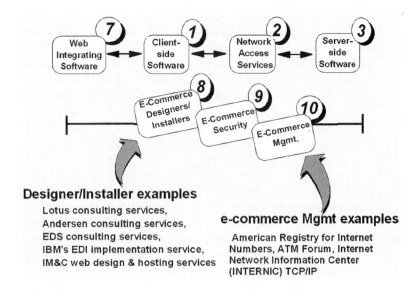

Designer/Installer examples

Lotus consulting services,
Andersen consulting services,
EDS consulting services,
IBM's EDI implementation service,
IM&C web design & hosting services

e-commerce Mgmt examples

American Registry for Internet
Numbers, ATM Forum, Internet
Network Information Center
(INTERNIC) TCP/IP

Figure 3.8   NE Support Services

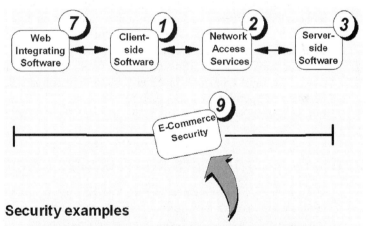

Security examples

Internet Security Systems (ISS) Intranet Scanner software,
CyberGuard Corp. Firewall 3.0, Bell Atlantic: Mobile Authentication
service, AT&T Secret Agent, U.S. government, Visa & Mastercard's
SET (Secure Electronic Transactions) standard, MIT's Kerberos,
Visionics' FaceIT, McAfee's antivirus software, Internet Privacy
Coalition,National Institute of Standards and Technology

Figure 3.9   NE Security Software and Services

3.3.2 Implications for Managers

Those who utilize and benefit from what the NE industry offers in the way of goods and services do not differentiate between routers and PCs. The hardware platform has become such a commodity that users apparently think of the industry rather broadly. If Cisco began assembling PCs or Dell began selling routers, this would not come as a surprise, apparently, to NE users. And there is the distinct possibility that they would also be ready to buy.

Software and services are fragmented and spread throughout the entire model, depending on purpose and fit between elements of the industry. Software is clearly the driving force, but services have a strong support role.

Services underly and undergird the entire structure, but payment services were singled out as being crucial for the ultimate success of e-commerce and appearing precisely at the intersection between the client and the server. Payment emerges as a critical provider function. Users perceive it as a major enabler (or disabler).

Security was the only category that included both services and software, and, like installer and designer services, was seen as an infrastructural capability for the entire industry.

Because e-commerce is such a rapidly changing phenomenon, managers in the industry need to make strategic decisions about their industry group and determine how to compete effectively in this industry. Not understanding the industry in which one competes could lead to lost potential and stymied growth.

It is clear that the future of the Internet will depend on how well it is governed. This structure indicates that only through cooperation of these various groups will a cohesive and comprehensive set of standards and regulations emerge. What is even more important, and clear in this emergent industry structure, is that no governance group should attempt to impose proprietary standards on e-commerce.

The model shows a fine balance between groups competing with one another and those who must cooperate in order for the industry as a whole to prosper. This balance between competition and cooperation, which has been termed "co-opetition" in the literature, will be expanded upon in the chapter on NE strategy.

3.4 STRUCTURE OF NET-ENHANCED SYSTEMS (NES) USAGE

User groups of Net-enhanced systems (NES) are at least as varied as the NE-provider industry groups. We have individuals accessing the Internet to purchase pet supplies, on the one hand; on the other hand, huge transportation firms like UPS are using it to monitor their worldwide package delivery and to give this information to businesses and individuals alike. Scope of activity or volume of transactions is certainly one dimension that could separate activities associated with usage, but another, perhaps more immediately helpful dimension, is type of user and the ties between them.

It is important to note at this juncture that firms can be both suppliers and users at the same time. Whether they are "pulling" products from the marketplace or "pushing" them to the marketplace depends only on which role they might be engaged in at any given time. So even firms that are supplying transmission capabilities and are part of the the infrastructure of the Internet, firms like ISPs, are also engaged in consumption of that same service themselves. At a specific time, though, they will either be providing or consuming, and it is in these different roles that we are interested in what they do and how they organize.

Entities utilizing the infrastructure offered by NE are shown in Figure 3.10, the Hex Model of NE. This model presents a stakeholder perspective on how technologies are applied, and it describes the fundamental interactions taking place between groups. The Hex Model is based on the work of Watson and Straub (2002).

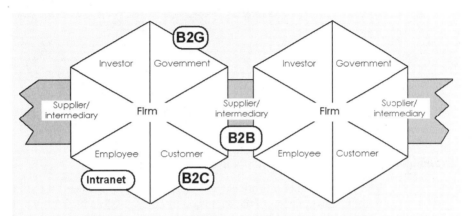

Figure 3.10   The Hex Model of NE, Adapted from Watson and Straub (2002)

The darkly shaded ribbon running through the figure is what most people would call the classic "supply chain" through which stakeholder firms exchange goods, services, and information electronically via networks. Intermediaries can also place themselves between any of the entities in this value chain. An intermediary such as a wholesaler will buy goods from a supplier, say computer components, and resell it to a firm assembling computers. The Hex Model also shows how each firm in the chain has suppliers and may be, at the same time, a supplier to another firm. Any firm in the chain, or any intermediary, can also deal directly through electronic connections with customers, employees, investors, or government.

The boundaries between the firm and the other stakeholders are intentionally open in the Hex Model to indicate the movement toward greater information exchange and the arising difficulty of knowing exactly where the boundaries of a firm are. If a firm is highly virtual and contracts many of its basic processes, then the information flows between partners are heavy. This blurs the traditional lines of distinction between firms with respect to who has the responsibility for building, inventorying, shipping, and servicing goods, and/or providing various services. The necessity for contracts to govern relationships between firms actually means that the boundaries of the firm are even more ambiguous than before the partnership, when it was clear that the firm itself was the only entity legally responsible for a certain process.

Not only are the boundaries more ambiguous between firms in the cyber world, but the relationships can almost be described as organic, as illustrated in Figure 3.11. The firm may be like the nucleus of a brain cell with its core DNA , but there are many other cellular bodies that cooperate with and help to nourish the cell as a whole. Without such partners as the mitochondria, the endoplasmic reticulum, and the Golgi apparatus, the cell would not survive.

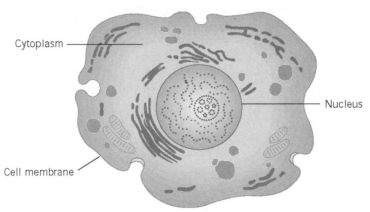

Figure 3.11   The Organic Exchanges between a Cell Nucleus and Its Partners as Metaphor for the Boundary-less Firm

3.4.1 Considering All Possible Interactions in the Hex Model

The Hex Model is a firm-centric model—that is, it focuses on the firm and its interaction with its stakeholders, to the exclusion of other possible interactions. Table 3.3 shows interactions with other stakeholders, both those that now exist and possible future interactions. Many of these go beyond the focus of the Hex Model, which tends to focus mainly on the firm itself. Please note that, from a business perspective, the linkage between businesses and government, noted in Table 3.3 as B2G, is extremely interesting to firms. If firms can exchange electronic forms and payments with the government through networks, there are huge efficiencies to be gained. But the linkage between governments their clientele (i.e., citizens), which is shown here as G2C, and that between governments and other governmental bodies, listed as G2G, are not the focus of the Hex Model. There is no suggestion that these interactions are not critical to society; it is simply that they are not a subject of inquiry in a textbook dealing with profit-making firms.

Table 3.3: Stakeholder Dyadic Interactions via the Internet[2]

		Receiver				
		Business/ employees	Suppliers/ intermediaries	Governments	Citizens/ customers	Investors
Sender	Business/ employees	Intranet	Extranet	B2G	B2C	B2I
	Suppliers/ intermediaries	Extranet	Extranet	B2G	B2B	B2I
	Governments	G2B	G2B	G2G	G2C	G2I
	Citizens/ customers	C2B	C2B	C2G	C2C or P2P	
	Investors	I2B	I2B	I2G		I2I

Legend	Past/ Present
	Future

---

[2]Based on Watson and Straub (2002).

Classes of Specific Interactions between the Firm and Its Stakeholders

Business to Business or B2B

As seen in Table 3.4, the firm's interaction with suppliers and industrial buyers is known as B2B, or business-to-business electronic commerce. B2B is extremely important in lowering the costs of goods and services and even in differentiating the firm's offerings. These exchanges can take place via several different mechanisms, as indicated in Table 3.4 and as discussed more fully in Chapter 11.

Table 3.4: Classes of Business Exchanges with Other Businesses

Class	Meaning	Description
B2B	Business-to-business exchanges of information	A broad term for all forms of electronic activity across networks between businesses; covers EDI, extranets, ETNs, and AFs
EDI	Electronic data interchange	A form of data exchange between businesses utilizing specific formats known as protocols (e.g., ANSI standard)
Extranet	"Extra-" meaning, literally, "coming from the outside" into a "-net" or network	Access by selected customers to a firm's internal Web-based information, usually controlled by passwords although other access control is possible
ETN	Electronic trading network	A Web-based network sponsored by a consortia of firms that pool purchases or sales to increase volumes and thus lower costs
AF	Application Format	Use of Internet by two or more clients whose application talk to each other (e.g., MySAP)

Sharing of transactional information has been transmitted over proprietary networks for decades. Through the traditional exchange, protocol is known generically as EDI. However, firms may purchase computers from a direct-to-purchaser Web site like Dell.com. At this site, SMEs have a designated part of the Web site where they can buy Dell's enterprise servers and other computer-related products.

Business to Consumer or B2C

Increasingly, firms are deriving revenues or cost savings from Web sites that connect them directly to their customers, who are ultimate consumers.[3] These sites were some of the first applications that drove the initial proliferation of the Internet itself. Sites like amazon.com and yahoo.com are world famous for their products and online services.

---

[3]Consumers stand at the end points of value chains. In most value chains, there are a sequence of buyers and sellers that precede the final sale in the chain. These are most often businesses, and the terminology in these cases is suppliers or vendors, and customers or industrial buyers. When a product or service reaches the final stage in the value chain, we are dealing with the ultimate parties who consume, hence "ultimate consumers."

▶ *CASE STUDY 3-2*

ATLANTIC BLUE CROSS CARE: SHOWING THE PROVIDER AND USER SIDES OF E-COMMERCE

Atlantic Blue Cross Care, formed in 1998 by Blue Cross of Atlantic Canada and Maritime Medical Care, is a leader in providing individual health, life, dental, and vision benefits; company group benefits; and travelers insurance. The organization processes some 40,000 drug claims per day, and, prior to its use of the Internet, these data were transmitted over private networks. By 1996, basic infrastructure was in place for Atlantic Blue Cross Care to develop a comprehensive Web site that could provide information, protect patient confidentiality, and allow for real-time processing. Today, Atlantic Blue Cross uses this technology to deliver exceptional service to customers and partners.

Atlantic Blue Cross Care uses NEXUS Network to deliver services across all regions of Canada. This centralized system allows Atlantic Blue Cross Care to reimburse and pay direct claims consistently and accurately throughout each province. Atlantic Blue Cross Care also implemented nine centers across Canada for quick-pay services. Customers can enter any quick-pay service where customer service representatives will enter the clients' identification and claim information into the system, and the claims will be processed within minutes. Almost immediately, the reimbursement check and explanation of payment are provided to the clients.

Another essential function of the Web site is to provide information on plans and products to the general public, potential customers, health care service providers, group benefit administrators, agents, and brokers. Each specific user group can enter a secure area and obtain information on new products and premium changes. User groups can request enrollment forms, brochures, and products. Transactions are performed in real time, and enrollment data is submitted electronically. Administrators are presented with only the fields of documents necessary to complete the task. This technology allows customer service representatives to quickly access all the information they need to provide accurate answers to benefit and coverage inquiries. If customers elect to call the toll-free customer information number rather than access information through the Web, they are asked to enter their client number and answer a few basic questions to determine the nature of their inquiry. When calls are transferred to the appropriate customer service representative, the clients' files are already open on the computer screen. Handwriting errors and missing information have been virtually eliminated.

The feedback from users has been positive. Roughly 850 companies have signed on to use the service, and 98% of pharmacies participate with the system.

Discussion:

1. Discuss the ways in which a centralized system has changed the business processes for customers, partners, administrators, and brokers.
2. Describe the essential functions of the Website.

Sources:

Jutla, D., et al. "Making Business Sense of Electronic Commerce." *IEEE*, March 1999.
http://www.atl.bluecross.ca
http://e-com.ic.gc.ca/english/stories/bluecrosssucc.html
http://www.atl.bluecross.ca/Website.nsf/Pages/Home

Business to Government or B2G

Firms need to communicate frequently with governmental bodies. Firms need to be able to access the regulations that govern their activities and communicate with government officials in matters related to the firm's interests. By the same token, governments need to inform firms about pending regulations and their changes, as well as collect tax revenue. Finally, a firm's interaction with the government can be dramatically affected by government Internet policy and statutes. All in all, this is a developing and important area of informational exchanges across networks.

Intranets

Finally, firms have built and are maintaining intranets for facilitating communication with and among employees. This has resulted in higher productivity and has provided the firm with new tools that can be of value to industrial buyers and agents, and eventually to end consumers. Intranets differ from internal e-mail and other applications that support collaborative work, such as Lotus Notes, and project management software in that they use Web-based interfaces. However, it is critical to understand that, unlike an extranet, an intranet does not imply or require that a firm be connected to the Internet. It is possible, although unlikely, for a firm to have an extensive intranet, but not enable anyone in the firm to actually access the Internet per se.

3.4.2 Classes of NE Activity

There are numerous useful ways to think about how and when e-commerce takes place and about the reach and range of NE. Table 3.5 gives four different perspectives, each taking a somewhat different focus. In Class #2, for example, the focus is on how organizations are involved in e-commerce as opposed to how individuals are involved. In Class #4, Internet capabilities coalesce around the concept of the informational exchange medium and its features. Each class is useful in that it highlights options available to designers and managers. NE offers many avenues for improving organizational performance and organizational life. These perspectives open up the black box of what is hidden so we can envision these opportunities.

Table 3.5: Types and Classes of NE Activity

Type	NE Perspective	Classes
1	Nets	(a) Internet, (b) intranets, and (c) extranets
2	Level of aggregation	(a) Organization-to-organization, (b) organizational unit–to–organizational unit, (c) organization-to-customer, and (d) individual seller–to–individual buyer for business purposes
3	Modes of interaction	(a) Computer-to-computer, (b) computer-to-human, and (c) human-to-human (Internet assisted)
4	Media	(a) Data, (b) text, (c) Web pages, (d) Internet telephony, (e) Internet video, (f) virtual reality, and (g) holograms

Focus on NE: PC-to-Phone Calls

Go2Call, a global PC-to-phone service provider, is the world's first Web-based PC-to-phone calling service. Go2Call provides service to over 200 countries and offers connectivity to both landline and mobile phone numbers. Go2Call saves callers up to 95% on calls and is available to anyone with a multimedia computer equipped with speakers, a microphone, and Internet access. Go2Call provides a variety of calling option plans and Go2Call's Basic Rate option starts at just USD $6 for 150 minutes of calling to the United Kingdom, Ireland, Canada, Germany, and the United States. Customers can begin making calls by using the organization's Web-based calling application. No download or installation is required. Customers select a calling plan by entering, on the home page, the name of the country they wish to call. Go2Call then presents the name and cost of the plan that includes that country. Once the plan is set up, customers can place one-click calls or send e-mail messages directly from the address book. John Nix, co-founder of Go2Call, says "Go2Call uses leading-edge technology backed by our private network of call servers and gateways to ensure a high quality calling experience. This combination of global coverage, great value and superior technology gives our customers the freedom to easily connect with friends and family anytime, anywhere in the world."

Sources:
http://www.business2.com/articles/mag/0,1640,41314,00.html
http://www.go2call.com/companyProfile.jsp

Type #1. E-Commerce Nets

A common way of categorizing e-commerce is through the classifications of intranet, extranet, and Internet. As shown in Figure 3.12, whereas intranets[4] take advantage of Internet technologies by using browsers and open protocols, communiqués and data exchanges on an intranet do not move beyond the boundaries of the organization. Internal e-mail is just one example of an application that can greatly improve efficiencies and that uses a technology that depends on Internet protocols. For multinational corporations (MNCs), this network can be worldwide, And the transmissions can be carried on proprietary networks and not on the Internet. The key distinction is that employees use standardized Web browsers to access Web pages that reside on internal corporation servers. The transmission protocol across at least part of the firm's network is an open protocol developed for the Internet. This current Internet protocol is named TCP/IP (there will be more on protocols in Chapter 4, "Basic NE Infrastructure").

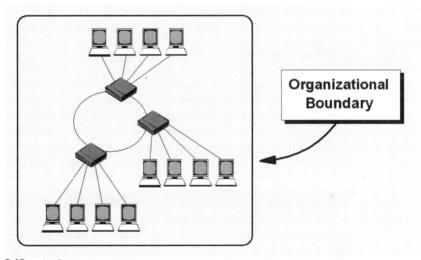

Figure 3.12 An Intranet

Extranets permit those outside to access an organization's internal network using open systems protocols like TCP/IP. The company's information is protected, however, by restricting access to legitimate users through passwords,[5] represented by the key in Figure 3.13. Extranets are ways for firms to allow selected customers access to specialized data, or, in fact, to the company's intranet, where product technical specifications may be found. Employees traveling away from company facilities may also use an extranet capability to gain access to the firm's intranet, as in Figure 3.14. Extranets are also used for subscription services like the *Wall Street Journal Interactive* edition (http://interactive.wsj.com). The Internet plays a key role in the transmission of information in an extranet, but a firm's internal information resources are not publicly available. Security systems act as filters to repel illegitimate use.

---

[4] From the Latin, "intra-," meaning inside or within.

[5] Or any other access control device, such a fingerprint readers. Passwords are now the usual method of controlling access through Internet technologies. This subject will be covered in greater detail in Chapter 6, dealing with security.

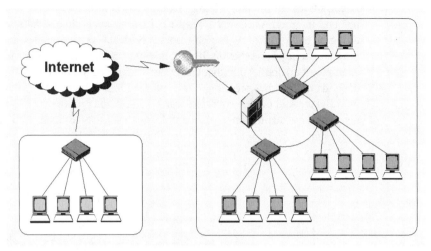

Figure 3.13 An Extranet

To ensure that valuable internal information is not revealed to the outside world, there are other security measures a firm can take to foil hackers and other antisocial actors. For the moment, it is sufficient to note that extranets show how Internet technologies can be styled so that firms take maximum advantage of the open (and inexpensive) nature of the Internet and, at the same time, create a virtual, closed system through the use of security. This gives optimal reach and range for chosen customers and selected activities.

Figure 3.14 A Recruiting Intranet Deployed by an Academic Department and Accessed Remotely via an Extranet Password Protection Scheme

The Internet itself has no built-in restrictions on access or on usage. A Web site can be accessed through any officially designated node on the Internet, as shown in Figure 3.15. Individuals and companies can visit the Web sites of other individuals and companies. There are no passwords required, and the only limitation to use is that embedded in the Web site application itself. The Internet is the most open communication and transactional concept ever invented. Its reach and range is enormous. It allows around-the-clock convenience and the conducting of business anywhere on the planet.

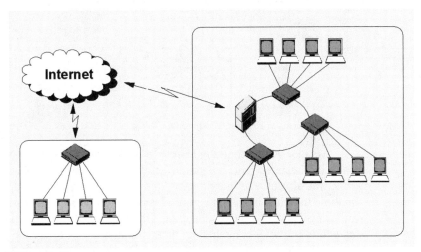

Figure 3.15   The Internet

Type #2: E-Commerce Levels

Table 3.6 depicts four levels of aggregation of e-commerce activity. Organizations are aggregations of business units within themselves, and business units are aggregations of individual employees. At the level of individuals are consumers or customers, who can interact with each other as individuals or interact with firms.

In level 1, organizations can communicate directly with each other, a set of exchanges common in B2B e-commerce. Traditionally, these forms of communication were called "interorganizational systems" or IOSs. Other traditional forms of firm-to-firm exchange are EDI transactions and EFT transmissions. The latter are typically carried out between banks, but this is only the historical way in which payments have occurred. Through e-commerce, it is possible for organizations to maintain their own payment and receipt accounts with customers and suppliers and to use information systems to manage the cyber-cash flows.

Extranets are, as just discussed, a form of communication between firms. The Web site becomes the method of exchange, and, hence, extranets are at the highest level of aggregation. Although individual employees may technically be accessing the extranet, they are frequently representing their business and, acting in this capacity, their transactions would best be described as B2B activity.

Table 3.6: Levels of E-Commerce Activity

1	2	3	4
Organization-to-organization (IOS, B2B, EDI, EFT, Extranet)	Organizational unit-to-organizational unit (Intranet)	Organization-to-consumer (B2C)	Seller-to-buyer C2C, B2B, B2C for business purposes

Another way of thinking about intranets is that the level at which they operate is typically the business unit. For purposes of streamlining processes, units need to coordinate order fulfillment, and individuals within these units need to cooperate with relevant information. Individuals are not acting as individuals in these circumstances but in the capacity in their roles within the organization. Of course, if the company intranet is also legitimized as a form of social communication, then individuals can use the intranet for personal purposes, but the primary and most critical function of an intranet is to support the role of the business unit.

The most widely recognized level of activity on the Internet is level 3, organization to consumer. A wide variety of Web sites allow individuals to interact with firms. Figure 3.16 shows the "front door" for the Lands' End site. At this site, individuals interact with the firm's Web application. As the consumer clicks on icons or text links, the firm sends the customer the requested information. Ordering and payment are also possible through the site, which give the firms extraordinary reach and range compared to traditional firms, or even compared to the traditional physical sales process for Lands' End.

Finally, it is important to recognize that some e-commerce activity at level 4 is between individuals acting for themselves as consumers or acting for their organizations in either a buying or selling role. A good example of sellers and buyers interacting is eBay, as illustrated in Figure 3.17. Here baby pacifiers are offered for sale and opened for bidding. The eBay model is an auction in which sellers offer, through the intermediary eBay, goods and services for sale. Buyers bid on an item and, at a certain point, bids are evaluated and a sale initiated. eBay stands as guarantor of the integrity of the transaction.

Individual proprietorships (businesses owned by individuals) can sell or purchase goods and services via the Web in this way. They can buy from consumers, and consumers can buy from them. Large firms can purchase from other large firms through electronic buying or trading exchanges. Individuals acting as sole proprietors can buy and sell to other sole proprietors through this online intermediary, also. Because all possibilities are present in this model, it can be said to encompass consumer to consumer (C2C) as well as B2B and B2C.

Figure 3.16 Typical Organization-to-Consumer Level of E-Commerce Activity (www.landsend.com)

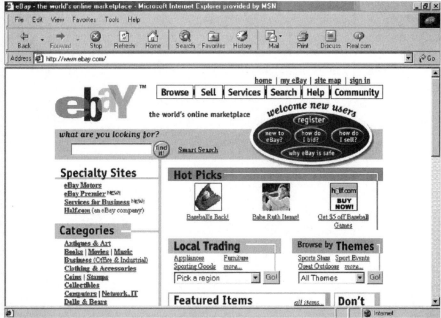

Figure 3.17 Example of Individual-to-Individual E-Commerce Level Activity through an Intermediary (www.ebay.com)

Type #3: E-Commerce Modes

One of the truly remarkable things about NE and e-commerce is the variety of modes of expression and interaction that are made available. From the standpoint of who can be senders and who can be receivers of information, all combinations of people and computers are possible, as shown in Figure 3.18.

Computers working alone can exchange information between themselves in an EDI transaction, or in a more sophisticated XML transmission. Orders can be made, inventories can be reduced, bills can be issued and paid, and reports on activity levels can be automatically generated. If a firm deals in digital goods or services, the product itself can also be sent. Figure 3.19 is a log account of a sample EDI message sent from sample firm Acme, Inc. to another sample firm, ABC Brands, Inc.

e-Commerce involves various technology-human modes of exchanges:
1. **computer-working-alone to computer-working-alone (little or no human intervention)**
2. **computer-working-alone to person-at-computer**
3. **person-at-computer to person-at-computer**

Figure 3.18   Three Modes of E-Commerce Interaction

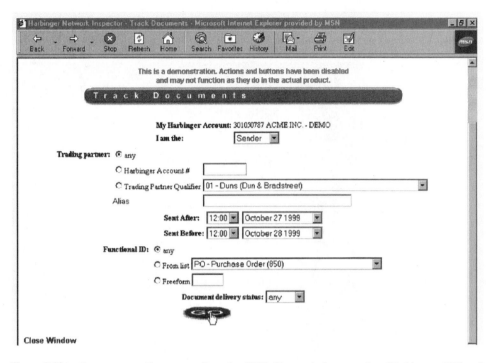

Figure 3.19 Computer-to-Computer Sample EDI Transmission at the Harbinger Web site (www.harbinger.com)

What is key in differentiating these modes of activity is the party that initiates the activity. If a computer can be set up to automatically initiate activity, then, for all intents and purposes, there is a computer at one end of the interchange. If a human being is required to initiate actions, as in a chat session, then we would conclude that a human was at that end of the communication.

A second form of interaction is between computers working alone and humans working alone. This is a very familiar format in that most online consumers are interacting with computer systems when they are seeking answers to questions, ordering goods, or simply being entertained. Human beings can initiate the downloading of software, for example, as in Figure 3.20, which shows the options available to download Nero Burning ROM's software for creating CDs. Once the software begins downloading, of course, we have a computer-to-computer exchange (which is still under the direct supervision of the human working alone).

Finally, the third mode of interaction is between two individuals working alone. The Web can be used for "chat" using intermediaries such as AOL or Web page-based services such as talkby.com. The latter permits company sales reps to answer questions having to do with the offerings on particular Web pages. Sales reps can also "push" new pages across the network to the customer. These pages may be more relevant to the customers' interests, and the dialogue can continue once the customer receives the new page.

Figure 3.20   Computer-to-Human Interchange at Nero Burning ROM Web Site (www.nero.com)

Type #4: E-Commerce Media

The kinds of media that can be transmitted over the Internet vary enormously. Table 3.7 shows just some of the possibilities. Among these are data, text, Web pages, audio, Internet telephony, Internet video, virtual reality, and holograms. These media differ on three critical dimensions: richness, social presence, and interactivity.

Table 3.7: Characteristics of Media Used in Internet Communications

Media	Media Richness	Social Presence	Interactivity
Data	Low	Low	Low
Text	Low	Low	Low for e-mail; medium for live chat
Multimedia Web pages	Medium	Low-to-medium	Low
Audio	Medium	Medium-to-high	Medium-to-high
Internet telephony	Medium	Medium-to-high	Medium-to-high
Internet video	High	High	High
Virtual reality	High	High	High
Holograms	High	High	High

With regard to richness, data and text sent over e-mail are said to be lean channels of communication in that they convey little in the way of a message other than exactly what the words, numbers, or special symbols mean. There is no doubt that the language in an e-mail can be ambiguous,[6] but the e-mail channel in single exchanges offers little more that can be sensed about the meaning of the communicator. Because of this potential ambiguity, happy face symbols like ":-)" are added to messages to enrich the meaning.

Both the senders of communiqués and the recipients sense that there is a certain social presence in the medium that conveys a human presence.[7] Media that convey a human presence and are expressive in revealing intonation and facial expression are said to be rich media. Face-to-face meetings are the richest form of communication. Telephones are leaner media because the visual presence of the speaker is lacking.

Data and text communicated over e-mail are limited in their expressive power. Web pages add a visual dimension and can also have audio and video components. The audio and video media add richness in that the visual channel is also present, but may or may not add a sense of social presence. If images of human beings are used in addition to their voices, then social presence on a Web site could also be pronounced.

Interactivity occurs when the medium permits immediate or real-time responses. Internet telephony, which permits senders and receivers to talk to each other over the Internet, is interactive. A static Web page is not.

Virtual reality and holograms are technologies that will, or could, convey a strong presence of human beings, as well as being visually and audio rich. If holograms occur in real time, they will be highly interactive. Virtual reality is generated by a computer program and, assuming sufficient computing power, can respond to a user very quickly. They can also be very realistic, and increasingly so as time goes by.

The mix of media a firm chooses to use in e-commerce settings is critical to how customers perceive responsiveness. Cisco has a click-to-talk capability that allows business customers to speak directly and in real time with a sales representative using the Internet. Companies support a wide variety of media choices for customers out of their call centers, and, although these investments may be expensive and labor-intensive, customer relationship management cannot be conducted without them. An illustration of how companies can spread their responses over these media is shown in Table 3.8. Chapter 11 will discuss these issues with regard to effective marketing over the Web and with B2B e-commerce.

---

[6]Daft and Lengel (1984).
[7]Short et al. (1976).

Table 3.8: Iomega Customer Support Matrix (www.iomega.com)

Contact	Web	E-Mail	Phone
Technical support	🌐	✉	☎
Returns and Warranty information	🌐	✉	
Product information and sales	🌐		☎
Customer Service	🌐	✉	☎
Express Customer Service			☎
Extended Protection Plan	🌐		
Fax-back			☎
Software download	🌐	✉	

The future capability of the Internet to be the channel of choice for certain applications was demonstrated at a conference in which Texas Governor Rick Perry's image was sent over the university test version of Internet2 from Austin, Texas to Dallas, Texas, a distance of some 400 kilometers (or 248 miles). The governor appeared to be standing behind a lectern next to the commentator and was able to answer questions in real time. The appearance of reality was said to be striking, as Figure 3.21 shows.

Figure 3.21   Image of Texas Governor Rick Perry (right) "Speaks" with Jim Adams, Retired Chairman of Board of Texas Instruments at Distance of 400 Kilometers[8]

[8] Graham (2001)

3.4.3 Managerial Implications of Media Choice

Managers have many choices in how to design customer response mechanisms. Using either e-commerce or traditional response mechanisms, the firm can favor Web-automated solutions or they can balance that with human agents who use the Web, e-mail, or other media for support of the customer relationship.

Human beings are expensive and error-prone. Their skills are essential for the effective running of corporations, to be sure, but whenever it is possible to exchange a computer for a person, the benefit of the substitution effects we have been discussing become realized. The physical processes performed by human beings are costly. When appropriate, computers can do repeatable and programmable processes much better and much cheaper.

The 24x7 capability of the Web and the sharing of virtual space with clients means that physical movement of customers to firms or firms to customers can be obviated, in certain situations. Face-to-face encounters are replaced with information, in some cases fairly rich information, for example, when talkby.com enables sales reps to direct customers around the firm's Web site and even to "push" relevant Web pages to the customers.

3.5 EXAMPLES OF E-COMMERCE APPLIED TO THE FRAMES

3.5.1 Successful Example

Examples of successful Web sites are easy to come by. There are many firms that are maximizing the value of their customer contacts through the Web. As shown in Figure 3.22, dell.com sells computers to individual consumers, SMEs, large corporations, branches of government, and nonprofits through its Web site, which suggests that it intends to service the broadest segment of the dyads in the Hex Model (Figure 3.10). On the supplier side, it provides hardware for the e-commerce industry, as indicated in Figure 3.22. Dell focuses on this market and has moved only marginally into tempting markets in other parts of the e-commerce industry structure.

Figure 3.23 likewise illustrates that Dell sales and service support utilizes several modes of interaction and a variety of media. E-Commerce call centers need to give customers latitude to contact the firm in whatever manner suits them, and at whatever time of the day.

Successful online firms like Dell Computer are engaged in many other forms of e-commerce that are not immediately obvious to the end consumer. They have a strategic relationship with UPS and other package delivery firms to coordinate the logistics of delivery to the last mile.[9] Monitors made by Sony are never delivered physically to Dell, but meet up with the rest of a customer order at the strategic partner's facilities. The customized package of components—monitor, computer, printer, and peripherals—can thus be brought to the customer at once. This replacement of physical movement of goods with information systems that track and coordinate the components is as much a part of the e-commerce revolution as the customer-facing Internet Web site.[10] This is the back-end B2B system that enables fulfillment of orders.

---

[9]Rangan (1999).

[10]Marketers and strategists sometimes divide the supply chain into supplier-facing and customer-facing sides of the value chain. The relative position is any firm, which has an upstream side facing the consumer or customer, and a downstream side facing the suppliers. See Robinson et al. (2000).

Figure 3.22 Dell Web site Indicating Its Target Market Segments

Figure 3.23 Dell Options for Customers to Contact the Firm

We can also be assured that Dell has an intranet that supports the internal communication that is required to formulate Dell's alliance strategies.[11] Extranets are a clear element of this strategy because they allow Dell's best customers to have access to information that is not available to the general public.

All in all, Dell illustrates a firm that capitalizes on all aspects of the frames we have enunciated.

3.5.2. Less-than-Successful Example

Just as with the successful examples, it would simple enough to list and describe firms that have had less-than-successful e-commerce strategies. The large-scale failures of dot.coms in the period from 2000 to 2001 provides ample numbers of firms that did not fully consider these NE frames.

The boo.com site is a celebrated failure in the high-fashion industry.[12] It burned through $125 million U.S. dollars of angel investment before announcing bankruptcy in May of 2000. The site was designed to appeal to the high-fashion–conscious European consumer by allowing users to see a simulated three-dimensional (3-D) view of what the selected clothes would look like on a model. The software on the server side was sophisticated, but apparently sufficiently bug-free that the visual impact was stunning to those who were able to access and use the site.

The designers of boo.com's strategy missed crucial elements of the provider industry structure, however. They did not consider the client-side hardware and software, nor did they consider the network access connections. Most users did not own high-end workstations or even the latest browser software, and this alone would have created problems for the site. The death knell was that the network access services could not support the high bandwidths required for effective performance. Consumers are just not going to wait a half an hour for a simulated 3-D visual to download.[13]

The brand was bought out of liquidation by Fashionmall, who used it to add the high-fashion niche to their repertoire of fashion offerings.[14] Figure 3.24 shows the boo.com site after it was acquired. As a brand asset, boo.com may be sold many times while its brand still has cachet.[15]

There are many other examples of firms that are not fully capitalizing on NE. Readers can perform an inventory of such firms on their own. There are some simple tests of the effectiveness of the site. When you go to the site, what can you find out about the firm's offerings? How easy is it to navigate to and through this information? Is the site intuitive or difficult to understand? If you wanted to purchase, how much of the sequence of purchasing events are supported on the Web? If you have purchased, how straight-forward is the after-sales support servicing? Which media are offered for sales and servicing? Are bail-out chutes available and obvious on every page of the site?

[11]Rangan (1999).
[12]DiSabatino (2000a and 200b); Rosier (2000).
[13]Rose et al. (2000).
[14]Tillett (2000).
[15]Weiss (2001).

Figure 3.24   The Reborn boo.com E-Tailing Web Site as of 2001

Industry-specific questions could be added to this inventory. Within a given industry like the insurance industry, we could try to find answers to more pointed questions. Go to any life insurance carrier's site. Ask yourself whether you would be able to find out what you need about the firm's offerings. Does the site have ways to answer your questions or does it simply relay you to its agents? If it can only relay your request to agents, does it provide e-mail addresses and URLs, or only surface mail adddresses and telephone numbers. If it presents information about physical addresses, does it have a way to assist you in driving to or taking public transportation to the agency? If the firm offers prices on its products, does it also tell you what its competitors are charging? These and other questions are extremely critical for interested consumers.

With a checklist of such possible interactions in hand, customers can assess how advanced a firm is in NE, at least at the obvious and overt level. What cannot be determined is the extent of NE activity behind the scenes. The extensiveness of B2B exchange activity is typically not as clear as B2C activity. Nevertheless, the reader can be assured that there will be major differences among firms in their NE readiness and deployment.

3.6 SUMMARY

This chapter has described the core body of knowledge of NE, an area that is growing and has certainly not firmed up yet. Using models, the chapter compares and contrasts: (1) the providers or industry side and (2) the user or demand side of e-commerce. After the NEIPS Model, which frames elements of the supplier side of the NE industry is the Hex Model. The Hex Model shows how partners interact on the user side of NE. The dynamic between industry and usage of e-commerce is a push-pull phenomenon common to technology-driven models. Demand for underlying technologies pulls the use of products by consumers, and innovation pushes development of new products in the industry.

The fundamental units of the e-commerce industry and the relationships within the industry are described in the NEIPS Model. The NEIPS Model describes 10 categories of providers within the industry. The relationships between them indicate that the central feature of the structure is a client-server model, with client software and hardware provided by the industry for users and server software and hardware provided for business Web sites.

Usage is as varied as the e-commerce provider industry groups. The Hex Model of e-commerce presents a stakeholder perspective on how technologies are applied and describes the fundamental interactions taking place between groups. There are several classes of specific interactions between a firm and its stakeholders, such as B2B, B2C, intranets, and extranets. Boundaries between the firm and the other stakeholders are open in the Hex Model to indicate the movement toward greater information exchange and the difficulty of knowing where the boundaries of a firm are. Other interactions do exist, but the Hex Model is firm-centric. Nevertheless, firms must consider all dyads in the Hex Model in order to create innovative systems.

Among the key terminology describing classes of NE activity are B2C, B2B, intranet, and so forth. These terms will be used in management meetings, and well-educated managers will need to understand them. Even more important, good managers will know how to apply them to firm actions. Many classes of specific interactions between a firm and its stakeholders exist. B2B, B2C, B2G, and intranets represent interaction between businesses and other businesses, consumers, and government.

Modes and means of interaction involve how NE connects people and machines, and there are critical managerial implications of each of these connections. Media richness is also a central element in carrying forward ideas for NE into practice. Nets, level of aggregation, modes of interaction, and media are useful ways to think about how and when e-commerce takes place and the reach and range of e-commerce. Each class is useful in that it highlights options available to designers and manager.

There are successful examples of NE that use strategic relationships with other services to provide customer support and fulfill orders promptly. There are also unsuccessful attempts, as evidenced by the large-scale failures of dot.coms from 2000 to 2001.

KEY TERMS

B2B: Business-to-business exchanges of information.

B2C: Business-to-consumer exchanges of information.

B2G: Business-to-government exchanges of information.

Client-side software providers: Software applications used by consumers or clients.

E-Commerce designers/installers: Third-party vendors that install corporate intranets, network hardware and software, EDIs, and Web-oriented software.

E-Commerce-related hardware anufacturers: These manufacturers include PC and server hardware, network computers, modems, and point of sale device makers

E-Commerce security providers: These providers offer security for clients and servers as well as Internet and EDI proprietary networks

Electronic data interchange (EDI): A protocol that permits data to be delivered across networks.

Extranets: In effect, the network accessed when connecting to an internal network from outside the organization.

Hex Model: A stakeholder perspective on how technologies are applied; the model shows fundamental interactions between stakeholders.

Intranets: An internal network through which communication with and among employees is facilitated

Level of aggregation: Unit at which a phenomenon is studied, organization to organization, organizational unit to organizational unit, organization to consumer, or seller to buyer.

Media: Data, text, Web pages, Internet telephony, Internet video, virtual reality, and holograms.

Modes of interaction: Computer to computer, computer to human, and human to human.

Nets: This term includes networks, intranets, extranets, and the Internet.

Network access services providers: These providers sell network and Internet access and include common carriers such as AT&T, British Telecomm, ISPs, and cable companies.

Providers of e-commerce management: These institutions and organizations manage the Internet and set communication protocol standards.

Server-side software providers: Software for network operating systems or administrative support that run only on a server.

Web-integrating software providers: These providers create software that allows user to convert documents, images, or multimedia to Web pages.

REVIEW QUESTIONS

1. What constitutes the supply side of e-commerce?
2. What constitutes the demand side of e-commerce?
3. What are the fundamental elements of the e-commerce supplier industry?
4. Describe a client-server model.
5. The underlying structure that ties firms together and is the most instrumental in the ultimate success of e-commerce in a firm is _____.
6. What are the classes of interactions between firms and stakeholders?
7. What are the classes of NE activity?
8. Which form of communication between firms has the highest level of aggregation?
9. Name and describe three modes of technology-human exchange.
10. What are the three critical dimensions of communications media?

TOPICS FOR DISCUSSION

1. The interaction between the supply and demand sides of NE create the dynamic technological transformations that make e-commerce possible. Compare and contrast the industry side of e-commerce with the demand side of e-commerce.

2. Technology-driven markets include a push-pull phenomenon. Demand pulls new products from the marketplace, and innovation pushes new products into the marketplace. Discuss the role of the user in stimulating innovation.

3. The relationship between the 10 categories of providers suggest that a central feature is a client-server model. Discuss why client-server architecture is ideal for e-commerce applications.

4. Certain services are principal intermediaries for both the client side and the server side. Discuss the types of services that are common to both sides and the types of applications that each requires.

5 Users perceive payment services as a major enabler and crucial to the success of e-commerce. Discuss the managerial implications of payment services within the supply structure.

6. In the Hex Model of e-commerce, boundaries between the firm and the other stakeholders are open to indicate greater information exchange and the difficulty of establishing boundaries. Discuss why boundaries are more ambiguous in e-commerce models.

7. The supply chain is the underlying structure that ties firms together and is instrumental in the ultimate success of e-commerce. Give an example of how a supply chain can be streamlined through an e-commerce application.

8. Interactions between firms and their stakeholders include B2B, B2C, and B2G relationships. Discuss unique characteristics of each and the challenges that accompany those characteristics.

9. Designers and managers may approach e-commerce with a variety of perspectives concerning NE nets, level of aggregation, modes of interaction, and types of media. What is the impact of each of these perspectives on the design of an e-commerce system?

10. A variety of media can be transmitted electronically and used in an e-commerce setting. Discuss the decision-making process, concerning media, that firms must address in deciding the mix of media to be used in their firms.

INTERNET EXERCISES

1. Visit the download.com Web site. Graph the number of downloads for the top 10 rated applications on the site.

2. Download the Internet Appliance Industry Report from http://www.corecom.com/ia/. Compare and contrast the characteristics of two Internet appliances.

3. Locate a client-side software provider and describe one product offered by the provider.

4. Locate a server-side software provider and describe one product offered by the provider.

5. Identify a firm that employs intranets, extranets, and the Internet within the organization. Write a one-page essay describing the purpose and uses of these technologies to the organization.

6. Locate Internet product reviews on Dreamweaver and FrontPage Web development software. Prepare a PowerPoint presentation on the features, similarities, and differences in the two products.

7. Locate a firm that offers Web design service. Outline the services offered by the firm and the cost structure of the design service.

8. Look up the Internet Society. Write a short essay on the purpose of the Internet Society. Join up with a free membership!

9. Find a community that has implemented online government services for citizens. Describe the services offered and the technology used to offer the services.

10. Locate and describe a system that uses computer-working-alone to computer-working-alone technology.

TEAM EXERCISES

1. The provider industry can be structured into 10 categories. Have team members delegate the categories and locate an example of an organization that fits into each of the 10 categories. Describe the characteristics, the service or product offered, the cost, and the purpose of the product or service. Then, have each team member pair with another team member and describe how the organizations they chose are related.

2. Locate a firm on the Internet that shows a balance between competition and cooperation. Prepare a report on how the firm achieves "co-opetition." Describe the advantages, the disadvantages, and the challenges that co-opetition involves.

3. Create a PowerPoint tutorial on the classes of business exchanges with other businesses. Include real-world examples and links to other resources.

4. Have each team member find a local organization that is one of the types or classes of e-commerce activity. Analyze the organization in terms of the four perspectives.

5. Prepare a slide show of Web site media richness. Choose organizations on the Internet whose Web pages range from one-channel (text) multimedia to full channel (all media elements). Prepare a table similar to the table on properties of different media (Table 3.7) in this chapter. Your table should categorize the degree of media richness, social presence, and interactivity of these selected Web sites.

INTERNET RESOURCES

Coopetition Interactive (http://mayet.som.yale.edu/coopetition/index2.html)—This site provides interactive java applets designed to understand the concepts of co-opetition.

Free 3-D Software (http://www.3dcgi.com/learn/free/free-3d.htm)—This site provides links to free downloadable 3-D software and animation programs.

IP Telephony Products (http://iptel.org/info/products/)—This site provides a listing on Internet Telephony products and reviews.

REFERENCES

Daft, R. L., and R. H. Lengel. "Information Richness: A New Approach to Managerial Behavior and Organizational Design." In *Research in Organizational Behavior*, L. L. Cummings, and B. M. Staw, eds., JAI Press, Greenwich, CT, 1984, 191–233.

DiSabatino, J. "Boo.com Failure Raises Questions About Online Boutiques." *Computer-World Online*, June 12, 2000(a). [Online]. Available: http://www.computerworld.com/industrytopics/retail/story/0,10801,45735,00.html.

DiSabatino, J. "Boo.com's Domain, Brand Names Goes to Fashionmall.com." *Computer-World Online*, June 2, 2000(b). [Online]. Available: http://www.computerworld.com/industrytopics/retail/story/0,10801,45628,00.html.

Rangan, V. K., and M. Bell. "Dell Online." Case no. 598116, Harvard University, Boston, 27.

Robinson, M., D. Tapscott and R. Kalakota, *e-Business 2.0: Roadmap for Success*, Addison-Wesley, New York, 2000.

Rose, G., H. Khoo, and D. Straub. "Current Technological Impediments to Business-to-Consumer Electronic Commerce." *Communications of the AIS*, 16, June 1999, 1–74.

Rose, G. M., D. W. Straub, and J. D. Lees. "The Effect of Download Time on Consumer Attitude Toward the Retailer in E-Commerce." *Proceedings of the Sixth Americas Conference on Information Systems*, Long Beach, CA, 2000, 1352–1354.

Rosier, B. "What Went so Horribly Wrong with Boo.com?" *Marketing*, 2000, 9.

Short, J., E. Williams, and B. Christie. *The Social Psychology of Telecommunications,* Wiley, London, 1976.

Tillett, L. S. "It's Back From The Dead: Boo.com." *Internetweek*, 2000, 11.

Storey, V., D. Straub, K. Stewart, and R. Welke. "A Conceptual Investigation of the Electronic Commerce Industry." *Communications of the ACM*, 43, 7, July 2000, 117–123.

Watson, R. T., and D. W. Straub. "New Horizons for ICT Research in Net-Enhanced Organizations." Working paper, University of Georgia, Athens, GA, 2002.

Weiss, T. R. "Fashionmall.com is Buyout Target of Online Marketing Firm." *Computer-World Online*, January 2, 2001. [Online]. Available: http://www.computerworld.com/managementtopics/ebusiness/story/0,10801,55732,00.html.

CHAPTER 4

BASIC NE INFRASTRUCTURE

UNDERSTANDING THE NE TECHNOLOGICAL INFRASTRUCTURE

Why do managers need to understand the underlying technology of the NE (r)evolution? Isn't this "technical" stuff something you hire others to know about for you if you are a high-level manager? It turns out that good managers must have a base-level appreciation of what technology can and cannot do in order to even begin to strategize. This chapter attempts to create a more level playing field between nontechnical persons who have set their sights on managerial positions and those who are already well versed in NE technology.

LEARNING OBJECTIVES FOR THIS CHAPTER

- To recognize the differences between levels of technology
- To describe the functions of telecommunications network
- To describe the features and purposes of TCP/IP
- To understand the construction of IP addresses and domain names
- To identify the roles of ISPs and common carriers
- To discuss the purpose of EDI, EFT, and proprietary networks
- To compare and contrast "open" versus "closed" networks

▶ *CASE STUDY 4-1*

NETWORKS FOR THE FUTURE

Sun Open Net Environment (Sun ONE) is Sun Microsystem's standards-based software vision for building and deploying services on demand. It provides a highly scalable and robust foundation for traditional software applications as well as current Web-based applications, while laying the foundation for the next-generation distributed Web-service computing models. With annual revenues of $6 billion, Sun Microsystems, Inc., provides solutions that enable customers to build and maintain open-network computing environments.

Widely recognized as a proponent of open standards, the company is involved in the design, manufacture, and sale of products, technologies, and services for commercial and technical networking. Sun's SPARC workstations, multiprocessing servers, SPARC microprocessors, Solaris operating software, and ISO-certified service organization each rank number 1 in the UNIX industry. Because computer use is quickly changing from centralized to decentralized processing, from single use to networking, and from closed to open systems, Sun envisioned that the open versus closed standards not only have different impacts on developing future technologies, but also in economic, political, and cultural realms. Open standards were largely responsible for the PC revolution and the development of the Internet. Sun realized that open standards are important because they specify formats or protocols, which are published and discussed, tested, improved, agreed to, and used by a large user base that would ultimately improve sales. A closed network, on the other hand, no longer accepts new providers. If a network closes, then the customer can choose only from the providers already on the panel. This situation can only be good for providers already on the network, who face less competition. Having a larger network usually increases the quality of services available, because the network is more likely to have a provider with expertise in needed areas. Closed networks almost always result in customer frustration because of difficulties and problems finding a local provider. Closed standards, such as many of those used by Microsoft (called "trade secrets"), make it difficult for others to interact properly with those systems. Sun ONE is based on an open, standards-based architecture for easier integration with the product portfolio, solving immediate business requirements.

Discussion:
1. Discuss the advantages and disadvantages of open networks and closed networks.
2. How can open standards impact quality of services available?

Sources:
Tillman, M. A. and D. C. Yen. "Systems Network Architecture (SNA) and Open Systems Interconnection (OSI): Three Strategies for Connection." *Communications of the ACM*, 33, 2, February 1990.

Sun Open Net Environment (Sun ONE) at http://www.sun.com/sunone/whitepapers.html

Phipps, S., Chief Technology Evangelist, Sun Microsystems. Commentary for *ZD Net*, Aug 20, 2002, http://zdnet.com.com/2100-1107-954484.html

http://www.sun.com/smi/Press/sunflash/1995-12/sunflash.951204.6754.html

4.1 INTRODUCTION

This chapter will discuss the basic infrastructure of enhancing network connections between firms and between individuals. Most of the stress will be on publicly accessible networks, that is, the Internet. However, there will be some discussion of private networks, both point-to-point and broadcast networks. The computers that run the network, and those that interpret, display, and store information will also be discussed, both from a s/w and h/w perspective.

4.2 LEVELS OF TECHNOLOGY

There are three levels of technology that, together, describe NE technology:

1. Basic NE infrastructure
2. Middleware
3. Applications

In this chapter we are considering infrastructure. The other topics will be covered in the next chapter.

What is the essential difference between these levels? One metaphor that is sometimes used is plumbing. In a home bathroom, the pipes that snake through the walls and floors of the home are part of the infrastructure that brings water from the city or rural sources and takes away the refuse. The sinks, bathtubs, and so forth are the middleware between you as a user and the infrastructure. They make it possible to use the infrastructure. Thus, they serve as an *interface* that allows you to perform various functions in the facility.

What would be the metaphorical equivalent of applications in a bathroom? Let us think about what you use a bathroom for? As can be seen quickly in Figure 4.1, you may use the bathtub to take a nice, soaking bath and relax after a hard day. If there is a whirlpool application available in your tub, you may decide to turn that on. Or, you may be in a hurry and decide to take a quick shower.

Figure 4.1   Bathrooms as Infrastructure, Middleware, and Applications
Photo courtesy of PhotoDisc, Inc./Getty Images

In the language of computing, the infrastructure includes the connections that route signals from one node computer on the network to another, or internally between subnodes. It may also include parts of the processors that are designed to interpret the protocols.

A fuller discussion of the nature of middleware and applications will take place in Chapter 5. It is sufficient for the moment that you understand the essential difference between these technological levels or layers.

4.3 TELECOMMUNICATIONS INFRASTRUCTURE

The basic infrastructure of a public telecommunications network depends on a combination of physical and microwave connections, as shown in Figure 4.2. To communicate either through voice or data between Miami and Los Angeles may involve a number of message switches and transmission through other cities (unlikely to be as many as are shown here, but the route of the message is determined according to available connections and capacity). Figure 4.2 illustrates many of the possible media. Cell or PCS transmission within a city and infrared transmission within a LAN are also possibilities unrepresented in this diagram.[1] Access to the Internet via cell phones is popular in Europe and growing slowing in popularity in the United States. In Chapter 5, more will be said about this topic, which is also known as m-commerce, for mobile-commerce.

With respect to computer data and the Internet, this telecommunications backbone operates via a set of translations from one medium to the next because some of the media work with frequencies (either digital or analog), some work with analog signals, some with voltages (digital only), and so forth. Information about these translations is carried along with the messages that carry Internet content. In this way, a message that is carried digitally through a LAN running Ethernet can be transferred over to a telephone wire through an analog signal. Naturally, there must be computer hardware devices and network software that implement this transformation at each point that the medium changes.

[1]PCS or personal communications services are the all-in-one wireless phone, paging, messagin, and data services being offered by numerous carriers. The technology is based on digital rather than analog signals.

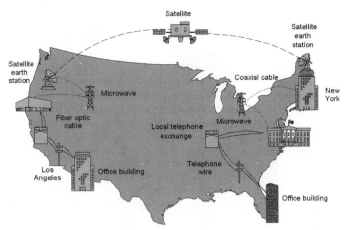

Figure 4.2   Physical, Satellite, and Microwave Connections in a Typical Telecommunications Connection

Most individuals come in contact with the issues having to do with basic infrastructure when they become involved in investment decisions, either organizationally or individually. The decision parameters are not terribly dissimilar, so we will explore this issue through an individual decision.

Suppose you want to access the Internet from home. The simplest connection would likely be use of a dial-up connection to an ISP or a value-added service such as AOL. A firm that provides you only with access to the Internet does not add value to your use. AOL, on the other hand, has a software interface and offers e-mail, community activities, news channels, and connections to preferred vendors. Value-added networks are sometimes referred to as VANs.

In order to complete your connection to the Internet, you need a device that changes the high and low voltages that represent digital bits in your computer into the analog signals that will be sent to the ISP or VAN over your voice-grade telephone line. The speed with which the computer can upload or download information from the Internet depends, for the most part, on the ability of your computer's hardware (modem) and software (Dial-Up Adapter in Windows 95-ME, 2000, and XP) to complete this translation. In the year 2001, the typical dial-up connection operated at about 56K baud, or 56 bits per second. Because there are 8 bits in a byte, and a byte is used to represent an alphanumeric character, a 56K connection will be able to maximally upload or download about 3K to 6K characters per second.

Focus on NE: DNS Hosting

There are many places you can host domain name system (DNS) records for your domain name. If you purchased a domain name, then DNS hosting might be included via your domain name provider. Your ISP or other service providers might also offer DNS hosting on a fee basis.

There are also free DNS hosting services available to the Internet community. One well-known free DNS hosting service is ZoneEdit.

ZoneEdit hosts reliable DNS servers, e-mail servers for e-mail forwarding, and Web servers for URL forwarding and parked domains. Zone Edit provides free hosting for up to five domain names and currently hosts 587,611 domains. ZoneEdit takes great pride in the value-added services offered at their site. Services provided by ZoneEdit include a Web-forwarding service, a mail-forwarding service, free starter Web page, and branded sites. Zone Edit also offers dynamic DNS support that allows users to run Web sites on their home PC through cable modems, DSL, and dial-up users. They also offer DNS monitoring and backup mail service. ZoneEdit provides a convenient single-location, integrated, Web-based domain manager for configuring all of their provided services.

Sources:
http://www.zoneedit.com/?ad=lookup
http://www.ids.org.au/main/tutorials/zoneedit_tutorial.php

4.3.1 TCP/IP

The translation mechanism that currently characterizes the Internet and, increasingly, LANs, is known as TCP/IP. Messages need to be sliced into certain sizes for transmission purposes. They also need to have header and trailer information that tells computers on the receiving end how to properly translate the message,

Known as "Internet protocol," IP was the original set of specifications designed for the Internet. It specified how information needed to be formatted in order for it to be interpretable at the receiving end. Unfortunately, the original IP did not have methods for dealing with errors in the transmission. TCP or transmission control protocol was, therefore, added to the IP to handle errors.

As Figure 4.3 shows, data to be transmitted may be thought of as traveling in units known as "packets." These boxes of data are transmitted to router computers or nodes, which are then sent on to other nodes until they finally reach the intended recipient. Nodes on the Internet are able to dynamically reroute packets if a node connection is lost or down. Each node maintains a database of possible intermediary nodes to which it can reroute the packet so that the loss of a single link or even multiple links does not incapacitate the entire system. This is why people say that the Internet is a "robust" network.

Data contents are labeled in the protocol with IP addresses so that the destination is known to all the network nodes that receive and forward the packet. IP addresses are actually sets of numbers identifying the computer (also known as "nodes" or routers) that originated the packet (the sender) and the computer intended to be the destination (the receiver). Figure 4.3 illustrates this as a "data" message being placed within an envelope that has "From" and "To" addresses.

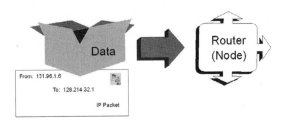

Figure 4.3   Data Packets and IP Addressing on the Internet

As strings of numbers, IP addresses are not user friendly, so "domain names" in alphanumeric Roman script were assigned to computer nodes as well as the numeric IP address. In the commercialization of the Internet using the World Wide Web, these domain names were critical so that users could locate nodes that held the information they were seeking.

One feature of TCP/IP was extremely important in the development of the Internet as a medium of communication. It was designed and implemented as an "open" protocol, available freely for use by any organization, institution, or person. There were many protocols in networking before TCP/IP. Most were "closed" systems in that they were owned and sold by commercial interests. IBM's networking protocol in this era was Systems Network Architecture (SNA), for instance.

Why is this fact critical in the evolution of the Internet? Begun as a "network of networks," its origin was in academic and defense circles for the free exchange of scientific information. By adopting a protocol that was available for free, the spread of the Internet was not hampered by commercial profiteering. It was readily adopted by all because of this openness.

▶ *CASE STUDY 4-2*

DELL COMPUTER CORPORATION

Dell Computer Corporation builds clients and servers for the NE infrastructure. They ship 20,000 PCs a day using the direct-to-consumer business model. By selling personal computer systems directly to customers, offering build-to-order systems, and providing solid service to back up its products, Dell has become one of the world's largest computer manufacturers. Based in Round Rock, Texas, Dell offers its products and services in more than 140 countries to customers ranging from major corporations, government agencies, and medical and educational institutions, to small businesses and individuals. The process has made Dell the world leader in direct sales of computer systems and has brought the company world recognition for its efficient business exchange model.

The company leverages the power of the Web to configure products in real time. Their NE system provides online order status, reduces order costs, and generates customized pricing and reports for corporate customers. A major design goal of Dell's Web e-commerce team was to create a site that could easily scale up in capacity as traffic increased. A data distribution scheme balances Web traffic by routing incoming Web requests through one of many front-end PowerEdge servers. Dell organizes information logically on the same servers rather than physically. Each server has a functional purpose. For example, Web servers run the presentation and business logic necessary for handling Web requests. Commerce servers handle the presentation and business logic needed to handle transactions. Dell has approximately 250 combination Web/application servers handling specific functions such as B2C commerce, B2B commerce, support, Premier Pages, and Gigabuys peripheral products site. Functional servers allow additional servers to be added without impact on online operations. It also ensures that customers can access the data they are looking for—such as pricing and model configurations—as quickly as possible with minimal waiting.

This parallel architecture gives Dell performance and stability. Objects are duplicated on Web/application servers and, in the event that a problem develops, the affected server can be removed or replaced without affecting all operations. The biggest key to Dell's success has been its ability to respond quickly to customer needs and to grow the business in pace with the burgeoning demand for PCs without overloading. Currently, 50% of Dell's Internet business revenue is generated by consumers and small businesses, but the company is rapidly increasing its corporate business because of its performance and stability.

Discussion:
1. Discuss the advantages to organizing server information logically instead of physically.
2. Discuss the impact of parallel architecture on performance and stability.

Sources:
http://www.microsoft.com/hk/solutions/ecommerce/dell.htm
http://www.microsoft.com/servers/evaluation/casestudies/dell.asp

4.4 WORLD WIDE WEB

Using TCP/IP as a basis, a graphical interface was created to be built on top of TCP/IP. The purpose of the original interface (known as Mosaic) was to permit an easy-to-use means of interacting with users. It supported multimedia for richer content and hyperlinks that encouraged simple choices through mouse clicks and radio buttons, selection boxes, and drop-down lists. The Mosaic browser was the immediate predecessor of Netscape's browser.[2]

Hypertext/hypermedia required its own freely available protocol, layered on top of TCP/IP; it is known as HTTP, or Hypertext Transmission Protocol.[3] With this protocol in place, software at the receiving end can ensure that hypertext and hypermedia can be displayed and "played" properly. We will discuss the software that sits in the middle between the HTTP infrastructure and the user applications in the next chapter. The software that interprets HTTP is known as a browser.

The combination of the Internet running via the TCP/IP protocol, the HTTP infrastructure, and browser software constitutes what is known as the World Wide Web (WWW), generally referred to as the "Web." The Web was the basic infrastructure (and middleware) that eventually allowed the development of commercial sites.

With the evolution of the Web, domain names were associated with numeric IP addresses, as shown in Figure 4.4, and these easy-to-remember addresses became one of the reasons for the enormous success of the Internet. Remembering "amazon.com" is simple compared to remembering a series of difficult-to-memorize and difficult-to-enter numbers.

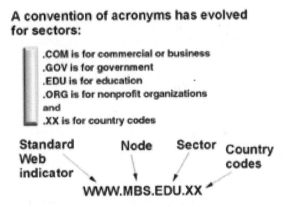

Figure 4.4   Internet IP Addresses as Domain Names

Not only are domain names such as "amazon.com" helpful in commercial situations, but Web servers, the computers that store and deliver the Web pages back to the client requesting the page, can also reinterpret the immediate URL placed in the locator line in the browser. As Figure 4.5 indicates, the Amazon server reinterprets "aMazOn.Com" as "www.amazon.com" to send back a page located on a subdirectory of the Amazon servers.

---

[2]Mosaic was the client-side software (browser) that interacted with the Web server and Web server software (such as Apache) through the HTTP protocol.
[3]HTTP is the graphical user interface (GUI) developed by Tim Berniers-Lee at CERN. It is the graphical display protocol that sits on top of TCP/IP.

Figure 4.5   Reinterpreted Domain Names at the Web Server Infrastructural Layer

4.5 CLIENT-SERVER NETWORK MODEL OF NET-ENHANCED COMMERCE

Clients and servers are also infrastructural elements. Servers respond to requests from clients for Web pages. As Figure 4.6 shows, the request is sent through the nodes of the Internet and answered in the same manner. From the standpoint of the client, the request is "uploaded," and the Web pages are "downloaded." The time to download is known as delay or wait time.

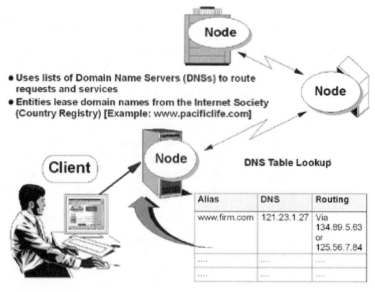

Figure 4.6   Client-Server Model and DNS Look-Ups

How does a node know where the requested Web page is sitting? Each node on the Internet has a table of DNS servers. These are listed by number and by alias, and a "table look-up" can check to find where the Web page is sitting. It also holds a routing that will eventually move the request to the destination. If that route is "broken" or "lost,"[4] it has alternate routes that can be used.

The availability of the alternative routes is what makes the Internet a robust network. Many links between nodes can be out of commission and the Internet will still function.

Clients and servers are the NE software elements that utilize the various network infrastructures. Naturally, each also requires hardware, and this hardware can be optimized for the particular function of each. So one tends to purchase heavy duty computing hardware for servers that are expected to engage in high volumes. Nevertheless, just to illustrate that clients and servers are primarily software, it is possible to set up a client and a server on the same piece of hardware and to actually access one's own node through the Internet. It is important for managers to recognize that software drives the development of NEOs. Hardware is primarily a commodity, with higher performance and lower costs with each generation. For this reason, the focus on NE development in firms should be on software rather than the latest hardware innovations.

4.6 ISPs AND COMMON CARRIERS

ISPs maintain large server nodes on the Internet and sell access to individual and firms. Cable companies provide this kind of service to be accessed through their cable modems, and Baby Bells[5] in the United States are frequently ISPs. Finally, many other firms have entered this market to provide Internet access and value-added services. In the latter category are Earthlink, AOL, and the like.

In the United States, common carriers include such firms as AT&T, Sprint, and the former Bell operating companies. Through ordinary twisted pairs of copper wire phone lines, they are now providing Internet access to customers from SMEs to large firms. Naturally, they also service the residential market. All-digital services include the older ISDN (Integrated Services Digital Network) and ADSL or DSL ([asymmetric] digital subscriber line). ISDN operates in the 124 Kbps (bits per second or baud) range, whereas DSL has a baud rate in the megabits.

4.6.1 EDI, EFT, and Proprietary Networks

It needs to be noted that some network applications between organizations run on proprietary networks and not on the Internet. EDI, which stands for electronic data interchange, is a decades-old technology/protocol that allows firms to send transactions directly over the network and to bypass physical processes. A firm that has established an EDI link with its suppliers can receive invoices over the Internet and pay them the same way. EFT, or electronic funds transfer, is another older technology that has been used for decades by banks to move money around electronically.

---

[4]Meaning that the connection is not available for some reason.
[5]The Baby Bells are the old AT&T operating companies, which were spun off when telecommunications industry was deregulated in the Unites States. These include firms like Bell South, Ameritech, and so forth.

Focus on NE: Secure TCP/IP

Telecommunication backbones are necessary for the basic infrastructure of a telecommunications network. MultiNet for OpenVMS is a leading TCP/IP that provides a reliable backbone for running mission-critical applications. MultiNet for OpenVMS is a suite of TCP/IP applications and services designed for Compaq's VAX and Alpha platforms. The system enables OpenVMS systems to participate as fully functional TCP/IP hosts. MultiNet enables a VAX or Alpha system to utilize all of the services and applications available on the Internet.

MultiNet provides several layers of security to protect against unauthorized network access and intruders from the Internet. Advanced security issues include Secure Shell v2 (SSH), Secure Copy Protocol (SCP), a Dynamic Host Configuration Protocol (DHCP) client, advanced Internet Printing Protocol (IPP) support, throughput statistics, and Simple Mail Transfer Protocol (SMTP) and File Transfer Protocol (FTP) accounting and statistical reports. Access restrictions also provide an additional layer of security to the network. Administrators can the applications local users can or cannot access. MultiNet also imposes incoming restrictions on the remote hosts' access to local services.

MultiNet is currently the running telecommunication backbone at the Department of Energy National Lab, General Dynamics, the University of Arizona and other major organizations.

Sources:
http://www.process.com/tcpip/multinet.html
http://www.process.com/tcpip/casestudy.html
http://www.process.com/tcpip/multinetds.html

Although these connections will be discussed in chapters that follow, it is important that readers know that they currently provide a great deal of the connectivity that is driving the Net-enhanced evolution away from physical connections. Over time, it is fairly clear that these connections will take place over the Internet. For the moment they are point-to-point dedicated connections for which firms pay service fees to the firms maintaining the telecommunicaitons infrastructure. There are security implications with respect to dedicated lines that will be discussed in subsequent chapters, but, for the present, it is sufficient to note that as popular as the Internet is, it does not fully describe the activity that has come to be known as e-business activity. Decades of sending messages via dedicated networks means that there is enormous momentum in this approach, and this represents a built-in resistance to changing to more-open, public systems.

4.6.2 "Open" versus "Closed" Networks

Figure 4.7 illustrates the difference between "open" and "closed" systems and networks. Point-to-point connections are closed in that no one other than the two parties involved in the transaction has access to what is, in effect, a private network. This is costly and difficult administratively because each link needs to be established beforehand, and the link needs to be maintained as a permanent connection.

Figure 4.7 NEOs Smashing the "Closed," Proprietary Links

Breaking away from closed systems means that NEOs will adopt an open systems architecture. There are many nodes on the Internet, and so a particular line does not need to be established in advance. In the chapter on security, we will see how firms use this basic infrastructure to create networks links that act as if they were private, one-to-one links.

4.7 SUMMARY

Managers need to understand basic NE infrastructure in order to rethink their strategies for the Networked Economy. This chapter will discuss the basic infrastructure of network connections between firms and network connections between individuals.

Basic NE infrastructure, middleware, and applications are the three levels of technology that describe NE technology. This chapter focuses on the basic NE infrastructure, the network connections between firms, and network connections between individuals.

The basic infrastructure necessary for a public telecommunications network depends on a combination of physical and microwave connections. The telecommunications backbone operates via a set of translations. Some of the media work with frequencies (digital or analog), some work with analog signals, and some with voltages. Computer hardware devices and network software are required for these translations to take place.

The translation mechanism that characterizes the Internet is known as TCP/IP. TCP/IP creates a "robust network" in that each node of the computer maintains a database of possible intermediary nodes to which it can reroute packets of information and data. The loss of a single link or of multiple links does not incapacitate the entire system. Data contents are labeled with an IP address that uniquely identifies the network nodes. IP addresses are given domain names so that users can conveniently locate nodes in the network. TCP/IP is a free, open protocol system and, because of these characteristics, has been readily accepted by all.

The World Wide Web is the combination of the Internet running on TCP/IP, the HTTP infrastructure, and browser software. The Web was the basic infrastructure that allowed the development of commercial sites. Basic infrastructure includes ISPs and common carriers, EDIs, EFTs, proprietary networks, open versus closed networks, and clients and servers.

KEY TERMS

ADSL or DSL: (Asymmetric) digital subscriber line, an all-digital service with a baud rate in megabits.

Browser: The software that interprets HTTP.

Clients and Servers: NE software that utilizes various networks.

.com: Acronym for the commercial sector of the World Wide Web.

Point-to-Point Connections: Closed connections that include only the two parties involved in the transaction. They are, in effect, private networks which are costly and difficult to administer because a specific link needs to be opened beforehand and maintained during the transmission.

Domain Names: User-friendly names in alphanumeric roman script assigned to computer nodes associated with the numeric IP address. The domain name is composed of various indicators which include respectively, the standard Web indicator, node, sector, and country.

Domain Name System (DNS): A process on a server that maps addresses to IP addresses and IP addresses to names.

EDI: Electronic data interchange, an old technology that allows firms to send transactions directly over the network and to bypass physical processes.

.edu: Acronym for the educational sector of the World Wide Web.

EFT: Electronics funds transfer, an old technology used by banks to move money around electronically.

.gov: Acronym for the government sector of the World Wide Web.

HTTP: Hypertext Transfer Protocol, which makes it possible for software at the receiving end to ensure that hypertext and hypermedia can be displayed and "played" properly. HTTP sits on top of TCP/IP.

IP: Internet Protocol, the original set of specifications designed for the Internet, which specified how information needed to be formatted in order for it to be interpreted at the receiving end.

IP Address: Sets of numbers that identify the sending computer that originated the packet and the computer intended to be the receiver.

ISDN: Integrated Services Digital Network, an all-digital service operating in the range of 124 Kbps.

ISP: Internet service providers who maintain large server nodes on the Internet and sell access to individuals and firms.

LAN: Local area network.

Mosaic: An early graphical interface for the Internet that was created to sit on top of TCP/IP. It supported multimedia for richer content and hyperlinks that encouraged simple choices through mouse clicks, radio buttons, selection boxes, and drop down lists.

Open Systems: An architecture characterized by the many nodes on the Internet, so that a particular line does not have to be established in advance.

Packets: Indivisible, discrete units of transmitted data.

Routers: Computing devices that route messages through to various other computers or nodes till they reach their final destination.

SME: Small-and-medium sized enterprises.

TCP: Transmission Control Prototcol added to IP to deal with transmission errors.

TCP/IP: Transmission Control Protocol/Internet Protocol, the translation mechanism that currently characterizes the Internet and, increasingly, LANs. It is an open protocol freely available for use by any institution, organization, or person.

Telecommunications Infrastructure: The basic infrastructure of a public telecommunications system of physical and microwave connections.

VANs: Value-added networks, such as AOL, which provide software interfaces, e-mail, community activities, news channels, and connections to preferred vendors in addition to a basic Internet connection.

World Wide Web: The combination of the Internet running on TCP/IP, the HTTP infrastructure, and browser software, also known as the Web.

.xx: Acronyms indicating country codes on the World Wide Web, for example, UK or uk for the United Kingdom.

REVIEW QUESTIONS

1. Describe the connections that a public telecommunications network depends on for basic infrastructure requirements.
2. How can messages be transferred from one medium to the next?
3. Identify some value added networks offered by Internet service providers.

4. What determines the speed of loading or downloading information form the Internet?
5. What is the transmission mechanism that currently characterizes the Internet?
6. How are messages translated over a TCP/IP?
7. Why is the Internet considered a "robust" network?
8. Define "IP address."
9. What is Mosaic?
10. What are the components of the World Wide Web?
11. How does a client know where a requested Web page is located?

TOPICS FOR DISCUSSION

1. Discuss the purpose of a telecommunications network and describe how the backbone of a telecommunications company operates?
2. Discuss the types of value-added services that an ISP may offer.
3. Discuss the importance and significance of TCP/IP.
4. Discuss the ways in which the Internet is a "robust" network? What would happen in a network that was not "robust"?
5. Discuss the impact of using open networks versus closed networks.
6. Describe the process that occurs when a Web site is requested from a client.
7. Discuss the origin and functions of ISPs and common carriers.
8. What are the primary functions of EDI, EFT, and proprietary networks?
9. Enumerate the characteristics of closed networks.
10. Discuss why clients and servers are considered software elements.

INTERNET EXERCISES

1. Identify your favorite ISP. Provide the Web page address and features of the ISP. Explain why this provider is your favorite.
2. Identify your browser of choice. Provide the Web page address of the browser and describe the functions and features of the browser.
3. Identify the advantage and disadvantages of open protocols. Find a related article through the Internet and summarize the contents.
4. What is VAN? Identify three VAN features in your ISP software interface and describe how these features affect your Internet use.
5. Find an example of closed protocol. Research related articles and provide a summary of your findings.
6. Design a personal Web page and upload it to the Internet. You may use free Web page building tools and a free space site such as http://geocities.yahoo.com/.
7. Describe and define the specifications of your computer. Include information about the brand, memory, RAM, ROM, and modem speed.
8. Locate a Web page address with a descriptive domain name. Describe the advantages of having a domain name and why it is important that the domain name reflect the purpose of the Web site.
9. What happened to free Internet service? Itemize the reasons free Internet service is no longer available.

TEAM EXERCISES

1. One of the telecommunication networks commonly used in business is a LAN system . Create a PowerPoint presentation regarding LAN systems. Include the following information:

(a) Definition of a LAN

(b) A diagram of LAN connections

(c) Describe ISDN, ADSL, and DSL applications

(d) Explain the advantages and disadvantages in implementing a LAN in an organization.

2. Create a PowerPoint presentation regarding the Internet evolution. Include the following information.

(a) Explain closed protocol and open protocols.

(b) Identify the users of different protocols.

(c) Provide an example of closed and open protocols and identify the advantages and disadvantages of each.

3. The Internet is called a "robust network." Compose an illustrated report to describe the features of the Internet that make it "robust." Provide examples and personal experiences and describe the advantages of this type of network.

4. Pick NE software of your choice. Make a PowerPoint presentation to introduce the software you choose including:

(a) Identify the strong points of the software.

(b) Identify the weak points of the software.

(c) Describe the advantages and disadvantages of the software.

(d) Explain how the software can be improved to maximize your business operation using a real-life scenario.

5. Create a PowerPoint presentation regarding different types of online connections including:

(a) The difference between analog and digital connections

(b) The strong points of each connection type

(c) The weak points of each connection type

(d) The cost of each connection type

INTERNET RESOURCES

HTTP Simulator (http://cne.gmu.edu/itcore/internet/Java/Module1.html): This site provides a simulation of HTTP. The simulation explains that a Web page is a series of requests and demonstrates the actions that take place to display the Web page.

Programs for Internet Access (http://odur.let.rug.nl/~bert/PROSA/rep-programs.html): The programs in this list are, at the moment, the most popular programs for accessing the various Internet services. There are several programs available for both Unix and MS-Windows.

CHAPTER 5

MIDDLEWARE TECHNOLOGIES AND APPLICATIONS

UNDERSTANDING NE MIDDLEWARE TECHNOLOGIES AND APPLICATIONS

Middleware is an essential linkage between infrastructure and programs that support user actions on the Internet. These actions are supported by endware or applications, which are themselves the lifeblood of NE. Without a basic level of understanding of how these work, a manager will never be able to follow the critical lines of strategic thinking that top managers pursue. Competitive advantage calls for managers who can see the future and move toward it. Increasingly, it is the managers who can speak a basic level of "tech" talk and who can bring about this transformation within their organizations.

LEARNING OBJECTIVES FOR THIS CHAPTER

- To define middleware and illustrate it through the client and server programs that characterize this class of technology
- To provide details about how client-side middleware browsers and HTML coding of endware Web pages interact on the World Wide Web
- To describe the role of server-side middleware programs, Web services, and databases in fulfilling user requests for Web pages
- To articulate the functioning of plug-ins in interpreting Web pages
- To describe at a high generic level the capability of client plug-ins such as encryption, m-commerce, FTP, e-mail, and so forth
- To differentiate World Wide Web applications by revenue models, including: (1) ad-based, (2) referral-based, (3) subscription-based, (4) sales-based, and (5) transaction-based.

▶ *CASE STUDY 5-1*

LONELY PLANET

The Internet travel industry is experiencing enormous growth, and predictions are that in the United States 14% of leisure travel sales will be made online by 2005. Lonely Planet™ is at the forefront of the online travel industry by providing guides to many locations around the world. Lonely Planet created CitySync™, a line of digital city guides designed for handheld computer devices, to assist travelers with information about destination cities. In January of 2000, CitySync launched the first five CitySync cities—Las Vegas, Los Angeles, Paris, San Francisco, and Sydney. There are now more than 20 CitySync modules available, and new cities are continually being added. CitySync can be purchased and downloaded directly from the Internet. The customer locates city maps and other information resident on the firm's servers. CitySync provides users with detailed street maps; hundreds of hotel, restaurant, nightlife, and attraction reviews; bookmarks and custom notes. Maps and text available through CitySync are fully integrated with the PalmOS Date Book feature so that users can access restaurants and then locate them using the scrollable maps. The program allows travelers to customize their own travel notes, and they can automatically record details of their travels and their likes and dislikes in their Palm Date Book.

One of the difficulties that Lonely Planet had to overcome when in the developing stage was the continuous evolution in handheld computers. When CitySync was first developed in 1999, the standard device memory was just 2 MB. Because each CitySync module requires 300–650 KB of memory, device memory was at a premium. Today 6–8 MB is more common. The effect of this is that the newer models can now more easily accommodate multiple city modules. Currently, the system requirements for CitySync are a PalmOS 3.0 or higher, a Macintosh or Windows desktop or laptop with sync cradle, Palm Desktop software 2.0 or later, and 300–650 KB available device memory per city.

Lonely Planet needed to develop significant middleware at their hosting site to service Web requests for the CitySync product. The server needs to match up the requests with the appropriate downloads and ensure that the transmission has been completed. It needs to be a secure transaction as well.

Over the next year, Lonely Planet will continue producing CitySync guides for major cities around the world and provide free updates to users who have already purchased and installed CitySync cities. Lonely Planet will also continue to investigate bringing services to all travelers, regardless of their mobile platform.

Discussion:
1. Discuss how m-commerce extended the services offered by CitySync.
2. Discuss the importance of the choice of platform for m-commerce applications.

Sources:
Weill, P., and M. Vitale. *From Place to Space Migrating to eBusiness Models.* Harvard Business School Press, Cambridge, MA., 2001.
Lonely Planet™, http://press.lonelyplanet.com/
CitySync™, http://www.citysync.com/about/about.htm
http://press.lonelyplanet.com/press/pr-palmpak.htm

5.1 INTRODUCTION

This chapter will discuss the middleware technologies that lie between the basic infrastructure and the endware applications with which users eventually interact. These middleware technologies provide the bridge between networks, which are hidden from users, and Web pages or applications in HTML code (and other language code) to which users are responding most immediately. These technologies have a life of their own, in the sense that they can operate separate from the network, although, clearly, their major functionality derives from the ability to communicate across time and space via the Internet. Designers can test their middleware programs independent of the Internet. When these programs are ready for production, designers turn them "on" for public use.

Middleware is the "glue" of the Internet, the layer of software between the network and the applications. Middleware occurs in obvious places such as browsers on the client side. But they can also be highly technical and not at all obvious to users.[1] Middleware can provide Web services such as identification, authentication, authorization, directories, and security. Because applications implementing these features could use very different technical approaches, open standards to which everyone can subscribe are extremely important in making the Internet accessible and competitive, and open Web services that can be downloaded and incorporated into applications will increase the ease-of-use of advanced network applications.

---

[1]For more on middleware, see http://middleware.internet2.edu/.

Focus on NE: PGP or Pretty Good Privacy

 Pretty Good Privacy (PGP) is strong encryption software that enables you to protect your e-mail and files by scrambling them so others cannot read them. You can use PGP to communicate securely about business plans; legal, financial, or medical matters; or any other personal matters that you would rather keep private. It also allows you to digitally "sign" your messages in a way that allows others to verify that a message was actually sent by you. PGP is available in freeware and commercial versions all over the world. PGP is one of the most common ways to protect messages on the Internet because it is effective, easy to use, and free. PGP is based on the public-key method that uses two keys — one is a public key that you disseminate to anyone from whom you want to receive a message, the other is a private key that you use to decrypt messages that you receive. To encrypt a message using PGP, you need the PGP encryption package, which is available for free from a number of sources. The official repository is at the Massachusetts Institute of Technology. PGP is such an effective encryption tool that the U.S. government actually brought a lawsuit against its author Phillip Zimmerman, for putting it in the public domain and making it available to enemies of the United States. After a public outcry, the U.S. lawsuit was dropped, but it is still illegal to use PGP in many other countries.

Sources:

http://www.pgp.com/

http://web.mit.edu/network/pgp.html

5.2 CLIENT-SIDE MIDDLEWARE

5.2.1 Browsers (and the Interpretation of HTML and XML Code)

The middleware that users are most familiar with are browsers. Browsers are computer programs that are designed to interpret Web pages (applications) sent via the HTTP over the Internet. If an opening page is not specified when opening a browser program, the browser opens a blank page. This illustrates how the basic program works. The browser is programmed to find and interpret the display characteristics of Web pages and to run small programs that can be incorporated into the Web page code. The Web pages may be accessed over the Internet, or they may be sought out on the local disk (hard drive) or LAN servers.

Designers create Web pages locally. As they write their HTML code or use a Web-integrating software package, such as Microsoft FrontPage, they can invoke the browser residing on their local disk and, with this middleware, test the look and functionality of their Web page applications. When they are convinced that their application is ready for prime time, they can upload it to the server and make it available for intranet, extranet, or public Internet use.

How exactly does a browser work? The principles are straightforward, although browsers have become more sophisticated over the years and now offer many sophisticated features. The essential characteristic of a browser is to allow a user to "browse" the World Wide Web of applications. The user interface display that appears before the user may be thought of as *endware* because the user enters information into the Web page on the screen, and these responses are transferred back to the server for processing. The application residing on the server comes to the user and is the major point of contact between the user and the system. That is why the browser may be thought of as middleware and the application as endware.

How does it do this? Browsers interpret Web pages written in HTML or XML downloaded from the server. Because these are two of the most common languages used in browsers, it is necessary to first understand what these markup languages are. Both languages use a tag system to indicate how a line should be displayed on the computer screen. For example, to display a line of content on the screen that is centered, bolded, italicized, and formatted by using the preset heading #1 font and font size, the HTML code would look like the following:

<H1> Home Page </H1>

When the browser receives a Web page from a server at a remote (or local) node with this HTML code in it, the browser is programmed to display the following on the screen for the user:

Home Page

Multimedia can also be displayed. The following command line calls for the display of a graphic of a businessman sitting on a beanstalk. The HTML code is: <img border=0 width=69 height=41src=businessman.gif hspace=10 alt="An Organic Firm">. Figure 5.1

shows what the image looks like. By default and unless specified to the contrary, the browser seeks out the source of the file in the same location as the Web page; the file name it looks for in this case is businessman.gif. GIF (graphical interchange format) files are frequently found on Web pages. If the source of the file requires the browser to download the file from the Internet, it will do this.

The code section beginning with alt indicates that the browser will display the words "An Organic Firm" in a box on the display screen if the user moves the mouse over the image. A border is not going to be displayed around the image ("border=0"), but the HTML code specifies the size of the image as it appears on the screen (in pixels).

More will be said about XML later, but the same capabilities for telling browsers how to display characters and symbols are also present in XML.

Figure 5.1   Graphical Image for "An Organic Firm" Presented through a Browser Downloading and Displaying the Source of the File

Browsers are not only limited to just displaying symbols, but also manipulate them. Within the HTML or XML code retrieved from the server can be small programs known as applets. These programs may be written using a language such as Java, JavaScript, or C++, and they are capable of manipulating user inputs called for by the Web page as it is displayed.

A JavaScript applet, for example, can send information about who is accessing the Web page to a public site.[2] The site then sends an increased-by-one "hit" number to a counter that is displayed on the user screen. The Web page owner can access the public site for overall statistics and other specific information on those who requested the page. The JavaScript code to accomplish this is shown below:

```
<script language=javascript><!--

s="";sc="";screencolors="";var xy = navigator.appVersion;xz = xy.substring(0,3);function

write(){document.write("<a href='http://[domain name of public site]/check.cgi?id=owner'
target='_top'>");
```

---

[2]These sites, which you can find by querying a search engine on the keywords "Web page counter," derive their revenues from advertising or from commercial licenses of the same service. Some of them do not charge for small firms with a limited number of Web pages requiring counters.

document.write("<img height='25' width='25' border='0' alt='[domain name of public site] - free statistic tracker'",

"src='http://[domain name of public site]/statz.cgi?id=dstraub&browser="+navigator. appName+"&version="+xz+"",

"&ref="+escape(document.referrer)+"&screen="+s.height+"x"+s.width+"& colors="+sc+"></a>");}

//--></script><script language="javascript1.2"><!--

s=screen;xy!="Netscape"?sc=s.colorDepth:sc=s.pixelDepth;

//--></script><script language="javascript"><!--

write();//--></script><noscript><a href="http://[domain name of public site]/ check.cgi?id=owner">

<img src="http://[domain name of public site]/statz.cgi?id=owner" border=0></a></ noscript>

The counter that is displayed on a professional Web page for an academic course is shown in Figure 5.2. The counter has advanced to 1174 hits, which also includes hits for the development of the Web site, in this case.

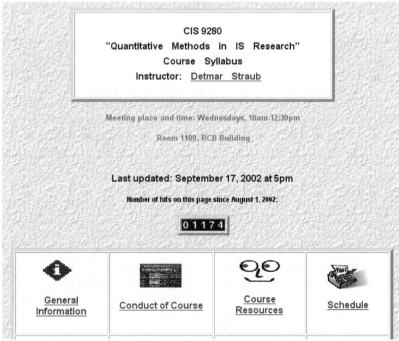

Figure 5.2   The Counter Increases by One via JavaScript Code Embedded in HTML Code Each Time It Is Accessed

5.3 SERVER-SIDE MIDDLEWARE

When servers receive requests from browsers via HTTP, the server software processes the request to retrieve the page. The page requested may involve manipulation of data or accessing a database for information. If there are parameters for these calculations or searches, that information will be sent to the server along with the name and location of the Web page (this is specified in the URL).

Servers are certainly hardware, and, as hardware devices, or central processing units, they are pretty much commodities that can be purchased according to anticipated volume of activity and sophistication of the Web site's response to customer requests. The most essential element of a server is its ability to compile and run designated server programming languages. There are a number of languages that can be used to program server responses. Singly or together, software programs written for the server work to fulfill client requests from the browser. Some of the most popular languages are ASP, CGI, Perl, PHP, and ColdFusion. Certain firms specialize in linking requests coming to servers from users to databases; products such as the Oracle database and SQL Server are databases that are adapted to fulfilling Web requests for information.

Let us explore a B2C Web application to see how server middleware would respond to a client request. If one were interested in finding a book on a certain subject, one might visit barnesandnoble.com, amazon.com, or borders.com. In reply to a user's initial request for the firm's site, the server will send an opening screen that allows one to enter search parameters. This screen also advertises books and allows the user to interact with a virtual community. If it can be detected that this is a return visit, the server might respond in a more pointed fashion. This potential will be discussed later.

The Web page that is retrieved from the online bookseller has been written in a combination of a markup language (e.g., HTML) and, say, a manipulation language such as Java, and these applets are embedded in the markup language code. When the client browser processes the page, some activities may be able to be processed locally, that is, on the client's machine. When the user enters purchasing information, for instance, an applet can process the entries to be sure that mandatory fields have been filled in. There are many other uses for distributed processing of which the Web designer can take advantage.

If a user is a return visitor, the server may be able to individually identify the user because the server has previously set a cookie on the user client machine. Cookies are short segments of data that are written on the user's hard disk. This action can be disenabled by the user, but the default on most browsers is usually that the cookie setting is enabled.

If one or more cookies have been set, the users' past behaviors and interests could be identified briefly in the cookies or sufficiently identified so that the server could relay a request to other firm computers. These computers could be what is known as *legacy system* computers, meaning that they are used to store and process basic accounting data, such as order and book inventory information. So if a user has purchased previously from the firm, the dates and book titles of these purchases could be made available to the server. One of the functions of the firm's Web application could be to inform the user that there have been new titles added to a subject area of interest of the customer.

This form of tailored response is a substitute for information from a physical phone call from a customer representative or even a personalized response in a physical store. If, for example, a firm's computers record that a user had visited the physical store before, and they identify the relevant customer subject areas through a credit card number that was recorded for a past physical purchase, the limitations of the physical store setting might inhibit the use of that information. During times when the sales clerks are busy just processing sales, there would be little time to even mention the new titles that might be of interest to the customer. But an on-site kiosk connected to the firm's home page could provide this service.

Cookies are a good way for firms to personalize responses. However, some users dislike the idea of firms placing information on their hard drives, and they disenable cookies. The identification of the visitor can still be accomplished, though. Alternatively, for instance, firms can have users log into their site and identify themselves through this mechanism.

5.3.1 Web Services

Among the technical middleware being touted today for the Internet are Web services such as CORBA (common object request broker architecture) and component-based engineering environments such as Sun's J2EE and Microsoft's .Net.

CORBA is an open, vendor-independent standard that computer applications use to coordinate processes across networks. Using the standard IIOP (Internet Inter-Orb Protocol), CORBA-based applications can interoperate with other applications from any vendor on any hardware and software platform as long as it uses CORBA. CORBA can also be used for server load balancing.

An example of a CORBA-based application would be server software that manages a shopping cart for a B2C Web site. Communications between the shopping cart on Web pages and authentication services, such as credit card companies, could be established through CORBA standards.

J2EE and .Net are frameworks or programming environments that facilitate middleware development. The idea behind them is that components can be built that would provide a standardized service such as security authentication of a message's integrity. When a firm needs to build server middleware, it can use the standards provided by these frameworks. Components can be rapidly assembled from different sources, and they will be able to interoperate with other servers.

5.4 CLIENT PLUG-INS

The Web page that is downloaded to the user may also rely on languages/applications that reside with the client. These languages or applications are known as *plug-ins*. This middleware works in harmony with the browser to present the Web page as it was intended to be presented to the user.

For example, a user can download Macromedia's Shockwave Player from www.macromedia.com, and install it on his or her client. This player enables multimedia content to be displayed as video, animation, and sound. It works in concert with the browsers whenever the Web page calls for it. Figure 5.3 shows a still version of the kind of content that this plug-in supports.

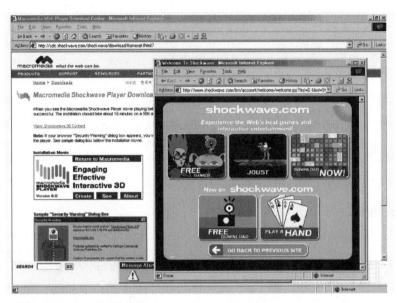

Figure 5.3   Example of a Plug-In

There are many other types of plug-ins, some that allow a user to subscribe to an online service, for example. Antivirus firms, such as McAfee and Norton, will alert a user through a browser pop-up screen that an update to the latest virus filters is available and will either proceed with an automatic update or prompt the user for approval. Figure 5.4 shows the McAfee Clinic for such updates.

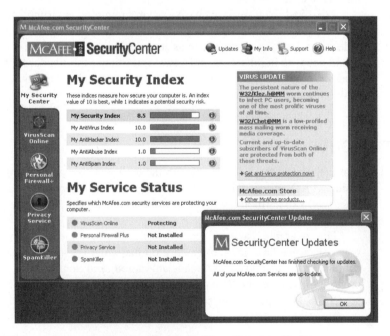

Figure 5.4   Antivirus Application Plug-In for Virus Signature Updates

5.5 ENCRYPTION (CLIENT AND SERVER)

Encryption is a middleware technology for securing the communications between parties from unauthorized access, interruption, and authentication. It will be discussed in greater detail in the next chapter, but it is critical to note at this point that, once again, encryption sits between the infrastructure and the user interface. Encryption (software) is middleware because it converts plaintext on one end of the transmission to an unreadable ciphertext and then, at the other end, translates it back into plaintext. Because of the need to encrypt and decrypt, encryption software is both a client and server middleware.

5.6 CLIENT M-COMMERCE AS MIDDLEWARE

Since middleware is the interface between users and the NE infrastructure, another set of middleware technologies that will grow and mature over the coming years is mobile commerce. Mobile commerce, or m-commerce, includes cell phones with Internet access and more intelligent interfaces such as PDAs (personal digital assistant). By a short extension of the logic, it can also include laptop computers with a cellular or PCS (personal communication services) connection to the Internet.

The key differentiating factor in this technology is the fact that it depends on a wireless infrastructure and wireless connection to the Internet. Radio signals have bandwidth limitations, but, even so, a large amount of information can be conveyed through this medium.

Why do people engage in m-commerce? M-Commerce has a distinct advantage over desktop machines and even laptops that require a hard line connection to the Internet, for that matter. These devices can be readily carried on a user's person or in small accessories like briefcases or purses. Their ability to access the Internet anyplace will transform organizational tasks and likely lead to huge productivity gains. Collaboration will be well supported because members of work groups will be highly accessible. The ability to bring closure to tasks is a key advantage of this form of media.[3]

The limitations of the compact m-commerce technologies are similar to their strengths. PDAs and cell phones, by their very nature, have small screens. Only so much information can be conveyed and displayed, and so Web pages have to be altered to suit the interface.

In fact, the connection between wireless devices and the Internet is also specialized by the protocol utilized. Currently, this protocol is called WAP (Wireless Application Protocol). The use of this protocol tells the server that the Web page to be delivered has to be altered to fit smaller screens. WAP is a substitute protocol for TCP/IP and may be a harbinger of newer protocols, which will eventually be used to convey messages across the Internet.

---

[3]Straub and Karahanna (1998).

5.7 WEB-INTEGRATING MIDDLEWARE (CLIENT)

It should be clear that the markup language code that is sent from a server resides on the server before it is transmitted over the Internet. Why then, in Chapter 3, is the software that is used to create this code designated as client-side software? The reason for this classification is that clients are typically where the applications in markup languages are written, so most participants in the GSU study saw them as associated with the client.

Does one have to be an expert in markup languages in order to design Web applications? Not necessarily, especially for simple Web pages. Some programs are able to generate markup language code even if the user is not conversant with these languages. Microsoft Word, for example, has an option to save the document as a Word (.doc) file, or a simple text (.txt) file, or as an HTML (.htm) file. Microsoft FrontPage and Dreamweaver are other integrating tools that generate the code. These forms of code-generation are WYSIWYG (what you see is what you get). If all goes as it should, the displays the user sees on the screen are exactly what one would see if a browser were the display interface. Clearly, then, in order to do this, these generators also have browser-like capabilities built into them.

In fact, the major browsers also have *composer* tools inherent in them to help users build their own Web pages. Each of these tools has different capabilities, but the only important thing to remember at this point is that code generators can make the job of designing Web systems much shorter and easier.

If a designer is unable to write code directly in tagged HTML or XML, many simple word processors are the middleware that facilitate the creation of the code. In this case, the designer must also open a browser to know how a browser will interpret the code.

Where does the application with which the designer is working sit? Does the application program reside on the designer's own client machine or on a Web server? The answer is that it can be on either. The browser will interpret the code that it is told to find by the URL, which is entered either by typing it in or by a Netscape bookmarked entry (known as a *favorite* in Microsoft's Internet Explorer browser). It is worth noting here that if a local disk drive is designated (such as the C: drive), the Internet "http://...." protocol is not appropriate. The format that is appropriate is simply "file::://...." followed by the drive, directory or directories, and file name. The designer can also access markup language code by choosing File | Open.

It is important that managers comprehend the fundamentals of middleware because good investment decisions depend on managers understanding how such systems work, at least at a high conceptual level. What should be clear to all readers at this point is that the client-server model describes reasonably well how Internet commerce works. Browsers are the primary vehicle for users, and servers process requests for pages (written in markup languages and, possibly, other languages).

PROGRESSIVE INSURANCE

Progressive Insurance, the fourth largest insurance company in the United States, launched its Web site in 1990, becoming one of the first major auto insurance companies with a Web presence and the number 1 rated auto insurance Web site. It is estimated that more than 1 million new visitors come to the site each month. The progressive.com site boasts traffic leadership over insurance company sites such as Allstate, State Farm, and GEICO. The company leads the insurance industry in consumer-friendly innovations with online auto insurance quoting and comparison rates, instantaneous online purchase of auto policies, and after-sale service.

Progressive was the first auto insurance company to offer real-time online sales of auto insurance to customers. Customers can buy direct online, over the phone, or through one of the 30,000-plus independent agents. Progressive's Web site allows customers to buy insurance online, manage policies by making payments online, change coverage at any time, make policy changes, and report claims.

Progressive is also the first auto insurance company to provide wireless Internet access to its Web site using WAP. WAP allows consumers to access general information about the company, find an independent agent in their neighborhood by inputting their ZIP code, and immediately connect to a direct sales agent. Existing Progressive customers can make payments via Web-enabled PDAs and connect immediately (via the phone) to Policy Services to make changes to their policy and/or report a claim.

Discussion:
1. Discuss the importance of having a Web presence on line. Describe the competitive advantage provided by having a Web presence.
2. Discuss the value added of WAP.

Sources:
Progressive Casualty Insurance, http://www.progressive.com/progressive/history.asp#3
"Insurance now offered on Web." *Insurance Systems Bulletin*, No. 6, 42(1), June 2002.
http://www.progressive.com/newsroom/number1_00.asp
http://portals.devx.com/SummitDays/Article/6665

5.8 MIDDLEWARE ABOVE AND BEYOND THE WORLD WIDE WEB

Millions of Web pages are available worldwide to users. This is both the triumph and downfall of the Web, as will be discussed under the topic of technological impediments in Chapter 13. But there are other forms of middleware that need to be discussed before we carefully sample from these millions of applications. This NE middleware is remarkable in its simplicity and, some would argue, has been largely responsible for the success of the Internet.

Web middleware uses HTTP, as we have discussed, and, therefore, the Web utilizes TCP/IP. But there are protocols besides HTTP that are based on TCP/IP and convey information across the Internet. Many of these antedated the Web. FTP, e-mail, Gopher, Archie, Telnet, and many other protocols were available on the Internet long before HTTP and the World Wide Web came online in 1989.

For illustrative purposes, consider FTP. This protocol will be discussed next.

5.8.1 FTP and Applications

FTP can be activated on the Internet itself or within browsers and the Web, the latter of which allowing Web sites to upload software or data upon user request. The protocol specializes in transferring files of any type. PDF files and self-extracting executable files are equally subject to the transfer so are document files such as Word files.

Specialized programs for utilizing FTP have been developed to display in separate parts of the window the sending and receiving directories. Figure 5.5 shows how these directories appear in WS-FTP (www.ws-ftp.com), which is one of these applications.

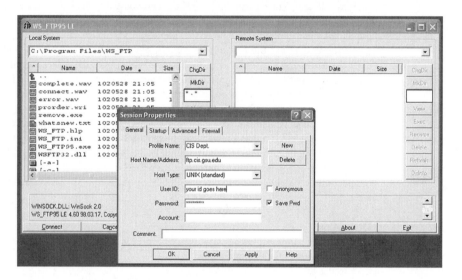

Figure 5.5   WS-FTP Application for Utilizing FTP

Please note that the remote system part of the window has yet to register a server directory because the connection has not been established with the CIS Department at Georgia State University. If the user has a legitimate account and password, the connection will be made over the Internet through FTP, as the dialog box specifies. In the terminology we developed in the last chapter, the local system is the client, and the remote system is the server.

Figure 5.6 shows the directory once the connection has been established. There are four files listed, one for each of the first three chapters of this book. Files can be uploaded or downloaded from the remote server to the local client. This allows Web designers, for example, to create Web pages on their clients and upload them to the production host system on the server when they are ready for user requests. Or, as in this case, it allows the textbook writer to store versions of the book chapters on an extranet directory that is accessible to the publishing staff and reviewers.

For an example of activating FTP, visit www.wiley.com/college/Straub_Chapter_15.html. Double click on Chapter 15. The file will be downloaded to a directory on your client machine that you specify through a dialog initiated and controlled by your browser.

One does not need a specialized program to create an FTP client.

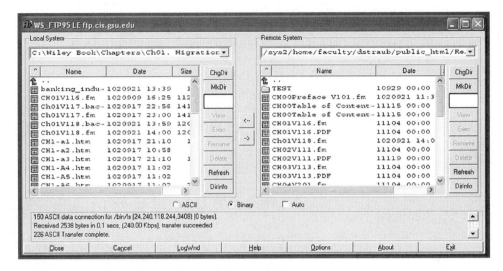

Figure 5.6   Local and Remote System Directories in WS-FTP

5.8.2 E-Mail Protocol and Applications

E-Mail is viewed by many as the "killer" application on the Internet. It employs its own protocol and has rapidly extended the use of the Internet to hundreds of millions of users. Historically, e-mail was limited to in-house company systems or to communities of interest. One of the largest of these communities of interest was BITNET, which was a large network for the U.S. Department of Defense's scientists and for educators.

When the Internet was created, the limitations of BITNET were removed and commercial and other types of organizational nodes were permitted. This allowed anyone and everyone to have an e-mail address associated with an IP address on the Internet.

E-Mail addresses follow the convention discussed in identifying nodes in Chapter 4. The portion of the e-mail IP address following the @ symbol is the node. That which precedes it is the unique identifier for the individual or other entity.

For example, the e-mail address of the author of this book is: dstraub@gsu.edu. The dstraub represents the individual e-mail account of the author, Detmar Straub. The node, gsu.edu, is the server for Georgia State University (gsu), which has a domain extension of edu for educational institutions in the United States.[4]

As we have seen before, there are protocols that sit on top of other protocols, or at least interact with them, as in the case of TCP/IP and HTTP. The same is true with e-mail. One e-mail protocol, for example, is SMTP. This protocol is a set of rules defining communication between e-mail servers around the world.

Figure 5.7 shows how e-mail can be used effectively in advertising and inducing sales on the Web. In this case, amazon.com has mailed a discount coupon to the author based on a prior interest (or purchases) of gardening books. This is an example of cross-selling, in that an interest in books is transferred over to trying to sell the recipient physical items that

---

[4]POPs (Post Office Protocols) are access points with unique IPs on the Internet. ISPs such as AOL have more than one point-of-presence on the Internet (see http://www.ietf.org/rfc/rfc1939.txt). There is no magic to having a POP, however. Many educational institutions have their own POPs, for example.

would go into a garden, such as mowers, pruners, and so forth. The e-mail is targeted in the sense that the recipient already has an expressed interest in the generic area, and Amazon is attempting to be a sole source provider for those needs.

E-Mail is low-tech in the sense that it has been around for decades. Ironically, it is under utilized by NE firms, though. The key to effective use is targeting. Most firms do not have systems in place that can do much more than broadcast ads to an e-mail list. In physical mail, this is known as *junk* mail. On the Internet, this is known as *spam*,[5] and this is not an effective way for firms to win over new customers. It may even be counterproductive.

Effective Use of E-Mail

From: "Amazon.com" <lawn-news@amazon.com>
Subject: $10 Spring Savings from Amazon.com
To: dstraub@gsu.edu

Dear Amazon Customer,

I have an extreme case of spring fever. And Amazon.com's new Lawn & Patio and Kitchen stores have a lot to do with it. Our Lawn & Patio store has everything you need to spruce up your yard. Weber grills, Black & Decker mulching mowers, Fiskars tree pruners--the selection is amazing. And if it's information you're looking for, we've got buying guides and articles that will turn brown thumbs green and green thumbs greener.

Best of all, if you shop before May 19, 2000, you can use the coupon below to save $10 off your Lawn & Patio purchase of $25 or more. Come explore:

http://www.amazon.com/lawnandpatio.

Figure 5.7   Use of E-Mail in NE Commerce

5.9 APPLICATION EXAMPLES BY REVENUE MODELS

The variety of applications that sit on top of the NE middleware and infrastructure is astonishing. To show the diversity of these business applications and to give readers a more in-depth understanding about how applications actually work, we can look at one example from each of five possible revenue models. These models, which are admittedly not definitive, are:

(1) Charges for advertisement
(2) Referral fees
(3) Subscriptions
(4) Product/service sales
(5) Transaction fees

[5]Originally called spiced ham. Named after the ham-based, high protein product developed by the Hormel Company in 1937. It was used for the U.S. army in World War II. Many people think that spam is foul-tasting; hence, its derogatory connotation on the Internet.

5.9.1 Ad-Based Applications

Many Web applications offer their services for free but make their profits (if they are profitable) through advertisements. This is a common communications media model. Newspapers do not charge a sufficient price to cover their expenses, usually. The remainder of the costs and the profits come from advertisements.

In Figure 5.8, the Web application is google.com. The ad is a subtle first line which allows a direct, click-through hyperlink to the Sprint Online Store. This ad appears at the head of a list of hits from a Google search engine query on e-commerce.

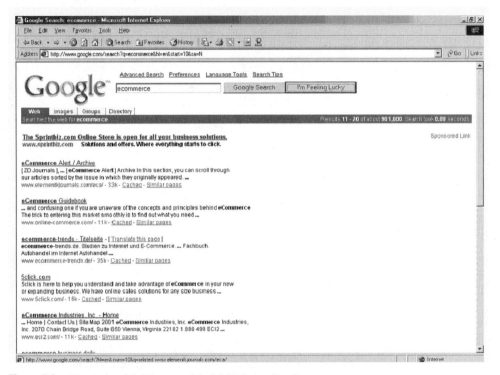

Figure 5.8 Example of Ad Revenue Model Web Application

How does this Web application work? The home page for google.com has a typical search engine dialog box, shown as Figure 5.9. The user enters a simple term (or through the Advanced Search hyperlink, more complicated Boolean terms). When the user clicks the gray rectangular box labeled Google Search, the request for a page is sent from the user client to the remote server. The remote server receives the data, the crucial part of which is the user-designated search term or terms. A database search is executed on the server, using advanced database technology and indices to rapidly locate all related Web page links. The indices themselves are based on the search terms appearing in the Web pages.

Where does the database come from? Google, like other search engine firms, spends a lot of its resources surfing the Web (only to a certain depth, it needs to be noted[6]). This surfing is automated and carried out by robots, or *bots*. Bots are intelligent agents, programs that are coded to look for pages and their embedded links. When a page is retrieved from another server by the bot, the Google server analyzes, or *parses*, the page and makes one or more entries into its database, depending on the number and kind of terms it finds on that Web page. The resulting database is huge, and this source of proprietary data is a great resource for search engine firms. It can be duplicated, but any new entrant into the search engine world needs to spend the money to build such a database before they can even begin to compete.

Figure 5.9   Google Search Engine Dialog Box

Back to the user query, the links that are found in the database search are prioritized according to a proprietary Google algorithm. All search engine firms have their own algorithms, and a competitive differentiator indicates to the user how relevant the returning, prioritized list is to the user's needs. What is actually returned to the user is a list of hyperlinks along with an opening passage from the Web pages (all of which are in the Google database).

Where does the ad fit into this scenario? The ad in this case is for Sprint, and the user clicks on that text within the colored, highlighted lines to directly access Sprint's Web store. Please note that it is possible and desirable to link the ad to the interest expressed by the user in the kind of search term entered. The term e-commerce is fairly broad and vague, but a more specific query, such as manufacturing shoes, returns information about how shoes are made, as well as a first advertising line for "Shoes at Banana Republic." Banana Republic is clearly a source of ad revenues for Google, in this case. The formula for fees can be based on: (1) the number of times an ad is returned to a user, (2) the number of *click-throughs*, and/or (3) user purchases. If the search engine participates in the sale itself, then the revenue model is not only an ad model, but also a commission model. If the revenue is based partly at least on click-through, then it is also a referral model.

---

[6]Pages stored by clients on AOL, for example, may not be accessible because of restrictions placed by the AOL node. Alternatively, the search engine firm can determine that it will not search certain directories.

5.9.2 Referral-Based Applications

Referrals derive their income from the fact that customers are "referred" to a Web site from another site. Sites that specialize in this are called *portals*. Others are mixed models, where they sell their own line of products as well. Amazon is a good example of this sort of Web site. As shown in Figure 5.10, Amazon has hyperlinks to other stores, one of which is merchandise sold under the rubric of zShops. These are firms with which Amazon has a strategic relationship. In such relationships where one partner refers customers to the other, the payment of fees can be based either on a fixed fee structure or a commission basis.

Figure 5.10 Amazon's zShops Referral Model

How does the application function? When customers entering amazon.com decide to click-through to a zShop merchant, the request is made to the merchant's server for a Web page (the main entry page, usually, but this can be determined through negotiation between the partners). The HTTP carries with it information about the referent, that is, the site that held the hyperlink, if any.[7] The online merchant processes the transaction. Their systems would capture the fact that the referral originated with Amazon, and fees could be paid accordingly.

5.9.3 Subscription-Based Applications

Subscriptions represent a fee-for-services model that is based on a flat fee, usually for a certain time period. In order to access the Web site and the capabilities of the Web application, a user must have access. This is often granted through an ID and password, although there are many other security options that could, theoretically, be implemented.

---

[7]Of course, the user could just type the URL, copy and paste it, or use a bookmarked-favorite hyperlink to access the merchant's Web site. If that is the case, then Amazon would not be the referred.

In effect, the subscription model is an extranet in which the firm sells its internal knowledge to a client base. One example is the Wall Street Journal (WSJ). With two pricing structures, one for current subscribers and one for nonsubscribers, the WSJ Interactive publishes online articles and features of the current day's paper as well as those in the archive. A searchable index is available for subscribers. Figure 5.11 shows the login dialog box for subscribers.

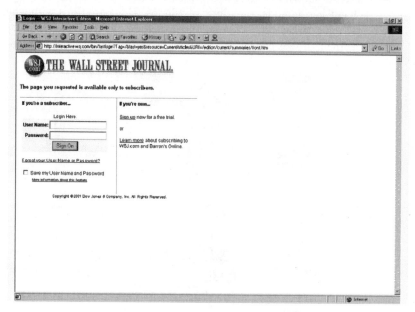

Figure 5.11   Login Dialog Box for WSJ Interactive (www.wsj.com)

How does the WSJ Interactive operate? In a manner similar to the Google search engine, the WSJ site receives the login information from the client. After verifying the ID and password in its database of subscribed users, the WSJ server presents the user with the page of its current issue, as in Figure 5.12. The assembling of these pages from individual article and images is a proprietary process that this newspaper uses. For our purposes, it is sufficient to note that the assembled HTML code is transmitted over the Internet from the server to the client browser, where it is interpreted and displayed.

Please notice also in Figure 5.12 that the WSJ does not use a subscription model alone. The rectangular ad on the right with the text inside that reads "helping millions of families achieve the American Dream" is a hyperlinked Freddie Mac advertisement.

5.9.4 Product/Service Sales-Based Applications

What we will later characterize as a direct-to-customer NE business model can also be seen as the revenue model of product/service sales over the Web. These sales can be to business customers or residential, that is, individual consumers. These applications can be simple brochureware in which the Web is used as just another channel for presenting information about products and services to customers. Or they can be a complete value chain site, where one can browse through the offerings, order them, pay for them, and, in the case of digital products, have them delivered online. After-sales support is also available at many sites.

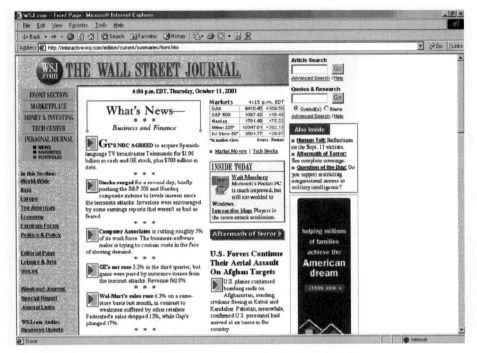

Figure 5.12   Accessing the Wall Street Journal's Web Application

An example of a firm that has a large sales volume over the Web is Progressive Insurance (www.progressive.com). As shown in Figure 5.13, the site adopts a multi-channel strategy for appealing to buyers. One can fill in information about one's driving experience and record online, get a quote, order and purchase the insurance, and have the policy bound. To deliver a verifiable copy of the policy requires a legal structure that recognizes digital watermarks and digital certificate authorities, so the policy itself may not be delivered online, but the insurance coverage can be in effect by midnight of the day purchased.

Alternatively, a consumer can purchase the insurance via the telephone or through independent agents, which are listed on the Web site.

In this case, the Web application needs to go beyond the back office accounting systems that accumulate order lines, process payments through credit or debit cards, and bind policies. These so-called legacy systems[8] handle the basic fulfillment process from the inception of order to the delivery of product/service and capture the customer information entered either via the Web or by telephone in the firm's databases.

---

[8]Legacy systems are true legacies. They represent significant investments in information systems over the years by firms, and, in a sense, they have been bequeathed by the firm for its own use as an NEO. A smooth interface between legacy systems and Web applications is often not possible because they represent different generations of software and in some cases, hardware. As legacy systems are replaced by newer systems for the underlying accounting and managerial applications such as ERPs, the linkage to the Web will be simpler and more straightforward. For the present, it is enough to recognize that these system are essential for the functioning of modern businesses.

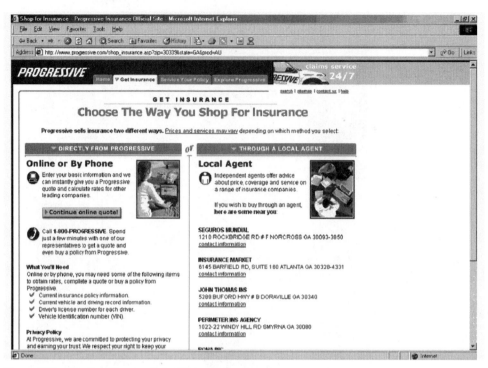

Figure 5.13   Product/Service Sales Web Application

This application must also present quotations for insuring the customer, not only from Progressive itself, but also quotations from other insurers. How does it do this? In the United States, insurance is a heavily regulated industry, and company rates for certain types and levels of insurance must be on file in the state regulator's office. This is publicly accessible information, and firms either gather this information directly or buy it from a broker for their rating engine. The rating engine calculates the dates based on the information that the customer has entered into the online screens. As a result Progressive can issue quotes from a set of other insurers such as Allstate or State Farm, as well as its own.

When the user finishes entering personal data, the capturing of that data on the server end of the transmission ceases, and the data is processed by a rating engine. The output of that program is then uploaded to the customer in the form of a comparative report.

Focus on NE: Search Engines

 In the beginning there were no charges, no cost, and careful choosing of keywords could land you a top ten ranking on a major search engine. Those were the good old days before the search engines developed business models to take advantage of the potential revenue stream. Every day there about 70 million commercial product searches conducted over search engines, and search listings are one of the most effective forms of online advertising. There are three basic types of models used for determining fees. The paid placement model is a straight bid for position. You must bid on a per click basis based on your keywords. The higher you bid, the higher you rank. Paid placement models are used on Overture, Find What, Kanoodle, and Google. With paid placement engines, you must work backward using average online sales amounts and visitor conversion ratios to determine the amount you are willing to pay for each visitor. For example, if your average online sale is $100, you have a 25% profit margin and you sell to one of every 100 visitors, your cost per click ceiling would be 24 cents. This is a starting point for setting per visitor budgets. The paid inclusion model requires that you pay a search engine to ensure that the site will be included in the search engine's index. A set price per URL is paid on an annual basis. The paid inclusion model is implemented by Lycos, Teoma, Inktomi, and AltaVista. The express submission model requires that you pay a flat fee that has no bearing on your ranking. The fee guarantees that an editor will review your site, but there is no guarantee that you will be included, although generally chances are good that you will be included.

5.9.5 Transaction-Based Applications

Firms can make money by charging a fee for each transaction. This model works best with information/knowledge-based products, which includes CitySync. CitySync is a service of Lonely Planet, the travel guide company based in Australia. Users of the service can purchase city-by-city information such as maps, lodging, restaurants, sights, and so forth. The information is downloaded to Palm Pilots so that users can easily retrieve the information even without a laptop.

CitySync requires a registration procedure before users can download the maps and other travel information. How does this application work?

Lonely Planet is a content provider, and if they derive revenues from selling that content directly to consumers, they have a viable business model. The various city maps and other information reside on the firm's servers. A customer purchases a city electronically and downloads an installer to a desktop/laptop. The installer puts the applications and databases onto the handheld device, where the content can be locally accessed.

5.9.6 Other Revenue/Income Models

There are other revenue/income models not covered here. There is the shared infrastructure model, for example, where the revenues can be derived from selling the use of a server-network infrastructure. The airline consortium Abacus (www.abacus.com.sg) comes to mind here. Or there is the fund-raising model, such as that used by the American Red Cross (www.redcross.org).

Both models will be covered in a later chapter, but the point in the current chapter is simply that there are a large number of ways that the Web can be used. Web applications can be purely informational, with more sophisticated transactions being conducted offline.

5.10 SUMMARY

This chapter discussed the middleware technologies (including browsers and server programs that process Web page requests) that lie between the Internet infrastructure and the endware applications with which users interact. It also covered Internet endware. Endware applications lie at the heart of NE.

Managers need to understand how these technologies work at a high level so they can make strategic choices about them. There are vastly different revenues models that can be used for Web applications. Some are based on sales; others are on a pay-for-service model. All of these models are supported to different degrees by the middle- and endware technologies.

Middleware technologies provide essential linkages between basic infrastructure and user applications necessary for NE. One major functionality of middleware derives from its ability to communicate across time and space. The middleware that users are most familiar with are browsers. Browsers are client-side middleware and are designed to interpret Web pages sent over the Internet. Another major functionality of middleware is its interoperability.

Server-side middleware is essential to the ability of a server to compile and run designated server programming languages. Popular programming languages are ASP, CGI, Perl, PHP, and ColdFusion. Some Web pages may also rely on languages/application resident on a client. Client plug-ins work with the browser to load the Web page as it was intended to be presented. Encryption technology, middleware for both client and server, secures the connections between parties from unauthorized access, interruption, and authentication.

Another set of middleware technologies that will grow and mature over the coming years is mobile commerce. M-commerce includes cell phones with Internet access and intelligent interfaces such as PDAs. The key factor of m-commerce is that it depends on wireless infrastructure and wireless connections to the Internet. The limitations of m-commerce technologies is that only so much information can be conveyed and displayed because of the size of the device, and Web pages have to be altered to suit the interface. The protocol for m-commerce technologies is called WAP.

Component-based standards include CORBA, J2EE, and .Net. The intention of these architectures and programming environments is to make middleware more interoperable and easier to build.

Web-integrating middleware is client-side software that allows the design of Web applications without expert knowledge of markup languages. Web-integrating middleware generates code automatically. Middleware supplements to the Web are also available and have been largely responsible for the success of the Internet.

A special protocol, FTP allows Web sites to upload software or data upon user request. The protocol specializes in transferring files of any type. E-Mail also has its own protocol. NE firms operate under five possible revenue models. These models are charges for advertisement, referral fees, subscriptions, product/service sales, transaction fees.

KEY TERMS

Applications: Computer programs that serve a specific need or solve a specific problem.

Ad-based applications: Web applications, such as google.com, that offer their services for free but make their profits from advertising.

Browsers: Computer programs that are designed to interpret Web pages sent using HTTP over the Internet. They are primarily tools for users.

Client plug-ins: Languages/applications that reside on the user's computer and work in conjunction with the browser to present the Web page as was intended by the designer.

Cookies: Short segments of data written to the user's hard disk that enables a server to recognize the user on a return visit to a Web site.

Endware: Applications running on the browsers that users have on their clients. Applications are what drive NE.

Encryption (Client and Server): A technology for securing communications between parties from unauthorized access, interruption, and authentication. Encryption software is middleware that sits between the infrastructure and the user interface.

FTP: File Transfer Protocol.

HTML: Hypertext markup language, which uses a tag system to indicate how a line should be displayed on a computer screen.

Microsoft FrontPage: Composing tool that generates HTML code.

Middleware: The interface systems and standards that lie between users and NE infrastructure.

M-Commerce: See mobile commerce.

Mobile commerce: Cell phones with Internet access, and more intelligent interfaces such as PDAs. Some definitions could include laptop computers with a cellular or PCS connection to the Internet. The chief differentiating factor of this technology is that it depends on wireless infrastructure and wireless connections to the Internet.

Product/service sales-based application: Sales to business customers or residential consumers through brochures, catalogs, or full service sites where customers can browse offerings, pay for them, and in the case of digital products, have them delivered online.

Oracle and SQL databases: Databases adapted to fulfilling Web requests for information.

Referral-based applications: Sites that derive their revenues from referring customers from one Web site to another.

Revenue models: Charges for advertisement, referral fees, subscriptions, product or service sales, and transaction fees.

Servers: Computers that process requests for Web pages.

Shockwave Player: Middleware that works in conjunction with the browser and enables multimedia content to be displayed as video, animation, and sound.

Spam: Broadcast ads or junk e-mail.

Subscription-based applications: A fee-for-service model that is based on a flat fee, usually over a specified time period.

Transaction-based applications: Fee-per-transaction model usually used with knowledge/information based products.

WAP: Wireless Application Protocol used for wireless devices.

WYSIWYG: What you see is what you get.

XML: Extensible markup language, which uses a tag system to indicate how a line should be displayed on a computer screen.

REVIEW QUESTIONS

1. What is middleware technology?
2. Describe the purpose of a browser.
3. Name four popular server programming languages.
4. Explain the purpose of a cookie.
5. Define encryption.
6. What is the key differentiating factor in m-commerce technology?
7. Discuss the limitations of compact m-commerce technology.
8. What is the protocol used for wireless devices and the Internet?
9. What is FTP?
10. Describe protocols used by e-mail on the Internet.
11. What is spam?
12. List and give examples of five NE revenue models.

TOPICS FOR DISCUSSION

1. Middleware technologies lie between the basic infrastructure and the applications with which users eventually interact. Discuss the function of middleware.

2. Browsers are the most familiar middleware to users. Describe how a browser interprets Web pages.

3. Cookies are short segments of data captured to collect data on past behaviors and interests of users. Compare the use of cookies to the physical means of tailored substitutes in the real world.

4. Discuss the purposes of client plug-ins and discuss some of the applications that are available for use.

5. M-commerce, includes cell phones with Internet access and other intelligent products such as PDAs. Discuss the special needs of m-commerce technology.

6. Web-integrating middleware helps users to build their own Web sites. Discuss the advantages and disadvantage of Web-integrating tools.

7. Discuss the reasons why managers need to understand the fundamentals of middleware.

8. Discuss the ways that e-mail can be used in advertising and inducing sales on the Web.

9. Compare and contrast revenue/income models for e-commerce.

10. Discuss examples of organizations and the type of revenue model implemented for the organization.

INTERNET EXERCISES

1. Interview someone who uses an m-commerce application, such as a PDA or a cell phone with Internet access. When interviewing, find out how they like it, how much they use it, and what if any problems they have and any suggestion that they might have to improve service.

2. Describe how businesses can use encryption to protect their customer information when ordering online. Find a business online that currently uses encryption and discover which encryption software package they use and any associated costs with using the encryption.

3. Using one of the Web-integrating programs such as Microsoft FrontPage or Dreamweaver build a home page for you and/or your family and post to the Web through one of the free services such as Tripod or GeoCities. Include on the page information about you and your hometown. Include at least three links to pages that interest you and one picture; it does not have to be of you.

4. Describe how use of e-mail has made the world a smaller place. Contact someone from a different country and interview him/her to find out how e-mail is making his/her life easier. The person should be associated with a business or with a university. Include their name, where they are from, and how often and why they use e-mail.

5. Using e-mail has made it easier for military personnel to stay in touch with their families. Contact one of the many deployed military groups through their ombudsman and discuss how the families are using e-mail to keep their family together through the tough times of deployment.

6. Discuss how online shopping has changed the way people shop for insurance and loans. Use one of the popular Web sites to shop for car insurance. Compare your current rates and the rates offered by the Web site in a spreadsheet. Report your findings and discuss whether the Web site offered you a savings.

7. Discuss how plug-ins allow users to communicate. For example, some chat rooms use Macromedia's Shockwave Player. How does this player enable users to exchange ideas and discuss relevant topics?

8. Interview someone who has accidentally downloaded a virus. How did he or she discover the virus? How did he or she correct the problem? Did he or she have an antivirus plug-in? E-Mail the customer service department of an antivirus software provider a question/concern about their software. Was the response timely? Did their answer help you? Do you think they could help you if you did have a problem?

9. E-Mail someone who has AT&T wireless services. Their e-mail address is their phone number@mobile.att.net. How long did it take for them to get the message? Were they able to e-mail you back? Was it easy to reply?

10. Research a trip using both a travel agent and an online travel Web site. Expedia and Travelocity are popular sites. Research airfare, rental cars, and activities. Which source provided more information? Which source provided the best deal? Have you ever booked a trip online?

TEAM EXERCISES

1. The purpose of this group activity is to build a workable e-commerce Web site that will utilize Web-based encryption. Build a simple one-page site that enables the users to enter their name and any communication that they wish to convey to the other users. This Web site will be used for conveying messages back and forth in all other group projects. The Web page should include a picture of each member, a chat area, and an area to post messages and files.

2. The purpose of this project is to determine the uses and effectiveness of e-mail in the workplace for communication among coworkers and customers. To start the project, begin by gathering current research data from the Internet on e-mail usage. The second step will include a group-developed questionnaire with at least five questions concerning the use of e-mail within an organization. Survey as many employees as possible and analyze the usage.

3. The goal of this project will be to understand how an organization can use the Internet and e-mail to generate revenue and to advertise their product. In order to do this, each group will decide on a company name and product to advertise. The group will decide on a marketing campaign and strategy for their product that includes e-mail advertisements, pop-up advertisements on other Web sites, and banner advertising. The project will also consist of a written report with research done on potential customers and costs of advertising, and possible revenues from (1) charges for advertising, (2) referral fees, (3) subscriptions, (4) product/service sales, and (5) transaction fees.

4. Plan a trip to a foreign country. The goal of this project is to obtain as much information as possible about traveling to the country. Research traveling to the country, traveling once you get into the country, extracurricular activities, where to stay, length of stay, and any other pertinent information. You may use any online resource, but *do not* contact a travel agent. E-Mail local students and tourist organizations, research online travel Web sites, or

any other online means to obtain the information. Write a one-page summary of the sources your group used and discuss the information you found.

5. Research the use of advertisements on popular search engines. Perform a few searches on Google and select an advertiser to contact. Find out the why the company chooses to advertise online. Find out how often their advertisements run. Ask how successful they believe their advertisements online have been. Ask how they track their results. Also ask the company about their traditional advertising methods. What advertising medium has been the most successful for them? Who is their target market? Does the Internet reach their target market? Write a three- to four-page summary of your results. Compare traditional marketing to online marketing.

INTERNET RESOURCES

Java Boutique (http://javaboutique.internet.com/stats/top_100.html): This site provides the top 100 java applets downloaded in the last 24 hours and tutorials on how to use them.

More Free Java Applets (http://www.free-applets.com/applets.html): Free downloadable java applets.

PGP (Pretty Good Privacy) (http://web.mit.edu/network/pgp.html): This is MIT's download site for the free PGP encryption key.

REFERENCES

Straub, D. W., and E. Karahanna. "Knowledge Worker Communications and Recipient Availability: Toward a Task Closure Explanation of Media Choice." *Organization Science*, 9, 2, March 1998, 160–175.

CHAPTER 6

NE SECURITY, TRUST, AND PAYMENTS

UNDERSTANDING NE SECURITY, TRUST, AND PAYMENTS

Why are security, trust, and payments important managerial issues for NEOs? Security gives managers the latitude to make future plans with less fear that the firm will be attacked so seriously it is put out of business. Part of the security that an organization engages in with outsiders is to create a trusting environment so that partners and customers will feel at ease working with the firm. Knowing that confidential information will remain confidential is part of this trust. All of this ties into payments options in an online environment because without security and trust, there will be no online payments. This crucial stage of the online value chain must be well designed and executed by managers, or the NE initiatives of the firm will never succeed.

LEARNING OBJECTIVES FOR THIS CHAPTER

- To explain the importance of security to an NE organization and identify steps to ensure that security
- To discuss the links between security, trust, and payments of an NE organization
- To explain the importance of security to an NE organization and identify steps to ensure that security. The student will be able to explain the links between security, trust, and payments of an NE organization.
- To describe the importance of establishing trust and be able to explain why consumers trust NE organizations
- To describe three trust-building mechanisms and understand how to use these mechanisms to build consumer trust in a Web site
- To list and explain the four required components for successful NE commerce
- To define the methods for securing network transactions, including the technologies of encryption, public key infrastructure, single-key security, and digital signatures

- To develop the ability to identify problems with adequately securing network transactions
- To articulate differences between two forms of public key infrastructure (PKI) and be able to explain the advantages and disadvantages of each
- To identify and explain how to secure the endpoints through the use of firewalls
- To enumerate five payment options for NE business transactions and explain the advantages and disadvantages of each

▶ *CASE STUDY 6-1*

FEDERAL TRADE COMMISSION

The Federal Trade Commission (FTC) settled its fraud case against a group that sold computers on several online auction sites and then failed to deliver them to buyers. The May 2002 court settlement fined the defendants $10,000 and forbade them to sell goods online.

The case against Auctionsaver and its executives arose out of the FTC effort to cut down on Internet fraud. The FTC monitored the actions of individuals who conduct business on online auction sites and discovered that scam artists build up their reputations over time at an auction site, then begin defrauding buyers on several different auction sites all at once. In this case the FTC alleged that in 1999 Auctionsaver advertised computers and related equipment on a variety of online auction sites including eBay, Amazon, and Yahoo. The FTC charged Auctionsaver with failing to ship merchandise or refund customers' money for computers it could not ship. The FTC said customers were cheated out of $90,000.

"Initially, they were fulfilling orders, then they ran into trouble filling orders but continued to take orders," said John Jacobs, an FTC lawyer on the case. Kevin Pursglove, an eBay spokesman, said eBay encourages users buying big-ticket items, such as computers, to use a payment escrow service, which ensures they receive their merchandise before payment goes through. Yet courts have consistently ruled that eBay is not liable for fraud that takes place through its site. The selling of illegal software, rare animal skins, and so forth, is a considerable risk for online auction sites. Sites such as eBay are very difficult to monitor and have suffered a rash of illegal auctions. In 2001, auctions for items such as 500 pounds of marijuana, a human liver, and an unborn baby were shut down.

The unregulated world of online auctions has led to a plethora of fraud complaints. In a recent report by the Internet Fraud Complaint Center (IFCC), the number one scam on the Internet is auction fraud. According to a report released by the U.S. Federal Bureau of Investigation (FBI) and the National White Collar Crime Center, Internet auction fraud was the problem in 64% of the complaints filed with the IFCC.

The IFCC is not the first agency to list auction fraud as the number one online consumer complaint. In October the U.S. Federal Trade Commission said that auction fraud topped the list of complaints received through its Consumer Sentinel database. Additionally, in January eMarketer released a report showing that auction fraud accounts for 87% of all online crime.

Efforts are being made to reduce the amount of Internet auction fraud and safeguard consumers. The FTC has begun an effort, Project Safebid, to help federal and state authorities better track and prosecute people who commit fraud on the Internet. Recognizing that the law is not specific to online auction transactions, and that the sellers are not always aware of their special rights, Auctionwatch.com developed the "Seller Bill of Rights." Online Internet sites such as abc.com, Internet Fraud Tips, and Nolo law provide consumers with valuable information about how they can protect themselves against the fraudulent activity that takes place on auction sites.

It is evident through this case study that there is a growing concern for Internet auction fraud. This type of controversy and negative publicity will inevitably adversely impact auction site providers such as eBay, Amazon, and Yahoo, to name a few. This case proves the impact that security, trust, and payments have on the success of an NEO.

Discussion:

1. Discuss the responsibility that eBay, Yahoo, and other auction site providers have in securing their sites and discouraging fraudulent sellers.

2. Consider the privacy policy of the eBay, Yahoo, and Amazon Web sites. Are there any ethical issues related to the fraudulent activity occurring on their sites and what they state in their privacy policy?

Resources:

Morrissey, B. "FTC Settles Online Auction Fraud Case." [Online] Available: http://ecommerce.internet.com/news/news/article/0,,10375_1031241,00.html. Accessed July 28, 2002.

Saliba, C. "Study: Auction Fraud Still Top Cybercrime." [Online] Available: http://www.ecommercetimes.com/perl/story/6590.html. Accessed July 28, 2002.

6.1 INTRODUCTION

This chapter will discuss security for NEOs. It will also discuss how security and perceptions of security affect the trust consumers and business customers have in NE vendors. A specialized form of security is applicable to payments over networks, and this will also be covered in this chapter.

6.2 THE LINK BETWEEN SECURITY, TRUST, AND PAYMENTS

Why do we devote such special attention—a full chapter, in fact—to information security, trust, and payment issues? And why are these topics in a unit on technology issues? The short answer to this question is that in a book this length, indeed, an entire chapter does need to be set aside to probe which technical security measures are available to NEOs and how payment systems can be implemented and secured. Without safe and efficient procedures and computer systems to facilitate business transactions over the Internet and other business exchange networks, the full potential of NE will not be realized. There are many studies that indicate consumers and businesses choose to engage in e-commerce depending on the ability of e-vendors to protect their sensitive information.[1]

Trust is a necessary precursor to online purchase[2] and may be the single most important factor directly affecting organizational and national prosperity and adaptability, including the acceptance of new IT.[3] Recent studies indicate that some form of user trust in the Web site and e-vendor may be increased by certain trust-creating characteristics of the Web site itself,[4] but the perception of secure transactions is likely to be another prominent factor. It is apparent that security and trust are intimately connected.

Moreover, security and payment issues are connected by virtue of the need to protect credit card information and other sensitive customer information that could be subject to fraud. The point of payment is that stage in the entire online business exchange at which customers share valuable information and need to be reassured that the vendor at the other end of the cyberspace transaction is legitimate. Clearly there is some information—both payment and nonpayment information—that does not need to be protected. But being careful with any data that could be used to compromise one's Web and EDI sites is critical if an NE initiative is to succeed. Customers, thus, have to be able to trust the payment system.

[1]Rose et al. (1999).
[2]Reichheld and Schefter (2000).
[3]Fukuyama (1995).
[4]Gefen and Straub (2001).

Focus on NE: Certificate Authorities (CAs)

 VeriSign, Inc., is the leading certificate authority for digital trust services. VeriSign's digital trust services strive to achieve a trusted environment in order to increase merchant, consumer, and industry awareness of the importance of authentication as the underpinning for secure transactions.

VeriSign provides several flexible and cost-effective solutions that protect brands, mitigate risk, and speed time to market, while allowing financial institutions to retain control of certificate issuance, access levels, and other key security policies. VeriSign also provides e-mail solutions that enable organizations to use e-mail to exchange confidential and high-value information. VeriSign guarantees tamper-proof and digitally signed messages, and reduces the costs of paper-based delivery. More than 7 billion communications and transactions are processed per day. VeriSign seeks to participate in the development of public policies around the world that affect its core business interests, the Internet, and e-commerce. As the company strives to be a good corporate citizen of the countries in which it operates, VeriSign also attempts to enhance its ability to operate effectively in those locations.

Sources:

http://www.verisign.com

http://www.aero.org/publications/GPSPRIMER/EvryDyUse.html

http://www.findarticles.com/cf_0/m1590/12_57/72868720/p2/
article.jhtml?term=%2BGlobal+%2BPositioning+%2BSystem+%2BUsage

6.3 WHAT IS THE SECURITY PROBLEM AND WHERE DO WE STAND?

The basic security problem is that NE commerce must be:

1. Safe
2. Secure from intentional violation
3. Secure from unintentional violation
4. Recoverable

6.3.1 Safe NE Systems

Systems must first be safe from disasters, both natural and not. It is important that managers can guarantee—at an acceptable level of risk—that flood, fire, sabotage, hurricanes, tornadoes, and so forth, will not render useless the computer systems that make possible the electronic transactions that lie at the heart of NE. In the security profession the term MTBU (mean time for belly up) is sometimes used to indicate an organization's survivability in the face of a disaster. MTBU is an indicator of how well a firm can survive an outage of its computer systems. It can be estimated in days, as shown in Figure 6.1, or in hours in the case of highly information-intensive and virtual businesses.

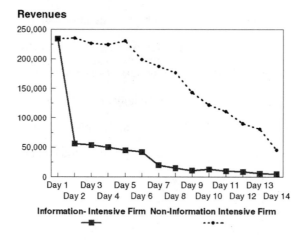

Figure 6.1   MTBU for Two Firm Types

Information-intensive firms such as insurance, banking, and securities firms are most vulnerable to loss of their transaction base, but even firms with traditional physical businesses, in which their business is not the information itself, cannot survive long without a continual flow of information and data, as the figure illustrates.

The interesting fact about MTBU is that such a metric has even been conceived.[5] It expresses the business orientation of information security goals. If a firm cannot effectively guarantee that it will be up-and-running again before MTBU, management has abrogated its managerial responsibility to its stakeholders, that is, the owners, the employees, and the public.

[5]The original source for this concept was likely from the team that wrote a widely cited 1978 working paper by the MIS Research Center at the University of Minnesota: Aasgaard et al. (1978).

There are two avenues typically taken to ensure that the firm will survive. The larger issues of determining what needs to be done to keep business operations running are dealt with in a document called a Business Continuity Plan. Also called contingency planning, this set of action plans lays out exactly how the firm will respond if a flood or any other major disaster wipes out certain operational units. It details where and how business will be set up on a temporary basis, how critical paper records and files can be retrieved, who notifies employees where and when to report for work, and so on.

Planning for how to deal with the loss of Internet connections, electronic data, records, and files, and the workstations, servers, routers, and printers that enable a distribution site to fulfill NE orders is frequently called just disaster planning or data disaster planning. In a certain sense, the distinction between these two types of planning is artificial because they are so interdependent. Nevertheless, there are separate, complex issues associated with the recovery of computer-related systems that may justify its distinct treatment.

As part of the planning, firms currently choose from three major options for restoration of the firm's operations: (1) cold sites, (2) hot sites, and (3) distributed computing with excess capacity at each distributed site. Each of these will be discussed in greater detail later in this section, but for the moment let us cover the needs of a firm experiencing a disaster.

When a disaster strikes, the recovery plans for the business and systems should be activated immediately. The plans should deal with: (a) hardware, (b) software, (c) data, (d) network connections, and (e) personnel and alternative work processes. Hardware can be made available through any of these restoration options. Software, along with data, should be stored in an archive on a regular basis and transported to an off-site location. Particular care must be given to data, as hardware and software can be repurchased or obtained from the original sources if necessary. Data, though, is unrecoverable without backups.

Network connections are critical to an NEO. Without them the business cannot truly operate. Current restoration options include network connections—this critical element means that firms will not lose business through an inability to respond to network requests. Computer systems do not really work independent of people and the regular ongoing processes that involve servicing online customers. So if a firm has alternative capacity for the systems elsewhere, there must also be facilities for at least the IT operations staff to interact with the firm's systems.

Business continuity planning should specify how the non-IT operations employees can continue their work. Temporary offices with phone lines switched from the old facility will take some time to set up, as will employee workstations. Given that all paper files are frequently lost in a disaster, the firm that has stored digitized images of its paper documents will be able to fully recover its business history. The firm that has no backup record-keeping capability will be hard-pressed.

Let's say that you are a manager for a firm that sells large volumes of plumbing supplies over the Internet. Moreover, let's say that one of your two main distribution sites has been flooded by rising waters on the Mississippi River in Missouri. The stock is flooded, but, even more problematic, the computer workstations, servers, robotic-retrieval systems, and most of the other computer equipment have been submerged and are likely a total write-off. Worst still, the main servers that respond to Web sales have been taken out along with the offices of the firm's IT staff.

You turn to your plan. You have a contract with a cold site disaster recovery outsourcer that will allow you to begin reorganizing your operations. Necessary network connections are present at this site, as well as backup copies of your software and data, but there is no computer hardware. The plan calls for bringing in rented equipment, including furniture, desks, workstations, and so forth, from a three state area. Contracts with these rental firms and other outsourcing firms specify that the requisite materials will be on-site and installed within 24 hours. Although the burden on the remaining physical distribution center will be severe, the main problem is the Web connection. However, with successful deployment of the plan, the firm can continue its computing within the MTBU limits.

Your company might have considered a more costly plan called a hot site. Hot sites also have duplicates of the hardware you are running, as well as the network connections. Hot sites (and cold sites) are shared; in the sense that if all clients of the outsourcer were in need of services at the same time, the facilities could not usually accommodate the demand. In other words, there is not a large room ready and waiting for a firm at the hot site, with the name of the firm stenciled on the door.

Cold and hot sites are contracted on the assumption that it is not likely that the occurrence of a cataclysmic disaster would necessitate servicing all of the contracted firms at once. There are many scenarios that threaten this assumption, for example, floods along a long stretch of river, devastating hurricanes, earthquakes, and, conceivably, terrorist attacks. Outsourcers specializing in disaster recovery may argue that their international resources can accommodate your needs, even if large areas are affected. What this means, however, is that the hardware, software, and networks may be in place, but without ready access for the personnel needed to continue operations. If the outsourcer has facilities in place in Canada, but the personnel are in Costa Rica, the solution is dubious.

The main alternative to hiring an outsourcer is to do it yourself.[6] The Internet provides an option for distributing computing through several locations and mirroring systems and data throughout the organization. In the event of a disaster, the prudent firms would have enough extra capacity to seamlessly pick up the processing at one of their other locations. The distribution of operations, personnel, and Web hosting is likewise a less risky option than depending on the fulfillment of a contract for the survival of the firm. Disasters are no[6]t merely inconvenient; they are firm-threatening events.

Is this approach costly? Yes, clearly it is but the prospect of going out of business is even more costly.

The technical problem with most disaster recovery plans is that they are not tested before a disaster actually occurs. Computer systems and networks are extremely delicate in the sense that the tolerance for incorrect configurations is limited. If just a few parameters are not set properly, either because the recovery procedure merely deployed all defaults and did not reinstitute altered parameters, or because the procedure did not reinstall crucial files, the firm's NE capabilities will not be restored.

In the wake of the September 11, 2001, terrorist attacks, managers need to carefully reexamine, both from a physical and informational point of view, their ability to rapidly recover their companies. Plans need to be periodically tested, and problems worked out well in advance of an actual event.

[6]Snow et al. (2003).

6.3.2 Secure from Intentional Violations

Web, Internet, and traditional networked systems need to be secure from computer abusers. As Figure 6.2 illustrates, the international character of the Internet means that attacks against a firm's computer systems, Web servers, and legacy systems alike can come from a host of international sources. Internal abuse is still the most likely possibility, even with hackers probing for entry points. Inside knowledge about the inner workings of a computer system, be it legacy or Web based, are still the surest avenue for penetration.[7]

Now Inter-National!!

Figure 6.2   Computer Abusers on the Internet

What exactly are abusers seeking? Aside from viruses—which appear to be simple, malicious acts by antisocial personalities—acts of abuse are motivated by personal gain or terrorist ideologies. Abusers seek:

1. Trade secrets
2. Strategic information
3. Private data (such as passwords and IDs)
4. Time-sensitive information
5. Credit card information
6. Electronic funds transfer data

Any one of these targets can lead to personal gain for the perpetrator. Trade secrets can be sold to competitors, as can strategic information. Criminals will buy private data, time-sensitive data, and credit card information. Finally, high-tech thieves can intercept and steal a company's funds. This last structure is likely the route through which terrorists can wreak the most havoc on the financial systems, and, thus, it is the most vulnerable to attack.

---

[7]See Straub and Welke (1998).

6.3.3 Secure from Unintentional Violations

Violations of security are not always intentional. Data can be altered by accident as well as purposefully. A thief or antisocial individual will have intentionality in the act. An honest employee making a mistake will not.

Nevertheless, NEOs must take steps to protect themselves from such violations. The recipe for changing the way the firm treats secure systems is well-known.[8] The difficulty is in getting firms to act.

6.3.4 Recoverable Systems

Prudent firms take steps to ensure that they are able to recover from limited problems as well as major ones. Disaster recovery is designed to protect computer systems in the event of a large-scale failure. But individuals can acquire a virus from the Internet and find that all of their data has been wiped out, and their hardware basically unusable.

It is for this reason that systems—legacy and Web based—must be recoverable with as little reworking as possible. This means that backup procedures incapable of restoring a computer's operation within a day or so of the disaster or violation is, by definition, not a recoverable system. One would have to say that it is partially recoverable, but certainly not fully recoverable.

6.4 SECURING THE NETWORK

There are two major vulnerabilities in NE systems. One critical vulnerability is obviously the network itself. As we have noted and as Figure 6.3 points out, the Internet inherently has "ears" at each node, and if these "ears" are compromised, they can hear things they are not supposed to hear.

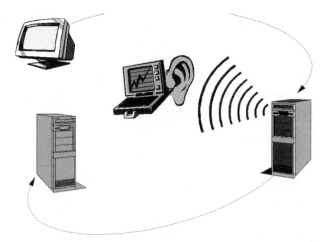

Figure 6.3   "Ears" Listening on the Internet

[8]Straub (1990).

The most pressing need for security is based on the threat of the transmission itself falling into the wrong hands and data being changed to ultimately benefit the abusers. This means that the data (or message) must be altered or scrambled so that if the abuser were to change the data, it would be noticed. The technique usually employed for this purpose—and one that has a high degree of security[9]—is known as encryption.

Besides assuring the integrity or confidentiality of messages in this manner, it is also important to *authenticate* the identity of the sender. In cyberspace there is a legitimate question about who is on the other end of a transmission. It is very possible for an abuser to masquerade as another person, a technique known as *IP-spoofing*.

Figure 6.4 shows an individual who has received a message from a second party claiming to be Kathy. But the first party has a legitimate concern that the sender may not actually be Kathy. An abuser could be misrepresenting himself/herself as Kathy by having intercepted the legitimate sender's IP and sending a different message through this IP address.

How can commerce take place across networks so that messages are confidential and identities are authenticated? Encryption might be the answer.

Figure 6.4 Establishing Cyber-Identities

Initially, one must know that encryption scrambles a message in such a way that it is extremely difficult for an abuser to accurately interpret a message while it may still be of use. Encryption is how most prudent organizations secure mission-critical transmissions.

The most effective encryption scheme for the Internet is known as Public Key Infrastructure, or PKI. PKI uses what is known as a public key scheme to make the encryption scheme both convenient and still highly secure.[10] Here is how it works.

The goal—keep in mind—is to secure the transmission across the Internet so that even if an abuser intercepts a message, he or she cannot either interpret the message or substitute it with a false message without being easily detected. Figure 6.5 illustrates how one part of the PKI solution transpires. PKI is known as a two key (public and private keys), asymmetric scheme.

The scrambling algorithm, or encrypting scheme, depends on changing the characters and symbols many times based on what is specified in a key. To exemplify this, we can take a simple transposition scheme. Let's say the key is ABC. The "A" indicates a particular manipulation of the data in a perfect mapping of the original, but not one that is immediately interpretable. If the original message was "The quick brown fox jumped over the

---

[9]Security that is made by man can be broken by man. The main issue is whether the breaking of security can be accomplished at a cost and in a timely enough manner to be of use to abusers.

[10]No method of security is completely unbreakable. We can only speak about relatively high levels of security versus relatively low levels.

lazy dog. $546.98," one transposition could be "Uif,rvjdl,cspxo gpy,kvnfe,pwfs,uif,mbaz,eph/ %657/09."

Can you guess what the transformation is? In this case, each alphabetic characters is substituted with the character following it in the alphabetic sequence; a "t" becomes a "u," an "h" becomes an "i," and so forth. A similar transposition is used for the numeric and special characters.

Now since the key has a "b" next in the full ABC key, a second algorithmic change would be applied to the already transposed message, for example, substitution using the second subsequent character in the alphabet, including the numeric and special characters. With the "c," we might skip three characters, and so forth.[11] The final ciphertext would bear no resemblance to the original plaintext, thereby preventing immediate interception and interpretation of the message by an abuser.

Although this transposition scheme is much too simplistic to stand up for a minute to a modern day hacker, it shows the basic principle behind keys and encryption. In practice encryption is elaborate and becomes stronger and harder to break when the allowable length of the key, the number of transformations, is extended. A key length of 64 bits is much shorter than one of 1024 bits, meaning the ciphertext of the longer key is computationally harder to break because the number of ciphertext transformations is much larger. If a hacker has the ciphertext, a brute force technique of multiple reverse transformations will eventually produce the plaintext (which can be identified automatically when it produces a common, recognizable sequence of letters and numbers). The more computing power that is assembled, the faster this will occur. But if the key cannot be broken in real time, firms can outwit hackers by using a different key for each new transaction. Thus, the danger of compromise is only for one transaction at a time. Even single transactions can be protected by a reverification scheme, so there are ways to thwart hackers even if they eventually break the key code and then try to reinitiate a new transaction.[12] Because the key has changed since the time they began the process of breaking the code and when they finally broke it, hackers would need to be able to decrypt in real time, which is a daunting task and unreachable at the present time.

Please note that each security countermeasure has a cost. More processing time, not to mention managerial coordination, is needed when firms employ different keys for each transaction and this trade-off of costs for higher security is not a trivial consideration. This is one reason many firms do not secure their systems as much as they might otherwise. Security costs money and it lowers productivity. There were widely circulated estimates that post-9/11 security measures had lowered productivity in the United States by as much as 8%, for example, and this may well be an underestimate!

What is more important with regard to PKI is the distinction between public and private keys. Private keys are exactly that—they are meant to be held privately. A single-key encryption scheme would use the key to scramble the plaintext at one end of the transmission and descramble the ciphertext at the other end. The same key must be available at both

---

[11]The examples here are overly simplistic to make the point. In fact, the three tanspositions given are the equivalent of only one transposition of symbols moving five positions to the right in the sequence and would easily be broken by a hacker through brute force. Transformation algorithms can be extremely complex, as long as the program for encrypting and decrypting is aware of the maping. Moreover, keys can be quite long, although this greatly increases the time to encrypt and decrypt. The so-called DES algorithm calls for 64 transformations.

[12]There is talk and experimentation going on at this time with quantum fluctuations that would be so unpredictable they would be unbreakable. But firms already have the edge in securing transmissions, if only some encryption is implemented! So further technical advances in encryption are not nearly as important as putting into practice currently available solutions.

ends for this to work. This poses a problem because in commerce you most likely would not want to share your key with other organizations since this would give any one of your partners access to all of your transmissions unless you had a separate key for each partner.

A second problem with this scheme is that it greatly complicates the exchange of information if one needs new keys for each new partner. Such information would also have to be coordinated throughout branches and divisions within an organization.

The public-private key, asymmetric system solves these problems. A public key is exactly that, a key that can be made public without a breach in security. In fact, public repositories on the Web can share information about the keys of any number of organizations. The keys can be long or short (relatively speaking), and it is not a critical matter.

Public keys are used by the sending organization to encrypt the message. In order to read the message, the receiver must have the asymmetric key, the private key linked to that public key, as shown in Figure 6.5. This means that anyone can intercept the encrypted message, but only the legitimate party issued the corresponding private key can read it. The sender can freely transmit a message across a network and not worry that a party can intercept and read the ciphertext. Even if an abuser were to guess the identities of the sender and the receiver and were to retrieve their public keys from the repository, an asymmetric scheme means that only a private key could unlock the message. So the public keys the abuser retrieved would be useless without somehow breaking the key code by brute force.

When a receiving organization is able to successfully decrypt and read a message, the organization can be assured with a high degree of certainty that the message has not be manipulated. However, they cannot be certain that the sending party is who he or she claims to be, because anyone can get the public key from the repository. In other words, they can be sure that the confidentiality of the message itself has not been breached, but they cannot be sure about the identity of the sender.

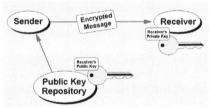

Figure 6.5   How PKI Works

PKI offers an ingenious solution to this problem. If the sender reencrypts the entire encrypted message with his or her private key, then the only way the entire enveloped message can be read is if the public key of the identified organization is used. In other words, if I use the XYZ sender organization's public key to first open the transmitted envelope, then I know with a reasonable degree of certainty that the sender organization has been authenticated as who it said it was. If, subsequently, I use my own private key to read the message within the envelope, I know that the message has remained confidential throughout its journey across the network.

Please note that the entire PKI infrastructure depends on trusted third parties. Although firms have no worry about the confidentiality (integrity) of the message if they can decrypt a message with their private keys, they could not be certain of the identity of the sender unless a third party can give them the precise public key that is definitely associated with a particular entity and with no other entity. Without this trusted link, the entire system breaks down."

6.4.1 Digital Signatures

When examining scenarios in which a vendor wants to verify that the customers are who they say they are (and vice versa), the terminology used is known as *digital signatures*. Digital signatures use a form of PKI and may be considered in that context. As illustrated in Figure 6.6, digital signatures ask the same questions about security asked in other uses of PKI.

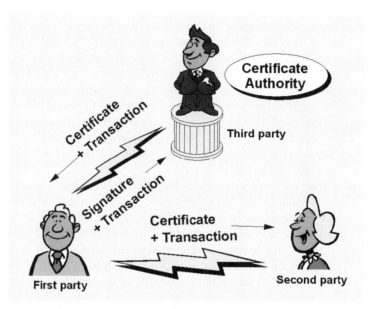

Figure 6.6   Digital Signatures

Digital signatures operate through a trusted third party, known as a certificate authority (CA). The CA issues linked public and private keys to parties when they establish their identities through traditional means. When an individual of one party wishes to buy something from an individual in a second party, the first party sends their digital signature to the CA along with the transactional information. In this manner, the transaction can be encrypted with the public key of the CA to ensure confidentiality of the transaction. If the CA can open, or access, the transaction, the first party and the CA know that the message has not been tampered with. The digital signature is, in effect, the private key of the first party, and if the CA can open the entire envelope with the public key of the reported sender, the identity of the first party has been authenticated. The CA issues a digital certificate, which is a warranty that the first party is who they claim to be. This certificate can be wrapped in an "envelope" with the public key of the first party and the transaction information. The second party opens the "envelope" with their private key, assuring themselves that the entire transaction has not been tampered with. The certificate can be checked through a separate inquiry to the CA.

The precise workings of PKI in NE commerce is of less interest than the bottom line, which is this: within a reasonable degree of certainty, transmissions over the Internet or through networks can be secured. Longer keys require abusers to spend more time attempting to break the encoding. One technique used by hackers, for example, is to subject the ciphertext—which is readily available to open ears—to the brute force of tremendous computing power. Multiple transformations of the ciphertext will eventually reveal the key that yields interpretable messages. The main issues are how much computing power can be used and the amount of time it takes to break the key. If this amount of intense computing breaks into a transmission worth $100 and it costs $2000 to break the code, there is clearly a poor cost-benefit for the abusers.

6.4.2 SSL and SET

SSL (Secure Socket Layer) and SET (Secure Electronic Transaction[13]) are two forms of security that are currently being used to ensure the confidentiality of transmissions—but, please note, *not* the identity of the sender—across the Net. The software used to enable SSL is built into browsers, and transmissions are secured (for confidentiality purposes) by a key generated for each session. Users can tell whether the message being sent to the server is encrypted by observing the protocol. If it is secured the protocol will be HTTPS rather than HTTP.

SET is a more advanced protocol than SSL. It has been advanced by a consortium of credit card companies including Visa and MasterCard. One of its major advantages over SSL is that the credit card number is scrambled when displayed to the vendor. Transactions can still be verified on all dimensions, but the vendor is never given access to the real credit card number.

▶ *CASE STUDY 6-2*

MCWHORTLE ENTERPRISES: COULD IT BE A REMARKABLE INVESTMENT?

Shaken by the September 11, 2001, terrorist attacks, and committed to supporting the American economy, Jane Doe decided to pull some money from her savings account and make new investments. She felt confident that companies working on biological defense mechanisms had significant opportunity for growth, so she began looking for investment options in this industry.

On January 26, 2002, Jane read an intriguing press release from McWhortle Enterprises. The established company claimed to have a solid track record and a "can't-miss product that customers are fighting to buy." In only four days, the company would go public, so she knew that she needed to make a quick decision. Jane spent time at the company's Web site, www.mcwhortle.com, and was pleased to read customer testimonials and even listen to a recent interview with McWhortle CEO and President Thomas McWhortle III.

Jane's excitement about McWhortle Enterprises increased when she read that the company was enjoying incredible demand from other investors. The Web site said that the pre-IPO investment program was oversubscribed, but explained that she could bid on the remaining shares that promised a return of 400% in three months. Although this sounded almost too good to be true, Jane was reassured by the detailed information on the Web site and the knowledge that her investment would be helping the economy.

Jane clicked on the link to post her bid and provide the required credit card number and social security number. To her surprise the link did not take her where she expected. The next Web page informed her that McWhortle Enterprises is a complete fabrication. This warning was posted by the

[13]See http://www.setco.org/ for site for the organization that manages the SET specifications.

Securities and Exchange Commission, the Federal Trade Commission, the North American Securities Administrators Association, and the National Association of Securities Dealers to alert investors to potential online frauds.

Although she certainly felt a bit violated, she was thankful to learn this lesson without financial loss. By reading the posted message and following the provided links, Jane learned how she can better research future investment opportunities and avoid being the victim of online fraud.

Discussion:

1. Discuss the McWhortle Enterprises Web site. Describe how the Web site is designed to gain the trust of investors. Discuss items that should make investors suspicious. Explore how the Web designers could have made the scheme even more plausible.

2. Discuss the role of the SEC in educating investors and warning them about scams.

Resources:

Bisset, S. "Protecting yourself." *Futures*. May (2002).

Keyt, R. "Regulators Launch Fake Scam Web Sites to Warn Investors about Internet Fraud." *Keyt-Law*. [Online] Available: http://www.keytlaw.com/sec/web_scams.htm. Accessed July 27, 2002.

McDonald, T. "Feds Set Online Scam to Warn Investors." *NewsFactor Network*, January 30, 2002. [Online] Available: http://www.newsfactor.com/perl/story/16069.html. Accessed July 27, 2002.

6.5 SECURING THE END POINTS

Given that transmissions can be reasonably secured, what are the main security vulnerabilities of NESs? From the beginning of the computer era, it has been clear that the ends of transmission lines are the weak links in security.[14] What does this mean? As shown in Figure 6.7, the client would be vulnerable to "fires" on the Net without a protective firewall (specialized software and/or hardware). Servers are also susceptible to such "fires".[15] They can be automated intrusions such as viruses and worms, or they can be attempts by hackers to penetrate a system.

Firewalls protect the endpoints of the system against unauthorized intrusions from the outside. They can be set up with access control lists to ensure that messages and requests sent to the server and client are legitimate and acceptable within the boundaries of company policies. These, like PKI, are "preventive" countermeasures meant to keep abusers from violating protected systems and data.

What is an access control list? An access control list tells organizational computers which computer operations are permitted to be executed by which users or processes. For instance, if a firm wishes to have an outside systems integrator automatically update certain software on their internal systems, the firm would have to authorize the integrator's updating processes to remove, add, and install files in the firm's internal systems.

Let's look at an example. A computer virus that is a potentially destructive, self-reproducing segment of program code is sent by an outside source to the server or via an e-mail attachment to the client. Firewalls typically contain virus protection software that isolates,

---

[14]Straub and Welke (1998).

[15]Please note that the server in this figure might be the firm's Web server, whereas the client would be the firm's purchasing arm. Thus, single or multiple servers and clients can be positioned on the firm's side of the organizational firewalls.

cleans, or deletes viruses. So, properly set up, the firewall protects the endpoints of the NES from this form of fire.

Access control lists and configurations of Windows or Mac operating system security should also be used to protect servers and clients from internal abuse. There are a large number of documented cases involving employees and ex-employees abusing internal systems. This threat is at least as large as the threat from the outside.[16] Hancock (2001) reports an incident where a GTE employee compromised the firm's internal systems for personal gain. This kind of incident—violation by a trusted insider—takes place across the world every day.

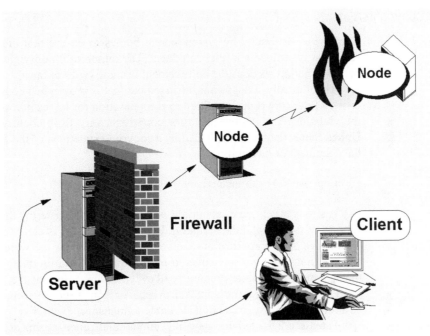

Figure 6.7   Firewalls to Secure the Endpoints

Endpoints can also be secured by deterring abusers from even contemplating an attack on organizational systems. We know from scientific evidence that abusers can be deterred by setting punishment levels high enough and having an active security effort to enforce compliance.[17] Organizations that take security seriously are willing to prosecute abusers and make this stance known.[18] The effectiveness of this positioning is seen in other areas of security, for instance, in retail stores. Stores that make it clear that they prosecute shoplifters regardless of the seriousness of the theft are examples of this. The intention is to warn potential abusers beforehand that they will be punished severely if they steal.

Finally, endpoints need to be secure from disastrous consequences should a security breach occur. Recovery of systems is an important element in the firm's disaster recovery planning. It may be executed on an individual, system-by-system basis whenever a system (server) has been compromised.

[16]Straub and Welke (1998).
[17]Straub (1990).
[18]Straub and Nance (1990).

6.6 PROTECTING INTELLECTUAL PROPERTY

Besides preventive (including PKI), deterrent, and recovery capabilities of security systems, there are two primary legal ways to protect Web systems and content. Such assets are known as *intellectual property* because they are products of the mind. Data, pictures, digital music, graphics, charts—all are generated by the mind of man and range from pure imaginative products to structured control signals. They all manipulate symbols as a critical aspect in their creation.

6.6.1 Copyrights/Patents

Copyrights are issued by governmental bodies to ensure that creators are able to get a return on investments in their products. The duration of copyright protection varies from nation to nation, as does the enforcement of these types of laws.

Theoretically, a copyright infringement that is proven in a court of law means that the owner of the copyright is entitled to compensation for losses in revenue and market due to the violation. The requirements for copyrights vary from country to country, but in the United States they are established by a copyright statement of the following sort placed on the document or medium.[19]

Copyright (c) by Detmar Straub, 2002. All rights reserved.

A stronger version of copyright is established by registering the creation with the U.S. Library of Congress in Washington, D.C. In any case, it is clear that software—including Web pages, server applications, server software, network software, and many other types of computer programs—is covered by these laws. As a product of the intellect, content that is not in the public domain is likewise covered. In that the financial compensation from a successful lawsuit helps a firm recover from a security breach, it can be thought of as a form of security protection available to managers.[20]

Patents are issued for new inventions, and, once again, are not consistent across nations. The idea behind a patent is to legally protect new concepts that are embodied in something useful to society. The implementation criterion has recently been loosened in the United States so that patents can now be issued for software and even for business models.

Copyrights and patents will be discussed later in the chapter on social and international issues, especially since there are so many global challenges to enforcement in these arenas.

6.6.2 Trademarks and Digital Watermarks

Besides trademarks, which are labels (in the United States trademarks are indicated by a "TM" superscript following the name, for example) that legally protect the name of a product or service, another primary way to protect intellectual property is with a digital watermark. Virtual watermarks—unlike intentionally visible watermarks on paper and

---

[19]In effect, the mere creation of a new work copyrights it, but there are varying strengths of copyrights, depending on how persistently the creator "advertises" the fact that the work is copyrighted. The copyright symbol, date, and other language are meant to reinforce the copyright.
[20]Straub and Collins (1990).

other products—are meant to be hidden from potential thieves. Bits that uniquely identify the product, the sellers, and the buyer are embedded in the file so they cannot be identified by a foreign party,[21] as illustrated in Figure 6.8. Of course, it is critical that the changed bits are not crucial bits, or the distortions would clearly reveal the watermark.

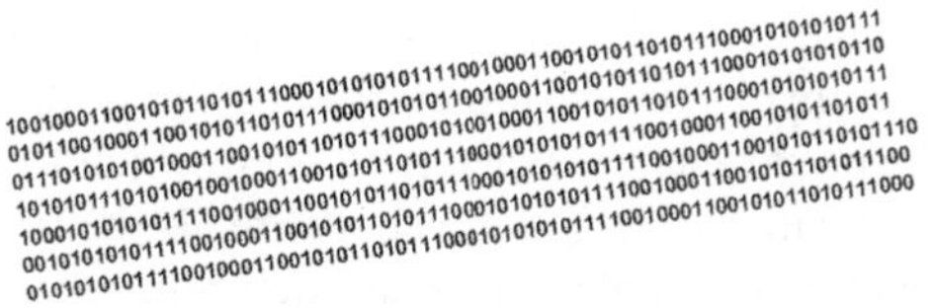

Figure 6.8 Bits Placed in Innocuous Locations in File to Serve as Digital Watermark

Only when the owner-key to the bits is presented can the identifying bits be unveiled. When the key is registered with a trusted third-party authority, the owner has the legal right to sue for any theft of the product or service.

Legal remedies allow firms to gain a measure of financial return on their intellectual property even when the up-front security measures have not worked (or could not work). Let's take an example. An unethical firm buys a gallery of digital photos from another firm, and then—contrary to the one-time user purchasing agreement—includes these photos in content that it sells over the Internet. By copyrighting and placing digital watermarks on the photo gallery sold for one-time use, the firm ensures that it can sue successfully. It needs to prove that the violating firm has indeed sold their protected products for substantial amounts and has affected the market for the products, according to U.S. law. What is more important than the specifics of U.S. law, however, is that there are legal remedies that can be effective in protecting e-property.

6.7 NE TRUST

The trust that consumers and business customers have in NESs is closely connected with the perceived—and actual—level of security of the online business environment.

Trust is a form of control and extended control. Human beings like to control their world, and when they need to deal with others in business exchanges they must necessarily pass part of this control to others. Trust is a mechanism for determining when and to whom to extend this control.

The bases on which individuals decide to give others control are numerous.[22] Some of them are purely related to circumstance. Others seem to be relatively stable and suggest how firms should interact with their customers in the long-term in order to maximize customer trust.

Trust is an ancient line of inquiry. Aristotle, in his major work *Rhetoric,* writes about the criteria we use to judge one another. These criteria are: intelligence, good character, and good will. Not surprisingly, these three characteristics bear a close resemblance to the reasons that we trust others, as discovered empirically by social scientists in the social

---

[21]Yeung (1998).
[22]Luhmann (1979).

psychology, marketing, and management disciplines. Aristotle's construct of intelligence corresponds to "ability," good character to "honesty and integrity," and good will to "benevolence."[23] A fourth aspect of trust that is sometimes cited is predictability.[24]

How does this work? In the circumstance in which we are primarily interested, a customer grows to trust or distrust an online vendor, depending on whether the promises being made by the vendor seem to be reliable. The aspects of the interaction being considered by the customer are, first, the ability of the firm to create and deliver quality. Consider the dilemma: if the customer has not had prior contact with or knowledge of an NE vendor, he or she has no experience from which to draw. Does the firm sell quality products, or is the online description vaporware? If the vendor is capable, and the customer believes the vendor is capable, either through prior experience or by reputation, then trust is high and the purchase is more likely to be completed. Dell, for example, has gained a reputation for quality products, and their online store is generating numerous annual sales as a result.

The second criteria for trust is integrity. The customer must believe that the vendor will stand by the promises made. If the customer feels he or she is being lied to, or given inconsistent messages from firm sales representatives or online material, this will erode trust. Indications that the firm is willing to stand behind its products and services, and accept and process financial returns are examples of signs that will help secure customers' trust in the vendor.

With respect to the third factor, customers assess the willingness of vendors to maintain a fair environment for business exchange. In labor negotiations, bargaining sides sometimes accuse each other of "bargaining in bad faith." This concept is similar to how customers in the NE world respond to vendors. If the customer feels there is "bad faith," they will avoid buying from a vendor. Good faith suggests a "benevolence" on the partner's part, and leads to a strengthening of the trust between the parties.

The fourth characteristic is predictability, which is self-evident. Erratic behavior on the part of a firm will turn off a customer. Lack of predictability sometime occurs when firms downsize, merge, or undergo a severe cultural change. A great deal of the healthy firm's behavior and learning concentrates on giving the customer a consistent set of messages, with reasonable policies steadily applied.

6.7.1 NE Trust-Building Mechanisms

Building trust in an online setting is difficult because the customer lacks the cues that are often ordinarily associated with a face-to-face or even a telephone purchase. Other than a vendor with click-to-talk Web capability, the customer knows only what she/he sees in the text and images or hears through a playable audio file on the site. NESs generally lack what is known as *social presence*. Social presence is the sense that a human being or human-like characteristics such as interactivity are involved in the exchange. Interactivity means that the vendor is responsive and willing to engage in an electronic dialogue with the customer.

Of course, many old and loyal customers trust an online vendor in spite of the uncertainty of not knowing who the party at the other end really is. But for the first-time visitor, the decision to buy is even more uncertain because they lack history with the vendor.

---

[23]Gefen and Straub (2002); Giffin (1967); Blau (1964); Schurr and Ozanne (1985); Rotter (1971).
[24]Mayer et al. (1995); McKnight et al. (1998).

So what can firms do to induce online sales even in the presence of all of these disadvantages? Perceived high security is part of the solution, as shown in Table 6.1. Trust in the vendor will increase if the customer trusts the *ability* of the vendor to secure the transaction itself and, therefore, the *integrity* of the transaction. The security mechanisms for accomplishing this have already been discussed in this chapter. Firms serious about conducting business via NE need to implement them.

Table 6.1: Ways to Increase the Perception of Trust in a Web Site

	Trust-Building Mechanisms
1	The perception of a well-secured Web site or EDI transaction
2	Third-party guarantors of transactional integrity
3	Responsiveness of vendor to customer inquiries
4	Heightened sense of social presence in Web site (likely related to interactivity of Web site)

Third-party guarantors of the transaction, firms like VeriSign (www.verisign.com—see Figure 6.9), offer alternate ways for the vendor to demonstrate its security *ability*. For customers concerned about the privacy of their data, a relationship with a third-party guarantor like TRUSTe (www.etrust.com) is helpful because it confirms that the vendor is complying with TRUSTe privacy standards.[25] Empirical research has found that third-party guarantors are instrumental in increasing the trust levels of customers.[26]

Figure 6.9 VeriSign's Home Page—Example of a Third-Party Guarantor

[25]Trust is also related to the percieved usefulness of an NES for both experienced Web users (Gefen, D., E. Karahanna and Straub (2003); Gefen, Karahanna and Straub (forthcoming, 2003).
[26]Gefen (1997).

Firm responsiveness is a third avenue for trust-building. When a firm responds quickly and competently to a customer inquiry, the impression made is a lasting one. Customers are given a sense that the firm cares, that is, it is acting in good faith with the customer. The issue is not that the firm always responds affirmatively to customer inquiries. If the customer asks for free samples, and the firm does not have a policy of doing this, then a competent response would be to suggest that the firm does have a liberal return policy. An incompetent response would be to just say that no free samples are allowed.

Why is a simple straightforward denial of a customer request not as effective as a redirection of the question? The customer is looking for assurances that the firm takes interaction with the customer seriously and is not off-putting. To build trust, the vendor needs to suggest ways that the customer can be reassured that they are getting additional value for their money and that the vendor is not a fly-by-night organization.

Even worse than a blunt denial is no response at all. In the ongoing Georgia State University study of NEOs, one large bank vice-president reported proudly to the researchers that the bank was receiving thousands of e-mail messages a week from their customers. When asked how they were able to field such a large number, the director replied that it was easy. They ignored them.

One of the keys to building customers' trust is responsiveness. One of the sure ways to lose trust is nonresponsiveness. In the NE environment, organizations must have human or automated quick-response mechanisms in place. Having a Contact Us click-on icon and no ready form of response will only create distrust.

How can firms both be responsive and indicate that they are responsive? If customers are sent signals that the firm is willing to interact in a variety of ways, and not just when the customer is purchasing, the customers are more likely to trust the vendor. Figure 6.10 shows how the bottom of the campmor.com home page has e-mail and phone contact points with the firm in addition to the Web site itself. These speak to the responsiveness of the firm. Please note that there are two third-party guarantors that also lend credence to the legitimacy of the vendor.

6.7.2 Creating Social Presence in a Web Site

The fourth trust-building mechanism is increasing the social presence of the vendor Web site. The reason is that trust, in general, is built through constructive interactions with *other people.*[27] Because human interaction with the trusted party, whether face-to-face or by any other means, is a precondition of trust, the perception of a high degree of social presence, implying direct or indirect human contact in the relationship, contributes to the building of trust. Certainly, deliberately avoiding the creation of a social interaction and making the relationship devoid of a social presence, such as showing a cold shoulder, reduces trust.[28] Trust in an NE Web site may be built through imbuing the medium of communication with a high social presence: the perception that there is personal, sociable, and sensitive human contact in the medium.[29]

---

[27]Blau (1964); Fukuyama (1995); Luhman (1979).
[28]Blau (1964).
[29]Short et al. (1976).

Figure 6.10   Example of Campmor NEO That Builds Trust by Giving Customers Numerous Options for Interaction

How can this work? NE commercial Web sites typically involve no actual human interaction. The firm must embed the sense of this contact in the site. Solutions include photos of sales representatives, customer contact personnel, and technical support staff people on the site to give a feeling of personal, sociable, and sensitive human contact. Multimedia is even more effective in this regard.[30] Pictures of smiling faces go a long way toward making a site home-like, and this is welcoming to a customer.

Personalization, discussed further in Chapter 11 on NE marketing, is another way in which a site will convey more than it is. With cookies, the server can learn who the customer is and welcome him/her by name. By accessing the site through a password, the firm automatically knows something about the user; this is another means of personalizing the responses.

A perceived higher social presence increases trust. We know, for example, that it has an impact on the extent of electronic communication in e-mail interactions.[31]

In conclusion, trust is not easily won from customers in NE environments. It needs to be built up over time through such firm behaviors as

1. A trustworthy track record of previous behavior[32]
2. A willingness to invest in a long-term relationship[33]
3. Investing beyond what is required by the initial contract[34]

---

[30]Daft and Lengel (1984).

[31]Gefen and Straub (1997); see Straub and Karahanna (1998) for a review of this line of research.

[32]Khmer (1996); McAllister (1995); Sucker (1986).

[33]Anderson and Narus (1990); Blau (1964); Deutsch (1958); Homans (1961); Kumar (1996); Morgan and Hunt (1994).

[34]Ganesan (1994).

4. Cooperativeness[35]
5. Staying in touch[36]
6. Not demonstrating opportunistic behavior[37]

In addition to the trust-building mechanisms, the firm that has a long-term view of customer trust and is willing to design NESs to accommodate trust building will win over customers in the final analysis. This insight is not widely known among firms pursuing NE strategies today.

6.7.3 NE Trust as a Temporary Problem?

Is lack of trust merely symptomatic of the early stages of a technological innovation, or will it always be a concern? One argument is that as those who grew up with computers become the driving force in buying economies, these fears will diminish. After all, the technology itself will be as familiar to people as driving a car, operating a television, or playing an audio system. So Web-savvy users will understand that the business exchange can be made safe and secure and they will trust the firms that are seriously dealing with the issue.

But in spite of growing knowledge of Web technologies, safety/security issues will likely not go away, and the relationship of two parties in a business exchange will continue to be of interest. Automobile technology, for example, has had a remarkable history over the last century. Cars of high quality can be produced in large numbers and increasingly custom-made for consumers. They incorporate computer technology to manage the engine and steering systems, and, more and more, will use global positioning satellites (GPS) to help people find destinations.

But no matter how advanced the technology of automobiles has become, questions about the endurance of tires or the tendency of a car to turn over can still arise to plague large, prosperous firms such as Firestone and Ford. Their crisis in consumer confidence hinged on two issues: the tendency of the tires to blowout and the car to rollover. The point is not whether either, both, or neither of these conditions prevailed in this situation. The point is that the crisis arose from a loss of consumer trust, and both corporate partners were drawn into the controversy. By the same token, NE firms will need to maintain a high level of surveillance on their security, or their partners will cease to trust them rather quickly.

6.7.4 Additional Aspects of Trust in an Online Environment

There are other technologies that impact user trust in NESs. Although security is clearly one of the most important of these factors, it is not the only one. There is growing evidence, for instance, that the structure of the interaction and the power of the brand have a bearing on the extent of trust. Among the modes of interaction we discussed in Chapter 3 were human-to-computer and human-to-human (e-mail or "click-to-talk"). In the case where a firm has no human contact available to customers online, it is especially critical that the Web site have a high social presence.[38]

---

[35]Crosby et al. (1990); Dwyer et al. (1987).
[36]Crosby et al. (1990).
[37]Morgan and Hunt (1994); Williamson (1985).
[38]Gefen and Straub (1997).

When firms have a feature for a live chat with sales representatives, high social presence is not simulated, but real. There is evidence[39] that even though click-to-chat sites are much more labor-intensive than a site that has only a machine response (or even allows sales representatives to batch process e-mail responses) they are still more efficient than a physical interaction. Live chat sales representatives can handle roughly three concurrent interactions, as opposed to the single person interaction to which a face-to-face exchange or phone conversation are limited.

Brand and Trust

Does the power of the brand carry over into the online environment? Although the issue is not entirely resolved,[40] it does make intuitive sense that firms that have engendered brand loyalty in the past will continue to profit from this in cyberspace. What are the technologies that reinforce brand? Clearly, NEOs that take advantage of their widely recognized logos, animate these so they become even more memorable and generally create an interest in a Web environment that could be unique to their brand. As opposed to the static print environment, the Web environment can take advantage of multimedia such as video and audio, and it has an edge on the one-way world of broadcasting because it can personalize Web content to match the needs and interests of the user. Personalization is a technology that we will discuss in the Chapter 11, on NE marketing, but, for the moment, it is relevant to mention that the sense of interactivity that can be conveyed in a Web site that is heavily personalized; it can lead to greater trust on the past of customers. Both the research to date and our intuition tell us that this must be the case.

Web-Site Design and Trust

Technical characteristics of Web sites may also affect how involved users feel toward an NEO. The jury is still out on the extent to which this is important,[41] but, again, it makes sense that users would respond to Web sites in the same way they respond to advertisements. An effective Web site will draw customers in the same way a good advertisement does.

6.8 NE PAYMENT OPTIONS

There are a host of online payment options for NE business transactions. But before discussing these, we need to understand what has to take place in any business exchange involving payments. First, at a relatively late point in the transaction, the buyer indicates that he or she wishes to purchase and needs a vendor warranty. The buyer undoubtedly wants some assurance that should he or she authorize the purchase (and the payment) that the goods/services will be provided by the vendor. If the vendor has a good track record or is a known brand, the buyer may be willing to trust that the vendor will deliver. This may be a sufficient warranty, especially in favorable legal circumstances. Guarantees of satisfactory performance are embedded in credit card law in the U.S., for instance, so that the credit card company will withhold payment (or demand a return of this amount) if the vendors defaults. In the same vein for eBay customers is a third-party escrow system. This is made available to both parties so that payment is escrowed, but will not be issued until the product or service is delivered.

[39]Yin (2002).
[40]Gefen (1997).
[41]Rose (2000).

The second issue is how the buyer will convey the payment. We will examine the options below, but both the buyer and the vendor want the payment part of the transaction to be completely secure. We have already covered the role of encryption in securing transmissions. Arguably, the payment information is the most crucial use of encryption in business exchanges.

Third, for the purposes of closure on the part of both buyer and seller, a confirmation that the transaction has been successfully completed and the transmission of confirmation numbers/transaction numbers to the buyer is a usual third stage in the payment cycle.

The payment options for NEOs are

1. Electronic funds transfer (EFT)
2. Credit cards
3. Debit cards
4. E-Cash

6.8.1 EFT

Business customers have the option of using EFT for payments in NESs. Figure 6.11 shows the elements of a successful execution of payment. Once the EDI payment options and invoicing cycles are completed, the payment is authorized by the purchaser. Some firms are experimenting with alternate steps in this cycle, but the point is that the transfer of funds in this scenario occurs from bank to bank. Because most B2C activity is low volume from the standpoint of the buyer, EDI is usually restricted to B2B where the organizations involved are either large firms or SMEs.

6.8.2 Credit Cards

Credit card payments are initiated by the buyer entering the card numbers either through data entry or through a swipe mechanism. The card numbers do not need to be verified online in the same manner that they are in the physical world because the customer is not carrying off physical goods. This allows the vendor to perform a more elaborate credit check if that is needed.

Credit cards are one of the preferred method of payment for online goods or services in the United States. Europeans generally prefer debit cards (or Smart Cards) for such transactions. The effective employment of credit cards in online purchases depends on having the regulatory environment that protects buyers. Because a credit card represents, in effect, a loan, actual payment is delayed to the vendor. Vendors would clearly prefer immediate, undisputed payment.

6.8.3 Debit Cards

Debit card numbers can be entered into an NE transaction in the same manner as a credit card. Debit cards are the opposite of credit cards in the sense that the authorization of the payment is immediate. Debits are automatically executed against the purchaser's account. The account with the funds may reside on the card itself, as in the case of a Smart Card, or in a bank. Unlike credit cards, purchasers using debit cards have a more difficult time recovering their funds if a vendor defaults. A strong regulatory environment might make this more acceptable, but it could be built into the nature of the payment device itself.

6.8.4 E-Cash

A fourth viable method of payment is electronic cash, or e-cash. In principle, it is straight-forward. A buyer has a bank account and electronically authorizes withdrawals from this account for goods and services. E-Cash has advantages over credit or debit cards in that there is no need for a physical card at any point, and it can deal with micropayments, which the current physical card system cannot. Micropayments are partial cent payments or charges that result in partial cents, such as interest calculations. There is no need for rounding to the nearest cent if an e-cash system is in place. To use e-cash, a purchaser needs to set up a bank account and obtain the appropriate software. If the vendor accepts e-cash, then the payment is authorized through the software for a certain amount. For the greatest security, encryption is used to protect the transmissions. A much lower level of security would require passwords from the payee.

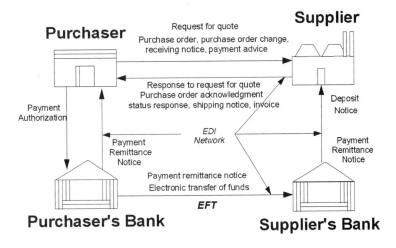

-Adopted from Senn (1996)

Figure 6.11   EFT and EDI Transactions

6.8.5 Online Public Transfers

The final means of paying for online transactions is through an electronically authorized transfer of funds over a public network like the Internet. It is clear that the Internet is less secure by its very nature than the dedicated telecommunications connections utilized for EFT. Any node on the Internet has "ears." To hear (and intercept) transactions on a private line an abuser needs to have fairly sophisticated inside help. No system is completely secure, and inside help can be forthcoming, but collusion on the part of perpetrators is the weak link for this form of abuse. For one reason or another, the fraternity of thieves (or even saboteurs) is an antisocial group filled with mistrust. It is inevitable that circumstances such as greed, paranoia, or dissatisfaction will lead to its being readily compromised.

The same is not true of the Internet, where abusers can work alone in relative anonymity, as long as he or she has undetected access to a node.[42] The Internet can be encrypted,

---

[42]An overwhelming percentage of computer abusers are men. Women have not, to date, been the primary perpetrators of abuse.

that is true, but codes can eventually be broken if they can be read. So a private connection significantly lowers one threat of interception in online transfers of funds from one account to another.

If an abuser has public access to a Web site where customers transfer funds, he or she does not need to intercept messages to steal someone's money.

Where do we see a large number of online public transfers? The NE securities markets are heavily involved in this form of payment. If a customer has an account at an online financial services firm, for example, he or she is likely logging in on a secured SSL link. This is obvious by both the "Security Alert" dialog box that appears (see Figure 6.12) and the protocol used to access the Web page from the server (HTTPS). Once the user clicks OK that he or she is aware that the transaction is taking place over a secure connection, the URL will switch to HTTPS.

Figure 6.12   Typical Security Alert Dialogue Box on Financial Services Web Site

SSL secures the transmission. What about the end-points? This requires authentication of identify. For this, securities firms vary in what they require by way of passwords, but it is important to note that password protection is generally less secure than digital signatures.[43] Password guessing can be used by an abuser to penetrate a user's personal security and defraud the user by stealing funds from their account. Various checks on the part of the securities firms, such as telephone calls to the client for large transfers and the mailing of withdrawals to established addresses, are intended to make this less risky, but there are vulnerabilities in this scheme. There can be no doubt that digital signatures would lead to more secure systems overall.

As long as vendors restrict user options to passwords, a double level of password protection is one viable solution for a relatively simple way to increase security. E-trade has both a login password and a password for actual trading. The first password allows the user to view past transactions and to monitor the balances on accounts. The second password is used for transference of funds. This requires an abuser to guess two passwords, which makes any criminal action that much harder.

6.8.6 Security and Payments

Payment schemes are only as good as the security levels maintained. EFT is very likely the most secure of these, because it is a proprietary networked solution, and banks are more security-conscious than the average large or small-to-medium-sized enterprise. Table 6.2 shows how relatively secure each of the payment options is.

---

[43]Please note that if your desktop or laptop holds your digital signature and is stolen (or misused), your identify could also be stolen along with the hardware. One assumption about the security of digital signatures is that your computing devices are physically secured or they are password-protected.

Table 6.2: Security of NE Payment Schemes

	Payment Scheme	Typical Security	Pros and Cons
1	EFT	Private key–encrypted transmissions over dedicated leased lines between banks or financial institutions	Highly secure, but limited in ease of participation by its closed, proprietary nature
2	Credit cards	PKI-encrypted transmittal of card numbers; SET hides card numbers from e-retailers; SSL does not	Regulatory environment can offer customer protections that will increase usage of online sites; lack of such an environment will inhibit commercial development
3	Debit cards	PKI-encrypted transmittal of card numbers; SET hides card numbers from e-retailers; SSL does not	Preferred by vendors because payment is immediate; creates hurdles for customers trying to recover from a fraudulent transaction.
4	E-Cash	In the most secure environment, PKI-encrypted digital signatures; in least secured, password-protected	Ease-of-use once installed; allows for micropayments; lacking automatic deposit or transference, requires some sophistication on part of user for transference of funds from other sources to an e-account
5	Online public transfers	PKI-encrypted digital signatures; password-protected	Digital signatures offer the greatest security in financial services sites; passwords are less secure, but can be mitigated by separate passwords for login and transactions

Focus on NE: Hackers

 Modern hacking was born in 1972 when John T. Draper, a.k.a. "Cap'n Crunch," discovered that he could make free long-distance phone calls by using the whistle out of a cereal box. Mr. Draper then distributed blue boxes that allowed others to access free long distance.

The first convicted hacker was Ian Murphy, who broke into the AT&T system and reset the internal clocks on the billing system. Rates were switched, and people calling at midday received discount rates and those who waited until midnight paid the highest rates.

In 1988, Robert Tappan Morris brought down one-tenth of the Internet by releasing the Morris Worm. The Morris Worm was an experimental, self-replicating, self-propagating program that replicated and reinfected machines at a much faster rate than anticipated. Ultimately, many machines at locations around the country either crashed or became catatonic. The worm caused $15 million worth of damage.

Kevin Mitnick has the distinction of being the very first person to be convicted of gaining access to an interstate computer network for criminal purposes. He was also the first hacker to have his face appear on an FBI Most Wanted poster. Mitnick stole at least $1 million of sensitive project data from computer systems, stole thousands of credit card numbers from online databases, broke into the California Department of Motor Vehicles database, and remotely controlled New York and California's telephone switching hubs.

In February 2000, a Canadian kid who went by the name MafiaBoy was arrested for launching a denial-of-service attack that brought down many of the Internet's largest sites. MafiaBoy crippled Amazon, eBay, and Yahoo during the weeks of February 6 and February 14 in the year 2000.

Source:

http://www.business2.com/Webguide/0,1660,22922,00.html

6.9 SUMMARY

This chapter focuses on how links between security, trust, and payment affect an NEO. Special attention is given to this area because, without safe and efficient procedures, the full potential of the NEO will not be realized, thus jeopardizing its success.

A basic security problem of NEOs is that they must be safe from disasters and have well-developed and tested disaster and business plans in place prior to the occurrence of an actual event. NEOs must also be secure from intentional and unintentional violation of their systems. Intentional violation is the purposeful act of violating a computer system, usually from computer abusers or hackers. Unintentional violations can innocently occur by employees of an organization and may result in data being altered or lost. Proper orientation and training programs must be implemented to prevent unintentional violation from occurring. NEOs must be able to recover quickly from problems and must design plans of action in anticipation of a violation.

NEOs must also take necessary action to secure their networks. This is accomplished by scrambling the data through encryption. PKI (public key infrastructure) is used to make encryption possible, convenient and secure. The two forms of PKI used are Secure Socket Layer (SSL) and Secure Electronic Transaction (SET). Digital signatures that use a form of PKI can also help NEOs secure their networks.

An NEO must establish trust with consumers and provide security for online businesses. The customer must feel that the promises the NEO makes will be fulfilled. The NEO must also be able to build, create, and deliver quality in their interactions with the customer at all times. The four criteria for trust that an NEO must establish with their customers are benevolence, integrity, good faith business dealings, and predictability. Four ways to build trust are through perceived high security of Web site or EDI transactions, third-party guarantees of transactional integrity, responsiveness of a vendor to customer inquiries, and a heightened sense of social presence in the NEO's Web site.

Different secured payment options must be available to meet the different needs and conveniences of the customers served. Examples of payment options are EFT, credit cards, debit cards, e-cash, and online public transfers. The NEO must take any necessary measures to secure the customers information and prevent any potentially fraudulent activity from occurring.

KEY TERMS

Access control list: A list that tells organizational computers which operations are permitted and by which users or processes.

Business continuity plan: A set of contingency plans outlining how to temporarily ensure operational continuity in case of a disaster. Focus is on paper records and files, as well as employee notification and deployment. See data disaster planning.

Certificate authority: A third-party authority that verifies credentials and issues digital certificates, which include linked public and private keys.

Cold site: Contracted outsourced disaster recovery facility that acts as a repository of a firm's backup data and software and has the capabilities to provide the firm with a temporary Internet connection. Hardware and other office equipment are rented from other outsourced firms. See hot site and distributed computing with excess capacity.

Ciphertext: Encrypted text.

Data disaster planning: See disaster planning.

Digital certificate: A warranty issued by a certificate authority that establishes credentials and identity.

Digital signature: An electronic signature used to authenticate the identity of the sender of a message.

Disaster planning: Plan dealing with the loss of electronic data, records and files, workstations, servers, and printers. Also called data disaster planning. See also business continuity plan.

Distributed computing with excess capacity: In-house alternative to outsource disaster recovery facilities through distributed computing and mirroring systems and data in different locations throughout the organization. See cold site and hot site.

Debit cards: Method of payment wherein authorization of payment is immediate. The funds may reside electronically in the card or in a bank account.

E-Cash: Electronic cash. Buyer automatically authorizes withdrawals from his or her account for goods or services. There is no physical card, and the transactions can deal with micropayments or charges that deal in partial cents.

EFT: See electronic funds transfer.

Electronic funds transfer: Transfer of funds from bank to bank through dedicated telecommunications connections, usually confined to business-to-business transactions.

Encryption: A security technique that protects the integrity of messages and authenticates the identity of senders by scrambling transmissions. See public key infrastructure.

Endpoints: The endpoints of network transmissions.

Fires: In Internet security terms, threats to servers and clients—unauthorized intrusions such as viruses or worms, or attempts by hackers to penetrate systems.

Firewalls: Software or hardware that protect endpoints of systems from unauthorized intrusion from the outside.

Hot site: Contracted outsource disaster recovery facility that not only has backups of data and software, but also provides network connections and necessary hardware. See cold site and distributed computing with excess capacity.

MTBU (mean time for belly up): A term in the security profession that indicates a firm's ability to survive an outage of its computer system, measured either in days or hours.

NE payment options: EFT (electronic fund transfer), credit cards, debit cards, e-cash, and online public transfers.

NE trust factors: Additional factors effecting the Web site aceptance besides trust are quality and reliability, integrity, good faith, and predictability as perceived by consumers and business customers.

Online public transfers: Electronically authorized transfer of funds over a public network like the Internet. Often used in transactions in the NE online securities market.

Plaintext: Original text form (or unencrypted form) of a transmission before being transformed by encryption into ciphertext.

Private key: In PKI, a key that is known only to the receiver and decrypts messages encrypted by either a public or a private key.

Public key: In PKI, a publicly known encryption key used in conjunction with a private key (known only to the recipient) to encrypt and decrypt messages.

Public key infrastructure (PKI): An asymmetric encryption scheme, using two keys (public and private), that prevents abusers from reading or altering transmitted messages. The scheme involves message transformation through the use of an algorithm that changes the characters and symbols from plaintext to ciphertext.

Secure Socket Layer (SSL): A form of PKI used to secure transmissions across the Internet, using browser-enabled software that secures transmission (for authentication purposes) by a key generated for each session.

Secure Electronic Transaction (SET): A more advanced protocol than SSL, using scrambling techniques, that verifies all transactions but prevents merchants and vendors from directly accessing actual credit card numbers.

Trust-building mechanisms: High perceived security of Web or EDI transactions, third-party guarantors of transactional integrity, responsiveness of vendor to consumer inquiries, and heightened sense of a social presence on the Web (likely related to the interactivity of the Web site).

REVIEW QUESTIONS

1. Define the point of payment.
2. What are the four basic security problems in NE commerce?
3. What does MTBU mean?
4. Define a business continuity plan.
5. Describe a disaster plan.
6. Distinguish between cold sites and hot sites.
7. List six items that computer abusers may be seeking.
8. How do organizations secure mission-critical transmissions?
9. What is the difference between public and private keys?
10. What is a digital signature?
11. Explain the role of a certificate authority.
12. List two forms of PKI used to secure transmission across the Internet.
13. What is a firewall?
14. Define an access control list.
15. List four trust-building mechanisms.
16. List five methods of payment.

TOPICS FOR DISCUSSION

1. Discuss the importance of trust to consumers.
2. Discuss two avenues that are taken to ensure the firm will survive.
3. Discuss the contents of a disaster recovery plan.
4. Discuss the differences between hot and cold sites.
5. Discuss sources of intentional and unintentional violations.
6. Discuss the significance of key length.
7. Discuss the problems associated with encryption schemes.
8. Discuss the role of a certificate authority in NE commerce.
9. Discuss the criteria for trust.
10. Discuss ways in which firms can establish trust.
11. Discuss the advantages and disadvantages of NE payment options.
12. Discuss the typical security methods associated with each type of payment option.

INTERNET EXERCISES

1. Find an NEO and summarize its privacy policy. Based on the information given in the privacy policy, how comfortable and secure would you feel in conducting business with the organization? Write a short essay expressing your findings.
2. Take the Cyber Security Test (http://www.staysafeonline.info/selftest.adp) and describe the results. How safe is your own personal computer?
3. Identify three certificate authorities. Compare and contrast their services in a spreadsheet.
4. Complete the Security Fundamentals Course (http://www.staysafeonline.info/enroll.adp). Summarize and present your experience in the course.
5. Consumer WebWatch (http://www.consumerwebwatch.org/) seeks to investigate, inform, and improve the credibility of information published on the World Wide Web. Pick an area of interest on this site and prepare a summary report of your findings.
6. Compare the differences between the programs and the meanings of the seals provided by BBBOnLine (http://www.bbbonline.org/) and TRUSTe (http://www.etrust.com/). Post your comments on which seal you believe would garner greater trust from consumers.
7. Find an article on the Internet from a free online magazine regarding any topic on the need for a secure e-commerce section and complete a synopsis of the article and what you learned from it.
8. Select a credit card of your choice and investigate the company's policy regarding card use and limitations for fraud when utilized in electronic transactions. From their policy, what can you infer about the risks involved when conducting commerce over the Internet?
9. Visit the Internet site of a digital signature CA. Summarize the steps necessary for an individual to obtain his or her own private digital key or digital signature. How much effort does this require when compared to securing a "real paper" certification by a notary public?
10. Go to a bank Web site of your choice and research the bank's offering of online services. Determine if they offer online banking with the electronic fund feature. Visit the Web site of your utility company or credit card company. Find out whether you can pay your bill online directly from a checking or savings account. Why do you think that electronic payment of invoices and bills has not become more common with the general public?

TEAM EXERCISES

1. Much of the focus on security in this module has been on the measures that NEOs in the United States are taking to secure their online organizations. Research the security measures that your group's assigned country is taking to secure its NEOs. Create a PowerPoint presentation of seven to ten slides introducing the country, discussing a variety of organizations that conduct business online, and describing how they ensure that their organizations are secure. Include a video or audio clip in the presentation.

2. Work with your assigned team members to develop a presentation in Microsoft Power-Point (five to nine slides) to educate your classmates about a topic related to trust in e-commerce. Prior to beginning work on the presentation, post your topic on the discussion board; do not duplicate topics. When you post the presentation, provide information on resources used so that your classmates have an opportunity to further extend their learning. Listed below are some areas you may consider exploring, but do not limit yourselves to these topics.

- How does consumer familiarity with e-commerce impact the importance of security?
- Explore the factors that a Web designer must consider when evaluating the value of partnering with a third-party guarantor.
- How do you create an effective social presence on a Web site?
- How can a company use interactions in bricks-and-mortar sites to build consumer trust for the company's online stores?

3. Each group will prepare a detailed outline of an IT recovery plan for a real or imaginary company of your choosing. You will post your company's plan on an actual Web site. The Web site should be posted on a free hosting site such as Tripod or GeoCities. You must detail the specific components or issues that would be addressed should your company flesh out the detailed contingency plan. (Remember, this is the outline or road map, not the final plan. It should contain what must be addressed but not the specific solutions.) Be creative and have fun with this assignment.

4. In earlier days, wiretaps and mail interception (authorized under court order) provided effective surveillance of individuals suspected of illegal activities. With the advent of high-level encryption, debate is raging on the need to allow government authorities to restrict encryption methods or to hold master keys to open encrypted messages. If the government holds such a master key, how can we be sure that such a valuable asset does not fall into the of unethical individuals? Prepare a report on the pros and cons of government master keys.

5. Choose a Web business and evaluate how the five payment options are used If some of the payment options are not yet available, please state that fact and post ideas on how the option(s) could be implemented by financial institutions and other companies. Your group's collective work will be presented as a Microsoft PowerPoint presentation with maximum of 10 slides. The content must include information about the payment options and references to where this information can be found by other students.

INTERNET RESOURCES

The ABC's of Security (http://www.cio.com/security/edit/security_abc.html): Discusses the important components of information security.

USA Today Article (http://www.usatoday.com/usatonline/20020227/3896905s.htm): Discusses the importance of securing the business network.

CSI/FBI Computer Crime and Security Survey (http://www.gocsi.com/press/20020407.html): Will help you better understand the importance for a NEO to implement security measures.

The Changing Nature of Information Security in the Department of Defense (http://www.cisp.org/imp/february_2000/02_00wells.htm): How the Department of Defense is securing information.

Homeland Security Bills (http://www.ieeeusa.org/releases/2002/042402pr.html): Two Senate Bills on Homeland Security.

REFERENCES

Aasgaard, D. O., P. R. Cheung, B. J. Hulbert, and M. C. Simpson. "An Evaluation of Data Processing 'Machine Room' Loss and Selected Recovery Strategies." MISRC-WP-79-04, University of Minnesota, 1978.

Anderson, J. C., and J. A. Narus. "A Model of the Distributor Firm and Manufacturer Firm Working Partnership." *Journal of Marketing*, 54, January 1990, 42–58.

Blau, P. M. *Exchange and Power in Social Life*. Wiley, New York, 1964.

Crosby, L. A., K. R. Evans, and D. Cowles. "Relationship Quality in Services Selling: An Interpersonal Influence Perspective." *Journal of Marketing*, 54, July 1990, 68–81.

Daft, R. L., and R. H. Lengel. "Information Richness: A New Approach to Managerial Behavior and Organizational Design." In *Research in Organizational Behavior*, L. L. Cummings and B. M. Staw, eds. JAI Press, Greenwich, CT, 1984, 191–233.

Deutsch, M. "Trust and Suspicion." *Conflict Resolution*, 2, 4 (1958), 265–279.

Dwyer, F. R., P. Schurr, and S. Oh. "Developing Buyer-Seller Relationships." *Journal of Marketing*, 51, April 1987, 11–27.

Fukuyama, F. *Trust: The Social Virtues and the Creation of Prosperity*. The Free Press, New York, 1995.

Ganesan, S. "Determinants of Long-Term Orientation in Buyer-Seller Relationships." *Journal of Marketing*, 58, 2 (1994), 1–19.

Gefen, D. "Building Users' Trust in Freeware Providers and the Effects of This Trust on Users' Perceptions of Usefulness, Ease of Use and Intended Use." Dissertation, Georgia State University, 1997.

Gefen, D., and D. Straub. "Gender Difference in the Perception and Use of E-Mail: An Extension to the Technology Acceptance Model." *MIS Quarterly*, 21, 4, December 1997, 389–400.

Gefen, D., and D. W. Straub. "Perceived Cultural Similarity and Technology Acceptance." Georgia State University Working Paper, 2001.

Gefen, D., E. Karahanna and D. Straub. "Inexperience and Experience with Online Stores: The Importance of TAM and Trust." *IEEE Transactions on Engineering Management*, (2003 forthcoming).

Gefen, D., E. Karahanna and D. Straub. "Trust and TAM in Online Shopping: An Integrated Model." *Mis Quarterly*, 27, 1, March, (2003), 51-90.

Giffin, K. "The Contribution of Studies of Source Credibility to a Theory of Interpersonal Trust in the Communication Process." *Psychological Bulletin*, 68, 2 (1967), 104–120.

Hancock, W. "GTE Employee Admits Guilt in Insider Data Corruption Case." *Computers & Security*, 20, 3 (2001), 190.

Homans, G. G. *Social Behavior: Its Elementary Forms*. Harcourt, Brace and Company, New York, 1961.

Kumar, N. "The Power of Trust in Manufacturer-Retailer Relationships." *Harvard Business Review*, November-December 1996, 92–106.

Luhmann, N. *Trust and Power*, John Wiley and Sons, London, 1979.

Mayer, R. C., J. H. Davis, and F. D. Schoorman. "An Integration Model of Organizational Trust." *Academy of Management Review*, 20, 3 (1995), 709–734.

McAllister, D. J. "Affect- and Cognition-based Trust as Foundations for Interpersonal Cooperation in Organizations." *Academy of Management Journal*, 38, 1 (1995), 24–59.

McKnight, D. H., V. Choudhury, and C. Kacmar. "Developing and Validating Trust Measures for E-Commerce: An Integrative Typology." *Information Systems Research*, 13, 3, September 2002.

Morgan, R. M., and S. D. Hunt. "The Commitment-Trust Theory of Relationship Marketing." *Journal of Marketing*, 58, 3 (1994), 20–38.

Reichheld, F. F., and P. Schefter. "E-Loyalty: Your Secret Weapon on the Web." *Harvard Business Review*, 78, 4, July-August 2000, 105–113.

Rose, G. "The Effect of Download Time on e-Commerce: The Download Time Brand Impact Model." Unpublished dissertation, Georgia State University, 2000.

Rose, G., H. Khoo, and D. Straub. "Current Technological Impediments to Business-to-Consumer Electronic Commerce." *Communications of the AIS*, 1, 16, June 1999, 1–74.

Rotter, J. B. "Generalized Expectancies for Interpersonal Trust." *American Psychologist*, 26, May 1971, 443–450.

Schurr, P. H., and J. L. Ozanne. "Influences on Exchange Processes: Buyers' Preconceptions of a Seller's Trustworthiness and Bargaining Toughness." *Journal of Consumer Research*, 11, March 1985, 939–953.

Senn, J. A. "Capitalizing on Electronic Commerce: The Role of the Internet in Electronic Markets." *Information Systems Management*, 13, 3, Summer 1996, 15–24.

Short, J., E. Williams, and B. Christie. *The Social Psychology of Telecommunications*. Wiley, London, 1976.

Snow, A., D. Straub, R. Baskerville, and C. Stucke. "The Survivability Principle: IT-Enabled Dispersal of Organizational Capital." Working paper #03-01 Georgia State University, 2003.

Straub, D. W. "Effective IS Security: An Empirical Study." *Information Systems Research*, 1, 3 (1990), 255–276.

Straub, D. W., and R. W. Collins. "Key Information Liabilities Facing Managers: Software Piracy, Proprietary Databases, And Individual Rights to Privacy." *MIS Quarterly,* 14, 2, June 1990, 143–158.

Straub, D. W., and E. Karahanna. "Knowledge Worker Communications and Recipient Availability: Toward a Task Closure Explanation of Media Choice." *Organization Science*, 9, 2, March 1998, 160–175.

Straub, D. W., and W. D. Nance. "Discovering and Disciplining Computer Abuse in Organizations: A Field Study." *MIS Quarterly*, 14, 1, March 1990, 45–62.

Straub, D. W., and R. W. Welke. "Coping with Systems Risk: Security Planning Models for Management Decision-Making." *MIS Quarterly*, 22, 4, December 1998, 441–469.

Williamson, O. E. *The Economic Institutions of Capitalism: Firms, Markets, Relational Contracting*. Free Press, New York, 1985.

Yeung, M. M. "Digital Watermarking." *Communications of the ACM*, 4, 7, July 1998, 30–33.

Yin, J. "Interactivity of Internet-Based Communications: Impacts on E-Business Consumer Decisions." Dissertation, Georgia State University, 2002.

Zucker, L. G. "Production of Trust: Institutional Sources of Economic Structure, 1840–1920." *Research in Organizational Behavior*, 8 (1986), 53–111.

CHAPTER 7

COMPETITIVE NE STRATEGY

▶ ## UNDERSTANDING NE STRATEGIC POSITIONING

How should managers position the organization to benefit from NE? Does traditional strategic analysis help or hinder in understanding this new world? Can firms achieve a sustainable competitive advantage through their NE initiatives? If so, how? To what extent will "bricks and mortar" continue to dominate this emerging marketplace? These are some of the questions about which managers of NE initiatives need to have a personal grasp. The competitive stances of their organizations could easily depend on it.

LEARNING OBJECTIVES FOR THIS CHAPTER

- To define the term *strategy* and how it applies to the Networked Economy
- To describe choices for strategic positioning of NEOs
- To define and elaborate on various organizational strategies
- To utilize tools for strategic analysis
- To discuss the electronic value chain
- To conduct a competitive analysis
- To recognize sustainable and momentary competitive advantage
- To understand the elements of environmental analysis

CHARLES SCHWAB

Launched in 1975 by Charles Schwab, the Schwab Corporation was created to grasp the market of individuals seeking a discount brokerage firm. It was sparked by the SEC's abolishment of fixed rate commissions on brokerage sales. Unlike full-service brokerage firms, Schwab did not actively manage portfolios, make investment recommendations, or sell proprietary research or actively managed products. Rather, it presented a wide variety of third-party investment alternatives and provided generalized investment advice. Through "self-directed" trading, Schwab's customers are able to research firms and make knowledgeable trade decisions on their own. Because the customer does not use a broker for specific advice, fees and commissions are greatly reduced.

As consumer interest in "self-directed" trading increased during the early 1980s, so did the number of competing firms within the discount brokerage business. As with any industry, competition instills efficiency and value within surviving firms. For Schwab, efficiency and value were found in the form of advanced information technology. Since the firm's foundation was built on providing information, not advice, to consumers, finding greater efficiencies was not a difficult task for Schwab. As the Internet-connected consumer base rapidly expanded during the late 1980s and early 1990s, Schwab honed its services to include StreetSmart—the first trading product designed for Microsoft's Windows computer program. Fully compatible with other financial software, such as Quicken, StreetSmart enabled consumers to conduct trading operations nearly autonomously— further reducing costs for Schwab.

Since the introduction of StreetSmart, Schwab has further enhanced its services through the use of advanced information technology by incorporating e-mail messaging as a means of consumer trade notification and marketing. One piece of it allows customers to subscribe to 35 e-mail alerts providing news, stock prices, and information on the portfolios of stocks and mutual funds they follow. MyClosingSummary, for example, has more than 300,000 subscribers. Subscribers can see clear Schwab branding, easy-on-the-eyes formatting, clickable links, useful columns and tables, and more.

Schwab has clearly set the bar for firms within the discount brokerage industry. In its early recognition of the demand for independent research, Schwab effectively built an information technology infrastructure designed to offer the right products to the right market. It has capitalized on the rapid expansion of the Internet and consumers desiring low-cost, but high-value, products and services.

Discussion:

1. Discuss the components of Schwab's first business model (pre-Internet) and their "high-tech model."

2. Describe the type of business model that best describes that used by Schwab today.

3. Where do you see technology taking this industry in the future, and how might that affect Schwab's business model?

Sources:
http://harvardbusinessonline.hbsp.harvard.edu
http://www.clickz.com
http://www.clickz.com/article.php/838411

7.1 INTRODUCTION

This chapter will discuss how managers should strategize for their NE initiatives. Firm strategy needs to respond in dramatic ways with the coming of organization-changing technologies. Creating strategy as if the world were still composed only of assembly lines and factory workers will not lead to success. Nor will pursuing the path of many of the dot.coms. Basic principles from traditional corporate strategy need to be adapted to the new economic realities.

7.2 WHAT IS ORGANIZATIONAL STRATEGY?

Leaders have been creating and executing strategy for millennia. There is nothing new about considering what you want to happen and planning sensibly for it. Military and civic leaders as well as business leaders have created such strategies since the beginning of modern civilization.

Individuals create strategy too. Every time you determine a path you want to take in your life or career, put in place the means to achieve those objectives, and then execute on them, you are creating a personal strategy and implementing it.

What would be a formal definition of business strategy? Alfred Chandler suggests, in his 1962 book, that strategy is "the determination of the long-run goals and objectives of an enterprise, and the adoption of courses of action and the allocation of resources necessary for carrying out these goals."[1] This is a good preliminary working definition for our purposes.

Developing the same themes as Chandler, the strategic management research tells us that there are at least four components of a corporate strategy. They are:

1. Mission
2. Vision
3. Tactics
4. Metrics for knowing to what extent one has succeeded in achieving the mission, the vision, and the tactics (see Figure 7.1)

A mission is a strong statement about goals of the organization, broadly stated to be sure. It could be a statement oriented toward traditional performance measures such as "To be the most profitable B2B intermediary connecting suppliers and customers in the music industry." A second example might be "We are the most successful pharmaceutical company in Europe, with Economic Value-Adds (EVAs) exceeding 30% of our gross sales."[2] Or, goals can be oriented toward an alternative set of measures, such as the mission of one of the new cell phone providers in Egypt: "To be the employer of choice in Egypt."[3]

---

[1] *Strategy and Structure*, Cambridge, MA: MIT Press.
[2] EVA is an accounting measure of performance that takes into account the use of investment funds compared to alternate investment opportunities.
[3] This mission was articulated by the CEO of Click GCSM in the year 2001 in one of the interviews in the ongoing GSU study.

Missions, or mission statements, tend to represent the present—that is, where the firm is now with respect to purpose and accomplishments, products/services, markets addressed, client base, geographic dispersion, and sources of revenue. Compared to the vision, mission statements are relatively short-term.

Missions send signals to all the stakeholders of the corporation about the purpose of the firm and how it should be evaluated. An investor who expects a firm to create value by moving into new markets would be foolish if he or she invested in a firm that had as its avowed purpose to stick to its traditional markets. Employees also need to know how to direct their efforts and whether the firm is one that aligns well with their personal values and ethics. Finally, a mission tells the customer what to expect from the firm. If the customer relationship is not part of the corporate mission, then a customer who notices this is forewarned and forearmed.

Visions are generally more long-term and futuristic and talk about new directions that the firm is considering as well as community endeavors. In the case of Dell Computers (www.dell.com), for example, their 2002 Web site talks about the history of the firm from its beginnings as a gleam in the eye of Michael Dell in 1984. Their vision emphasizes projects in the Tennessee Valley as well as customer satisfaction goals for the future.

Vision, or vision statements, tend to be oriented toward the future—that is, where the firm will be in five to ten years with respect to purpose and accomplishments, products/services, markets addressed, client base, geographic dispersion, and sources of revenue. An example of a vision might be "Maintaining high EVAs, our long-term vision is to dominate markets in Asia as well as Europe by offering lowest cost, highest quality drugs to Asian communities that have previously not been adequately served by regional providers."

Figure 7.1   Sample Metrics for Determining the Success of NE Strategies

7.2.1 Time Dimensions and NE Strategy

Strategy is key to maintaining the momentum of the firm in future directions, but it is executed in the present, as shown in Figure 7.2. Goals, objectives, and plans represent things to aim for. Making the best use of present resources and managing the current business are how a firm plays its strategy out in the present. When these are well aligned, there is a greater likelihood that the firm's strategy will be successful. What is important for managers to recognize is that the best plan in the world is just that, an abstraction about what could be done. The action side of the equation is the critical follow-on for a good strategy. So the only good strategy is one that informs the present and retains the sense of direction for employees and other stakeholders.

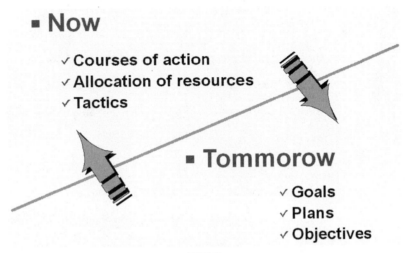

Figure 7.2   Present and Future Dimensions of NE Strategy

7.3 STRATEGIC ANALYSIS

In order to understand how to capitalize on the e-commerce technologies that have been covered in the last two chapters, it is critical that we review certain intellectual tools for thinking about and analyzing a firm's competitive position. We will cover several standard approaches that have been in use for several decades, but we will adapt them to the new phenomenon of NE or e-commerce. The fact that these tools can be successfully adapted to this dramatically new environment shows that they can stand the test of time and have an enduring character. The tools are:

1. Porter's Three Producer Strategies
2. Porter's Five Forces Model in the NE Era
3. Electronic Value Chain
4. Competitive Analysis

Focus on NE: eBay's Strategy

 Online auction site eBay has taken another bold step in attracting more customers with the creation of Online "Trading Assistants." Trading Assistants are experienced eBay sellers who have indicated their willingness to sell items for others for a fee.

The Trading Assistant Directory, which launched in February 2002, contains a list of sellers who want to sell for others. Clients can search the Trading Assistant Directory to find someone to sell for them. The terms of service are to be negotiated between the Trading Assistant and the seller.

The online Assistants provide the opportunity for individuals who have items to sell but do not have the time or know-how to sell on eBay. This service allows novice sellers to hire an experienced eBay member to sell for them. With this service, eBay is creating additional revenue-generating opportunities for itself and for its experienced buyers. This will also help to create additional customer loyalty.

Doree Klassen, an eBay seller, shared some of her success with the Trading Assistant program. She stated that 40% of her sales come through the Trading Assistant channel. "The market for trading assistant services is huge right now," she said. "As computers become more prevalent in our society, buying as well as selling opportunities will expand, whether on eBay or the rest of the Internet. Offering services such as Trading Assistant is another way to include more people in the huge Internet market."

Sources:
http://www.testwareinc.com/resources/articles/Web-siteCookieTesting.pdf

7.3.1 Porter's Producer Strategies

As a background to discussing the five forces and competitive analysis, the landmark book by Michael Porter of Harvard (1979) on the nature of competition is extremely useful and widely known. Porter argues that firms can combine or use singly up to three strategies when they enter a competitive marketplace:

1. Low cost provider/producer (LCP) strategy
2. Differentiated product/service strategy
3. Niche market strategy

The nature of a **low cost provider/producer strategy** is, perhaps, intuitively obvious, but just to articulate it, this strategy requires that firms constantly seek out and implement ways to reduce costs in order to offer pricing that is attractive to customers. These firms usually must develop economies of scale in order to drive down costs. Competing with Intel to make chips, for example, requires the know-how, first, and then an over U.S. $1 billion capital expenditure for each state-of-the-art chip plant capable of making competing products.

On the services side, Accenture has a huge staff of consultants, and they can bring to bear highly specialized talent on difficult problems. Their economies of scale are in their human capital, but the concept remains the same.

How do economies of scale operations translate into e-commerce concepts? As we have seen from Chapter 2 on the principles of the Networked Economy, business exchange costs should be much lower because of networked connections. Likewise, production costs for information businesses should also be able to take advantage of these scale economies. We will see later how aggregators like amazon.com have substituted systems for physical aggregation of book content and driven down the costs of providing buying opportunities for their millions of customers.

The second major strategy a firm can pursue is known as a **differentiation strategy.** Customers are willing to pay a premium, it has been found, if the product or service has a value-added component that makes it different (and better) from what is being offered by the competition. Firms differentiate in so many ways that it would be difficult to enumerate them. Otis Elevator charges a premium for their elevator servicing because they have a reputation for technical expertise that is unparalleled in their industry. Customers who hire a value-added service expect that the maintenance and proactive servicing of the utility will allow them to direct their managerial attentions onto their core businesses, so they are willing to pay.

The third strategy applies only to firms that have a narrow market focus and, therefore, employ a **niche strategy** to concentrate their marketing efforts on a particular market segment. This strategy depends on the buyers needing the goods or services of the niche producer and on the provider forming relationships that are either deep and long-lasting or short-lived and at arm's length. The extent of rivalry in the niche industry will determine which of these is more likely. Competitiveness can vary from being nonexistent or low, as in monopolies and oligopolies, to hypercompetitive environments.[4]

[4]Zohar and Morgan (1996).

7.3.2 Porter's Five Forces Model Revisited in the NE Era

One of the most useful models for thinking about competition is the famous Five Forces Model stated by Porter (1979). As can be seen in Figure 7.3, there are five "forces" that enter into any strategic analysis of a firm's position in an industry. The ***rivalry*** within an industry is the first item for consideration. It is possible, for example, that a start-up in e-commerce has found a niche that is not already full of competitors. At one time, for example, amazon.com was in that position. If there are few limitations that would keep a rival from entering exactly the same e-commerce business, then it can be said that the ***barriers to entry*** are low and the ***threat of new entrants*** is high. If, on the other hand, a major physical capital or human capital investment is required, then the barriers to entry are high, and it will take a longer time for rivals to enter the business. Technological barriers to entry are an interesting additional area for study. For example, the Web is based on both back-office and front-office systems for inducing and following up on sales. This could significantly raise barriers to new entrants, although it is clear that these barriers can never be so high that no competitors are willing to attempt to overcome them. Nevertheless, we will see later, in Chapter 8, "Business Models and Strategic Planning for NE," it is seldom possible to depend on technological advances to sustain a competitive advantage.

Figure 7.3   Porter and Millar's Five Forces of Industry Competitiveness (Porter, 1985)

The next force that Porter speaks of is the ***threat of substitute products***. This force is often misunderstood and mistaken for the products of a true competitor. In fact, what Porter means by this force is the possibility that a buyer will switch, for one reason or another, to a product/service that is similar, but not identical. In the emollient products group, a person may decide to switch from butter to margarine because margarine is much less expensive. Or a traveler may decide to switch to a bed and breakfast from a hotel because he or she enjoys the quaintness.

Bargaining power comes in two forms: supplier and buyer. The ***bargaining power of the supplier*** is the pressure that the supplier can exert on the firm for lower prices and contractual terms. If the supplier is in a relatively weak position, as many suppliers to the auto industry are, then its bargaining power is said to be low. Prices are usually at the margin for these suppliers.

Bargaining power of the buyer is the last of the Five Forces. This force addresses the question of how costly it is for the buyer to switch to a firm's competitors. Analysts will frequently discuss the "switching costs" for one of the firm's customers to move to a competitor. If the Web interface of a competitor is perceived by the customer to be more difficult to navigate, the switching cost may be too high to move to the competitor. These are critical questions for firms that are low price providers.

Porter's model has had a long and successful run, but it fails to embrace the more cooperative and sharing atmosphere that characterizes many contemporary NE relationships. In certain cases, as we shall see, even competitors are working together in order to expand the entire market and to lower costs throughout the industry. Moreover, relationships with customers are also being conceptualized on a new basis. NE firms are interested in creating trusting relationships that lead to lifelong, loyal customers. The older view of customers as pawns that firms must manipulate in order to retain their business is being replaced by the concept of "customer relationship management," which will be discussed later in the chapter on e-marketing.

The value of the model is that it continues to show how forces in the marketplace can be analyzed by these constituent parts. For NE firms, though, the model neglects the absolutely critical element of strategic partnerships. The boundaries of the corporation are becoming more fluid, as Peter Drucker has noted, and successful enterprises are becoming highly dependent on the success of dynamic networks of firms that join together to deliver products and services. Therefore, we would propose a model of six forces to amend the Porter model for the NE era. It is shown in Figure 7.4.

The new entity is depicted as a relationship with a partner. Partners can be complementors, or firms whose products and services enhance the value of your offerings to your customers. These are firms with whom you have an alliance, possibly what has become known popularly as a "strategic alliance." Strategic alliances are formed when you have joined synergistically with these partners to offer an attractive "bundle" or "package" to the customer. It could be the joining of Microsoft and Intel to create PCs that work well together. Or it could be the offer of a computer from one vendor and an accompanying installation and maintenance contract from another. Generally speaking, complementors are not in direct competition with you, either directly in product line or as substitutes for your products/services.

Partners can also be outsourcers, or firms that you hire to assist with your operations, with your components, or with assembly.

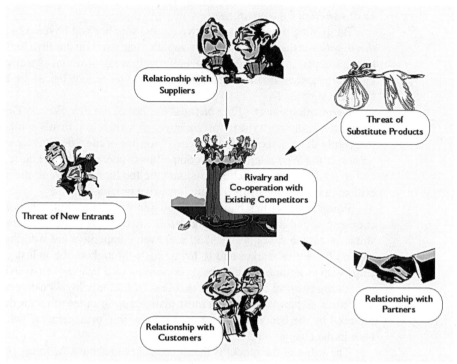

Figure 7.4   Six Forces Model for the NE Era

Partners can also be competitors, Note that firms experience both rivalry and cooperation with their competitors. Increasingly today, NEOs are finding ways to create a larger bargaining unit, for example, in seeking lower prices on standardized supplies. The electronic trading network formed by the Detroit automakers, Covisint, is a good example of this. Threefold increases in sale sizes for such items as standard car radios should drive economies of scale to the point where all of these competitors can save costs. Cooperating on shared infrastructures on the customer-facing side, such as Orbitz, is another case where rivals in most venues can be partners for the greater good of the industry.

7.3.3 Electronic Value Chain

Businesses fulfill their orders for goods and services through a series of activities. These are to some extent a lockstep sequence, and to some extent iterative. As seen in Table 7.1, Porter also visualized the value chain of a firm. (Porter's focus most often seems to be on the manufacturing sector, and he generally ignores service industries.) This conceptualization has elements similar to those in the general systems theory of the firm, in which inbound logistics are similar to "inputs," operations are similar to "transformation processes," and outbound logistics are similar to output. Marketing is envisioned by Porter as an activity that is an essential or line function, and even though it appears after outbound logistics in the chair model, it is clearly ongoing and in a real sense precedes the purchase of raw materials and the manufacture of product. Finally, service is after-sales support, such as product maintenance, aftermarket parts supply, and so forth.

Table 7.1 also shows the so-called staff functions of firm infrastructure, human resources (HR), technology, and procurement. The argument is that these functions are not directly in the value chain in the sense that they do not contribute immediately to the creation of products. Their contribution is more indirect. The phrases in the cells, such as "planning models" or "automated scheduling," are examples of information systems that support each of these functions.

	Inbound Logistics	Operations	Outbound Logistics	Marketing	Service
Firm Infrastructure	Planning models			Sales forecasting	
HR Management	Automated scheduling			Automated scheduling	Automated scheduling
Technology Development	CAD	Electronic markets	Electronic commerce delivery of digital products	Database targeted marketing	
Procurement	Links to suppliers				
Line functions	Automated warehouse	Robots	Shipping DSS	Telemarketing	Remote monitoring

Table 7.1: Porter and Millar's Value Chain (1985)

Whereas it is possible to criticize Porter's model as being too focused on manufacturing and for its perhaps artificial distinction between line and staff functions, the application of these concepts to NEOs is by its very nature more integrative and avoids some of these critiques.

So, as useful as they have been over the years, Porter's models need to be replaced by new ways of looking at corporate strategy in the Networked Economy. The limitations of Porter's approaches in this context are shown in Table 7.2. Among the main limitations are that Porter tends to focus on manufacturing, to the exclusion of the services, intermediaries, and retailers that largely dominate the Networked Economy. Thus, it is not clear what the value chain for a services firm is, nor how it differs, if at all, from a manufacturing firm; likewise for the other firm types, such as intermediaries (which includes wholesalers) and retailers.

Other Porter models are limited in terms of the entities they see as being a critical part of the firm's environment, and in the nature of these relationships. It is likely that entities such as complementors and outsourcers were not included in the original models because they were not viewed as important to competitive advantage, or, possibly, that they were not important, period. Whatever the reality, there can be no doubt that firms are taking on different partners in the Networked Economy and that even suppliers and customers are thought of in a different light than they have been in the past. It is time for new models of these emerging relationships to be used for managerial thinking about how to create wealth in NEOs.

Table 7.2: Limitation of Porter Approaches in NE Environments

Area	Limitation
1. Scope of model coverage	Tends to be more applicable to manufacturing than to services, which are key to the Networked Economy
2. Distinction between line and staff functions	Over time, some staff functions, such as IT, have become integral to core processes for delivery of goods and services; not a clear line between line and staff
3. View of relationships with customers and suppliers as always being adversarial	Emphasis in Networked Economy seems to have shifted to cooperative relationships
4. Five Forces include only entities of rivals, suppliers, and customers	Complementors, outsourcers, and strategic partners are not considered

One possible model is the "NE Value Chain" Model (Figure 7.5) which emerged from e-commerce firm data collection in the GSU research project. It is intended to capture the basic processes of NE businesses, both B2C and B2B.

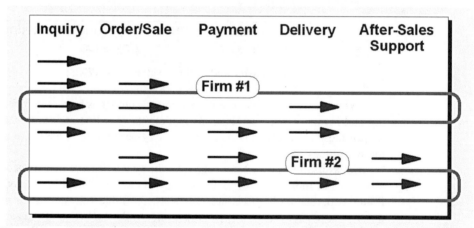

Figure 7.5   NE Value Chain Model

There are five basic steps in the interaction between a firm and its customers (B2C) or suppliers (B2B). First, there is the inquiry stage, in which information about products and services is sought out by customers. For large volume purchases between the firm and its suppliers, the inquiry stage could also include negotiations and contracts, but the stage may be generally thought of as all activities that precede a sale. The order/sale stage is self-explanatory and is usually closely connected with payment and delivery, although the exact sequencing of these steps is variable. Finally, the support that firms offer after sales is represented in the model.

The model applies equally well to manufacturing, intermediary, retail, and services firms. All of these firms have customers to whom they are expected to deliver a good or service. There is a sales process, and support is expected after the sale, even in arm's-length transactions. In the United States, for example, sellers warranty what they sell, by law. The extent of these guarantees is likewise limited by law, but "caveat emptor" is not the standard business rule. Since much of the commerce taking place over the Web today is being developed and promulgated by American businesses, and purchasers worldwide are coming to expect after-sales support, it is likely that after-sales support will become a necessary component of NE business.

Implementation of Stages of the NE Value Chain

Figure 7.5 also illustrates that there are numerous configurations of the stages that make up the entire NE value chain. Firm #1, for example, has opted not to go online with payment and after-sales support. These essential processes would be handled through traditional means. Firm #2, on the other hand, has made a decisive move into virtuality. All parts of the process are being handled through networked communications. The fact that delivery can take place online indicates that at least part of the firm's offering is a digital good or service.

Clearly, the firm that has implemented all five stages of the value chain will experience the lowest business exchange costs. Customer responsiveness can also be high, as there are no physical barriers to quick response. Some forms of online payment eliminate float, which is a benefit to the firm.

For a firm that is an aspiring NEO, what is the best order of implementation of these stages? Figure 7.6 shows that the inquiry stage is clearly what most firms begin with. Placing the firm's products and services online is no more than an electronic sales catalog, although having this in an electronic form rather than a physical form has the advantages that it is searchable and that alternative arrangements of the inventory are possible and intriguing to customers. Virtual Vineyards (www.virtualvinyards.com) is presently an online mall for a variety of items, but it was at one time a wine shop where the wines were organized by variety and by price as well as by name. Imagine a physical wine shop that had its inventory duplicated in three places in the store in this manner. Truly unimaginable, except as something a terribly inefficient bureaucracy would do!

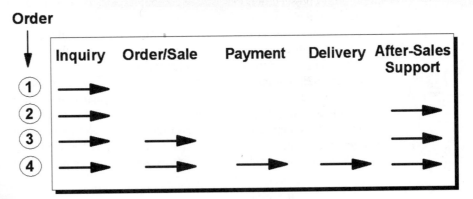

Figure 7.6   Recommended Order of Introduction of Stages in NE Value Chain

The inquiry stage has many subcomponents that could make the introduction of inquiry a major effort for an aspiring NEO. To the firm's peril, some of these elements may not be initiated before the firm moves on to the other stages. For example, a life insurance carrier wants to allow potential customers to connect with its agents, in addition to selling insurance online, perhaps. If the firm has no capability for processing sales on the Net, then the agent link-up is especially critical. A "brochureware"-like listing of agents, addresses, and telephone numbers has few advantages over the Yellow Pages, other than that it can be updated in real time and does not have to wait for the annual hard copy publication. An agent locator is a more sophisticated sales tool. It can find the agents closest to the customer (in the United States, the search algorithm usually uses zip codes), and allow the option to download a map and set of directions from the customer's location to that of the agent. Partnerships with firms like MapQuest are a natural so that some of this capability can be outsourced. Finally, agents can be e-mail-accessible, and there can also be a simple clickable icon to encourage e-mails to the agents.

All of these elements can go into the inquiry stage of the NE value chain. Each stage has a similar set of potentially elaborate components. The order/sales stage, for instance, can be made more convenient for the clients if the vendor "remembers" the client invoicing, shipping, and payment information so that the client has to engage in as little data entry as possible and finds the site visit a more enjoyable experience. This is the personalization concept behind amazon.com's "OneClick" and the "Double-Click" of its competitors. This has sometimes taken the form of an "electronic wallet," where even credit card information is kept securely so that customers have little to do other than to click on radio buttons and fill quantities in.

In which order should a firm introduce the stages of the value chain? Since each stage has many possible subelements, we can specify a recommended overall plan of introduction. The key thing to remember is that the firm needs to create a reliable site that performs as expected, irrespective of the total number of site functionalities. A site that truly works well with two features is preferable to one that works poorly with 25 features.

As mentioned above, inquiry is usually the first stage that is put up. Customers need to have access to the firm's offerings before any kind of meaningful exchange can take place over the Net. Firms that wish to create a strong site will consider the multifaceted approach to presentation that we see in popular sites such as amazon.com or yahoo.com. Menus and clickable icons allow users to navigate the site to the exact information they wish. Both have ways of identifying the individual user, and the sites are tailored to a certain extent with that information. In amazon.com's case, the site responses are personalized, based on past interests and purchases.[5]

In the B2B and intermediary spaces, the inquiry stage can range from pure electronic markets or auctions on one end of the spectrum to malls and electronic trading networks on the other. Whether the buyer places a request and the vendors bid on the work, or the buyer is given comparison prices for various goods and services from different vendors, is not nearly as important as to recognize that the stage is essentially the same as in a B2C site. Customers are inquiring and, perhaps, negotiating on price and conditions of sale.

---

[5]The essential features of good Web site designs have been studied in the scientific literature. See particularly Palmer (2002) and Agarwal and Venkatesh (2002).

From the standpoint of the economics that seem to be driving the NE business environment, we recommend that firms introduce after-sales support as the next stage. This may seem like a third- or fourth-level consideration at first blush. But firms that develop specialized knowledge of their customers need to use this information as soon as possible to differentiate their support of the customer's purchase. This can lead to a competitive advantage, as we shall see later in this chapter. Customer support can be as simple as e-mail and as complex as holograms (see Chapter 5) and live chat. The point is to provide an avenue for the customer to air grievances, request further products and services related to their initial purchase, and develop trust. Customer responsiveness is a differentiator in the Networked Economy.

Having the capacity to accept an order is the next in importance. It is not necessary to couple this tightly with complete fulfillment of an order. Delivery is not that difficult in the world of digital goods and services, but it is vastly more complicated in the physical world of factories, logistics firms, and warehouses. Deploying the order process means that firms need to gather requisite information about the customer and to confirm pricing and shipping data. Online ordering gives the firm a much better grasp about sales related to the Net as opposed to those made through traditional processes involving field reps or bricks-and-mortar stores. The major problems with introducing order capabilities is that the Web systems need to be integrated with legacy systems of the firm. Legacy systems are the traditional accounting systems that handle order fulfillment. Eventually, sales online must end up on general ledgers; for this to take place, there must be a movement of the online data to the accounting systems that the firm has been using for traditional, physically oriented orders.

A complete implementation of the value chain brings online delivery and payment. Delivery can be partially or fully implemented earlier in the NE initiative if the goods and services are digital, as remarked above. Delivery of physical goods requires a tracking capability so that customers have online, real-time information about where in the cycle their order(s) are. Many firms are outsourcing this capability to logistics specialists, like UPS. By outsourcing this subelement, the site can quickly be more customer-responsive at a small additional cost to the firm. As long as there is a sufficient after-sales support function on the part of the firm, the Web-based tracking system can be used to address customer complaints or simple queries, as easily by the support reps as by the customer himself or herself. Moreover, the logistics firm's tracking system can be overlaid with the vendor's logo so that it appears as if the customer is actually dealing with your firm. Customers can input tracking numbers and find out which stations have already processed the order and what the likely arrival date and time will be.

Firms could develop the expertise to build such a tracking system in-house, but in most cases this is not a core competency of the firm and would, therefore, be a waste of resources. We will discuss the implications of these kinds of decisions later in this chapter and throughout the rest of the book.

Finally, payment systems are the last stage to implement, because they involve a "leap of faith" on the part of the customer, and if the other elements are not in place and working, customers could be unfavorably impressed with a payment system that was far superior to the delivery system, the after-sales support system, or the inquiry system. The international legal environment is still developing in this arena as well. Digital signature statutes need to be in place to verify transactions and to build broad-scale consumer and firm-supplier trust. Like the delivery and order systems, payment systems need to be closely integrated with the firm's legacy applications. This places one more hurdle in the path for full implementation of the NE value chain.

7.3.4 Competitive Analysis

Firms are intended to make wealth for those that own them and to provide employment for their official families. The creation of wealth is good for society, so corporations are protected by governments through laws. Part of this protection is to maintain a competitive environment for the sake of an industry itself. Monopolies, like bureaucracies, are not efficient uses of resources, because they do not have to be.

What is competitive advantage? It is basically producing products and services that customers prefer to those of your competitors and, thus, winning in the marketplace. Winning in the marketplace must be a strategic goal of profit-making firms. It is the only way they can continue to hold their share of the market and bring in revenues. Whereas a firm may choose to have market share as one of its strategic goals, the shareholders are going to be more interested in profits and the increasing value of the company in the long run. So profitability must also be a strategic goal of firms, whether this is explicitly stated or not.

Competition can be analyzed from an internal or an external perspective, as Figure 7.7 shows. We have already seen Porter's Five Forces model, which takes into account both internal and external characteristics. In this unit, we will analyze these separately.

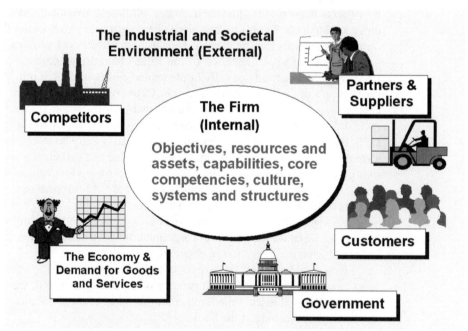

Figure 7.7 Internal and External Characteristics for Competitive Analysis

Modern strategic theorists believe that there are internal characteristics that are conducive to market success. Most of these theories talk about firm resources and how the firm uses these resources. Rapid response to external characteristics is also thought to be a key to success, but the difficulty with attempting to "sense and respond" to the environment is that the firm has much less control over these. Firms maintain lobbyists in seats of government power to influence the broader legal, social, political, and economic settings, even though the ability to have a direct impact on the outer environment is limited.

An analysis of one's industry, however, can tell managers how to position the firm strategically to take advantage of marketplace conditions. Each of these topics will be discussed in turn.

Competitive advantages are either "momentary" or "sustainable." A "momentary" competitive advantage is any means by which a firm acquires a temporary, short-term advantage over rivals. It can be the result of a product innovation or a dramatic improvement in costs. Long-term advantages, that is, ones that last more than a few months,[6] involve things the company does that sustain the advantages over time, and are, hence, sustainable. Most competitive advantages are momentary.

Why are most competitive advantages momentary? The answer to this question lies in two theories that describe why some firms are more profitable than others. One theory is known as the resource-based view (RBV) of the firm. The other is known as firm capabilities (FC) theory.

► *CASE STUDY 7-2*

AMICA: BUILDING MARKET SHARE WITH THE NEW TECHNOLOGY

As the oldest mutual insurer of automobiles in the United States, Amica's hallmark has been providing superior customer service. Increased competition in the insurance industry and the willingness of customers to shift providers for lower rates influenced Amica's strategy to increase customer loyalty through new technology.

Amica's main strategy for growth has been a major advertising campaign designed to expand Amica's profile across the United States. Recognizing the need to expand its range of channels, Amica has adopted the Internet as a significant new distribution and communications channel. The use of Internet technology posed both a strategic opportunity and a challenge to the company. It was decided that the Web would function as a "virtual branch office" for Amica. Amica's Web-based solution, known as Access Amica (www.amica.com), represents the company's main platform for interacting with both existing policyholders and the general public. In addition to company information, nonpolicyholders accessing the general Amica site can view information designed to support their insurance decisions as well as consumer safety information. Amica targets its policyholder community with a range of advanced services collectively known as "Policyholder Express." Amica customers using Policyholder Express can gain access to a variety of services including detailed billing and account history information, bill pay, and online claim reporting. Amica has recently added the ability to obtain auto, homeowner, and excess liability insurance quoting online to its Policyholder Express system.

Amica's e-business solution was developed in three phases. The first phase, begun in July 1999 and launched in November 1999, introduced Amica's newly designed Web site. Amica's Policyholder Express and online quoting features were also introduced during the first phase. In January 2000, Amica broadened its online quoting capabilities and added the ability to view account history. Amica's Web solution is designed as an extension of Amica's traditional, highly personalized approach to customer contact. Since introduction, the company has experienced a dramatic increase in Web site traffic. In the first month following the introduction of Access Amica, the number of site requests rose 170%, while the number of visits increased by 145%.

---

[6]It would heartening to believe that a firm could readily achieve sustainable competitive advantages that last years, if only it were smart enough. But short of patents and other legal monopolistic rights, sustainable advantages need to be revitalized on a regular basis, or they will cease to be competitive edges. This seems to be particularly true in the cyberworld, where one's edge is displayed for all to see on the Web site and imitation begins immediately.

By providing a rich array of services and information via the Web, Amica expects to strengthen its customers' satisfaction even further, which is consistent with its mission of being a completely customer-focused insurance provider. Amica also believes that its Web initiatives will appeal to prospective customers who see the Web as an ideal tool for making informed decisions about insurance.

Discussion:
1. Discuss the impact of the Internet on Amica's distribution and communication channels.
2. Describe Amica's strategy in implementing Internet services.

Sources:
Choi, Soon-Yong, and Andrew B. Whinston. *The New Service Economy*, Center for Research in Electronic Commerce, The University of Texas at Austin, 2001.
The Amica companies, http://www.amica.com/aboutUs/annualrpt/annua

Resource-Based View, Firm Capabilities Theory, and Core Competencies

RBV theory maintains that firms are superior to other firms when they possess superior resources (and exploit them).[7] Figure 7.8 shows some of the generic resources that firms have at their disposal. Please note that some of these resources are physical assets, like money and buildings. Others are intellectual in nature, like patents. Finally, the human resource may be the most important of all of these resources.[8]

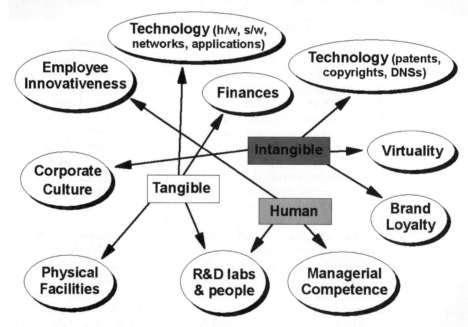

Figure 7.8 Sample Corporate Resources

---

[7]Barney (1996); Peteraf (1993); Robins (1992); Wernerfelt (1984).
[8]Quinn and Hilmer (1994).

Not all resources can be used to create and sustain above-average economic returns.[9] Only "strategic" assets or resources qualify in assisting a firm in sustaining a competitive advantage. Strategic resources are valuable, rare, imperfectly imitable, and/or nonsubstitutable.[10] An example of a valuable resource is a patent. It may or may not be a "rare" resource, in that other firms may acquire similar or substitutable resources. Amazon.com's OneClick patent, for example, allows them to exploit this competitive advantage (assuming that customers prefer a simpler interaction with less data entry on their part). If a similar capability on the part of other firms selling similar products and services is perceived to be a substitute by customers, then having a patent is not a major resource advantage.

Just having or holding resources is vastly different from the intelligent use of these resources. Firm capabilities, defined as the capacity to "perform an activity as a result of organizing and coordinating the productive services of a group of resources,"[11] permit the deployment of resources in a way that brings a competitive advantage. When a firm can perform an activity better than its competitors, that capability becomes a competence. This is the essence of FC theory.

Thus, capabilities that are embedded in a firm and can be thought of as its "core competencies" can lead to competitive superiority. Interest today in core competencies was likely reinvigorated by the far-reaching success of Peters and Waterman's *In Search of Excellence* (1982). In this work, the authors argued that successful firms develop areas of distinctive competence or excellence. Firms excel in expertise or processes, but the critical element in their continued success is that they persevere in having a strategic focus. The American idiom used to describe this management strategy is "sticking to one's knitting."

In the 1990s, this thesis was further developed specifically using the term "core competency."[12] Core competencies are what make an organization "unique" in its competitiveness.[13] It is the knowledge that the organization has gained about its own processes that allows it to compete with the best in the world. An organization that possesses a core competency can integrate "core" technologies and governance processes, realizing performance and customer service levels that exceed those of its competitors.[14] Core technologies are a critical enabler of this capability. To compete globally, firms need to ask whether retaining a resource within the firm and exploiting it will improve its ability to perform an activity at a level comparable with the best of breed.[15]

RBV, firm capabilities theory, and the core competencies literature stress the need for firms to capitalize on their unique assets and to develop management strategies to exploit the advantages from strategically positioned resources. Because of these similarities, the terminology of core competencies for all lines of thought will be used in the remainder of the book.

A model that indicates how managers can analyze their resources and capabilities in order to move them into production is shown in Figure 7.9.

---

[9]Amit and Schoemaker (1993).
[10]Barney (1991).
[11]Tsang (2000, p. 216).
[12]Prahalad and Hamel (1990).
[13]Quinn and Hilmer (1994).
[14]Prahalad (1993).
[15]Drtina (1994).

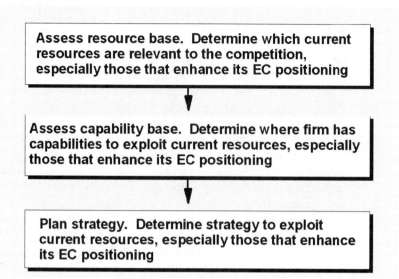

Figure 7.9 Strategic Analysis of Resources and Capabilities

It is clear that developing the strategy of a firm in the physical or online environment necessarily involves several stages. Let's take the case of a firm that already has a Web presence but wants to expand its value chain, as we discussed earlier. We could say that this was a strategic objective of the firm. Its current inquiry site has a set of linked pages for its products, but no internal search engine for customers to query about products that they cannot readily find. In assessing the current resources, the management team lists physical resources like servers, network routers, and telecommunications links, but it also lists the server software it has for satisfying user requests. Human resources include the systems development personnel who could be assigned to the project.

Once the resources have been inventoried, the capabilities of each of these resources is assessed. Servers have a capacity as do people. With the human resources, one usually evaluates the ability of the developers to enhance the Web site in the manner intended. If the internal expertise is present, then it is possible to develop the systems in-house. This decision has many dimensions, however, and will be covered in a later chapter on outsourcing and virtual organizations.

The last step in a strategic analysis is to decide on the strategic position, that is, whether to move ahead with the value chain extension or not. If the decision is a "Go," then strategic planning will follow.

Analysis of a large-scale NE initiative can lead to a business model that lays out the specific resources and the competitive advantage to be achieved, including benchmarks. The components of this model will be covered in the next chapter on business models and strategic planning.

Creating New Resources for an Online Bookseller

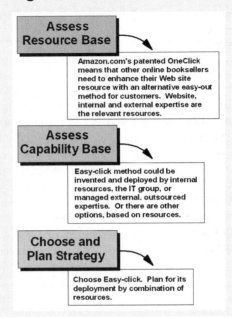

Assess Resource Base

Amazon.com's patented OneClick means that other online booksellers need to enhance their Web site resource with an alternative easy-out method for customers. Website, internal and external expertise are the relevant resources.

Assess Capability Base

Easy-click method could be invented and deployed by internal resources, the IT group, or managed external, outsourced expertise. Or there are other options, based on resources.

Choose and Plan Strategy

Choose Easy-click. Plan for its deployment by combination of resources.

Companies create new resources that help them to compete with other firms in their industry. Once firms decide to create new resources, they must then be sure they can deploy them using their internal capabilities and core competencies. If they have both assets and ability, they can proceed to deploy.

Unsustainable Competitive Advantage through NE Systems

To what extent can a firm achieve a long-term, or sustainable, competitive edge through the technologies that are powering the NE evolution? Proponents of the basic theories acknowledge that a firm's resources include its ability to implement and exploit valuable information technologies[16] such as Web technologies. Application of the theory to IT suggests that it may not be the technologies *per se* that confer competitiveness.[17] First of all, systems that are commercially available are unlikely to convey competitive advantage as resources alone. Since all of your competitors can purchase the same systems, there is nothing special about the resource that would allow your firm to win in the marketplace.

An Enterprise Resource Planning (ERP) system that is commercially available from a vendor cannot in itself bring about a competitive advantage, for instance. You and everyone else in your industry can purchase this resource. The vendor is not likely to restrict purchase without a special arrangement for which you would have to pay a huge premium.

Nevertheless, some firms are better at exploiting systems than others, and these capabilities could become a competitive advantage. But to date, the extent to which IT capabilities differentiate firms in the NE space is not clear.

Why does ownership of certain IT resources *not* make the firm inherently more competitive over time? If the resource is on the market, it is not rare, but commonplace. Moreover, even "home-grown" software systems are readily imitable, copyright and patent notwithstanding.[18]

---

[16]Barney (1991).

[17]Clemons (1986); Clemons (1991); Clemons and Row (1991).

[18]As long as a firm creates its own code (or hires someone to do so for it), there is nothing in U.S. statutes that is usually considered to be proprietary about the idea behind a computer application. Within the last few years, though, patents have been issued for business models such as Priceline's reverse auction. It is not clear yet whether the patenting of ideas will be upheld in the courts. If so, then a patent and copyright could be inimitable resources for the firms holding them.

Unless the firm's brand is so powerful that it is difficult to overcome this resource edge (e.g., amazon.com), firms can see what their competitors are doing on their Web sites and rapidly imitate it.

Brand can make a difference in this equation. Ownership of the Windows franchise and ownership of the Intel franchise give these respective firms today a huge resource advantage. By maintaining the brand alone, these firms have continued to dominate the marketplace. Before this domination in PC operating systems took place, Apple had a vastly superior graphical interface in its Macintosh system. Microsoft copied the idea of graphical folders, use of the mouse, and so forth, and grew its Windows software largely through imitation. So the software itself did not prove to be a resource that could sustain a competitive edge.

Beyond software, hardware and network connections are equally duplicable, and for decreasing amounts of money. The architecture of a firm's entire infrastructure may be a competitive advantage if it is well done, but this is more closely related to the ability of its designers than to the boxes, chips, and cables. Under unusual circumstances, it is possible to envision hardware that has unique capabilities that lead to a competitive advantage, but this is the exception rather than the rule. A proprietary token-exchanging security device, for instance, might be imagined to lead to highly secure exchanges in very sensitive cases. The internal workings of the hardware and its protected software could conceivably be protected through legal and physical means, but this is not a common occurrence with most companies.

Sustainable Competitive Advantage through NE Systems

Where does sustainable competitive advantage come from if not from software and hardware? In keeping with RBV, Ross, Beath, and Goodhue (1996) argue that it comes through exploitation of three resources, as shown in Figure 7.10.

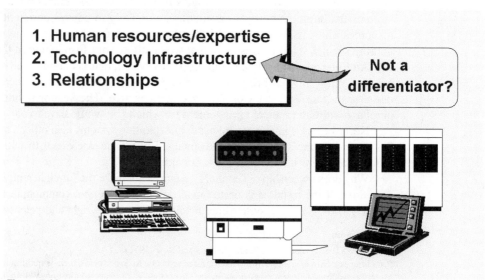

Figure 7.10   IT Resources Leading to Sustainable Competitive Advantages

The question has already been raised as to whether easily imitated systems ("technology infrastructure") are a differentiator for firms. Some commentators argue that the creation of a highly complex infrastructure is a differentiator,[19] but others do not view technology itself, even in sophisticated configurations, as unique.[20] In fact, the resource base in IT may not differ that much within industries, and this means that it is difficult to sustain a competitive advantage through technology.

A way to resolve this question may be to examine the other two resources: expertise and relationships. Expertise is a core competency of the firm in connection with Web systems when it involves some of the distinctive characteristics of a networked organizational structure. For example, if the firm believes that increased telework, e-mail, and the movement of major tasks to extranets will have a dramatic effect on the bottom line, then the intellectual capability to turn the firm's IT resources into a viable employee support system could lead to a competitive edge. Since this competency is primarily internal, it is possible that competitors will not be able to readily duplicate the combination of support technologies and even, possible, the training capabilities of the firm.

Public systems such as new features on a Web site cannot be kept proprietary, by definition, so there may be little that could be a sustainable advantage in the public-facing system without legal protections. On the server side, though, a transactional capability implies that the Web systems are integrated with the firm's legacy systems, and this is a nontrivial task. This integration and the creation of a smooth and seamless interface with the customer (consumer or business customer) may constitute a core competency of the firm.

Relationships are a broad-brush resource. They can involve some entities that are external to the firm, and, in this sense, we are engaged in a miniature form of environmental analysis every time we interact with a customer.

This resource could involve relationships among the firm's top managers, which would lead to the creation of NE innovations. It could involve relationships among the various stakeholders that the firm cultivates—customers, suppliers, and partners. In the traditional business setting, relationships with customers are why the sales force is often seen as the critical element in the firm's success. But in the networked world, it is the coordination of all stakeholders that spells the difference between traditional firms and NEOs and could be a differentiator among NEOs. Figure 7.11 illustrates how coordination among these entities could be (and likely is) a primary core competency of NEOs.

There is one other resource related to relationships that can be highly proprietary and a source of competitive advantage. But before making the case for the importance of this resource, we need to discuss how managers tend to view the strategic changes that their firms are experiencing with e-commerce.

[19]Weill and Broadbent (1997).
[20]Clemons and Row (1991).

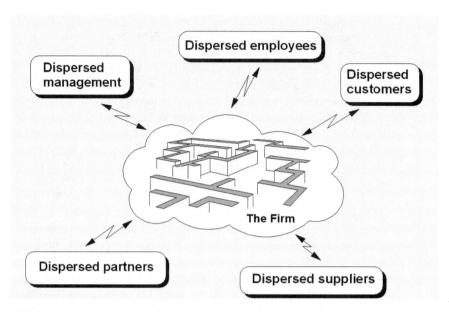

Figure 7.11   Coordinating among Dispersed Stakeholders in NEOs

Alpha, Beta, and Gamma Effects in Measuring NE Strategic Success

The GSU study of NE strategy inquired into managers' strategic thinking about the changes that they expected to experience as a result of NE initiatives.[21] Figure 7.12 depicts the three levels of benefits that managers anticipated. Straub and Klein (2001) designate these as alpha, beta, and omega changes. First-order changes are expected to be lower costs and productivity improvements. With a competent NE strategy, soon afterward will come expanded markets and other growth effects. These are basically short-term effects, however, and will not allow the firm to maintain a competitive edge over the long term. Omega changes are long-term changes in benefits to the firm that are quite different from alpha and beta changes. These changes come about when the firm views the process of NE strategy as a learning process in which they look for ways that they exploit information advantages over competitors. The heart of the NE (r)evolution is substitution of information for physical processes, as we have discussed. But if firms do not exploit this substitution, they will not win in the marketplace. If they do exploit what they know about their business more than their competitors, Straub and Klein (2001) call this a peer-level "information asymmetry." This differs from the kinds of information asymmetries that are frequently discussed with respect to parties that are not peers, like stockbrokers and investors, or salespersons and buyers.

---

[21]Straub and Klein, 2001. The analysis in this paper is highly dependent on the thinking in Zmud and Armenakis.

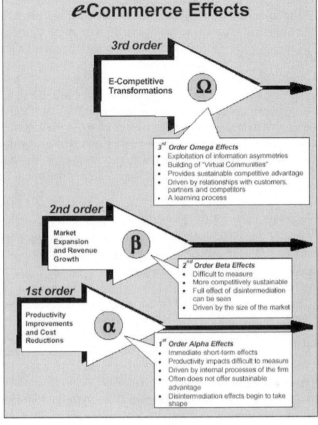

Figure 7.12   Three Levels of Strategic Effects from e-Commerce Initiatives (based on Straub and Klein, 2001)

Let's look at an example of an online firm that profits from such information advantages. Amazon.com has developed a large databank of information about its customers. When a customer visits the Web site, the firm attempts to individually identify the user. This can be achieved with cookies or through a sign-in procedure, but the important point is that the firm uses past information it has about the customer to induce sales. Armed with knowledge of who the customer is, the server returns not only the standard interface to the customer, but a personalized set of suggestions for other books that might be of interest. How does the firm do this? Past transactions, whether completed or not, contain invaluable customer preference data, which amazon.com exploits. Firms can create a profile for a customer that indicates the kind of products they prefer, what they view as credible sources of information,[22] and other highly useful information that has been integrated from external databases.

[22]Volkov (1999).

Why is this an omega change in benefits, and why is it sustainable? First, we need to keep in mind Porter's Five Forces model, our extension of this model, RBV, and what they tell us about strategic advantage in the marketplace. In the long run, the only resources that matter in competition are those over which you have a proprietary control. If they are publicly available or readily copied, these resources will not allow you to differentiate yourself. If you have something your competitor does not have, and cannot easily get, you can develop a long term advantage in that you make use of that difference.

Information or data about customers, as in the case of amazon.com, meets all of these criteria. First of all, it is proprietary in the sense that amazon.com has information on a large number of customers that its competitors does not have. Because ownership of this data is retained by the firm, competitors must develop completely independent sources of information. This takes a huge investment. The barriers to entry in this case are sizable.

Second, whereas rivals can duplicate the technology amazon.com introduces tomorrow,[23] it could take years to build up the client list that amazon.com has, and during these intervening years, amazon.com will, presumably, be building its customer base as well.[24] So time and finances are both in amazon.com's favor and could help it to exploit this resource as a sustainable competitive advantage.

Creating and maintaining a competitive advantage over a period of time is possible if firms gather and creatively use their proprietary customer data, it is argued. This is the resource that relates most clearly to the three Ross et al. resources discussed earlier. As Figure 7.13 shows, proprietary information about any of the entities the firms deals with is, in essence, the third resource for gaining competitive advantage. Whereas it is doubtful that technology itself can provide a long-term edge, intellectual capital and proprietary data can, or so the argument goes.[25]

What are the steps managers should take to dominate the relationship with customers in the NE world? There are three strategic actions that will lead to this position. These represent, in effect, the firm's capabilities to deliver value on the resources it possesses.

First, there must be a commitment to collecting data about customers in spite of the costs incurred. When there is a viable use of customer data that can be purchased from outside marketing databases, this should be done and integrated with the firm's database.

Second, you need NE systems that leverage this information by playing off of customer characteristics and preferences when the customer arrives at your Web site. This is the personalization concept that will be repeated many times in this book. It is extremely important as one of the waves of the NE future.

---

[23]Keep in mind the caveats we introduced earlier about new directions in patenting scope in U.S. law. This may not hold over time, so it is more useful to think about this from an historical perspective.

[24]It is interesting to note that amazon.com also tracks all of its interactions, which amount to over a terabyte of data annually. This amounts to a huge source of information asymmetry that could be exploited for competitive advantage. The analysis of these patterns is still an art form rather than a science, but over time, firms will learn how to utilize this treasure chest of information.

[25]Straub and Klein (2001) make this argument, but see also Evans and Wurster (1998), who have a similar line of reasoning.

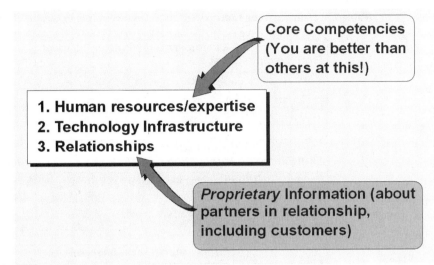

Figure 7.13   Proprietary Data as Resource That Captures Relationships

Finally, customers can be sent information, or "pushed" information. This will be much more effective if, indeed, the information is not an electronic version of direct, third-class mail but is targeted at what the customer needs. Customers will respond favorably if the information being "pushed" to them is, indeed, targeted to their needs and not just broadcast. These steps are the capabilities that firms need to develop in order to take advantage of the resource of proprietary data.[26]

Environmental Analysis

As shown in Figure 7.7, firms have external forces to deal with in the NE world just as in the traditional commercial world. A process of analysis of these forces can help managers decide how best to compete or cooperate.

The first task in an environmental analysis is to determine exactly what business you are in. This is not as silly as it sounds. There are several dimensions of competition that may give you different answers to this question, and so the firm needs to see its position clearly across all three dimensions before it truly knows and understands its markets. Through this analysis, firms may discover not only who they currently compete with, but who they might be competing with.

Table 7.3 indicates three traditional dimensions in the middle column.[27] If a firm focuses on customers, the industry it is in depends on customer preferences and what they deem to be substitutes. Let's assume you are Rolls-Royce. If the customer base you are appealing to would not substitute a truck for one of your cars because of attractive pricing, on average, then you can safely believe yourself to be in the automobile business and not in the truck business. If they start to feel, down the line, that some new specially equipped trucks are adequate substitutes for your vehicles, then you may have to consider moving into the truck business as well. At that point, you might redefine your business as the motor vehicle business.

[26]Straub and Klein, 2001.
[27]These three perspectives are thoroughly discussed in Grant (2000), for instance.

Table 7.3: Defining Your Industry (derived from concepts in Grant, 2000)

Firm Example	Customers substitute on basis of price......	Industry
Rolls-Royce	Unwilling: trucks for cars	Automobile
Lexus	Willing: luxury car for SUV	Luxury car

Firm Example	Firms substitute on basis of production capability.....	Industry
Ferrari	Unable: luxury cars for mass market cars	Luxury car
Maytag	Able: refrigerators for dishwashers	Appliance

Firm Example	Firms substitute on basis of global availability.....	Industry
GE	Able: global brand for national	Global jet
"SovietCar"	Unable: global brand for national	USSR car

Lexus was in a prime position in the luxury car market as long as customers did not see an SUV as a substitute for a luxury car like a Lexus. When lower prices for luxurious SUVs started to limit Lexus sales, then we can say that customers became willing to make the substitution. At this point, Lexus redefined itself as something other than just a luxury car maker and began making Lexus SUVs.

The ability of a firm to change their production runs, or to make changes in the runs of their suppliers, can determine what business a firm is in. Because of the large amount of hand crafting in a Ferrari, it is not really possible for them to think of themselves as being in any business other than the luxury car business. They cannot tool up for mass markets without a major change in their production capabilities. Maytag's washer line, however, calls for factories that are able to jigger production runs by themselves or their partners to produce refrigerators, dishwashers, or other large appliances. This suggest that Maytag should think of itself not as a washer company but as an appliance company.

In certain specialized cases, products (and services) are geared for a national or regional market. If the ability to go global is simply not there, because the firm is restricted in some way to producing only on a national or regional basis, then the regional nature of the industry must be captured in thinking about what business the firm is in. GE makes jet engines, but these engines can go on many types of aircraft, from airliner manufacturers like Boeing or Airbus to luxury aircraft firms like Gulfstream. Since the market is global, GE has no real regional restrictions. Some nationalized industries, like the auto manufacturers in the old Soviet Union, were restricted to selling cars only within the national boundaries. It was necessary for managers in those firms to see their business as the Soviet car business, therefore.

NE Variants on this Environmental Analysis   Many NEOs can still be analyzed by these three traditional dimensions. It is instructive to see whether Yahoo and AOL are in some of the same industries even though AOL is an ISP as well as a "portal." Firms that have simply extended their current business definition into the NE world are clearly still subject to this analysis. Landsend.com and REI.com[28] still compete for the same kind of customer in their virtual stores. They may not be perfect overlaps, but they are still trying to appeal to similar customers in their "outdoor" line of clothing. Their production capabilities would tell them more about the extent to which the other is a direct and immediate competitor.

There is at least one dimension in NE that goes beyond these considerations. Firms compete in the cyberworld on the basis of information as a value-added product/service. Is the information (or transactional capacity) that firms use to differentiate their products so valuable to customers that they will develop a loyalty to one provider over another? The online financial industry offers a ready example. Fidelity.com and vanguard.com offer similar information services, but they may not be in the same industry, as argued in Table 7.4. How do customers feel about these features? If one or more features are distinct enough that customers will move to that firm in large numbers, then these firms may cease to be in the same business and may no longer be competitors.

Let's say that one of the two decides to become a full-service financial broker, a one-stop shop for all of a customer's financial needs. Suppose one could invest in stocks, bonds, and mutual funds; buy any and all kinds of insurance; pay one's bills; and bank. The difference between the firms is so marked now that they are surely no longer in the same industry, but the basis for differentiation is not price, production capability (the other firm may have the expertise and the servers), or regional restrictions.

Table 7.4: NE Definition of an Industry for Environmental Analysis

Firm Example	Customers substitute on basis of information value-added......	Industry
Lands End	Unwilling: regular clothes for outdoor-styled clothing	Outfitter
Fidelity	Willing: complete financial services for mutual funds	Full service broker

Simple Test of Industry

An alternate, and simple, identification of industry competitors is to place yourself in the position of your customers. Then think of another firm's products and services. If the customer would perceive these products and services as being substitutes for yours, then that firm is a rival. If the customer would see these as complementary to or synergistic with yours, then that firm is a potential strategic partner.

Stakeholder Analysis

Given that a firm knows what its industry is, the next analysis that managers should perform with respect to the environment is an assessment of stakeholders. This assessment is an interpretive evaluation of the entities, their position in the market, and their current or potential relationship with the firm.

---

[28]REI stands for Recreational Equipment Incorporated. It is a cooperative that sells clothing and equipment for outdoor use.

Customers   One way of understanding this stakeholder is to carry out market research on customer preferences, customer history, and customer requirements. The firm needs to have a clear understanding of market demand, price elasticities, and the set of features customers require. In this regard, environmental analysis becomes a critical element for a successful marketing strategy for a NEO as well as a traditional firm.

Suppliers   Having a set of trusted suppliers is essential for carrying out business online. The firm needs to be able to multisource its needs so that it is not dependent on a single source. Even if the bulk of the firm's business in a certain area is sole-sourced, there need to be contingency plans in case a catastrophic failure in supply occurs. An updated stakeholder analysis of suppliers tells decision-makers who is able to meet current and future needs, the scale of provisioning that is possible, and the pricing for each level of provision.

Outsourcers   The firm cannot and should not carry out all the activities that are involved in the fulfillment process. Knowing who is available to carry out some of the critical activities is part of this analysis. A sense for what is a core competency of the firm and what is not is part of a more detailed analysis of "do" versus "hire" decisions. Much more will be said about outsourcers and their central importance to NEOs in Chapter 10.

Partners   NEOs tend to be engaged in more cooperative arrangements than traditional firms are. The partnerships that are formed make the firm's products and services more valuable to customers and, thus, partnering is a win-win proposition.[29] Which partners are of greatest value to NEOs? Part of the answer to this question lies in which business the firm wishes to be in. If the firm decides to move into selling servers, for example, it may want to partner with a firm that installs and services servers. Other firms that create software for servers are other potential partners.

Government   Governments regulate business. In some cases they clearly overregulate, but there can be little doubt that they are important stakeholders, both as setters of the standards under which business will be conducted and as purchasers of goods and services themselves. Most large firms maintain lobbyists in government centers to monitor the changes in the environment that are initiated by government entities, and even small firms belong to trade associations that perform this function. Government Web sites are likewise sources of data for staying in touch with this stakeholder's interests.

Foreign Countries   Firms that wish to trade abroad must understand the conditions of foreign markets and the requirements for actually carrying out business in a foreign culture. No strategic thinking can take place without knowing these basics. If a firm wants to begin a branch operation in Egypt, for example, it is critical to know the costs of custom duties for the firm's products, the regulations regarding employees, the level of infrastructure development, the capacity for distribution, and so forth. The overall stability of the country in political and economic terms is also critical.

[29]Brown et al. (1996).

Focus on NE: Strategic Choices for Selling Online

Not all products can be sold on the Internet. Some products may be better suited for online sales than others, and others may not work on this new commercial medium at all. According to an Ernst and Young study, the most popular online purchases are computer related products (40%), books (20%), travel (16%), clothing (10%), recorded music (6%), subscriptions (6%), gifts (5%) and investments (4%). The kinds of products and services that sell best on the Internet are those that take advantage of the convenience of the Net. Online businesses allow people to shop any hour of the day or night at any site without the inconvenience of crowded stores and irritating sales clerks.

To increase your chances of success in e-commerce, products and services should exhibit certain characteristics: Offbeat or unusual products and services often sell strongly and attract attention. Items such as gourmet items, rare tobacco products, diamonds, and other specialty items are example of such products. Items that do not have high shipping costs associated with them are more likely to move. Information-based products are also good movers. Products that are used to communicate, entertain, educate, and research are popular items. Nonperishable, information-intensive products such as computers, software, books, travel, electronics, magazine subscriptions are the most popular online products. Services such as hotel reservation, air travel, and investments have also successfully translated themselves to the Internet.

Sources:
http://www.powerhomebiz.com/vol12/kindsofproducts.htm

7.4 NE POSITIONING

To position the firm strategically in NE, managers need to seek out unique advantages that the firm can exploit. A strategic analysis that tells the firm (1) who its competitors are, (2) what industry it is currently in, and (3) which industry it could be in is a useful and valuable exercise that few firms conduct.

It may sound strange to analyze one's own industry. After all, if we do not know what business we are in, who could? That is, in fact, exactly the point, since no one else can or should do this analysis. Firms who hire others to formulate their strategy are probably forsaking their own core competency, because strategy has to be revisited on such a regular basis that a complementor who spent that much time on your site, with your managers, employees, and customers, would give you more value for your investment if he or she were simply part of your own organization.

Businesses who go on assuming that they are in a line of business and never in another will be threatened in the NE world. Amazon.com is a case in point. Its core competency in developing an online storefront has allowed it to take this core competency to the marketplace, even selling their systems and management ability to its competitor, Borders.

There is growing evidence that the source of ideas for new NESs will, in fact, drive corporate strategic positioning more than top executive planning will. Emerging technologies make certain strategic changes inevitable in cyberspace. Amazon.com introduces a new and easier way for customers to purchase online. The "one-click" innovation is so threatening to Barnes & Noble that the latter placed little effort in challenging amazon.com's patent on OneClick and moved forward with a technology it calls "double-click."

Let's imagine a vibrant Net-enhanced industry for selling clothes online. Some sites offer splendid pictures of garments, while others offer to blend digital pictures of customer's torso and faces into the images of the clothes so the potential buyer can visualize what he or she would be purchasing. It is not hard to imagine that firms with the latter sites are picking up market share at the expense of the former. It is well known in the industry that this cause-effect interpretation is descriptive of what is happening.

One of the former, laggard firms decides not merely to imitate the competition, but to leapfrog it with new and better technology. They hire a super-designer who uses proprietary algorithms to create a pseudo-three-dimensional image of the clothes on a potential buyer and allow the user to rotate the image and see it from all sides.[30] To ensure that the site does not take forever to download at the low bandwidths that most people have in their homes, a routine is devised to download data to a user site in 10% of the time that previous technologies would have taken.

When the site is introduced in the marketplace, customers flock to it. It takes a lot of the guesswork out of buying online, because now it offers as much as or even more than a visit to a physical storefront, and it takes so little time, once the digital image has been uploaded and permanently stored in the firm's database for future use. Market share begins to move in favor of the innovating firm, at first slowly, then later more dramatically as word-of-mouth kicks in.

---

[30]In fact, this scenario is not far from what the e-tailer Boo.com planned to do in its online store. See Rosier (2000) and Tillett (2000) for a description of why and how this business failed.

What do you suppose happens soon afterwards in the executive penthouse of competing firms? Top managers see the connection between the technological innovation and increasing market share and make a decision to duplicate or to one-up the invention. So what is occurring in the executive suite is that corporate strategy is being altered by the existence and successful exploitation of emerging technologies. In short, corporate strategy, especially in a world where net-enhanced businesses are challenging the status quo, is being driven by technology, as argued by Straub and Klein (2001).

The Straub-Klein argument that corporate strategy must align itself with opportunities presented by emerging technologies has been elaborated by Wheeler (2002) in his Net-Enabled Business Innovation Cycle, shown as Figure 7.14. Wheeler develops each of the stages in detail, with choosing the technologies as the first stage.

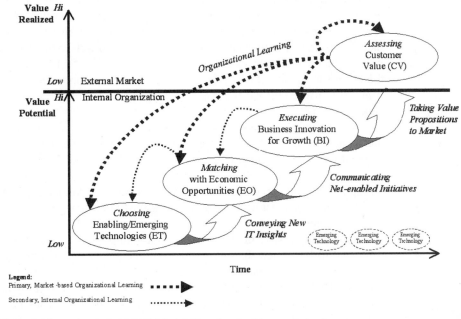

Figure 7.14 Wheeler's NeBIC Model [Reprinted with permission]

The second stage is a matching with economic opportunities that leads to the articulated strategy. This is the stage where top managers that include the IT leader make the determination to proceed with the innovation. The executing and assessing stages are deployment stages and need not concern us here, except to say that, once again, the use of resources is as important as having the resources to begin with. One cannot make a cake without eggs, but blending the eggs with the flour and baking it properly are equally critical parts of the process.

That technology does or should lead strategy is a controversial interpretation of NE strategic positioning. Not all commentators agree that this is the best description of how strategy is made. Moreover, if even if the interpretation is correct, has it always happened in organizations and is just being fully realized today? Or have times changed? We do not know the answer to these questions, but there is no doubt that well-educated managers need to be aware of the debate and be able to take a stand themselves on these matters within their own organizations.

7.5 SUMMARY

Net-enhanced business is business with an added element of value. But the same core business principles are at work in a bricks-and-mortar firm as in an Internet startup. A company must have a corporate strategy if it hopes to keep its doors open. The mission, vision, tactics, and metrics of an organization define the company. Similarly, strategy is the motivating force of the enterprise but must be translated into action in order to be effective.

The tools that we use for strategic analysis are the same tools that have been used for decades, but they need to be modified to reflect the new landscape of cyberspace. Examining Porter's producer strategies will allow us to define our place in the competitive world. Another tool provided by Michael Porter that can prove useful in examining our competitive environment is the Five Forces model. In order to use this model in a Net-enhanced business, it is helpful to consider strategic partnerships. The value added of these partnerships in an e-commerce system is sufficiently large to merit inclusion in the original model. The concept of a "value chain" also translates well to the cyberworld. A firm must implement, although not sequentially, each of the links of this chain in order to maximize the benefit to its operations. As with any other process that adds value to a product, the firm must ensure that the customer's perception of each link in the chain inspires confidence and trust.

A company must identify ways to earn a customer's business. Competition with other companies should be closely examined from multiple perspectives. Both internal and external forces act on a firm, and the firm must isolate the force or forces that give it an advantage over its competitors. That advantage may be sustained or momentary, but either way, it is critical that the company have the means to maximize productivity.

The business must have the ability to identify the strategic resources that it can use to create a competitive advantage. It should also have the ability to apply those resources in order to actually realize the benefit. An important point to note is that an advantage that is perceived to be gained through the use of technology is actually due to the company's application of that technology, such as the use of proprietary data gathered through their systems. Their ability to apply these principles allows them to enjoy an advantage, albeit momentary in most cases, over a firm that has not been rigorous in the development of their strategy.

A portion of strategy development must be devoted to recognizing the benefits to be gained from a Net-enhanced business. E-commerce can have positive strategic effects on an organization, and it is useful for the firm to spend some time considering what type of benefit they expect. These benefits range from the initial productivity improvements and cost reductions through revenue growth, but ultimately to competitive transformation.

Through environmental analysis, a firm should also determine its industry and learn what this implies. Environmental analysis as applied to conventional firms involves determining the firm's place within three dimensions of substitution. This analysis can be extended to Net-enhanced firms by considering the informational or transactional capacity of the company as a differentiator.

Positioning a firm within the world of e-commerce involves applying many strategic tools that are familiar. NE can be viewed as extending the playing field of the company, but the basic ground rules remain.

KEY TERMS

Bargaining power of the buyer: The force addressing the question of how costly it is for the buyer to switch to a firm's competitors.

Bargaining power of the supplier: The pressure that the supplier can exert on the firm for lower prices and contractual terms.

Business strategy: The determination of the long-run goals and objectives of an enterprise, and the adoption of courses of action and the allocation of resources necessary for carrying out these goals.

Competitive advantage: Producing products and services that customers prefer to those of a firm's competitors.

Core competency: Knowledge that an organization has gained about its own processes that make it unique in its competitiveness.

Differentiation strategy: A firm offering a product or service that has a value-added component that makes it different (and better) from what is being offered by the competition.

Low cost provider/producer strategy: A strategy requiring that firms constantly seek out and implement ways to reduce costs in order to offer pricing that is attractive to customers.

Mission: A strong, broad statement about goals of the organization.

Niche strategy: Where firms that have a narrow market focus concentrate their marketing efforts on a particular market segment.

Strategic resources: Assets that are valuable, rare, imperfectly imitable, and/or nonsubstitutable.

Sustainable competitive advantage: A competitive edge that enables the firm to exploit its unique resources and deployment of those resources; usually not a long period of time for online firms.

Vision statements: Goals generally oriented toward the future with respect to purpose and accomplishments.

REVIEW QUESTIONS

1. Define a business strategy.
2. List the four components of a corporate strategy.
3. Define an organizational mission.
4. What is the purpose of a mission statement?
5. What is a vision statement?
6. What are the characteristics of a good strategy?
7. Name four tools for strategic analysis.
8. What are the three strategies for entering a competitive marketplace?
9. Enumerate and describe the five forces of Porter's model that have an impact on the strategic analysis of a firm's position in an industry.
10. What are the five basic steps in the interaction between a firm and its customers or suppliers?
11. What is the major problem of introducing order capabilities?
12. What is competitive advantage?
13. What is the resource-based view of the firm? Why is it also called a theory? State the relationships implied in the theory.

14. State the steps in strategic analysis and elaborate on each.
15. What three resources produce competitive advantage?
16. What is an environmental analysis?

TOPICS FOR DISCUSSION

1. Two components of a corporate strategy are a mission and a vision. Discuss the purpose of each and how they differ from each other.

2. Michael Porter of Harvard developed one of the most useful models for thinking about competition and strategic analysis. Discuss the value of Porter's model.

3. The main focus of Porter's model of Five Forces is manufacturing and services. Complementors, who largely dominate the Networked Economy, are excluded. Discuss the limitations of Porter's model as it applies to NE environments.

4. Describe how relationships with stakeholders can be a primary core competency of a firm.

5. Discuss how proprietary data can improve competitive advantage.

6. Discuss the strategic actions that managers can take to dominate the relationship with customers in the NE world.

7. Discuss the purpose of an environmental analysis and describe the tasks involved.

8. Discuss the dimensions of competition and the impact on an organization.

9. Discuss Wheeler's Net-Enabled Business Innovation Cycle and how its acceptance would impact corporate strategy.

10. Discuss all of the elements that should be considered for an environmental analysis of a Net-enhanced organization.

INTERNET EXERCISES

1. Pick two companies with Internet presences, one manufacturing and one service. What are their corporate strategies? Which of Porter's producer strategies have they adopted? Document your findings on the group discussion site.

2. Select two of Porter's six forces for the NE era. Provide a link to a Web site that demonstrates a specific application of each.

3. Examine the organizational chart for a company of your choosing. Discuss the divisions between line and staff functions.

4. Provide an example of one firm at each stage of the NE value chain. Does the firm's implementation make sense? Does it need to add further stages?

5. Find three firms that possess a competitive advantage in their fields. Are these advantages momentary or sustainable? Why?

6. Examine a failed "dot.com" business. Using the tool developed in this chapter, "Strategic Analysis of Resources and Capabilities," discuss why this business failed.

7. Using a business news service, find an example of each of the three levels of strategic effects.

8. Discuss, with specific examples, the competitive advantage gained by a firm using proprietary information.

9. Define the industry for a company that you do business with online.

10. Identify a firm that is using emerging technologies to its advantage.

TEAM EXERCISES

1. Create a dummy e-commerce business and identify a company/product that could qualify for each of the adapted Six Forces Model for the NE Era. Identify the key challenges for this company to be successful.

2. Pick a company and identify three ways that the company could use e-commerce to reduce cost or improve the company performance (increased efficiency or reduced turnaround time). Highlight a brief implementation plan for each of the three e-commerce opportunities.

3. Pick three e-commerce sites in the same general market and compare and contrast recommending improvements for each site.

4. Create a scenario and product not amenable for qualification by the Six Forces Model for the NE ERA. Are there generic products and areas of commerce not amenable to e-commerce?

5. Give three examples of services a physician, dentist, or similar professional could offer that could be offered through e-commerce within the adapted Six Forces Model.

INTERNET RESOURCES

The Entrepreneurs Guide Book (http://smbtn.com/books/gb21.pdf): How to write a mission statement.

Strategic Planning for Profit and Not-Profit Organizations (http://www.mapnp.org/library/plan_dec/str_plan/str_plan.htm): This site provides a comprehensive coverage of creating a strategic plan for your organization.

Myth & Realities (http://www.informationweek.com/712/12iumyt.htm): This site deals with barriers to entry in the e-commerce area and other myths about e-commerce.

REFERENCES

Amit, R., and P. Schoemaker. "Strategic Assets and Organizational Rent." *Strategic Management Journal*, 14 (1993), 33–46.

Agarwal, R., and V. Venkatesh. "Assessing a Firm's Web Presence: A Heuristic Evaluation Procedure for the Measurement of Usability." *Information Systems Research*, 13, 2, June (2002), 168–186.

Barney, J. B. "The Resource-based Theory of the Firm." *Organization Science*, 7, 5 (1996), 469–469.

Brown, C. V., E. R. McLean, and D. W. Straub. "Partnering Roles of the IS Executive." *Information Systems Management*, 13, 2, Spring 1996, 14–18.

Chandler, A. *Strategy and Structure*. Cambridge, MA: MIT Press, 1962.

Clemons, E. K. "Information Systems for Sustainable Competitive Advantage." *Information & Management*, 11, 3 (1986), 131–136.

Clemons, E. K. "Evaluation of Strategic Investments in Information Technology." *Communications of the ACM*, 34, 1 (1991), 24–36.

Clemons, E. K., and M. C. Row, "Sustaining IT Advantage: The Role of Structural Differences." *MIS Quarterly*, 15, 3, September 1991, 275–292.

Drtina, R. E. "The Outsourcing Decision." *Management Accounting*, 75, 9, March 1994, 56–62.

Evans, P. B., and T. S. Wurster. "Strategy and the New Economics of Information." *Harvard Business Review*, 75, 5 (1997), 70–82.

Grant, R. M. "The Resource-based Theory of Competitive Advantage." *California Management Review*, 33, 3 (1991), 114–134.

Grant, R. M., *Contemporary Strategy Analysis*. Blackwell, London, 2000.

Palmer, J. "Web Site Usability, Design and Performance Metrics." *Information Systems Research*, 13, 1, March 2002, 151–167.

Peteraf, M. A. "The Cornerstones of Competitive Advantage: A Resource-based View." *Strategic Management Journal*, 14 (1993), 179–191.

Porter, M. E. *Competitive Strategy*. Free Press, New York, 1979.

Porter, M. E. and V. E. Millar. "How Information Gives You Competitive Advantage." *Harvard Business Review*, 64, 4, July-August 1985, 149–160.

Prahalad, C. K. "The Role of Core Competencies in the Corporation." *Research-Technology Management*, 36, 6 (1993), 40–47.

Prahalad, C. K., and G. Hamel, "The Core Competence of the Corporation." *Harvard Business Review*, 68, 3, May-June 1990, 79–91.

Quinn, J. B., and F. G. Hilmer, "Strategic Outsourcing." *Sloan Management Review*, 35, 4 (1994), 43–55.

Robins, J. A. "Organizational Considerations in the Evaluation of Capital Assets—Toward a Resource-Based View of Strategic Investment by Firms." *Organization Science*, 3, 4 (1992), 522–536.

Ross, J. W., C. M. Beath, and D. L. Goodhue, "Develop Long-term Competitiveness through IT Assets." *Sloan Management Review*, 38, 1, Fall 1996, 31–42.

Rosier, B. "What Went So Horribly Wrong with Boo.com?" *Marketing* (2000), 9.

Straub, D. W., and R. Klein. "e-Competitive Transformations." *Business Horizons*, 44, 3, May-June 2001, 3–12.

Tillett, L. S. "It's Back from the Dead: Boo.com." *Internetweek*, October 23, 2000, 11.

Tsang, E. W. K. "Transaction Cost and Resource-Bases Explanation of Joint Ventures." *Organizational Studies* (2000), 215–242.

Volkov, S. "Personalized Content Aggregation at Web Portals: Tailoring the Content Bundle Based on Content Provider's Credibility." Unpublished doctoral dissertation, Georgia State University, 1999.

Weill, P., and M. Broadbent. *Leveraging the New Infrastructure: How Market Leaders Capitalise on Information Technology*. Harvard Business School Press, Cambridge, MA, 1997.

Wernerfelt, B. "A Resource-Based View of the Firm." *Strategic Management Journal*, 5, 2, September-October 1984, 117–181.

Wheeler, B. "NeBIC: A Dynamic Capabilities Theory for Assessing Net-enablement." *forthcoming in Information Systems Research*, 13, 1, March 2002.

Zmud, R. W., and A. A. Armenakis. "Understanding the Measurement of Change." *Academy of Management Review*, 3, 3 (1978), 661–669.

Zohar, A., and G. Morgan. "Refining Our Understanding of Hyper-Competition and Hyperturbulence." *Organization Science*, 7, 4 (1996), 460–464.

CHAPTER 8

BUSINESS MODELS AND STRATEGIC PLANNING

UNDERSTANDING MODELING AND PLANNING ISSUES FOR NEOS

What are the possible business models that managers can use to design an NE initiative? What resources does the firm own with each model, and how can this be exploited for competitive advantage? What planning models are applicable to traditional businesses as they migrate to NE? These critical strategic issues will be addressed in this chapter.

LEARNING OBJECTIVES FOR THIS CHAPTER

- To define the concept of a business model
- To identify the components of a business model
- To classify atomic business models
- To express the capabilities of each model and its limitations
- To articulate the strategic advantages accruing from owning resources available in each atomic model
- To give examples of each atomic model and discuss the flow of information, products and services between relevant entities
- To assess hybrid models

▶ CASE STUDY 8-1

AMAZON.COM: ITS BUSINESS MODEL

Amazon.com began in Jeff Bezos's garage in Seattle in 1994. Bezos, recognizing the potential of the Internet, left his lucrative job on Wall Street and began his Internet startup company. Bezos's vision was to create a virtual bookstore that would hold more volumes than any existing bookstore in the world. When amazon.com opened its virtual doors in 1995, books were shipped to more than 45 different countries in the first 30 days. By 2001, sales amounted to $3.1 billion.

In its eight years of operation, amazon.com has grown from a dedicated bookseller to a distributor of a wealth of diversified products such as CDs, cookware, toys, games, tools, and hardware. It also operates the Internet Movie Database (imdb.com), which holds more than 300,000 movies and entertainment titles. Moving into other product categories allowed Amazon to be thought of as a dominant retailer. In addition to expanding into new product categories, Amazon proceeded into two new directions. The first initiative was to partner with e-tailers who sold products that Amazon did not carry and did not plan to carry. The second one was to host several small businesses as part of the zShops initiative. With each of these initiatives, the company leveraged its reputation and minimized its risk.

Amazon needed a system that would give the company real-time alerts for troubleshooting and also provide the ability to conduct root-cause analysis. These features would allow Amazon to tune the system and avoid bottlenecks during peak traffic periods. Amazon also wanted a solution that would not add overhead to the system or slow down the rate of information to customers.

Today, amazon.com is one of the most common e-commerce models. It is a client-server application supported by product databases and shopping cart capabilities. It allows customers to accumulate and store lists of items as they shop. They sell their own products directly to consumers and also serve as brokers for others. Many refer to them as content aggregator and portal for this reason.

Discussion:
1. Describe the type of business model that Amazon operates.
2. Discuss the model resources that Amazon possesses.

Sources:
Center for Advanced Spatial Analysis, July 1999, http://casa.ucl.ac.uk/amazon.pdf
http://www.rice.edu/projects/reno/rn/20000914/Templates/amazon.html
Amazon.com Inc., Company Information http://www.amazon.com/exec/obidos/subst/misc/company-info.html/002-4986275-3239237

8.1 INTRODUCTION

This chapter will discuss how managers can create a business model for their NE initiative. Each atomic business model calls for a separate analysis of resources, and the combination of models is another important consideration. Finally, strategic planning requires consideration of a host of other issues, such as revenue models, marketing models, financing models, and implementation or project planning. These issues will all be discussed in this chapter.

8.2 THE CONCEPT OF A BUSINESS MODEL

The phrase "business model" has been bandied about since the beginning of the World Wide Web revolution by consultants, practitioners, and academics as a substitute for the concepts of strategy, strategic planning, other typical plans, business cases, architectures, and blueprints. It grew into prominence with the Internet and e-commerce era and may be connected with some of its distinctive features.

Although many people use the term as a synonym for such older concepts as strategic planning, we can (and should) ask whether there is there anything new about the business model as a concept. If there is, then it makes sense to develop the concept more fully and use it where appropriate.

A recent use of "business model" should be sufficient to see what is new. Consultants, practitioners, and academics see the term as referring to a unique aspect of the way business is conducted.[1] They differentiate these unique ways, organized by value stream for business partners, buyers, revenues, and logistics. One way these unique models play out is with descriptors that allow one to see the ways in which the model being proposed will differ from traditional "bricks and mortar" operations and how it will make money.

Dating from the diffusion of graphical user interfaces (GUIs), such as Mosaic and Netscape, business models have been used heavily by entrepreneurs to propose their ideas to venture capitalists (VCs), and in this sense, they are also fairly extensive expressions of ideas. Complete business models include at least the elements noted in Table 8.1.

[1]Mahadevan (2000).

Focus on NE: Angel Investors

Need money for that "can't miss" idea? Maybe an angel investor will come to your aid. Angel investors are financially sophisticated individuals with a high net worth, willing to provide seed, start-up, and growth capital, on high-risk companies for an expected large return on their investment.

Angel investors look for companies with high growth potential, exciting products or services, and proven management. The term *angel* was originally coined to describe wealthy individuals who backed Broadway shows in exchange for the privilege of rubbing shoulders with theater personalities. Some cities have organizations such as venture clubs where companies and angel investors meet. An example of such an organization is the Rockies Venture Club in Denver, Colorado. This club has a membership of several hundred and has a dinner meeting each month with between 150 to 250 attendees. However, even at such meetings it is difficult for the angel investor to locate companies that meet the criteria for investment. Most angel investor organizations have methods of introducing companies to the investor. Introductions are often done by giving the investor a simple summary of the company rather than a full business model, thus leaving it up to the investor to determine his or her level of interest in pursuing the investment possibility, requesting the business plan, and doing all of the necessary due diligence on the company. The angel organization usually charges the entrepreneur a fee for this service, thus limiting the investment opportunities to only those companies who are aware of the organization and willing to pay the fee.

Sources:
http://www.angel-investors.com/investor.html
http://www.venturevest.com/angelInvest.html

Table 8.1: Components of a Fully Articulated Business Model

	Component
1	Mission and other strategic statements
2	Diagrammatic or schematic view of relationship with stakeholders
4	Revenue model
5	Projected financial statements
6	Marketing model
7	Investment decisions for partners, complementors, and supplementors (Chapter 10)
8	Implementation plan and timetable (strategic planning)
9	Exit strategy

The mission and other strategic statements are the high-level positions that are part of a strategy. They give the organization direction but lack the details of a planning document. Diagrammatic views of the enterprise are meant to show how the firm relates to the primary stakeholders. In other chapters in this book, we argue that there are many more stakeholders of the firm in a NEO than in a traditional firm. These diagrams are intended to present a holistic view of the various stakeholders, including customers, suppliers, partners, and even competitors. They represent flows of goods, information, and money.

Submodels include the revenue model, which basically states how the firm anticipates deriving income from the venture. An important part of the business model, as far as VCs are concerned, are prospects for profitability. The firm's projected financial statements relating specifically to the NE initiative are another part of this argument. Because NEOs tend to take on relatively high proportions of partners in their projects, making the investment decision for bringing in outsiders is also critical. This decision is so important that we have dedicated Chapter 10 entirely to this topic.

Marketing models include the methods that the firm will use to attract and retain customers. It could include a prototype of the Web site and other features that are unique to this business model. Once details for marketing the concept are articulated, a full-blown implementation plan can be developed. A schedule of when the Web site will be built, when it will be inaugurated, and so forth are all items in the plan. In Porter's work,[2] marketing is viewed as a downstream activity, but in this book it is discussed as a set of strategic issues in Chapter 11. In this sense, the marketing model is a strategic plan that takes into account how to market the firm's offerings.

Many start-up business models include prospects for making an initial public offer (IPO) to a firm, selling the firm, or moving it to a new level. The equivalent of such plans for an SME or large firm would be a section on future developments.

[2]Porter and Millar (1985).

8.2.1 Models, Strategies, and Strategic Planning

For the purposes of this book, the concept of a business model will incorporate strategies and strategic planning. The concepts apply both to initiatives inside large firms and to start-ups. Initiatives for start-ups are typically captured with the term *entrepreneurship,* whereas those inside a firm are called *intrapreneurship.* The business model for GE's latest B2B NE initiative, for example, might have all of the elements listed above, including the goal of the initiative, its financial impacts, and a schematic of how it affects stakeholders and the firm's ownership of resources. GE managers who are proposing the initiative have internal processes that would lead to approval or rejection of the new business model. Their model may not be an exact replica of the standard components of a business model listed in Table 8.1, but top managers will expect answers to the kind of questions examined in each of these areas before launching the initiative.

A start-up firm or a small firm would also have a business model for their first foray into NE. This business model might be more extensive than the one used by an established, old-line firm that has well-established investment decision procedures because they would need to raise capital from the outside. The added risk of not knowing the players should mean that VCs and even angel investors[3] will demand a higher burden of proof.

A business model, thus, is a management tool for making decisions. The firm will make a considerable investment in NE projects, and a procedure with reasoned set pieces will make the process more systematic and, hopefully, less risky.

8.3 TYPES OF BUSINESS MODELS

Weill and Vitale (2001) articulate eight types of business models that they believe are "atomic." Their scientific work is the best evidence we have to date of the types of business models that managers can combine into full-blown NE strategies. These models lie at the heart of our new understanding of NEOs and what will make them successful.

What do they mean by "atomic"? Just as atoms build into molecules and molecules build into more complex physical entities in the real world, business models are argued to be composed of essential, underlying elements. Just as water is composed of hydrogen and oxygen, and as H_2O, in a two-to-one ratio of the former to the latter, most businesses will end up being complex combinations of atomic models. One or more atoms could make up the bulk of the molecule, but it would not be accurate to describe the firm's business as if it were composed of a single atom.

The eight models and short descriptions are shown in Table 8.2. After previewing the nature of each and the resources they command, we will discuss each one in detail, with examples.

---

[3]Angel investors are private parties who invest in a firm's e-commerce efforts. These private investors are usually not incorporated, as are VCs.

may have explicitly handed this activity off to a host. Thus, in such a case, an outsource is the actual "owner" of the transaction, but the "owner" of the relationship would still be the brand. What is important is who the customer thinks they are conducting transactions with, electronically speaking. If a customer only knows how to get to a retailer through the Z-shops at amazon.com, then Amazon owns the relationswhip, but likely not, in this case, the transaction. Some data having to do with how the customer navigated the site to find the retailer may be owned by Amazon. But the exchange of transactional data would be handled by that retailer and perceived as such by the customer. It is not handled by Amazon, so Amazon would not even own this transactional data. Weill and Vitale (2001) attribute the transaction to the firm that receives transaction fees, which is particularly relevant in certain industries such as online brokers but applies also to many other situations. Please consider such lines of thinking when making your own assessment about who owns the transaction.

The transaction itself is the least important resource. It can even be separated from the relationship, and from the data, with little loss. Another firm could handle the transaction processing for the firm, for instance, while branding the interaction as if it were occurring directly with itself. Logistics handled by UPS, for example, could be branded for the individual retailer so that the customer would believe that they were interacting directly with the firm. In this case, the firm would own the transaction and not UPS, even if UPS were actually handling the Web inquiry.

In the physical world, ownership of the transaction is most often tightly coupled with the data generated by that transaction and the relationship with the customer. The only time this does not occur is when there is an intermediary, such as a wholesaler or retailer. Compaq does not know who is purchasing their computers because this is proprietary data controlled by intermediary firms such as CompUSA or Best Buy. NE allows firms to establish direct links to their customer base and bypass intermediaries. If they can do this, they can gain ownership of more resources.

Schematics allow managers to configure their business models in such a way as to maximize effectiveness. They are also helpful tools in understanding the model and in convincing others about the investment potential. The symbols that will be used in the schematics are shown in Figure 8.2.

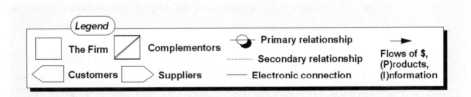

Figure 8.2 Graphical Symbols for Interpreting Business Model Schematics

As the legend indicates, the firm itself will be represented within a rectangle or square. Other firms that are seen by customers as enhancing the firm's products are known as complementors, and these are shown with a diagonal line drawn through a rectangle or square. Customers are in a five-sided figure with the point facing left, and suppliers are represented with the reverse image of this, that is, a five-sided figure with the point facing right. Flows of money, products, and information are shown by the "$" or the capital letters "P" or "I" on the lines with the arrows. These lines will be solid or dotted, depending on the nature of the relationship. Primary relationships will have a shadowed circle placed on the line, whereas secondary (nonelectronic) relationships will be dotted lines. Solid lines also convey the sense that the relationship is electronic or Net-enhanced.[--pb--]

8.4.1 Content Provider

Content providers were one of the earliest users of the Web. Major TV networks such as CNN (cnn.com), publishers like Ziff Davis (ziffdavis.com), and newspapers like the Wall Street Journal (wsj.com) used the Web to induce subscribers to cross over to some of their other services. Some of them, such as the Wall Street Journal Interactive, provide partial access through the public Web site and subscriber access through their extranet, which is, of course, password protected.

The basic schematic for this model is shown as Figure 8.3. All schematics in this book will use Weill and Vitale formats, although our models may be simplified at times for expository purposes.

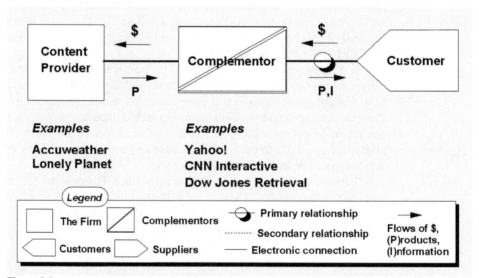

Figure 8.3   Type 1: Content Provider Schematic

When the firm is a content provider in NE space, it typically has a relationship with a complementor who, in turn, has a relationship with the customer. AccuWeather or MapQuest, for example, work with CNN and Yahoo to provide content for CNN and Yahoo customers. The business model for the complementor may be represented by a number of atomic models. That issue will be dealt with in time. The point here is that content provision does not allow a firm to connect directly with the ultimate customer.

The revenue model for content providers is simply the fees it charges the complementor, as shown in Figure 8.3. Although the content being provided is all digital, and in this sense is data at least, Weill and Vitale (2001) conceive of this as the content provider's product. Information, for Weill and Vitale, is what might accompany the direct product and serve as value added to the main product (as in the case of the complementor-customer relationship). When a client is willing to pay for content, then what they are paying for is product.

Content providers are not in a strong competitive position. Because they have no direct connection with the ultimate customer, they do not own the relationship, the transaction, or the data. Unless their content is unique, the complementor can drive costs down by playing one content provider against another. On the surface, managers need to be extremely suspicious of content provision as a revenue source. Most firms provide a great deal of content on their Web site for customers, but this is an enhancement of the general offering and not the offering itself. Table 8.4 highlights the resources owned by the content provider.

Table 8.4: Content Provider Resources

Resource	Ownership Considerations
Relationship	Content providers tend not to own the relationship with the customer. They provide information to complementors, who resell their services to customers for subscriptions, as in the Wall Street Journal Interactive. However, they may sometimes share the customer relationship with the customer if they brand their content, as in the case of Lonely Planet's branded content on Yahoo.
Data	Rarely do content providers have direct access to customer data, but a strategic partnership could realize this potentiality.
Transaction	Customers perceive that they are dealing with CNN Interactive. Even if the content is branded, customers know with which Web site they are working, and, hence, do not have a clear and defined sense that the content provider is handling the transaction.

8.4.2 Direct-to-Consumer

Many people think of the direct-to-consumer model as being the quintessence of e-commerce. In many ways, this is true. This model allows a firm to interact electronically with customers. Firms such as Dell have become immensely profitable in the World Wide Web era by using this model.

Direct-to-consumer models pose some problems, such as channel conflicts for firms with an extant distribution chain, a conflict which will be discussed later in Chapter 11, on e-marketing. For the moment, it is enough to note that in this model business exchange costs are extremely low for the firm as well as for the consumer. Search costs are low for the consumer because it is not difficult to compare pricing between Web sites or even visit sites such as epinions.com, where comparisons also include reviews. For the firm, this model eliminates the physical costs of retail stores or even, in certain cases, warehousing costs.

Figure 8.4 shows the schematic for the direct-to-consumer model. Customers visit the Web page of the firm and browse its offerings. Whether the transaction is carried out completely online or not, the Web site can be said to be the origin of the sale, or the means by which customer preferences can be amassed. It is easy to see that even if a customer does not make a purchase, the customer's navigation through the site could be instructive. With its virtually infinite capacity for capturing information, NE permits a firm to create a strong electronic and symbolic connection with the customer. The movement of digital products (P) across the network, as in the case of E*Trade (etrade.com), can be accompanied by value-added information (I). E*Trade offers information for investors about stock trends, which, incidentally, it purchases from a content provider.

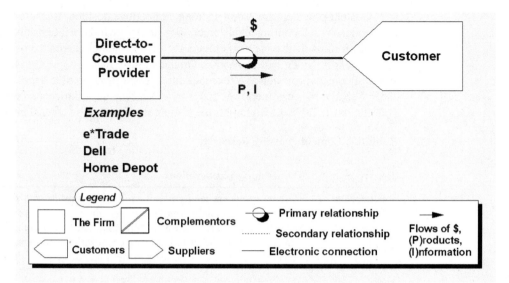

Figure 8.4 Type 2: Direct-to-Consumer Schematic

Dell is an example of a firm that is firmly committed to the direct model. From the very beginning, the firm pushed a new way of selling computers. The electronic value chain is fully implemented at Dell, and has been for a long while. Technical questions and troubleshooting (after-sales support) are handled on the Web site as well as are ordering and payment. Online tracking of shipments is another capability. Dell pioneered this concept among computer manufacturers and achieved an initial competitive advantage from these basic services.

Table 8.5 enumerates the resources owned in this model. It is one of the strongest models in that the firm owns and controls all three of these key resources. A firm such as amazon.com has some direct-to-consumer characteristics, but it is a reasonable interpretation that they are also deploying other models, discussed later as the intermediary and value net integrator models.

As noted earlier in this chapter, Amazon exploits other atomic models as well as the direct-to-consumer model. Therefore, it is fair to say that it is a hybrid or molecular model formed by several atomic models. We will illustrate this concept later in this chapter.

Table 8.5: Direct-to-Consumer Resources

Resource	Ownership Considerations
Relationship	Direct-to-consumer models own the relationship because they are the firm of record for all services and good dispensed to the customer.
Data	This model also owns the behavioral data related to the customer purchases and after-sales interactions.
Transaction	Customers perceive that they are dealing with Dell or E*Trade, for example. Even if the hosting of the transaction is outsourced, the URL of note is that of the firm. This is a very powerful model for e-commerce, with respect to resources.

8.4.3 Full-Service Provider

This model has not completely emerged in the marketplace yet, although there are definite signs that it will continue to develop. It is characterized by going beyond the firm's own offerings to include those of a host of partners. In the interest of completely serving the needs of its customers, it may, in fact, carry the products of its competitors. In the example in Figure 8.5, we theorize what the business model of fidelity.com, the Mutual Funds financial firm, would look like if it worked with complementors like Schwab to sell stocks and with insurance carriers like Aetna to sell insurance. These firms would pay a commission for leads and sales, but might, conceivably, carry out the transaction themselves. Could Fidelity, starting in, say, the year 2002, also forge a partnership with another major mutual fund firm like Vanguard? A full-service provider of financial services would also have to consider offering banking to its clients. Thus, a virtual firm like NetBank (http://www.NetBank.com) could also be viable candidate for this model at some future time. They already service significant segments of customers' financial needs. The concept of full service is to deal with as many needs of a customer as possible in one important area of their lives, their finances.

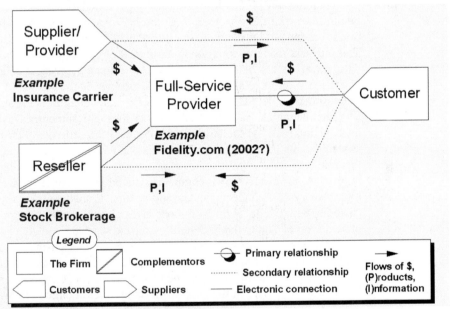

Figure 8.5 Type 3: Full-Service Provider Schematic

The danger of this model is that customers will forsake the firm and make a direct connection with the reseller, complementor, supplier, or competitor in subsequent transactions. The entire point of a full-service provider is that they supply brands other than their own. Therefore, customers know exactly whose products or services they are buying. The full-service model owns the data resource and the transaction, but it is possible that the data, in particular, may have to be shared. The more these resources are owned or appropriated by others, the more likely it is that the firm can lose the primary relationship.

Table 8.6 lists the assets of this model. It is as strong in the data and transaction resources as the direct-to-consumer model, but suffers from the relationship drawback mentioned previously.

Table 8.6: Full-Services Provider Resources

Resource	Ownership Considerations
Relationship	Full-service providers own the primary relationship with the customer, although nothing prohibits the customer from interacting directly with a supplier or a reseller. There are few examples of mature firms in this category, but Prudential's Advisor and Bank One's Wingspan are close. Fidelity would be a likely possibility for initiating this model in its full-blown form.
Data	They also own the data and share with suppliers or resellers only to the extent that there are mutual benefits accruing from the partnerships.
Transaction	Customers perceive that they are dealing with the full-service provider. Even if the content is branded, customers know which Web site they are working with.

8.4.4 Intermediary

Intermediaries are similar to full-service providers in that their Web site forms the primary relationship with the customer. With the intermediary business model, the actual transaction is carried out by suppliers or complementors in the way Weill and Vitale conceive it. This business model is common in traditional physical systems as well in cybersystems, as with travel agents or real estate brokers, although physical intermediaries sometimes maintain the direct relationship with the customer. In the NE world, this would be a direct-to-consumer model, where the wholesaler or manufacturer is the supplier.

Intermediaries, or cybermediaries as they are sometimes called, make the proper introduction between the buyer and seller, and the seller-supplier or complementor actually carries out the transaction. EBay is a good example of an auction Web site that fulfills this role. The online travel agents expedia.com and travelocity.com are other examples. In Figure 8.6, the Jango search engine associated with Excite is an example of a pure-play intermediary that connects buyers and sellers. It shares a primary relationship with the customer with Excite. Selling of goods takes place through the supplier, and a commission of some sort is paid to the intermediary for the service.

What are the resources owned by the intermediary business model? The schematic in Table 8.7 shows that this model owns the relationship but has limited access to data and no ownership of the transaction. On the face of it, the most important relationship belongs to the intermediary and, in the case of the Jango search engine, knowledge of the customer evaluation process (i.e., what search terms they use, what results they get, and which vendor they choose). The lack of ownership of the transaction itself is not that critical, as we have discussed. Intermediaries should be prospering. Is this the case or not? We will investigate the profitability of the models later in this book, but, for the moment, we can say that the jury is still out on the overall successfulness of this model. There are some sterling examples of success, such as eBay, but the B2B auction sites have not always enjoyed such success.

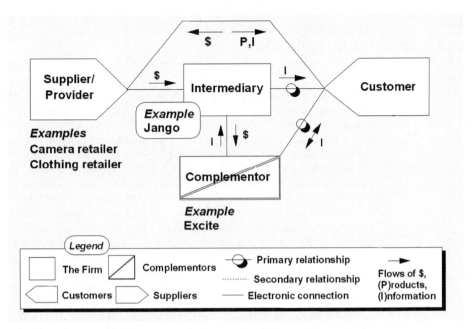

Figure 8.6 Type 4: Intermediary Schematic

Cybermediaries represent an organizational design that is unique to the Web. They did not exist before the rapid diffusion of the Internet. They have a high degree of virtuality in their designs, and they are exemplars of substituting information for physical processes in their business exchanges. This model is so important that it calls for a chapter in its own right, duly following this chapter. If it can become clear why intermediaries succeed or fail, this information will benefit managers in other settings. They are, in a way, the clearest case of a pure NEO, and can lead the way forward for all other firms in this arena.

Table 8.7: Intermediary Resources

Resource	Ownership Considerations
Relationship	Intermediaries are the primary contact point with the customers, so they own the relationship. Secondarily, they refer customers to suppliers or complementors, who do not own the relationship with the customer.
Data	In fact, intermediaries can learn a great deal about customer comparison shopping behavior, but they may or may not have access to the customer purchasing behavior data. That data may be retained by the supplier.
Transaction	The supplier conducts the transaction at their site, and the customer is well aware of this when they hyperlink away from the intermediary to another site.

▶ *CASE STUDY 8-2*

ATOMIC MODELS AND ISWORLD NET

ISWorld Net (ISWorld.org) provides scholars and practitioners in information management and information systems (IS) with a single point of contact to resources pertaining to information technology. The purpose of ISWorld Net is to foster the development of an international information infrastructure to improve the use of information systems for creating, disseminating, and applying knowledge. Membership includes about 5,000 researchers and educators in colleges and universities throughout the world. Over 2,000 members subscribe to the ISWorld discussion list. Other participants include undergraduate, masters, Ph.D.-level students, and thousands of IS professionals around the world. Some 24 countries have contributed Web pages to ISWorld Net.

ISWorld provides a variety of resources to the global IS community. It serves as an important knowledge repository, providing access to information for research, teaching, and professional activities. Information on undergraduate and graduate IS programs in the United States and abroad are available. Bibliographic databases, including ProCite, EndNote resources, and ISBib (http://readable.eci.gsu.edu:8080/examples/servlet/isbib), are available for access. ISWorld is an invaluable outlet of research resources. Research subject areas, research methods, and research services are offered to members. The site also contains archives of research papers from past national and international conferences. A faculty directory is available as well as listings of IS journals, research centers, and conference information. Professional services such as placement services, professional organizations, faculty development, and information about careers and trends in the IS profession are also available. ISWorld Net offers information on IS education, including IS courses, pedagogy, online cases and courses, and IS programs.

ISWorld Net's objectives are to foster learning through worldwide availability of examples, summaries of phenomena, explanations, and discussions as well as to be at the forefront of a networked global world through action research. ISWorld Net also seeks to provide common goals, structures, and tools, while leaving implementation to individuals or institutions. ISWorld Net is committed to drawing universities, governments, and the private sector more closely together while striving for equal access to information.

Discussion:
1. Discuss how communications in the IS community has changed because of ISWorld Net.
2. Describe the characteristics of the atomic model(s) employed by ISWorld Net.

Sources:
http://www.isworld.org
http://readable.eci.gsu.edu:8080/examples/servlet/isbib

8.4.5 Shared Infrastructure

Shared infrastructures involve entities (or members) sharing a site for their mutual benefit. All members participate in the transactions conducted through the site, but they may or may not have an equity position in the shared infrastructure firm itself. Shared infrastructures can be for the benefit of supplier-members or customer-members. We can look at the supplier schematic, depicted as Figure 8.7, first.

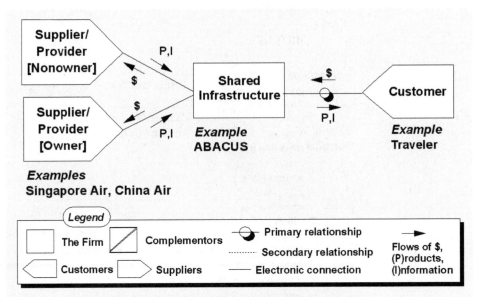

Figure 8.7   Type 5: Shared-Infrastructure Schematic for Supplier-Members

In the schematic, Orbitz is the supplier-member shared infrastructure that provides its members access to the traveling public through its Web site. The advantage to the traveling public is that they get comparison routing and pricing information from the shared infrastructure that would not be available at a single airline site, such as delta.com. The abacus.com site is an example of another airline shared-infrastructure atomic model.

This model clearly benefits the customer, but does it help the supplier-members? The idea behind the model is that many Web customers are already savvy about using the Web for comparison shopping, and the firm cannot pretend that this competitive reality is not affecting customer buying decisions. In short, not playing in this game is even more dangerous than playing in it. The cost of the shared infrastructure is shared among members, and owner-members also have the advantages conferred by their equity positions. Nevertheless, this subtype has some obvious drawbacks.

The opposite variation of this model is the customer-member model. Figure 8.8 shows the relevant schematic.

In this subtype, the customers band together to ensure supplies and drive down supplier prices. In Porter's classic model, this should reduce the bargaining power of the supplier by allowing customers to form a larger-scale buying unit. Covisint, the electronic trading network (ETN) formed by the large automakers GM, Ford, and DaimlerChrysler, draws in suppliers of all varieties to offer their wares.[5] They expect revenues of $300 billion within a relatively short time, which shows the potential power of this model for certain ventures.

[5]Kestelyn (2001).

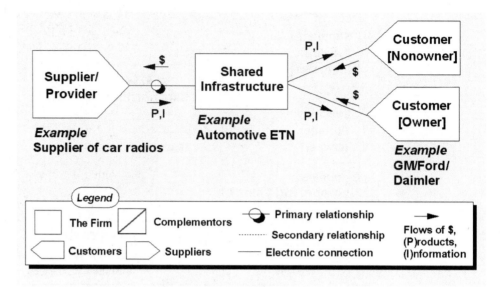

Figure 8.8   Type 5: Shared-Infrastructure Schematic for Customer-Members

This is a very complex model from the standpoint of ownership, as seen in Table 8.8. Owners negotiate among themselves as to sharing of data as well as the extent to which the relationship with the individual owners or nonowners should be revealed to the customer or supplier, and when that relationship should be revealed. The concept of sharing of the infrastructure is to create a single cybermarket in order to create benefits for the owners. But the needs of the nonowner members have also to be considered, or the cybermarket will be perceived as too narrow and of lesser value.

Table 8.8: Shared Infrastructure Resources

Resource	Ownership Considerations
Relationship	The shared-infrastructure models have several advantages, but owning the relationship is not one of them. In fact, from the standpoint of an individual owner firm, it is advantageous that the buying or selling party identifies with them rather than with the infrastructure. Were it otherwise, this model would not work.
Data	The owners of the shared infrastructure own data relating to their own activities. The shared-infrastructure owner firm may or may not give nonowners access to its data. These can be negotiable terms for membership.
Transaction	In Orbitz, a traveler eventually knows that the ticket is being purchased from Delta Airlines, for instance, but the transaction is most often handled by the shared-infrastructure entity. Owning the transaction has little benefit because the relationship is with the supplier in the final analysis. Neither owner nor nonowner really cares who owns the transaction, as long as the data is shared.

To make the cybermarket attractive to suppliers or customers, depending on which model variant we are talking about, nonowners need to join. If they perceive themselves as being at too much of a disadvantage by not being owners of the infrastructure, they will not join. So a balance needs to be set. Owners derive immediate benefits from the infrastructure in their sales relationship and in the data that is being amassed. A high-level view of how competitors are using the trading network could be valuable for firm strategy, and, for this reason, this data may not be available to the owners. On the other hand, nonowners may feel they have little choice but to join in spite of this competitive disadvantage.

An analogous circumstance occurred in the early days of the Apollo (United Airlines) and Sabre (American Airlines) customer-reservation systems. Nonowners joined because these systems had critical mass in placements with travel agents. The infrastructure favored owners in many ways, however, and nonowners were at a disadvantage for years, until the playing field was leveled by the U.S. court system.

How did this happen? The results of a search for flights on certain dates at certain times gave preferential display (initial or opening positions) to flights of the owner airline. Primacy theory in psychology says that initial stimuli are better received than later stimuli, and the truth of this theory played out in this case in the form of higher sales for the owner airlines.

Moreover, owning the transaction is not nearly as important as the data generated by that transaction, and this, too, is subject to negotiation in shared-infrastructure models.

8.4.6 Value Net Integrator

Value Net integrators (VNIs) take advantage of their central position on the Internet between suppliers, complementors, and ultimate customers. With the suppliers, they coordinate ordering and stocking of goods and services for their complementors, who, in turn, deal mostly with the ultimate consumer or business customer. VNIs may exchange information with the ultimate customers, but this is solely for the purpose of better coordination of capacity and stocking. They are a true "cyber" business, who, like cybermediaries, did not exist before the coming of modern networks. In a sense, they are a pure "management" function because physical actions are being handled by the complementors and suppliers. Some people have referred to this model as "outsourcing with attitude," and there is a great deal of truth in this humorous characterization.

Figure 8.9 shows the schematic for the basic VNI model. It might be easiest to understand if we follow it through with the 7-Eleven example. The 7-Eleven franchise stores in Japan are convenience stores that are highly specialized within local markets. They tend to be small operations and most lack computer sophistication. Without outside help, their capability to order just in time and to avoid the expense of large inventories and stock-outs is limited, therefore. The firm that is the 7-Eleven Japanese Net integrator, however, has the economies of scale that allow it to manage the specialized needs of individual stores. The Internet connects all parties and the coordinating systems at the Net integrator, places orders, queries ultimate customers for forecasts, and so forth.Money flows from the complementors to the Net integrator and from the Net integrator to the suppliers, but the Net integrator never touches physical products.

Focus on NE: Atomic Model for Activeworlds?

Activeworlds, Inc., provides software products and online services that permit users to enter, move about, and interact with others in a computer-generated, three-dimensional virtual environment using the Internet. Unlike a two-dimensional environment, which permits movement on a computer screen only along horizontal and vertical axis (up, down, left and right), a three-dimensional virtual environment enables users to move in three dimensions by allowing them the added capability of moving forward and backward. Because Activeworlds is primarily an Internet-based platform, the potential market for Activeworlds-based products is global. There are currently over 1.5 million individual users worldwide. There are more than 1 million hits on the site per day, and more than 1000 new users download the browser each day. To date, more than 40,000 users have registered to be a "citizen" of the Activeworlds universe. These fee-paying users receive enhanced capabilities in the Activeworlds environment. Users who do not pay the annual fee are called "tourists." The market for three-dimensional interactive Internet technologies is growing due to both an increasing demand for interpersonal interaction between Internet users and an expanding interest in Internet-based applications. Activeworlds' robust architecture, ease of use, speed, reliability, and scalability have attracted users worldwide. Three-dimensional Internet applications provide enhanced richness that would be of interest to users developing Internet-based advertising, distance learning, training, entertainment, e-commerce, chat, and other online activities.

Sources:
http://www.activeworlds.com

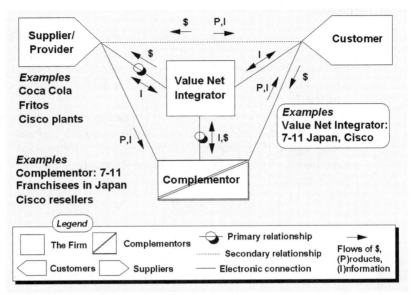

Figure 8.9 Type 6: Value Net Integrator Schematic

What are the resources owned in this model? As shown in Table 8.9, VNIs own the relationship with the complementors, who are, in effect, the single type of customer of the VNI. The relationship with the ultimate customer, either consumers or commercial customers, is handled by the complementor, although the VNI shares information with these parties. Complementors use their data sparingly, trusting the VNI to manipulate it for their use. It is in the interest of the VNI to do this well because it leads to profitability of the complementor and continued use of the services of the VNI. Because the VNI can batch large orders, they have economies of order and can negotiate good prices from the suppliers. This serves the interests of the supplier, because they have to deal with only one professionally operated VNI, and the complementors who do not usually have the expertise to manage the supply chain this effectively. The transaction is likewise owned by the VNI.

Table 8.9: VNI Resources

Resource	Ownership Considerations
Relationship	VNIs are cybermediaries with few physical assets. They coordinate the flow of goods and, hence, own the relationship with the complementors (who pay for the integration) but not the relationship with the ultimate customer.
Data	VNIs specialize in managing information, including data about the customer purchasing behaviors and supplier and complementor capabilities. This is their core competency. They own the data.
Transaction	The transaction with the complementor is owned by the VNI, who shares the information with the complementor and the ultimate customer. The VNI's customer perceives the transaction to be with the VNI. The ultimate customer perceived the transaction to be with the complementor.

8.4.7 Virtual Community

Virtual communities capitalize on the interests of a group of Internet users, as shown in Figure 8.10. The community forms or is formed around a topic, like fishing or traveling. In the case of the examples listed, suppliers or providers financially support the virtual community either for commissions, referral fees, or because they are an appendage of the business itself.

It is difficult to see how virtual communities could be a large revenue generator in their own right. They own the relationship with the customer (see Table 8.10), but one of the reasons the customer visits the site is to participate freely and for no charge in the community. Were a subscription to be levied, the number of users would likely drop precipitously.

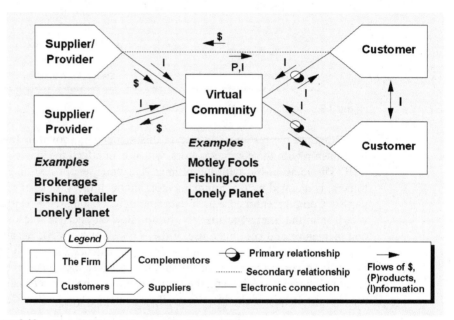

Figure 8.10   Type 7: Virtual Community Schematic

Within the community itself, the navigation patterns of the users can be captured by the virtual community. For privacy reasons, community members often do not approve of entities selling data about their activities.[6] This limits the extent to which virtual communities can resell this data. As long as the data is used to advance the interests of the community members, this data can be exploited.

---

[6]eToys.com sold its customer data when they went out of business, and there was a universal outcry about this in cyberspace. Firms need to be sure that they will not degrade the entire commercial environment by such acts, even if there are no legal proscriptions against so doing.

Table 8.10: Virtual Community Resources

Resource	Ownership Considerations
Relationship	Virtual communities are most often free services that aggregate information for customers, but they may also serve as an appendage for a business, as in the case of Lonely Planet, Amazon, MetLife, and so forth. The primary relationship in the model is between customers and the virtual community.
Data	Data about customer interests resides with the virtual community. This could be a source of information for making the site more valuable to the customer.
Transaction	There are no transactions to speak of with this model. Organizations use virtual communities as value-added differentiators. They receive money indirectly, through their other sales channels, but not through this firm.

8.4.8 Single Point of Contact[7]

Single point of contact (termed "Whole of Enterprise" in Weill and Vitale 2001) is a model that gives entry to an entire cornucopia of offerings or services. The Victoria State Government in Australia is one of the few examples of this model, although the U.S. government is attempting the same thing (http://www.firstgov.gov). The concept is that users come to the site with a need or question. The single point of contact acts to direct them to the business (or agency) units that can solve their problems.

Almost every large firm in the world has a Web site whose domain name reflects the corporate identity. Although many of these have menu bars and other icons to try to redirect the inquirer to relevant divisions of the company, it is not immediately obvious to a user which of these can deal with their problem. On the General Electric site (accessed in November 2002), for example, the menu bars give the user access to the company's structure, business and personal financing options, and solutions for home and business (see Figure 8.11). However, it might not be clear to a consumer where to go among these menu choices if they have a problem with a product.

Single-point-of-contact models are not oriented toward the firm, but toward the user. The relationship between the firm and the user is driven by the firm's ability, through this single Web site, to solve the user's problem, as illustrated in Figure 8.12. If the need is for after-sales support, then a *problem analysis* engine could help the user discover where in the organization a particular problem could be solved.

[7]Weill and Vitale (2001) call this atomic model "Whole of Enterprise." Because a number of their examples are governments, we are focusing on a different feature of the model in the term *single point of contact*. This term can apply equally well to private- and public-sector organizations.

Figure 8.11   GE's Single-Point-of-Contact Home Page Site

As seen in Table 8.11, this model owns all the resources, unless the site is set up so that some transactions are handled through secondary sources. As an organizational principle for complex firms, it makes a great deal of sense. If a potential customer cannot figure out where to go on the site to purchase or seek remedy, then the firm's image will suffer and that customer may be a lost customer.

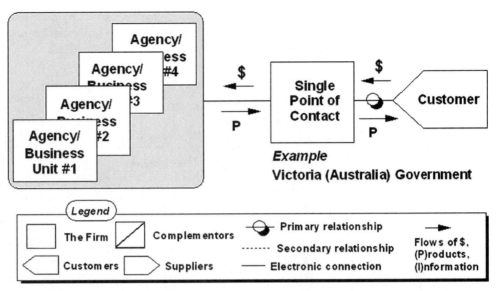

Figure 8.12   Type 8: Single-Point-of-Contact Schematic

Table 8.11: Single-Point-of-Contact Resources

Resource	Ownership Considerations
Relationship	Single point of contact shares some of the characteristics of the direct-to-consumer model. It owns the relationship, since that is, in fact, the entire idea behind the model. Customers should not have to seek beyond the single point of contact to have their needs met. There are few mature examples of this model.
Data	Naturally, data is owned by the single point of contact, who attempt to answer questions and direct customers to the products and services they seek.
Transaction	Customers perceive that they are transacting with the single point of contact, and that the Web site is their access point.

8.5 HYBRID MODELS

Few companies exemplify pure forms of the atomic business models. Most, as in the microscopic world, combine atoms into molecules. A direct-to-consumer model for Delta Airlines (delta.com) will be introduced in the next chapter, but it is readily apparent that Delta is also driving business through its ownership of orbitz.com. The latter shared-infrastructure model complements the direct-to-consumer model while creating no channel conflict in the process. Channel conflict will be dealt with in Chapter 11, "Strategizing for E-Markets," but for the moment, it is important to note that the real world is rarely as simple as academic models would have it.

Weill and Vitale (2001) are sensitive to the viability of hybrids in the e-business space and cite Lonely Planet as an example. Figure 8.13 shows the business model for this popular travel book company, headquartered in Melbourne, Australia.

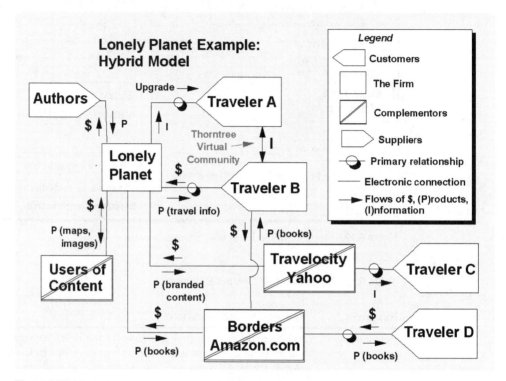

Figure 8.13   Lonely Planet as a Hybrid (Molecular) Business Model Composed of Many Atomic Models

Lonely Planet's traditional business is represented at the bottom of Figure 8.13; they have been enormously successful in selling travel-aid books through complementors such as Barnes & Noble and Borders. The retailer, through its physical stores, acts as an intermediary and resells these books to travelers. Like other traditional intermediaries, booksellers' value-added proposition, as we shall see in the next chapter, is to break bulk by buying in large quantities and passing on these economies-of-scale savings to consumers and businesses.[8]

When Lonely Planet decided to move into cybermarkets, they faced a serious challenge: Their distribution partners, such as Borders, would not appreciate their opening up a direct-to-consumer connection to the ultimate customer. Nevertheless, Lonely Planet viewed it as a strategic necessity and began selling directly to travelers, such as Traveler B in Figure 8.13.[9] Their sales were both original and complete travel books as well as updates, which were not in the same category of competition with their channel partners because it was not really feasible for print book shops to sell printed inserts with updated

[8]Westland and Clark (1999).
[9]Weill and Vitale (2001).

material. To slightly mute the channel conflict, some of the content they are selling electronically is through their CitySync Web site, which is intended to download to PDAs.

Another form of new sales for Lonely Planet was to offer content through portals such as Yahoo. Although they also decided to sell content to in-flight magazines (content provision shown in the left-hand side of model), the content they sold to Yahoo was branded. Lonely Planet reasoned that they would be less vulnerable to loss of the asset of the customer relationship if the customer was made aware of the fact that Lonely Planet was the source. So in this particular case, Lonely Planet engages in both branded and unbranded content provision and is handicapping their vulnerability by gaining some control over the strategic resources.

Lonely Planet also supports a virtual community called Thorntree. This community allows travelers to share information about touring and traveling, and, because Lonely Planet has access to these exchanges, it is not unreasonable to think that there may be a value-add from this. An insightful reading of these exchanges could lead the firm to devise new travel products and services, perhaps. In any case, the virtual community draws users to Lonely Planet's Web site and may induce crossover sales.

Table 8.12 shows the atomic components for Lonely Planet. It is a true hybrid model—one that has not resolved all of its channel conflicts, but one where many assets are still owned by the firm.

Table 8.12: Hybrid Model for Lonely Planet

	Lonely Planet Atomic Components	Relationship	Data	Transaction
1	Content provider			
2	Direct-to-consumer	X	X	X
7	Virtual community	X	X	

Had the firm chosen to provide content only to organizations such as Yahoo and to continue selling through physical intermediaries, they would have risked being sidelined by more innovative travel information companies. Short of a bold, even daring, move into a model such as full service, it is difficult to see another strategic direction they could have taken that was more appropriate. The virtual community could conceivably contribute valuable customer requirements for both the content provision and direct-to-consumer models. Like Dell Computer's transition from selling computers to merchandisers to selling computers to consumers, Lonely Planet may find that there are attractive margins associated with an immediate connection with customers. After all, their writers are already creating content in digital formats, and the overhead of the Web site is trivial compared with the expense of the physical printing. This would allow Lonely Planet to move more forcefully toward a virtual model over time and to take advantage of increasing returns to scale.

Lonely Planet is branching out into other media, and this is, likewise, a good experiment with their core competency as creators of specialized travel information. They host syndicated TV programs that feature low-cost, behind-the-scenes glimpses at cultures around the world, in keeping with the theme of their books. It is easy to see how this exposure can help to create a sense of brand for the other products that they sell through other media, such as through their Web site. We will explore such deployment strategies in the next module of the book.

8.6 BUSINESS MODELS AND ATOMIC MODEL SCHEMATICS

In creating an NE-strategic plan for a firm, the business model must be put forth. The derived business model is what will sell or will not sell the case to top managers in the case of an intrapreneurial project or to VCs in the case of an entrepreneurial project.

Managers and their assistants can use the concept of atomic models to first determine the firm's core competencies and then build the schematic that represents the direction to be taken by the NE initiative. Most likely, the derived business model will be a hybrid that will combine approaches, hopefully in a synergistic way. If not, then there will need to be a plan to deal with or overcome channel conflict. The revenue model for the initiative is implied in the schematic, but this can be elaborated with information about the potential market, and so forth.

Projected financial statements for five years, typically, may be the most difficult part of the exercise. Projecting revenues is hard enough in well-understood product lines in long-time established firms. For new business models implied in an NE initiative, there are a lot of uncertainties about who will buy and how much they will buy. Nevertheless, without this information, there is not a good way to see if the effort will ever become profitable. There are upfront costs associated with building and setting up the systems, of course. In the long run, the marginal cost of adding a customer will be near zero, and the profits should be seen in the latter years of the projections. If increasing returns to scale is an accurate description of this initiative, then profits would soar in the next five-year period, but most business models do not project out this far.

The marketing and implementation plans deal with subjects that we will cover in later chapters. For the moment, it is enough to say that it is likely that both of these areas have been neglected to the great detriment of dot.com businesses. Systems were built and may have been capable of delivering value, but without customers they languished. In some cases, the entrepreneurs built a good company but did not turn it over to professional managers soon enough to convert the start-up into a medium-sized enterprise. The point here is that care and brilliance in the front end could come to no avail if the execution is not up to par. Firms need meticulous management throughout the cycle to be successful.

8.7 SUMMARY

The term *business model* has become popular since the beginning of the Internet and e-commerce revolution. It has been used as a substitute for the concepts of *strategy* and *strategic planning*. But what exactly is a business model?

Business models are used heavily by entrepreneurs to present their ideas to VCs when starting an Internet business. Also, companies such as GE have been using business models when changing to an NE strategy. Groups in established firms that utilize business models may be referred to as *intrapreneurs*. A business model includes elements such as the following:

- Mission statement
- Revenue model
- Marketing model
- Projected financial statements
- Implementation plan
- Timetable

All these elements jointly give the organization direction and illustrate the bigger picture to the VCs when making the presentation. Thus a business model is a management tool for making decisions. Different types of business models exist today and are proven to be the best when managers are making the decision to move to an NE strategy and to execute such a strategy. The models identified by Weill and Vitale (2001) are as follows:

- Content provider
- Direct-to-consumer
- Full-service provider
- Intermediary
- Shared infrastructure
- Value Net integrator
- Virtual community
- Single point of contact

Hybrid models are not only possible but likely for most firms. Hybrids combine features of two or more models. Some intermediary models, such as Yahoo, also support their user community by allowing the user to search his or her directory and communicate via e-mail or instant messenger. Being able to create a business model for a NEO helps with the strategic planning for e-commerce initiatives.

KEY TERMS

Business model: A basic description of the way a business is to be conducted or is currently being conducted.

Content provider: When the firm typically has a relationship with a complementor who, in turn, has a relationship with the customer.

Direct-to-consumer: This model establishes a direct cyberlink between the producer (or assembler) and the ultimate customer or consumer.

Full-service provider: A model for a NEO that gives access to a range of services originating through itself or complementors (including competitors).

Hybrid model: A combination of two or more atomic models to form a molecular business; hybrids are most effective when they are synergistic.

Intermediaries or cybermediaries (Weill and Vitale view): A service provider that makes the proper introduction between the buyer and seller but facilitates a seller-supplier or complementor who actually carries out the transaction.

Marketing model: The plan for how the NEO will create brand through other media or otherwise create a customer base for its offerings.

Revenue model: States how the firm anticipates deriving income from a venture.

Shared infrastructures: Entities (or members) sharing a site for their mutual benefit.

Single point of contact: A model that gives entry to an entire cornucopia of offerings or services within an organization.

Value Net integrator (VNI): Highly virtual firms specializing in managing information, including data about customer purchasing behaviors and supplier and complementor capabilities.

Virtual community: Sites that capitalize on the interests of a group of Internet users and are formed around a topic, such as fishing or traveling.

REVIEW QUESTIONS

1. List the elements of a business model.
2. Define a revenue model.
3. What is a marketing model?
4. Distinguish between entrepreneurship and intrapreneurship.
5. List eight types of business models.
6. Apply the resource-based theory of the firm to atomic business models.
7. What is a content provider?
8. Why don't content providers achieve a strong competitive position?
9. Define the direct-to-consumer model.
10. Describe differences between the full-service provider model and the direct-to-consumer model.
11. Define the intermediary model.
12. List characteristics of a shared-infrastructure model.
13. Describe the distinctive competence of a value net integrator.
14. What intermediary characteristics do we find in full-service, intermediary, and shared-infrastructure models and VNIs?
14. Define a virtual community.
15. Describe differences between the single-point-of-contact model and the full-service provider model.
16. Why do most NEOs employ a hybrid model for their strategic positioning?

TOPICS FOR DISCUSSION

1. Discuss the importance of choosing a business model.
2. Discuss the importance and significance of schematics to business models.
3. Content providers are not in a strong competitive position. Discuss the reasons why this is not the case.
4. Discuss the ownership considerations of relationships, data, and transactions for the content-provider model.
5. Discuss business exchange costs for the direct-to-consumer model.
6. The direct-to-consumer model is one of the strongest models in that the firm owns and controls the relationship, data, and transactions. Discuss the considerations of ownership for these three resources.
7. Discuss the primary threats to the full-service provider.
8. Discuss ownership considerations of resources, data, and transactions for the full-service provider model.
9. Discuss the ownership considerations of resources, data, and transactions for the intermediary model.
10. Discuss the complexity of the shared-infrastructure model from the standpoint of ownership.
11. Describe the resources owned and the ownership considerations for the VNI model.
12. Why is the virtual-community model seldom a stand-alone model?
13. Describe the ownership considerations of the single-point-of-contact model.
14. Discuss the essential characteristics of hybrid models.

INTERNET EXERCISES

1. Locate two mission statements for high-tech companies. Compare the strategies of the mission statements.

2. Identify which NE model is used by the following organizations:

   a. American Red Cross

   b. FedEx, specifically Logistic Services

   c. The Official Site of Texas Tourism, traveltex.com

3. Find mission statements from three companies on the Internet. Identify the primary stakeholders referred to in the mission statements. Analyze the mission statement, primary stakeholders, and the Web site of each company.

4. Locate three companies from different industries. Identify the revenue model used by each company and discuss how you were able to identify it.

5. Search the Internet and find an example of a firm that incorporates one of the revenue models. Find an example for each model.

6. Choose an e-business on the Internet. Write a two-page synopsis of their business model. Be sure to explain what type of model it represents and how and why you think the firm chose that particular model. Explain what you would do differently if you managed the firm.

7. Search the Internet for an example of a full-service provider or a firm that appears to be headed in this direction. Write a one-page description of the firm. Make constructive comments about your impression of the firm, its business model, and its Web site.

8. Search the Internet for an example of a firm that uses a hybrid of models. Write a one-page description of the firm. Make constructive comments about your impression of the firm, its business model, and it Web site.

9. One of the elements of a firm's business model is the marketing model or plan. This element is extremely critical to e-business firms because Internet users can control their ad viewing more easily than, say, a viewer of television. Go to the site yesmail.com and learn what this firm offers its clients. Write a two-page response discussing how this firm can help or hurt the marketing plan of an e-business firm. Include your comments on where you think marketing for Internet firms is going in the future.

10. Visit a Web site such as nbc.com or another content provider and browse through the Web site to find out what other types of services they are offering in the Web site besides the "news."

TEAM EXERCISES

1. Use a chat room to discuss current events of your choosing with your fellow teammates/classmates. Makes notes about the usability of the chat room along with notes about your discussions. Why does the chat room you chose to utilize exist? Is there a profit motive behind the sponsor?

2. A four-person team should pick a virtual community to explore. One person should act as the coordinator and assign the other three members the following tasks:

   a. Describe the ease of use of the virtual community.

   b. What is the purpose of the selected virtual community?

   c. Provide a detailed description of the "average" profile of a regular user of this virtual community.

It will be the coordinator's responsibility to collect the data from other three team members and prepare a one-page summary of the findings.

3. A five-person team should visit the site ebay.com and compose a two- to four-page report detailing the following information as it relates to the Web e-tailer:

    a. How does eBay attract capital?

    b. What model, as described in Chapter 8, does eBay employ?

    c. How does eBay encourage customer loyalty?

    d. How does eBay manage the investment community?

    e. How does eBay define unethical behavior?

    f. How does eBay handle unethical transactions?

4. A four- or five-person team should identify one real-world Net-enhanced company (not a company mentioned in this textbook) that fits one or more of the following NE strategic planning models: content provider, direct-to-consumer, full-service provider, intermediary, shared infrastructure, VNI, virtual community, single point of contact, and hybrid.

5. A five-person team should pretend that they are a management team that will be approaching VCs for funding of the NE project following the content-provider model. Utilizing the information provided in Chapter eight, the students should develop a PowerPoint presentation that will encourage the VCs to invest in their idea.

INTERNET RESOURCES

Strategy Quotient (http://www.strategy4u.com/sq.php): You can learn your company's Strategy Quotient right now. The assessment below just takes two minutes, but the benefits could last a lifetime. Answer the following questions truthfully—honesty is the starting point for change. Your answers should reflect how your business works today, not how you wish it were. You'll immeiately receive a free report with suggested remedies to get you headed in the right direction.

Business Models on the Web (http://digitalenterprise.org/models/models.html): This is one attempt to present a comprehensive and cogent taxonomy of busniess models observable on the Web.

REFERENCES

Kestelyn, Justin. "The Big Bang-Covisint." *Intelligent Enterprise*, 4, April 16, 2001, 30–35.

Mahadevan, B. "Business Models for Internet-based E-commerce: An Anatomy." *California Management Review*, 42(4), Summer 2000, 55–69.

Porter, M. E., and V. E. Millar. "How Information Gives You Competitive Advantage." *Harvard Business Review*, 64(4), July-August 1985, 149–160.

Straub, D. W., and R. Klein. "e-Competitive Transformations." *Business Horizons*, 44(3), May-June 2001, 3–12.

Weill, P., and M. Vitale. *From Place to Space: Migrating to eBusiness Models*, Harvard Business School Press, Cambridge, MA, 2001.

Westland, J. C., and T. H. K. Clark. *Global Electronic Commerce: Theory and Case Studies*, MIT Press, Cambridge, MA, 1999.

CHAPTER 9

INTERMEDIATION AND CYBERMEDIATION

UNDERSTANDING INTERMEDIATION ON THE WEB

Among the organizational designs covered in Weill and Vitale's atomic business models, intermediation (cybermediation) is very important because a firm can be heavily information-based as a intermediator. Intermediators meet our central criteria for NEOs, that is, they have a minimum of physical processes and focus these processes on information as their value-add and core competency. Predictions that intermediators and intermediation on the Internet were not going to disappear and, in fact, would remain extremely important have proven to be true. Why is this the case? What are the various forms cybermediation can take and what are the value-adds of each type? How does a manager structure cybermediation in order to be successful? What are the limitations in cybermediary atomic business models and how does a firm overcome these? These and other questions will be addressed in this chapter.

LEARNING OBJECTIVES FOR THIS CHAPTER

- To define the concepts intermediation and cybermediation
- To be able to elaborate on the fundamental qualities of intermediation and cybermediation
- To distinguish between disintermediation, reintermediation, and cybermediation.
- To articulate one theory of intermediation
- To recognize and argue for the value-add of intermediaries
- To identify intermediary roles in NE
- To compare and contrast atomic model and cybermediaries

▶ *CASE STUDY 9-1*

INTERMEDIARIES TAKING THE HARD OUT OF HARDWARE

The computer hardware industry has drastically changed its means of delivery and its distribution channels over the last few years. Stores like Best Buy, Circuit City, and CompUSA are having a hard time keeping up with sites like www.ebay.com and www.pricewatch.com. Now, it is easier than ever to find hardware for computers at discount prices.

Acting as an intermediary, eBay has thousands of listings of computer hardware that can be found for prices much less than for what retailers are selling. Somehow, people are finding ways to get the hardware at discounted prices or sell the hardware for which they have little or no use. The prices on eBay are actually higher now than they used to be a year ago but are still more competitive than what you would usually find in the retail stores. Not all prices on eBay are competitive, but a majority of them are.

Pricewatch has an interesting site that allows a consumer to pick a category of hardware, select the specifications, and view a listing, sorted by price, of where they can find it online. You can find every type of hardware imaginable at discount and hard-to-believe prices. This intermediary actually provides information to consumers about products for sale from discount and smaller scale online stores. The search produces a list of hardware with detailed information on part numbers, model numbers, specifications, and so forth. Once you find the price you like, you can usually click on the seller's Web address to order the part and obtain more detailed information on the product. All of the seller's contact information is listed, regardless of whether or not they have a Web site.

These sites are an incredible resource for the individual who builds computers for sale, or wants to build a computer for personal use. With access to these sites, a consumer can build a powerful computer for much less than what they are sold for in retail stores. Most of the hardware sold on these sites has some sort of warranty.

Intermediaries are clearly having a major impact on taking the hard out of hardware.

Discussion:
1. Discuss why computer hardware sites are intermediaries in terms of atomic models.
2. Discuss how computer hardware sites affect competition and prices for consumers.

Sources:
http://www.pricewatch.com
http://www.ebay.com

9.1 INTRODUCTION

This chapter will discuss how managers should strategize for intermediation. Many businesses make intermediation the sole purpose of their business and others find themselves serving in the role of intermediaries, whether or not it is central to their main business model. What is intermediation and who are typical intermediators on the Web? After examining these issues, we will explore why certain forms of intermediation will persist in e-commerce in spite of some who have predicted the death of middlemen. The value-adds that these businesses can bring to the table are what will make them successful in the long run. What are these? The more managers know about intermediation, the more they will be able to develop it effectively for their own firms.

9.2 WHAT IS INTERMEDIATION?

On the surface, intermediation would seem to be easy to define. It is any business process that lies between the endpoints on a value chain. Business units that dig raw minerals out of the ground are not generally thought of as intermediators, therefore. On the other end of the chain, the final consumers of a product or service are likewise not intermediators. In a classic sense, then, any entity that adds value to a product/service is intermediating. Wholesalers and retailers are other examples of intermediation along these lines. There are, for example, brokers who serve a critical role on the supply side. In the aircraft parts industry, brokers help the airlines locate critical components when an aircraft has broken down.[1] Finding these parts quickly and flying them to the destination keeps the fleet in the air. A grounded fleet loses a great deal of money, as was painfully obvious after the September 11 terrorist attacks.

In common usage, the term *intermediators* also has a more restricted role as entities who serve a market by bringing together multiple buyers and sellers.[2] A stock exchange is one example of intermediation in this vein. The terms *brokers*, *traders,* and *agents* are usually found in this context.

Figure 9.1 depicts a classic value chain with brokers/agents being designated as intermediators. In this case, the firm that is manufacturing the goods has not been labeled as an intermediator, even though it technically stands in an intermediate position on the value chain. Creators of goods and services are often seen in the same light as suppliers of raw materials and content. Their value is not primarily information-based, and, therefore, they are originators more than they are intermediators. This is particularly true in the cyberworld, and because we are focusing our attention on this phenomenon, it is appropriate that we make distinctions along the lines of information.

---

[1]Choudhury, et al. (1998).
[2]Spulbler (1999).

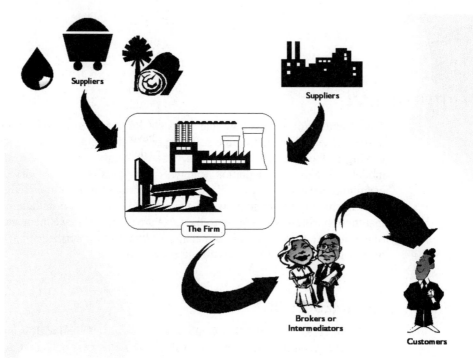

Figure 9.1   Intermediaries in a Value Chain

Thus, the essence of intermediation is that the intermediary very often has an information-based service (not a product, as in a content provider). When a line of business takes place on the Web, it can be called *cybermediation*.

One can think of two major types of intermediaries. As shown in Table 9.1, they either (1) do not take ownership of products or services (virtuals) or, at least, (2) may own but do not produce or even assemble the products or services themselves (aggregators). It is truly the case that both virtuals and aggregators fall somewhere other than at the endpoints of the value chain. Their role is to use information to match the needs of buyers and sellers and to transition goods and services quickly through their operation.

Table 9.1: The Types of Intermediaries

Type	Description
Virtuals	Purely information-based; do not own the products and services they resell
Aggregator	May own, but do not produce or assemble goods and services; use information to match buyers and sellers

9.3 BRICKS AND CLICKS INTERMEDIARIES

Many makers of products and services require market-makers in some part to deal with the demand side. The reasoning for this is clear enough. To focus on core competencies, a firm may allow others to handle logistics and other parts of its marketing function. GM is an example of a firm that supplies cars to consumers worldwide but does not have a direct relationship with the ultimate users of its products. Intermediaries, its large network of dealerships and distributorships, deal directly with the consumer. The insurance industry is similar with respect to firms that do not have so-called *captive* agents. Firms such as State Farm Insurance hire their own agents to deal with the customer. Other firms, such as MetLife, use independent agents. A captive agent structure, thus, gives these insurance carriers direct access to the ultimate consumer. An independent agent structure places intermediaries in the value chain between the carrier and the ultimate consumer.

Intermediation is difficult for firms that have had an established traditional presence in the marketplace. If they now wish to forge direct links to their ultimate customers, they are in conflict with the intermediaries that have supported them in the past. In the last chapter, this was called *channel conflict*. This can impede or limit a firm's entry to the Web world. In cyberspace, intermediaries can be easily bypassed, and so they must provide other capabilities to prove their worth. So cybermediation and straightforward channel conflict are issues that confront many firms that have and will continue to wrestle with its implications.

9.4 DISINTERMEDIATION, REINTERMEDIATION, AND CYBER-MEDIATION

It is important that managers understand the differences between breaking off with their intermediators (disintermediation), reintroducing mediation into their value chain (reintermediation), and forming a virtual unit to serve as a Web presence (cybermediation). A firm can clearly engage in one or more than one of these activities. Let's take the example of Delta Airlines and define these concepts through this example. Figure 9.2 shows how Delta disintermediated its travel agents by encouraging customers to call the airline directly. Delta saves the travel agent commission of 5% to 15% when a customer books a seat directly with the firm. It is easy to see why Delta would prefer direct-to-consumer models, whether the channel is Web-enabled or not.

In Figure 9.3, we see that Delta next adds a channel for its ultimate customer by creating a Web site where electronic tickets can be sought and bought. Delta, in fact, had to purchase this domain name (delta.com) from another firm of the same name that had already commandeered this cyberturf. This reinforces the point made earlier in the book that cyberspace is closely akin to the greatest land grab of the nineteenth century, the Louisiana Purchase in the United States. That is why many firms that are entering the Web world late are making up names such as Accenture so that they can claim the domain name and establish their brand from this point forward.

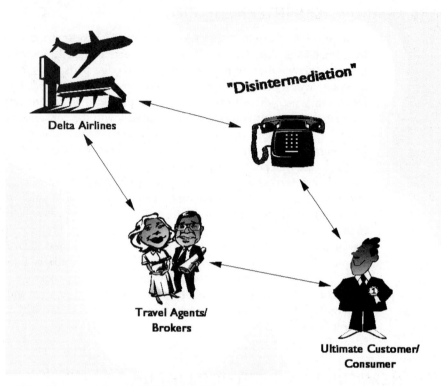

Figure 9.2   Disintermediation via Traditional Channels

Reintermediaton is the action of firms to reinsert themselves electronically into the value chain in place of its brokers or agents. In short, they are taking over the job of the brokers via a direct connection. Figure 9.3 illustrates this in the case of Delta. The customer interface in this case works directly with the customer reservation system that the airlines share. However, the business model itself is a clear example of a direct-to-consumer model in Weill and Vitale's scheme.

If the customer ordered a ticket from Delta through Orbitz, then the model would be different, although the result would be the same. The business model would be a shared infrastructure, and Delta, along with its competitors, would be reintermediating and displacing its agents.

Before discussing the theory behind intermediation, we need to talk about why airlines are able to deal head-on with the channel conflict in this case. How can the airlines be so indifferent about the huge loss of business for their traditional intermediaries, the travel agencies?

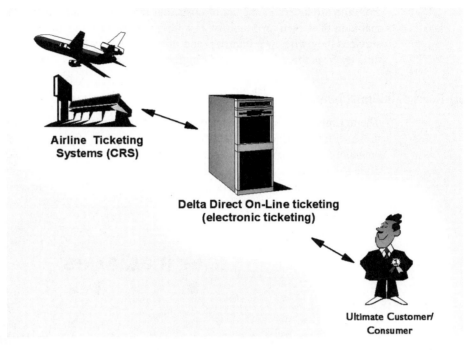

Figure 9.3   Reintermediation of Delta into the Value Chain

Research indicates that much of what travel agents have been doing for the airlines is routine and transactional in nature. When the customer simply needs to buy a ticket and can make the decision by himself or herself about which airline, which route, and which price is acceptable, then a travel agent adds little value to this process.[3] Useful information provided by the travel agent is minimal, and the only service is access to the customer reservation system to make the booking. Once customers were able to purchase such commodity services themselves over the Web, the eventual demise of this part of the travel agent's business was foreseeable. There are areas of value-add where intermediation in travel is still important and necessary. We will examine these once more after considering the theory of intermediation.

9.5 THEORY OF INTERMEDIATION

If we examine a theory related to the effect of the Internet on intermediation, we can better understand the role of mediation in the cyberworld. Economic theory suggests that purchases and transactions that are the least costly will be preferred in the marketplace. This is particularly true when the product or service being offered is a commodity, that is, economies of scale and low pricing is what is important to customers. If there are many intermediaries in a value chain that drive up the price needlessly in the eyes of the customer, then that value chain will not be as efficient as one in which there are fewer price hikes. Intermediaries add cost, as Figure 9.4 illustrates. The costs the intermediaries received

[3]McCubbrey (1999).

from the producers is one set of costs, but they have to add their own charges in order to maintain their own profitability. In addition, consumers incur costs in locating the goods/ services they wish to purchases, and this adds cost, whether they are searching these out directly from the producers or through intermediaries.

9.5.1 Roles of Intermediaries

The arguments of economic theory are also interesting with regard to established firms, those with huge bricks-and-mortar investments. These firms are characterized as *supplemented intermediaries*. Firms such as Delta Airlines, become, in effect, their own intermediaries through the reintermediation process. In other words, they use the Internet to reinforce the existing channels of their ticketing branches and airport sales.

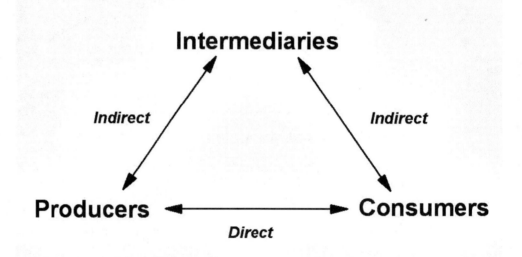

Figure 9.4   Producers, Consumers, and Intermediaries

An example might help to show all the costs involved. Suppose the year is 1990, and you want to buy a ticket to fly to Alaska. You could call every airline that flies to Alaska and compare their prices and flight schedules, or you could go to an intermediary who has access to all airline information. That intermediary would be a travel agent. What are the costs involved? The airline picks up the costs of the travel agency by paying a commission on the price of the ticket. The customer saves on his/her costs by not having to contact each possible airline. But, overall, the customer prefers to go through a travel agent-intermediary because the personal costs in time to him or her are lower.

After the advent of the Internet, when cybermediaries such as travelocity.com and expedia.com made flight information available online, this equation changed dramatically. Today customers can choose their own flights without having to rely on or wait for travel agents. If a customer wants to make a reservation at 10 P.M. on a Saturday night, they now can, even though their travel agents are likely closed in countries in which Saturday and

Sunday are considered to be the weekend.[4] Costs after the Internet are lower for many customers, and so they go to cybermediaries for their business.

Figure 9.5 shows how Sarkar, Butler, and Steinfield (1995) theorized the pre- and post-Internet possibilities for intermediaries. Their predictions have been remarkably accurate and are worth discussing for that reason. When many of the early observers[5] predicted that most intermediaries would become irrelevant in the cyberworld, these insightful researchers argued that intermediation would change, but it would never become irrelevant.

	Pre-Internet	
Post-Internet	Direct $ < Indirect $	Direct $ > Indirect $
Direct $ < Indirect $	**Direct marketers** (Foster & Smith Mailorder Pet Supplies)	**Threatened Intermediaries** (Traditional travel agents, life-auto insurance agents)
Direct $ > Indirect $	**Cybermediaries** (amazon.com, Expedia)	**Supplemented Intermediaries** (Barnes & Noble; Walmart; Delta Airlines)

Figure 9.5   Intermediation Pre- and Post-Internet

They predicted that there would definitely be a group of intermediaries whose value-add would be challenged. The travel agent example we have just explored is a classic case of this. These are the *threatened intermediaries* in Figure 9.5. Before the Internet, they offered services that both the airlines and customers valued, partly because costs were lower for customers, and the airlines had no direct channel to the consumer.

---

[4]Alternatively, they could interact directly with airlines by going to their online sales channel. This is less demanding than calling and trying to understand the many choices over a phone line.
[5]Benjamin and Wigand (1995); Malone et al (1987).

But other intermediaries, such as Expedia and Travelocity, insert themselves into the value chain and make the indirect less expensive than the direct, they posited. As Figure 9.5 shows, these firms are, in effect, serving the role of *cybermediaries*, which is like an electronic producer-to-consumer channel because their marginal costs approach zero. As virtual organizations, they have few physical assets and amortized over millions of transactions, even when the overall costs of the systems themselves rapidly move to zero. Direct costs are higher than indirect costs (which would favor traditional intermediaries) because firms are using the Internet to drive down business exchange costs. They either become their own intermediaries or a new form of intermediation by being virtual firms, offering products and services with incredibly low costs to cover the transaction itself. Once set up, a Web site has no storefront or other expensive physical overhead.

Supplemented intermediaries are those organizations that assume the role of intermediaries themselves, such as Delta Airlines. By reintermediating its Web system in place of the travel agents, the firm reinforced its tickets office channels. Sarkar and colleagues predicted that these firms would succeed with their intermediation because their channels would feed each other, rather than detracting from each other.

In short, this theory says that firms cannot compete in the commodity business if they do not become their own electronic intermediaries or move convincingly from physical models (like bricks-and-mortar travel agents) to electronic ones.

9.5.2 Differentiated Products and Services

Whereas commodity products and services compete primarily on price, differentiated offerings compete on useful services and embedded information. Customers are willing to pay more for something if there are such value-adds. The airlines industry provides a good example of this principle.[6] Travel agencies can compete and remove themselves from being disintermediated by avoiding areas where economies of scale are critical. In short, they need to stop trying to compete against computer systems that can provide more completely basic information better than human agents. They need to rethink how they can differentiate themselves from these systems.

9.6 THE VALUE-ADD OF INTERMEDIATION

For traditional intermediaries that are not producers taking on these roles themselves, as in Sarkar et al.'s model, the lessons of the Internet are that they need to increase their value-add or they will cease to exist. Travel agents are a good case to consider before examining the principles of value-added intermediation.

Will all travel agents disappear or are there important roles they will continue to play? An interesting study to this effect was conducted several years ago.[7] Providing evidence for Sarkar et al.'s prediction, this study found that many functions of travel agents will, indeed, disappear. Frequent, simple transactions, that is, those requiring high economies of scale, will be taken over by cybermediaries and the airline's direct online channels. Even

[6]McCubbrey (1999).
[7]McCubbrey (1999).

low frequency but complex transaction will be diverted to other channels, as travel agents, with their low markups, cannot afford to spend time on one time complex transactions. The result is that travel agents will increasingly focus on frequent, complex transaction such as tour packages and negotiated corporate travel.

What are the underlying aspects of a business that favor cybermediation and direct online sales? Clearly, simple commodity-like goods and straightforward services are susceptible to computer interaction between the firm and the customer. The more complex the transaction, the less capable current systems are to handle the task. Future systems may have enhanced intelligence that will allow for more sophisticated interactions, but for the moment, these will mostly be carried out by human intermediaries using mostly physical processes.

Cybermediaries are also able to handle transactions that travel agents can no longer afford to conduct, such as low frequency, complex transactions.

The general rule seems to be that if the product or service requires more information and analysis than can be conducted through a Web site, then physical intermediation still has a role to play. It is important to remember that as firms facilitate online expert systems and online chat and live talk, the Web will be the medium through which these sales are concluded. There will be a physical component, but the primary channel will be the Internet.

Commentators have added some additional reasons why intermediation in both physical and electronic forms will continue to be important in business life. Ultimately if an intermediary can offer economies of scale or scope to other entities in the value chain, they will survive.[8] Specific roles have been enumerated by many authors,[9] but Table 9.2 covers many of their value-added services.

Table 9.2: Value-Added Roles of Intermediaries and Cybermediaries

Role	Description	Cyber Examples
Search efficiencies and information management	Use knowledge of how to procure items and services; create trading floor for buyers and sellers	expedia.com ebay.com
Routinizing and guaranteeing transactions	Handle complex transactions; insure payments and shipments	ibm.com amex.com
Logistics	Delivery of goods, locally or globally	ups.com
Aggregating demand/ negotiating prices	Gather orders and negotiate prices with client(s)	priceline.com ETNs like Covisint
Creating packages	Break bulk through large-volume purchases, and reassemble into packages	dell.com

---

[8]Alderson (1954); Coyle & Andraski (1990).
[9]Sarkar et al. (1995); Westland & Clark (1999); Wareham & Klein (2002).

9.6.1 Surviving Intermediary Roles

Search Efficiencies and Information Management

Intermediaries fulfill a valuable function when they know more about markets than most buyers and sellers, and they are compensated for this knowledge. Kelley Blue Book (kbb.com), for example, gives potential car sellers information on the trade-in value of their used cars. Sites that offer comparative pricing of a product—such as the auto insurance quotes offered at progressive.com—are other cyber examples of this function. At the Kelley site they also act as a switching yard for sellers of cars, some of these services being referrals to other intermediaries like autobytel.com. If potential buyers choose, they can buy a car directly at carsdirect.com or link to auto dealer sites.

Routinizing and Guaranteeing Transactions

Firms often do not have core competencies to efficiently handle transactions that underlie their business. Traditionally many of these activities have been outsourced to other firms, such as banks and credit card companies in the e-payment arena. The economics of NE favor this transference as well. Moreover, there is empirical evidence that more of such functions will be taken over by intermediaries in cyberspace.[10] IBM routinizes transactions for its clients as an outsourcer; they will host a Web site, build the systems, maintain the databases, and provide a call center. Also known as securitizing the transaction, other intermediaries will ensure that there is no defaulting on either end of the buying channel. The premium they charge is an insurance policy that each end buys.

Logistics

Delivery of goods has always been a major value-added capability of intermediaries. In the case of Dell Computer Corp., for example, logistics intermediaries such as UPS fulfill this role by gathering together monitors from Sony, workstations from Dell, as well as other peripherals from other suppliers and coordinate the delivery of the entire package to the ultimate customer. It is obvious that there are few firms who can handle this level of doorstep distribution. Logistics firms now provide online tracking services so that customers can monitor the processing and delivery of their orders.

Aggregating Demand/Negotiating Prices

Relating to buyers and sellers in a many-to-many relationship, some intermediaries represent the interests of numerous entities by coalescing demand and negotiating prices. The reverse auction model used by priceline.com is a good example of this approach. Priceline aggregates the demand for airline seats by attracting many people to its Web site. Negotiation of the prices is also handled by its engine, which, in effect, joins together the airlines and the flying public. Another example of this model is the electronic trading network. Covisint aggregates the demand of automobile companies for parts and supplies. Bidders for large orders are expected to pass along economies of scale to the purchasers.

---

[10]Storey et al. (1999).

Creating Packages

Intermediaries can purchase goods in large volumes and offer these for sale in assortments that would be extremely costly for buyers to put together on their own. In our discussion of the travel agency business earlier, we indicated that there needed to be value-added services provided, or these intermediaries would be supplanted by cybermediaries. A classic example of such an assortment would be a package offered for tourists. Bundling airfare, tours, rental vehicles, and cruises together and selling these to tourists would be one case where intermediaries cannot be easily replaced. The more commodity-like the products or services, the less likely that these packages can be put together by online providers, but in the online business, the agencies that learn how to exploit the Web for these services will capture a lion's share of business. Firms such as Rosenbluth Travel are trying to do just this (www.rosenbluth.com).

9.7 ATOMIC MODELS AND CYBERMEDIATION

Our discussion of intermediation is slightly at variance with Weill and Vitale's concept of intermediation in their atomic business models, and it is important to make this clear. They define the intermediary atomic model as bringing together buyers and sellers via such services as search engines and auction sites. But the intermediary function as we have developed it in this chapter extends beyond search and auction to include several other atomic models, as shown in Table 9.3. Our notion of intermediation is closely related to intermediaries and intermediation in the traditional bricks and mortar world. Some intermediaries own inventory, and some do not, as we indicated at the beginning of this chapter.

Table 9.3: Intermediary Roles in Atomic Business Models

Weill & Vitale Atomic Model	Intermediary Role Characteristics
Intermediary model	Search efficiencies and information management
Shared infrastructure	Aggregating demand and negotiating prices
VNI	Information management; routinizing and guarantying transactions
Full-service provider	Creating packages; logistics

As seen in Chapter 8, shared infrastructures such as Abacus or Orbitz aggregate the demand of customers for airline seats. From the consumer's point of view, comparison pricing makes these sites as desirable as those of intermediaries such as expedia.com. The reason the airlines created and owned the shared infrastructure is to better control their distribution channels and to not abandon this part of their market to third parties such as Travelocity and Expedia. We are seeing a number of firms moving activities up and down the value chain to take advantage of the new electronic linkages offered by the Web.

VNIs are pure information managers and are highly virtual in their organizational design. They make transactions, such as procurement and distribution, ordinary and allow the franchises, branches, or customer firms to focus on their own core competencies. Their assets are primarily informational, and their value-added is much higher than the atomic intermediaries. This is a form of intermediation that has immense appeal, especially because it tends to lock in complementors.

Finally, full service providers can be highly virtual, especially if they do not own inventory and if they are in information-intensive businesses such as financial services. They offer customers a one-stop service, but unlike the single-point-of-contact model, from multiple and competing providers. They may even coordinate logistics but not handle this themselves and, thus, remain essentially virtual. Firms such as Fidelity are moving aggressively in this arena, and we may see fully functioning examples of this model in the near future.

▶ *CASE STUDY 9-2*

THOMPSON ELECTRONICS AND VENTURA CAPITAL

Bill Thompson walked out of the office of Ventura Capital happier than ever. His electronic equipment company had just received more investment capital to expand and move beyond supplying parts to regional manufacturers. Now, he had several decisions to make.

Thompson Electronics makes batteries for computers. They make the type of battery that provides power to the PC when it is not plugged in. Thus, the system always retains a certain amount of information. They have stable business partners in the region, but now he had the chance to expand. The Internet was really making waves and some of his competitors had recently begun offering their products online. He wondered if this is what he also should do.

Bill knows that Thompson Electronics can provide more value for their shareholders. He thought of several ideas that he might pursue now that he had the cash.

One idea was to begin purchasing the other parts for a PC and manufacture the remainder of the unit in their facilities. He could source the other parts and begin selling directly to consumers via the Internet. In short, he would be creating packages from components.

A second plan centered on the idea that Thompson should harness the knowledge that his company currently has about the electronics market and create a Web site and an emerging business division in the process that would offer comparisons and information about other computer components. The site would offer the company's customers as much information as they needed to make decisions about components.

In addition to creating packages or providing information, Bill thought that Thompson could create an electronic components marketplace. The Web site could offer components from several manufacturers. Each of these would be for sale in an auction style setting on the Web. This was already being done in the auto industry, and he thought that it could work in the electronic component industry as well. The consumers or purchasing companies would win because the savings obtained by economies of scale would be passed to them.

Bill has a meeting at 8:30 A.M. the next morning to discuss the direction for the company with the Board of Directors. Traditionally, the board has agreed with Bill's recommendations. The pressure is enormous. The future of Thompson Electronics is in the balance.

Discussion:
1. Discuss the options Bill is considering. Decide which would be the best alternative and the issues that Bill will have to face to execute the plan.
2. Discuss the effect that Thompson Electronics's e-business will have on stakeholders, business partners, and customers.

9.7.1 Portals and Content Aggregators

How would one categorize the business models of pure play firms such as Yahoo and Amazon? In Weill and Vitale's scheme, they are, at least in part, intermediaries. Yahoo receives content from others such as maps, news, financial quotes, shopping site links, and so forth. Among the many products and services offered at amazon.com are links to its book sales' affiliates, as well as links to its other online shops. The intermediary models that these sites are exploiting have also been called a *portal* or *content aggregator*, and each of these terms describes some of the functionality of these complicated business models. To a large extent, these sites are classic intermediary switchyards.

But these firms are hybrids in that they also offer direct-to-consumer sales. Yahoo sells hosting services. Amazon sells books and other products directly to the consumer as if it were always from its own stock and not being supplied by other parties. What is of greatest interest in all of these analyses, perhaps, is that these Web firms are heavily based on information. They use information to run their enterprises, and they are providing it throughout the site as well. There are physical aspects to the business, to be certain, but the value of the business lies more in the replacement of physical processes with information than in their traditional properties.

As can be seen, portals and content aggregators in the Web world are quintessential cybermediaries. Let's imagine what these businesses would look like if they had a physical manifestation, which will help us understand the extent of the transformation into a company with information-based coordination and provision. Say Yahoo is a retailer such as Wal-Mart. It has a huge distribution system through its corner convenience stores, some of which are franchised and many of which are company-owned. It sells printed information such as maps and newspapers, and it also has a physical ticker for the financial information that many of its patrons value. In another corner of the store is the mailing service, similar perhaps to a Mail Boxes Etc. store. There are many other products and services offered, including greeting cards and the logistics needed to mail them. These few elements are represented symbolically in Figure 9.6. Yahoo actually offers a great deal more than this, but even these reduced set of business activities make the point convincingly. In fact, with Yahoo none of these physical activities is needed because, as an information-based intermediary, Yahoo handles these processes through its systems and through its manipulation of information.

They are a cybermediary, for the most part, and their future success depends on the nature and extent of the overall transition to e-commerce. If the traffic is there, then Yahoo, and those who challenge Yahoo for dominance in this market niche, should have a place in the digital economy.

Figure 9.6   Physical Activities Required for a Yahoo Physical Storefront

9.8 SUMMARY

Intermediation plays a large role in the business world today. Some intermediaries make intermediation the sole purpose of their business, although others find themselves serving in the role of intermediaries, whether or not it is central to their main business model. Intermediaries can be either virtuals or aggregators. Virtuals do not manufacture or own the products or services that they resell. Aggregators may own the products or services, but they do not manufacture or assemble the products or services that they sell. Intermediaries may be involved in disintermediation, reintermediation, or cybermediation.

The discussion of the theory of intermediation states that for commodity purchases and transactions, those that are the least expensive will be generally preferred in the marketplace. Saving the cost of their own time is why consumers prefer to make travel arrangements through intermediaries such as travel agents and travel Web sites. Consumers choose to use an intermediary, such as priceline.com, to book their travel arrangements instead of calling the airlines directly or even using their reintermediated Web sites because of money that can be saved. In return, airlines compete by offering discounts for the use of their online booking services.

Consumers choose intermediaries because of the value-add that they provide. Depending on the service being provided, each intermediary plays a different role in the marketplace. Some intermediaries, such as expedia.com and ebay.com, are known for their search efficiencies and information management. Ibm.com and amex.com routinize and guarantee transactions. Ups.com provides value-add in its logistics. Priceline.com is able to negotiate prices between airlines and customers. Dell.com is able to create packages for consumers. As long as intermediaries can offer economies of scale or scope to other entities in the value chain, they will be successful. If they specialize in a differentiated service or product, then they need to continue to offer something more than what can be acquired over the Web.

Atomic business models explain how intermediaries, such as yahoo.com and amazon.com, bring together buyers and sellers on the Internet. These intermediaries use information to run their businesses and are providing information as a service. These sites have become very popular over the years and will continue to be effective well into the future, as long they are able to bring together buyers and sellers for commodity products and services.

Predictions that intermediators and intermediation on the Internet were not going to disappear and would remain extremely competitive have proven to be true. As long as intermediaries are able to focus on their core competencies and provide pricing or invaluable information to buyers and sellers, they will continue to be successful in the marketplace.

KEY TERMS

Aggregator: May own, but does not produce or assemble goods and services; uses information to match buyers and sellers.

Channel conflict: The clash that occurs when two channels are providing the same service; when, for instance, an organization wishes to drop its intermediary and deal directly with the customer instead of through their intermediary.

Cybermediation: Forming a virtual unit to serve as a Web presence.

Disintermediation: Breaking off with former intermediators.

Intermediators: Entities who serve a market role by bringing together multiple buyers and sellers. Alternatively, an intermediator is any firm or organization that sits at an intermediate position on the value chain, meaning that it does not sit at either end on an end-to-end fulfillment process.

Reintermediation: Reintroducing a mediation into the value chain.

Supplemental intermediaries: Organizations that use the Internet to reinforce existing channels and become their own intermediaries.

Threatened intermediaries: Before the Internet, these organizations offered services that customers valued because their costs were lower; after the Internet, this system was no longer true.

Virtuals: Purely information-based; do not own the products and services that they resell.

REVIEW QUESTIONS

1. Define intermediation.
2. What are intermediaries?
3. Define the two major types of intermediaries.
4. What is a captive agent?
5. What is an independent agent?
6. What is channel conflict?
7. Define disintermediation, reintermediation, and cybermediation.

8. Discuss the meaning of the theory of intermediation. Why were people predicting the death of intermediation with the advent of the Internet?

9. What kind of transactions will likely be taken over by cybermediaries?

10. What are the value-added services provided by intermediators in either the Old or Networked Economy?

11. What is the difference between the atomic models of intermediators and cybermediators as discussed in this chapter?

TOPICS FOR DISCUSSION

1. Discuss the role of an intermediator.

2. Discuss why intermediaries often have information-based services.

3. Discuss the role of virtual and aggregator intermediaries.

4. Distinguish between captive and independent agents.

5. What effect can intermediaries have on organizations that use their services.

6. Discuss the role of mediation in the context of economic theory.

7. Discuss pre-Internet and post-Internet intermediation.

8. Discuss the value-add of intermediation.

9. Discuss the value-added services provided by intermediaries.

10. Discuss the significance of intermediary roles in the Weill-Vitale atomic business models and in cybermediation as conceptualized in this chapter.

INTERNET EXERCISES

1. Call a travel agent and ask for a ticket price to the destination of your choice. Check on the Internet for the same trip and compare the prices.

2. Prepare a spreadsheet comparing the features of expedia.com and travelocity.com.

3. Enter your car information into the Kelley Blue Book site (http://www.kbb.com/) and investigate the value of your car.

4. Go to priceline.com. Explore the site and determine what are the value-adds that would allow this intermediary to compete.

5. Go to the rosenbluth.com site. Explore the site and determine what value-adds would allow this intermediary to compete.

6. Compare the Abacus and Orbitz sites. Compare the services offered.

7. Research Dell's process of creating packages. Write a brief report on the process. Describe how this process has disintermediated traditional firms such as retailers and wholesalers. Is there reintermediation in this process? What would that be?

8. Consider a publishing firm. Express your opinion of the publishing business as a threatened intermediary.

9. Locate an Internet firm specializing in search efficiency and information management and describe its intermediary role.

10. Find an example of a Internet-based full-service provider and describe the range of services offered. Using the theory of intermediation and the value-adds of these roles, you can address the question of whether they can sustain their competitive advantage?

TEAM EXERCISES

1. Buying a Used Car with the Help of Internet Intermediaries

(a) Go to a used car dealer and find a car that your team would be interested in purchasing. Find out all of the specifics about the car—that is, make, model, year, mileage, and price. Also, see how much information the dealership is willing to give you about the history of the car.

(b) Go to edmunds.com to see if the car is listed on the Web site, and if so, does the information the dealership provided your team match the information on the Web?

(c) Go to Kelley Blue Book to see what the value is for the car your team is interested in purchasing.

(d) Finally, go to carfax.com and conduct a free record check to see if the vehicle the dealer is trying to sell your group is a deal or a dud.

Was the information your team found on the Internet more than what the dealership offered you? Was it consistent with what the dealer told you? Prepare a group presentation on your findings.

2. Planning a Vacation with the Help of Internet Intermediation

(a) Choose a location where you want to travel to. Be creative. You can travel anywhere in the world! Call a local travel agent to request information and price your trip—make sure to include airfare, hotel, and rental car.

(b) Now choose an airline that you would like to use to get to your destination and look at the airfares listed on the airline's Web site. Some good examples are Southwest Airlines, American Airlines, and Continental Airlines but feel free to choose any airline.

(c) Now choose a hotel at which you would like to stay. You can check out Marriott, Days Inn, or Radisson. Stay anywhere you like!

(d) Pick a car rental company that you would like to use and pick out your car. Some good sites are Avis and Hertz, but there are many from which to choose.

(e) Finally, go to expedia.com and build your own trip. Let Expedia choose your airline, hotel, and car for you.

(f) Which method of travel planning do you prefer and why? Which trip costs less?

3. Planning and Buying a Computer Online

(a) Your team needs to come up with a scenario in which you are looking to buy a computer for your business, department, school, organization, and so forth.

(b) Use the Internet to do research on what types and configurations of computers are available to you.

(c) Determine as a team what you are looking for in a computer to meet your computing needs.

(e) Determine a budget for this purchase.

(f) Find different models of computers that fit within your budget, and satisfy your needs via the Internet.

(g) Decide, as a team, which computer you are going to purchase.

    1) Explain your team's scenario.

    2) Explain how your group approached each step as well as the results of each step and provide the information you gathered as a result of your research.

    3) Tell us what computer you decided to purchase, and why.

    4) Post the challenges, insights, and benefits of doing this activity online.

4. Intermediaries—Are they helpful to the consumer?

(a) Determine the five most popular Web portals and visit each site.

(b) Discuss the differences between each of the five Web portals. What do these intermediaries offer? How do they benefit the consumer?

5. Atomic Models

(a) Based on the types of atomic models presented in this chapter as being essentially intermediary (Intermediary Model, Shared Infrastructure, Value Net Integrator, Full Service Provider), find three intermediaries that play the role or represent the characteristics of each model.

(b) Give an explanation of why your team chose the intermediaries that you did and describe what characteristics led you to your choices.

6. Value-Added Services

Compare some traditionally customer-oriented businesses and decide how well they handle value-added services.

7. Online trading:

(a) Choose any two online trading companies. Which two did your team choose?

(b) What additional services (besides stock purchasing) did they offer?

(c) Which provides the best value-added services?

8. Another method of providing additional services is through cybermediation, that is, acting as a go-between to provide another business's services to the customer. Compare and contrast the Web sites homeportfolio.com and improvenet.com. If you were remodeling your bathroom, which service would you most likely use and why?

INTERNET RESOURCES

Ding Dong, Web Calling (http://www.business2.com/articles/mag/0,1640,14266,FF .html): Learn how Avon is assisting their sales people in an e-commerce initiative.

The Role of Intermediaries in the Development of Trust on the WWW: The Use and Prominence of Trusted Third Parties and Privacy Statements (http:// www.ascusc.org/jcmc/vol5/issue3/palmer.html):

Abstract: "Developing trust between suppliers and consumers is critical for the continued growth of Internet commerce. This article presents an empirical investigation into how firms promote trust by exploring the use and prominence of Trusted Third Parties (TTPs) and privacy statements. The Web sites of 102 publicly held firms with predominantly Inernet based businesses were examined for their use of TTPs and privacy statements, the number of links, currency of the Web site, length of time the Web site had been operating, traffic, and financial performance. Surprisingly, only 17 of the firms utilized trusted third parties and only 45 had privacy statements. The article presents a methodology for the analysis of four propositions that explore the relationship of embeddedness and a firm's length of time online to use and prominence of TTPs and privacy statements. The exploratory data in this article clearly supports the proposition that the use of TTPs and privacy statements increase with the embeddedness of the Web site. The article then discusses the potential reasons for this finding including how TTPs strategically solicit firms and why trusted firms may be more likely to be embedded. The remaining three propositions show mixed results but provide insight into the strategic use of TTPs and privacy statements. One key insight is that TTPs and privacy statements are actually used quite differently by firms to promote trust in Internet commerce.

REFERENCES

Alderson, W. "Factors Governing the Development of Marketing Channels." In *Marketing Channels for Manufactured Products*, R. M. Clewett, ed. Richard D. Irwin, Inc., Homewood, IL, 1954.

Benjamin, R., and Rolf Wigand. "Electronic Markets and Virtual Value Chains on the Information Superhighway." *Sloan Management Review*, 36, 2, Winter 1995, 62–72.

Choudhury, V., K. S. Hartzel, and B. R. Konsynski. "Uses and Consequences of Electronic Markets: An Empirical Investigation in the Aircraft Parts Industry." *MIS Quarterly*, 22, December 1998, 471–507.

Coyle, J. J., and J. C. Andraski. "Managing Channel Relationships." *Proceedings of the Annual Conference of the Council of Logistics Management*, 1990, 245–258.

Malone, T. W., J. Yates, and R. I. Benjamin. "Electronic Markets and Electronic Hierarchies: Effects of Information Technology on Market Structure and Corporate Strategies." *Communications of the ACM*, 30, 6, June 1987, 484–497.

McCubbrey, D. "Disintermediation and Reintermediation in the U.S. Air Travel Distribution Industry: A Delphi Study." *Communications of the AIS*, 1, 18, 1999, 1–39.

Sarkar, M. B., B. Butler, and C. Steinfield. "Intermediaries and Cybermediaries: A Continuing Role for Mediating Players in the Electronic Marketplace." *Journal of Computer Mediated Communication*, 1, 3, 1995, 1–14.

Spulbler, D. F. *Market Microstructure: Intermediaries and the Theory of the Firm*. Cambridge University Press, Cambridge, U.K., 1999.

Storey, V., D. Straub, K. Stewart, and R. Welke. "A Conceptual Investigation of the Electronic Commerce Industry." *Communications of the ACM*, 43, 7, July 2000, 117–123.

Wareham, J., and R. Klein. "Intermediation in Five Inclusive Stages: Estimates of Fiancial Performance and Growth Strategies." Working paper, Georgia State University, 2002.

Westland, J. C., and T. H. K. Clark. *Global Electronic Commerce: Theory and Case Studies*. MIT Press, Cambridge, MA, 1999.

CHAPTER 10

STRATEGIC PARTNERING, OUTSOURCING, AND VIRTUAL ORGANIZATIONS

▶ UNDERSTANDING PARTNERING ISSUES AND BUILDING VIRTUAL
ORGANIZATIONS

How do managers design their organization to benefit from NE? What is a virtual organization, and how does it differ from firm designs built around physical processes? What are the relationships the company forms to become more virtual, and how do managers make decisions about the value of these linkages? Can one really cooperate with competitors? How and under what conditions? These and other issues will be covered in this chapter.

LEARNING OBJECTIVES FOR THIS CHAPTER

- To distinguish between physical and virtual organizational designs
- To detail types of virtuality in the partnering continuum
- To identify the relationship between managerial control, core competencies, and selective sourcing
- To articulate reasons for making the sourcing decision
- To use cost/benefit analysis tools
- To explain the three levels of decision making in partnering
- To discuss the objectives and effects of information visibility

▶ *CASE STUDY 10-1*

ORBITZ.COM: ALLIANCE OF COMPETITORS

In 2001, orbitz.com was founded by five airlines—American, Continental, Delta, Northwest, and United—as a joint venture. Orbitz currently offers airfares from over 450 airlines, along with options for hotel reservations, car rentals, and vacation packages. Orbitz receives over 6 million visits per day and is selling over 300, 000 tickets per day. In less than a year, Orbitz became the third largest travel site in United States and is growing at a rapid pace.

Orbitz is a very unique company because it is a joint venture of five competitors. The biggest strength of Orbitz is that these various airlines all agree to give the lowest airfare to Orbitz, meaning that Orbitz always has an advantage over supply compared to its competitors.

However, Orbitz is not without its problems. The partners involved are competitors, and it is likely that they will disagree on the strategy of the company. Similarly, partners may not always want to give the lowest fares to Orbitz—they may want to sell them directly to the consumers themselves, because most also have ticket-selling services. Also, proprietary sales information may become available to partners through the Web site's operation. These potential risks may undermine the success of Orbitz in the future.

Orbitz can solve the problem if the airlines involved are coordinating with each other in routes and airfare prices. Such an action may solve the internal problem in Orbitz but may lead to the accusation of harming competition. Already, the Department of Transportation (DOT) has been investigating the business of Orbitz. Although the DOT has not been able to find evidence of any illegal action, they may put restraints on Orbitz's future growth. It will be interesting to see how the business structure of Orbitz evolves in the near future with the challenge of coordinating among competitors without forming an alliance that harms competition.

Discussion:
1. Discuss the ways in which participating in this strategic alliance could lead to a loss of competitive edge?
2. Describe the ownership of resources in this business model.

Sources:
http://www.orbitz.com/

10.1 INTRODUCTION

This chapter expands on issues having to do with strategizing for e-commerce by looking at the partners needed to carry off any traditional business, let alone an e-business. The quality of the relationships with these partners and the mutual profitability that the relationship brings is one of the most strategic issues one could imagine. What is interesting in this is that a modern manager must think beyond the old ways of thinking and extend boundaries to include traditional competitors.

Focus on NE: eBay's Partners

In 1995, Pierre Omidyr developed eBay, which is now one of the leading online marketplaces for the sale of goods and services. The company offers more than 18,000 categories to many individuals and businesses. eBay generates its revenue through listing and selling fees, and the community includes 49.7 million registered users. It is considered one of the most popular Web sites for shopping. The rapidly growing company offers new services that include wireless access for phones, PDAs, and pagers to a variety of wireless applications, such as used cars auctions. They are expanding into new countries (Australia, Brazil, Spain, Switzerland, and Taiwan) through joint ventures, site launches, and acquisitions.

The community involves diverse groups of people. They include individual buyers and sellers, small businesses, and some Fortune 100 companies. Some of the features of the Web site include a discussion and chat board and "Neighborhood Watch." The discussion and chat board allows users to meet other members to chat. If someone has questions or concerns, they can get feed back from other members of the community. Members in the community share information on vacations, products, collectibles, vendors, service, and a variety of other topics through use of the discussion boards and chat rooms. "Neighborhood Watch" groups, formed by members, make sure that the company's guidelines and policies are being met throughout the site. eBay offers different sources and features online. Billpoint is an online payment service that allows customers to pay through a credit card. The community offers half.com, a fixed pricing trading online. The sellers set a fixed price for items at the time that the item is listed. The half.com site offers high-quality, previously owned mass-market goods. With these options, eBay Stores are able to provide traditional and fixed styles of auctioning.

There are many countries that represent eBay internationally. eBay is continually expanding its services all over the world. Currently they have specific sites in Austria, Australia, Canada, France, Germany, Ireland, Italy, Korea, New Zealand, Switzerland, and the United Kingdom.

An automotive marketplace has opened on eBay, featuring such products as auto parts, cars, and motorcycles. They also provide services such as auto insurance, escrow, financing, inspections, lemon check, title and registration, and vehicle shipping.

eBay offers professional services by providing a destination on the Web site to find professional and freelancers for all kinds of businesses.

The company offers special features called Buy It Now, Local Trading, and Live Auctions. Using Buy It Now, the buyer can purchase an item without waiting until the end of the auction. The sellers get to sell their items quickly through this feature. eBay has 60 markets throughout the U.S. Customers can use Local Trading to find items they are interested in that are near their location. This feature gives customer an additional convenience with items such as furniture, automobiles, and appliances. The Live Auctions feature allows millions of online buyers to bid in real-time on items being sold on the sales floors of auction houses.

Sources:
http://www.ebay.com/aboutebay/releases/index.html

10.2 THE CORPORATE FOOD CHAIN

Before discussing the organizational design issues associated with partnering, it is important that a relevant range of corporate structures and goals be established. In this book we are focusing on informational versus physical processes as one of the key distinguishing features of NE and e-commerce. Firms that focus extensively on informational processes and minimize their engagement with physical processes are known as "virtual" firms. The more virtual a firm is, the more it is dependent for profitability on its intellectual assets as opposed to its physical assets.

We need a brief definition of *virtual* design to use in this chapter. It is shown in Figure 10.1. "Virtual" firms are those that transfer noncore physical processes to contractual or even informal arrangements. They also tend to move away from co-location of assets, including human resources. They are highly decentralized, therefore. Please note that inherent in the design of the firm is an assumption that electronic connections will be substituting for such things as on-site managerial monitoring of work processes, daily face-to-face meetings, and (of course) physical processes.

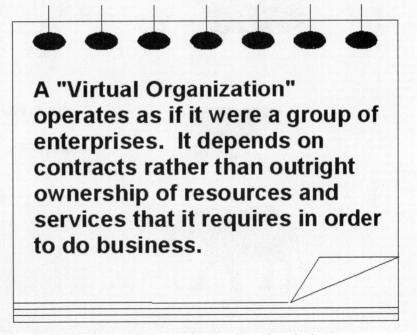

Figure 10.1   Working Definition of a "Virtual" Design for an Organization

Varying in the extent to which they are committed to physical processes as core competencies, corporations are similar to the ecological food chain, as illustrated in Figure 10.2. Firms that are lower on the food chain consume more physical resources to survive. Their "food supply" is directly linked to physical processes, similar to the linkage between animals and to the earth itself and its products, such as grass, leaves, and plankton. Animals lower on the food chain tend to be larger but, like elephants and water buffalo, cannot move with the quickness of those higher up on the food chain. The same observation might be made about physically oriented versus virtual firms.

Animals high on the food chain cannot volume-process physical resources, such as grass, in and of themselves. They must have this processed by animals lower on the food chain. Although they depend on the animals lower on the chain as their food source, they can never completely deplete this resource or they themselves will perish. The stronger and healthier the lower parts of the chain are, the healthier and stronger are the higher parts of the food chain.

Similar to the animal realm, firms on the lower end of the food chain process large volumes of physical resources as their stock-in-trade. Thus, these firms are likened to grass-eaters in natural settings. The bulk of an elephant's diet is vegetative, and, because of the food value of these resources, it takes a huge quantity to maintain life.

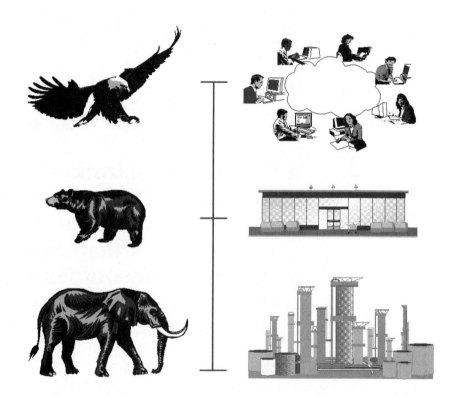

Figure 10.2   Ecological Food Chain Compared to Corporate "Food Chain" for NE

By the same token, physical processes in a business tend to be labor and capital intensive, requiring large quantities of raw materials, as in the oil industry example on the right side of Figure 10.2. To take another case of a physically resource-intensive industry, the vehicular industry, on the whole, regards the manufacturing of automobiles and trucks as their core competency. The complexity of this enterprise is reflective of a vast array of physical processes required for the design, assembly of raw materials and parts, and the manufacturing of the finished product.

Midway up the food chain are animals and firms that are not as focused on physical volume. Omnivorous animals such as the bear are part way up the food chain in that they are both eaters of vegetation like berries and predators on salmon and other animals. To the extent to which their diet is based on the flesh of other animals, they are higher up on the food chain. Because they do not have to make protein internally, as it is present in their food, they have a more efficient intake of food than grass-eaters.

Firms somewhere in the middle of the corporate food chain are like the bear in that they do not have an organizational design that is completely physical in its orientation, nor is it completely virtual. The scope of core competencies for such firms is usually narrower than for firms that focus on physical processes. Many of these processes have been out-sourced or are being handled by partners. The firm may still have a fairly large physical presence, as in the case of the large insurance carriers in the United States. Connections with agents are largely virtual, but insurers (carriers) are still heavily into co-location and campus-like structures. For this reason, they may be thought of as being partway up the corporate food chain toward virtuality.

In nature, the top of the food chain is the predator, an animal like the eagle. An eagle's diet is resource lean in that it subsists completely on the protein provided by other animals. In this sense, they need far less volume in their diet.

Cybermediaries on the Web are examples of an industry that is largely virtual. Firms such as Yahoo have low inventories of physical objects (for sale or for internal supply) and have fewer physical processes than a traditional intermediary, such as a wholesaler. How can the cybermediaries pull this off? The answer, in large part, is through partnerships and outsourcing, topics that lie at the heart of this chapter.

The ability of a cybermediary to be profitable is not necessarily related to how virtual it is, however. As we saw in the last chapter, many cybermediaries are still trying to find areas of profitability within the business model. The point is more that a virtual design makes sense for these firms in that their business is basically information, and the need for physical processes is (and should be) low.

The food chain metaphor has some usefulness and some limitations. It is useful to realize, for example, that even in e-commerce there must always be some entities engaged in processing physical resources. Moreover, until robotization succeeds in removing the bulk of labor from manufacturing and assembly processes, the greater part of organiza-tional entities will still be engaged in these activities. As discussed above, firms that are good at physical processes can still automate and informate these processes and offload physical processes to machines. But, although this moves them higher on the food chain in this dimension, it does not completely eliminate physical processes, even in these specific areas.

As an example, the automobile industry may lower the number of physical processes through robotics. Nevertheless, these robots have to be created, programs have to be built for them, the robots have to be installed and maintained by workers, and the process of building automobiles must still be managed and coordinated. In some cases, the firm is moving higher on the food chain by depending on others to create the technology needed to build automobiles. Yet the robotics firms have moved in at the bottom of the chain, to a large extent, with a new set of physical processes.

From an industrial and social standpoint, this is not a one-for-one replacement. Over time, the greater productivity resulting from the use of robotics in the automobile industry reduces the overall need for physical processes, certainly by human beings, and, because of its efficiency, even by machines. Even adding up the physical processes required to build robots in the robotics factory (which itself can employ robots for greater productivity, of course) results in a net gain for the industry and the society. Fewer physical resources are consumed to make automobiles, in the final analysis.

Virtual organizations are bound together through their electronic connections, as in Figure 10.2. Their core competencies lie in their abilities to manage relationships with firms that take care of the physical components in the value chain. There are, undoubtedly, few firms that are completely virtual, but there are many firms, even large firms, that are anchored in or moving toward this end of the food chain. These firms own few physical assets and employ their talents in acquiring intellectual assets when and where they need them. They depend heavily on the skills of their employees to innovate and differentiate themselves from their competitors in terms of their leanness.

In Figure 10.3, physical organizational designs are compared and contrasted with virtual designs. As noted in our discussion of food chains, virtual firms rely on systems and people more than on physical assets. Physical assets are needed to conduct physical processes and so the needs of the two types of organizations are different. In Chapter 2, we described the decreasing returns to scale that are inherent in traditional industrial models, and noted that firms heavily engaged in exploiting physical processes are subject to these limitations. Associated with these limitations are the fact that large pools of employees are costs that are high, even in good times, and hard to displace in bad times. The focus on physical assets means that there are huge capital investments involved, and these are not readily moved into new business production. A chip factory is not easily converted to a factory that makes shoes.

Physical Design ("Bricks and mortar")		Virtual Design ("Clicks")	
Characteristics		**Characteristics**	
1	Focus on physical processes as core competencies	1	Focus on informational processes as core competencies
2	Main resources required: (a) raw materials, (b) machine tools, (c) funds for investment in physical assets, (d) facilities, (e) coordination and control systems, (f) technical and managerial skill sets	2	Main resources required: (a) coordination and control systems, (b) technical and managerial skill sets, (c) funds for investment in human assets
3	Liabilities: decreasing returns to scale; lack of HR flexibility; slow movement into new businesses	3	Limitations: lack of business history or experience with this design; branding issues; requires higher skill levels; loss of intellectual capital can be devastating
4	Strengths: requires lower skill levels as percentage of employee base	4	Strengths: can lead to higher margins from increasing returns to scale; HR flexibility; rapid movement into new businesses

Figure 10.3   Physical versus Virtual Organizational Designs

Virtual firms are managed through the Internet. Their employees may or may not be physically co-located. They are often physically dispersed, needing only occasional face-to-face meetings and on-site observations. They have the advantage that they can command high margins if they are able to capitalize on their intellectual assets and to own intellectual properties that create economic rents (profits), or if these assets allow them to innovate and move decisively into new markets and business ventures. The need for extremely bright people is a disadvantage to virtual firms in that bright people are well paid and are sought after by others, including competitors. The loss of major players in a virtual firm can have a greater effect than in traditional firms where their influence is not so profound or where they do not make up such a large percentage of the workforce. As illustrated in Figure 10.4, they maintain extensive electronic connections with their stakeholders.

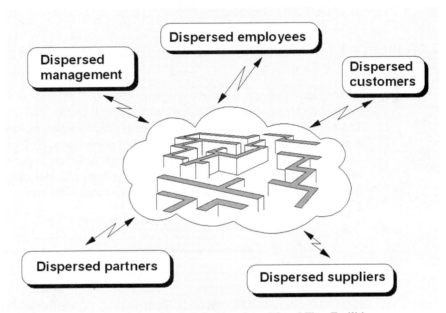

Figure 10.4   Virtual Connectivity with Stakeholders from Virtual Firm Facilities

10.3 AFFINITY BETWEEN VIRTUAL ORGANIZATIONAL DESIGNS AND NE

Besides the obvious implication of the need for electronic network connectivity in virtual firms, what is the underlying affinity between NE and virtuality, if any? NEOs seek to substitute information for physical processes, and they need information processing and networks to accomplish this. So it is no surprise that a virtual organization depends heavily on client-server network architectures.

In the GSU study that is the empirical basis for much of this book, respondents reported that they saw a close affinity between virtual organizations and e-commerce. They stressed their movement away from co-location of workers. Indeed, e-commerce allows firms to promote telework. NE also encourages sales-at-a-distance, which removes the need for the traditional breadth and depth of retail channels. Finally, disintermediation of traditional intermediaries is a natural outgrowth of NE. In all cases, the firms are able to economize on their employee base while increasing productivity.

What was extraordinary about the responses from this study was that many respondents, especially those from the insurance industry, were not enamored with the idea that their firms were becoming more virtual. In some cases, they were personally disenchanted with the prospect. But no one that we spoke with felt that the change was anything but inevitable. Virtuality was a natural by-product of a firm's move to NE, according to even the most skeptical participants.

Given that virtual organizational designs are important in Net-enhanced organizations, what are the ways in which a firm becomes more virtual? Clearly, the firm must reduce its involvement with physical processes. This means that other firms must take over some of these activities for the firm.

10.4 SOURCING TO ARM'S-LENGTH VENDORS VIS-A-VIS STRATEGIC PARTNERS

Before discussing the decisions that managers must make about outsourcing their activities and finding partners for initiatives, we need to outline the choices that are available. There are a range of options for the nature of the partnering relationship, in addition to an arrangement with competitors, which will be covered later. As Figure 10.5 indicates, firms can invest in individual transactions, on the one hand, or they can form a partnership or strategic alliance, on the other.[1] These anchor opposite ends of a continuum that ranges from little involvement between the firms to a strategically critical interaction.

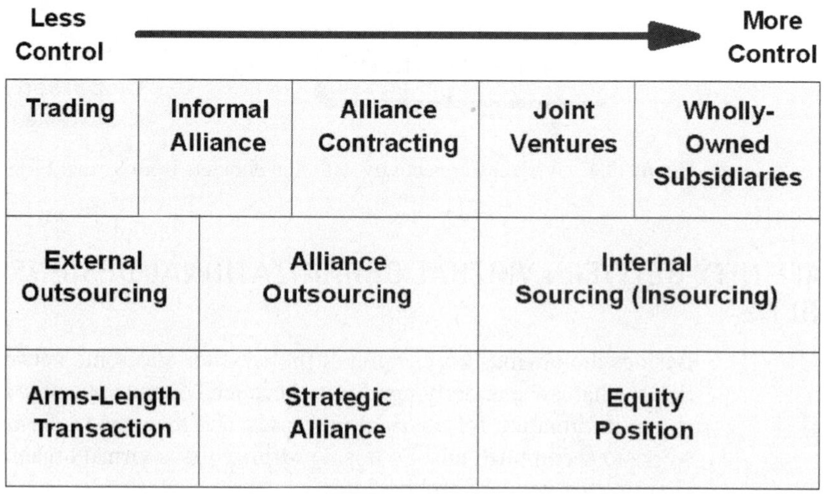

Less Control				More Control
Trading	Informal Alliance	Alliance Contracting	Joint Ventures	Wholly-Owned Subsidiaries
External Outsourcing	Alliance Outsourcing		Internal Sourcing (Insourcing)	
Arms-Length Transaction	Strategic Alliance		Equity Position	

-Based partly on: *Heeks, 1996*

Figure 10.5   The Partnership Continuum

[1]Heeks, 1996.

In an arm's-length transaction, the firms involved are interested in the short-term mutual benefits of the exchange. One firm is being hired to provide commodities or commodity-like services. There may or may not be contracts that are more than the built-in contracts that occur with any purchase. An example of such an arm's-length transaction is the purchasing of hardware. Let's say that a firm visits Compaq's Web site and purchases some heavy-duty servers. The implied contract (or warranty) is that the servers will work as advertised. If the purchase specifies a main memory of 10 GB, the servers that are delivered must have this feature.

From the standpoint of the firm, there is no necessary, further connection between the purchaser and vendor beyond the sale itself. Installation and maintenance is the responsibility of the firm unless this value-add is also purchased from the vendor. Beyond laws that require vendors to warranty manufacturing specs, the arm's-length relationship is concluded.

The opposite end of the continuum is not technically an outsourcing or partnering arrangement at all. Firms can use their own hierarchy to carry out an activity, known as *insourcing,* or they can buy other firms, which gives them an equity position in the firms' products and services. This form of vertical integration was common in the robber-baron era when, for example, Andrew Carnegie bought the railroads and shipping lines to transport his iron ore from Minnesota to Pennsylvania across the Great Lakes. Physical integration of firms is the exact opposite of virtualizing the organization, and so this end of the continuum must be scrutinized carefully by firms who are trying to focus on their core competencies.

The central position on the partnership continuum is the strategic alliance. This is the relationship that allow firms to exert medium levels of control over outcomes while still abandoning the physical side of corporate activity. The legal and technical relationship can be through informal arrangements, such as simple business plans, or they can be through formal legal contracts. Kodak's outsourcing arrangements with its partners, IBM, DEC, and Businessland, were based on informal plans.[2] Other organizations have well-specified contracts that lay out exactly what each party is required to do.[3]

10.5 AN EXAMPLE OF PARTNERING IN TELECOMMUNICATIONS

How should managers determine that a complementor is a desirable partner in an initiative, particularly an e-commerce initiative? NE Principles should tell us how and when one should form relationships with complementors, even in the absence of any other established ways of analyzing the decision. As we have already discussed, organizations need to find ways to substitute informational processes for physical processes in order to derive the great potential benefits of e-commerce. How does this happen when we open up the possibility that the firm does not have to always source all processes internally?

We can approach this crucial managerial option by examining a case in which a firm outsources its telecommunications to a partnering firm. If the firm has always managed its own internal telecommunications network, why would it be desirable and what would it look like if the firm decided to allow external firms to provide these services? E-commerce Wannabee Company (EWC) has a staff of five persons handling their telecommunication networks. These people make decisions about purchasing or leasing the routers and

---

[2] Applegate and Montealegre (1995).
[3] McFarlan and Seger (1993).

telecommunication preprocessors and postprocessors that the firm requires in order to efficiently process network traffic, both for those processors that originate from inside the organization and for those that seek entrance from outside. They also design the entire internal network so that new LANs are either on the company backbone, or have gateways that allow them to directly transact business with the outside world. In e-commerce, they would also be responsible for the Web servers that will service page requests from outside the organization. Some of these servers may be straightforward, servicing with no sophisticated capabilities beyond HTML. Others may be Java servers that need to be able to process potentially hundreds of thousands of lines of code quickly for a rapid response to customers.

There are many physical processes that are involved in such an internal operation. Hardware such as routers and servers must be brought in and configured for the devices and gateways that each needs to talk with. Cabling needs to be strung. Access to external networks and the establishment of this physical connectivity needs to be negotiated, signed off on, and paid for. Maintenance of the internal network is an ongoing challenge.

Deciding to shed its internal networking capabilities is a complex decision, but firms that have adopted NE Principle #1 (that is, *Substitution of Less Expensive, More Effective Information-Driven Processes for Physically Driven Processes*) will see the value of doing this in the case of telecommunication departments. Assuming for the moment that the many other considerations for outsourcing make sense, the firm should move in this direction because it removes one additional set of physical processes that impede the firm's flexibility and rapid movement into new businesses.

Organizations cannot simply shed processes that they were either acceptably or marginally good at without replacing this skill base with another core competency. The core competency that replaces the knowledge and capabilities of working physically with routers, cables, servers, and the software that is resident on these devices is the ability to manage others who, in turn, do this for the firm. In short, intellectual capital in the form of management of the outsourcing relationship must be built in order to shed the physical processes,

Substituting information—which means people, intellectual capital, and human capital—for physical capital requires a new level of coordination.[4] It also requires new design skills in many cases. If one moves up the food chain, the pure virtual organization is a pure management organization. Like the VNI, it coordinates everything. Resembling an intellectual holding company, it owns nothing other than investments in other people's firms. It manages an array of activities that eventually lead to a customer, but does not itself take on the day-to-day management responsibility.

10.6 MANAGERIAL CONTROL, CORE COMPETENCIES, AND SELECTIVE SOURCING

It would be the height of irresponsibility for firms to outsource firm activities and then to exercise no managerial control over these activities. How does a firm maintain its oversight over other firms while continuing to focus on its core competencies? The argument in this text is that managing-systems integrators and outsourcers, whether these are strategic alliances or simply arm's-length transactions, are (and must be) core competencies of

---

[4]Crowston (1997); Malone and Crowston (1994).

the firm. Fortunately, the control that the firm maintains is not complete control; it is a partial but sufficient control.

In order to understand what control firms retain when they outsource, it is important to realize that there are two forms of control: outcome control and process control. Outcome controls are measures that a manager can take with respect to performance. Process controls are the day-to-day task assignments and oversight exercised by operational level management. Outsourcers undertake process controls while the firm itself needs to be aware of and act on outcome controls. Reports on performance or, in the case of information systems contracts, service-level agreements (SLAs), are required by most outsourcing contracts and are, hence, available to the firm's managers.

Thus, in virtualizing its activities, the firm reduces its managerial responsibilities by hiring agents to do this. Strategic partners or outsourcers take over the responsibility for controlling the everyday carrying out of necessary tasks. Part of why the firm is paying the partner is intended to ensure that this control is exerted.

For firms that are displacing more and more of their traditional physical actions to others, the question arises as to how this displacement helps firms concentrate on their real core competencies. Let's take an example of a firm that ceases to manufacture its products, and focuses instead on assembling components created by others. The manufacture of components needs to meet certain specifications, and the firm's managers will now be given reports by the outsourcers on quality control checks on these specifications. The firm's managers must have the ability to recognize where and when quality is slipping, if it is, and to take corrective action quickly with the outsourcer. Therefore, the outcome controls that are retained by the organization become core competencies when a firm virtualizes.

This argument will be made in other contexts, but it is important to recognize at the outset that all entities that play a role in the firm's electronic value chain must be controlled and coordinated. If the firm lacks this capability, it should never outsource, and thus never virtualize.

Before closing this topic, it is interesting to note that suppliers can be viewed as firm activities that have not been vertically integrated, and that these should also fall into the category of a necessary firm core competency. If a firm decided to vertically integrate completely, it would supply its own electricity, its own water, and so forth. In this event, it would be necessary to ensure that the infrastructure operated properly and consistently. Firms would again have to exert process controls as well as outcome controls over the provision of water and electricity.

Let's assume that the firm later decides to outsource these services. At this point, it would be outsourcing the electricity service and the water production to utilities and must oversee the performance of these outsiders. The fascinating point of this scenario is that suppliers, outsourcers, and strategic partners are all subject to the same analysis. The basic underlying question is whether the firm chooses to carry out an activity itself or whether this is provided by another organization in which it has no equity position.

The essential issue, in short, is a sourcing question that basically destroys distinctions between suppliers and other provisioners, including competitors. The ultimate questions for the firm are whether a given activity is a unique, distinctive skill for the firm and the related question of who should do it in the event that the firm cannot or should not.

If the argument for retaining in the firm core competencies and outsourcing non-core competencies is accepted, then the firm will be more often engaged in *selective outsourcing* rather than *total outsourcing* of certain functions. Consider the case of Web application development. A firm may not feel that the creation and enhancement of computer applications is related to their marketing innovativeness, which is their perceived core competency. But, in fact, the firm gains a real-time advantage by converting its marketing ideas into applications and using their Web site to attract new customers. So the applications that execute the marketing vision is inextricably bound up in what the customer responds to. Could this activity be outsourced? Sure. Would the firm experience the risk that the outsourcer would not be able to dedicate the time and talent necessary to rapidly integrate new marketing approaches into the Web site? Sure.

Firms need to be prudent in not outsourcing their core competencies, which are the origin of their competitive advantage. Straub, Weill, and Stewart (2002) have found evidence that managers are sensitive to this issue and tend not to over-outsource.

10.7 MAKING THE SOURCING DECISION

When should an NEO source a component, service, or process beyond its boundaries? When should it go to the marketplace to carry out some of its essential activities? This is the rudimentary "buy versus make" decision that firms have been making since the beginning of commerce and trade. The thinking on this has been helped in recent years, however, by theories about when it is advisable and when it is not. Table 10.1 shows the four basic reasons for sourcing outside the organization.[5]

Table 10.1: Sourcing Decision Factors

	Reasons for Sourcing Outside the Organization
1	The activity under question does not concern strategic assets of the company, nor is it a core competency; outsourcing would allow the firm to focus more on its core capabilities.
2	The cost to go outside is considerably less than doing it internally.
3	There will be an increased flexibility in personnel because the services can be acquired as needed; costs move from being fixed to being variable.
4	Other organizations are outsourcing this function, and this encourages the firm to follow suite.

[5]Much of this reasoning is derived from Lacity and Hirscheim (1993).

10.7.1 Reason 1: Achieving Strategic Focus

Managers should always make important decisions for strategic reasons, and the best reason to outsource a process, in and of itself, is to allow the firm to focus more on what it is really good at. Most organizations are not experts, nor want to be experts, at preparing food for their employees. So this is a function that distracts the firm from its real purpose and its "talent." Figure 10.6 illustrates this critical point.

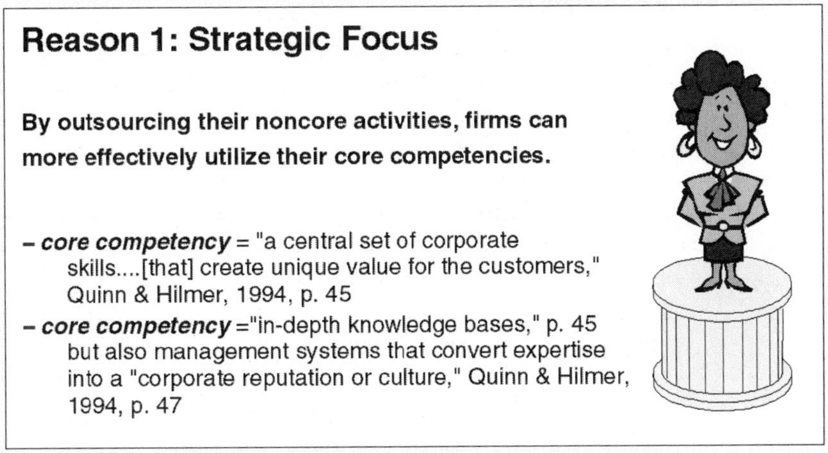

Reason 1: Strategic Focus

By outsourcing their noncore activities, firms can more effectively utilize their core competencies.

– *core competency* = "a central set of corporate skills....[that] create unique value for the customers," Quinn & Hilmer, 1994, p. 45
– *core competency* ="in-depth knowledge bases," p. 45 but also management systems that convert expertise into a "corporate reputation or culture," Quinn & Hilmer, 1994, p. 47

Figure 10.6   Outsourcing Reason 1

There are cases in which it makes sense *not* to hire an external organization to prepare food for employees. Chick-fil-A is a large fast-food franchised corporation headquartered in Atlanta, Georgia. Their stock-in-trade is serving delicious chicken-based fast-food entrees. In this case, it makes sense for the firm to handle the preparation of food for employees internally. Employees can be used to test new products, and new procedures and technology can be tested out before moving them to the field. But, for most organizations, the employee cafeteria is not a core competency.

In the technical arena, there are numerous examples of outsourcing that come to mind. In the late 1980s Kodak decided to outsource their data centers because they distracted the firm from their mission.[6] It is difficult to argue with this logic. Kodak is a film and image company that also has synergistic interests in chemicals. They are not data processing specialists.

If Kodak had determined in their strategic analysis of their businesses that they had a special talent for data processing and that this could become a major income source for them, then it would have made sense to continue to provide for these services in-house. Many NEOs find themselves in this position in that the creation of the Web site and the integration of the site with legacy, back-office systems is an expertise that the firm has painfully acquired. Some firms, such as Amazon, decided to capitalize on this systems development capability and to market it to others. Ironically, one of the firms that has bought Amazon's handling of customer transactions is one of their competitors, Borders.

[6]Applegate and Montealegre (1995).

Later in the book we will discuss the question of whether this was a good decision for either Borders or Amazon, but for the moment it is sufficient to notice that there were strategic elements in thinking through this decision for these firms.

Strategies only work if they can be executed and the other reasons for outsourcing may have a bearing on whether a strategic decision to insource or outsource is implementable. So, in a sense, this decision is always a holistic decision. No single reason could or should dominate the decision.

10.7.2 Reason 2: Cost Savings

Cost is the second major reason for having someone else provide a service or product for your use, as depicted in Figure 10.7. If your organization does not specialize in janitorial services, for instance, it is unlikely that having your own janitorial staff can be very cost-effective. Firms achieve economies of scale and economies of expertise when they focus their energies on a limited set of tasks and, under these circumstances and in the case where these economies achieved by the outsourcer are passed on to their clients, it makes sense to outsource. Cost should not be the driving factor, however, if the asset is strategic.

Reason 2: Cost Savings

By outsourcing activities that cost more to privision internally, firms can save money and displace fixed costs with variable costs.

Vendors argue that they can recapture scale because they can specialize in a fuctional speciality and lower costs because of volume discounts, sharing of resources and expertise, etc.

  ▶ **Their savings, they argue, are passed on to their clients**

Figure 10.7   Outsourcing Reason 2

Suppose that Intel outsourced the processes that are used in their factories to make chips. Even if another firm could do this less expensively, would it make sense for Intel to suppose that another firm without their reputation for quality would be able to deliver the equivalent product? Moreover, what would happen to the intellectual capital that had been built up around chip making? It is certainly conceivable that Intel might conclude someday that they are chip designers and not chip makers, which is the decision Sun Microsystems has made, but as long as they consider themselves to be consummate chip makers, they should not outsource this process to others, even if the price were right.

Cost is a dominant consideration for many managers, so much so that it is stronger predictor of the choice to outsource than any other single factor.[7] When we think of these kinds of costs, we are referring to what are known as *production* costs. These are the costs that are directly relevant to carrying out the activity. There are other costs as well. These are the costs of searching for, deciding on, and negotiating the contract for a complementor, as shown in Table 10.2. They also include the ongoing costs of monitoring the complementor. What is critical in calculating the cost advantage offered by a vendor is what this advantage looks like once the sometimes-large transaction costs are taken into account. After all, top management time is a precious commodity, and every minute spent considering how to structure a strategic alliance subtracts from the cost advantage of going to the marketplace. These transaction costs are often called "friction," and they represent the hassle of "going to the market."

Table 10.2: Transaction Costs Involved in Moving to the Marketplace

	Sample Transaction Costs
1	Preparing RFPs
2	Evaluating bids
3	Travel expenses for user sites
4	Management reviewing and decision time
5	Preparing and negotiating contracts
6	Insuring or bonding against contractor nonperformance
7	Ongoing monitoring of work of the complementor

Ang and Straub (1998) studied the relative role of production cost and transaction costs in managers' thinking and found that they were both important, but that production costs were overwhelmingly the major factor. This stress on unadjusted cost savings to the detriment of real or actual cost savings could lead to significant management errors.

Let's say that the cost advantage of hiring outsiders to maintain Web servers for a large firm is U.S. $500,000 per year. And, for the sake of argument, let's say that the transaction costs are U.S. $700,000 one time costs and U.S. $200,000 per year ongoing monitoring and bonding costs. It is clear that if the client managers also consider the time value of money, the cost advantage of this bid may not lead to a positive cash flow for some time to come. If the reason for outsourcing is that the activity is not in the realm of the firm's core competencies, then the firm may decide to use the complementor irrespective of the cost equations. The point here is that the cost estimates need to be as accurate as possible to inform the strategic focus issues. Poor information can lead to poor decisions, and, for this reason, transaction costs need to be carefully tabulated and subtracted from the nominal cost savings.

[7]Ang and Straub (1998).

10.7.3 Reason 3: Staff Flexibility

Managers are able to achieve flexibility in their workforce with selective outsourcing (see Figure 10.8. Selective outsourcing means that the firm hires others to undertake certain functions for it while retaining the strategic assets it needs to compete. Well-formed contracts give the firm flexibility to hire on extra talent from the complementor when it is needed and dispense with it when it is not, without penalty. Thus what were formerly the fixed costs of full-time employees become the variable costs of contractors once a functionality is outsourced. The movement from fixed to variable costs gives the firm financial flexibility as well as flexibility in human capital.

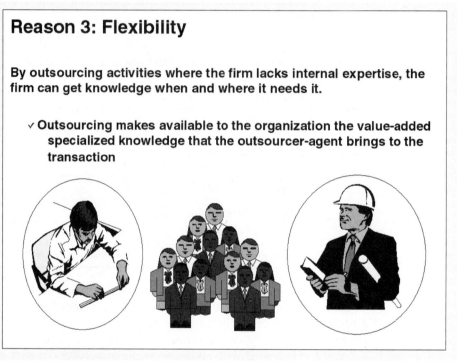

Reason 3: Flexibility

By outsourcing activities where the firm lacks internal expertise, the firm can get knowledge when and where it needs it.

 ✓ **Outsourcing makes available to the organization the value-added specialized knowledge that the outsourcer-agent brings to the transaction**

Figure 10.8   Outsourcing Reason 3

Contrast this with the situation of a firm that still retains many of its own noncore processes. A staff of janitors and cafeteria workers may have nothing to do with the firm's genius, which lies in attacking the niche market of corporate travel. If the firm needs to cut costs in tough economic times (e.g., disintermediation of the travel industry as a result of online travel agents such as travelocity.com and expedia.com), it is painful and demoralizing to reduce staff levels to a large extent. Because the firm still needs these services, some personnel will have to be retained unless and until the services are sourced to outsiders.

Suppose we have the additional confounding factor of unions? If the teamsters have unionized these workers, the firm has more constraints in terms of who can be laid off, who can be fired, and when this should occur. In the case of unionized or nonunionized workers, there are social payments that may have to be made to the workers (in the United States, these are called unemployment benefits). In short, the fixed costs of the labor force can be a major liability for a firm seeking to be agile and innovative in tough economic times.

The situation is even more challenging when a firm has not become more virtual by finding complementors for noncore processes, because the areas where they should cut are in the noncore areas. Although firms may be able to reduce expenses in noncore areas without significant loss of competitive energy, they frequently begin to cut into programs or processes for which the degrees of freedom may not be as limited as with nonprofessional employees. When they begin to cut into these processes, such as research and development, firms end up euchring themselves.

When noncore processes are contracted, firms may choose to use a minimal amount of these resources with little to no disruption of their internal routines and without the disorienting effects of large-scale lay-offs. There are certainly times when even core assets must be reduced, but this option should be the court of last resort. Strategic sourcing permits this prioritization.

10.7.4 Reason 4: Imitation

At times, companies imitate leaders in their industry without going through proper due diligence. This form of imitative behavior is well documented in the outsourcing literature,[8] and illustrated in Figure 10.9. Of the four reasons that undergird a move to the market, this is the worst reason. It is not based on an analysis of the firm's strategic needs, its costs, or its need to remain agile in its workforce. It is based on a nonintellectual approach to management. Consumers should not follow fads for the sake of the fads themselves, and firms, in particular, are not exercising good managerial judgment when they slavishly imitate.

Lacity and Hirscheim (1993) call this the *bandwagon effect* because firms are joining in through some sort of spirit of rivalry. The mindlessness of imitation, even when the move to outsourcing makes no sense for a particular firm, is what must be avoided at all costs. Prudent managers will take note of the bandwagon, of course, but will follow their own reasoning to determine which, if any, assets to outsource.

10.7 DECIDING ON NE: COST-BENEFIT ANALYSIS

If we divide the world into small and large contracts, it becomes clear that wholly different selection procedures are relevant in each case. If a purchase of goods or services can be expensed in your firm, it is being treated not as a long-term asset that must be amortized, but as an operating expense that is reported for tax purposes on an annual basis. These limits have to do with where the firm's top management sets the upper bounds on the funds that different managers can spend without external scrutiny and layers of authorization. Let's say it is U.S. $10,000. For small investments, the selection of a vendor needs to be efficient and effective. Comparison pricing using online stores and other digital sources may be the best way to determine options and criteria for specification. Industry-specific sites are becoming more commonplace (see later chapter on e-marketing for some of these URLs). Responsible managers use their contacts to determine what success others have had with vendors, and these judgments become part of the rapid assessment.

[8]Ang and Cummings, 1997; Loh and Venkatraman, 1992.

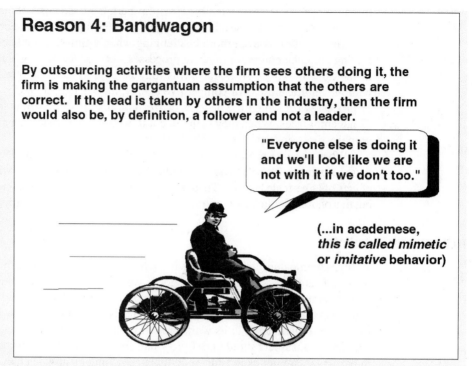

Figure 10.9   Outsourcing Reason 4

Longer-term investments that call for significant funding require a more detailed investigative process. Suppose a firm wants to initiate a full-scale transactional Web site for its products. This could be a sizable investment that involved large-scale hosting as well as the development of an intricate online architecture and programs that can accept parameters directly from customers and process them. As discussed earlier, the site could be even more complex if delivery, payment, and after-sales support are involved.

But the first question in deciding to virtualize is even more basic than "Who?" It is "Whether?" Should the organization virtualize the process? Does a shift to an electronic channel to the customer make sense? Or are traditional channels better strategic choices? This question is tied in with the high-level strategic analysis that was recommended in Chapter 7, "Competitive NE Strategy."

Certain quantitative techniques are helpful in analyzing this decision from a financial standpoint. One such technique is *cost-benefit analysis*. Table 10.3 shows a spreadsheet expression of the costs and benefits that a firm hopes to achieve from computerizing an engineering firm's project management system and making it Web enabled. This sample spreadsheet is available in your online course materials at http://www.wiley.com/college/straub.

Table 10.3: Sample Cost-Benefit Analysis for E-Project Management System

	Quant.	Price	2003 Year 0	2004 Year 1	2005 Year 2	2006 Year 3	2007 Year 4	2008 Year 5	2009 Year 6
File servers	3	$ 50,000	$ 150,000						
>>maintenance				$ 10,000	$ 10,000	$ 10,000	$ 10,000	$ 10,000	$ 10,000
PCs	100	$ 3,000	$ 300,000						
>>maintenance				$ 10,000	$ 10,000	$ 10,000	$ 10,000	$ 10,000	$ 10,000
Network cards	100	$ 500	$ 50,000						
Scanners	6	$ 1,200	$ 7,200	$ 1,200	$ 1,200	$ 1,200	$ 1,200	$ 1,200	$ 1,200
Fax boards	100	$ 250	$ 25,000						
Gateways	2	$ 8,000	$ 16,000						
>>maintenance	1	$ 400		$ 400	$ 400	$ 400	$ 400	$ 400	$ 400
Cabling	1	$ 100,000	$ 100,000						
e-Projects System			$ 52,000	$ 121,000	$ 6,000	$ 6,000	$ 6,000	$ 6,000	$ 6,000
Network	1	$ 10,000	$ 10,000						
>>upgrades	1	$ 2,500		$ 2,500	$ 2,500	$ 2,500	$ 2,500	$ 2,500	$ 2,500
Groupware	100	$ 500	$ 50,000	$ 1,000	$ 1,000	$ 1,000	$ 1,000	$ 1,000	$ 1,000
Windows	100	$ 99	$ 9,900	$ 3,960	$ 3,960	$ 3,960	$ 3,960	$ 3,960	$ 3,960
Engineers' Network Training	54	$ 400	$ 21,600	$ 21,600	$ 21,600	$ 21,600	$ 21,600	$ 21,600	$ 21,600
General Training	300	$ 100	$ 30,000	$ 30,000	$ 30,000	$ 30,000	$ 30,000	$ 30,000	$ 30,000
Director	1	$ 100,000	$ 100,000	$ 110,000	$ 121,000	$ 133,100	$ 146,410	$ 161,051	$ 177,156
Technical Specialists	4	$ 50,000	$ 200,000	$ 216,000	$ 233,280	$ 251,942	$ 272,098	$ 293,866	$ 317,375
Training Specialist	2	$ 30,000	$ 60,000	$ 63,600	$ 67,416	$ 71,461	$ 75,749	$ 80,294	$ 85,111
Annual Investment			$ 770,100	$ 150,060	$ 35,060	$ 35,060	$ 35,060	$ 35,060	$ 35,060
Annual Costs			$ 1,181,700	$ 591,260	$ 508,356	$ 543,163	$ 580,916	$ 621,870	$ 666,302
Running Costs				$ 1,772,960	$ 2,281,316	$ 2,824,479	$ 3,405,396	$ 4,027,266	$ 4,693,568
Depreciation			$ 128,350	$ 153,360	$ 159,203	$ 165,047	$ 170,890	$ 176,733	$ 182,577
1. Billing enhancements			$ 300,000	$ 400,000	$ 500,000	$ 600,000	$ 600,000	$ 600,000	$ 600,000
2. Reduced apprentice engrs			$ 25,000	$ 25,000	$ 25,000	$ 25,000	$ 25,000	$ 25,000	$ 25,000
3. Reduced clerical			$ 25,000	$ 25,000.00	$ 25,000	$ 25,000	$ 25,000	$ 25,000	$ 25,000
4. Reduced messenger			$ -	$ -	$ -	$ -	$ -	$ -	$ -
5. Reduced telecommun			$ 10,000	$ 10,000	$ 10,000	$ 10,000	$ 10,000	$ 10,000	$ 10,000
6. Engineer efficiencies			$ 120,000	$ 240,000	$ 360,000	$ 480,000	$ 600,000	$ 600,000	$ 600,000
Annual Benefits			$ 480,000	$ 700,000	$ 920,000	$ 1,140,000	$ 1,260,000	$ 1,260,000	$ 1,260,000
Running Benefits				$ 1,180,000	$ 2,100,000	$ 3,240,000	$ 4,500,000	$ 5,760,000	$ 7,020,000

On the right side of the spreadsheet are six metrics that sum up the results of the cost-benefit analyses. These statistics basically answer the question: Is this a sound investment for the firm?

Let's examine these in order. First is payback analysis, as shown in Figure 10.10 (Part 1). Payback analysis (cost-benefit statistic #1) asks how long it will take for benefits from the investment to completely offset the up front costs. The statistic is in years, and managers have a sense for what period of time is acceptable for a payback period. It has been common to think of many internal IT investments in terms of a three-year payback, for example. Since the advent of the Web, these periods have shrunk. Web systems are easily imitable, as discussed in Chapter 7. To cover costs for a short-term strategic advantage, these paybacks need to be in months rather than years.[9]

The payback calculation looks only at the initial investment. This is a weakness of the statistic in that ongoing costs can be substantial, and they are not accounted for. Payback is the single most popular statistic, however, and this is likely because the statistic is intuitively satisfying and easy to understand.[10]

---

[9] One has to be careful not to let the numbers dominate the decision. Cost-benefit analysis should be used as a quantitative aid, rather than as the main rationale. Strategic decisions should depend more on the ultimate goals of the organization. Even if a cost-benefit analysis determines that a course of action will lose money for the firm, it could well be that the firm will still proceed. Some actions are strategically necessary to meet the competition irrespective of costs.

[10] Hinton and Kaye (1996).

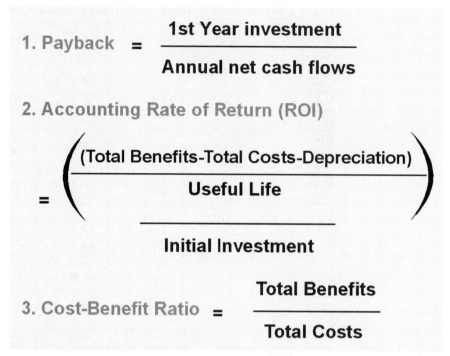

Figure 10.10   Cost-Benefit Analytical Statistics (Part 1)

Unlike payback, the accounting rate of return, or what is known by managers as ROI (return on investment) takes into account costs beyond the first year and even the depreciation of the asset, as seen in Figure 10.10 (Part 1). The ROI (cost-benefit statistic #2) is thus comparable to banking interest rates or returns on stocks. The question the manager can answer with an ROI is whether this investment would net the firm more than any other investment that might be made with the same funds. If an ROI is 5%, for example, and the money market rate is 6.5%, the firm would be better off financially by leaving the money in a more liquid form, all things being equal.

Cost-benefit ratios (cost-benefit statistic #3) are simple calculations of the total benefits divided by the total costs. If the ratio does not yield a number greater than 1, then the investment will result in a loss for the firm.

None of the first three statistics reviewed takes into account the fact that money is worth less (or more) from year to year, depending on the economy. If the inflation rate is 5%, for example, money is worth 5% less in the year following the investment. This means that for the same money, the firm can buy 5% more in year 2. Present values (PVs) are calculations that account for the fact that money has a time value, as shown in Figure 10.11.

4. Net Present Value (NPV)

$$= \begin{array}{c} \textbf{Time-discounted value of} \\ \textbf{net cash flows (Present Value or PV)} \end{array}$$

$$\textbf{- 1st year investment}$$

5. Profitability Index $= \dfrac{\textbf{Present value}}{\textbf{1st year investment}}$

6. Internal Rate of Return = the interest rate that will equate the present value of the future cash flows with the 1st year investment

Figure 10.11   Cost-Benefit Analytical Statistics (Part 2)

Cost-benefit statistic #4 recognizes that the benefits or the net cash flows from the investment are worth less as the years go by. By subtracting the first-year investment from the value of these cask flows in the PV, we can know how much money that investment brings into the firm by investing in it today. In the example in Table 10.3, the net present value (NPV) is $103,519. This can be interpreted to mean that the firm will be $103,519 richer by making this investment today. NPVs do not compare this investment with other investments the firm could make. And they only use the first-year investment as the base for the calculations. They are conceptually straightforward and, at the same time, are considering discounts for money over time. For this reason, they are a popular measure with many managers.[11]

The profitability index (cost-benefit statistic #5) divides the PV by the first-year investment rather than subtracting it. Similar to the cost-benefit ratio, if the result is greater than 1, the investment will yield a profit. Although this ratio is a more sophisticated rendering of the time-value concept, it is not as popular as the simpler cost-benefit ratio.

The final cost-benefit statistic (#6) takes into account both the time value of money and the alternative internal investments that the firm could make. The IRR, or internal rate of return, gives the firm a comprehensive assessment of the value of the project. It is only relevant against the IRR of other firm projects, however.

[11]Hinton and Kaye (1996).

10.8 SELECTING BETWEEN COMPLEMENTORS AND INTERNAL SOURCING AND AMONG COMPLEMENTORS

There are two additional levels of decision making that are necessary before the firm can contract with a complementor. Figure 10.12 shows the three levels of decision making that take place when, say, a partnering decision for computerizing a process is being considered (this level is a basic decision to make a change or not). The initial decision (Level I) is whether NE is the correct strategic avenue. The other decisions are whether to insource or outsource and who to hire.

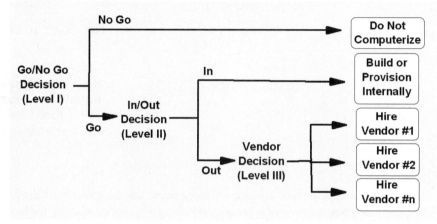

Figure 10.12   Three Levels of Decision Making in Partnering

Assuming the firm has decided to engage in NE, the Level II decision is whether the firm should hire outsiders to provide the goods and services that the firm needs. This is a strategic matter and should be analyzed in the way we discussed earlier.

Figure 10.13 presents the components of the decision and the likely managerial choices. If the asset (resource) being considered for outsourcing is not strategic for the firm, the firm has no internal expertise in this area, and the cost-benefit analysis is encouraging, the natural choice is to outsource.

The opposite quadrant tells of the circumstance where the asset is strategic and is integral to the firm's core competencies. If the financial analysis says that the decision is a "go" to computerize or Webize, for example, then the firm should retain the resource and provision it internally. Irrespective of how financially attractive it would be to outsource this asset, whether the firm would have an NPV of $100,000 a year or $10 million by outsourcing, it is this unique capability of the firm that makes for success. To outsource the system is to risk complete disaster—it should never be outsourced.

Sun Microsystems is a good example of a firm with a clear sense of its core competencies, what they should insource, and what they should outsource. They outsource nearly everything in their value chain except the design of hardware and software. They think of themselves as an "intellectual holding company" because their manufacturing and logistics are all handled by complementors. No Sun employee every touches one of their products before it is sent out. The core competency of Sun Microsystems is to design high-end computers. They have focused on this distinctive competence and prospered through this clear-cut strategic control.

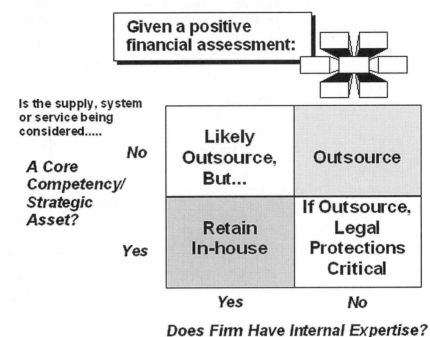

Figure 10.13 Insource versus Outsource Decision (Level II)

There is growing scientific evidence that firms that selectively outsource and retain strategic control are high performers. One study by Straub, Weill, and Stewart (2002) has found that 27 large multinational companies attained higher performance levels when they carefully outsourced. If anything, the study found that more could have, and should have, been outsourced to better allow firms to build their core competencies.

Generally speaking, the firm should also outsource even if it has the internal expertise, because this will allow it to focus more on its core competencies. There are always contingencies that would grant degrees of freedom in such cases. Suppose the firm now has a critical mass of employees in a strategic area related to the function being outsourced. The loss of employees in the one area could jeopardize the attractiveness of the firm in retaining employees in the other. Suppose also that the firm's internal bid for the work is highly competitive. It may be a good strategic choice for the firm to retain this resource even if most indicators argue for outsourcing it.

Finally, firms may be motivated to outsource when the asset is strategic but the firm does not currently have the in-house expertise to fully utilize their internal talent. All things being equal, firms can outsource in this situation, being extremely careful to protect themselves with well-wrought contracts. Figure 10.14 shows some of the legal steps that firms can take in the United States under conditions where software is the resource in question. If the system is public, then trade-secret laws do not apply, but the software can be copyrighted and patented, either by the outsourcer or the firm itself. Clearly, it is preferable for the firm to own such a strategic asset, but there are conditions under which the firm might take an exclusive lease from the outsourcer for a certain period of time. When the outsourcer is a partner in the development of the software, for instance, and both have an equity position in the software, the firm could use the software exclusively as a beta test site, and once the initial competitive advantage had been achieved, the software could be released for commercial sale.

	Intellectual Property Rights Specified in Systems Contract	Conditions	Best Form of Further Legal Protection
Strategic Assets	**Company Owns: System Integrator Builds**	**System is public**	Copyright and/or patent
		System is not public	Trade secret; non-disclosure clause in systems contract
	Company Leases; Systems Integrator Builds and Owns	**System is public**	Systems contract specifies that integrator must hold copyright and/or patent
		System is not public	Systems contract specifies that integrator must protect the trade secret
Non-Strategic Assets	**Company Licenses; Systems Integrator Builds and Owns**		Systems contract specifies number of copies sufficient to meet firm's present and future needs

Figure 10.14   Legal Protections for Outsourced Assets

There are many other circumstances that would allow for variants on the general rules of thumb for when to source. If the firm is thinking in a strategic way, this decision will be taken very seriously, and the eyes will still be on the prize.

10.9 CONTRACTING FOR WEB SITE DEVELOPMENT, HOSTING, MAINTENANCE, LOGISTICS, AND PROVISION OF PRODUCTS

An NEO needs to utilize networks, the Internet, and other proprietary networks to connect with its stakeholders. Software is the glue that binds the network together and presents content that makes it worthwhile for stakeholders to deal with NEOs. The entire client-server internal network must be integrated if the firm wishes to automate the electronic value chain.

Focus on NE: Depth of Partnering

 As the industry moves towards an automated sales environment, many high-tech companies are discovering just how difficult that transition can be. Most have made enough investments in e-commerce to understand the potential, and the difficulties, associated with this new channel. Even vendors that are heavily dependent upon partners for market reach and revenue growth see the benefits of e-commerce. However, channel companies are also beginning to understand their need to address the softer issues of "e-partnering" before their e-commerce ambitions can be realized.

How does your company compare to the industry? Judge your e-partnering progress on the following scale:

DEPTH LEVEL ONE—ALMOST NO E-PARTNERING:

E-mail is working, but most or all partner programs are still handled manually. The partner Web site is a shell, and a lot of the information is out of date. Partners get what they need through relentless telephone calls and an occasional face-to-face meeting.

DEPTH LEVEL TWO—RUDIMENTARY E-PARTNERING:

The partner Web site is functional, but constantly fighting for resources to keep information current. Marketing materials (in PDF format) are occasionally e-mailed out after arguments with legal departments and consultations with MARCOM, which supplies safety training and regulatory compliance products to organizations in order to comply with government regulations and create safer workplaces. Webinars, or Web-based seminars, sound interesting and may be tried soon. There are discussions about automating soft-dollar programs, training, and lead management, but the budget is not approved.

DEPTH LEVEL THREE—CREDIBLE E-PARTNERING:

Your company's Web site contains up-to-date and useful information, and it allows basic partner matching with opportunities, some lead distribution, and literature fulfillment. Functional extranet includes all partner e-mail addresses, and "push" communication activities have started. Webinar technology is embraced and popular. Basic training capabilities are online with expansion plans in place. Partner relationship management software is being evaluated with approved plans for a partner portal this year.

DEPTH LEVEL FOUR—COMPREHENSIVE E-PARTNERING:

Partner relationship management capabilities are in place, including active extranet, business planning, partner recruiting, forecasting, soft-dollar management, training and certification, order processing, lead generation, lead management, and sales support. Your company is looking at Web-based incentive programs and collaboration software to enhance partnerships. A partner portal provides administrative services such as order processing, lead-time information, configuration, pricing, and other asset management capabilities.

Source:
http://www.tc-group.com/tc/TCaccess/News/news38.htm

This is a tall order. For a firm with a major Web presence and substantial EDI activity, there is a huge investment in hardware as well as software.

Let's take the case of a start-up with a particular service or product line and reason out the design of the firm, with respect to what makes the firm Net-enhanced. The mission of this U.S.-based firm is to provide digitally-enhanced or rendered images for the graphic design industry. The images the firm creates are used in advertising and other forms of promotion. The firm is a spin-off created by some of the most innovative players on Madison Avenue.

What kind of partnerships should the firm form? What kind of internal expertise is required that will still allow the firm to be a virtual organization?

Consciously or unconsciously, the firm principals plan the organizational design through their sessions on the corporate strategy and their discussions of what is core to their business and what is not. In their planning meetings, they decide that their business is distinct because of their professionals' abilities to work with images. They need to maximize the creativity of their staff and make their products known to the customer base in order to be successful. Their personal contacts will go a long way to ensure the firm can be launched, but expansion to Asia and Europe is critical to succeed in the long run. They are keenly aware that this is a niche business, and that there will be a global demand that the firm must address.

What is the wish list to make this firm Net-enhanced? A fairly extensive internal client-server network is needed to allow the highly skilled renderers to share work among team members. Good connections to the outside world serve the goal of making the firm's products better known, as are the firm's growing repository of images, which can be viewed on the Web site. Incomplete versions of these images can be downloaded by potential customers, but the firm needs to protect its complete versions from pirating, especially in certain foreign markets. The firm has developed preliminary software to digitally watermark the images; the software also makes the images time-sensitive and capable of self-destruction after the contracted lifespan. They are anticipating other means of protecting this intellectual property using Web linkages.

Which firm activities are vitally connected to the firm's mission? It should be clear from even this short description that the firm needs internal legal and security expertise to be able to sell its products worldwide and to expand into new markets. Please note that the physical alternative to the electronic ordering and distribution channel that is envisioned is a sales force and physical versions of the digital images burnt onto CDs. What was most troubling to the organization's top management was the sizable investment in physical and human assets to go global in a traditional manner. The firm would have needed to set up branches and find sales persons in each of these countries who know the local advertisers. Travel expenses to allow sales personnel to maintain contact with widely dispersed customers would have been large as well. The security issues involved in securing CDs would be too difficult for local staff to handle, and so these CDs would have to be surface-mailed with the inevitable time delays.

The choice to invest in the electronic channel means that the firm should have internal expertise in processes intimately associated with its products, but not functions that are only peripherally related. The firm did not have expertise among its initial employees in running large server "farms" to handle the traffic on the Web site. Maintaining a firewall between the firm's internal systems and the Internet was also not a capability that the firm had developed. The decision was made, therefore, to hire a well-financed, value-added ISP to provide Web hosting and firewall security. An iron-clad contract gave the firm assurances that their intellectual property would be protected from theft and other security violations, or else substantial penalty clauses would kick in. This firm also provided the hardware, software, and maintenance for the firm's internal client-server network.

The creation of methods to watermark and secure the firm's products from pirating was believed to be a firm core competency. This security was, therefore, developed and implemented by internal developers. The provision of new content for the Web site was also viewed as an internal competency. Content creators were given tools that allowed them to upload new products to the Web site without intervention, and this brought about an immediate and one-to-one connection between the firm's professionals and potential customers.

Figure 10.15 shows the dimensions that were insourced and outsourced. It also suggests that this firm hired the ISP to manage their internal client-server network ("facilities management" and "maintenance"). Clearly, not all firms will hire hosting services. Firms that are into some computer services businesses should be viewing this as their core competency and that which drives their strategy. They are likely running their own hosts. In fact, the value-added ISP that our image design firm has contracted with is one such firm, most probably. The only time this would not be true would be if the ISP saw itself as a marketing firm and outsourced the physical hosting and security to others.

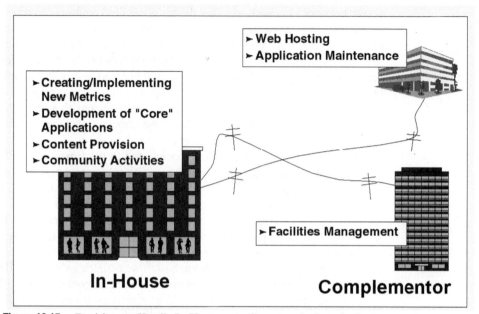

Figure 10.15   Decisions to Handle In-House or to Outsource in Sample Case

Firms that capitalize on their core competencies are good at something internally, such as hosting, and this is part of what they sell to the outside world. IBM became an expert at e-business (in fact, inventing the term) before they began to promulgate the value of NE to other companies.

Logistics and provision of products are also elements of the value chain that firms should consider for outsourcing. Delivery of product from the end of the production line to the destination is not the core competency of most firms. Companies such as UPS have spent billions of dollars perfecting machine and computer systems that can move goods efficiently and effectively. It is the height of arrogance by most firms to believe that they can transport goods better than such specialists.

UPS, for example, has an entire division set up to enable an e-commerce solution for firms. Online tracking capabilities for the firm and for customers are one of the offerings that can even be established under the firm's logo. This will allow the firm to maintain its relationship with the customer even through the delivery cycle that they are not physically involved with.

When suppliers of goods that are part of a package deal are involved, these logistical partnerships become even more important. In the case of Dell, for instance, the monitors that are part of a package sale of a Dell computer are provided by Sony. Dell employees never physically handle the monitors.[12] Transport firms are part of the partnership that

[12]Rangan and Bell (1999).

allows Dell computers, software peripherals, and monitors to be gathered together near the local destination and delivered as a package, through the initiating of the firm that handled the transaction, in this case, Dell.

Let's say that Dell saw its core competency as assembling a world-class package that included its own processors and products of its competitors, in some cases. Hewlett Packard (HP), for example, competes with Dell on workstations, but Dell might view HP's printers and CD-RW device as state-of-the-art. So besides its partnerships with, say, Sony and UPS, it might also partner with HP. Figure 10.16 in Section 10.11 illustrates this scenario, one that is becoming even more commonplace in the Net-enhanced space, where boundaries between firms are not as clear-cut as they are with physically oriented firms.

10.10 WHY WORK WITH SUPPLEMENTORS (RIVALS)?

Clearly, there are situations when those firms that supplement activities, that is, your competitors, should be considered as partners in the Net-enhanced world. In their seminal book on this subject, Brandenburger and Nalebuff (1996) talk about co-opetition in the modern age. According to their book, the splitting of the world into competitors and those firms that can help you is a simplistic and inaccurate view of the world. There is actually some scientific evidence that firms have increased their collaboration with competitors.[13]

A specific example in which competitors joined together in order to nurture their individual businesses is Pinnacle Alliance. Pinnacle Alliance was a corporate partnership to service the IT needs of J. P. Morgan Bank. Members, and ordinarily competitors, were: Computer Sciences Corp., Andersen Consulting, AT&T Solutions, and Bell Atlantic Network Integration. The deal was for U.S. $2 billion and for seven years.

Why did these competitors join together? Because it was in their mutual self-interest. J. P. Morgan wanted an organization to which they could selectively outsource one-third of all their IT functions. They did not believe that any one firm could handle these functions, but they were willing to accept the services of a strategic alliance.

The choice for the partners was to share in $2 billion worth of business or to be out of the action entirely. Co-opetition can clearly be profitable, in special circumstances.

Another case in point is the ETN set up by the automakers for supply of component parts. A joint B2B enterprise (shared-infrastructure model) between such major players as GM and Ford, the firm deals electronically with suppliers for common auto parts. Known as Covisint, the business model has been successful enough that there are plans to move the network to other industries.[14] The success of the venture is indicated by the fact that automakers not in the strategic alliance are banding together into alternative ETNs for their own protection.[15]

Why would a firm engage in a cooperative venture with its rivals? The answer is, again, money. Firms are duty-bound to make money for their shareholders and to prosper for general social good. If assuring quality supplies and component parts can result from a joint venture with competitors, this benefits the industry. In point of fact, it probably also benefits the supplier industries in that it regularizes purchases, allows many

---

[13]Lado et al. (1997).
[14]Frook (2001).
[15]Bauer (2001).

formerly disenfranchised suppliers to participate, and encourages those with economies of scale to prosper.

Before moving off the subject of co-opetition, it is important to make two observations. NEOs are particularly receptive to the virtues of strategic alliances because they are inclined to be virtual organizations anyway. Alliances with rivals allows a firm to reduce process control on the supply chain. It likely also results in lower costs for the firm.

The second observation is that forming an alliance with a competitor can be a dangerous proposition. Sharing strategic information directly with a competitor, for example, is something that would be anathema for most organizations, but this may occur, unwittingly, if care is not exercised. The final discussion in our chapter on virtual organizations and outsourcing is on this subject.

10.11 SHARING INFORMATION AND INFORMATION VISIBILITY

The concept of sharing information between complementors and supplementors in cyberspace is known as "information visibility." The basic idea is that as products and/or services move up the value chain from supplier to the firm to the customer, the process will be more efficient and more effective if there is a concerted effort by the parties to share information.[16] The design of a virtual organization is intimately connected with the amount and kind of information that is being shared. Firms can extend their boundaries by capitalizing more about downstream and upstream events on the virtual value chain. They will be more limited to their physical boundaries if this information is not made available to them.

▶ *CASE STUDY 10-2*

RURAL INTERNET ACCESS AUTHORITY: INFORMATION SHARING IN NORTH CAROLINA

In the year 2000, North Carolina's General Assembly passed a wide-ranging law to expand IT infrastructure statewide within three years and to prepare North Carolina citizens to take full advantage of the information-sharing opportunities provided by the Internet. The Rural Internet Access Authority has been charged with carrying out this agenda. The Authority is based at the North Carolina Rural Economic Development Center, a nonprofit organization that works to develop, promote, and implement sound economic strategies to improve the quality of life of rural North Carolinians. The Rural Internet Access Authority has a huge, complex, critical, and time-sensitive mission ahead of it. To accomplish what it is charged by law to do, it had to find a way to enable all 21 commissioned members and 170 volunteers—spread out across the state and split into eight committees—to communicate quickly and easily and work together effectively. To facilitate communication and information sharing, the authority has set up a SharePoint Team Services–based Web site. Through the site, all members can stay in touch with each other, work together within their committees, and keep track of how the authority is progressing. In this way, the authority has been able to move quickly toward its goals.

The North Carolina General Assembly has charged the Authority with providing local dial-up Internet access to all citizens of North Carolina within one year and providing high-speed Internet access at competitive prices to all North Carolinians by the year 2004. This is happening in a state

[16]Straub and Watson (2001).

that ranks forty-fifth in households with computers and forty-sixth in the percentage of households using the Internet.

"This is a massive undertaking," says Elaine Matthews, vice president for communication and development of the North Carolina Rural Economic Development Center, where the Rural Internet Access Authority is housed. "This group is under extreme pressure to roll out the delivery system. In the process, they have to do an inventory of all existing infrastructure, and they also must meet the challenge of creating demand among individuals. The public has to want to gain access to the Internet. On top of it all, the press is following the authority's progress, the leaders are following it, and the public cares."

"A tremendous amount of communication has to happen for us to reach our goals," points out Jane Patterson, the executive director of the Rural Internet Access Authority. A solution to this need was proposed by one of the commissioned members of the Authority, Ed McDaries, chief operating officer of the Internet-hosting company Advanced Internet Technologies (AIT). AIT is a registered member of the Web Presence Provider program for Microsoft FrontPage Web site creation and management tool and SharePoint Team Services. McDaries proposed that the authority use SharePoint Team Services from Microsoft, a communication and information-sharing tool that he envisioned would help the Authority reach its goals.

The Authority decided to implement SharePoint Team Services as a central focal point for information and communication. Considering SharePoint Team Services features—such as a calendar that allows the Authority members to keep up-to-date with their many meetings and deadlines and a comprehensive contact list—the authority looked to SharePoint Team Services as a way to help it get the job done quickly and efficiently.

The Authority implemented SharePoint Team Services with the aim of improving discussion. "One of the goals that we have is to get people into more of a discussion format with each other, so that they meet and talk in virtual space more than they could in physical space," says Matthews. "Most of the commissioned members come from different backgrounds and haven't necessarily worked with each other before. So it's important to get a shared space where people can come together around a goal and learn to work together. This will help us move this project faster, and move it in a more effective way." Using SharePoint Team Services, the Authority members work together on documents through the document libraries, stay on top of deadlines and meetings with the calendar, stay in touch through the contact list, and engage in discussions through the discussion board.

Discussion:
1. Discuss how information sharing between the stakeholders in the Rural Internet Access Authority increases efficiency of operations.
2. Discuss the importance of a virtual environment to information sharing capabilities.

Sources:
http://www.microsoft.com/frontpage/evaluation/casestudies/ria.htm

An example of "information visibility" would be the UPS tracking system. Once an order is placed, the suppliers, the firm, and the customers can all access logistical information about delivery. But if this is all the firm is capable of, this would not qualify as an example of "full information visibility" in this domain. Let's assume that parts of an order are back-ordered and the packages are being held in a supplementor warehouse until completed. In this case, the delivery cycle would not have begun and, thus, not all parties would be aware of the status of the order. There are many cases where more complete information up and down the supply side and customer-facing side of the electronic value chain will help in forecasting and planning. Cisco had such a system in place, and this system was responsible for Cisco's systematic progress in the marketplace until some assumptions in the system proved to be its undoing. One could argue that the principle of information sharing was not the problem for Cisco, but rather the problem stemmed from fatal flaws in the planning models that used this information.

But is "full information visibility" always desirable? Although often touted in the trade press,[17] it may not be desirable in all cases. Sharing strategic information with close partners who have signed nondisclosure, noncompete, and confidentiality contracts with one's firm is risky enough, but clearly information about strategic plans or, more specifically, anticipated production volumes could place one in a decidedly poor competitive position if one's rivals were privy to this information.

Figure 10.16 shows the value chain and visibility strategies by vendors and clients. The same logic applies when we consider other partnerships, whether they are with complementors or supplementors, but the vendor-client relationship is basic and critical in information visibility scenarios.

The blue bars in Figure 10.16 indicate information shared by the vendor, and the green bars are information shared by the client. The strategies depicted in the top set of bars (*visibility seeking*) show that there is an imbalance between what the vendor is sharing and what the client is sharing. Over time, there needs to be a perceived equity or fairness in sharing, as in the lower set of graphs, lest one or the other partners pulls out of the relationship. The strategies shown in the bottom set of bars is more symmetric (*symmetric sharing*) and, it can be argued, more conducive to long-term partnering and longevity.

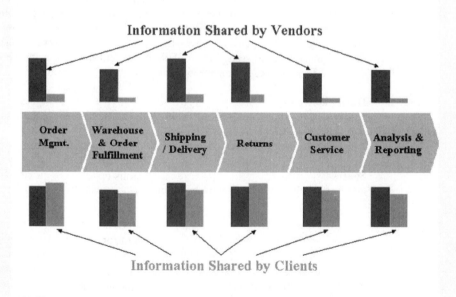

Figure 10.16   Information Visibility (Reprinted with permission of Klein, 2001)

[17]Slater (2000); Taninecz (2000); Webb & Gile (2001).

There are a number of scientific theories that have a bearing on this issue. One of the most important is game theory, invented by John von Neumann, the famous Princeton mathematician and computer scientist.[18] It was subsequently researched by John Nash, of MIT and Princeton, who won a Nobel prize for this work.

Game theory says that when parties compete, the system as a whole may end up with suboptimal results, whereas benefits will be optimal with cooperation. The difficulties come with game theory when parties do not trust each other and end up being opportunistic in order to maximize their own welfare. In that case, only one will profit and the other will lose. Overall, this will be a suboptimal result, but the short-term thinking of the winner does not take that into calculation. An example of how game theory works is shown in Figure 10.17.

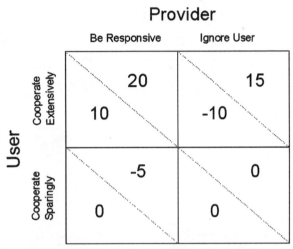

Figure 10.17   A Possible Outcome Matrix for Information Sharing (Reprinted with permission of David Gefen [1997])

If both the vendor (provider) and client (user) share information ("Cooperate Extensively" and "Be Responsive"), as in the first quadrant, they maximize the overall benefits in the system (20 + 10 = 30). No cooperation produces zero gains, but there is an imbalance when either does not cooperate. The most egregious case is when the client does not share, but the vendor does. In this case, the vendor's outcome is negative (–5) because it costs something to share information and there are no benefits accruing to the vendor.

Why should a vendor be responsive (10) when they could achieve higher gains if they ignore the user (15)? Game theory assumes rationality on the part of all participants, and if the client sees that they are losing (-10) because the vendor is not being responsive, then they will pull out of the relationship. So a short-term benefit may result to one party, but the relationship will be destroyed by this opportunistic behavior. If both cooperate, however, there is mounting evidence that the value of increased information in the system will result in higher performance for all.[19]

---

[18]von Neuman and Morgenstern (1953).
[19]Chen et al. (2001).

Trust is clearly a part of the equation in all cases. If the vendor and the client do not have a minimal level of trust and some agreed upon basis for cooperation (contractual or not), then they will not cooperate and there will be no benefits to either party, as in the fourth quadrant.

Even though partners basically trust one another, there are theories that say that the partners must still protect themselves from some natural opportunistic behavior on the part of the other. Agency theory says that principals, or parties hiring an agent, need to monitor the other party to prevent the party from taking advantage. Other ways to protect oneself include contracts, insurance, and so forth, so the principal must also pay "bonding" charges, such as insurance. These costs are represented figuratively in Figure 10.18.

Figure 10.18   How Partners Protect Themselves in Information Sharing

In this figure, we have a depiction of costs to one party for protection, but, in fact, both parties are protected by contracts, and both parties can include nondisclosure clauses in these contracts. So agency theory applies in the partnerships we are discussing by suggesting what each partner should do. Trust in the extent and nature of mutual information sharing is desirable, but the contract specifies what happens if the relationship breaks down.

The issue of how much information should be shared between firms in strategic alliances is not yet resolved. We will return to the question also in the chapter on e-marketing. The key point here is to remember that sharing certain information is built into the nature of outsourced arrangements and the virtualizing of firms. The real questions are: What kind of information? and How much information?

10.12 SUMMARY

Every corporation and every member in the business world is part of the food chain in the lifecycle of business. Some businesses, by the virtue of their industry, are at the bottom of the food chain, and other businesses are at the top. Informational versus physical core processes is a distinguishing feature in determining the location of a firm in the business food chain. Businesses committed to physical processes are lower in the food chain because they consume more physical resources to survive, similar to animals like elephants that consume so much energy and cannot move as quickly as those higher on the food chain. The same observation can be made for "virtual" firms.

Virtual firms are those that minimize the physical process and focus extensively on informational process. Cybermediaries on the Internet are an industry that is largely virtual. They rank higher on the food chain because they have low inventories of physical objects. Cybermediaries minimize their physical process through partnerships and outsourcing. Partnerships and outsourcing are the keys to staying lean and on top of the food chain, but a firm's kingdom is only as good as the partners on the lower parts of the food chain. It is extremely important to choose the partners wisely and select the right companies for outsourcing.

Managers need to use systematic analysis in order to determine where the firm should virtualize (or outsource) and where it should retain these resources inside the organization. The key reasoning elements are (1) maintaining strategic focus by only outsourcing noncore competencies, (2) outsourcing where the firm is at a comparative cost disadvantage in doing the work internally, and (3) going outside of the firm when they need flexibility in expertise. Firms should not outsource just because everyone else in their industry is doing so.

There is a systematic and analytical process for determining whether to seek out contractual (and even informal) relationships with partners. Managers use such intellectual tools as payback, ROI, cost-benefit ratios, NPV, profitability ratios, and internal rate of return to determine whether there is a comparative cost advantage to outsourcing. It is also important to realize that there are transaction costs associated with going to the market, and these costs need to be subtracted from the production cost advantages to outsourcing.

With respect to Net-enhancement, firms should determine how their core competencies align with the many functions required to put up an effective Web site. When the Web site is intricately connected to their strategic core competencies, they should do it themselves, in general. When this is not feasible, they need to minimize risk through contracts and other protective mechanisms.

A key issue with regard to working in strategic alliances is how much information to share and when. Research indicates that this should be at high levels in deep strategic alliances and it should be relatively symmetrical. This leads to high levels of trust and to higher performance for both partners.

KEY TERMS

Accounting rate of return (ROI): A metric for measuring IT investments; considers account costs beyond the first year and depreciation.

Agency theory: Principals, or parties hiring a agent, need to monitor the other party to prevent the party from taking advantage.

Cost-benefit ratio: A metric for measuring IT investments; total benefits divided by total costs.

Information visibility: The concept of making information "visible" between complementors and supplementors in cyberspace.

Internal rate of return (IRR): A metric for measuring IT investments; considers both the time value of money and the alternative internal investments.

Net present value (NPV): A metric for measuring IT investments; considers the time value of money.

Payback analysis: A metric for measuring IT investments; considers how long it takes for benefits from the investment to offset the up front costs.

Profitability index: A metric for measuring IT investments; present value divided by the first-year investment

Selective outsourcing: Selective outsourcing means that the firm hires others to undertake certain functions for it while retaining the strategic assets it needs to compete.

Strategic alliance: The center position on the partnership continuum.

Virtual firms: Firms that focus extensively on informational processes and minimizing their engagement with physical processes; heavily outsourced firms; firms with a minimal physical infrastructure and a lean set of resources dedicated to exploiting the firm's core competencies.

REVIEW QUESTIONS

1. Delineate the core competencies of a virtual firm?
2. What are the quintessential characteristics of a virtual firm?
3. What kind of architecture does a virtual organization depend most heavily on?
4. Define the two forms of control need to be considered when managers outsource.
5. List, explain, and give specifics of four basic reasons for outsourcing?
6. What is the strongest predictor of the choice to outsource?
7. Enumerate the six metrics used for a cost-benefit analysis?
8. Define game theory.
9. Explain agency theory.
10. What kinds of costs does the principal incur to be sure that the agent is exercising process control?

TOPICS FOR DISCUSSION

1. Virtual firms rely on systems and people more than on physical assets. Physical assets are needed to conduct physical processes; for this reason, the needs of the virtual and bricks-and-mortar firms are different. Discuss the similarities and differences in virtually oriented organizations and physically oriented organizations.

2. The partnering continuum has firms on one end of the continuum that operate through arm's-length transactions. On the other end of the spectrum are firms that insource or own the resource outright. Discuss the impact of the partnering continuum on an organization and discuss examples of organizations and where they fit on the continuum.

3. To contract with a complementor, firms must make decisions about their partnering strategy. Discuss the three levels of decision making and the outcomes that are possible at each level.

4. When should a NEO source a component, service, or process beyond its boundaries? Discuss the source decision factors that should be considered and explain the impact of each of the decisions.

5. Cost is a dominant consideration for many managers who are considering moving to the marketplace. Discuss the transaction costs involved in moving to the marketplace.

6. Discuss the importance of the cost-benefit analytical statistics and how they should be used.

7. Under what conditions would a firm need legal protections for outsourced assets?

8. Discuss reasons why firms may want to work with supplementors or rivals.

9. What are some of the effects of visibility-seeking strategies?

10. Discuss the impact of game theory and agency theory on process control.

INTERNET EXERCISES

1. Explore the Kodak site. Describe the range of services and products offered.

2. Locate Internet firms that outsource shopping carts for online order capabilities. Investigate the cost involved and the services offered.

3. Go to the Project-Manager site (http://www.project-manager.com), use the Direct Map link, and take both of the quizzes from the Personal Skills section. Summarize your results and write a brief report on the implications.

4. Go to the ETN site (http://www.etn.nl). Compare the services offered with Expedia.

5. Go to the borders.com Web site. Compare to amazon.com to get some sense for the extent to which they are moving toward virtuality and amazon.com's model. It may be that you will conclude that they are not.

6. Locate an article on transaction costs for NE firms. Summarize the article and write a brief report.

7. Investigate the services of a Web-hosting service. Describe the services offered and the costs involved.

8. Find a financial statement for a NE firm. Report on the six analytical cost-benefit statistics for the organization.

9. Visit the Covisint site (http://www.covisint.com). Go through the demo. Describe your experience and your impressions.

10. Research the biography of John Von Neumann. Write a brief report on his accomplishments and contributions to the computer field. In what sense is von Neumann the "father of virtuality"?

TEAM EXERCISES

1. Find a company that offers permission e-mails and one company that offers banner advertisements. Contact them and inquire about their average click-response rate. Find out the price they charge for their marketing program, and calculate the cost per click-through.

2. Discuss the advantages and disadvantages of outsourcing the billing and order processing function for a company that is going online. Specifically, comment on the product types, the size of the firm, the firm's general business strategy (e.g., cost leader versus differentiation), and their potential impact on decision of outsourcing. Find one company that provides outsourcing billing and processing function for others, and comment on their service.

3. In a virtual organization, a company may have a different structure compared to a traditional organization. In a traditional organization, it may be divided into manufacturing, marketing, research and development, and other functional departments. How will a virtual company organize itself? Find a virtual company and describe its organizational structure.

4. In a virtual organization, employees may be dispersed all over the world. Discuss the advantage and disadvantage of this dispersion as related to control and monitoring of employees and organizational learning.

5. Find one strategic alliance between two companies that enables a traditional company to go online. Discuss how you see this alliance may benefit both companies and the potential problems of this alliance.

INTERNET RESOURCES

E-commerce outstanding services compare-o-matic (http://www.nwfusion.com/ecomm2001/ecomm0226compare.jsp): The compare-o-matic lets you compare two or more E-commerce outsourcing services based on criteria you set. Select two or more providers and whichever criteria you are most interested in, and the system will create a comparison table. Note: While you could select every app and every criterion, that would result in a table roughly the size of Rhode Island. Also, Internet Explorer 3.x and Lynx do not display the results tables properly.

BricksorClicks.com (http://www.bricksorclicks.com): The BricksorClicks game puts you in the role of CEO at a traditional toy manufacturer. The company, called ToyBlocks Inc., must confront the challenges of launching an online sales channel while managing and maintaining their current traditional sales channels. The Kellogg Case Simulation Team, Knowledge Dynamics, and Powersim Corporation have partnered to develop BricksorClicks.com for the DFC 2000.

REFERENCES

Ang, S., and D. W. Straub. "Production and Transaction Economies and IS Outsourcing: A Study of the U.S. Banking Industry." *MIS Quarterly*, 22, 4, December 1998, 535–552.

Ang, S., and L. L. Cummings. "Strategic Response to Institutional Influences on Information Systems Outsourcing." *Organization Science*, 8, 3, May-June 1997, 235–256.

Applegate, L. M., and R. Montealegre. "Eastman Kodak Co.: Managing Information Systems Through Strategic Alliances." Case Study 192030, Harvard Business School, 1995.

Bauer, M. "Covisint: An Evolving Story?" *Automotive Industries*, 181, November 2001, S7.

Bers, J. S. "Growing Trend to Create Virtual IT Organizations." *Bank Systems & Technology*, 33, 6 (1996), 40.

Brandenburger, A. M., and B. J. Nalebuff. *Co-opetition and the Death of Competition: Leadership Strategy in the Age of Ecosystems.* Currency/Doubleday, New York, 1996.

Chen, Y., C. Naradimhan, et al. "Individual Marketing with Imperfect Targetability." *Marketing Science*, 20, 1 (2001), 23–41.

Crowston, K. "A Coordination Theory Approach to Organizational Process Design." *Organization Science*, 8, 2 (1997), 157–175.

Frook, J. E. "Exchanges Ready If Enlisted." *B to B*, 86, 1, October 2001, 17.

Gefen, D. "Building Users' Trust in Freeware Providers and the Effects of this Trust on Users' Perceptions of Usefulness, Ease of Use, and Intended Use," dissertation, Georgia State University, 1997.

Heeks, R. "Global Software Outsourcing to India by Multinational Corporations." In Palvia, P., S. Palvia, and E. Roche, eds. *Global Information Technology and Systems Management: Key Issues and Trends*, Ivy League Publishing, Nashua, NH, 1996, 365–392.

Hinton, M., and R. Kaye. "Investing in Information Technology: A Lottery?" *Management Accounting-London*, 74, 10, November (1996), 52.

Klein, R. "The Effect of e-Business Enabled Symmetric Information Sharing Practices in Vendor / Client Relationships." Dissertation proposal, Georgia State University, 2001.

Lacity, M. C., and R. Hirscheim. "The Information Systems Outsourcing Bandwagon" *Sloan Management Review*, 35, 1, Fall (1993), 73–86.

Loh, L. and N. Venkatraman. "Diffusion of Information Technology Outsourcing: Influence Sources and the Kodak Effect." *Information Systems Research*, 3, 4, December (1992), 334–378.

Malone, T. W., and K. Crowston. "The Interdisciplinary Study of Coordination.," *ACM Computing Surveys*, 26, 1, March (1994), 87–119.

McFarlan, F. W., and K. N. Seger. "General Dynamics and Computer Sciences Corp.: Outsourcing the IS Function (A) and (B) (Abridged)." Case Study 193178, Harvard Business School Press, 1993.

Quinn, J. B., and F. G. Hilmer, "Strategic Outsourcing," *Sloan Management Review*, 35, 4, (1994), 43–55.

Rangan, V. K., and M. Bell. "Dell Online." Case Study #598116, Harvard University, March 26, 1999.

Slater, D. "The Integrated Enterprise: The Whole... Is More than Its Parts" *CIO*, 13(2000), 116–122.

Straub, D., P. Weill, and K. Stewart. "IT as a Core Competency of the Firm: A Test of Selective Outsourcing Theory." Working paper, Georgia State University, 2002.

Straub, D., and R. Watson. "Transformational Issues in Researching IS and Net-Enhanced Organizations." *Information Systems Research*, 12, 4, December (2001), 337–345.

Taninecz, G. "Value Chain IT Infrastructure." *Industry Week*, 249 (2000), 33–38.

von Neumann, J., and O. Morgenstern. *Theory of Games and Economic Behavior.* Princeton University Press, Princeton, NJ, 1953.

Webb, J., and C. Gile. "Reversing the Value Chain." *The Journal of Business Strategy*, 22, 2 (2001), 13–17.

CHAPTER 11

STRATEGIZING FOR E-MARKETS

▶ UNDERSTANDING MARKETING ISSUES FOR NEOs

How should managers think about marketing the organization's products and services to benefit from NE? In short, how should managers strategize about markets in cyberspace? It is likely that cyberspace differs from traditional physical spaces, and this implies very different views of what markets are and how they function. But exactly in what ways do those views differ? How do B2C marketing strategies differ from B2B marketing strategies, and what are the critical strategic implications in these distinctions? What are the marketing strategies that make sense for firms that are hybrids, either in the atomic business models that they are employing or in the mixing of traditional physical capabilities and virtual capabilities? These are some of the key questions addressed in this chapter.

LEARNING OBJECTIVES FOR THIS CHAPTER

- To describe the unique capabilities of Internet technologies
- To differentiate between vertical and horizontal marketing channels
- To utilize marketing tools and strategies in case applications
- To point out the advantages and disadvantages of online firms
- To discuss the characteristics of customer relationship management (CRM) systems
- To explain the critical pricing issues related to cyberspace

▶ *CASE STUDY 11-1*

HARRAH'S

The role of an effective customer relationship management (CRM) system is to identify, attract, develop, and retain customers and to generate sustainable and profitable growth. CRM is really a management principle that stresses customer-driven goals for the firm. CRM systems support the entire customer relationship lifecycle with applications for marketing automation, sales force automation, customer support automation, and knowledge management.

The global CRM market has suffered a sharp downturn partly, as a result of the extended depressed economic conditions and market uncertainty created by the terrorist attacks of September 11. As a result, the value of CRM software and services markets fell to $6.75 billion in 2001. In spite of the economic downturn, there is expected growth within the CRM for the market to rebound from these setbacks over the next five years and grow to $10.4 billion by 2006.

One company looking to strengthen their CRM effort is Las Vegas-based gaming and hotel giant Harrah's Entertainment, Inc. Harrah's was founded in 1937, when Bill Harrah opened a bingo parlor in Reno, NV. Harrah's grew quickly, building and acquiring properties throughout Nevada and beyond. In 1973, Harrah's became the first casino company listed on the New York Stock Exchange. With 18 casinos in eight U.S. states, Harrah's Entertainment, Inc., is the most recognized and respected brand name in the casino entertainment industry.

Harrah's CRM solution gives Harrah's a better understanding of its customers and the activities they enjoy at Harrah's properties. Harrah's is forming closer relationships with its millions of guests who eat, sleep, watch live shows, and bet at the company's casinos. During the next two years, the system is expected to electronically tie together Web and e-mail campaigns, front desk services, and even slot machines. For instance, if a customer played a slot machine for four hours in the afternoon, the system could advertise a lunch special on the machine's screen.

Harrah's produces more than 20 million customer offers for free entertainment, vouchers for food and accommodation, and points redeemable for merchandise annually and tracks each offer to determine when and how offers are redeemed. With NCR's (formerly the National Cash Register Company) Teradata warehouse, Harrah's can analyze hundreds of customer attributes to determine likelihood to visit, predicted spending, opportunities for cross-sell, and much more. This allows Harrah's to target promotions and mailings to individual customer preferences. For example, Harrah's might award hotel vouchers to out-of-state guests and provide free show tickets to customers who make day trips to the casino.

"Our NCR customer relationship management solution helps us analyze each customer's preferences and predict what services and rewards they'll want in the future. As a result, we can offer them a more enjoyable experience each time they visit our casino," says John Boushy, Harrah's senior vice-president of Information Technology and Marketing Services. "Harrah's has the only system in the industry for recognizing and rewarding its customers on a national basis, across all of our properties. Knowing our customers better differentiates us from our competitors."

Harrah's has recently been recognized by *Forbes* and *Business Week* as a market leader, due in large part to its mission to "build lasting relationships" with its customers. Harrah's achieves this mission through operational excellence and technological leadership that enables Harrah's to manage each customer relationship individually.

Discussion:
1. Describe the purpose of an effective CRM systems module.
2. Discuss how the current economy has impacted the diffusion of CRM systems.

Sources:
http://www.computerworld.com/industrytopics/travel/story/0,10801,61654,00.html
http://www.ncr.com/repository/case_studies/data_warehousing/harrah.htm
http://www.isourceonline.com/article.asp?article_id=2811
http://www.pcworld.com

▶ 11.1 INTRODUCTION

Marketing is critical in any business, to ensure that the exchanges that the firm depends upon with customers and suppliers take place. The side of the firm facing toward the suppliers is called business-to-business, or B2B, and the strategies employed for this part of the business are different than those for downstream customers, and the final consumers of the goods/services. But these two types of channel have always existed for firms. In what ways are these exchanges distinctive in the cyberworld? This question will be addressed here as will the question of how physical systems differ from virtual systems that depend on network-delivered information.

Focus on NE: Nature Network's Stimulation of the Senses

What is Nature Network (http://www.orca-live.net/)? The idea of Nature Network is to relay live imagery and sound from cameras set up in nature throughout the world. "My hope is to bring people closer to Nature without disrupting her," writes Dr. Spong. (Please read the "Message for OrcaLive by Paul Spong.") At this very moment, all over the world, a variety of organisms are beaming with life. Wouldn't it be wonderful if there were medium through which people could get a sense of this? If a window could be opened up that would trigger city dwellers' memories of the rhythms of nature, the way in which we view the world and our way of being are bound to change. That hope, too, lies within. One night some 20 years ago—when the ocean was still and a full moon lit the sky—Dr. Spong heard the breath of the passing orcas. He felt that if only the whole world could share this moment, it would surely change people's sense of the world. This moment inspired the concept of the Nature Network: Stations set up in nature that transmit live images and sound to people around the world. Implementing the concept, which at the time was technically very difficult, becomes much more feasible with the widespread use of the Internet. This site has been conducting a variety of experiments since 2000 toward realizing Nature Network. Visit this amazing site!

Sources:
http://www.orca-live.net/

11.2 STRATEGY AND E-MARKETS

Marketing is an analysis of exchanges, especially the types of channels employed and how the exchanges are priced. What channels does the firm have to effectively bring raw materials and subcomponents together on the supply side and/or to flow these products and services to brokers and customers on the demand side. Logistics on either the supply or demand sides have long been part of the study and practice of marketing because logistics is essentially a matter of channel efficiency and effectiveness. Relationships with complementors such as value-added resellers have clearly been in the domain of traditional marketing, but coordination with joint venture partners has, in the past, been more a central concern of strategic-level management. Handling all vendor, complementor, and supplementor relationships is a challenge for a firm that goes beyond the boundaries of traditional marketing, but there is no reason why such topics should not be discussed as if they were just other highly innovative channels.

An important area of study in marketing is how firms develop new channels, and so the linking of strategy and marketing is a natural linkage. When firms move toward greater virtuality, they are exploring channels outside the box. An order fulfillment process that is handled online is quite different even from a telephone system manned by a call center. Advertising on the Web has a wholly new set of parameters for managers. Where and when should such channels be employed? That is the big question.

Finally, channel conflict is a critical issue in marketing because channels need to complement each other whenever possible. If channels begin to contend with each other, the entire fulfillment process, B2B as well as B2C, begins to suffer. The clearest case of this is when a firm decides to disintermediate brokers, such as travel agents. When the industry as a whole reintermediates with individual firm Web sites (e.g., www.delta.com or www.ual.com), the conflict is more manageable for the firm because brokers lose tremendous power when the industry as a whole adopts a practice that does not favor the intermediary. Nevertheless, it is still a bone of contention and travel agents could start to steer their value-added business segments to non-American carriers, if, for instance, the American carriers were strong advocates and leaders in the push to disintermediate agents.

Resolution of channel conflict is one of the most important aspects of e-marketing because new channels made available through the Internet are at the least cannibalizing older channels, or at the most replacing them. The firm needs to strategize to find ways to introduce new channels to minimize such conflicts. Weill and Vitale (2001) offer a range of suggestions as to where channel conflicts tend to arise between atomic models and how to handle some of these problems.

Pricing at all levels of the supply chain will undoubtedly change as a result of NE. In what ways? Some are predicting that consumers will gain power in the cyberworld. Others see equal or superior advantages for sellers. We will discuss each of these points-of-view and see why there is likely to be a dynamic that will level the playing field.

11.3 STRATEGIC MARKETING ISSUES RELATED TO THE NOVELTY OF E-MARKETS

Because the Web enables new forms of business where it is not practical or possible for traditional business forms to succeed,[1] there are extremely important strategic implications for e-marketing. Consider the following innovative capabilities in Table 11.1. All of these are realized through Internet technologies.

Table 11.1: Unique Capabilities of Internet for E-Marketing

	Cyperspace Versus Physical Space	Examples
1	Online auctions permitting geographically remote participants to bid on items and interact in communities based on similar areas of interest	eBay
2	Exchanges enlarging the market for suppliers and buyers regardless of size	Freemarket Covisint
3	Live chat, instant messaging, and voice-over-IP (VoIP) enabling individuals to communicate in real-time with each	qvc.com
4	Broadcasting through Web cams and sharing of real-time activities	ICU
5	Peer-to-peer applications that allow individuals to share digital information without requiring a centralized database	WinMX
6	Commercial sites that connect to the rest of the Web world	grc.com
7	New pricing models such as reverse auctions for expanding market opportunities	Priceline Mobshop
8	Novel ways of sorting products and services, such as by price or size, in ways that go well beyond the limitations of physical store displays	wine.com
9	Personalized services and configuration of offerings to vast numbers of concurrent customers	e*Trade fidelity.com dell.com

---

[1]Straub, Hoffman, Weber, and Steinfield (2002).

Each of these capabilities has strategic implications for marketers. Let's examine them one at a time.

11.3.1 Unique Capability Number One: Online Auctions

Because an auction can be structured to favor either the buyer or seller, firms need to create online auctions that maximize revenues at the lowest possible cost to the firm. There is no comparable to this capability in the physical world because e-bidders can come from anywhere on the planet so long as they have connectivity. Physical commerce cannot gather individuals from the far reaches of the planet at a given time and run the overall auction continuously. This is the perfect case of the substitution of information for physicality, discussed as the distinctive feature of NE in the opening chapter of this book.

The marketing challenge for online auctions is retaining user interest and liveliness of bidding so that both buyers and sellers return frequently to the site. If users never win a bid at a price they view as comparatively low, they will likely not return as often. The marketing strategy of sellers, therefore, is to offer enough volume of commodity-like products at an opening bid that is viewed as a bargain. If the buyers bid up the price to higher values, then that is, of course, advantageous to the seller.

eBay is an intermediary because it owns none of the inventory. For intermediaries, as we have seen, the difficulty is that buyers will begin to disintermediate you after connecting with the seller. This interpretation assumes that there will be future sales of a high enough volume to make this worthwhile. eBay avoids this complication in their marketing strategy by focusing on one-time transactions. By serving as a marketplace for individual buyers and sellers who are treating each exchange as a unique transaction, buyers and sellers have to return to eBay for each new good being purchased. eBay is undoubtedly being disintermediated by buyers and sellers who engage in higher volumes of transactions, whether they are individual consumers or businesses so this unique business capability has some positives and negatives.

11.3.2 Unique Capability Number Two: Web Exchanges

Online exchanges, whether they are auctions or not, can theoretically reach a global market at a fraction of the costs involved in bringing together the same buyers in the physical world. This represents an unprecedented expansion of markets. Consider the case of Covisint, the shared infrastructure of the automobile industry. As long as the conditions of sale can be met, buyers and sellers on this network are counting on worldwide competition for components. Especially for commodities, a large automobile manufacturer is most concerned with cost, once it is assured through detailed specifications that the quality of the product meets its needs.

Let's take car radios. An automaker wants lots composed of different types of radios, each of which has different characteristics, for instance, the difference between a plain AM-FM radio and one with a built-in CD player. By issuing the RFB (request for bids) on an online exchange, the features of each lot of product would be specified, and the bidders (the suppliers of the stereos) could come from anywhere on the planet, assuming they qualify as bidders.

Therefore the bidders get business that they would have ordinarily been frozen out of and the buyers get new bidders, whether or not they are capable of delivering the product and service. The process of determining the quality of the bidder looms larger in the cyberworld, perhaps, because of the larger numbers of potential merchants online, but a tried and true method is to accept bids, monitor fulfillment, and place more business with reliable suppliers over time.

The online exchanges favor multisourcing over sole sourcing because the advantages of the exchanges derive from their reach. If a firm identifies itself as the sole source of a product or service, for a variety of reasons, then online exchanges do not meet the profile.

11.3.3 Unique Capability Number Three: New Communications Media

Media enhancements offered through Internet technologies affect nearly all marketing channels. Live chat enables sales representatives to "talk" via text exchanges with customers in real-time, as shown in Figure 11.1. This interactive response can be a powerful tool in strengthening customer relationships.

Figure 11.1   Beginning of a Live Chat Session with Sales Representative at qvc.com

What makes this a unique capability for NEOs? In the physical marketspace, a sales representative can only deal with one customer at a time, for all intents and purposes. In the cyberworld, sales representatives seem to be able to maintain contact with three customers at a time! This is a threefold increase in productivity that is hard to match in most processes in physical organizations.

Instant messaging, actualized by voice-over-IP (VoIP) technologies, goes even further in terms of simulating the social presence of a human being. Digital versions of the analog signals that carry voice over telephone lines can also carry voice over the IP. For customers who need a close interaction with a sales representative, for example, VoIP offers another conceivable channel.

11.3.4 Unique Capability Number Four: Web Cam Broadcasting

Using a technology known as *video streaming*, broadcasts of live action (or nearly live, meaning that the screen is refreshed less than what would give the impression of a moving image) over the Internet can give customers a strong association with the most influential brand images of the organization. The comparable physical storefront capabilities would be videos of product lines, manufacturing processes, installation procedures, and so forth. But the novelty of the Internet is that these images can be delivered anywhere at the customer's convenience. Figure 11.2 illustrates how information about traffic patterns can be made easily accessible through Web cams.

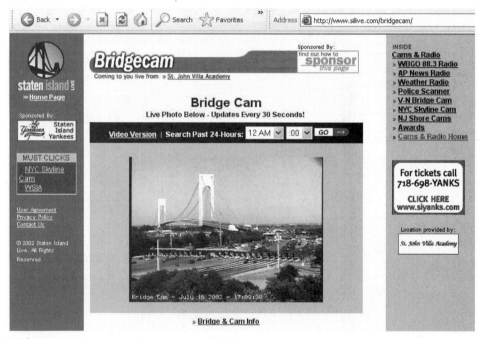

Figure 11.2 Real-Time Traffic on Verrazano Narrows Bridge

Whereas most of the applications of Web cams to date have been in public service or nonprofit venues, small stretches of the imagination can visualize how the technology can be applied to profit-making organizations. Live shots, just like live talk or live text exchanges, capitalize on a sense of immediacy that is important when establishing customer involvement.

11.3.5 Unique Capability Number Five: Peer-to-Peer (P2P) Communications

Peer-to-peer, or P2P, technology allows entities to exchange data directly without the intervention or control of third-party Web server sites. The software that enables this employs a search capability to determine where data or information is located and then establishes a direct connection through the Internet to that IP address.

This decentralized mode of operation gave rise to a huge number of file-sharing sites, some of which like Napster, have been challenged in courts of law because of the sharing of copyrighted material. The business press has argued that, from a practical standpoint, the entertainment industry cannot contain P2P sharing, and they need to devise value-added strategies so as to incorporate P2P in their business models.[2] Legally, there may be a case for digital goods industries, but there are too many avenues for P2P exchanges over the Internet, which will only increase with higher bandwidth channels. For the moment, this technological innovation is being heavily used. How it can be appropriated by organizations is uncertain but needs to be explored. Without a creative view of new VANs, digital goods industries are just going to lose more and more ground every year.

There is no question that the scale of the changes resulting from the sharing of physical media is monumental. It is vastly different than traditional processes. Copying a vinyl record to an audio tape, for example, is an extremely labor-intensive process. The digitalization of content and the ability to share this content over networks has overturned the traditional physical constraints hampering organizations and made new business propositions viable.

11.3.6 Unique Capability Number Six: Global Reach and Range

One of the most obvious and dramatic characteristics of publicly-accessible Internet Web sites is that they are globally accessible. There is nothing remotely similar to this reach in traditional business forms. Range can be achieved with an extensive inventory, much of which is supplied by affiliate members, as in the amazon.com model. Amazon can offer millions of books because of their Web-coordinated capability of aggregating content from their own and other people's sites.

Figure 11.3 shows that the entrepreneurial firm grc.com (Gibson Research Services) offers services to protect PCs from unauthorized access. With millions of downloads of the site's free advice for protecting PCs (Shields Up!!), this site demonstrates that there are huge opportunities for cross-selling other firm services.

The global reach of such a site is impressive. If translated variants of the site were made available, there would not even be linguistic barriers to using it. Because the services the firm offers are designed for WinTel platform machines, the market is potentially enormous.

What is even more extraordinary about marketing over the Web is that products and services can be offered to the public on a worldwide basis without a prodigious physical infrastructure. Adequate technology platforms are required, to be sure, but the investment is not remotely comparable to a large internationally dispersed sales force for dealing with millions of potential customers.

---

[2]Harmon (220).

Figure 11.3   GRC's Shields Up!! Information and Software Security Site

11.3.7 Unique Capability Number Seven: New Pricing Models

Electronic auctions conducted over the Web represent a movement of traditional auction structures to the new medium. From the standpoint of scale and scope, online auctions are unique. But the pricing model itself is not unique.

Priceline and other variant auction forms have actually changed underlying pricing model by reversing the roles of buying and selling and taking advantage of the global presence of the Web (Figure 11.4). The price of a service in Priceline is initiated by the buyer's and the seller's bids, in effect, on the offer. Moreover, it is a lowest price for the buyer model, which is uncommon in most auction formats.

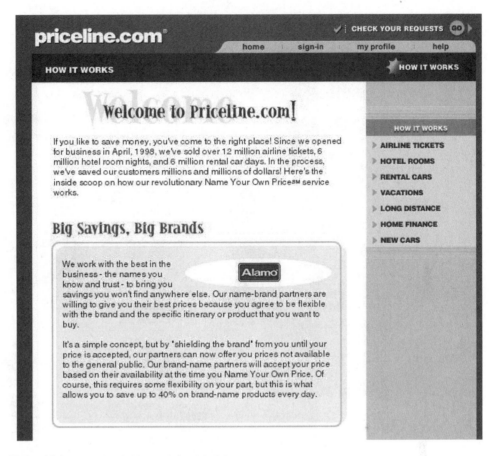

Figure 11.4 Priceline's New Pricing Model

Figure 11.4 shows Priceline's information about how reverse auctions work. The firm has moved across industries and takes an intermediary position in other hospitality and travel industry groups.

11.3.8 Unique Capability Number Eight: Novel Display Capabilities

The Web allows firms to present their goods and services to customers in unique ways. The consortium wine.com's shared infrastructure site offers a case in point (Figure 11.5). Wine in the consortium's inventory can be viewed by type, region, and winery. Clearly, a physical inventory can be displayed in only one way. It is possible to enhance a physical site with information that would allow customers to conceptualize the inventory in different ways, through indices, and so forth, but any one item can only be physically present in one place. In cyberspace, each way of displaying the inventory is equally valid because the physical processes of display have been supplanted by information.

Moreover, there is no limitation to new ways of thinking about the firm's offerings and designing systems to incorporate these innovations. An obvious extension of this logic would be to display the inventory by price.

Figure 11.5 Novel Display Features at wine.com

11.3.9 Unique Capability Number Nine: Personalization and Recommender Systems

The Web can be programmed to treat customers as individuals. The most profitable way of doing this is by exploiting customer data that the organization already owns. When a customer identifies him or herself to the site or is identified by cookies set on the customer machine, this underlying intelligence can be used to effectively respond to customer needs. At amazon.com, for example, returning customers are prompted with book selections that match their previous profile of buying.

Recommender systems that assemble and process customer needs can personalize organizational responses by utilizing customer utility functions. Netflix.com is an example of this approach. The firm recommends DVDs for purchase, based on general customer reviews and the individual customer's own past preferences. Until the individual has a history from which to draw, the profile will be thin at best. But as time goes on, the system should be able to predict more precisely.

What is the physical counterpart of the recommender system and its personalization? Let's say you go to a Blockbuster store to rent a video and that you are a regular customer. Indeed, you are so well-known that the clerk may recognize you and suggest a new title related to your previous rentals.

How is this different in the Web world? First of all, a single powerful server can deal with hundreds of thousands of customers at once, unlike the physical store. And assuming that the technology platform is adequate and the server software is not flawed, the Web site will not be distracted by a flood of sudden customers and thus unable to respond personally. Physical stores have major surges in demand offset with lulls that make it extremely difficult to maintain consistently good service.

11.4 REPRISE: B2B VERSUS B2C

Marketing channels are traditionally divided into business-to-business versus business-to-consumer channels. What is the main difference? If the organization finds itself dealing with another business as a customer, then the relationship has the potential to take a different form than if the relationship is with the ultimate consumer. Procter & Gamble deals with grocery chains in a B2B manner, whereas the grocery chains serve in the intermediary capacity as retailers to the ultimate consumer.

For these reasons, B2B is sometimes referred to as industrial or commercial purchasing. Although not completely mutually exclusive from B2C, B2B relationships tend to be higher in volume and less cash-driven. Levels of trust must, therefore, be high in that a firm's cash flows could otherwise be seriously impacted by large bad debts on the part of nonpaying customers. The structure of procurement processes and intermediary handling of the goods and services in the supply network are dramatically different from selling to consumers.

Because of such differences, marketing departments in business schools typically have a group of professors who specialize in consumer behavior. The psychology of ultimate consumers, who are typically not making business purchases, is focused on product quality; service, including on-time delivery; and price. For individual buyers, trust in the product and vendor is inordinately important, and building a long-term relationship with the vendor is not generally as critical because transactions may be infrequent and sales values relatively small.

11.5 VERTICAL CHANNELS

Traditional B2C channels include entities such as wholesalers, intermediaries, distributors, logistics carriers, and retailers. B2B channels include suppliers at different levels of the chain, otherwise known as *tiers*. Suppliers can be manufacturers of products and/or service providers, or they can be involved in value-added activities such as component assembly. Figure 11.6 illustrates how these entities may be viewed from a *vertical,* or within-industry perspective. The firm is placed illustratively between two sets of intermediaries, but keep in mind that a given firm could fall anywhere along the chain.

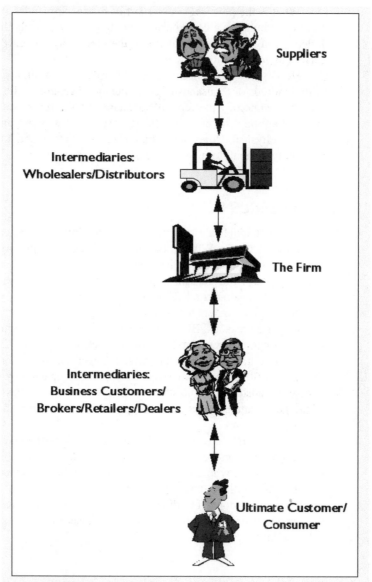

Figure 11.6 Vertical Marketing Channels

Channel partners who are contributing directly to the movement of goods and services from end to end along the chain are said to be part of this vertical. They are said to be part of the *supply chain*. What is extremely important to recognize is that in Net-enhanced organizations we are increasingly interested in horizontal partners as well. A horizontal perspective broadens the base of entities with which the firm needs to work. Net-enhanced organizations are learning to work effectively with this wide range of stakeholders and partners.

11.5.1 Horizontals

Figure 11.7 depicts how firms are using horizontal-level partnerships to support their value chains.

We will examine below how even competitors are contributing to the bottom line for NEOs. For the moment, it can be noted that firms need a co-opetitive as well as a competitive relationship with rivals. Figure 11.8 illustrates this concept.

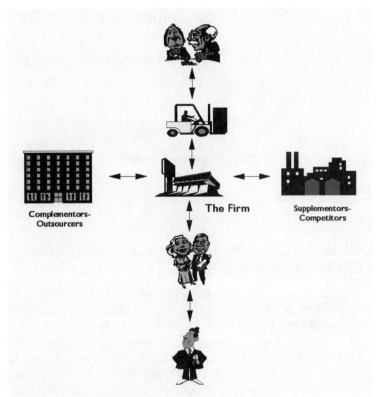

Figure 11.7   Horizontal Partnerships in the Marketing Channels

Moreover, it is not always that easy to differentiate when firms are cooperating and when they are competing. If customers view the products and services of two firms as reinforcing (complementary) then the firms are not competing in that particular activity (product line, setting industry standards, etc.). They are cooperating in bringing a better product or service to the marketplace. HP and Dell appear to be fierce competitors, which they are, most of the time. But both firms participate in industry technical groups that determine the standards for interoperability of WinTel systems. Please note that by not participating in these standards, another firm like Apple, could be viewed as a competitor in this same scenario. Apple sets different standards for its hardware and software and only cooperates in making its systems emulate the WinTel platform so that users can copy files and perform other actions that make the Apple platform more valuable.

■ **Complementor**
- **Customers value your product/service more when they also have access to that of the complementor**

■ **Competitor**
- **Customers value your product/service as substitutable with that of a competitor**

✓ **HP and Dell <u>compete</u> in selling PCs**

✓ **HP and Dell <u>cooperate</u> in PC standards**

Figure 11.8   Criteria for Determining Competitors and Complementors

11.6 PRE-NE ERA TOOLS FOR REACHING OUT: DATABASE MARKETING, DATA MINING, AND DATA WAREHOUSING

In order to reach out to their vertical and horizontal partners or customers, firms need data, and they need information. Traditionally, data is thought of as the raw signals emerging from the environment. Such signals can be captured and stored by computer systems. Data is then said to be processed into information according to the firm's managerial standards. This information can then be fed back into the firm's processes, as shown in Figure 11.9. This figure depicts this process as a system, in accordance with the General Systems Theory (originally articulated in the 1930s) and the derived General Systems Model of the firm.[3]

Information serves to reduce uncertainty about threats to the firm and to give insight into new opportunities to pursue. Information about customer satisfaction with the firm's services, for example, could tell managers how to adjust the incentive system to improve the internal responsiveness. Subsequent information, which confirmed that the satisfaction ratings had gone up, would reduce uncertainty about the effectiveness of these managerial actions.

The ability of a NEO to gather more and varied information than competitors is critical to the mission,[4] especially because the cycle time in the NE era is so much shorter. Nevertheless, the use of extensive data storage and search and manipulation capabilities is nothing new. The three technologies—database marketing, data mining, and data warehousing—are being heavily used in networked enterprises that have developed over the last 20 years.

[3]Bertalanfy (1936).
[4]Straub and Klein (2001).

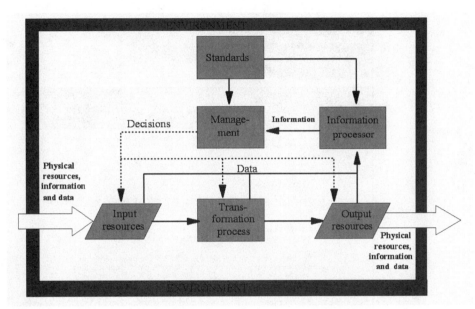

Figure 11.9   Information and Data in the General Systems Model of the Firm

11.6.1 Database Marketing

Marketing departments have been collecting information about customers and potential customers and analyzing it via market segments for a long time. Third-party providers of such services, such as the firm in the Web site shown in Figure 11.10, gather data from a variety of sources and aggregate it for resale. Creating information composites that did not previously exist is protected by copyright laws in many countries, such as the United States, so in many cases the information composites are aggregated from private and public sources. If the contract between the third-party provider and the original content provider does not specifically rule out the creation of a composite, then the activity is most likely legal and itself protected by copyright. This proprietary aggregation can occur as a result of the resources owned by the third-party content provider (in this case, the aggregator). This changes the stakes regarding the competitive advantage offered by the content provision atomic business model. In brief, a database marketer offering access services to its database over the Web can continue to own the data, just as it does in the physical distribution of data.

What does the Web offer a database marketer? The Web gives the firm an enormously expanded markets for its services, opportunities for the collection of fees in real-time, and the ability to repackage services and cross-sell them to patrons, to whom one is connected by e-mail.

Figure 11.10   Database Marketing Firm's Home Page on the Web

Use of Database Marketing Services by NEOs

NEOs use the databases acquired through third parties in much the same way they always have. The value of this information is that it allows the firm to segment its markets and its marketing efforts. If the data shows that the customer group attracted to product X is in a certain age group, then the advertising designed to market product X needs to appeal to this age group. It is obvious that a sizable segment of the beer drinkers in the United States are young people who watch sporting events, and this is the reason most of the advertising is targeted to this group.

Firms can also combine external data acquired through third party sources with their internal transactional data. The transactional data acquired through online ordering is extremely powerful, especially in B2C contexts. Many or most B2B transactions individually identify the customer, particularly because a large proportion of this business takes place on credit and generates an accounts receivable journal entry. In B2C settings, though, the consumer is identified only if she or he uses a debit or credit card or check. If the transaction is in cash, the individual customer transactional data is often lost.

The desire to capture such information is obvious. Airlines popularized frequent flier programs, in part, to tap into such data. Frequent buyer programs have been carried out in many other industries to try to learn who the firm's customers are and what they want.

An online B2C environment has the advantage of requiring customers to individually identify themselves. For one thing, there must be a means of payment, and this requires individual identification. For another, there must be a shipping location in the case of physical goods or services. Even when the firm offers trial versions, as in the case of software, the customer is identified at least by an FTP address, and an addition to this can be an email address. Figure 11.11 shows a hypothetical dialogue between a customer and Nero.com illustrating the trial software process. When the customer clicks on the hyperlink to download this software, the vendor server, through its upload of the Web page request from the customer, can capture the FTP address of the customer. Customer email addresses are usually closely associated with the FTP address. and the firm can either deduce these or ask the customer directly for this information.

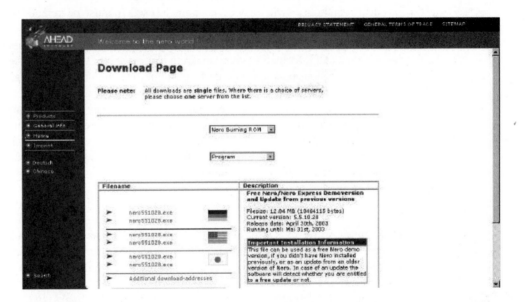

Figure 11.11   Capturing of E-Mail Addresses through Uploads

The data that relates to the entire online transaction process is known as *clickstream data*. It is basically a recording of the interaction between the user and the server. Requests for downloads are just one of these possible requests. If a given user clicks through on various hyperlinks on a Web page, the server can time stamp and store this data about the interaction itself. We discuss the use of clickstream data later in this chapter. For the moment, it is sufficient to note that transactional data, as well as data about transactions, as discussed by Weill and Vitale,[5] could be far more useful and far better used by the vast majority of NEOs than is currently the case.

---

[5]Weill and Vitale (2001).

What should NEOs do with the enormous amount of clickstream data from a technical standpoint? It is clear that this data is related to the behavior of individual customers and, if analyzed, could tell the firm a great deal about customer preferences. Suppose a NEO wants to understand why certain potential customers abandon the Web site. The exact pages requested and the time likely spent on each page might reveal patterns that could characterize abandonments, so the analysis of huge quantities of this data could dramatically improve the firm's marketing.

To do this, the data needs to be combined so that the times visited, the patterns of usage during those visits, and the events that led to a purchase (if any) are linked to the basic customer data such as name, address, e-mail address, and so forth. The result of such a combination and the use of this data is better discussed under the next section on data warehousing.

11.6.2 Data Warehousing

The underlying concept of a data warehouse is, obviously, a warehouse. It is as if data were sitting in bins and shelves where it could be retrieved and further utilized. Unlike a physical warehouse, where once an item is used it must be remade and resupplied to inventory, information can be duplicated and used an infinite number of times. The binary digital original is never depleted by copying. This is the distinct advantage of symbols, such as data and information, over concrete objects and physical processes.

Data warehouses combine data from numerous sources into a single repository that can be utilized to address management issues and questions. It is critical that managers realize that these databases are derived. They are combinations. They are not intended to be production databases for use by servers to directly answer customer questions or to provide a basis for transactions and ledger entries. They are compilations that can be searched and queried, mined with data mining software, and probed for new perspectives on how to market to customers through the channels.

11.6.3 Data Mining

Data mining software is a set of tools that allows managers to view data in new ways. The process of finding patterns in underlying data can be automated or manually controlled. Although managers in virtually all functional areas can profit from this software, marketing applications offer the most obvious benefits.

Figure 11.12 shows rows and columns of data for U.S. banks. In Cognos's PowerPlay data mining software, a single value such as Bank of America's consumer finance interest rate of 17.21% can be highlighted in its row and column. If a manager wishes to compare this rate with those of the competitors in the database, the data can be sorted. Selections among all banks, so that the comparison is with other large banks, is also possible. Finally, the manager can *roll up* (move to a higher level of aggregation) or *drill down* (move to a more detailed level). In the latter instance, clicking on the consumer finance column produces a new screen with rates for the same banks under column headings of Gold Card and Standard Card.

Data mining software typically has graphical display capabilities as well as a unit of preset reports and the ability to save ad hoc reports so they can be readily reused at a later time. With such report capabilities, the voluminous data that is generated in Web transactions and browsing can be filtered according to the information needs of management.

	Auto Finance	Home Finance	Consumer Finance	Unsecured	All Credit Products
AmSouth Banco	9.08	7.70	15.97	12.85	9.92
BB&T Corporati	9.68	8.17	13.64	14.78	9.95
BOK Financial (	9.25	7.63	15.48	14.71	9.21
Banc One Corp	9.50	8.03	15.87	14.15	9.68
BancorpSouth,	9.14	7.85	14.13	17.17	9.25
Bank Of Montre:	8.47	7.66	17.22	15.67	9.17
Bank of New Yo	10.17	7.87	14.43	13.87	9.52
BankAmerica C	10.16	7.71	17.21	15.60	9.78
BankBoston	9.90	7.61	12.23	14.83	9.04
Brenton Banks,	9.68	7.73	17.94	13.50	9.31
CPB, Inc.	12.29	6.91	15.41	13.75	10.25
Chase Manhatt:	9.81	7.89	16.26	14.41	9.77
Chittenden Con	9.61	8.18	15.88	14.94	9.91
Citicorp	9.57	7.69	16.72	17.25	9.53
Comerica, Inc.	10.19	7.89	16.41	15.90	10.48
Commerce Bar	8.70	7.77	14.55	13.08	9.32
CoreStates Fin:	10.21	7.59	16.23	12.49	9.57
CoreStates Fin:	10.21	7.60	16.23	12.49	9.58
Crestar Financi	9.08	7.68	16.69	13.99	9.54
Deposit Guarar	9.01	7.89	na	10.00	8.38
First American (	9.01	7.91	12.29	14.25	8.90
First Chicago N	9.44	7.65	17.18	14.54	9.48
First Commerce	9.28	7.59	16.57	14.50	9.32
First Commerci	10.00	7.67	13.93	10.00	8.86
First Hawaiian,	11.72	7.50	15.93	11.50	10.20
All Bank Familie:	**9.73**	**7.84**	**15.71**	**14.16**	**9.61**

Top menu bar: All Bank Families | All Credit Products | All Months | All Regions | All Financial Institutions | All Income Levels

Figure 11.12   Data Mining in Bank Interest Rates

Let's take an example in order to understand how the Web presents new challenges as well as new opportunities for smart managers. Suppose potential buyers are identified by offering online inducements such as trial versions or loss leaders. Even better, suppose their e-mail addresses have been requested and captured. Clickstream data has also been collected on the one to many visits the potential customer makes to the site. By rapidly linking up this initial firm-owned specific information with data purchased from a database marketer, the combined data can be placed into a data warehouse. Now the firm is in a position to learn about its online target market segment.

Data mining reveals that a particular premium product line with high margins was visited heavily by teens and retired people (who also owned two cars), but that they generally did not purchase. The firm's marketing manager moves quickly to find out from a sampling of users with these characteristics why they did not purchase the product via an e-mail survey. The enticement to participate is a free sample of one of the firm's less expensive, commodity products or a discount for future purchases.

The manager finds out that price is part of the problem, but a bigger issue is that the Web page does not answer questions about product features. Several of the hyperlinks are not working, as well. The sampled users expressed high interest in the product but did not know or trust the firm enough to take a chance on the fairly expensive product not suiting them.

To see if these are truly representative issues, the manager makes some adjustments to price but also has the Web site redesigned for responsiveness. Sales surge ahead in this product category and in the particular brands where more information about product features appears to be critical.

Please notice that firms such as Amazon, with millions of online users, can institute fairly large surveys and still be able to later present all users with improvements and inducements that result from the experimentation. Experimentation lies at the heart of e-marketing. Not only is it feasible on the Web, but it is a part of the repertoire of tools that a competent manager will exploit in cyberspace.

The Web has been called the largest marketing focus group in history, and there is a lot of merit in this *bon mot*. Now traditional technologies such as database marketing, data warehousing, and data mining create unique capabilities for firms that are attempting to exploit the inherent characteristics of the cyberworld. NEOs have to adapt to this dynamic environment with new experimental approaches to answering questions. Those NEOs that do will lead their industries and can dramatically alter the shape of these industries.

11.7 B2B MARKETING STRATEGIES

B2B marketing stresses connections between channel participants who are businesses. These exchanges are either in the mode depicted in Figure 11.6, where there is an ultimate consumer at the end of the chain or where a business is itself the end of the chain. If Business A buys office supplies from officedepot.com, for example, there may be ultimate consumers who are customers of Business A, but it is equally possible that Business A sells only to other businesses, such as Business B. There is a generally held view that B2B transactions and relationships are qualitatively different from B2C and other dyadic connections, and for this reason, we consider it separately. This section deals with the setting of B2B goals in an organization.

11.7.1 Supply Chains and Electronic Trading Networks

An exciting development in NE with respect to B2B interactions is the ETN. These are business exchanges that bring together multifarious sellers and buyers. These are typically either intermediary or shared infrastructure atomic models. Examples include Covisint, the automobile industry exchange owned by GM, Ford, and so forth (see Figure 11.13). Other examples are Omnexus,[6] the plastics industry exchange for resins, and Manheim Auctions,[7] an exchange for used auto dealerships. Other examples include ForestExpress, an exchange for forest products originated by Georgia Pacific and others. These exchanges are technological innovations and, as such, will experience the success or failure rates that are typical with new ideas.

[6]See the case by Rai, et al. (2000).
[7]See the case by McKeown and Watson (1999).

Figure 11.13 Covisint Electronic Trading Network Home Page

An ETN strategy needs to take into account the relatively weak position of intermediaries and shared infrastructures. When Omnexus entered the plastics electronic exchange marketplace in 2000, for example, there were well-entrenched competitors, e-firms such as GetPlastics and PlasticsGrid, already in place. How can a newcomer compete in such a market?

Omnexus chose to seek backing from the major resin suppliers, firms such as BASF and Dow. They also formed strategic partnerships, again with equity position, with firms such as IBM. In short, they chose the greater involvement of a shared infrastructure model to attempt to bring give their company enough clout in the market. Their marketing strategy was to move vertically in the plastics industry and horizontally to related industries such as chemicals. Whether ETNs such as Omnexus ultimately succeed in the marketplace, the strategic goal of using the synergies of a developed and operational ETN to branch out from this launch point and to tackle whole new market segments makes sense.

How does an ETN affect the supply chain? If products can be purchased online, with ordering, settlement, and delivery arranged electronically, the supply chain becomes *seamless*. Omnexus wanted to become the end-to-end fulfillment channel for the suppliers of raw materials such as resins all the way through to manufacturers who were purchasing plastics for their products.

The clear effect on a supply chain is to make it more efficient. The costs of business exchanges include search costs,[8] negotiating, legal, and insurance against default. All of these costs can be much lower to somewhat lower in the electronic environment.

[8]Malone et al. (1989).

How? Let's take the example of search costs and explore it in greater detail to show how this can occur in reality. A buyer has been acquiring services that the firm needs on a regular basis from two suppliers. She has a growing suspicion that the cost of these services is not as low as it should be, especially with development of new technology over time, and that the quality is not what it should be. The service is standardized and can be specified in boiler plate service level agreements. An example of such a service might be courier services.

The buyer goes online and finds an ETN that specializes in the services the firm needs. A variety of providers in the firm's region are indicated, several of which are in addition to the firm's two current suppliers. The ETN allows the buyer to specify needs/service levels and to accept bids online from sellers. The buyer receives several bids, including lower pricing with higher service levels from its current suppliers.

Of course, if the firm does achieve lower costs for higher quality, then there are benefits from the ETN that go beyond the electronic connection in that they could be achieved through physical processes. What is distinctive about the ETN is that the buyer has access to information about potential suppliers that could have not very easily been available otherwise. In some of the ground-breaking work by Nobel Prize Laureate Herbert Simon, he showed that information searches result in a *satisficing,* or sub-optimal behavior. Searchers, in effect, give up seeking new information after a period, and this very often results in choices that are not the result of complete information.

In using an ETN, a buyer has at her fingertips information on firms that are interested in bidding for her business. Her search costs are, therefore, lower, and the serendipity is that the search is likely more complete. It may be the case that some critical bidders are missing from an ETN. Nevertheless, in an ideal case, this will not be true.

▶ *CASE STUDY 11-2*

DATA MINING AT ASPEN TECHNOLOGY CORPORATION

E-commerce organizations have invested large amounts of money in information technology to help them manage their organizations more effectively and to gain competitive advantage. A popular tool is data mining, which helps customers to leverage their data more effectively and obtain insightful information that can give them a competitive edge. Aspen Technology Corporation has invested significant resources into implementing data mining.

In 18 years of selling software products, the company had many economic problems because of the current situation; however they were trying to allocate resources and find a way to keep investing in the company. Aspen Technology needed to measure the effectiveness of their Web banner advertisements using the metric, the number of click-throughs, and thus fail to take into account the sales generated by each visitor. The goal was to sell more and attract buyers to the Web site in order to sell the software products more effectively. The best ways to get these kinds of results were to measure a mix of multiple data sources.

They used the analysis component that provided an integrated environment for decision support, utilizing data mining, which allowed the system to transform, report, and be visualized. The complexity of the available data gave the analysis a great advantage over horizontal support tools. This automatically helped the system to know the type of each attribute; in other words Aspen Technology could know when each customer has a Web session and that each Web session includes page views and orders. This also helped to identify the customers and to make sure that the customer set has been adequately determined because customers are the main concern on any businesses (e-commerce).

By utilizing data mining in their company Aspen Technology was able to bring more customers into the Web site and also determine relationships among different factors such as price, products, customer satisfaction, and external factors such as competition and customer location. This information helped the organization to determine the impact on sales and corporate profits. Aspen Technology's sales increased 8.6% in comparison to the last year total sales, which showed that it was a good move.

In conclusion, this technology helped the business discover hidden patterns in the data and also helped them understand the effectiveness of their Web banner advertisements and helped to increase the sales. The company worked hard to implement this technology, and the results were great. The company had the opportunity to bring more people into the business and have a better opportunity to sell their software products.

Discussion:
1. Discuss the benefits of data mining in customer service.
2. What is the importance of multiple data sources in the data mining process?

Sources:
http://www.mindleaders.com/catalog/ecom06.html
http://dmoz.org/Business/E-Commerce/Consultants/Software_Developers/
Microsoft Data Mining: Integrated Business Intelligence for E-Commerce and Knowledge, 1999, 354–378.

11.7.2 Development of Buying Networks rather than Pure One-to-One Auctions

Buying networks are being developed rather than one-to-one auctions in part to create information visibility in the supply chain. Traditional auctions are one-time transactions that remain at arm's length. Buyers and sellers have little reason to cooperate other than on a negotiated price and other terms of sale. Long-term relationships do not fit neatly within the auction model.

ETNs encourage strategic alliances. Bids may be set up for long-term supply at fluctuating prices, for example. Terms can also be renegotiated over time. Such process customization and process sharing can still be accommodated within an ETN.

11.7.3 B2B Information Visibility

As partners work together more and grow to trust each other, they can extend themselves by sharing information about forecasts, strategy and future needs. This kind of information visibility can theoretically reduce the variation in the flows and stocks of the traditional supply chain. Figure 11.14 shows how changes in orders from the auto industry had a dramatic effect on the machine tool industry in the United States from 1961 to 1991. Because the machine tool firms were not given access to information about demand for automobiles and likely production schedules, they suffered from huge underproduction and overproduction. This is known as the *bullwhip* effect.[9]

[9]Lee et al. (1997).

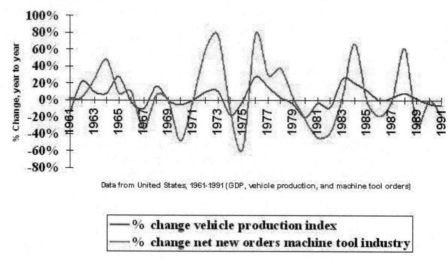

Data from United States, 1961-1991 (GDP, vehicle production, and machine tool orders)

———— % change vehicle production index
———— % change net new orders machine tool industry

Figure 11.14   Bullwhip Effect from Information Invisibility in the Supply Chain[10]

Buying networks also create flexibility by contracting dual sourcing and multisourcing arrangements. Some envision *virtual switching* between suppliers depending on pricing[11] and other factors, but it is not necessary to have such a well-oiled switching mechanism in place to enjoy the benefits of information visibility. Sharing transactional information about upstream flows and stocks can greatly help all downstream partners estimate demand and adjust production. This information can be aggregated and placed into seasonal patterns.

More strategic sharing of information, naturally on a need-to-know basis, benefits both parties. Rather than just transactional data, firms can share their own interpretations and estimates, for example. This helps all parties in provisioning and providing superior service. Logistical suppliers are a good example of how beneficial this can be. There are extremely strong relationships between B2B partners who share at high levels as well as share equally. Such relationships are characterized by trust and long-term perspectives. Partners receive both tangible and intangible benefits from their strategic partnerships.

11.7.4 Changes in Distribution Channels and Logistical Failures

Where can B2B buying networks fail? The supply chain can break down at numerous points. The bullwhip effect results from poor (or no) information flowing up and down the supply chain, and the inability to deal with uncertainty in the marketplace. There can also be outright failures in the distribution channels and logistical failures that, occurring near the end of the cycle, invalidate everything that precedes it. We argue that higher levels of appropriate information visibility can reduce bullwhip, even in the presence of out-and-out physical failure.

Let's take a sample case. Suppose a key supplier suffers a major weather disaster and has its manufacturing plant wiped out by a flood. This physical failure can have devastating

[10]From Fine (1998).
[11]Moschowitz (1997)

implications for the supply chain unless the network has been operationalized to be robust against such failures. An extremely intelligent contingency or disaster recovery plan for the supply chain would have alternate sources that could be cranked up quickly to replace the lost capacity.

Here again, information visibility could alleviate an incipient problem. Knowledge about the place of the failed supplier in the network and the likely repercussions can help to put in motion adequate replacements. Once the network has been reset, the continuing flow of information can provide the information to allow adjustments that will keep the system in equilibrium. Figure 11.9 shows how feedback from information can be used to adjust inputs, processes, and outputs in the General Systems Model of the Firm. This kind of adjusting feedback is known as *cybernetics*.

11.7.5 Long-Term Channel Conflicts in Atomic Business Models

As long-term strategic marketing issues, channel conflicts may not result in immediate points of failure, but they can degrade the network performance over time. Typically, channel conflicts occur when a firm is able to substitute information for one of the value-added traditional links in the chain. This is often a replacement of a physical process in the cyberworld.

Channel conflict is when the partners have different goals and cannot or have not resolved this discrepancy. An obvious case is when a firm forms new network connections directly to a lower supply tier or directly to the consumer. We have discussed this phenomenon as *disintermediation*.

Weill and Vitale (2001) discuss channel conflicts between the atomic business models. These are noted below in Table 11.2 as CON, or channel conflicts. Synergies, or SYN, are also noted as are cautionary or questionable combinations ("?").

Table 11.2: Channel Conflicts in NE Business Models (Based on Weill and Vitale 2001)

	Model Type	1	2	3	4	5	6	7	8
1	Content Provider	--------							
2	Direct-to-Consumer	CON	--------						
3	Full Service Provider	?		--------					
4	Intermediary	?		SYN	--------				
5	Shared Infrastructure		CON	?	?	--------			
6	Value Net Integrator	CON		?	?		--------		
7	Virtual Community		SYN	SYN			SYN	--------	
8	Single Point of Contact		SYN		SYN	?	?		--------

It is redundant to discuss every point of interest in this table. Let's talk instead about one conflict and one synergy so you understand the underlying principle. The direct-to-consumer model conflicts with the shared infrastructure because both are trying to establish an immediate connection with the customer and to own the customer relationship. Delta Online and the other airline direct-to-consumer sites are in competition with their own shared infrastructure, Orbitz. Inherent conflicts can sometimes be resolved by offering a different set of products, services, or pricing. This seems to be how the airline owners of Orbitz are handling this conflict.

Full service providers, on the other hand, utilize intermediaries in their model by using them to transfer or service business. Full service providers are by their very nature extending themselves beyond the boundaries of the firm and including partners such as intermediaries and suppliers in their network (SYN). As depicted in the schematic, there is the possibility that the full service provider will lose business to the supplier or intermediary, but their proposition to the customer is that they can satisfy all needs in a certain category and that they aggregate the information that allows for this switchyard function.

There are cautionary notes in the combination of shared infrastructure and full service provider, again because both are trying to own the customer. Nevertheless, there may be circumstances where a shared infrastructure can derive revenue from the full service provider by serving the role of content provider or intermediary. This business may come from customers who would not visit the shared infrastructure Web site, in any case, and the marginal returns from such business would, therefore, be valuable.

11.7.6 B2B Intermediaries

There are numerous B2B third parties whose own business models depend on serving an intermediary role in flowing goods and services through the supply network. Microsoft's Biztalk, for instance, has a generic electronic market floor where buyers and sellers across industries can interact. Figure 11.15 shows the variety of industries that this site is attempting to link.

Figure 11.15   Microsoft's Biztalk B2B Intermediary

Other firms, such as i2 Technologies, Apache, Ariba, SAP, and Web Methods, provide middleware for firms to make the electronic connections to their downstream and upstream partners. In the long run, even SMEs will likely have a mixture of internal systems such as Web EDI and external systems such as Biztalk and firms providing middleware. We will examine some of these issues in the next chapter on deployment of NE solutions.

11.7.7 A Network, Not a Chain

Although we represent B2B and B2C relationships between parties as chains, following Porter,[12] among others, this may be outmoded thinking in the NE era. The evolving relationships among firms, partners, and customers is better described as an intricate network of interconnections. Although each segment of a supply network can certainly be thought of as a chain, this is not the holistic perspective, which may be required to plan and execute NE systems. Nevertheless, we are probably forced to continue using the chain metaphor in many circumstances until we better understand the nature of business networks and networked enterprises, both from a scientific and practical point of view.

Why do we say that supply networks are more accurate descriptions of NE relationships among stakeholders? Foremost among the reasons is that NEOs are participating more and more in networks rather than simplistic supply chains. In the computer goods industry, for instance, the end-to-end fulfillment of a consumer order was traditionally a movement of goods in one direction up the chain, handed off from Tier 3 to Tier 2 to Tier 1 suppliers/distributors to the retailer, in this case CompUSA,[13] as shown in Figure 11.16.

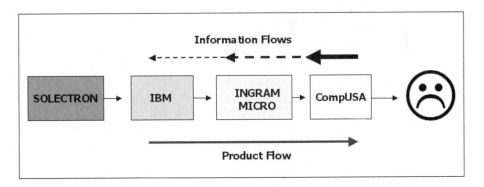

Figure 11.16   Former Traditional Supply Chain for CompUSA

Information flows back through the chain, with CompUSA gathering information about likelihood of future purchases from customers, demand forecasts by CompUSA to Ingram, but decreasing amounts of information about demand and preferences from Ingram to IBM, and so forth. The result of this process is an unhappy customer because the information that flows back through the supply chain is incomplete and

[12]Porter, Michael E., *Competitive Strategy*, Free Press, New York, 1979.
[13]Malhotra et al. (2000) describe how this supply network has evolved.

inaccurate by the time it reaches the first tier. As an intermediary or distributor, in fact, Ingram served as a buffer and was unable to buffer effectively because of variation in production down the chain and variation in demand up the chain. Costs go up because of over- and understocking, delays enter the system, and products are unavailable or late.

Product flows are also cumbersome in that each tier must handle the product. The very term *tier* suggests the nature of the problem. There are multiple tiers in the channel, and this undercuts the timely fulfillment of customer needs.

Networks differ from chains in that each node on the network may (or may not) be connected to each other node. This potential for complete interconnectivity (which can be dynamically adjusted in sophisticated networks) means that information can be spread throughout the network wherever it is needed and that the participants in the channel only handle the goods or perform the service if it is required that they do so.

Dell Computer's partnering with Sony and UPS offers a straightforward example of the effective strategizing and execution of interconnectivity in a supply network.[14] Dell itself does not make or assemble monitors. These are purchased and resold from vendors such as Sony. For this reason, Dell does not need to handle a monitor destined for a consumer (and should not), but it is critical that information about a given transaction involving a monitor purchase flow to Sony from Dell and to a logistics provider such as UPS. The goal of this coordinated network is to have UPS manage the assembly of peripherals for an order at a regional location near the customer delivery site and to deliver the goods together so that it appears as if Dell has served effectively in their role as single point of vendor contact. It is in the interests of Sony and UPS to work with Dell as strategic partners to make the network efficient and effective. All of their future business depends on it. This common goal diminishes the possibility of opportunistic behavior.

The evolution of CompUSA's supply chain into a supply network demonstrates these strategic marketing principles more completely, as graphically depicted in Figure 11.17. To improve order management, goods were delivered by Ingram to both the retailer and the customer directly, depending on the situational needs. This speeds up delivery to the customers and reduces CompUSA's inventories. Just as important is the flow of information to only the parties that needed it (need-to-know criteria), in this case IBM, the OEM or reseller, and Solectron, the manufacturer.

Figure 11.17 shows how the network changes when we consider the need for introducing new products. Here information from the customer flows to both IBM and CompUSA, and IBM distills this to send information about new products or product features to Solectron, the manufacturer. Again, Ingram serves as the distributor and is not concerned with product development *per se*, so they are not a bottleneck in the loop.

[14]Rangan and Bell (1999).

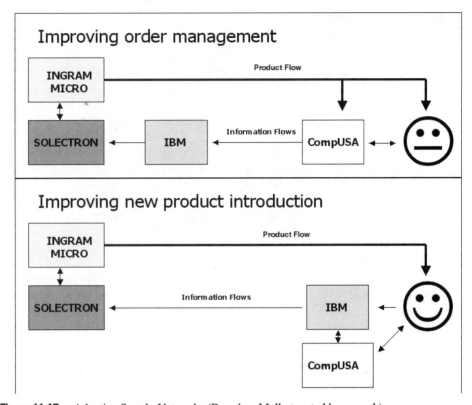

Figure 11.17   Adaptive Supply Networks (Based on Malhotra et al.'s research)

If we abstract from the details of this network and look only at the generalized nodes and links, as in Figure 11.18, it is easier to see how a network functions. Nodes are connected with other nodes but not all other nodes. Information can flow in one or both directions. Some connections represent a one-way flow; others are a two-way flow. A good network design would be presumably connections that are optimal for the performance of the overall network. Information visibility is selective between partners, but there is far more information shared at higher levels than in the traditional supply chain.

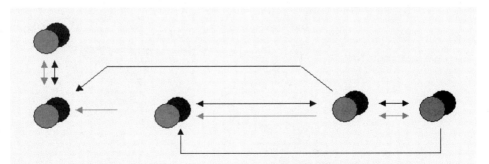

Figure 11.18   Nodes and Links in the CompUSA Information Flow Supply Network (Legend: Orange is for order management; blue is for new product development.)

11.8 B2C MARKETING

Marketing to end-consumers in traditional marketplaces differs from B2B marketing in these ways. Long-term relationships exist in the sense that brand depends on the existence of a loyal customer, but consumer purchases are not long-term in other meanings of the term. Consumers typically do not buy in volume. Even volume purchases by a consumer at a retailer such as Sam's Club are dwarfed by B2B orders. A family stocking up on diapers may buy several gross, but distributors will be buying in lots of hundreds and thousands of gross.

For another reason, consumers are more prone to one-time purchases and to be induced into sales by spur-of-the-moment impulses. Long-term buying with contracted and negotiated prices is atypical of the consumer world.

So how should Web vendors, often called e-tailers, think about creating a sales channel that will drive sales? This section tries to answer this question to some extent.

11.8.1 Models of Cues in B2C

Over the last half decade, there have been numerous studies for why consumers buy online. A full review of these studies is not necessary for the purposes of this introductory text. What is important for managers to know is that the Web world is different, and there are different factors in play for the hearts and the minds of the e-consumer.

Let's sample a few of the scientific studies that have looked at why e-consumers buy online. In Sayrac's work,[15] shown in Figure 11.19, traditional marketing variables such as the characteristics of the product are examined along with factors unique to the Web environment, such as the ability of the e-consumer to navigate the Web pages (Web expertise).[16] Both turn out to be important in encouraging sales.

Factors that are distinctive about the Web, such as the time it takes for a page to download to a client, have also been studied for effects on how consumers view the product. Not surprisingly, Rose et al. (2000) have discovered that the longer it takes for a Web page to download, the less interested the consumer is.[17] Web pages are equivalent to advertisements in print media, and the more user-friendly they are,[18] the more interested potential buyers are.

---

[15]Sayrac-Yaverglu (2002).
[16]See also Koufaris (2002).
[17]Rose (2000; Rose et al. (2000); Rose and Straub (2001).
[18]Palmer (2002).

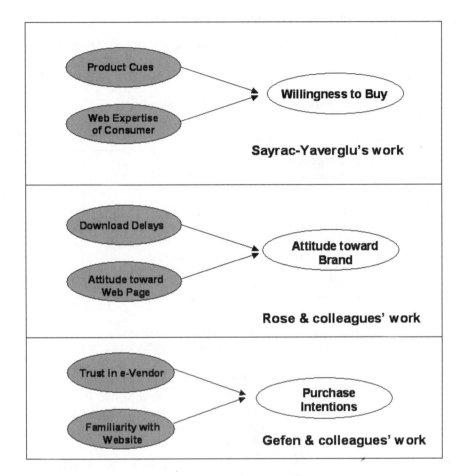

Figure 11.19 Reports on Why E-Consumers Buy Online[19]

Trust, security, and privacy are major areas for motivating online B2C sales.[20] Gefen et al. (2002) have been studying and reporting on the importance of this connection for years.[21] Knowledge of the Web and e-vendors that are trustworthy is an important reason for why some feel comfortable online, and others do not. Firms must build trust in consumers, a point which will be expanded later in the chapter. Interactive marketing is one way to do this.

[19]Sayrac-Yaverglu (2002); e.g., Rose et al. (2000); e.g., Gefen et al. (2002).
[20]See also Torkzadeh and Dhillon (2002) and McKnight et al. (2002).
[21]Gefen (1997); Gefen and Keil (1998); Gefen (2000); Gefen and Straub (2002); Gefen et al. (2002).

11.8.2 Inherent Deficiencies and Advantages of Online Shops

In order to carefully strategize for NE, marketers must consider some of the built-in incentives and disadvantages of B2C Web sites as electronic storefronts. These are shown in Table 11.3.

Table 11.3: Built-in Pros and Cons of Web Storefronts

Feature	Pro	Con
1. Goods and services displayed through multimedia	Offerings can be made as attractive as possible through stimulation of different visual and aural senses.	Lacking the sense of touch and feel for products and face-to-face contact in sales can have negative impacts.
2. No immediate delivery of nondigital goods and services	Inventory appears even when there is none in stock; stock-outs may be hidden from the customer.	Customers may choose to shop where there is immediate availability.
3. Potential for dynamic pricing	Rapid, program-initiated algorithms can maximize margins on given items.	Customers may be frustrated by changes in online pricing between visits.
4. Automatic capturing of customer data	Transactional data and clickstream data are automatically collected on each customer, including ship-to information.	The intrusiveness of the Web may irritate some customers for privacy reasons.
5. Shopping where you are	Convenience is one of the strengths of the Web, assuming Internet connections and an access device are readily available.	Consumers need to have an access device and a network connection.
6. Search engines	Keyword indexing is so much more powerful than topic alphabetization in physical search directories, such as the Yellow Pages.	Web searches have many false hits and voluminous lists of responses.
7. Opens up new communications channels	E-Mail and FTP run on the same underlying connection as the Web.	These applications can overwhelm a firm's resources.
8. Push-pull	As a pull phenomenon, the Web means it should be easier to sell to those who visit.	How to push users to visit is a difficult problem for many Web sites, especially late entrants.

Feature #1

Web sites can present the consumer with visually and aurally stimulating information to induce sales. They suffer compared to physical stores in that they cannot yet emulate the sense of touch. Trying on a pair of jeans in a store has no counterpart in a Web store. Online clothing stores such as boo.com attempted to use 3-D simulation technology to show what clothes would look like on a model. But even if boo.com's technology had not been difficult for most users to utilize, which was the reason for the failure of the site, the experience of feeling the jeans fit was not present even in this innovative site.

Feature #2

Digital stores cannot yet transfer physical offerings directly to customers, and this actually creates an advantage because the Web vendor can attempt alternate sourcing before the customer learns the product is out of stock. The inventory that appears on a firm's Web page is what the vendor carries, not necessarily what the vendor has in stock. When something is out of stock, it is much harder to hide from a customer in most storefronts, especially if all the stock is known by the customer to be on display.

On the contrary, Web stores may not even see some customers because the customer needs the good right away and can acquire immediate ownership in a traditional storefront. The advantage that Web stores have in this regard is that customers have to physically transport themselves to a bricks-and-mortar shop (i.e., a physical store). In an age of larger and larger congested urban areas, shopping at home or in one's office has a major appeal.

If a customer needs a product immediately and can locate and purchase the product online, there can be tremendous synergies for firms that have a physical storefront. Customers of Barnes & Noble might be able to purchase online and pick up the book at the closest physical store. This speeds the process of check-out and takes advantage of both channels. This is a case where the Web *supplements* the physical pre-Internet channel as described by Sarkar et al. (1995) and reported in Chapter 9 on intermediation.

Feature #3

The potential for dynamic pricing has not been heavily exploited by firms to date. Although changing the prices in a store with physical price tags is a major task, it is simple and programmable in a Web store. Pricing can be tied to demand, so that as the purchasing levels increase for popular items, so do the prices. If the price is elastic, consumers will still be willing to pay premium prices.

For the electronic vendor, the downside risk is that customers who return to the site shortly after first inquiring may find that the price has gone up. Some subset will also likely find that their price has gone down, but this does not offset the frustration of the customer with a higher price to pay. This situation can be rectified technically if the user allows cookies to be set. The firm can store off the prices displayed for a customer who has recently been visiting. This form of customer responsiveness would require some database storage but may fit with a firm's commitment to customer satisfaction.

Feature #4

On the Web, customers enter their own data. This reduces error and increases efficiency. Moreover these systems can be simplified for the customer by storing individual transactional and shipping information, as in Amazon's One-Click system. In addition, data about where the customer went on the firm's Web site can be captured as clickstream. Clickstream and transactional data together can give the firm insight into patterns of buyer behavior, both on an individual and market segment level.

By the same token, the amount of data that is being captured by Web sites may cause more customers to restrict tracking mechanisms, such as cookies, and to undermine the firm's marketing in this respect. Customers in many countries have concerns about privacy and their unwillingness to share personal information may keep them from shopping on the Web at all. It is interesting that bricks-and-mortar firms are attempting to get customer data at the point-of-sale (POS) terminal for those customers who do not use a credit or debit card by either asking name and address (Radio Shack) or ZIP code. They undoubtedly meet the same resistance as Web stores for the same reasons.

Feature #5

When customers shop via online stores, they can be located anywhere, so long as they have access to the Internet. Online stores also allow customers to shop at any time. With this "anywhere, anytime" capability, the Web gains a clear advantage over physical stores. The value proposition is not entirely clean, though. Devices to access the Net are needed as is an ISP. A wireless connection to the Internet eliminates the need for a landline connection but also may increases the risk of a security violation by hackers.

Feature #6

Search engines are both the boon and bane of Web stores. Even highly tuned search engines such as Google yield false hits to the user, which can be upsetting when an inquiry for shoes in Cincinnati returns, say, 66,789 links. The positive side of search engines is that they open the world up to Web markets. One does not need to have local knowledge to learn where to find rare books in Brisbane, Australia. As search engines improve, gain in intelligence, and enact interactive querying capabilities, the negative aspect of this feature may diminish.

Feature #7

E-Mail and FTP are applications that run on the Internet in conjunction with the Web. These are potential channels of communication that accompany Web sites and have no correlation in the physical world. E-mail addresses, in particular, are a valuable means of communicating with customers for after-sales support, upgrades, new products, and so forth. FTP can be used to send large files, with, for instance, specification. It essentially duplicates the attachment feature of most e-mail client software. What is the downside risk of this capability? Many firms institute e-mail replies to customers without committing to the volume of response that may be entailed. One bank manager in the GSU study told us proudly that he received 50,000 mail messages a week from customers. When we asked him how he processed this many, he indicated that he could not, because of the high volume. It should have been clear that this lack of customer responsiveness would not serve the firm well in the long-term.

Feature #8

The Web is a pull rather than a push phenomenon, as in the case of many physical sales channels. Other than users browsing completely at random, e-vendors can assume that visitors to their Web site are already half-sold. Potential customers have some reason to believe that the firm is stocking items or services that they might wish to purchase. Whereas firms that already have significant Web businesses are in a strong position, those trying to gain entrance are not. Firms need to learn how to create a Web brand so that they have a loyal group of Web buyers. This is not a trivial problem for firms going online.

11.8.3 Personalization, Mass Customization, and Markets-of-One

When marketing B2C, strategists need to be conversant with the ability of a firm's Web site to tailor its responses to the specific individual who is visiting. When people speak about the end of mass markets, this is the general idea to which they are referring. Personalization is a unique capability of electronic storefronts, as we noted at the beginning of the current chapter.

In the futurist Steven Spielberg film *Minority Report*, the hero walks through malls several times (see Figure 11.20) where each of the colorful billboards calls out his name as he approaches them. By reading the retina prints in his eyes with lasers, the mall computer system is able to identify the hero and then tailor visual and aural ads specifically for him. At one point, the audience hears in the background that the hero bought something last time he was in the mall, coupled with a rapid attempt to cross-sell to him.

Figure 11.20   Billboards in Futurist Mall Tailor Their Ads to Movie Protagonist

Personalization takes many forms in the Web world. There are at least three manifestations: (1) tailored offerings, (2) recommender systems, and (3) configuration engines.

Tailored Offerings

The Spielberg film is one example of tailoring offerings to customers based on prior information about the customer. By pushing information about products related to prior purchase, amazon.com exploits this capability. Let's say that you have purchased numerous gardening books from amazon.com in the past. When you revisit them, they may try to sell other gardening books to you, or they may try to cross-sell to you with gardening-related products. These are the basic principles behind tailored offerings.

Recommender Systems

Recommender systems are Web applications that accept general preference information from individuals and then try to match these interests with products or services. The systems can be fairly general and simply present consumers with review or evaluation-type information as in epinions.com, shown in Figure 11.21, or they can be more specific, using previously acquired personal preference data to make recommendations.

Figure 11.21   Reviews of Products at epinions.com

Configuration Engines

Configuration engines personalize by offering customers their choices of features on products or complementary products. More sophisticated engines will note when there is a conflict between choice, as in computer peripherals that will not function together. Dell Computers pioneered the concept and began selling directly to customers, both business and home clients. After one chooses a product category, elements that are typically purchased together, such as a PC and monitor, are offered to the consumer, each with choices of model, size, speed, power, and other product attributes. The PC, for example, will have a choice of main memory size and processing speed. Monitors will offer choices of flat panel screens or cathode ray tubes (CRTs), and 17-inch or smaller screens. More sophisticated configuration engines not only not point out conflicts between consumer choices, but also suggest ways of resolving the conflict. Certain speakers systems only work with certain PC models, for instance, and the configuration engine uses its built-in rules to suggest models that will work with each. Dell's engine refuses to place the order until all such conflicts are resolved, thus saving both the customer's and sales representative's time.

11.8.4 E-Branding and Spiral Branding

How do cyberfirms make their products and services known? How do they establish a reputation for their offerings? These are traditional branding issues, which are even more important in B2C than B2B settings. Businesses have legacies of information about suppliers, distributors, and other members of the supply channels. Most of these channels are well worn, and reputations have already been established. Breaking into these channels is also a matter of establishing brand, but advertising is more targeted and limited, in general. Mass media is not used nearly as much as it is in B2C.

Branding for cyberproducts and services seems to be taking the direction of spiral branding. Different media promote different channels to the firm. Voicemail systems mention that the customer can move to the firm's Web site for certain types of information. Web sites provide information for telephone contact. Television and radio likewise promote the Web site and call center contact numbers in a spiraling fashion where each medium mentions the others so that customers can reach the firm in numerous ways.

One of the clearest cases of firms not fully exploiting the NE media is when Web sites do not have obvious, readily available contact numbers (e-mail, telephone, and fax) and addresses. These are known as *bail-out chutes* (as in parachutes) and are absolutely essential for maintaining a continuous thread of contact with the customer. Once the customer gets frustrated and leaves the firm's presence, physical or virtual, he or she may well be lost. Spiral branding ensures that one or another avenue of contact is always before the customer.

Test this out yourself. Go to any firm's Web site and navigate through it. Are there pages where, if you ready to bail-out, you would not have a chute? There needs to be a clickable link to Contact Us or even banners with numbers obvious on the page. When you click Contact Us, do you see ways of reaching the firm by e-mail, phone, fax, or mail? If not, the site is lacking in spiral branding capabilities. It could be a serious deficiency in customer relationship management for this firm.

Focus on NE: Monster.com's Communication Channels

Monster.com has a database of more than 11 million resumés and has over 400,000 job postings from a listing of over 100,000 employers. There are over 16 million job seeker accounts and in May of 2001, there were over 26.9 million visits to the site. In June of 2001, Monster.com also announced an important ongoing partnership with the United States Department of Labor that will analyze trends in the workforce, workforce statistics, global job classifications, and skills requirements. Monster.com is the largest US online job board and encourages job seekers, employers, and other career professionals to actively communicate with each other. Chats, boards, and newsletters provide opportunities for everyone to sound off on topics that are related to job searching and career development. Participants can feel free to share questions, concerns, and knowledge about a wide variety of topics concerning job placement. Professional consultants are available through networking services to offer advice and counseling on interview tips, resumé tips, career planning, diversity issues, and industry issues. Monster.com incorporates the use of spiral branding by using different media to promote different channels to the firm. Television and magazine advertisements direct users to the site and Internet search engines point to the home site as well as to specific categories within the main site. The Web site provides information for multiple forms of contact and illustrates good customer relationship management for the firm.

Sources

http://www.skillsgapconsortium.org/Archives/DOL%20Monster%20Partnership.pdf

http://www.monster.com

11.8.5 Clickstream Analysis of Consumer Transactions

The electronic B2C channel is distinctive because it can be set up to capture a great deal of information about customer interactions with the Web site. Among other interesting interaction data, HTTP carries with it information about the originating site link (before the request to the vendor's server) and the operating system of the client. If the client allows cookies to be set, the vendor can track the movement of a user through their Web site, time stamp these URL requests, and store them. This is what is known as the *clickstream*.

What should firms hope to gain by analyzing this clickstream? Let us imagine a firm is storing this data and wants to exploit it for inducing sales. Amazon stores about a terabyte worth of such data every year and is an example of a firm that is in exactly the position to do this. Which parts of the site are the most popular? What is the average length of time a user lingers on a page? Such descriptive statistics are suggestive of which parts of the site are profitable.

Once managers move beyond simple, but informative descriptives, they can begin to explore linkages between data. Where do they tend to come from prior to visiting this site? Where do they go next? Analyzing patterns and correlations, such the high incidence of purchases of both product D and product V indicates good cross-selling opportunities.

Once basic information is extracted from the clickstream, the data can be combined in a data warehouse with demographic data, gathered from the firm's internal customer information sources or purchased from third-party vendors. Having detailed information about customers' attributes next to their behaviors on the Web site can be an unbelievably powerful data source. Marketing research can predict what age groups and other such market segments are buying which products and combinations of products with the details of past behavior and demographics.

The ability of managers to learn about consumers is so much greater for Web vendors that some have predicted that it will be a sustainable competitive advantage for the best of breed of NE firms in decades to come.[22]

---

[22]Straub and Klein (2001).

11.8.6 Interactive Marketing, Including CRM

Interactive marketing is taking advantage of the ability of a Web site to respond to a consumer in multiple ways. Businesses that have Web sites should always make it clear to customers how to contact them via the Internet, but also by phone and regular mail. Customers should have access to bail-out chutes at every point in the Web site. Suppose a customer gets frustrated with navigating the Web site but would be willing to e-mail the firm. Sending such an e-mail message should be a click away. Suppose the customer wants to speak with a person immediately, either through live chat or VoIP? Again, these choices should be just a click away.

The window at the bottom of Figure 11.22 shows a live chat vendor, talkby.com, whose software permits a firm to be assigned as host of its own Web site and to conduct multiple live chat sessions between its sales representatives and visiting users. If IBM were to sign up to be the host for their own home page, the live chat windows at the bottom of the page would appear in user screens and allow users to interact in chat format with IBM sales representatives.

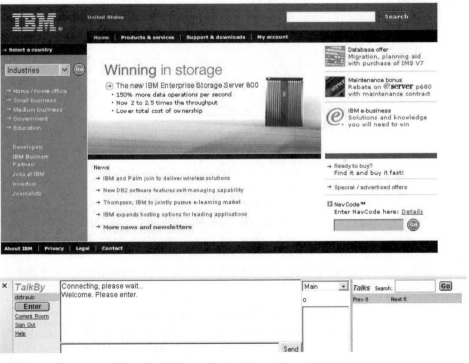

Figure 11.22　TalkBy Live Chat Associated with IBM's Home Page

Thus, human sales representatives may use the Web as a mediating channel through either asynchronous or synchronous formats. The asynchronous format is e-mail. The synchronous format is live chat (pictured in Figure 11.22) or VoIP. The key to an interactive Web site is that the customer perceives that the Web site is highly responsive and that questions can be answered, problems resolved, and after-sales support rendered.

The Web site itself can simulate interactivity by making it appear as if an intelligent entity is responding to customer inquiries. Even compared to e-mail and live chat, dynamic, hyperlinked Web pages can create a lot of excitement for customers.[23]

How else does one create an effective interactive marketing channel? One major way is to carefully manage the relationship with customers through computer-supported systems. These systems typically maximize the company's handling of a set of issues related to customers. Table 11.4 shows a typical set of the working applications that make up these systems.

Table 11.4: Applications That Make Up CRM Systems

Customer Relationship Management System Modules	
1	Acquisition module
2	Profitability by customer and customer segment module
3	Retention module
4	Loyalty module
5	Service module

Let's look at just one of these modules, #2, profitability by customer and customer segment. If a firm can answer the question "Who are our best customers across product lines?", it is in a much better position to allocate resources to pleasing these customers. Knowing the needs of such customers can maximize future sales and/or profits. Best customers can be defined as revenue or by margins and may define different parties. Clearly, high margins are more critical than revenues, and the firm that has this information in hand is in greater control of its destiny.

ScoutSolutions

Figure 11.23 is an example of a commercial CRM that demonstrates some of these properties. In Figure 11.23, we see that scoutsolutions.com specializes in the contact and prospect management side of customer relations. This Web-based software gives employees access to contact and sales prospect information from the field. This gives traveling employees a much better grasp of all of the possibilities of the channel.

Call Centers

We end this section with a mentioning of the humble, traditional, time-worn, and highly successful call center. As one of the bail-out chutes for interactive, Web-based marketing, telephone contact with the firm will remain a critical marketing tool. In fact, customers will continue to use it for ordering, complaints, service, and sharing information with the e-firm. It is hypothetically possible for an e-firm to accept only e-mail correspondence from customers and prospective customers (Will this work, though?). However, bricks-and-clicks firms, which have both a physical and an online presence, have already established a pattern of phone availability, and customers will expect it to continue. For SMEs, call centers may become a requirement for competitive reasons. Over time, call centers may be less of a requirement, but for the moment, they are still very much in the repertoire.

[23]Yin (2002).

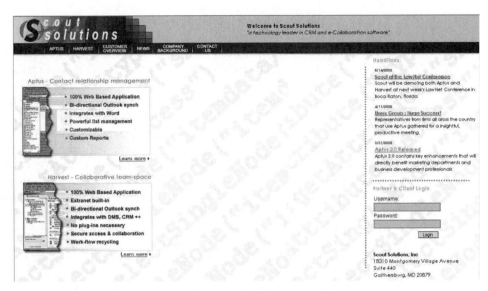

Figure 11.23 Customer Relationship Management Software Vendor

11.9 PRICING ISSUES IN CYBERSPACE

How does pricing between and among Internet vendors differ from that of traditional physical businesses? If search costs are lower, then prices should theoretically also be lower. Empirical research to date has not found this to be true,[24] but we are early in the game and more mature, sophisticated users should, over time, have a dramatic impact on pricing.

There are two sides to a price. The seller wants to enjoy the highest prices possible while the buyer wants exactly the opposite. A price, though, is an economic equilibrium point that represents a compromise between buyers and sellers. Prices are said to be elastic when this range of compromise is broad and inelastic when this range is small.

For long-term B2B relationships, the agreed-upon price will benefit both parties, with a minimum of opportunistic behavior on either part. It is not in the interest of either party to see the other fail. The primary impact of the Internet on this process is to make the buyer more broadly aware of purchasing options. If the buyer is able to consider a larger number of bidders for new or renewed work as a result of information available over the Internet, then the good/service finally delivered and the pricing should improve for buyers.

---

[24]Online car purchasing in Japan has resulted in higher prices (Lee (1998).

Sellers have an equal opportunity for premium pricing because they are more likely to reach buyers willing to pay their price with a larger marketplace for their bids. It is obvious that not all participants can increase their economic rents so there will be poor performers with respect to exploitation of the Web, and these firms will suffer from the standpoint of pricing.

B2C pricing issues are also interesting. As discussed earlier, dynamic pricing is a potential marketing advantage for Web stores. Changing the physical pricing labels, even on the bins and not the items, is a daunting task for any retailer. The Web changes all this by making one change in the database that is reported online thereafter whenever that a customer inquires about that item. The degree of freedom this gives management is a huge advantage.

Moreover, pricing can be programmed, based on immediate demand conditions and other factors, and in this way higher volumes or higher margin goods or services can be sold. Again, only a change to the database is required. The customer reservation system of the airline has worked effectively with pricing over the last several decades. Thousands of changes in prices are made daily to reflect this response to and manipulation of demand.

The airlines use this dynamic pricing mechanism in their yield management systems. Less expensive seats are sold far in advance, and tickets at the last minute are generally much higher because those who travel at the last moment are usually business travelers, and they have more price elasticity than leisure travelers. The goal of these systems is to maximize profits by manipulating the number of seats sold at varying prices to different sets of clientele.

Consumers are theorized to have more power on the Web due to the availability of price comparisons. Economic theory suggests that prices are higher when consumers do not have full information about competitor prices. With the wide availability of comparative pricing on the Web, there is every reason to believe that prices will favor the consumer, in the long run.

What is happening in the European Union is a telling example of how the Web can result in lower prices for consumers. With the advent of the common currency, the euro, even confusion over currency conversions has been solved. European consumers can now see quickly how much a given product costs, irrespective of where it was made. Easy-to-use currency converters on Web sites make this even more of a global phenomenon.

There is little doubt that pricing will be subject to new pressures with Internet vendors. Time will show us which of these theoretical predictions will prove to be true.

11.10 SUMMARY

In this chapter, we learned that there are characteristics of cyberspace that impact markets in ways that would not be possible in a traditional business setting. The Web enables online auctions that give sellers and buyers geographically the opportunity to bid on items and participate in communities for different categories. Web exchanges can reach global markets at a fraction of the cost involved in bringing buyers together in traditional businesses. New communications media allows sales representatives to talk with customers in real-time through live chat. This type of communication can enhance customer satisfaction between sellers and buyers. Video streaming is just one technology to allow the transmission of customer brand images over the Internet. In P2P technology, entities can now exchange data directly, without the control of a third party. People all over the world can access the Web as long as they have Internet connections. Companies now have new pricing models that are unique. These new prices are now reversing the roles of buying and selling and taking advantage of the global presence of the Web. One example is Priceline, which is initiated by the buyer, and the sellers bid.

Marketing channels are traditionally divided into two channels: B2B and B2C. B2B are transactions connecting businesses on the Web. B2C are transactions connecting ultimate customers and businesses on the Web. Businesses can increase product quality and save costs by working with suppliers through a supply chain. At different tiers, or stages in the flow of products through the chain, suppliers develop long-term relationships that must be built on trust. B2B relationships are also usually higher in volume and less cash driven. Channel partners who contribute directly to the movement of goods and services from end to end along the chain are part of this vertical.

Pre-NE era tools for reaching out along the vertical include: (a) database marketing, (b) data mining, and (c) data warehousing. Database marketing is when marketing departments collects information about customers or potential customers and analyzes it via market segments. Data mining allows managers to view data in new ways. Data warehousing combines data from numerous sources into a single repository that can be utilized to address management issues and questions.

The setting of B2B goals in organizations involves considerations of: (a) supply chains and ETNs, (b) the development of buying networks rather pure one-to-one auctions, (c) information visibility, (d) changes in distribution channels and logistical failures, and (e) long-term channels conflicts in atomic business models, intermediaries, and networks.

B2C marketing differs from B2B, partly through the differing cues in B2C. Web pages, for example, are equivalent to advertisements in print media. Potential buyers are more interested in making purchases online when pages are more user-friendly. There are three manifestations of personalizations. They are (a) tailored offerings, (b) recommender systems, and (c) configuration systems. Tailored offering are usually based on prior information about the customer. Recommender systems are Web applications that accept general preference information from individuals and then try to match these interests with products or services. Configuration engines personalize by offering customers their choices of features on products or complementary products. Firms market products and services through e-branding and spiral branding. B2C systems can gather information about customer interaction through collection data from the clickstream. Interactive marketing gives a Web site the ability to respond to consumers in multiple ways.

KEY TERMS

Business-to-business (B2B): Transactions connecting businesses on the Web.

Business-to-consumer (B2C): Transactions connecting customers and business on the Web.

Channel conflicts: Problems of duplicative efforts occur when a firm is able to substitute information for one of the value-adds in the traditional links of the chain; in such cases, the channels conflict because one or another channel can be disintermediated.

Clickstream: The sequence of clicks that creates user patterns at a Web site; when a client allows cookies to be set, the vendor can track the movement of the user through their Web site, time stamp these URL request, and store them.

Configuration Engines: Personalize by offering customers their choices of features on products or complementary products.

Database marketing: In cyberspace, databases that match Web-gathered transactional data with external demographic data; marketing departments collect information about customers or potential customers and analyze it via market segments.

Data mining: Software that allows managers to view data in new ways.

Data warehouse: Typically large-scale databases that combine data from numerous sources into a single repository that can be utilized to address management issues and questions.

Disintermediation: Substitution of one or more parties in a value chain; in cyberspace, when a firm is able to substitute information for one of the traditional links in the chain.

Electronic training network (ETN): Business exchanges that bring together different sellers and buyers.

Interactive marketing: Marketing that appeals to the senses by taking advantage of the ability of a Web site to respond to a consumer in multiple ways.

Peer-to-peer communications (P2P): Internet-specific software that allows entities to exchange data directly, without the intervention or control of third-party Web servers.

Personalization: Marketing to the individual; when a customer identifies him or herself to a site or is identified by cookies set on the customer machine, this intelligence can be used to respond in a custom-made way to customer's needs.

Recommender Systems: Web applications that accept general preference information from individuals and then try to match these interests with products or services.

Supply chain: Channel partners who are contributing directly to the value-add and movement of goods and services from end to end along the vertical.

Tailored Offerings: Custom-made offerings that are based on prior information about the customer.

Tiers: B2B channels include suppliers at different levels of the chain.

Vertical channels: Channels seen from an industry perspective.

Video streaming: Broadcasts of live action (or nearly live) over the Internet can give customers a strong association with the most influential brand images of the organization.

REVIEW QUESTIONS

1. In what ways will pricing at all levels of the supply chain change as a result of NE?
2. Marketing channels are traditionally divided into what two channels?
3. True or False: Is it easy to differentiate when firms are competing?

4. Firms need _____ and _____ to reach out vertically and horizontally.
5. What three technologies are being heavily used in networked enterprises?
6. Define the term clickstream.
7. Discuss data warehousing.
8. Explain what data mining is.
9. When do channel conflicts typically occur?
10. Why do we say that supply networks are more accurate descriptions of NE relationships among stakeholders than supply chains?
11. Name at least three manifestations of personalization taking place in Web world.
12. Define personalization, mass customization, and markets-of-one.
13. Explain the features of recommender systems.
14. Define configuration engines.
15. What are two types of branding?

TOPICS FOR DISCUSSION

1. What are the differences between B2B and B2C channels?
2. What are vertical market channels?
3. Discuss the differences between complementor and competitor.
4. What does the Web offer a database marketer?
5. Discuss the use of clickstream.
6. Discuss data marketing and its importance.
7. Why are buying networks being developed rather than one-to-one auctions?
8. When do B2B buying networks fail?
9. How do networks differ from chains?
10. Discuss the advantages and disadvantages to online auctions.
11. What is ETN? How does it affect the supply chain?
12. What are P2P communications?
13. Discuss how pricing between and among Internet vendors differs from that of traditional business.
14. When do channel conflicts typically occur?
15. Why is global reach so unique in cyberspace (versus a traditional business)?

INTERNET EXERCISES

1. Visit the Gibson Research Corporation Web site (http://www.grc.com). Choose one of the products and write a review.
2. Go to http://www.qvc.com. Write a report on the technologies used in the site for customer communication.
3. Locate a Web cam on the Internet. Describe the subject, the purpose, and any other pertinent information you can find concerning the site.
4. Locate articles that address the selling of wine and tobacco products on the Internet? Present the advantages and disadvantages and give your opinion on the subject.
5. Sign up for amazon.com. Explore the site. Log in a second time and see what information the site has collected about you.

6. Go to the talkby.com site. Investigate the services and write a report on the advantages of using such a product.

7. Go to the Epinions Web site (http://www.epinions.com/). Critique the Web site after describing the strategy indicated by the design.

TEAM EXERCISES

1. Have each team member choose one of the unique capabilities of the Internet for e-marketing. Locate an example of each item on the Internet. Discuss the advantages to the capability and how the organization uses it for marketing.

2. Locate two firms on the Internet. Find one that uses vertical marketing channels and one that uses horizontal marketing channels. Compare and contrast the supply chain and diagram the organizations.

3. Prepare a PowerPoint presentation of the inherent deficiencies and advantages of online shops. Include the advantages and disadvantages of each and provide real-world examples of each.

4. Investigate the ways that 3-D is used in marketing. Locate as many sites as you can that sell products that are demonstrated with 3-D technology.

5. How does pricing between and among Internet vendors differ? Go to the MySimon site (http://www.mysimon.com/index.jhtml) and choose five different types of products. Compare the range of prices for each item and compare the deviation in the ranges to the types of products. Report your findings.

INTERNET RESOURCES

Internet Chat with KoKo the Gorila (http://www.geocities.com/RainForest/Vines/ 4451/KoKoLiveChat.html): This is the transcript of the AOL Live Chat with KoKo the gorilla, which took place on April 27th, 1998, at 7 p.m. EDT, in honor of the month-long celebration of Earth Day. This event was the first ever live interspecies Internet chat with Koko the gorilla.

The Telegarden (http://www.usc.edu/dept/garden/): This tele-robotic installation allows Internet users to view and interact with a remote garden filled with living plants. Members can plant, water, and monitor the progress of seedlings via the tender movements of an industrial robot arm.

REFERENCES

Fine, C. H. *Clockspeed: Winning Industry Control in the Age of Temporary Advantage.* Perseus Books, Reading, MA, 1998.

Gefen, D., and M. Keil. "Developer Trust-Building Behavior and User Perceptions of Perceived Usefulness: A Social-Exchange Perspective." *DATA BASE for Advances in Information Systems*, 29, 2, (1998), 35–49.

Gefen, D. "Building Users' Trust in Freeware Providers and the Effects of this Trust on Users' Perceptions of Usefulness, Ease of Use and Intended Use." Dissertation, Georgia State University, 1997.

Gefen, D. "E-Commerce: The Role of Familiarity and Trust." *Omega: The International Journal of Management Science*, 28, 6 (2000), 725–737.

Gefen, D., E. Karahanna, and D. Straub. "Building Consumer Trust in Online Shopping and TAM: An Integrated Model." Drexel University, 2002.

Gefen, D., and D. Straub. "Managing User Trust in B2C e-Services." *eService Journal*, 2, 1 (2002), forthcoming.

Harmon, A. "Music Industry in Global Fight on Web Copies." *New York Times*, 7 October 2002, A1, A6.

Klein, R. "The Effect of e-Business Enabled Symmetric Information Sharing Practices in Vendor / Client Relationships." Dissertation, Georgia State University, 2002.

Koufaris, M. "Applying the Technology Acceptance Model and Flow Theory to Online Consumer Behavior." *Information Systems Research*, 13, 2, June 2002, 205–220.

Lee, H. G. "Do Electronic Marketplaces Lower the Price of Goods?" *Communications of the ACM*, 41, 1, January 1998, 73–80.

Lee, H. L., V. Padmanabhan, and S. Whang. "The Bullwhip Effect in Supply Chains." *Sloan Management Review*, Spring 1997, 93–102.

Malhotra, A., O. El-Sawy, and S. Gosain. "Rethinking Value Chain Processes for e-Business Applications." Presentation at University of Minnesota, November 3, 2000.

McKeown, P. G., and R. T. Watson. "Manheim Auctions." *Communications of AIS*, 1, June 1999, http://www.terry.uga.edu/~rwatson/estrategy/mol/mol.html.

McKinney, V., K. Yoon, and F. Zahedi. "The Measurement of Web-Customer Satisfaction: An Expectation and Disconfirmation Approach." *Information Systems Research*, 12, 3, September (2002).

McKnight, D. H., V. Choudhury, and C. Kacmar. "Developing and Validating Trust Measures for E-Commerce: An Integrative Typology." *Information Systems Research*, 13, 3, September 2002.

Moschowitz, A. "Virtual Organization." *Communications of the ACM*, 40, September 9, 1997, 30–40.

Palmer, J. "Web-site Usability, Design and Performance Metrics." *Information Systems Research*, 13, 1, March 2002, 151–167.

Rai, A., B. Weinlein, J. Wareham, and M. Keil. "Omnexus: The ePlastics Marketplace." 2001, http://www.coba.usf.edu/departments/isds/faculty/abhatt/cases/Omnexus.pdf.

Rangan, V. K., and M. Bell. "Dell Online." Case Study 598116, Harvard Business School Press, March 26, 1999.

Rose, G. "The Effect of Download Time on e-Commerce: The Download Time Brand Impact Model." Unpublished dissertation, Georgia State University, 2000.

Rose, G. M., D. W. Straub, and J. D. Lees. "The Effect of Download Time on Consumer Attitude Toward the Retailer in E-Commerce." *Proceedings of the Sixth Americas Conference on Information Systems,* Long Beach, CA, 2000, 1352–1354.

Rose, G., and D. W. Straub. "The Effect Of Download Time On Consumer Attitude Toward the E-Service Retailer." *E-Service Journal*, 1, 1 (2001), 55–76.

Torkzadeh, R., and G. Dhillon. "Measuring Factors that Influence Internet Commerce Success." *Information Systems Research*, 13, 2, June 2002.

Sayrac-Yaveroglu, I. "The Relative Effects of Price, Brand Name, and Store Name on Buyers' Product Evaluations in Online and Offline Markets and the Moderating Role of Web Expertise." Unpublished dissertation, Georgia State University, 2002.

Sarkar, M. B., B. Butler, and C. Steinfield. "Intermediaries and Cybermediaries: A Continuing Role for Mediating Players in the Electronic Marketplace." *Journal of Computer Mediated Communication*, 1, 3 (1995), 1–14.

Straub, D. W., and R. Klein. "e-Competitive Transformations." *Business Horizons*, 44, 3, May-June 2001, 3–12.

Straub, D. W., Donna Hoffman, B. Weber, and C. Steinfield. "Measuring e-Commerce in Net-Enhanced Organizations." *Information Systems Research*, 13, 2, June, 2002, 115–124.

Torkzadeh, R., and G. Dhillon. "Measuring Factors that Influence Internet Commerce Success." *Information Systems Research*, 13, 2, June 2002, 187–204.

Yin, J. "Interactivity of Internet-Based Communications: Impacts on E-Business Consumer Decisions." Unpublished dissertation, Georgia State University, 2002.

CHAPTER 12

DEPLOYING NE SOLUTIONS

UNDERSTANDING IMPLEMENTATION TACTICS FOR NEOs

What are the tactics that managers employ to bring NE solutions to their organizations? What resources does the firm own with each business model, and how can these be exploited for competitive advantage? What are the distinctive characteristics of B2C and B2B deployment that managers need to know? How should intranets and extranets be introduced? What planning and development models are applicable to traditional businesses as they migrate to NE? These are some of the key issues we will deal with in this chapter.

LEARNING OBJECTIVES FOR THIS CHAPTER

- To apply the core competencies for each of the atomic business models to NE implementation
- To recite the stages of the implementation process and explain each of these dimensions
- To explicate the terms B2B, B2C, intranets, and extranet in the context of NE deployment
- To analyze Web usability
- To argue for the importance of content in B2B and B2C Web sites
- To describe the repair and maintenance needs of NE systems
- To describe how to move from strategy to deployment
- To distinguish between centralization and decentralization in IT development and operations

▶ *CASE STUDY 12-1*

NOVEL 3-D VIDEO (HOLOVIDEO) DISPLAY TECHNOLOGY

Computer graphics are confined chiefly to flat images. Images may look three-dimensional (3-D), and sometimes create the illusion of three dimensions when displayed. Nevertheless, when viewing an image on most display systems, the human visual system sees a flat plane of pixels. Volumetric displays can create a 3-D computer graphics image, but they fail to provide many visual depth cues (e.g., shading, texture gradients) and cannot provide the powerful depth cue of overlap (occlusion). Discrete parallax displays (such as lenticular displays) promise to create 3-D images with all of the depth cues, but are limited by achievable resolution. Only a real-time electronic holographic ("holovideo") display can create a truly 3-D computer graphics image with all of the depth cues (motion parallax, ocular accommodation, occlusion, etc.) and resolution sufficient to provide extreme realism. Holovideo displays promise to enhance numerous applications in the creation and manipulation of information, including telepresence, education, medical imaging, interactive design, and scientific visualization.

Elizabeth Downing, a graduate student of Stafford University, developed a prototype video display (or "holovideo") with the help of electrical engineering Professor Lambertus Hesselink. The holovideo can produce 3-D images in a wholly new way—by creating actual 3-D color images inside a solid cube of fluorescent glass. This technology, although still rudimentary, has a number of potential applications:

- Physicians could use it to gain a more complete view of images of the human internal organs via magnetic-resonance imaging, computer-aided tomography, or ultrasound.
- Air traffic controllers might use it to track aircraft positions in three dimensions.
- Engineers could find the technology useful for product design and for viewing products created with computer-aided tools.

Downing considers medical imaging to be the most natural application. She estimates a 10-in. prototype display would cost about $80,000, but expects that price to fall rapidly once the concept is commercialized.

The technology is unique in that "it doesn't create an image that appears to be three dimensional, it actually produces an image that is drawn in three dimensions," Downing says. "As a result, there are few restrictions on the viewing angle and a number of people can view the images at the same time Also, the images are emissive—they glow rather than reflect—so they can be seen easily in ordinary room light." The technology also has limitations. The objects that it forms are transparent, not opaque, and so additional processing would be required before it would be suitable for entertainment purposes. It also takes 500 times as much data to construct a 3-D object as it does to draw the same object in only two dimensions.

Downing envisions a different future for computer monitors, TVs, and other equipment relying on an image to present information. She demonstrated how the concept could produce a 3-D color image inside a cube of clear glass. The cube is surrounded by lasers, scanners, and the other components of a prototype video display that creates images a whole new way—by creating actual 3-D images inside the solid piece of glass. In that demonstration, the glass was about the size of a sugar cube, but Downing is confident that the concept can be scaled up to handle a variety of commercial applications. To pursue that potential, she has founded 3-D Technology Labs.

One of the advantages of this 3-D display are that it does not require any special 3-D glasses. It provides a more naturalistic perception of depth, thus does not cause viewer fatigue, and it can be built from existing components that are readily available. A 3-D display based on the new perception mechanism would clearly have enormous potential for supporting image communications that convey a more realistic sense of presence. This capability is now being experimented with 3-D television and games, all sorts of simulators, electronic museums and exhibits, and many more potential applications. Using the prototype 3-D display system, research will continue to seek a better theoretical understanding of the new physiological depth cue, while investigating ways to achieve sharper resolution, create larger screen sizes, and exploit monocular movement parallax and other depth cues.

The patented technology has been licensed exclusively to Stafford University for novel display technologies. The team at Stafford is working with other companies on other commercial and military applications. Though promising, it is a lengthy process to the marketplace. There are huge costs involved, and every new idea has to punch through the inertia of the existing technology base. Whatever the risks, the Novel 3-D video display technology continues to evolve and explore novel ways to display and interact with the real world.

Discussion:
1. Discuss potential applications for Novel 3-D video display technologies.
2. Differentiate the restrictions on video system applications from those on Novel 3-D video display technologies.

Sources:
NTT. "NTT Discovers a New 3-D Perception Mechanism for displaying 3-D Images." [Online] Available: http://www.ntt.co.jp/news/news00e/0005/000530.html.
ITCom. "Three-Dimensional TV, Video, and Display," 2002. [Online] Available: http://www.spie.org/conferences/calls/02/itcom/confs/IT105.html.

12.1 INTRODUCTION

Careful strategizing can create stupendous opportunities for NEOs to gain competitive advantages over their rivals. Prudent managers need to engage in best practices to deploy those NE solutions that make sense and create dynamic capabilities for the firm from its resource base.

Deployment tactics first require an examination of the intent of the systems. Matching these goals, business processes, and core competencies with the available technologies is the next step. There will clearly be a difference in how computer-to-computer systems, such as Web-EDI, XML, third-party handling of transactions, application formats, or computer-to-human systems such as Web pages will be constructed.

Focus on NE: ELIZA

ELIZA was meant to be a hoax. The name comes from a flower-selling girl in *My Fair Lady* who pretends to be more than she is. Why is ELIZA interesting? For a brief explanation, here is a quote from the *The New Hacker's Dictionary*: "ELIZA effect: / *-li:'z* *-fekt'/ [AI community] n. The tendency of humans to attach associations to terms from prior experience. For example, there is nothing magic about the symbol "+" that makes it well-suited to indicate addition; it's just that people associate it with addition. Using "+" or "plus" to mean addition in a computer language is taking advantage of the ELIZA effect.

The term comes from the famous ELIZA program created by Joseph Weizenbaum. This program simulated a Rogerian psychoanalyst by rephrasing many of the patient's statements as questions and posing them to the patient. It worked by simple pattern recognition and substitution of key words into canned phrases. It was so convincing, however, that there are many anecdotes about people becoming very emotionally caught up in dealing with ELIZA. All this was due to people's tendency to attach to words meanings which the computer never put there." The ELIZA effect is desirable when writing a programming language, but it can blind you to serious shortcomings when analyzing an Artificial Intelligence system. You give it a try! See if ELIZA (http://www.nu-woman.com/eliza.htm) can help you! When you are done with ELIZA try out the John Lennon Program (http://triumphpc.com/johnlennon/index.shtml)!

12.2 MATCHING NE APPLICATIONS TO BUSINESS PROCESSES AND CORE COMPETENCIES

The planning process for implementation begins actually as part of the strategy. Domain navigation is one of the explicit charges for a business strategy, and this addresses the issue of how the strategy should be executed. A firm must take into account its core competencies, both in its formulation of strategy and in its implementation of this strategy. The plans form the "tactics" of the strategy.

We have already covered how NEOs should think about aligning the firm's resource base with its competitive initiatives. This chapter focuses on deploying those capabilities and realizing the benefits of its strategy.

12.2.1 Planning New Business Models: Emerging Technologies and Core Competencies

Wheeler's model of strategic planning for networked organizations, originally displayed in Chapter 7, is repeated here as Figure 12.1. The execution phase of the model is the phase we are now focusing on. The firm has presumably already determined that an emerging technology can be exploited for certain economic opportunities and that the firm has core competencies to bring the technology online. The model also shows this as a continuous process as new technologies are developed and made ready for exploitation.

Let's consider a situation where the firm encounters a new technology they are considering for exploitation and see how they might execute on it. Suppose a firm specializes in expert judgments on estate planning and sells their advice and legal services to well-to-do clients. The firm's expertise is physically distributed between offices in New York, Miami, and Los Angeles. Clients tend to be traditional in that they prefer to see and hear their advisors in person.

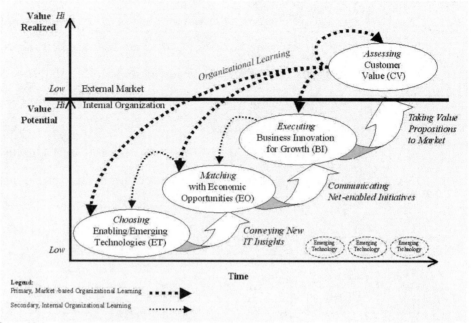

Figure 12.1   Wheeler Model of Planning for NE Systems

The fascinating new technology the firm is considering involves full-scale model images in real time, sent over the Internet (see the brief discussion and illustration of this technology in Chapter 3). They believe that they can gain a competitive advantage by being able to bring in their remote partners as "virtual" advisors on subjects that require sophisticated knowledge of certain aspects of estate planning. The "virtual" advisor will meet with the client along with the local, physical advisor in a specially equipped room.

The firm has no technologists who are knowledgeable about full-scale model images (this is an extremely new technology, after all). In addition, they are using a computer services firm to provide access to the Internet and host the firm's Web site and, so, do not really even understand the dynamics of high-speed bandwidth for any applications.

How should they go about executing this strategic initiative? The firm has developed a core competency in coordinating with such partners, and they even have some arrangements in which they cooperate on special projects with competitors in cities where they do not have physical offices.

The firm sees no strong connection between the introduction of this new technology and its current core competencies, but it also believes that the technology could give it a leg up on competitors. The decision is therefore made to hire a complementor—in this case, a consultant (one of the Big Four accounting companies) to integrate the system into the firm. One of the firm partners will serve as the manager-in-charge of the project and work closely with the complementor (systems integrator).

A time table for implementation is established and a team composed of the manager-in-charge, selected members of the internal systems group, and the systems integrator begins the planning. The integrator focuses on making the technology as easy to use as possible, given that there will not be internal IT specialists who are fully versed in the technology.

The system is rolled out in phases, between Los Angeles and New York first. Technology rooms are built to be comfortable for clients and still capable of clear projection of the images. High-speed fiber bandwidth is acquired and installed to the technology room.

The initial rollout is a limited success, wherein the full-scale model image projection software works well, but the quality of service on the fiber optic line is not adequate. Adjustments are made by the network provider and the systems then performs acceptably. The audio system is redone to assure that all parties can hear well in the technology room.

Tests with clients indicate that once the initial shock of talking to human-sized image has subsided, the client begins to warm to the concept and appreciate the interaction of the firm's experts in planning her or his estate. Exit interviews indicate that, as planned, switching costs have been raised significantly for the customer by this technological innovation.

The use of the Internet by a traditional firm such as these estate-planning advisors uses the Internet in a remarkably traditional way. It enhances the way they have always done business. In this hypothetical example, computer systems and networks achieve a competitive advantage by improving internal processes and offering this value-added service to its customers. It would qualify as NE because it involves the substitution of information (full-scale model images) for physical processes (traveling to other cities for face-to-face conferences. Indeed, if the system is as effective as planned, it would allow partners to move effortlessly from city to city in cyberspace in a manner that could not be duplicated through flying, even by the most inveterate business traveler.

12.2.2 Core Competencies and Capabilities Required for Atomic Models

But what about e-firms and NEOs? When major parts of a firm's transactional business depend heavily on the Web or the Internet, what core competencies are required? Core competencies, as we saw in Chapter 7, are the ability of the firm to utilize its resources to create value. They are relevant skill sets as well as the ability to retain these skills, and not just smart people.

Core competencies for NEOs depend on their having core competencies related to NE, which clearly differ according to their atomic model or hybrid model. As Weill and Vitale (2001) point out, firms need to recognize where their intellectual capital lies so that they do not attempt to execute strategies in ways that do not play to their strengths. The estate-planning firm knew that they were not experts in image technology nor would hiring that expertise make sense, because it was at odds with their skills in estates and working with well-to-do clients. So they sourced this outside the firm, and focused on their own expertise in aiding their estate clients.

Table 12.1 shows the core competencies associated with each of the atomic business models. To deploy the models will require minimal capabilities in at least these basic core competencies. To excel will require mastery.

Table 12.1: Atomic Business Models and Core Competencies (Based on Weill and Vitale, 2001)

	Model Type	Core Competencies
1	Content provider	a) Providing leadership in content field b) Handling content for multifarious forms of distribution c) Marketing expertise about content
2	Direct-to-consumer	a) Forming supply chain strategic partnerships b) Using customer data to understand customer needs c) Marketing through allies d) Integrating online and offline customer processes e) Being low-cost provider
3	Full-service provider	a) Managing relationships with customers and other parties in the value network b) Understanding customer segments and matching firm abilities to deliver new offerings to these segments c) Managing business complexities through IT infrastructure d) Developing brands
4	Intermediary	a) Collecting and analyzing information about products, prices, and markets b) Balancing service completeness with customer volumes c) Analyzing customer data for positioning new services
5	Shared infrastructure	a) Delivering IT infrastructure services to deploy model b) Coordinating a coalition of competitors c) Attracting new participants
6	Value net integrator	a) Managing relationships with customers and other players b) Managing coordination of nodes by analyzing the information in the network c) Developing and managing the brand d) Utilizing levers of influence rather than control mechanisms
7	Virtual community	a) Building a sense of community b) Sourcing or creating attractive content that is not expensive c) Discovering member needs
8	Single point of contact	a) Understanding life events in customer and designing Web site accordingly b) Providing leadership to move NEO to whole -of-enterprise viewpoint c) Showing ability to manage complex IT environment d) Negotiating agreements among divisional and business unit (BU) senior managers

12.3 DEPLOYING NET-ENHANCED SYSTEMS THROUGHOUT THE VALUE CHAIN

In Chapter 6, we discussed the NE value chain and the recommended order of implementation of modules. Figure 12.2 repeats that graphic.

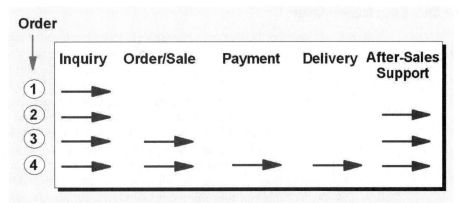

Figure 12.2   Recommended Order of Introduction of Stages in NE Value Chain

This value chain applies to either the supply or customer side of the value chain, because the processes are generic enough to consider deployment issues separate from this context. At a detailed level there will, of course, be differences, and some of these critical differences will have separate treatments later in this chapter.

Next, we cover the deployment problems that have surfaced in the GSU study data and offer some solutions and for managers. The first stage in the implementation is *inquiry*. What are the major hurdles in this deployment?

12.3.1 Inquiry Stage

Inquiry is where most firms begin their NE effort. The primary issues for deployment appear to be lack of alignment between the firm's overall strategy and the presentation on the home page. Firms reported to us in the GSU study that they were not clear as to what image they should convey on this key introductory element. The more high-level management was involved in articulating the impression they wished to convey as to the strategic mission and direction of the firm, the more successful the inquiry stage.

There are many possible subelements that can be introduced to satisfy customer inquiries. The online inventory of goods and services is one approach, with search capabilities being an important adjunct. For those items that have high independent ratings available, a link to these can be highly effective. Major advances in displayed inventory include comparison prices with competitors. Needless to say, this makes more sense if firms know that they are the lowest-cost providers on commodity items.

For firms that do not directly interact with the ultimate customers, a locator service to physical distributors, brokers, or dealerships is useful, especially with hyperlinks and e-mail connections.

The most sophisticated forms of inquiry capability can return information about the availability of products and services at physical sites and a reservation system for these (reservations are not the same as orders). For customer convenience, online maps to physical retail (or service) locations are another strong feature.

12.3.2 After-Sales Support Stage

Although not necessarily the norm, after sales is the recommended second stage for development. Retaining customers is a critical aspect of marketing that can be well supported through the new, powerful channel of NE. Economic theory indicates that firms can differentiate themselves from their competitors by gaining more information about customers and exploiting that information.[1] Servicing existing customer accounts is an obvious area for firms to differentiate themselves from their rivals via the Web and the Internet.

An example of where this has been effective may help to explicate this point. The mcafee.com site sells online security services that involve downloading an initial software package for real-time virus filtering. An initial database of virus signatures tied to the product is used to filter out viruses in e-mail attachments or Web downloads. Updates to this virus database are the after-sales support offered for McAfee's software. Customers are constantly aware of the McAfee service by being asked if they wish to upgrade their systems for the new viruses that have been spotted. A graphic showing the risk from each of these new viruses (Figure 12.3) is also presented to induce sales.[2]

McAfee calls their updating capability a *Web service*, which is a concept being pushed by Microsoft, among others. This is a component-based approach to delivering Web systems more rapidly. In an indirect sense, McAfee's upgrade service is also a Web service in that it may be component-based. For our purposes, it is sufficient to take note of these emerging technical phenomena.

Figure 12.3 McAfee Dialogue Page for Upgrading Customer Virus Protection over the Internet

---

[1]Straub and Klein (2001).

[2]Although McAfee sells an online clinic in which the package includes such upgrades for a year, the principle that this is really supporting initial sales is clear.

Interactive Marketing and After-Sales Support

The discussion of interactive marketing and the wide range of bail-out chutes that firms need to offer online customers was laid out in the previous chapter. What we can say here is that implementing an e-mail answering service and especially a live chat service is a nontrivial expense, but one that has economic advantages. (These observations certainly apply to after-sales support, but it needs to be noted that they apply equally to the inquiry and order stages.) First, a live-chat sales representative can handle up to three chat sessions at a time. This contrasts with a phone interaction or VoIP in which the sales representative can only service one customer at a time. So live chat is three times more efficient than voice contacts. Moreover, a call center that allows employees to switch off between voice- and Web-inquiry answering duties would likely enrich employees' jobs and improve quality of service.

If the NEO chooses to offer e-mail responses, there is a major advantage to using speech recognition software that can create text from voice. Sales representatives can answer a larger number of after-sales inquiries if they have this software assistance.

Finally, the Web site itself can be used for effective after-sales support with FAQs (answers to specific questions) and other clearly linked information. In fact, this dynamic response of Web sites to inquiries leads customers to believe that the site is highly interactive,[3] which makes the site attractive or "sticky" with customers. It encourages customer loyalty and retains the customer among the firm's frequent purchasers.

Monitoring live chat and e-mail is also a more efficient operation than voice-only call centers. Reviewing the tapes of phone interactions is a tedious process, and managers can only examine a small portion of actual sessions. Reviewing the logs sessions of e-mail and chat, however, can take advantage of quick reading techniques, enabling managers to have a wider and more in-depth understanding of call-center employees' performances. Reviewing the live-chat and e-mail sessions with employees as part of a quality control and improvement process will be much easier with text-based systems such as e-mail and live chat. Finding the place in question and forwarding or backing up a tape recorder to the appropriate event is a difficult and time-consuming process. Although this can be digitized, the search process is still trickier than text with the current technologies.

12.3.3 Order/Sales Stage

B2C sales usually involve a process in which B2C consumers find what they want and place it in an online "shopping basket." The metaphor is appropriate in using a physical analogy of a store and choosing what one wants at given prices. B2B deployment takes different forms, although making a purchase over the firm's direct-sales Web pages is certainly an option. Figure 12.4 shows this B2B option for Dell Computer. Using B2B exchange hubs, or ETNs, is another option, and Web-EDI is a third.

Dell's B2B site can be accessed by the firm's human procurement agents, or the HTML code that selects certain options can be prepared and the firm's client software can interact with the Dell site without human intervention. Some of the firms in the GSU study were employing the latter approach, to their advantage.

---

[3]Yin (2002).

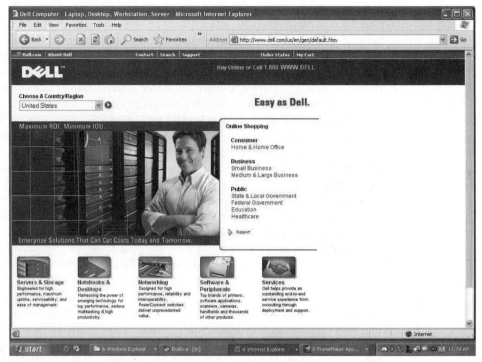

Figure 12.4 Dell's B2B Order Capabilities ("Business" in Clickable Link Above)

Order capabilities for both Web B2C and B2B are primarily an IT issue. In established firms, they must be integrated with back-end, legacy systems. This meshing of older and newer systems is a daunting task, because the older technologies have different technical architectures than the newer ones. Nevertheless, the only alternative for established firms is to begin their Web initiative with a wholly owned subsidiary which handles its accounts through its own, newly created systems. This delays (perhaps indefinitely) the need to integrate with legacy systems. It also has the benefit of permitting the subsidiary to explore virtual organizational designs.

12.3.4 Delivery Stage

Setting up delivery systems for digital goods may appear to be relatively straightforward. The firm needs to host or to outsource hosting of what is known as an FTP site. FTP requires industrial strength servers, depending on the volume of requests, of course. But this infrastructure and the Web dialogue boxes that accompany delivery functionality are pretty standard by this time.

Where are the implementation hurdles for delivery? The major issues center around intellectual property rights and protection of the firm's assets. Piracy, or illegal transference of digital products or services to other parties, represents a huge loss for firms involved in digital commerce. The danger is that the firm sells one copy and the remainder are illegally copied and uploaded to nonpaying recipients. Firms can clearly not survive if they sell only one copy of their offerings. This is a serious implementation issue because the extent of losses internationally from piracy are staggering.

The Napster P2P network is a good example of the devastating effect this kind of piracy can have on an industry. Users basically shared copyrighted music with each other by setting up direct connections with other users through Napster. Although Napster itself was first highly constrained by U.S. court rulings, then bought by the Bertlesmann entertainment conglomerate, and finally slipped into bankruptcy, there were many other sites that filled this market position. Sharing of MP3 and other file formats is a brisker business today than it was when Napster was in its prime.

As discussed briefly in Chapter 6, copyrights in U.S. law are automatically available for new works bearing requisite copyright language, including software, presentation graphics, digital images, literary works (such as product brochure copy), and so forth. Managers should be certain that the firm's digital goods bear such imprints. Agreements for licensing are most often appended to installation wizards, and the purchaser's acceptance of these terms, again, helps to protect the firm from a legal standpoint.

Under special circumstances, there are other legal issues that the firm may need to consider. Insurers may send policies over the Internet and have them take effect (the "binding" time and date as they say in this industry) at a set moment. The difficulty is in proving in a court of law that the client and the insurer are both bound by the same contract. Because the document is digital, it would be relatively simple for either to change the terms of the policy to favor themselves, and so there must be a legal way of determining which was the original transactional agreement.

There are a number of technical solutions available, including digital watermarks or documents marked with digital signatures. In both cases, there must be a trusted third party who can state in a court of law that a given policy was, indeed, the policy that bound the parties on a certain date. Where insurance is heavily regulated and subject to well-drawn legal parameters, the components of this delivery system can be worked out. In the absence of regulation, the consumers may not trust the insurers enough to engage in online buying, and the industry may never develop. This could be particularly true in developing countries.

Value-Added Services rather than Legal or Technological Protection

Given the continuing, rampant violation of intellectual property in the Napster case mentioned, firms need to think of other ways to derive revenues from their creations. Some editorials in the trade press have taken the position that legal solutions are not the best strategy for deployment of digital goods and services. Technology solutions are equally suspect because they are so readily compromised. This line of argumentation focuses on the online setting as a value-added setting. If the initial pricing of the item is in the range where most users would choose to pay rather than seek out illegal copies, then margins could be forthcoming from increased volumes. Where appropriate, online sales could also be tied to value-added services that involve an updating of files or innovative offerings that are only available on a one-time basis to registered buyers. The trick is to experiment with online sales and find ways to derive incremental revenues over a longer period of time.

When a buyer has purchased a product for what is considered to be a reasonable investment, then updates are a clear avenue for incremental revenues. Improved versions of software and updates to image, audio, picture, or video files lock the customer into the concept of enhancements. Smaller fees over a longer period of time may be able to substitute effectively for an initial "sticker shock" pricing that will drive a lot of buyers to underground sources and the piracy market.

It could be equally true that some of these digital goods and services industries will lose intermediaries and restructure themselves so that the suppliers become connected directly with consumers. Distributors in the record industry could be disintermediated in a setting where artists set up sites themselves or send their works to cybermalls and sell directly to consumers, passing the savings in business exchanges costs and transactions costs onto the consumer. Consumers may be more than willing to pay several U.S. dollars for a new album directly to the artist rather than US $15+ for a digital version of a CD that is priced in this range.

12.3.5 Payment Stage

Very few firms have electronic payment core competencies. Financial institutions would be an exception, but most NEOs will choose, quite rightly, to outsource this capability. The approaches that can be made are described in Chapter 6. As we saw in Chapter 3, the NE supplier-side industry is already organized to provide these services.

The more options that Net-enhanced organizations make available to clients, customers, and consumers, the better. Keeping that in mind, some will be more readily acceptable under the pragmatic and legal conditions prevailing in a particular community and country. For example, debit cards and smart cards may be more prevalent in Europe and so Web sites that detect an inquiry from this area may be designed to present a different screen than an initial request from a North American site, where credit cards may be more common. E-cash or receivables options may be highlighted in countries where plastic cards are less frequently used.

The legal environment will have a major impact on the acceptability of online payment. If the downside risk is bottomless on credit cards, which is true in many non–North American environments, customers will be reluctant to acquire the cards in the first place or to use them in the second place. A healthy credit card setting for online purchasing is one in which holders of cards are protected by law against unlimited charges, fraudulent or not, against the card.

12.4 B2B DEPLOYMENT

Although our discussion on the electronic value chain covers a lot of the ground regarding B2B and B2C deployment issues, there are special conditions in each of these areas. For example, shared infrastructures such as Omnexus[4] and Covisint are typically B2B exchanges and, as such, have different hurdles to overcome than the creation of an e-vendor Web site. As Weill and Vitale (2001) point out, there is a requirement for core competencies in IT infrastructure and managing information in order to build and maintain the ETNs themselves. These capabilities can be hired, which was the choice at Omnexus in hiring IBM and Accenture, but then the legitimate question arises as to what exactly is the skillset of any ETN. Without internal expertise in building and maintaining the shared infrastructure, this skillset is reduced to being a marketing core competency. This is, perhaps, not an impossible position to be in, but many of the atomic models require a technical agility that is often not reliably available through outsourcers.[5]

---

[4]Rai et al. (2000).
[5]The reason this position is troublesome is because of the inability to specify contracts that can warrant that the outsourcer is up-to-date on new technological innovations. The theory that articulates this is known as "incomplete contracting theory." See Richmond et al. (1992).

12.4.1 Open-Buying Internet–EDI, and XML-EDI (Web-EDI) Compared to Traditional EDI

Whereas launching a B2B ETN or business exchange means that a firm should have a core competency in Web design and applications, using the Internet to link to partners in the supply network via Web-EDI means that the firm may need to design and build computer-to-computer links. This is also a technical agility, in this case in XML. XML permits more-flexible data fields in that the definitions of the data are included within the Web page. Firms wishing to deal with each other via exchanges on the Web can learn quickly what format the data will be in.

Some standards, known as open-buying Internet (OBI) standards, may assume a prominent place in this exchange, and promote the evolution toward EDI transactions being conducted over the Web. Figure 12.5 shows the new technologies and NE solutions that have evolved since EDIs overtook VANs and those that will be evolving in the future to deal with B2B exchanges.

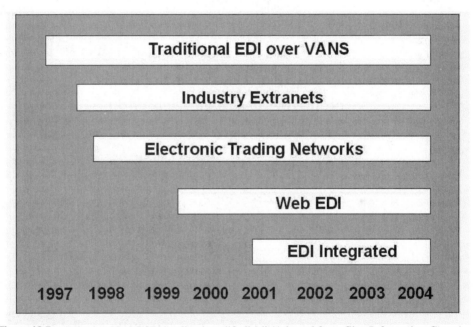

Figure 12.5   Bringing New B2B Applications "Online" (Adapted from Giga Information Group)

The traditional EDI is now a fairly primitive technology that has been in place for 20 years or more. It specifies rigid protocols or formats for certain kinds of transactions, for example, a purchase order. All firms that use the protocol need to comply with the size and type of data fields. EDI typically transmits over proprietary networks such as VANs, which are simply enhanced forms of common carrier data communications services.

Historically, EDI has focused on a transaction. It is a one-time exchange of information. A payment is made from firm A to firm B. For firm A, the mirrored transaction is an offset to accounts payable and a debit to cash. For firm B, money is received and becomes an offset to accounts receivable and a credit to cash. Other transactions between the same firms, even if the exchanges are related, are also handled on a one-time basis. A transaction that is clearly related to this one is a purchase order, because that is what generated the accounts payable (firm A) and accounts receivable (firm B) to begin with. Firms relate to each other through fulfillment processes, but traditional EDI could only handle one part of this process at a time.

A new concept of process in EDI exchanges has been called *EDI integrated*. This view ties the single transactions together with a series of expected exchanges that can be matched and coordinated, as depicted in Figure 12.6. Whether a firm uses rigid EDI protocols or more flexible Web-EDI protocols, this integrated view could be the future.

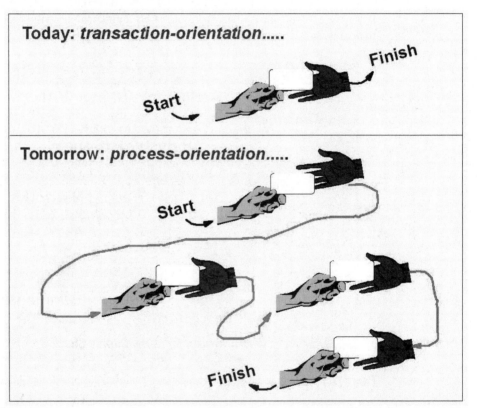

Figure 12.6   Movement from Traditional EDI to EDI-Integrated (Adapted from Giga Information Group)

Over time, NEOs will be moving to B2B exchanges, third-party intermediaries, and Web-EDI. SMEs, in particular, will find these solutions feasible and within their budgets. The waning of traditional EDI over VANs and the growing use of ETNs and Web-EDI for B2B solutions is depicted in Figure 12.7. The role of extranets in this multichannel environment will be discussed along with intranets later in this chapter.

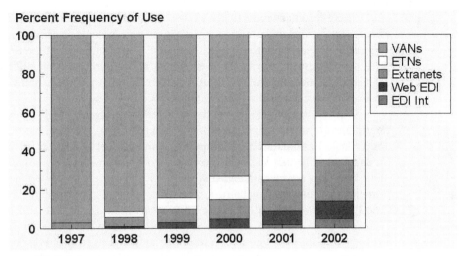

Figure 12.7   NE B2B Deployments (Adapted from Giga Information Group)

12.4.2 Alternate B2B Deployment

Interacting with ETNs is one solution to seamless B2B exchanges; EDI is another. A third implementation option is application formats. Application formats allow firms to exchange information between and across similar software packages. Two firms running ERP systems, for example, may use these applications to send and receive data. Compatibility is an issue here, not only between different versions of the same commercial program but also between different vendor products.

What will likely occur in the evolving B2B environment is that individual firms will deploy a variety of solutions, including ETNs, third-party intermediaries, Web EDI, application formats, and other Web-based approaches as well as paper-based options to interact with firms that are not now NEOs and unlikely to be so in the near future. Over time, one or two of the options may come to dominate the marketplace, but that eventuality is not presently obvious.

12.4.3 Deploying Less than Full Information Visibility in the Supply Chain

We saw in the last chapter that information visibility was selective in the case of the CompUSA supply network. There were some processes that needed information exchanges between partners A, B, and D but not C. There were others that involved A and C but not D. Depending on the process being supported, different information exchanges were optimal.

That being said, there are huge benefits accruing to NEOs that engage in strategic information-sharing with their partners. In a study of 3PL (third-party logistics), a recent scientific investigation has discovered that a high degree of sharing on a partner-by-partner basis leads to higher performance overall. [6] What is even more interesting is that if the sharing is symmetric, that is both partners share roughly the same degree of information, the benefits are even more striking.

---

[6]Klein (2002).

These results suggest that we have accumulating evidence that information visibility in the supply network is highly desirable. Seamless flows of goods and services are nearly equivalent to seamless flows of information. The boundaries of the firm are extended, in a real sense, into the processes of its partners, outsourcers, competitors, and even its customers. The more information that is present where it is needed and when it is needed, the more likely the process will function as smoothly as possible.

Why is this the case? What is the underlying logic or theory? Information is the symbolic form of objects in the real world. An individual item in inventory, for instance, can be represented by its SKU number, or unique identification numbered assigned by the manufacturer. It can also be represented by graphical images, either sketches or photos, and by design-type documents that specify its measurements down the thousandths of millimeters, its shape, the machine tool settings that will craft the item, and so forth. It may be represented by information about its exact manufacturing date and time, when it passed into a wholesaler's inventory and at what price, and when it left that inventory. It can likewise be tracked throughout its history of storage, transport, and display.

Symbols describing the sale of an individual item can include the name and address of the customer, and the sale of this particular item can be placed in the context of sales of this product to a given customer and across all customers. In short, information is perhaps even more important than the physical representation of the item itself. Managing goods and services symbolically allows the firm's offerings to be manipulated so as to minimize inventories and maximize the sale of these items. One example of inspired use of this information would be the personalization of customer relationships that we have discussed throughout this book.

A clarion call for this view of information as the fourth resource (besides the classic trio of men [people], machines, and money) was introduced into management studies over 15 years ago, and the power of this proposition is even more obvious in cyberspace. The Internet allows information to be effortlessly and inexpensively linked between and across servers, to be manipulated and passed onto partners, and to support personal communications. The careful deployment of systems that reinforce each of these areas can dramatically affect bottom lines, a value proposition that we are now beginning to see in the B2B space.

12.5 B2C DEPLOYMENT

Putting B2B Web systems in place involves a detailed understanding of consumer behaviors, as we discussed in the last chapter. In many situations, these systems can serve both consumers and one-time or infrequent business purchasers, as the Dell site indicates. Small businesses and consumers are very similar in their buying profiles, and the parts of the site that prove to be "sticky" for them are similar.

Web design is the critical success factor for sites that work. The area of research that studies what makes a good Web design and what makes a less effective design is known as *usability*. If users find the site attractive, we can say that it demonstrates "stickiness," and visits to the site should be long and frequent. In short, the site has something of substance that draws consumers to it.

DEPLOYING NOVEL SOLUTIONS: INSTANT MESSAGING AND VoIP

NEOs are vitally interested in improving the methods they use to reach customers. Live services or real-time communication such as live chat, instant messaging, and VoIP are some of the methods that firms are investing in to improve customer service. These have been helpful in ensuring that customers complete purchases and have access to the information they are seeking.

Instant messaging (IM) facilitates e-commerce sites in acquiring potential sales. FaceTime Communications has introduced an instant messaging system focused on call centers; it works with networks from AOL, Microsoft, and Yahoo. A Problem that IM presents is that most companies are not prepared to handle large amounts of simultaneous messages. IM is growing very fast and is gaining popularity. It is estimated that by 2004 more than 400 million clients will be generating 2 trillion instant messages among consumers and businesses. Forrester Research estimates that the average cost of a contact center call is about U.S. $33, whereas an instant messaging session costs about U.S. $7.33. By 2005, IM will go beyond the use of e-mail as the main way in which customers interact electronically. Also, IM will be incorporated into 50% of businesses customer-interaction applications.

Lands' End (a catalog clothing company) has implemented new technologies on its Web site such as online chat to maintain return customers. One of the strategies they have is "Shop with a friend," which offers real-time online chat with a personal shopper who helps customers find the items they want to purchase.

Another service that e-commerce companies use to talk with their customers in real time is "Push to Talk." This service will have a large effect on B2B e-commerce, as well as with B2C e-commerce. eFusion has its own private VoIP network that performs calls using Internet protocols. eFusion's new service works by allowing the e-tailer to place a "Push to Talk" button on the site. When a customer pushes the button, a small Java-based program is downloaded to the customer's PC. The program looks at the PC's capability to determine the best way to route the customer service call. If the customer has a PC with speakers and a microphone, the call is placed immediately to the company's customer service department. The Web page that the customer is viewing is displayed on the service representative's screen, so that both are in sync.

1-800-Flowers also uses a technology called Net2Phone that allows customers to talk to a service representative during a transaction. One of their advantages is that clients have the ability to look at merchandise images on their screens while they talk to the customer service representative.

eStara, a Web voice service provider, has a service called Click2Speak. A partnership between eStara and CyberRep (a customer relationship management company) established a call center, which allows CyberRep to offer Click2Speak technology to its Fortune 1000 clients. The program contains HTML code that initiates a call through a PC over the Internet. That call then is transferred to a contact center over a regular phone network. A customer service representative receives the transmission as a normal call.

These new technologies will improve overall e-commerce operations. All of these technologies are based on great customer service and strong human interaction, they offer a very valuable opportunity to e-commerce companies to offer a better customer service and enhance customers' online shopping experiences.

Discussion:
1. Describe the value-added services that technologies such as VoIP and IM provided to customers.
2. Discuss the advantages and disadvantages of real-time communication.

Sources:
http://www.ecommercetimes.com/perl/story/10246.html
http://www.ecommercetimes.com/perl/story/2376.html
http://www.ecommercetimes.com/perl/story/12187.html
http://www.ecommercetimes.com/perl/story/16483.html
http://www.ecommercetimes.com/perl/story/18378.html
http://www.ecommercetimes.com/perl/story/17345.html

12.5.1 Web Site Usability

What are the features that constitute "usability" in a Web site? There are two scientific studies that have taken prior work in the usability of computer systems and applied it to Net-enhanced systems. The features that these studies found to be important are shown in Table 12.2.[7]

Table 12.2: Web Site Usability Features that Managers Need to Be Aware of

Palmer's Validated Features	Agarwal and Venkatesh's Validated Features
Download delay	Content
Navigation/organization	Ease of use
Interactivity	Promotion
Responsiveness	Made for the medium
Information/content	Emotion

Managers, both general managers and IT managers, have to ensure that their Web site incorporates these features into the design. Most organizations have only an intuitive grasp of how to go about this. They hire people with various expertise in order to cover the bases, but a systematic management approach, with usability tests before releasing new Web pages, is the best practice.

Promotion

How can managers institute this? Hiring the right people to do the job is clearly part of a solid implementation plan. Let's take the case of the "Promotion" feature before passing on to the other characteristics. There can be no doubt that the ability of the site to promote products and services is critical, as noted in Table 12.2. The Web site serves partly as an advertisement[8] and is a primary vehicle for inducing sales. Therefore, it needs to have the characteristics of good ads, for which there is a voluminous literature in marketing and complete curriculum in many universities. So the promotional feature of a Web site calls for talented people who can combine artistic and aesthetic design with a psychological need. The usability characteristic of "Emotion" is also related to the promotional ability of a Web site. There needs to be drama in visiting a Web site, and this is another way for creating site "stickiness."

[7]Palmer (2002); Agarwal and Venkatesh (2002).
[8]Rose (2000).

Technology experts can give support to the advertising efforts on Web sites. Besides giving marketers information about the latest advances in Web technologies, they can establish technologies such as "push" technologies. Known as "pop-up" windows, these can be sent to the user as an unsolicited window with special offers. An example of this is seen in Figure 12.8. The realestate.com site links customers to agents and mortgage brokers, and this pop-up window in red advertises mortgage financing possibilities as part of its regular offering.

Figure 12.8   Special Mortgage Offers in Pop-up Window at realestate.com

Pop-ups can actually be sold as advertising space to other firms, in a manner similar to "banner ads" on a Web page. An example of a sauna company selling a pop-up "push" window to a credit report service is shown in Figure 12.9. The inclination of the target audience to absorb a certain number of these windows should govern the timing and frequency of unsolicited "pushing" to the customer, but this technology can be a powerful marketing tool beyond those Web pages specifically requested by the user.

These areas of promotion alone call for experts in the following: (a) artistic design, (b) consumer psychology (people who can run ad campaigns), (c) Web design, (d) emerging and established B2C technologies, and (e) project management or coordination skills.

Navigation and Ease of Use

The way a site is organized will make it easy or hard for a user to find what she or he needs. The same thing can be said about a single Web page within that site. Navigation is extremely important in encouraging system use, a relationship supported in many scientific studies for on-task activities.[9] These studies have found that when the user thinks the task is important, the ability to navigate the interface becomes crucial.

---

[9]This theme has been studied in the IS Technology Acceptance Model literature, a stream of research originally begun by Davis (1986). A review of the findings can be found in Gefen and Straub (1999).

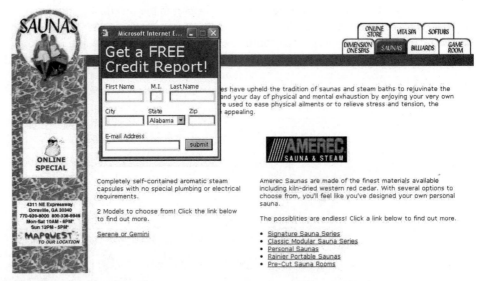

Figure 12.9   Pop-up Window Advertising Credit Reports at Sauna Web Site (URL: www.atlan-taspa.com)

Let's say you are browsing the Web site, but you want to contact the firm by phone because you are having trouble interpreting what is shown as specifications for a sauna unit. Neither through the menu bars nor through the Web pages you browse can you find a telephone number. It is actually buried under one branch of the site tree where you would have to have already purchased a product before you see the screen. There are e-mail addresses to use on every page, but you are in a hurry and want to use the phone.

We would have to classify this as two failures. First, the designers of the site did not realize how critical it is to have bail-out chutes on each page for users, so that the firm will not lose contact with a potentially interested party. Second, the navigational characteristics of the site design were such that it was difficult to find the telephone number unless you knew where to look.

The fact of the matter is that consumers do not have patience with a firm that does not make a site easy to navigate. Their switching costs are low, and they will move quickly to another site that they can understand and follow easily. Switching costs are low for e-consumers in that they can just click on the next Google entry (or that of another search engine), and they are connected to the next e-vendor.

What are the core competencies a firm must have to implement easy-to-navigate sites? Web designers with an understanding of simple, clean pages and intuitive appreciation of what the site has to offer and what the hyperlinks mean are clearly crucial. Market researchers with a grasp of how customers in the market segment think about the firms offerings and are likely to respond to future offerings are another helpful group. The point that needs to be kept in mind is that the creation of a Web site is a team effort and will be accomplished best with the input of numerous parties.

Download Delay

Although it is a truism that no one likes to wait, it is particularly true on the Web. Research has discovered that there is a strong causal connection between users being frustrated by long download times and their attitudes toward brands and inclination to purchase.[10] This effect seems to hold worldwide, even in countries that are more laid back about timeliness.[11]

In the next chapter, we will discuss hurdles to implementing systems that are based on the Internet. Download delay is a prominent problem, and we will review it in greater depth at that time. This is a managerial issue: Firm managers need to articulate guidelines to the Web designers about how to reduce download delay under prescribed circumstances.

Interactivity and Responsiveness

Web pages are best if they give the user the sense that the system or a person at the other end of the communications channel are in contact with them. The Web channel needs to have either a real "social" or human presence or at least the perception of a social presence.[12] The more that consumers sense this presence, the more they are inclined to buy online.[13]

What are users expecting? The site should seem to respond to their individual needs, even when we know that, in fact, it is a computer system that has been programmed for response. In the 1970s, a computer program that was written and made available by the University of Pittsburgh attained quite a bit of popularity. The program, called ELIZA, simulated a psychologist interacting with users over the network. For its day, it was pretty ingenious, and many users came away from using the program thinking they had spoken with a person. This program passed what has become known as a *Turing test* in computer science. When a machine or program passes a Turing test, it means that a user cannot tell whether they are interacting with a human or a machine. This feature is considered to be the ultimate capability of a computer application.

Web systems need to adopt this same attitude toward the creation of a Web site. It needs to be dynamic and full of options for the user without being confusing. That is the trick.

Let's take a simple example of an interactive site that is trying to give the impression that it is responsive and highly interactive (two-way). First, the responses are rapid, partly because the number of graphics is kept to a bare minimum for low bandwidth users. Next, the explanations are detailed and pinpointed to show the user how to operate the site. If a data entry element is incorrectly entered by the user, then the system responds by explaining as exactly as it can what the problem is. The programming is linked to a table of common mistakes for each data entry blank, and if the user entry matches this list, there is an informative error message to accompany the Web server response.

A general message such as "you did not fill in some field on the form" is going to be received as cold and unfriendly by the user. However, a system that identifies and highlights, in an alternate color or in some other manner, which blanks still need to be filled in will be seen as far more responsive than one that merely says that there is some mistake somewhere on the data entry page.

---

[10]Rose and Straub (2001).
[11]Rose et al. (2002).
[12]Yin (2002).
[13]Yin (2002).

In fact, to show how interactive a site can be, Web page designs could include a feature where only those fields that were incorrect were presented again to the user for fixing. At the end of the transaction, the system could summarize and present in a readable form the data that had been collected, by field, through the site's Web system. Once again, in case there are errors in the information given by the user, they need to be given a chance to respond and make further corrections.

The level of interactivity to be incorporated into the Web site is a managerial decision. Resources are required to staff a call center for live-chat sales responses as well as to answer e-mails. Being able to design the site to give the appearance of human presence is a Web design talent.

Made-for-the-Medium

The feature of B2C Web site design that is known as *made-for-the-medium* has to do with ways in which the unique capabilities of the Internet, some of which we covered in Chapter 11, have been captured in the Web site. One feature, which is also a stand-alone atomic model, is incorporating a virtual community into the site. Allowing users to connect to other users can be reinforcing for a B2C firm. User groups of technology can enthusiastically promote the product and help the firm determine desirable features for new products or services. Microsoft's usability guidelines also include "refinement," which is making recent trends or offerings more prominent on the Web site.

There are different skills involved in forming or shaping the site to take advantage of the unique capabilities of the Internet. Installing a Webcam feature, for instance, requires a technical understanding of this video technology and the ability to apply it to the site. Each of these unique characteristics involves a different set of skills.

Content

It hardly needs to be said that consumers come to a Web site with expectations that they will find information on products or services they are searching for. This area is so critical that we will devote a whole section to it later. For the moment, it can be acknowledged that good content with hyperlinks to further information will bind users to the firm, whereas poor content with thin back-up information will drive them away.

What would be examples of good content versus poor content? Under the "About Dell" link, Dell Computer (www.dell.com) has a hyperlink that scrolls a company history slowly across the screen, using a technical plug-in that can simulate this moving image. Displaying dates of significant events in the firm's life, the Web page effectively captures the key events and promotes Dell as a company with an illustrious past. It uses multimedia to visually highlight the PC and laptop innovations that have distinguished the firm.

Although this content does not directly sell computers, it gives the customer the sense that the firm is reliable, conscious of quality in its products, and envisioning a prosperous future. Contrast this with an insurance Web site (which shall remain anonymous) that offers no information about its life insurance products. Clicks on its "Life Division" take one to sites that talk about the organizational structure of this division. There are hyperlinks to agents of the firm, but none of these has an e-mail address, only street addresses and phone numbers.

The latter site is a content disaster. Its content actually conveys a worse impression of the firm (a firm out of touch with the modern Internet world) than if it had no B2C Web site at all. Creating, uploading, and maintaining content calls into play the firm's core competencies, and deserves concentrated treatment later in this chapter.

12.5.2 Personalization Systems and Systems for Markets-of-One

Having a site that is usable means that customers like the site and respond favorably to its form, images, and linking capabilities.

Web sites that wish to strongly appeal to consumers will need to implement systems that can recognize the consumer as a past customer and customize responses to that individual. This is known as creating and delivering to "markets-of-one."[14] Amazon has pioneered a number of these concepts, as shown in Figure 12.10. This customer has ordered gardening books before from the Web site, and the cross-selling discount in this e-mail message is for lawn and garden furniture, which the amazon.com systems determined would be a related product to gardening books.

Dear Amazon Customer,

I have an extreme case of spring fever. And Amazon.com's new Lawn & Patio and Kitchen stores have a lot to do with it. Our Lawn & Patio store has everything you need to spruce up your yard. Weber grills, Black & Decker mulching mowers, Fiskars tree pruners--the selection is amazing. And if it's information you're looking for, we've got buying guides and articles that will turn brown thumbs green and green thumbs greener.

Best of all, if you shop before May 19, 200x, you can use the coupon below to save $10 off your Lawn & Patio purchase of $25 or more. Come explore:

http://www.amazon.com/lawnandpatio.

Figure 12.10 Personalization of E-mailings to Customers by amazon.com [Graphics Added for Effect; Year Altered to 200x from Original Date]

This customer has also bought cookbooks from Amazon in the past, and this customer service e-mail hits on this interest coupled with the interest in gardening. The e-mail continues with the sales pitch in Figure 12.11. It makes sense that someone who has purchased cookbooks might also be in the market for kitchen appliances.

---

[14]Gilmore and Pine (2000).

Figure 12.11   Continuation of Personalized Message from amazon.com [Graphics added for effect]

The concept of personalization is to make the customers feel that they are not interacting with a computer but with a salesperson who can make personal suggestions to them. Good salespersons, for example, are observant and can play on that knowledge to induce sales. If they have a long-standing relationship with the customer, this knowledge comes even more into play.

The equivalent of a long-term relationship in Web systems is the database holding proprietary data about the customer. If, in prior visits, a customer has preferred certain kinds of information, such as ratings by independent parties, but not ratings by other customers, then the default display for this customer should respect these preferences. There should be an easily available option to reinstate the other options, but what the customer sees should be what the customer wants.

Marketing-to-one is a philosophical orientation that few firms have adopted as of yet. The more a NEO thinks and acts this way, the more it will gain a competitive edge. Customers like to be treated like persons, and Web systems can be designed to give this impression. Order-of-magnitude substitutions of servers for human communications that the customer perceives as being interactive will lead to stronger bonds. A rack of powerful servers can serve the role of millions of sales or technical representatives. This represents the substitution of information for physical processes on a grand scale, and we are seeing this enacted every day by competent NEOs in cyberspace.

No one has the mistaken belief that customers think they are dealing with humans rather than computers. Consumers realize they are dealing with computers, but are impressed (and willing to suspend disbelief) when the computers demonstrate even a modicum of simulated intelligence. As mentioned above, the famous computer scientist Turing argued that when the behaviors of computers are so close to the behaviors of humans that people cannot tell the difference, then systems designers have achieved their ultimate goals.

12.6 CONTENT AS KING IN B2C AND B2B

The bottom line for Web site deployment is to have content on sites that appeals to users. The buzz in the trade press that has conveyed this viewpoint is that "content is king on the Internet." Good content can overcome a lot of other drawbacks to a Web site, including a less-than-stellar interface. The content needs to be up-to-date, complete, and to take advantage of multimedia capabilities; that being said, users will return to a site that offers them something of value, especially to a site where that value is not static.

Where does content come from? Let's say that the firm is introducing a new product. Who has been involved in this innovation? In a traditional hierarchical organization where the research and development division has designed the product and operations division has built it (or outsourced its manufacture), the sales force brings the product to the attention of possible buyers. Features of the product that would appeal to customers must be highlighted, and then they must be incorporated into the Web site. It has been determined from studies that the more relevant this information is to the customer, the more likely they will buy.[15]

In short, the provision of content on a Web site is the core competency of the firm. Which roles in the firm should be the providers of this content? There is no straightforward answer, because it depends on the nature of the content and the type of business. A general answer would be "domain area experts," but who, for instance, might qualify under this rubric? Consider an industry trade association that provides its members with legislative updates on bills that are pending or have passed. This legislation could be at the local, provincial, or federal levels, and it could be broken down into many categories of interest. In this case, the domain experts are the firm legal staff, lawyers and paralegals, who follow such legislation and can interpret the impacts of the statutes on the industry. They might also track regulatory changes, but the key point is that some background in the tracking and interpretation of laws and regulations is one of the things that distinguishes this trade association from other trade associations. Industry firms become customers of this trade association to the extent to which the information on the association Web site (password-controlled extranet, in this case) is useful in their own struggle against rivals.

Suppose the provision of content is passed off to another group hired by the trade association. What skills would they have to have to be able to follow the legal trends, spot new regulations and bills, and then bring them to the attention of the trade association members? They would need legal and paralegal skills! So what is a firm that outsources nearly everything, including the core competencies associated with a given business? It is a shell of a real company, and its major skillsets are managing its investments in other firms, including outsourcers and strategic partners. Some call it a "holding company" and others call it the extreme form of a "virtual" organization. There is no doubt that holding companies are viable enterprises, and their capabilities in investment can be prodigious. But some firm has to have the core competencies that allow content to be uploaded to the Web. Therefore, the core business of the firm is being represented on the site via this provisioning.

[15]Palmer (2002); Agarwal and Venkatesh (2002).

In short, it is difficult to see how content provision can be effectively outsourced. It is possible to outsource the hosting services and networks connections, certainly, and possibly maintenance (as we shall see below), but the uploading of new information that keeps a Web site vital and interesting to users is what makes a firm unique with respect to its competitors. How can a firm outsource this essential differentiator?

Because this is an important point, let's look at another type of firm. Amazon has a model in which they have their own inventory of books that they sell over the Web, but they also serve as consignees of the books of their associates and, in this sense, are "content aggregators" of books. Managing these two kinds of products is clearly different, but it is all being driven through the Web site and, therefore, is subject to the same issue regarding core competencies. If Amazon is able to stimulate sales through the addition of new volumes, some of which are from their own inventory and some that are available through associates, it is transparent to the users. The users want choice, and whatever happens in the background to create this choice is all to the good.

Product offerings at amazon.com are displayed as advertisements, "pushed" books, or as the result of a user-initiated query, as shown in Figure 12.12. A user asks if there are books on traveling in Nepal, and the database of all books, owned and consigned, is searched for these keywords. Some of these books are in Amazon's inventory; others are in the inventories of the associates. It is not obvious from the site which is which, nor does it matter to the user.

Figure 12.12   Results of Amazon Query for Books on Traveling in Nepal

Where are the core competencies in this process? First, with regard to the associates, Amazon needs to carefully manage its relations with them to ensure that they are up-to-date in providing the latest book availabilities and accurate pricing. Entries into the database can be undertaken by Amazon, by the associates with access privileges to protected parts of the main database, or by a hired third party. From Amazon's perspective, it is clearly beneficial to have associate's inventory appear on the site. The risk is that the associate will not have mastered the skills to enter the data properly. If managing the Web site is crucial from a competitive standpoint (it most likely is), then Amazon may wish to handle the data entry itself. Problems with the data could lead to late or canceled orders, or losses if the pricing is not accurate. Managing the data on books on the site becomes, therefore, a competitive issue.

Amazon can have employees on staff who enter new offerings from their own or others' inventories, change pricing, and delete out-of-print items. These persons are product-knowledge workers in the sense that their inputs and outputs are both in the form of information.[16] Where do they get their information about books? Publishers have this information available once a book is for sale. This information is then made available in electronic form to retailers such as Amazon. Nowadays, digital forms of the pictures or images on the book cover are also available for advertising the wares.

Amazon's core competencies in this process, thus, are to acquire information about books being stocked and to have this information available on the Web site as soon as possible. Handling this process efficiently and effectively is a strategic necessity, if not a competitive advantage. If Amazon's competitors are not quite as good at this as Amazon, then it could translate into superior sales and profits. So, once again, the domain area experts are those who have the skills to bring the firm a competitive edge, or, at least, allow them to stay even with their rivals. In this case, marketing analysts and product-knowledge workers would be the content providers. Their capabilities make the resource base for the running of the Web site—including the server software and hardware, the network, and the Amazon Web site application and database—valuable. Without this dynamic capability, the Web resources would be shortly become useless.

What about the technical creation and ongoing maintenance of the Web site itself? Is this a core competency of a firm, or can it be hired out? This is a critical question for managers of NEOs to address.

12.7 BUILDING AND MAINTAINING NE SYSTEMS

Does a firm need to have Web design skills inside the firm or can these be hired out? And how does this relate to core competencies?

The trade-off of hiring versus internal provisioning is, again, relevant to core competencies. In the case of Amazon, their Web site and its continuing innovation was such a competitive advantage that they became the envy of the industry. The "One-Click" ease-in-shopping innovation is an example. For registered users, the One-Click feature means that all the data on name, shipping address, credit card numbers, and so forth could be pulled from the customer database, and there is no need for the user to reenter data. The convenience of this approach led to Barnes & Noble imitating the concept in their "Double-Click" feature, which was necessary because Amazon had patented the "One-Click" idea in the United States.

This continuous introduction of new Web site capabilities was a major reason why Borders hired Amazon to build the Borders Web site. Without doubt, it is unusual to hire your competitor to create a primary customer interface, but it does show the extent to

---

[16]Davis et al. (1993).

which Amazon's technological innovation had placed them in such a dominant position in site stickiness.

Ordinarily it would not be in either Borders's or Amazon's best interest to engage in such an outsourcing arrangement. Borders can achieve competitive parity if and only if Amazon transfers the same technical capabilities to their site that Amazon uses on its own site. Although competitive parity may be an acceptable goal for many firms, it cannot lead to a competitive edge, obviously. The only way this can be done is if Borders itself or its outsourcers creates new ways of appealing to customers.

Amazon is also placed in a potentially conflicting role if it is both competing and cooperating with another firm in the same solution domain. Should it withhold certain technical functions from the rival's Web site until it has derived its own first-mover advantages? If not, what happens to its competitive edge? These are not easy issues to resolve, and the firm could find itself in a compromising position when, in fact, there may be little gained from a competitive standpoint.

Borders may view its core competencies as being the management of its physical stores and supply chain or in its marketing. In this case, competitive parity for its Web site may be a good strategic choice, at least for the short-term. If Amazon's online sales start to seriously erode Borders's physical store sales, then Borders's not viewing its Web site as a core competency would have to change. Only time will tell on how the book market in e-tail and retail develops.

If it comes to pass that Borders does change its strategic position in this area, then the recognition that the Web site is a critical competitive edge means that they will need internal expertise. This can, and should, be built at this point. Being able to capitalize quickly on new ways of presenting the firm's content offerings is the edge needed.

Amazon is another matter. As a cybermediary, they already view their site as the source of their competitive advantage and insource their own systems development. But why then would they transfer their hard-earned knowledge to their competitor's advantage? Amazon may view "bricks-and-clicks" firms like Borders as not being competitors in the same way as varsitybooks.com (see Figure 12.13). If a bookstore only sells books online, then its sales are directly impacting Amazon's market share. A purchaser of a book at Borders's physical store may not have purchased online in any case. And it is also conceivable that their use of the Borders's Web site is in a kiosk within the physical store, simply checking on locatability of a volume.

Nonetheless, a book purchase on the Borders site does directly impact Amazon's bottom line, unless the Borders customer is motivated strictly by loyalty.

For Amazon, the trade-off is the exercising of a new business model in which they provide Web site development skills to others, going beyond books sales, for example. In this, they are capitalizing on their core competencies and should never outsource these skills. They may rethink their handling of the Borders' account, but the decision to retain internal IT skills in NE systems represents sound strategic positioning.

Figure 12.13   VarsityBooks—Amazon's Competitor in Cyberspace

12.7.1 Maintenance of NE Systems

Maintenance of NE systems, just as with traditional systems, takes on at least two forms: repairs and enhancement.[17] Repairs to systems can be systems-life threatening, where the system aborts or cannot perform a critical function, or they can be cosmetic. In the high-need category, customers will interpret the loss of functionality as a lack of responsiveness on the part of the e-vendor. This can be serious because there could be, potentially, millions of affected customers. Cosmetic repairs do not require emergency surgery.

The primary issue for NEOs with respect to maintenance of Web systems is whether this activity should be insourced or outsourced. Regardless of whether the firm has hired an outsourcer to build the system, these same developers will know the system well and could, conceivably, make emergency repairs rather quickly. Unfortunately, most information services functional areas separate new development from maintenance, with the former being the more prestigious and considered to be more interesting work. In such

[17]Swanson and Beath (1989); Swanson (1988).

cases, there is a slight advantage to having outsiders build and maintain the system in that the contract can require the continued involvement of the developers. Most major repairs on the system will occur within the first six months, and thereafter it is possible to have trained a group of maintainers who were not part of the original development team.

Enhancements are very different from repairs. Feedback from users will tell the maintenance manager that major or minor changes need to be made to improve the functioning of the system. These keep the system "living" and not relegated to the category of a "dead" system, meaning that it no longer meets the needs of the users.

Focus on NE: Pop-ups

Take a peek behind the browser window you're using now. How many other windows does your browser have open? More than you thought? Congratulations: You've been popped. You can find pop-up ads all over the Web. They're bothersome, for sure, and with their prevalence increasing, online consumers are getting more fed up. A Jupiter Media Metrix study conducted in June found that 41% of respondents cited pop-ups as an annoyance that would affect their decision to revisit a site. When the same study was conducted in 1999, only 23% responded that pop-ups would be a factor in their decision to return to a site. Seizing on this anti-pop-up sentiment, EarthLink (ELNK) announced in August 2002 that it would include anti-pop-up features in the latest version of its software, Total Access 2003. The move marks the first time a major ISP will include anti-pop-up software in its connection package.

Sources:
http://www.business2.com/articles/web/0,1653,43050,FF.html

12.7.2 NES Technical Environment and Firm Core Competencies

Making systems adaptable so they can be rapidly changed to address changing requirements of users is sensible for a NEO. Modern tools and development environments can speed this process up, and the best of breed practice among professional IT staffs will allow this to take place. An in-depth discussion of this technical capability is beyond the scope of this book, but it needs to be noted for general managers that if NE systems are built and/or maintained inside the firm, then the firm has determined, de facto, that this is a core competency of the firm. In short, for the firm to capitalize on its resource base, it must be able to deliver on its Web and EDI systems in the shortest possible time frame and to create highly dependable systems to boot.

A critical success factor for deploying systems rapidly in such a case is to use rapid application development (RAD) techniques. These tools allow a prototype of a system to be created within a short period of time so that users can react to the "look and feel" of the system before it is programmed in the language of production. The large computer vendors, such as Sun and Microsoft, have been heavily supporting this area with the concept of component-based architectures. This means that pieces of the application would be reusable modules that would be, in effect, "plug and play," just as in the client hardware and software environments.

12.8 DEPLOYING INTRANETS AND EXTRANETS

Intranets and extranets are closely related, we would argue. Much of the information provided by an intranet could, at some point, be extended to parties external to the firm. These would include strategic partners and customers. When the firm opens up its systems to these parties, it is, in a real sense, blurring the boundaries between itself and the environment for competitive reasons.

Not all the features of the intranet can be extended to extranets; however, many can. In Table 12.3, both customers and business partners would find a firm's telephone directory useful. They could readily use the lists and descriptions of the firm's products and services, as well. The firm will want to keep sales reports private, and although they might be willing to allow the firm's logos to be downloaded, it is unlikely that they would be that useful, even to partners, and would just clutter up the extranet.

Table 12.3: Features Typically Available on Intranets and Extensibility to Extranets

Feature	Extensible to Extranet?
Firm telephone directory	X
Sales reports	
Product/service information	X
Logo repository	
Public financial statements	X

12.9 IMPLEMENTING INTRANETS, EXTRANETS, AND PROACTIVE E-MAIL (INTERACTIVE MARKETING)

There are several major implementation questions regarding intranets, extranets, and e-mail, which is a "killer" application for the Internet and, thus, closely connected to the deployment of intranets and extranets. How should a NEO introduce these, and what is the relationship between them?

E-mail is the most natural entry point for a start-up firm. Even without an intranet or extranet, e-mail enhances intra- and inter-firm communications. E-mail has been used by most large- and medium-sized firms for decades, long preceding the Internet. With the Internet, the range of possible communicants has been greatly enhanced.

The ability to attach documents and, for most of client e-mail applications, to interpret HTML, much like a browser, is making e-mail clients more versatile. For purposes of interactive marketing, hyperlinks within e-mail messages can be hotlinked, and message recipients can immediately activate an Internet browser and request the firm's designated Web page. With multimedia graphics and sound, they can even serve in a B2B or B2C after-sales support capability, as discussed in Chapter 11.

As a communications and sales tool, e-mail is still greatly underutilized, in our opinion, even with the incredible levels of worldwide usage that we are seeing. The automation of e-mail messaging is feasible and yet not that widely implemented. First, there are the distributional advantages: Groups can be set up through database queries of demographics, group membership, or interests. These can be dynamic so that no one need receive an irritating e-mail and have their right to privacy violated. E-mail can be automated in many ways, including personalized advertisements. The cost of a regular sales campaign is incredibly low, with millions of e-mails sent at a fraction of a fraction of the cost of a paper-based or alternate media-based campaign.

Whether the firm has completely exploited the capabilities of e-mail or not, intranets give the firm the advantage of making information widely available, which is crucial to the internal operations of the firm. Let's take the air crew bidding systems that the major airlines use for connecting pilots and flight attendants to the scheduling of their flights. Intranets can present a user-friendly front to a complicated back-end that prioritizes bids on the basis of seniority, randomness, or any other firm-determined algorithm. Such a system allows employees to tailor their flying schedule to their personal needs and is certainly desirable from an employee point of view. But it also serves the firm by eliminating paper bids, data entry (with its attendant errors and complaints), and published paper schedules. Placing the bidding process month-in and month-out on the intranet can be automated so that very little is required in the way of staff supervision. Once the interface between the bidding subsystem and the flight schedule is completed, for example, the change to a new month is just a matter of flipping the calendar, either manually or automatically. Moreover, all of this data is entered in a timely manner into a complete flight database, which can be used by the management for decision-making purposes.

Let's continue with the implications of having created this intranet application. If an airline has a strategic alliance with other carriers, as many carriers do these days, there may be good reasons for extending access to the completed flight database—with ports of call, gates, times, aircraft, and crew information—to partners. Partners would access the database through a password-controlled extranet and could better plan their own offerings by understanding the full capabilities of their strategic partners.

Clearly, intranets may be built with features that could be useful to partners and carried forward into an extranet. In the GSU study, a large electrical cable manufacturer found that the intranet they had built for their field sales representatives was easily extended to their best customers so they could view the latest inventory online. When the manufacturer introduced online order functionality for the sales representatives, there was a natural transition of the system to their best customers.[18] This was initially a limited online presence. Payments were still handled through the paper-based accounts receivable–accounts payable (AR-AP) systems, and there was no special provision for online tracking of purchased goods. But the movement from intranet to extranet allowed the firm to get double mileage (synergies) from the same resource. It increased sales and dramatically reduced paper and publishing expenses by half.

There is a dynamic between e-mail, intranets, and extranets that firms need to strategize about and plan before deployment. The worst possible case would be to allow these systems to be implemented without having taken a holistic view of these three approaches and coordinating them for maximal advantage.

12.10 INTERNET TIME AND MOVING FROM STRATEGY TO DEPLOYMENT

One of the main tenets of the Internet age seems to be that time and space are changed by this medium. Internet time, in particular, is believed to cycle rapidly, so rapidly, in fact, that first-mover advantage can only lead to a competitive edge if the builder is already developing the next technological innovation. If this is true, what are the implications for strategizing the firm's NE position and implementing NE systems?

One of the clearest indications that things are different is that Web sites for many B2C sites seem to be in the constant state of flux. The navigational process has been altered (one would hope to the good), the graphic design has been changed, and the layout of the site, as indicated by the site map, rearranged. This kind of constant and drastic shifting may represent a need to respond to customer needs, as one would wish, or it may represent a panicky feeling that Internet time requires this level of activity.

What should change regularly on a firm's Web site and on other NE systems? Content. The value added from a Web site that is already well designed comes from having new products and services more than presenting them in constantly new and different ways.[19] All systems that lead to fluid and accurate content provision should receive the highest priority in NEOs. Other usability features are important, certainly, but are of secondary importance.

In other NE systems, change is clearly hard with protocols that operate most smoothly when they are standardized. Traditional EDI, for instance, absolutely depends on lack of change, and Internet time cannot alter the need for the tight coupling of these systems for

---

[18]Many firms handle the channel conflict of disintermediating the sales representatives by giving them credit for sales within the territory, whether carried out over the Net or not. Over time, NEOs will have to reduce or eliminate these sales commissions, or they will never realize the full cost savings from the Net. But this approach does seem to work in the short-term.

[19]Collis and Montgomery (1995).

efficient operation. Changes in such industry protocols is a long and laborious process that is political as much as it is technical.

With Web EDI, there is some flexibility gained by XML data definitions being embedded in the transferred code. Nevertheless, there will be a need to adapt such changes at both ends of the flow, and this still takes some time.

Once again, changing content is what B2B data exchange systems are best set up for. Each order is different and so is each customer, but the major difference as far as the systems is concerned is in the content, or data. Internet time may have an impact on NEOs, but the concept needs to be much more carefully defined and its implications demonstrated before it can be taken as much more than a consulting buzzword.

We would argue that Wheeler's model of thoughtful application of emerging technologies to the firm's already existing core strengths, and the rapid creation of NE systems to capitalize on these strengths must certainly cycle through relatively quickly, especially compared with traditional development and implementation cycles. But it needs to be shown scientifically that NE requires that this cycle occur at Internet hyperspeed rather than just "faster." It may be the case that hypercompetitive environments are differentiating firms in this way. Capability theory even today argues that the implementation of strategy is what distinguishes some firms for long-term competitive advantage. And this may be another such time.

12.11 EFFECTIVE IMPLEMENTATION THROUGH NE MANAGEMENT

How should firms manage online NE systems? First, if Internet time is truly different, then long, drawn out systems development projects will not work. Earlier in the chapter we mentioned the emerging rapid applications environments that are component- and prototype-based, and we considered the CORBA, J2EE, and .Net component-based environments in Chapter 5. All of these examples are indications of the need to rapidly develop and deploy online NE systems.

Creating the systems is only one part of the equation, though. The overall management of the Web site—its goals and objectives, its construction, its enhancements, and its ongoing updating and operation—is the key to success. And the central issue for organizing the firm to deliver NE systems is an age-old set of questions: (1) Who owns the site or parts of the site? (2) Who should be creating and updating the content for the site? (3) Who is responsible for the technical infrastructure of the site, including the servers and applications? and (4) How shall this overall effort be organized (i.e., centralized or decentralized management)?

We have seen that content provision is central to a successful site. Content provision is in the province of non-IT personnel, for the most part, and yet the IT personnel, either in-house or outsourced, need to be tightly coupled to the business units in learning how to rapidly implement good ideas. For this reason, some would argue that applications development of mission-critical applications is a core competency of a NEO.[20]

---

[20]Straub et al. (2002).

12.11.1 Business Unit Participation in IT Development and Operations

There is a long history of debate as to how much and when business professionals should be involved in systems work.[21] When businesses first used computers to solve business problems, information processing was carried out solely by the IS department, but with the increased availability of microcomputers, tasks traditionally handled by IS professionals were dispersed to non-IS personnel. These users (termed "end-users") began to create their own small applications such as spreadsheets, database reporting systems, as well as actual production-geared, department-level programs. End-users were defined as those who had immediate, personal control over all stages of the computing activity and who used computers autonomously for their own information-processing needs. The capability of end-users to directly control their own applications and computing methods has been defined as end-user computing (EUC).[22]

Some end-users became so adept that they earned the title "super-user." In this capacity, they began to function as a mini, nonofficial IT department within their departmental units. Most end-users were nontechnologists, though, and yet still grew in their understanding and knowledge of PCs and how they could aid the organization. Later, when client-server technology became popular, they learned to work directly with the mainframes and large servers through their PC and workstation clients.

As nontechnologists, NE content providers within the firm today are in a remarkably similar position to end-users over the last two decades. Therefore, what we have learned about EUC—such matters as roles, responsibilities, and division of management control—should be applicable to NESs.

Applicable Characteristics of End-User Computing[23]

Among the groups involved in the EUC phenomenon were the following: nonprogramming end-users, application end-users, programming-level end-users, and end-user programmers. Typically, EUC started with small applications on a microcomputer platform. These small applications may or may not have been developed by end-users themselves, but the end-users controlled the inputs, processing, and timing of outputs of these applications.

For an effective EUC effort, it was discovered that a balance of managerial activities was needed to promote and, at the same time, contain EUC. As we saw in discussing Nolan's Stages of Computing Growth Model[24] in Chapter 1, an uncontrolled spreading of computing in the organization can be thought of as a "contagion," and this lack of standardization and budgetary responsibility can lead to unfortunate consequences.

In general, strategies for expansion and strategies for control implemented at the right time have been found to most effectively orchestrate the firm's EUC effort. Early in the history of EUC, there were few managerial activities in place to support or control the small systems that were owned and controlled by end-users. Firms typically operate in a laissez-faire mode in this early stage. Later, firms managed EUC through a greater number and wider range of expansionary and controlling activities. As EUC evolved in the firm, we began to see conscious efforts to manage growth.

---

[21]See, for example, Hartwick and Barki (1994).
[22]Davis and Olson (1985).
[23] Works to consult for points raised in this section are Rockart and Flannery (1983); Davis and Olson (1985); Huff et al. (1988); Brancheau and Amoroso (1990); and Brancheau and Brown (1993).
[24]Nolan (1973).

Managing NE Implementation

Best-of-breed practice strikes a balance between decentralization (or expansion) and centralization (or control). As with EUC, the goal of effective management is to promote NE as a dynamic force for change in the organization without choking it or permitting it to grow in an uncontrolled fashion. Business unit managers, content providers, and superusers all need to be given latitude to introduce new ideas, but there needs to be some overriding strategic control of the Web site. The Weill and Vitale (2001) "single point of contact" atomic business model exists because firms want customers and strategic partners to see the firm through a unitary vision. If each division has its own Web page design, method of navigation, and format for content display, then the impression that a user will have of the overall site is that it is fragmented and terribly disorganized, perhaps just like the firm itself. This is distinctly the wrong impression.

Ineffective NE management occurs far too often, with the result that the opportunity for critical innovation is lost as managers struggle with their strategic positioning or fail to recognize the need to change strategy over time. When a radical technological innovation of the dimension of NE is first introduced, organizations must plan for and later initiate a fairly complex infrastructure to support NE activities. As the innovation becomes internalized and routinized, this infrastructure can (and should) be opened up to reflect the new conditions. Later, as organizations learn how to profitably employ innovations, less formal, cooperative relationships may replace rule-based relationships and centralized management with its heavy dose of standards. These informal but cooperative arrangements will also prove to be better than a laissez-faire style, which is no hands-on management at all.

That being said, Web sites need to give a strong impression in cyberspace of the goals and central thrust of the firm. Some centralized control over that impression should always be continued. In the GSU study, one senior vice-president of e-commerce confided that his first official act upon being brought in from another industry was to shut down the firm's Web site. The "face presented to the world" on the Web site was so poorly implemented that he felt that it was a misrepresentation and an embarrassment. Three months later, the new site was inaugurated with a unitary theme and a clear indication that impression management was important.

Web systems blur the distinctions between users and developers by bringing online the systems that are related closely to the core competencies of the firm.[25] These groups must be managed so that they each have assigned responsibilities but, at the same time, are given license to promote and bring forward new ideas. It is a delicate balancing act for managers of NE, but one that is crucial for the future prosperity of the firm.

12.12 SUMMARY

Careful strategizing can create new opportunities for NEOs to gain competitive advantages. Deployment tactics first require an examination of the intent of the systems. Matching the goals, business processes, and core competencies with available technologies is an important part of strategy.

[25]Bansler et al. (2000).

Core competencies for NEOs differ according to their atomic model or hybrid model. Net-enhanced systems can be deployed throughout the value chain. The order of stages in the NE value chain are inquiry, order/sale, payment, delivery, and after-sales support.

Special conditions exist for B2B and B2C deployment issues. B2B involves a detailed understanding of consumer behavior.

Web sites should be designed for usability. Usability issues include download delay, navigational and organizational capabilities, interactivity, responsiveness, and information or content. Web sites can also appeal to consumers through personalization and markets-of-one. The bottom line for Web site deployment is to have content on sites that appeal to users. Maintenance of NE systems consist of repairs and enhancement. Repairs can be systems-life threatening or cosmetic.

Deploying intranets and extranets in firms should also be coordinated with an e-mail implementation. E-Mail is the first Internet technology that the firm needs to carefully intro-duce. There are many benefits to be gained in binding the firm more closely to customers and partners. Intranets can lead into extranets with partners or selected customers. Once again, the effective introduction of these technologies can strengthen the firm's strategic position.

Building systems at Internet speed may become a prerequisite for a NEO. What is crucial to remember is that involvement of users in content provision is essential for gain-ing a competitive edge. The management of this effor is analogous to the choices that have been made over the last two decades in end-user computing. This managerial approach may change over time as NE systems become more widely understood within the firm.

KEY TERMS

3PL: Third-party logistics

EDI integrated: A new concept of process in EDI exchanges that ties the single transac-tions together with a series of expected exchanges that can be matched and coordinated.

EUC: End-user computing.

FAQ: Frequently asked questions to which the Web site provides answers.

Open-buying Internet (OBI): An open-systems, Web-based EDI apporach to establish-ing computer-to-computer links to link with partners.

Web service: A component-based approach to delivering Web systems more rapidly.

REVIEW QUESTIONS

1. What are the stages of implementation?
2. What are the primary issues for deployment?
3. How can firms gather transactional data?
4. What are the economic advantages of an e-mail answering service or live-chat service?
5. What are implementation hurdles for delivery.
6. What are the disadvantages of traditional EDI?
7. What is the difficulty with Web-based application formats?
8. List the Web usability features that managers need to be aware of.
9. What kinds of maintenance are required on NE systems?
10. What is a critical success factor for deploying systems rapidly?

TOPICS FOR DISCUSSION

1. What are the differences between B2B and B2C channels?
2. What are vertical market channels?
3. Discuss the difference between complementor and competitor.
4. What does the Web offer a database marketer?
5. Discuss the use of "clickstream"?
6. Discuss data marketing and its importance?
7. Why are buying networks being developed rather than one-to-one auctions?
8. Where can B2B buying networks fail?
9. How do networks differ from chains?
10. Discuss the advantages and disadvantages to online auctions.
11. What is ETN?   How does it affect the supply chain?
12. What are P2P communications?
13. Discuss how pricing between and among Internet vendors differs from that of traditional businesses.
14. When do channel conflicts typically occur?
15. Why is global reach so unique in cyberspace versus a traditional business?

INTERNET EXERCISES

1. Go to the McAfee Web site. Investigate the virus hoax section and summarize one of the entries.
2. Go to the Borders Web site. List as many similarities to the Amazon site as possible.
3. Locate a virtual advisor on the Internet. Describe the services offered.
4. Locate two Web sites in the same industry. Compare the type of introductory information offered on the home page.
5. Go to amazon.com. Describe the after-sales support offered by this firm.
6. Look up a speech-recognition software. Describe the capabilities of the application.
7. Choose a music file download site. Why is it operating and Napster is not?
8. Go to eBay and investigate the payment options offered to customers.
9. Go to Web Design With An Edge. Choose two of the suggestions for improving Web design and summarize.
10. Choose two pop-up killer applications. Compare the features of each application.

TEAM EXERCISES

1. Find a company that offers permission e-mails and one company that offers banner advertisement. Contact them and inquire about their average click response rate. Find out the price they charge for the marketing program, and calculate the cost per click-through.
2. Discuss the advantages and disadvantages of outsourcing the billing and order processing function for a company going online. Specifically, comment on the product types, size of the firm, and general business strategy (e.g., cost leader versus differentiation) and their potential impact on decision of outsourcing. Find one company that provides outsourcing billing and processing function for others and comment on their service.

3. In a virtual organization, a company may have a different structure compared to a traditional organization. A traditional organization may be divided into manufacturing, marketing, research and development, and other functional departments. How will a virtual company organize itself? Find one virtual company and describe its organization.

4. In a virtual organization, employees may be dispersed all over the world. Discuss the advantages and disadvantages of this dispersion as it pertains to control and monitoring of employees and organizational learning.

5. Find one strategic alliance between two companies that enables a traditional company to go online. Discuss how you see this alliance may benefit both companies and what may be the potential problems of this alliance.

INTERNET RESOURCES

Analog X and POW! (http://www.monster-hardware.com/articles/computerutilities.htm): Kill those pop-up windows!

CGI Programs (http://www.katsueydesignworks.com/cgi_index.htm): Load your own pop-up ads!

REFERENCES

Agarwal, R., and V. Venkatesh. "Assessing a Firm's Web Presence: A Heuristic Evaluation Procedure for the Measurement of Usability." *Information Systems Research*, 13, 2, June 2002, 168–186.

Bansler, J. P., J. Damsgaard, R. Scheepers, and E. H. J. Thommesen. "Corporate Intranet Implementation: Managing Emergent Technologies and Organizational Practices." *JAIS*, 1, 1 (2000), 1–23.

Brancheau, J. C., and D. L. Amoroso. "An Empirical Test for the Expansion-Control Model for Managing End-User Computing." Proceedings of the Ninth International Conference on Information Systems, Copenhagen, Denmark, 1990, 291–304.

Brancheau, J. C., and C. V. Brown. "The Management of End-User Computing: Status and Directions." *ACM Computing Surveys*, 25, 4, December 1993, 437–479.

Collis, D. J., and C. A. Montgomery. "Competing on Resources: Strategy in the 1990s." *Harvard Business Review*, July-August 1995, 118–128.

Davis, F. "Technology Acceptance Model for Empirically Testing New End-User Information Systems: Theory and Results." Dissertation, MIT, 1986.

Davis, G. B., R. W. Collins, M. A. Eierman, and W. D. Nance. "Productivity for Information Technology Investment in Knowledge Workers." In Banker, R. D., R. J. Kauffman, and M. A. Mahmood, eds. *Strategic Information Technology Management Perspectives on Organizational Growth and Competitive Advantage*, Idea Publishing, Harrisburg, PA, 1993.

Davis, G. B., and M. H. Olson. *Management Information Systems: Conceptual Foundations, Structure, and Developments*, McGraw-Hill, New York, 1985.

Gefen, D., and D. Straub. "The Relative Importance of Perceived Ease of Use in IS Adoption: A Study of E-Commerce Adoption." *Journal of the Association of Information Systems*, 1, 8 (2000), 1–29.

Gilmore, J. H., and B. J. Pine. *Markets of One: Creating Customer-Unique Value through Mass Customization*, Harvard Business School Press, Boston, 2000.

Hartwick, J. H., and H. Barki. "Explaining the Role of User Participation in Information Systems Use." *Management Science*, 40, 4, April 1994, 440–465.

Huff, S. L., M. C. Munro, and B. H. Martin. "Growth Stages of End User Computing." *Communications of the ACM*, 31, 5, May 1988, 542–550.

Klein, R. "The Effect of e-Business Enabled Symmetric Information Sharing Practices in Vendor / Client Relationships." Dissertation, Georgia State University, 2002.

Nolan, R. L. "Managing the Computer Resource: A Stage Hypothesis." *Communications of the ACM*, 16, 7, July 1973, 399–405.

Palmer, J. "Web-site Usability, Design and Performance Metrics." *Information Systems Research*, 13, 1, March 2002, 151–167.

Rai, A., B. Weinlein, J. Wareham, and M. Keil. "Omnexus: The ePlastics Marketplace" 2001. [Online] Available: http://www.coba.usf.edu/departments/isds/faculty/abhatt/cases/Omnexus.pdf.

Richmond, W. B., A. Seidmann, and A. B. Whinston. "Incomplete Contracting Issues in Information Systems Development Outsourcing." *Decision Support Systems*, 8, 5, September 1992, 459–477.

Rose, G. "The Effect of Download Time on e-Commerce: The Download Time Brand Impact Model." Dissertation, Georgia State University, 2000.

Rose, G., R. Evaristo, and D. Straub. "Culture and Consumer Responses to Web Download Time: A Four-Continent Study of Mono- and Polychronism." *IEEE Transactions on Engineering Management,* forthcoming, 2002.

Rose, G., and D. W. Straub. "The Effect Of Download Time On Consumer Attitude Toward the E-Service Retailer." *e-Service Journal*, 1, 1 (2001), 55–76.

Straub, D. W., and R. Klein. "e-Competitive Transformations." *Business Horizons*, 44, 3, May-June 2001, 3–12.

Straub, D., P. Weill, and K. Stewart. "Strategic Control of IT Resources: A Test of Selective Outsourcing and Resource-Based Theory." Working paper, Georgia State University, 2002.

Swanson, E. B. *Information System Implementation*, Irwin, Homewood, IL, 1988.

Swanson, E. B., and C. M. Beath. *Maintaining Information Systems in Organizations*, Wiley, New York, 1989.

Yin, J. "Interactivity of Internet-Based Communications: Impacts on E-Business Consumer Decisions" Dissertation, Georgia State University, 2002.

CHAPTER 13

CHALLENGES TO IMPLEMENTATION

UNDERSTANDING NE IMPLEMENTATION CHALLENGES

The dominant drivers behind NE are likely to be irresistible over time. Yet there are many obstacles to the full realization of the vision. What are the reasons that NE is impeded and/or resisted? There are at least six major technical areas that have been identified in the literature, and there are many other social reasons that are perhaps self-evident although unconfirmed in the scientific literature. A critical technical problem, for instance, is the download delay of Web pages. Other impediments are organizational in nature or emerging from the environment. An example would be lack of trust in the e-vendor, which is often paired with lack of trust in the e-consumer. How should managers understand and deal with these impediments? Being able to work around these impediments is critical for advancing the firm's interests. Once again, managers need to find solutions to NE implementation bottlenecks and push for their adoption. Otherwise, the benefits from NE will be hampered for years beyond what is necessary.

LEARNING OBJECTIVES FOR THIS CHAPTER

- To explain why security is the key issue in Internet commerce adoption
- To describe security barriers to use, both from a consumer perspective and an organizational perspective, and to briefly describe solutions to the problems faced
- To explain how to deal with the security issue
- To explicate why download delay is a major factor in online purchasing, even while bandwidths are increasing in many countries
- To make a case for why search problems are a major issue and what can be done to resolve them
- To describe the value of metrics, the need for better metrics, and how to get them for the Web

- To overview interface limitations and how to possibly deal with them
- To discuss how managers can overcome the varying standards emerging on the Web
- To describe a set of social issues, such as: (1) fear of consumers in buying or transacting business over the Web, (2) lack of brand awareness, (3) management/cultural problems in instituting e-business practices and ideas, (4) lack of firm experience in doing e-business, (5) organizational fear of doing business over the Internet, (6) migrating to Internet computer-to-computer linkages from more familiar electronic data interchange (EDI), (7) lack of well-accepted or understood e-cash on the part of consumers or organizations, and (8) ambiguous or hostile legal or regulatory environment for NE

► **CASE STUDY 13-1**

TAXATION OF INTERNET TRANSACTIONS

The emerging online marketplace has generated debate over the taxation of transactions on the Internet. Policymakers and other stakeholders deliberate on whether cyberpurchases should be subject to the same sales taxes levied on brick-and-mortar retailing. At present, online buyers pay no sales taxes, but the supersonic growth of the sale of goods over the Internet shows that there is plenty of money at stake, and government is scrambling to get a piece of the action.

The growth potential of e-commerce is stupendous, as the number of people connected to the Internet increases. Forrester Research estimates that 56.3% of households in the United States alone will be on the Internet in 2003. The Direct Marketing Association says online sales will reach $31.1 billion in 2004 compared to $75.5 billion in catalog revenue, although a few others believe that Internet revenue will surpass catalog revenue by 2004. Though figures and estimates vary widely, one thing is clear: Electronic commerce will grow to account for hundreds of billions of dollars a year in sales. E-commerce is poised to take off as consumers take advantage of comparison shopping, niche markets, and, importantly, the tax-free status of goods bought and sold over the Internet.

The debate over Internet taxation started several years ago, when Internet was in its earliest stages. In 1998, the U.S. Congress passed the Internet Freedom Act, which imposed a three-year moratorium on new Internet taxes. Presently, states can still tax income earned through Internet service providers. States can also apply local business license taxes to a service provider when it is located in the same jurisdiction and collect sales taxes on products bought over the Internet, if the taxes are imposed in the same manner as taxes on mail-order products. The Internet Freedom Act also set up the National Advisory Commission on Electronic Commerce to recommend a course of action for Internet taxation. As of November 28, 2001, President Bush renewed a ban on Internet taxes, ensuring that the country's 130 million Internet users will not face new taxes for at least another two years.

Sources:
http://www.powerhomebiz.com/vol4/internet-taxation.htm

13.1 INTRODUCTION

NE facilitates or creates the opportunities for a vast number of new commercial ventures. These need to be seen as *order-of-magnitude opportunities*,[1] meaning that we are on a completely different plane of activity than with traditional businesses. If your business has been communicating with millions of consumers previous to NE, the potential customer base is now in the hundreds of millions. At some point in the not-too-distant future, it will be in the billions.

The picture is not entirely rosy, though. Although the growth of the Internet has been impressive, to say the least, the dot.com bust in 2000 to 2001 has spawned an atmosphere of doubt in which fewer investments in new ventures were subsequently being made. In the long run, this may lead to entrepreneurial activities that are more sustainable. But in the early years of the twenty-first century, it has led to significant hurdles for innovation.

This chapter deals with challenges. These challenges are either technical in nature, that is, they are built into the way the Internet, the World Wide Web, or current applications on the Internet function, or they are social. Social challenges have to do with the way society (citizens, and in their buying role, consumers), business, and government interact. It has to do with what they believe (true or not) and how they consciously or unconsciously act in dealing with the Internet.

Focus on NE: Bots

Whether you want to optimize your investment or save $1.50 on a CD, you can do it with a *bot*. Bots (short for robots) are also called autonomous agents and consist of small pieces of code that are sent out over the Internet to bring back information, such as the best price on a product. Early bots crawled the Web for information. One widely used bot named Archie looked for software available through the Internet's FTP. The World Wide Web Wanderer and

---

[1]Watson and Straub (2002).

its successors scoured the Web for sites to list on search engines. Bots can auto-

mate time-consuming tasks, and e-business can improve customer service by giv-

ing more consumers what they need much faster than with human intervention.

Sources:
http://www.isi.edu/teamcore/inquirerbackup.htm

13.2 TECHNICAL AND SOCIAL CHALLENGES TO IMPLEMENTATION

Technical challenges to the acceptance and full use of the Internet have been studied in the scientific literature.[2] Much of the material in this chapter, in fact, is adapted directly from the work by Rose, Khoo, and colleague.[3] As commented on throughout the book, it is vastly better for managers to base their best practices on what has been discovered by real-world oriented research. This work may (or may not) ultimately prove to be true in a firm's experience, but it offers a fresh, relatively objective perspective for change in a world of vested interests, salespersonship, and entrenched positions.

It is also important to note here at the beginning of this chapter that although technical limits have been researched holistically, this is not so with respect to social limits. Social, legal, regulatory, and business hurdles also affect the adoption of NE business practices. These social challenges are organizational or environmental in nature. Table 13.1 shows the hurdles under both categories.

Table 13.1: Technical and Social Challenges to NE Implementation

	Nature of Challenge
Tech-1	Security weaknesses
Tech-2	Download delays
Tech-3	Search problems
Tech-4	Inadequate measurement of Web site success
Tech-5	Limitations of the interface
Tech-6	Lack of Internet standards
Social-1	Fear of consumers in buying or transacting business over the Web

[2]Rose et al. (1999).
[3]Permission to use material granted by the Association of Information Systems. Thanks also to my coauthors, Dr. Greg Rose and Huoy Khoo for their cooperation.

Table 13.1: Technical and Social Challenges to NE Implementation

	Nature of Challenge
Social-2	Lack of brand awareness—significant penetration of the total market for specific products by companies
Social-3	Management/cultural problems in instituting e-business practices and ideas
Social-4	Lack of firm experience in doing e-business
Social-5	Organizational fear of doing business over the Internet
Social-6	Migrating to Internet computer-to-computer linkages from more familiar EDI
Social-7	Lack of well-accepted or understood e-cash on the part of consumers or organizations
Social-8	Ambiguous or hostile legal or regulatory environment for NE

Both technical and social challenges present large and complex management problems for NEOs. Some can be solved through the intelligent application of best practice and a thorough understanding of the challenge. Later, we discuss many cases where managers can make decisions that reduce the negative effects of an obstacle, or even completely mitigate it. As we shall see, there are ways to deal with the fact that your customers may not have high speed connections to the Internet and your current Web pages take an inordinately long time to download. A redesign and customer interface options are some of the remedies proposed.

Others are beyond the firm's control, for the most part. Whereas individual firms may try to impact the Internet standards picture and to improve these standards for the benefit of all, this is a consensual evolution from nation-based Internet societies and, strictly speaking, beyond the firm's control. Colloquia of Internet Society representatives, provider and supplier industry representatives, and societal groups will lead to buy-in on standards. Firms should definitely cooperate with these influential groups and do what they can to influence desirable outcomes, however.

13.2.1 What Makes Obstacles to Internet Adoption So Different?

Why has the firm lost influence over adoption in the Internet environment? A primary reason is that sellers provided or controlled key methods for access in the past, but no longer do. Consider the following historical situations (Table 13.2) where organizations were more in charge:

Table 13.2: Underlying Changes in Ownership of Access

Medium	Ownership of Access
Telephone	Public Telephone and Telegraph (PT&T) services
Cinema	Distributor-owned movie houses
Electric/gas	Infrastructure provided by monopolies
Cable	Infrastructure owned by cable companies
Retail	Retailer storefronts

What is so different in the modern era is that half or more of the Internet access tools are now owned by the end users, whether they are individuals or businesses. Contrast this to a situation in the not-so-distant past when the telephone companies owned all the technology, when even telephones were leased, in the United States at least. In the case of some access tools, such as TVs, the United States has not experienced conditions in which the equipment was leased or licensed from broadcasters, unlike the UK; it is still true that control over the presentation of TV programming has basically been in the hands of the content providers from the beginning until now.

The Internet has opened this up. Most content on the Web is free-of-charge today, but without guarantees as to accuracy or levels of service. One can pick and choose what kind of content to access and when to access it. Other than nodes on the Internet, which are still leased by the majority of users, the equipment or software of access is locally owned. The Internet is a highly distributed, decentralized operating model. Business customers and individuals are in control of their own access tools, from LANs that batch requests, to printers, to PCs, laptops, workstations, PDAs, and cell phones for reaching out to the Internet.

This difference in ownership in access tools changes things dramatically for firms wishing to do business via the Internet, and it poses some thorny technical challenges.

13.3 TECHNOLOGICAL CHALLENGES

Internet technologies were responsible for enabling networked enterprises and their connections to customers, and they, in part, disenabled it. The highly decentralized nature of the Internet is both responsible for its success and for its limitations.

It is important to remember that the Internet is essentially a decentralized client/server network, as we have pointed out many times in this book. Web applications use the Internet as do e-mail and FTPs. Many other applications beyond these can and sometime in the future will use the Internet as their infrastructure.

Why are there built-in limitations to the applications that run over the Internet? Partly, this is due to historical evolution. Because the original infrastructure of the Internet was used for information sharing in government and academic areas, security and payment were not high on the agenda of the developers. Also, because the early applications such as e-mail were primarily asynchronous (lag times between sending and receiving not being very important), the Internet had not been optimized for the later multimedia applications that came on board.

Commercial needs differ greatly from the more straightforward information sharing needs of government officials and academics. So when the Internet was released for commercial use in the mid-1990s, it became immediately clear that some of the features of the Internet that made it so attractive for unrestricted information sharing were drawbacks in the commercial arena.

The second main characteristic of the Internet that made the transition to commercial use troublesome was that its original charter was nonprofit. Changing the mentality of users so they were ready to pay for valuable services and to accept security and other restrictions that would make it a viable exchange medium for a buying and selling milieu required time.

There is every reason to believe that the growth in the Internet can be measured with the most sensitivity by measuring the extent to which the challenges discussed in this chapter are overcome. Simply adding new nodes, new Web pages, and new users at astonishing rates is not the issue. For the Internet to become entrenched in the commercial fabric of the world will require the solution, in part at least, of these impediments.

Implementing NE has enough deployment challenges without the negative impacts of impediments that come from the very utilization of NE technologies themselves. What are technical, rather than managerial/behavioral impediments to the development of NE? To make sure we know what a technical obstacle is, let's take a clear example and examine it briefly.

Web pages take time to download. These times are not lengthy if the user has a high bandwidth connection. However, the vast majority of households and even SMEs not only in the United States, but around the world operate at slow speeds like 28.8 Kbps (or what is known as the *baud rate*). At these speeds, a Web page that has a lot of images and animated GIF files,[4] for instance, takes considerable time to download, irrespective of the internal processing speed of the client machine and software. Many Web sites could take over a minute to completely download.

What is the impact of such slow downloads on customers? They become impatient and basically bail out of Web sites.[5] Sites that have fast-to-download Web pages experience more positive attitudes toward products and a greater inclination to purchase. Numerous scientific studies have verified these discoveries.[6]

Managers are confronted with a difficult scenario. Given that many of their potential customers are operating with limited bandwidth, what should they do? The impediment is technical and cannot be remedied by higher processor capacity on the server side, nor can it be remedied with a wider transmission channel. Until the customer buys greater transmission capacity, the e-vendor or e-supply manager has to figure out how to deal with this obstacle.

For now, there are workarounds, and, in the long run, such problems will be solved by the dissemination of broadband. For the time being, though, the prudent manager will take whatever measures will suffice. These we will cover in this chapter.

---

[4]These are the moving image graphics that appear on Web pages.
[5]Rose and Straub (2001).
[6]Rose et al. (2002); Rose et al. (2000)

13.3.1 Relative Importance of Technological Impediments

With respect to the technologies that power the Internet, how important are each of the technical hurdles listed in Table 13.1? Analysis is highly suggestive that they should be considered in the order in which they appear in Table 13.3 below. Possible solutions to the problems which are also enumerated will be discussed later in the chapter.

Table 13.3: Prioritizing and Coping with Impediments to E-Commerce

Impediment	Design Choices that Minimize Impact	Workarounds	Emerging Solutions
Tech-1 Security	Encrypt sensitive information; stress internal security on Web site; fully activate firewalls	Offer bail-out parachutes for patrons, that is, toll-free numbers, faxes, mail; promote the fact that one's Web site is secure	Improved firewalls; better intrusion detection software from deeper understanding of hacker psychology; better virus software
Tech-2 Download delay	More and speedier servers; client give-aways; text-only options	Push technologies working during lagtimes	Bandwidth improvements; Internet 2; faster CPUs
Tech-3 Search Problems	Purchase company intuitive domain names at almost any cost	Buy related domain names; spiral branding; buy portal links	Intelligent agents
Tech-4 Inadequate metrics	Cookies	Nielsen opinion surveys (physical or electronic)	Pentium ID tracking or equivalent (if ever approved)
Tech-5 Interface Limitations	Animation; virtual reality modeling language (VRML)	Mail physical samples of products	New sensory-capturing and -sending devices; advanced virtual reality
Tech-6 Lack of Internet standards	Drop down one generational level on Web site; use lowest common denominators	Mail plug-ins to consumers	New browsers able to work with different generations of technology

Tech-1

Security has been and will probably continue to be the most serious problem for firms wishing to do more and more business over the Internet. Well-publicized security break-ins and attacks on NEOs only hint at the extent of the problem. An orchestrated denial of service (DOS) attack by hackers on major content aggregators like eBay, Yahoo, and Amazon a few years ago showed just how vulnerable e-firms can be. Some of these sites were closed down for many hours, and loss of business and customer confidence is incalculable.

Unfortunately, there are few studies that reveal the depth of the problem. Nevertheless, we can be certain that hackers and other antisocial individuals will continue to disrupt the process of online business unless security is taken on as a high priority management goal.

Tech-2

Second only to security is download delay. As we shall see, there is a huge variance in bandwidths in current use. Firms are in a tricky position because they cannot assume that their customers are operating at low or high speeds, when the true answer is that they are using both. At low speeds, many interactive Internet applications such as click-to-talk or multimedia advertisements work poorly and turn off customers.

Tech-3

If users cannot find out where and how to shop online, they will not do so. There is a critical need for search engines to become sophisticated to the point where users get exactly the information they need and not more than they need or can process. Locking down intuitively obvious domain names is only one of the many ways firms can deal with this problem.

Tech-4

Being able to measure success is surely one of the most central tasks of managers. Without good information on performance, for instance, there is no feedback against which to measure management e-initiatives. Did such-and-such investment work or not? The effects of change are also unknown.

Metrics are important, and it is only because we have some previous measures from traditional business settings that it is not even higher on the agenda. Which traditional metrics work and which are no longer applicable to NEOs? That is the rub.

Tech-5

Sensory limitations of the interface constrain the levels at which customers can be reached, but these are not terribly different from other common media. Other than face-to-face meetings, most media lose richness in one dimension or another.[7] E-mail, for example, is an extremely limited communication channel. Its impact is restricted to visual textual symbols, but in this regard it is no different than print media (without illustrations). Click-to-talk increases the richness with its auditory channel but does not generally have an accompanying visual channel, which would augment richness. Again, this makes it no more or less limited than the radio.

[7]Daft and Lengel (1984).

Tech-6

Standards drive the rate of technological innovation and when standards are nonexistent or not evolving to keep pace with change, they can impede progress. Although there are task forces that work to develop Internet standards, some changes have been slow in coming. Standardization on the browser interface is just one example of an area where complete standards have not yet emerged. Yet, it is clear that the Internet is functioning. Consumers order goods and make payments, business customers engage in electronic trades, and firms move sensitive data across virtual private networks (VPNs).

Because the standards currently governing the Internet are functioning, the reason that they deserve attention is to allow aggressive movement forward in the future. Among the technical factors, this is important but not of immediate critical concern.

13.3.2 Tech-1: Security Weaknesses

Although hackers take heed of holes in Internet technology to press their advantage, countermeasures such as encryption can protect the transmission itself. The possibility of hackers or other antisocials intercepting transmissions, decrypting and reading them, substituting in parameters, and reaping financial benefits are remote if available security countermeasures are implemented.

Even with encryption, there are security weaknesses because endpoints of the transmission are extremely vulnerable, and breaches at either end are much more dangerous than breaches in the middle. The ends are uncertain because the Internet is such an open system, with the overall security of the entire network being no more secure than the weakest link. If one node has been compromised, then entities on that node can masquerade as others by pretending to be their IP. This technique is known as *IP-spoofing*. Please note that it is not the transmission that has been compromised, but the end, or node.

The ways in which the Internet is insecure are primarily managerial in nature. Within acceptable levels of risk, there are technologies that can control access to PCs, sites, and servers. If managers are serious about security, they can institute security controls and own a relatively secure site, and they can institute managerial controls, for example, that require that their business partners are relatively secure.

Some of these are designed to identify the originator. Conversations are transmitted across a variety of links for each packet sent. Furthermore, these packets may be relayed via some unscrupulous or poorly protected nodes. On the Internet, messages are being passed in a shared domain. Anyone with access to that domain can simply view all messages that are being sent. Under these conditions, it is best to assume that unauthorized people are able to view any packet transmitted. Therefore, nodes that seek privacy need to speak in a fashion analogous to using code words. As long as any eavesdroppers do not know the secret code, they can listen in but cannot understand. Internet technology is also no better or worse than telephone technology in guaranteeing that the person on the other end of the line is who they claim to be.

Short of having a guarantor analogous to a thumbprint or signature, one cannot be sure with whom one is dealing. To secure Internet computing, technology has been created to conceal messages and guarantee the identity of people on each end of the transmission. Digital signatures, secure electronic transaction (SET), and similar technologies covered in Chapter 6 can act as guarantors for the transaction, assuring interested parties that the signatories involved currently exist and are who they claim to be.

With regard to concealing messages, two primary techniques are available. The first is to send nontext files. The other is to send text files that are jumbled via cryptography. With respect to the first technique, managers should know that sending unencrypted plaintext (ASCII) files, is terribly insecure. Users transmitting text messages across the Internet should consider them to be no more secure than a postcard. Anyone with access at any routing node can listen in to a text fragment and read that fragment without special software. By contrast, a weak security technique can be employed by avoiding text files and sending nontext files such as picture or application data files (for example, a Microsoft Excel document). These require picture readers or other applications to interpret them. Typically speaking, files that require an application to interpret cannot be read without the intact file. Furthermore, if file extensions are altered, it is not necessarily clear which application is needed to read the file even if it can be captured. As a result, multiple hurdles stand between a would-be spy and confidential information.

Although picture and application files are somewhat more difficult to read and interpret, they are far from being entirely secure. A motivated snoop can still capture the entire datastream and analyze the files to find which application (typically off the shelf) is needed to interpret them. By contrast, encryption of messages, or Technique 2, offers far better protection against all but the most highly motivated criminal interceptor when used correctly.

As noted in Chapter 6, encryption technology uses cryptography to scramble messages. Different strategies are available that can secure either or both ends of a data transmission. Furthermore, digital signatures use the same technology to assure that one is dealing with only the individuals with whom one wants to deal. Digital signatures are assigned by a certified Internet authority. Unique passcodes of digital signatures identify individuals in much the same way as a physical signature or password. Of course, digital identities can be physically stolen.

However, mechanisms are available that make identity-theft extremely difficult. Examples include having identities hard-coded onto a smart card and using biometrics such as retina scanners to confirm identities prior to authorization of use.

By using such technologies, managers can be assured that transactions across the Internet can be made more secure than many traditional transaction processes. If current technologies are implemented, the biggest dangers to security occur before or after data is transferred. Security threats exist even if a legitimate e-consumer sends data to a legitimate e-tailer without that data being intercepted.

Threats to Security from the Physical World and Hackers

Getting the transaction to the recipient can be made safe, but the transaction information is not as safe once it reaches the destination. Clearly, within organizations, there are threats that exist in the intraorganizational electronic and physical worlds from rogue employees. Security on the Internet cannot prevent abuse within corporations any more than a secure phone line can prevent someone with access privileges at the telephone company from retrieving and publishing an unlisted number residing on the customer database. The security of the transactional communication medium in that case is not the issue. Threats occur from the wrong people accessing corporate databases from within, not on the way to the company.

Threats from rogue employees exist regardless of whether the retailer is conducting business on the Internet. However, unlike non-Internet commerce, e-commerce has many millions more people with potential access to those corporate databases. Hackers are a clear security threat to e-tailer servers, for instance. Because many corporations store data that is accessible online, any hacker on the Internet has the opportunity to steal data from corporate databases.

Although sophisticated firewalls and other security measures exist, hackers appear to be one step ahead of available security. Risks are real and worrisome in their scope. For instance, one survey of 1700 corporate and government Web sites found more than 60% had "serious potential security vulnerabilities."[8] In addition, examples of successful computer hack-ins show just how potentially damaging these security breaches can be. In one instance alone, a hacker broke into a database of a San Diego ISP and stole 100,000 credit card numbers using well-known hacking techniques.[9]

Besides inadequate utilization of available firewall features, a major technological limitation of most firewalls is that they must be equipped to identify a line as belonging to a particular IP address. If not, IP-spoofing can allow hackers access to internal networks.

Apparent Threats to NE

Transaction security is a technical problem for NEOs because the Internet has so many places where hackers can penetrate. Moreover, managers do not recognize the solutions available to them, nor do they apply them. Retail customers are not yet comfortable with sending personal information across the Internet. The irony is that the Internet can be at least as, if not more, secure than a phone transaction as long as encryption is used, the caveat being, as we have seen, that a transaction is only secure if appropriate technologies are used. This issue extends beyond technology and represents a failure in the human and managerial domain. The real threats to security lie outside the transaction. To some extent, threats exist because people are not utilizing the existing technologies. If people conduct business transactions with unscrupulous vendors or if sensitive information is stored on unsecured databases, security threats exist even when data is perfectly secure in transmission.

Although hackers can attack servers and steal sensitive data from outside the organization, client-side vulnerabilities are limited for the present. Currently, clients seldom have permanent IP addresses because these are dynamically assigned at the node or by the ISP. The threat of hackers will only grow worse when customers begin to have Internet clients with permanent IP addresses. Sensitive data will then be vulnerable to attack from the client side as well as the server side.

In spite of existing technologies, millions have been victims of e-commerce fraud or related credit-card misuse. What percentage of these problems could be eliminated simply by utilizing existing security technologies is not clear. What is clear is that security is a serious problem for NE. Transactional security is mostly a managerial rather than a technological problem. However, areas such as firewall vulnerabilities, simplistic intrusion detection software, and server flooding problems (DOS attacks) remain technical issues.

---

[8]Lohr (1997).
[9]Gurnon (1997).

Designs and Solutions—Security

Designs and solutions allow managers to deal with this impediment, even if the organization's systems are not set up to accommodate security. Table 13.3 highlights these solutions for security and the other impediments.

In the case of security, for example, customers can be offered bail-out parachutes such as call centers or fax communications if they do not wish to trust their credit card data or other sensitive information to the Internet. Moreover, organizations need to promote safety features of their Web site even if the site has not been thoroughly secured. If customers are willing to transact business with the organization even though they have been informed about those features that have been activated (and, implicitly those which have not), then the company may be considered as to having legitimately informed the consumer of the risks.

One design tactic, for example, that can minimize actual security violations is encryption. When used, encryption should eliminate essentially all hacker interpretation of the transmission itself. Managers also need to ensure that the firewalls they now have protecting their internal systems are fully functioning and robust to attack. If they are not, greater attention needs to be placed in this area.

Technologies on the horizon will solve some of the current security problems. Firewalls are being given more intelligence and will eventually be able to duplicate many of the enlightened security decisions of a human monitor. Virus software is likewise improving and available as a Web service, although it has proven hard to keep pace with the insidious inventiveness of hackers.

Finally, we need deeper insights into hacker psychology to improve technological solutions. Such insights can emerge from academic researchers with sufficient funding from sources such as government and corporations, and the deeper knowledge that this research will produce can assist us in designing technology that prevents and detects computer abuse. This kind of software, called *intrusion detection*, will, no doubt, advance from its current, relatively primitive state to a level of greater sophistication through deeper understanding of hacker motivation and behavior.

13.3.3 Tech-2: Download Delays

Download time is the amount of time it takes for a Web client machine to receive and display a data file requested by the client and transmitted by a Web server. Download delays impede the development and use of Internet applications such as multimedia. For example, technology exists to show a television ad on a Web page. However, the amount of wait time required before such an ad can be downloaded and run is prohibitive, and, thus, is not often used. Download delays are responsible for the virtual absence of television-style 30-second audio and video advertising over the Web. For the most part, the practical limits of multimedia use are established by what users think is acceptable download time. Under normal computing conditions, end-users find it objectionable to wait more than a few seconds between computer processing cycles (such as the amount of time it takes to load a Web page upon requesting it). Waiting more than half a minute is considered intolerable. As a result, there are limits to the use of multimedia communication that require longer download times.

Download time is primarily a function of: (1) the size of the data files being transmitted; and (2) the technological configuration of nodes, the network infrastructure, and the bandwidth connection between nodes and infrastructure. Compared to simple HTML pages (typically 1 to 10 KB in size), many existing Internet multimedia technologies require relatively large data files to be transmitted and displayed. Examples of these types of media include: (1) video or pictures (which vary in size between 10 KB and several megabytes), especially those in color and with a wide color spectrum, (2) video or picture files with a large display area, (3) sound files, and (4) files that contain applications or applets.

In addition, traditional desktop application data files, such as PDF, Microsoft Word, or Microsoft Excel files are often shared in Internet client/server computing and can often be larger than 1 MB in size. As a result, many of these types of communications become impractical on the Web, depending, of course, on the technological configuration. Furthermore, when considering the combination of multiple data files for use in one hyperdocument, compromises between optimal communication and reasonable download time need to be considered.

Download time differences can be significant for even small file sizes. Table 13.4 shows tests of delay data obtained for loading a 10.5 KB file and a 6.3 MB file. The baud rate is a bits per second transmission rate.

Table 13.4: Download Times at Different Communication Speeds

Communication Speed	10.5 KB file (Source: Netmechanic.com, 1998)	6.3 MB file (Source: Ozer, 1999)
14.4 KB baud	7.83 seconds	
56 KB baud	3.84 seconds	23 minutes, 13 seconds
128 KB baud (ISDN line)	2.66 seconds	16 minutes, 17 seconds
1.5 MB baud (T1)	2.06 seconds	
500 KB baud (Cable)		1 minute, 34 seconds
1.5 MB baud (DSL)		45 seconds

Clearly, a delay of over 23 minutes at 56 KB baud would be considered excessive by most people. Interface design requiring files of this size have to be carried out with this delay in mind.

Technological Conditions That Increase Download Time

Many multimedia technologies require prohibitively long download times depending on the node or infrastructural technologies in use to request, transmit, and display the files. A file that would be considered quite large under one set of conditions could be considered completely practical (that is, sufficiently small) in another. Therefore, file size in and of itself is not an impediment to Internet computing. However, the technological conditions that increase download time are impediments. Delays in download time can occur on the server side, in transmission, or on the client side. The potential for bottlenecks in each of these areas is shown in Figure 13.1.

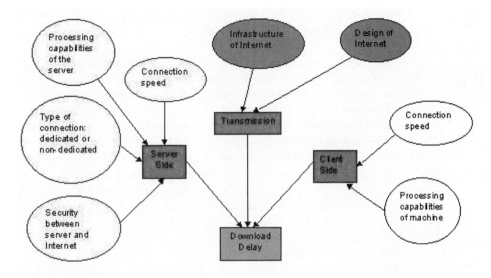

Figure 13.1 Elements of Download Delay

Server-Side Download Time

Assuming that a request for hypermedia was sent via a URL to its appropriate server, the technological configuration of that server can increase download time in three ways: (1) in the connection between the server and the Internet, (2) in the processing capacity of the server itself, and (3) in the security system between the Internet gateway and the server that is processing requests and retrieving files.

Server and the Internet Connection   A server can be set up as either dedicated or non-dedicated and with a low or high throughput connection. If a server is not available to receive Internet requests at all times (i.e., it is a nondedicated connection), responses from the server will clearly be delayed until the server can be accessed. If a server has a narrow bandwidth connection (such as a 56 KB modem connected to a phone line), it can serve only a few client requests at a time and will have a difficult time transmitting very quickly even one request for files larger than a few kilobytes. Therefore, a server with a nondedicated connection at 56 Kbps will exhibit extremely high download times. By contrast, a dedicated T1 connection at 1.5 MB baud can theoretically transmit more than 50 times more data than a dedicated 56 KB modem and has the capacity to handle many requests for files many MB in size.

Processing Capacity of the Server Itself   Even if the Internet connection can transfer 1.5 Mbps, sufficient numbers of requests, each only 1 KB, can overwhelm the processing capacity of a server. Although a relatively small amount of bandwidth capacity would be used in this condition, the server would be unable to respond to any more requests, and download time would be increased for all subsequent requests. Therefore, depending on the volume of individual requests, a higher capacity server or even multiple, parallel servers may be needed to meet demand.

Security Systems between the Internet Gateway and the Server This delay is by design. Security software and hardware need to be set up as a firewall between a server and the outside world to restrict access to those clients or file transfers deemed acceptable. The very nature of this security process is to have the computer check requests, user domains, passwords, and so forth. As a result, processing time is required to check these users and files against a specified list of acceptable users, nodes, or processes. As the number of requests increases, the amount of processing time also increases both for processing a user (to confirm their requests are acceptable and to provide the data requested) and for processing all subsequent users. Any one of these three technical points related to servers has the potential to be a data transmission bottleneck and, therefore, contribute to increased download time.

Transmission Download Time

The network infrastructure lies between the client and the server and carries the communication between them. Transmission delays or limitations with regard to this infrastructural element increase the download time.

There are limitations in the infrastructure of the Internet itself. Average download times for corporate sites vary drastically between certain cities and certain weeks of the year. Much of this variation is caused by infrastructure delays.

The public tends to assume that technological systems are perfect when they are not. The Internet infrastructure is generally considered to be robust and reliable and is expected to improve as router technology improves. However, shutdowns do occur, albeit rarely. Much as an occasional power or telephone disruption, regional sections of the infrastructure have shut down.[10]

Slow transmission across the Internet may be a product of its design. Especially when dealing with large files, the very nature of the Internet can lead to communication difficulties. By design, the Internet and TCP/IP break up large data into small packets. Individual packets do occasionally get delayed (and, less frequently, lost). Naturally, the larger the file, the greater the number of packets. A consequence of having many packets is that the larger the file, the greater the chance of having one piece of the total file delayed or lost in transmission. This limitation in the infrastructure for handling very large data transmissions, in fact, inspired the creation of Internet2. Internet2 is a project to develop a parallel Internet that would allow for high speed transmission of extremely large data files. Examples of data files of this size would be corporate databases, virtual reality video, video conferencing, and television-style broadcasts or movies. Internet2 is being projected as a pay-as-you-use system for business. This approach differs from the Internet where no charge is levied for the transmission of data packets between destinations within the United States.

Currently, the only charges for e-tailers and customers are for transmitting the message to and from the Internet itself. Paying for Internet transmission will change the nature of Internet client/server computing but will allow for dependable and faster large file transfer.

---

[10]Wagner and Gaudin (1997).

Client-Side Download Time

The client side of Internet computing suffers from the same two basic limitations as the server side: the connection and the processor.[11] With regard to the connection, client machines in a typical residential computing environment in the United States consist of a 14.4 Kbps to 56.6 Kbps modem connection via the telephone. As a result, even if data is transferred out of the server through a T3 line (45 Mbps) and across the Internet at a brisk pace, this data cannot be accepted by the client machine any faster than the receiving modem allows. Consequently, client-side connection bandwidth is often seen as the biggest source of download time in Internet computing.

In addition to bandwidth, plain old telephone service (POTS) is generally acknowledged to provide unreliable connections.[12] Problems can include busy and no answer signals, as well as failure with modem connections once the call goes through. Connection problems can also be an issue when the client has a dedicated line. Anecdotal evidence indicates that cable services are disrupted with some regularity.

In spite of these limitations the availability of higher speed connection alternatives such as cable modems, dial-up modem computing is the norm in U.S. households at present as well as throughout much of the rest of the world. Average residential users are extremely price sensitive. Dial-up access has fairly inexpensive monthly costs with no startup costs beyond the modem in the United States. These fees are far more costly in countries outside the United States. Costs are low in the United States because existing phone lines can be used at no additional charge and modems are very inexpensive (U.S. $25 to $100). By contrast, high-speed alternatives known as *broadband* can cost several hundreds of dollars more initially, and $10 to $40 more each month, than dial-up computing.

Even if high-speed alternatives were the same cost as slower dial-up connections, these alternatives will not be universally available in the near term. Only 60% of the United States is projected to have broadband available by 2004. Therefore, 40% of U.S. households will not have these broadband alternatives available to them at any cost. Although satellite connection is, in theory, available to the remaining users, this service is currently available only to those with clear southern exposure and is seen as a lesser alternative even when available. Satellite is currently recognized to have more limited capabilities and drastically slower data transfer speeds than DSL or cable.

Regardless of price, however, the demand for high-speed access is not universal. Surveys of users currently online have found that fewer than half are interested in having a high-speed connection. In addition, customers may be wary of using dedicated Internet connection for security reasons. Unlike dial-up connections, dedicated connections assign permanent Internet addresses to client machines. As a result, clients with dedicated lines are significantly more vulnerable to computer hackers. Appropriate firewall software costs approximately U.S. $500 and cannot guarantee protection from attack.

Whatever the reason, broadband penetration worldwide is not expected to be universal anytime soon. As a result, slow connection speeds for client-side computing at the residential level will very likely persist in the near future and beyond. In addition to slow connection speed client-side processing, limitations can increase download time. Older

---

[11]Client-side security is another possible delay. Most clients likely do not have a personal firewall at this time, but when these become more common, this is another conceivable point of delay.

[12]Snyder (1997).

and slower machines do not have the processing capabilities or memory capacities to interpret and display large graphical or application files rapidly. Furthermore, underconfigured machines may find it particularly difficult to open hyperdocuments while multiple browsers or other desktop applications are running. Clearly, the slower the computer processor, the lower the memory capacity, and the larger the number of concurrent applications being run, the longer the download time.

Apparent Threats to NE

Threats with regard to download time are most apparent on the client side of e-commerce. Server side download time limitations are completely within the control of the party that owns the server. With enough money and prudent server administration, there is no reason why the server side would have to be a bottleneck. Impediments to improved server delay are basically economic. Firms can make decisions on how to overcome these delays at a known cost. The decision, if made rationally, is affected by the estimate of the increase in business that faster response time would bring. It is also unlikely that the Internet infrastructure will be the primary bottleneck in the near future. Improved routers and the forthcoming Internet2 may eliminate much of the infrastructure delay. Even with the traditional Internet, it is unlikely that a typical NE application will have its primary download time difficulties occur within the Internet infrastructure itself. However, some predict that if broadband computing leads to larger files being transferred, the Internet infrastructure will become the source of significant download time. But until broadband is universally adopted, bottlenecks should occur primarily at the client end.

Unfortunately, there is no good way for a retailer to control the hardware configuration being used at the client side, short of buying equipment and connection bandwidth for customers. Because customers will vary in processing and bandwidth capabilities, it is difficult for retailers to effectively accommodate every user. Moreover, telecommunication infrastructures and computer technologies are less robust outside the United States, especially in the developing world. If a retailer is trying to reach customers across global markets, the differences in download time may be even larger.

Currently, Web user connection speeds are disparate but fairly slow. One survey of Web users found a wide distribution across a sample of more than 7000 people in the United States (Figure 13.2). Respondents were asked about the speed of their primary connection to the Internet. Because the survey did not discriminate between home or work connections (where employers may restrict Internet use to business activities), the data may not be representative of typical connections. Presumably, actual connections would be slower for home than for work connections.

As a result of disparities in download times among customers, retailers need to be careful in devising their NE strategy. Hypermedia development needs to have the right balance of content and file size to communicate effectively to all customers without excessive delay. In addition, user-selectable versions of the same messages should be created to accommodate different capacities. For example, some users may choose to reduce their own download time by selecting a text-only version of the hyperdocument transmission.

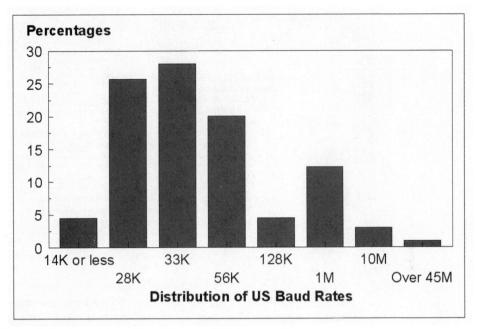

Figure 13.2   Slow Average Baud Rates for U.S. Internet Usage

Currently, few retailers appear to be utilizing the preferential option. However, some companies have adopted this dual strategy. Among nonprofits, isworld.org, the Web site for IS professors, offers a text-only site, presumably for faculty with slower connections.

Designs and Solutions—Download Delay

What are possible solutions? Table 13.3 highlights these. On the server side, organizations can ensure that there are minimal delays in node access to the server and retransmission of Web pages. If processing on the server is needed, then delay can be minimized with sufficient investment in powerful server hardware, software, and telecommunication gateways. More and speedier servers are the obvious solution to the server side of the problem.

The solution on the client side is complex. If consumers are not willing to rent or buy cable modems, purchase faster client software and hardware, or download and install the latest generation of browser software, then companies are hamstrung. Text-only options will reduce download delay on the client side, certainly, and this option should be made available on the e-firm's home page. Web pages can also be split up, as demonstrated in Figure 13.3.

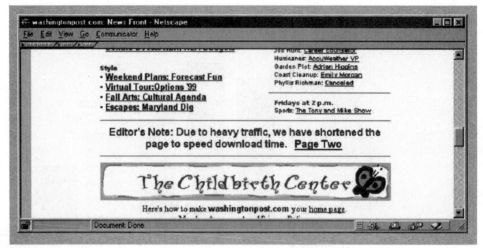

Figure 13.3   Cutting Content to Speed Downloads (www.washingtonpost.com, September 16, 1999)

The only other immediately obvious solutions are client giveaways. Giving away PCs or network computers (NCs) may be an economically justifiable solution. Risk-taking firms have been doing this over the years under the assumption that free computers will generate enough Web business to more than cover the expense. Computers that are given away can be configured for minimal download delays and for automatically receiving new upgrades online as they become available. These qualities can be hardwired so that users cannot reconfigure the units. Although this sales technique has not been a gigantic success to date, these firms are strategically correct in assuming that this is the only way to truly control download at the user end.

Over time, some download delays will be solved by wider bandwidth availability, such as Internet2, cable modems, and so forth. Faster CPUs will also reduce delay. But, ironically, as bandwidths increase, so do the requirements of Web applications. More firms will opt for livening up their Web pages with multimedia and applets, animated GIFs, and so forth, in such a way that added bandwidth may be absorbed as fast as it is created.

13.3.4 Tech-3: Search Problems

Creation of content and ability to transmit that content are not in and of themselves enough to communicate a message. Assuming limitations to hyperdocument content development and delivery can be overcome, communication will not occur without customers finding those documents. Current technological limits in Internet technology hinder requests for hypermedia.

Hypermedia are requested by Web clients through the use of URLs. URLs are typically invoked three ways: (1) by manually typing in the URL, (2) by recalling a URL from a list of bookmarks stored on the client machine, and (3) via hyperlinks.

Hyperlinks are either hard coded into a hyperdocument or are generated dynamically from user input. Search engines such as Yahoo and AltaVista are examples of user input creating a dynamic page of hyperlinks. Bookmarks and manually typed addresses require that a user has previously visited a page or recalled a Web address. Limitations affecting how people can hear about a Web address are mostly not technological in nature. Word of mouth, spiral branding, or promotional strategies create an awareness of URLs. Hyperlinking to invoke URLs, however, is often a product of existing technologies. As a result, limitations in these technologies can lead to a restricted ability to find appropriate URLs.

Therefore, there are technological difficulties in finding URLs both with regard to hard coded hyperlinks and with dynamically created hyperlinks. When a URL is hard coded into a Web page, there are technological problems dealing with the persistence or existence of these links. Because the hyperlinks are static and written in HTML code, they can become outdated. As Web pages move, are replaced or deleted, the hard coded URLs can point to incorrect or nonexisting content. This problem is chronic across banking Web sites, for example. Although technology such as client-pull exists for forwarding browsers to new links from the original addresses, implementation of this strategy may become impractical for all but a few links such as those found on home pages.

The technology for finding outdated links across the Internet is currently not available. Thousands upon thousands of Web pages pointing to obsolete addresses reside currently on servers around the world. In addition, even if all of these outdated links could be found, they could not be updated by any single individual or organization. Servers where a user does not have security access would not allow outsiders to update resident HTML files. Because technological security measures can themselves impede the maintenance necessary for maintaining accurate URL links, the ability of content providers to have their messages found is impacted by current Internet technologies. Even without such security and managerial limits, however, the problem would still exist. Under the best of current conditions, with dynamic link creation and search engines, the task of updating Web links is untenable. Automated search engine robots with the power to scan the entire Internet, even those with security clearance, chronically suffer from inaccurate link data.

With search engines such as AltaVista, dynamic links are created from databases of Web page locations. Large search engine databases are updated on a regular basis by search agent *know-bots*, programs designed to find and report on the contents of Web pages. Intelligent search agents scour the Internet discovering Web pages and collecting content and corresponding URLs. Data about page content and addresses are stored in large databases. When a search is requested, the address in the database is used to create a hyperlink on a dynamic page.

Suppose you were in Tokyo, Japan, on business and wanted to buy some shoes while you were there. You access the Internet and type in a URL for a search engine such as altavista.com. Figure 13.4 shows that a search for shoes in Tokyo returns such a dynamic page of hyperlinks, including some feasible entries and some that seem to be more related to Japanese cuisine than shoe purchases. In short, the page has some entries that are related to your needs, and some that are likely not related. The latter we would refer to as *false hits*. Too many false hits is a problem that overloads the user with unuseful information.

Figure 13.4 Likely and False Hits on Search for "Shoes in Tokyo"

By using search agents, existing pages can be reconfirmed periodically, and data about those pages can be updated. As a result, a dynamically created page of hyperlinks will be typically more accurate than a static page of links. Although this solution overcomes many of the limitations created by static Web pages, it is not without its own limitations. Each year, millions of new host Internet computers are being added to those already registered. As a result, hundreds of millions of pages exist at any given time. Computing technology to date finds it impossible to collect and maintain a perfect database of Web page addresses and content for such a huge population. Unfortunately, even if a perfect database could be created and maintained, the sheer number of pages make it difficult for client-side users to find appropriate pages. Even with the improvements in search engine technology represented by engines such as google.com, search engine queries are not yet sophisticated enough to be entirely effective. There are still too many false hits.

Current search queries are based on keyword searches. Keyword queries consist of a user entering a list of keywords. The search engine uses this query in its database to search for pages containing those words. Often these searches result in hundreds of thousands of matching pages—far too many to be useful in finding the specific information sought. Worse still, unknown thousands of other pages that could be applicable to the user are missed because they do not contain the particular keywords chosen by the users, but only synonyms of the keywords requested. In short, current search engine technology provides both too much and too little information. Although it does aid in helping users find specific hypermedia, it is still severely limited.

One way to avoid difficulty with search engines is to acquire an intuitive URL. Web pages such as www.microsoft.com make it easy to find Microsoft without a search engine. Pages with less intuitive URLs are presumably at a disadvantage. Further difficulty comes from organizations that own URLs that would seem to be logical addresses for other larger and better known firms, sites such as www.delta.com. This Web page once belonged to Delta Comm Development, not Delta Airlines, as apparently 15,000 people per day believed. Consumer confusion is evident in the delta.com home page (of Delta Comm Development) which stated:

> We apologize for the lack of pretty graphics—you'll find those within the links above. 15,000 of you per day are looking for an unrelated company, so we have been forced to make this page as sparse as possible to prevent server overload. If you are one of those, please use a search engine to find the travel company you were looking for. If you're looking for information about Telix, or our Internet services, please come on in.

After Delta Airlines purchased the domain name for itself, this search problem disappeared.

Although some similarly named Web pages do provide links to the likely candidate page, such as www.bic.com (the Brookhaven Instruments Corporation), which gives a link to the razor manufacturer at www.bicworld.com, others such as Delta Comm Development would not. Goodwill cannot be relied on and so it can be said that Delta made a good choice in purchasing the DNS.

From the Delta example, as well as the literature, it appears that customers experience difficulty in finding organizations without an intuitive URL. Retailers with URLs that cannot be guessed easily are presumed to be at an apparent disadvantage at being found because search engines are imperfect tools. Search engines, however, can be manipulated by retailers. Specifically, retailers can pay to have their pages appear closer to the top of search engine query results and in portal listings. With enough available resources, companies should be able to overcome some of these technological limitations.

To empirically test the difficulty of finding pages for organizations with the largest financial resources, a simple, limited experiment was conducted by Rose et al. (1999). Ten Fortune 500 companies whose URLs were not www. + the company name + .com were chosen as a convenience sample. The names of the companies and their associated industries were read aloud to allow subjects to misspell the names as they would naturally do in their own searches. The industry type was provided for use both as a search criterion as well as a verification tool that would allow students to find the correct organization. Subjects were asked to spend up to five minutes trying to find each home page. Table 13.5 lists the firms that subjects were asked to find:

Table 13.5: Firms That Were Searched for on Web in Simple Experiment

Fortune 500 Companies Subjects Were to Find on Web	Industry	Fortune 500 Corporation Industry Home Page URL
1. Owens-Illinois	Glass and plastics	http://www.o-i.com
2. Procter and Gamble	Consumer goods	http://www.pg.com
3. H.F. Ahmanson	Banking	http://www.homesavings.com/ home.shtml
4. Omnicom Group	Advertising	http://www.omnicommny.com

Table 13.5: Firms That Were Searched for on Web in Simple Experiment (Continued)

Fortune 500 Companies Subjects Were to Find on Web	Industry	Fortune 500 Corporation Industry Home Page URL
5. Dayton Hudson	Retail	http://www.dhc.com
6. Johnson & Johnson	Health care	http://www.jnj.com
7. AMR Corporation	Airline	http://www.amrcorp.com
8. Federated Department Stores	Retail	http://www.federated-fds.com
9. Minnesota Mining & Manufacturing (3M)	Consumer and industrial goods	http://www.mmm.com
10. United Technologies	Technology	http://www.utc.com

Findings from this study give a glimpse into what would be the lower bound of difficulty in finding Web pages. Results reinforce the belief that customers have problems in locating Web pages on the Internet. Of the 130 total pages searched for in the study (10 pages and 13 subjects), 31 pages (24%) were not found after 5 minutes of search time. Of the remaining 99 pages, an average search time of 1 minute and 37 seconds was required to find a page. Delays are known to cause anxiety and delays as little as 1 second are known to have significant negative impacts.[13] The results show that current technological and human search capabilities can be a threat to successful B2C NE under even the best of conditions.

Apparent Threats to NE

The inability of clients to locate an appropriate URL is a most difficult challenge for NEOs. When seeking information, consumers and even business customers will generally stop looking for alternatives fairly quickly, that is, after putting in a relatively limited amount of effort on each alternative.[14] If a content provider's URL is buried among 100,000 other URLs, it is unlikely that a user will be motivated enough to find a specific address. Furthermore, if users receive a message indicating that a Web page does not exist, they are quite likely to seek an alternative vendor whose URL is readily retrievable. Some vendors, knowing that they are competing for the top spots on the search engines, use techniques such as *spam-dexing*. Spam-dexing is a strategy to put keywords in HTML headers that will put that page up near the top 10 listing for common search strings. A side effect is that individuals who do not attempt to manipulate the search engines, even those that are more legitimately related to the search string, are left out. A risk is that, if caught by managers of the search engine, spam-dexers may have their Web pages removed entirely. Therefore, it is difficult to say if spam-dexing is a good managerial design strategy.

[13]Shneiderman (1998).
[14]Capon and Burke (1980).

Efforts to counteract these problems can be made. Strategies such as paid advertising on the Web allows vendors to pay for pages on other servers to have up-to-date hyperlinks. Unfortunately, because of limitations in Web metrics (discussed next), the success rates of these advertisements is unknown.

▶ *CASE STUDY 13-2*

CERT AND SECURITY

The CERT Coordination Center (CERT/CC) is located at the Software Engineering Institute (SEI), a federally funded research and development center at Carnegie Mellon University in Pittsburgh, PA. After the Morris Worm incident, which ground to a halt a disturbingly high percentage of computers in November 1988, the Defense Advanced Research Projects Agency (DARPA) charged the SEI with setting up a center to coordinate communication among experts during security emergencies and to help prevent future incidents. Since then, the CERT/CC has helped to establish other response teams, and incident handling practices have been adapted by more than 200 response teams around the world. CERT security practices provide concrete, practical guidance that helps organizations improve the security of their networked computer systems. These practices address the most pervasive problems, as reported to the CERT/CC.

The role of CERT has expanded over the years. Each year, commerce, government, and individuals grow increasingly dependent on networked systems. Along with the rapid increase in the size of the Internet and its use for critical functions, there have been progressive changes in intruder techniques, increased amounts of damage, increased difficulty of detecting an attack, and increased difficulty of catching the attackers. To better manage these changes, the CERT/CC is now part of the larger SEI Networked Systems Survivability Program, whose primary goals are to ensure that appropriate technology and systems management practices are used to resist attacks on networked systems and to limit damage and ensure continuity of critical services in spite of successful attacks.

In the area of survivable network technology, CERT focuses on the technical basis for identifying and preventing security flaws and for preserving essential services if a system is penetrated and compromised. Approaches that are effective at securing bounded systems are not effective at securing unbounded systems such as the Internet. Therefore, new approaches to Internet security must be developed. They include design and implementation strategies, recovery tactics, strategies to resist attacks, survivability trade-off analysis, and the development of security architectures.

CERT's understanding of current security problems and potential solutions comes from their analysis of security incidents, intrusion techniques, configuration problems, and software vulnerabilities. Since CERT was organized, they have received more than 596,525 e-mail messages and more than 21,015 hotline calls reporting computer security incidents or requesting information. More than 173,725 computer security incidents and more than 8,250 vulnerability reports have been received.

Discussion:
1. Discuss the difference in security needs for bounded versus unbounded systems.
2. Discuss the ways in which the role of CERT is liable to expand in the future.

Sources:
http://www.cert.org/meet_cert/meetcertcc.html

Designs and Solutions-Search Problems

Among possible solutions are: (1) buying intuitively clear as well as related domain names, (2) spiral branding, and (3) portal links. Originally, Delta Airlines pursued a related name strategy with www.delta-air.com because www.delta.com was owned by another firm, Delta Comm. However, this strategy was not as strategic as owning the intuitively obvious name, www.delta.com. So Delta Airlines purchased this domain name for its own use and in doing so, made a good strategic move.

Another solution is spiral branding. As discussed in Chapter 11, spiral branding is the use of alternative media to advertise a firm's URL. URLs appear regularly on television and radio as well as in print media. This approach, no doubt, has some effect on consumer's habits in accessing an URL. Portal links, costly as they may be, stake out heavily visited cyberspace, and, therefore, positioning on their site is worth a good deal. Some argue that the market values of Yahoo, Excite, and even Amazon are directly attributable to their familiarity with customers and their ability to sell that space through portaling to other sites.

Technological solutions to search engine deficiencies are being touted every day. Perhaps the most vociferous of these claims is intelligent agents. When these work well, agent technology should be able to parse a natural language user request for information and determine the sites most appropriate for that request. A request for physical shoe stores in Tokyo should not have listings for virtual shoe stores or for anyone who lives in Tokyo and happens to mention shoes on their personal home page high up. And it should return many fewer false hits than is presently the case with search engines. As search engines improve, agent technology is likely to be at the heart of this change.

AltaVista's Prisma feature is intended to be one of these technical improvements resulting in fewer false hits. Figure 13.4, shown earlier, returned a list of links on a search for shoes in Tokyo that can be refined by clicking on one of the categories appearing at the top of the page, categories such as "bowling shoes," "brand," and "Italian shoes." This refinement automatically changes the key words searched, as shown in Figure 13.5. Now the keywords used in the search are "shoes," "Tokyo," and "Italian shoes."

13.3.5 Tech-4: Inadequate Measurement of Web Site Success

Measuring the success of a Web page or a Web site is very difficult. The core issue is that we do not know what makes an appropriate metric of success for a hypermedia application. Commonly used measures such as number of times a Web page is viewed (called "hits") can be misleading. Hits are used because they are easy to capture; however, they are very hard to interpret as a measure of success. Why? Aside from hits recorded by those who blunder onto the site and have no genuine interest in their content, search engines routinely add to site counters through their "know-bot" intelligent agents, discussed above. Moreover, multiple visits by individual potential consumers cannot be discriminated from single visits by separate potential consumers. Each visit to the Web site is counted, irrespective of the client requestor.

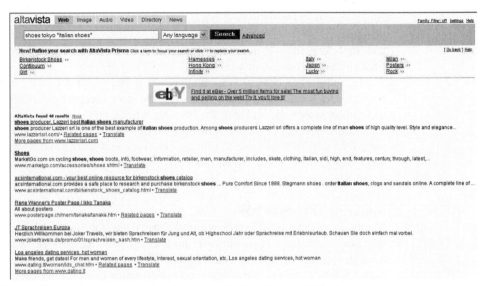

Figure 13.5 "Refined" AltaVista Search for "Italian shoes in Tokyo"

What is even more critical, however, is the fact that viewing a site does not clearly represent a level of interest. Interest will range from "no" interest whatsoever to "highly" interested, but the site owner has absolutely no knowledge of the nature of the frequency distribution of interest level through this gross measures of hits. The metric content providers should be trying to gather is best described as: Who is looking at my content, how many times are they visiting, and for how long?

Unfortunately, current Web technology does not allow servers to obtain a clear picture of who is looking at its pages. Typically, Web servers are only aware of the Internet gateway being used by a client. For example, a server can detect that numerous hits have come from clients attached to AOL (www.aol.com), but nothing more. Furthermore, some gateway machines act as proxy servers for groups of clients. These proxies may capture a Web page once per day and show a copy of it to anyone else on the local network requesting that Internet page. For instance, 100,000 hits to a site local to the proxy would add just one hit to the actual server where the original resided.

One final unwanted source of inaccuracy in hit data is from internal sources. Every time employees view a page for reference, maintenance, or updating, a hit is registered. Again, these hits should not be used in evaluating the success of e-commerce implementation.

The final technological limitation with regard to metrics is the inability to measure how long a client is viewing a page. Web browsing is a client-server process in which the actual viewing is done on the client machine. How long a page is viewed could only be known by monitoring the client machine, which is not an option for most content providers.

Some of these limitations can be overcome by the use of "cookies." As reviewed earlier in this book, cookies are data files that the server places on the client's hard drive. These files can keep track of data that has been entered on the Web page as it is viewed by the client browser. The cookie file can then be uploaded by that Web page's server. Such cookies are being widely used to monitor user preferences and keep track of demographic information. However, client Web browsers can be configured so as not to allow cookies, and, therefore, there is no guarantee that all customers will be able to be monitored and tracked through the use of cookies.

In addition to cookies, this technological impediment can be overcome by buying metrics. Organizations such as Media Metrix (now owned by comScore) perform offline and online sampling similar to the Nielsen ratings for television (see Figure 13.6 for the Web page on some of their metrics products). In addition to finding out who is visiting your Web site, they are able to find out the frequency of the visits, what parts of the page were viewed and clicked on, and times of day of the visits. These data are critical for selling to Web advertisers who are buying ad space and time on your pages.

Apparent Threats to NE

Limitations to measuring success are key for NEOs. One reason for this is that advertising is expensive (average costs of attracting a single customer may exceed U.S. $30). If useful measures of success are not available, how can an organization assess gains from advertising? Another reason is that startup and maintenance costs for Web server applications cost dearly. Without useful metrics, it is difficult to know how a Web-based strategy is performing relative to other media and channels.

Alternatives to hits are feasible, although some have other disadvantages. Firms with a Web ordering capability are clearly able to measure the volume of sales generated by that Web site. Organizations that launch a Web site to develop a new line of business have an unconfounded source of metrics, but those with a traditional ordering process in addition to the virtual ordering process cannot be certain whether the Web sales merely cannibalize their traditional sales process. This confounding affects many firms engaged in NE.

Options to hits, cookies, and Web sales revenues would include measures of loyalty. Loyalty to a firm and its products and services are akin to belonging to a community. Feelings of community and attitudes can be monitored and evaluated using the Web itself, if e-tailers use the sales event as an opportunity to also gather customer opinion and demographic data. It is not necessary to gather large amounts of data during each contact. Data gathering can be accomplished in an incremental fashion that is less annoying to customers. This data allow a firm to profile customers and to determine whether the mix of customers differs in major ways from their traditional customer base. This information will, in turn, lead to new strategies to market to the changing customer profile.[15]

Designs and Solutions—Metrics

Metrics are crucial for all new ventures, but especially for business transformations such as NE. If an organization cannot adequately measure its business benefits from a course of action, then it is extremely difficult to know how much of an investment is justified in this arena. The Web is still relatively new, and metrics are not as great a problem as they may be later when expenditures cannot be as easily justified on the grounds of experimentation or imitating competitors.

---

[15]Straub and Klein (2001).

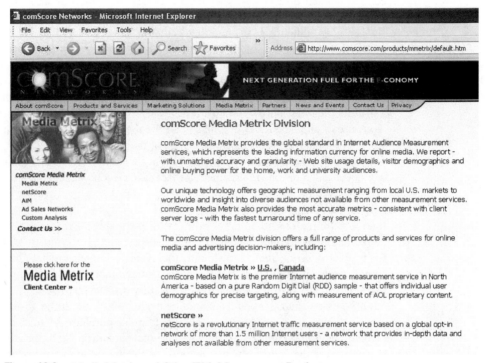

Figure 13.6 Media Metrix and Other Web Measurement Products

The Web is severely limited in its ability to measure and track consumer cyberpatterns. Hits are nearly as gross a measurement as Internet sales. Other than post hoc analysis of customer-entered data, the only marginally acceptable way to design measures to determine customer navigating patterns is through cookies. When and if browsers make the "disabling" of cookies the default (rather than the current default, which is "enabling" of cookies), the problems become even more difficult. For the moment, many consumers are not aware that firms are writing cookies to their hard drives. Until such time as they are generally aware of this (and may rebel by disabling cookies), firms would be well advised to exploit the valuable information cookies provide.

13.3.6 Tech-5: Interface Limitations

Even if practical limitations could be eliminated by improved download time, there are physical limits to Internet interface technology. Although Web GUIs are generally seen as attractive and easy to use, they do fall short when compared to alternate communication media. The Web browser is one of the richest electronic interfaces ever developed. It allows for full-spectrum color images, video, and stereophonic sound. However, it has serious physical limitations.

One obvious problem with all electronic communication media is that a customer cannot touch and feel a product over the Web. The marketing literature indicates that lack of touch is a problem with direct marketing of all sorts, electronic or otherwise. Electronic communication also lacks a mechanism to transmit smell or taste. Both of these senses have been shown empirically to directly impact consumer buying behavior.[16]

Another limitation of the interface is in 3-D imaging. Current personal computer display systems cannot display holographic images, but someday may be able to do this. Technologies that simulate three dimensions on a two-dimensional monitor already exist. These technologies are not truly 3-D and are not yet commonly used by NEOs. As discussed earlier in the book, boo.com attempted to give users the ability to rotate sample clothes on mannequins a full 360 degrees, but were hamstrung by user bandwidth, among other things. An ingenious use of simulated 3-D graphics is on the thebanmappingproject.com site. Commercial ventures should consider such approaches for their offerings.

Until electronic communication can replicate the five senses and produce 3-D displays, it will not be a one-for-one replacement for face-to-face communication or traditional commerce.

Apparent Threats to NE

Interface limitations to Internet computing pose special threats to NE applications. In noncommercial applications, two interested partners are trying to share data. Toleration for problems in the interface should, therefore, be much greater than in a typical consumer-vendor relationship. A B2C online outlet cannot hope to compete against vendors in the physical world if a buyer requires a fully sensory experience in order to buy. Without a 3-D view, many products cannot be evaluated. Without the ability to hold an object, many products lack the ability to generate impulse purchases. Under these circumstances, technological impediments are much more incapacitating for those attempting to conduct business over the Internet than for those using the Internet for noncommercial applications such as internal communication or messaging to partners.

With regard to competition between NEOs, practical limitations in the interface create other difficulties. Because a vendor cannot hope to include a complete multimedia message within the limits of tolerable download time, some of the preferred message must be eliminated. Otherwise, the preferred message will send an additional, unintended cue of delay and aggravation. In an online retail application, this interface problem could create a bias against a company versus its competitor. Thus, there is a potential for confusion in the message sent. Where confusion in a noncommercial application might lead to a follow-up question via an e-mail, confusion in a B2C application could lead to purchase of a competitor's goods and services. As a result, finding the appropriate balance between media-rich hyperdocuments and tolerable download times appear to be more difficult and important for those engaged in B2C NE.

Designs and Solutions—Interface Limitations

Solutions are rather restricted by what can be presented via the computer. Potential customers can be mailed physical samples of products in certain cases. The future looks brighter, but that does not help with immediate solutions. Rudimentary computerized devices that send impressions of touch and taste are technically feasible and should eventually reach the marketplace. Holographic and 3-D images are, likewise, technically feasible and may be deployed at some point in time. For the moment, simulated 3-D is a reasonable option for firms. In this vein, advanced forms of virtual reality are also being explored by companies such as Microsoft. The language that is used to program these applications, VRML

---

[16]Johnson et al. (1985).

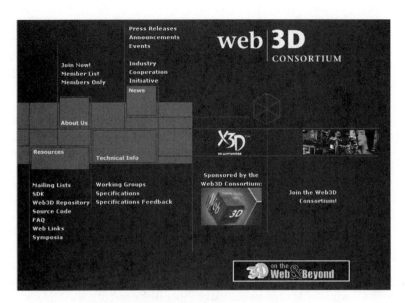

Figure 13.7   Web 3-D Consortium Home Page (www.vrml.com)

(virtual reality markup language), has good industry consortia support such as that featured in Figure 13.7, and so we can expect that this will be a vibrant arena for future development.

Even if practical limitations could be eliminated by improved download time, there are physical limits to Internet interface technology. Web GUIs are generally considered to be attractive and easy to use, although they do fall short when compared to physically encompassing communication media such as television and movies. The Web browser is a rich medium now, and can be even richer with new technologies coming on board every year. We can look forward to an interesting period of innovation in this area.

13.3.7 Tech-6: Lack of Internet Standards

The final technological impediment to wider diffusion of Internet computing comes from the absence of well-established and agreed-upon Internet standards. Internet standards are used as guidelines for the development of software that conforms to generally accepted rules for communication between applications. For example, by conforming to standard protocols, a browser developer can know the format needed to request, receive, and interpret HTML files. Using this format allows that browser to communicate with all Web servers, which also conform to the same standards. Problems occur when there is either an absence of a standard or when an existing standard is augmented or added to. In the case where standards are augmented, multiple parties are often augmenting the original standard in proprietary ways to meet a new perceived need. The difficulty is that many solutions to a single problem may coexist simultaneously without an agreed-upon standard. The best illustration of this phenomenon is in extensions to HTML.

HTML went through several accepted revisions. Between revisions, however, competing browser manufacturers extended HTML to perform new functions. Past examples have included displaying different types of graphics files. At one point in time, some browsers could display graphics files of type .gif, .jpg, and .bmp, whereas others could only display .gif and .jpg files. Content developers could create pages that included .bmp files but could not be assured of the files being displayed correctly by all browsers. As a result, content had to be developed twice: one version developed without the .bmp file, and one developed with .bmp files that would be displayed as an error message on certain browsers.

HTML is rife with examples of extensions that followed this pattern of differences between browsers that is ultimately caused by a lack of standards. One recent troubling pattern is the seemingly purposeful divergence of certain competing standards. Netscape and Microsoft have long waged a "browser war" to compete for the Internet software market. Part of the strategy in fighting this war included the creation of proprietary standards for each browser with the goal of differentiating one browser at the expense of the other. A significant instance of differentiation was applet and applet-script standards.

Microsoft has developed a set of standards (ActiveX) for running applets and applet script on its browser. ActiveX was put forth to compete with the Sun Microsystems Java language. Netscape adopted Java standards and further extended them with a proprietary scripting language called JavaScript for running on their browser. The implied and stated goals were to entice users to develop Web pages that adopted one standard over the other. Upon doing so, all clients who would communicate with those sites using that standard would need a compatible browser.

Apparent Threats to NE

Different standards and protocols for Web computing and the Internet infrastructure exist in such areas as encryption, electronic currency, and multimedia. Netscape and Microsoft use different standards for these functions critical for NE. Purveyors of Web content need to be aware that the browser market is fragmented into the browsers Internet Explorer, Netscape, and proprietary browsers like that of AOL.

Customers further complicate things through the use of any number of different generational versions of these browsers. Furthermore, certain browsers are not compatible with older operating systems. Many of the latest browsers that contain the most recent HTML extensions can only be run on a 32-bit operating system. A customer running a machine with Microsoft Windows 3.1 is limited in what HTML code can be viewed correctly on that early model software and hardware. Under these conditions, it is difficult to predict which browser application or version will be interpreting an e-tailer's Web page at any given time.

Client technology is beyond the control of the content provider. Different browser protocols and standards are used by different browsers and vary as to which files they can interpret. Therefore, developing a firm Web site that is readable by all or most customers is challenging.

Designs and Solutions—Lack of Standards

Although inability to standardize on a certain version of browser software creates inconveniences for users, its impact is perhaps the least of the six obstacles. Firms need to reduce the sophistication of their Web sites so that they can be interpreted by most clients. Most clients can read frames at this point in time, but may not accept XML. Firms would be advised to keep this in mind and to seek out lower common denominators to be able to reach the majority of customers.

Working around this problem is not simple. Plug-ins can be mailed to users, either electronically or physically, but it is not clear that users want or would accept this service. Download delay for these plug-ins alone may be enough to deter customers from selecting an upgrade. As browsers and other hardware and software advance and knowledge of downloading new software becomes better understood, some problems in this area may diminish.

Focus on NE: Internet2

Watching a movie off the Internet and having a telephone conversation that seems like a face-to-face meeting, remain potential technological promises that are, as of yet, unfulfilled. But a brand new Internet network, dubbed Internet2 (I2), may bring Net denizens closer to those pipe dreams.

Abiline, one of the many networks that will make up I2, is up and running, connecting 150 universities and research centers with high-speed fiber optic cable. It is 45,000 times as fast as the average modem, which means it could transmit the entire Library of Congress in just 20 seconds. The I2 network design, which will remain compatible with the current Internet, will provide a pathway for higher-bandwidth traffic. I2 uses Internet Protocol version 6 (IPv6) instead of the current Internet Protocol, IPv4. IPv6 uses a different package scheme; the advantage of this scheme is that it incorporates native multicasting, high reliability, and high capacity along with QoS (quality of service) controls. IPv6 will allow applications requiring high bandwidths to coexist with each other. However, I2 is, as of now, off-limits to the general public. Those developing the project say they need to reserve and retain the network's capacity in order to complete their research. But eventually, the new technologies developed on I2 are expected to trickle down for use by the general public. With corporate and government backing, networks around the world will soon link up with I2, sharing research and turning knowledge into commercial products.

Sources:
http://www.internet2.edu/
http://www.cnn.com/TECH/computing/9902/24/internet2/
http://www.technologyreview.com/articles/tynan0710013.asp

13.4 SOCIAL (ORGANIZATIONAL AND ENVIRONMENTAL) CHALLENGES

Although the technological hurdles for a digital economy are formidable and easily imagined, there has not been as much codification or systematization of these problems in the social arena. The importance implied by the order of discussion to follow, which may be intuitively appealing, does not have the benefit of rigorous analysis that characterized the technical issues.[17]

For this reason, our discussion of these issues is much briefer than with the technical issues. There is no question that these issues are of critical importance. The lack of holistic, analytical reasoning in the scientific literature is why we need to be circumspect. As we learn more about their prominence and relative importance, these challenges can be further elaborated.

13.4.1 Social-1: Consumer Fear of Buying or Transacting Business over the Web

Customers fear buying over the Internet. Whether the e-vendor's systems are secure or not, users believe that their confidential and transactional information may not be well protected. This lack of trust in the general security of the Web and NE systems undermines usage. Although the underlying problem may be the actual security of the systems, customers' perceptions and fears are the immediate social issues.

As pointed out in earlier chapters, this primarily affects the payment phase of the NE value chain. There may be concerns that transactional data is vulnerable, but when credit and debit card numbers are at stake, these concerns are greatly magnified. Large-scale fraud using the Internet as the vehicle of transference remains a viable but improbable threat when firms institute state-of-the-art security measures. But little is being done to inform consumers about the extent of the security effort, and fear, therefore, is high even when it should not be.

Related but slightly different from security concerns is a legitimate concern about the privacy of personal data on the Web. Customers worry that they have not been informed about the intended use of their data and its being sold to others who could engage in spamming or worse.

13.4.2 Social-2: Lack of Brand Awareness—Significant Penetration of the Total Market for Specific Products by Companies

One of the major difficulties of Internet marketing is that the first-mover advantages are formidable and hard to overcome. The ability of amazon.com to control the books-plus online market is one example of this. Moreover, across industries, firms that already have brand awareness are able to capitalize on their past by purchasing (or having purchased) a domain name so that customers can find their online operations as easily as their physical operations.

Why is this different from the importance of brand in traditional marketing? Does this suggest that the barriers to entry are higher for new firms entering cyberspace? This may indeed be the case. Traditional marketers have a far larger number of venues at their disposal

---

[17]Rose et al. (1999).

to make customers aware of their brand. First, they can position themselves on key traffic routes, whether these are physical locations, as in retailing, or at trade conventions, as in B2B operations. The equivalent of this in the cyberworld is thought to be portals, but portals have become so crowded that it is not clear that one can get the attention of customers on sites such as Yahoo or Amazon.

In traditional markets, branding can occur through a variety of media, but the Web is a "pull" medium, and customers can easily resist inducements to buy by just moving to another page or closing a "pop-up" advertisement. Consider how difficult it is to resist advertisements on television, radio, or other "push" media while partaking of highly desirable content, such as popular television or radio shows. The Web, thus far, does not have this kind of compelling content draw, except for specific buying purposes. The delivery of entertainment over the Web has not yet found its voice, and so the spiral branding that might occur for other Web brands is not nearly as effective as it is for traditional media.

13.4.3 Social-3: Management/Cultural Problems in Instituting E-Business Practices and Ideas

This hurdle is a classic problem. People (and managers) resist change. New ways of thinking about the customer-firm relationship and the need to make wholesale changes in how the firm does business are anathema to many managers. A relatively small part of the employee population is attuned to abstraction and experimentation, and this has a devastating effect on instituting new processes for NEOs.

The classic solution to this problem is to foster a climate of innovation. Reward and incentive structures need to be aligned with fulfilling this goal, so that employees are not punished for attempting innovation and failing some of the time.

This mismatch between having a strategic vision and being unable to execute the vision has been one of the key findings in the ongoing GSU e-commerce study. Managers were asked if they believed that firms that were successful in e-commerce would also have to become far more virtual in their designs. There was a strong consensus on this issue that focusing on core competencies and outsourcing noncore processes was critical. Some participants elaborated on what needed to happen for the firm to really change to becoming a NEO.

Ironically, when the follow-up question was asked as to whether managers believed their firm was becoming more virtual, the answer was generally "no."

Firms may see the need to change, but those that are actually able to accomplish this level of change are unusual. Many organizations change processes on a superficial level, and, in doing so, do not "stress out" their culture or significantly alter routines. Although this may result in a conflict-free environment, the end result is likely to be a firm that falls far short of "best of breed."

13.4.4 Social-4: Lack of Firm Experience in Doing E-Business

There is evidence that there are sizable first-mover advantages among those who have been exploiting the power of the Internet. Part of these advantages accrue from learning the unique characteristics of the Web and focusing on these. A few of these at a higher level were highlighted in the Chapter 11 on e-marketing.

Firms that have not developed this experience, covering both successes and failures, are, frankly, at a considerable disadvantage. The obstacle is in realizing that the firm is behind in the game and mobilizing the resources to catch up and even leap frog the competition.

A good example of a CEO coming to this realization, and drastically reorganizing the firm so as not to fall even further behind, is Microsoft. In the late 1990s, CEO Bill Gates realized that stand-alone and within-firm client-server computing were not nearly as important as networked computing in the future, and he had to initiate changes in the entire culture of Microsoft, including their project priorities in new product development, to respond to this realization.

13.4.5 Social-5: Organizational Fear of Doing Business over the Internet

Complementors
To engage in contractual relationships and partnerships is one of the heralded advantages of the Internet. E-mail alone is a "killer" application in its ability to link individuals within and between organizations. Group mailings serve the purpose of large-scale information dissemination at an absurdly low cost.

Suppliers
An even more powerful argument for use of electronic connections in place of physical processes is for supply-chain efficiencies. Sharing information up and down the chain on a need-to-know basis can smooth out product flows and prevent massive over- and undersupply.

In cases of either horizontal (complementor) or vertical (supplier) integration, the firm needs to be assured that the information it is sharing is not being openly shared with competitors. Theft of industrial secrets and its sale to competitors is already a worldwide problem, one that could be aggravated by widespread disclosures. In a major turn of fate, the very capability of Internet applications to share information between legitimate and approved parties is also the same vehicle that could be used for abuse.

What keeps the advantages of networked connections from being realized as soon as possible is, in many cases, the fear that data is not being held confidential. In one sense, firms, like individuals, learn to trust each other by virtue of seeing others act in trustworthy ways.[18] This problem is being solved over time, in this way.

Other solutions are contractual solutions. Nondisclosure clauses with partners and suppliers will give the firm legal recourse in case of defalcation. This is never the preferred course of action, but may be necessary when, by happenstance or bad judgment, the firm has partnered with an untrustworthy partner. There is no doubt that this is a key hurdle to the evolution of NE in that it deeply affects the willingness of other firms to engage in electronically oriented partnerships.

13.4.6 Social-6: Migrating to Internet Computer-to-Computer Linkages from More Familiar EDIs

Firms have sunk huge amounts of money into EDI. These investments have paid off well for firms such as Ford. For example, personnel who were performing the manual processes

---

[18]McKnight et al. (2002); Gefen and Straub (2002).

of data entry in accounts payable were replaced by computer-to-computer exchanges. Staffs were reduced by, in some cases, 95%.

The movement of these systems to XML or application formats such as MySAP will take some time because firms are still trying to recoup the benefits from past EDI expenditures. Transferring over to ETNs means that virtually none of the legacy systems will interface well with the data from the ETN, and, in these situations, new software and possibly new database schemas will be required.

New technology often brings with it new levels of complexity. It may mean running the Internet systems alongside EDI and other business exchange systems. And if the firm chooses to go with an ERP and to connect with suppliers and partners through these application formats, this implementation can be extremely complex.

Managers avoid launching endeavors that make their lives more complex. As indicated earlier, there are strong psychological factors that lead to acquiescence. Creating more work that will ultimately lead to a more efficient and effective firm takes visionary leadership and competent follow-up; not all firms do this well.

13.4.7 Social 7: Lack of Well-Accepted or Well-Understood E-Cash on the Part of Consumers or Organizations

E-cash will facilitate business on the Internet by regularizing the payment process. The proper identification of buyer and seller and the exchange of electronic funds for goods or services will lead to a secure payment system that speeds delivery and assures financial fairness. Figure 13.8 shows the architecture of a typical e-cash settlement. Why is it not happening faster?

Electronic payment systems are just beginning to be accepted by NEOs and their customers. There are a wide variety of such systems, and so it is taking a while for the emergence of standards and development of a critical mass of customers. Even the transition from SSL to SET is taking a lot longer than originally predicted.

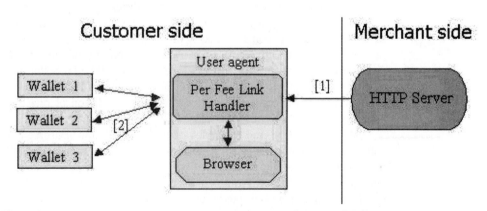

Figure 13.8   Architecture of Typical E-Cash Settlement (Reprinted with permission of ecash.com)

Part of the difficulty may be that we are dealing in a world of symbols in cyberspace, one in which there are no good physical surrogates. When paper money was introduced, it took some time before people were ready to accept it in place of specie. When the backing for paper money, the gold in repositories around the world, was abandoned as a monetary standard, the value of the paper was backed up by a trust in governments to guarantee this money as a medium of exchange. Both of these processes took a long time for people to accept, but they eventually came to pass.

Such gradual transitions are different from e-money because we are completely divorced from a requisite physical representation. Let's take a simple case where a family banks through an Internet bank that processes charges against their account when given a proper digital signature. The family may even be having their paychecks deposited automatically into their Internet bank account, so they never see any representation of their worth except for the online reports they request, or through statements or reconciliations. It is not hard to see why this exchange and manipulation of symbols that constitute a family's livelihood would not be comforting to all.

Firms who are in the e-payment spectrum, this includes banking and other financial services as well as firms specializing in e-payment software and services, need to create an atmosphere of interest and trust in these innovations. Free training in their systems would be one obvious avenue for creating these, but testimonials from satisfied customers using the major media is also needed.

13.4.8 Social-8: Ambiguous or Hostile NE Legal or Regulatory Environment

The social environment as regulated through statutes or government agencies needs to encourage Internet business. If cyberspace is overtaxed or regulated in ways that do not increase confidence in areas of weakness, it can be counterproductive. For example, what is really crucial are international regulations that establish standards for digital signatures and third-party certificate authorities. The full mechanism of global law and regulations will heighten confidence in transactions over the Internet. "Once burned, twice cautious" is not an experience that governments want to have to legislate against, so this work needs to be put in place as soon as humanly possible.

We have discussed examples of overregulation throughout this book. In our opinion, the Internet should not be censored. Governments will be far better off in achieving conditions of moral and economic sanity for their citizenry if they educate rather than regulate. Free markets and free speech go together, and regulation of one or the other will have long-term deleterious consequences.

We have also offered examples of useful regulation. Enforcement of copyrights on software is important because it not only encourages internal and direct foreign investment, but it also supports the creation of a native software industry. An example of an ambiguous regulatory environment is when countries have copyright laws on the books, but, for all intents and purposes, never enforce them. It would be better to drop the pretense of supporting the protection of intellectual property and forthrightly and honestly send a message to the international community that the government takes no position on intellectual property, rather than this ambiguous and confusing message.

SUMMARY

NE facilitates or creates the opportunities for a vast number of new commercial ventures. This chapter dealt with the technological and social challenges in implementing NE. These include:

Technical Challenges:

1. Security weaknesses
2. Download delays
3. Search problems
4. Inadequate measurement of Web site success
5. Limitations of the interface
6. Lack of Internet standards

Social Challenges:

1. Fear of consumers in buying or transacting business over the Web
2. Lack of brand awareness–significant penetration of the total market for specific products by companies
3. Management/cultural problems in instituting e-business practices and ideas.
4. Lack of firm experience in doing e-business
5. Organizational fear of doing business over the Internet
6. Migrating to Internet computer-to-computer linkages from more familiar EDI
7. Lack of well-accepted or well-understood e-cash on the part of consumers or organizations
8. Ambiguous or hostile legal or regulatory environment for NE

Managers need to be aware of these barriers to use as well as the workarounds that will allow the firm to capitalize on Internet technology for the present. In the long run, many of these limitations and impediments will be solved through new technologies. For the foreseeable future, though, they represent challenges to designing an effective Web initiative.

KEY TERMS

Contractual solutions: Any contractual clause that solves the problem of an Internet adoption impediment; one example of these would be nondisclosure clause with partners and suppliers.

Download time: The amount of time it takes for a Web client machine to receive and display a data file submitted by a Web server after that file was requested by the client.

IP-spoofing: Disguising oneself as another; when one IP masquerades as another, adopting the IP address.

Keyword queries: Search queries based on a user entering a list of key words.

Know-bots: Programs designed to find and report on the contents of Web pages.

Spiral branding: The use of alternative media to advertise a firm's URL.

REVIEW QUESTIONS

1. Why has the firm lost control in influencing user adoption in the Internet environment?
2. Why are there built-in limits to applications that run over the Internet.
3. Name the technological impediments to B2C commerce.
4. What are two techniques used to conceal messages?
5. List two elements that affect download time.
6. How can a technological configuration of a server increase download time?
7. What are the limitations of the client side of Internet computing?
8. How can delay be minimized on a server?
9. How are URLs invoked?
10. Which metrics are difficult to generate for Web activity?
11. How can firms reduce apparent threats to NE?
12. What are the limitations to interfaces on the Web?
13. What are the social challenges to e-commerce?

TOPICS FOR DISCUSSION

1. Discuss the technical and social challenges that affect implementation of NE organizations.
2. Discuss the characteristics of the Internet that make the transition to commercial use difficult.
3. Argue for the importance of technological impediments.
4. Discuss solutions to the threat to security from the physical world as well as from hackers.
5. Describe all the dimensions of download time.
6. Discuss why cable is less secure than phone lines.
7. Elaborate solutions to download delays.
8. Discuss how hit counters can be inaccurate.
9. What is the impact of lack of Internet standards? Lead a discussion on this topic.
10. Discuss ways in which consumer fear can be lessened.

INTERNET EXERCISES

1. Locate articles on the Internet referring to the breaches at eBay, Yahoo, and Amazon. Write a report on the incidences and the outcomes.
2. Locate a firm that offers firewall protection. Write a report that describes the services provided by the firm.
3. Locate an Internet article on e-commerce fraud. Summarize and present your findings.
4. Find an article on the psychology of hackers. Prepare a PowerPoint presentation on types of hackers and the explanations of their behavior.
5. Run Speedtest (http://bandwidthplace.com/speedtest/) on your computer. Summarize your test results in a spreadsheet.
6. Search the Internet for an example of Internet2 in action. Write a paper describing the capabilities of Internet2 and describe the way that your site has utilized these features.

7. Locate an example of a firm on the Internet who implements spiral branding on their Web site.

8. Locate a firm that offers Web-tracking statistics. Investigate the Web page and describe the services offered.

9. Choose an e-commerce Web site. Investigate the credit card protection offered by the firm.

10. Investigate how to find cookies on your computer. Check your own computer and report your findings.

TEAM EXERCISES

1. With respect to the technologies that power the Internet, prioritizing and coping with impediments in B2C e-commerce is an important consideration of managers. Have each team member investigate one of the technological impediments to B2C e-commerce. Prepare a PowerPoint presentation presenting the design choices, solutions, and emerging solutions of each element. Include real-world examples of each element.

2. Have team members investigate the work of hackers and describe instances that have occurred. Create a timeline of well-known break-ins and criminal activities. Explore the legal issues and the punishments that have been handed down for violations.

3. Investigate applications which have been developed for Internet2. Describe how IPv6 affects Internet2 and the value of using the new protocol. Describe several of the applications that have been developed, and develop your own idea of an appropriate application for Internet2.

4. Investigate Jakob Nielsen's ideas on Web usability (http://www.useit.com/). Prepare a PowerPoint presentation on the elements of usability and describe the impact of each element on Web design. Summarize the basic philosophy of Web design according to Nielsen.

5. Investigate the impact of social, organizational, and environmental challenges on a digital economy. Locate real-world examples where these social issues have had an impact on the acceptance of technology.

INTERNET RESOURCES

The Bot Spot (http://www.botspot.com): The spot to download bots!
Internet 2 (http://www.internet2.edu): The official site of the Internet 2.

REFERENCES

Anonymous "Keynote Business 40," 1998. [Online] Available: http://www.keynote.com.
Capon, N., and M. Burke. "Individual, Product Class, and Task-Related Factors in Consumer Information Processing." *Journal of Consumer Research*, 7 (1980), 314–326.

Daft, R. L., and R. H. Lengel. "Information Richness: A New Approach to Managerial Behavior and Organizational Design." In Cummings, L. L., and B. M. Shaw, eds. *Research in Organizational Behavior*, 6, JAI Press, Greenwich CT, 1984, 191–233.

Freed, L., and F. J. Derfler. "Fast Connections." *PC Magazine Online*, 18, April 20, 1999.

Gefen, D., and D. Straub. "Managing User Trust in B2C e-Services." *eService Journal*, 2002, forthcoming.

Greene, T. "What's Winning: Cable or DSL?" *Network World*, 16, 9 1999, 59.

Gurnon, E. "Credit Card Theft on Net Is Not Rocket Science." *San Francisco Examiner*, 1997.

Johnson, S. L., R. Sommer, and V. Martino. "Consumer Behavior at Bulk Food Bins." *Journal of Consumer Research*, 12, 1 (1985), 114–117.

Lohr, S. "Go Ahead, Be Paranoid: Hackers Are Out to Get You." *New York Times Online*, March 17, 1997.

McKnight, D. H., V. Choudhury, and C. Kacmar. "Developing and Validating Trust Measures for E-Commerce: An Integrative Typology." *Information Systems Research*, 13, 3, September 2002.

Ozer, J. "High-Bandwidth Options: ADSL vs. Cable." *PC Magazine Online*, 18, March 23, 1999.

Rose, G., H. Khoo, and D. Straub. "Current Technological Impediments to Business-to-Consumer Electronic Commerce." *Communications of the AIS*, 1, 16, June 1999, 1–74.

Rose, G., R. Evaristo, and D. Straub. "Culture and Consumer Responses to Web Download Time: A Four-Continent Study of Mono- and Polychronism." *IEEE Transactions on Engineering Management*, forthcoming, (2002).

Rose, G., and D. W. Straub. "The Effect Of Download Time On Consumer Attitude Toward the E-Service Retailer." *eService Journal*, 1, 1 2001, 55–76.

Rose, G. M., D. W. Straub, and J. D. Lees. "The Effect of Download Time on Consumer Attitude Toward the Retailer in E-Commerce." *Proceedings of the Sixth Americas Conference on Information Systems*, Long Beach, CA, 2000, 1352–1354.

Shneiderman, B. *Designing the User Interface: Strategies for Effective Human-Computer Interaction*, Addison-Wesley, Reading, Massachusetts, 1998.

Snyder, B. "Carrier Checkup." *Telephony*, 232, 17, April 28, 1997, 38.

Straub, D. W., and R. Klein. "e-Competitive Transformations." *Business Horizons*, 44, 3, May-June 2001, 3–12.

Wagner, M., and S. Gaudin. "While E-commerce Firms Sweat Out Shaky 'Net Reliability." *Computerworld*, 31, 30 1997, 14.

Watson, R. T., and D. W. Straub. "New Horizons for ICT Research in Net-Enhanced Organizations." Working paper, University of Georgia, 2002.

Credits

Figure 3.16	© 2002, Lands End, Inc. Used with permission.
Figure 3.17	© Ebay Inc. All rights Reserved. Used with permission.
Figure 3.19	© 2002, INOVIS Inc. Used with permission.
Figure 3.20	© Ahead Software / Nero Burning. Used with permission.
Figure 3.21	© Teleportec, Inc. Used with permission.
Figure 3.22	© Dell Computer Corporation.
Figure 3.24	© Boo.com. Permission requested.
Figure 4.5	Courtesy of Amazon.com, Inc.
Figure 5.2	© Macromedia, Inc. Used with permission.
Figure 5.3	© McAfee, Inc. Permission requested.
Figure 5.7	© Google.com. Permission requested.
Figure 5.8	© Google.com. Permission requested.
Figure 5.9	Courtesy of Amazon.com, Inc.
Figure 5.10	Reprinted by permission of The Wall Street Journal, © 2002 Dow Jones Company, Inc. All Rights Reserved Worldwide.
Figure 6.8	Reprinted with permission of VeriSign Inc.
Figure 6.9	© Campmor.com. Used with permission.
Focus on NE	Angel Investors, page 238 – courtesy of VentureVest Capital Corporation.
Case Study	10-1, page 320 – Used with permission from Microsoft Corporation.
Focus on NE	Depth of Partnering, page 315/316 – courtesy of Technology Channels Group, Inc.
Figure 11.1	© QVC.com. Permission requested.
Figure 11.3	© Gibson Research Corporation. Used with permission.
Figure 11.4	© Priceline.com. Used with permission.
Figure 11.2	© 2003 SILive.com. Used with permission.
Figure 11.5	© Wine.com. Used with permission.
Figure 11.10	© SPSS, Inc. Permission requested.
Figure 11.11	© Ahead Software / Nero Burning. Permission requested.
Figure 11.13	© Covisint. Permission requested.
Figure 11.20	© Twentieth Century Fox. Permission requested.

Index

Pages with "W" prefixes are available online at www.wiley.com/college/straub